*Major Problems in
the History of
the Vietnam War*

MAJOR PROBLEMS IN AMERICAN HISTORY SERIES

GENERAL EDITOR

THOMAS G. PATERSON

Major Problems in the History of the Vietnam War

DOCUMENTS AND ESSAYS

THIRD EDITION

EDITED BY
ROBERT J. McMAHON
UNIVERSITY OF FLORIDA

HOUGHTON MIFFLIN COMPANY
Boston   New York

Editor in Chief: Jean L. Woy
Senior Development Editor: Frances Gay
Associate Production/Design Coordinator: Christine Gervais
Senior Manufacturing Coordinator: Priscilla Bailey
Marketing Manager: Sandra McGuire

Cover image: *Jungle Column* by Samuel E. Alexander. Courtesy of Army Art Collection, U.S. Army Center of Military History.

Printed in the U.S.A.

Library of Congress Control Number: 2002106480

ISBN: 0-618-19312-X

6789-MP-08 07 06

To my students

Contents

C H A P T E R   4
Dwight D. Eisenhower and Vietnam: Deepening the Commitment
Page 87

C H A P T E R   5
John F. Kennedy and Vietnam: Incremental Escalation
Page 123

C H A P T E R   6
Lyndon B. Johnson's Decisions for War
Page 158

C H A P T E R   7
U.S. Military Strategy
Page 206

CHAPTER 14
The Paris Peace Accords of 1973 and the Fall of South Vietnam
Page 475

CHAPTER 15
Legacies and Memories of a War
Page 510

Preface

U.S. intervention in Vietnam grew slowly in the first years after the Second World War—almost imperceptibly so to most Americans. But an ever-deepening commitment soon became evident. By the early 1950s the United States was underwriting about 80 percent of the bill for France's colonial war against Vietnamese nationalists; and following the collapse of French rule in 1954, Washington became the principal source of support for a new, struggling South Vietnamese government. By the early 1960s the United States was providing that regime with thousands of military advisers in an effort to check a renewed guerrilla insurgency. In 1965 American ground troops joined the fray, only to become bogged down in a major land war.

In the ten-year period bracketed by the introduction of American combat forces in 1965 and the collapse of the U.S.-backed Saigon regime in 1975, the Vietnam War dominated political, social, cultural, and intellectual life in the United States. Probably no issue since the Civil War has divided Americans more deeply than the Indochina conflict. Certainly few, if any, episodes in contemporary history have had a more profound impact on American society or compelled a more searching examination of America's role in the world. A complete accounting of the war's deeper costs, however, remains elusive. The passions it unleashed have not yet ebbed, nor has the nation fully absorbed or overcome its many consequences.

Indeed, the divisions opened by the Vietnam War have resurfaced in numerous guises ever since 1975, especially during presidential political campaigns and foreign policy debates. In 1992, for example, political opponents questioned Democratic presidential candidate Bill Clinton's evasion of the draft during the 1960s just as, in 1988, political opponents had questioned Republican vice-presidential candidate Dan Quayle's military record. The fact that both men avoided service in Vietnam, and that both appeared to use either subterfuge or family connections in the process, became more important in the ensuing swirl of charges and countercharges than their dramatically different positions on the conflict. Moreover, each time the United States intervened, or considered intervening, abroad over the past quarter-century—whether in Iran, Lebanon, Grenada, Libya, Central America, Somalia, Bosnia, or Kosovo—critics and interventionists alike drew lessons from the Vietnam experience. After the American-led coalition's victory over Iraq in the Persian Gulf War in 1991, President George Bush proclaimed triumphantly that the United States had finally overcome "the Vietnam syndrome." His assertion, however, appears to have been an expression more of wishful thinking than of careful contemplation.

U.S. military action against the Taliban regime in Afghanistan and its al Qaeda supporters prompted troubling Vietnam analogies and memories once again—despite the overwhelming public support for the war against terrorism. "As Americans fight the war against terrorism, we assure ourselves that this conflict is completely differ-ent from the one we carried out a generation ago in Southeast Asia," editorialized the *New York Times* at the height of that conflict. "Yet Vietnam ghosts are still here," it added. "They do not tell us that our current fight is less than just or necessary. But they steal away the old certainty that the end will inevitably be triumphant. And Americans of a certain age will always shiver when the debate turns to the use of ground troops in far-away, inhospitable lands."

This third, completely revised edition of *Major Problems in the History of the Vietnam War* reflects the wealth and abundance of new work on the Vietnam War that has appeared in recent years. More than half of the essays in this edition are new, most of them only published after the second edition came out in 1995, including selections from Michael Hunt, Mark Bradley, Fredrik Logevall, Robert Brigham, Qiang Zhai, and Lewis Sorley. Several chapters also feature fresh docu-ments: some are recently declassified government records; others are drawn from newer personal reflections or memoirs. These include a revealing, tape-recorded conversation between President Lyndon Johnson and Senator Richard Russell, a personal recollection of his Vietnam experiences from Secretary of State Colin Powell, two eyewitness accounts of the My Lai massacre, and documents relating to women's role in the antiwar movement and to the Chinese–North Vietnamese rela-tionship. This edition also features an entirely new chapter—Chapter 8, "Americans in Combat," which investigates how the peculiar nature of warfare in Vietnam was experienced by the ordinary Americans called by their government to serve in that distant land.

The impressive outpouring of Vietnam-era reflections in the United States in recent years testifies both to the continued public preoccupation with the war and to the absence of a broad consensus on its meaning. A proliferation of movies, television series, documentaries, novels, and memoirs has competed for the pub-lic's attention with books and articles by scholars, policy analysts, military offi-cers, civilian policymakers, and journalists. The viewpoints expressed in these diverse efforts have varied as widely as the lessons drawn. Significantly, this con-tinuing fascination with the Vietnam years has not been confined to those with vivid memories of that turbulent time. College students, most of them born after the collapse of the Saigon regime, continue to flock to the hundreds of Vietnam War courses taught in universities both inside and outside the United States. Per-haps they are simply curious about an episode central to their parents'—or, in some cases, grandparents'—generation. Or perhaps they are trying to understand how and why events that reached their denouement on the battlefield nearly three decades ago still reverberate with such force across the political and cultural land-scape of contemporary America.

This volume addresses these issues and questions. It seeks to stimulate critical thinking about the Vietnam War and its long-term meaning for Americans. The essays and documents in this book, like those in the other anthologies in Houghton Mifflin's Major Problems in American History Series, introduce students to the main controversies and debates surrounding the subject. Because the Vietnam War represents a pivotal episode in the American national experience, the principal focus of these readings is on three America-centered questions: Why was the United States drawn into the Vietnam War? How did the nation seek to accomplish its goals in Vietnam from the 1940s to the 1970s? And what have been the lessons and consequences of the war for the United States?

The war, of course, forms a chapter not just in American history but in the history of modern Asia—and the world. Nor was the United States the only significant actor in the drama. In an effort to present students with a balanced perspective on the war and with the context necessary for understanding American decisions, I have included three chapters that deal exclusively with Vietnamese topics—and that feature Vietnamese voices. In each chapter, the essays and documents place U.S. policy in the broadest possible framework. The book's primary focus remains, nonetheless, the *American* experience in Vietnam.

Each chapter opens with a brief introduction to the topic at hand. The introduction is followed by a series of primary documents and two or three interpretive essays by historians, political scientists, participants, or other authorities. The documents reveal the flavor of the time and the range of contemporary issues and retrospective assessments. The essays present the most significant debates and controversies generated by the war. Readers are encouraged to assess evidence carefully, to weigh conflicting arguments, and to form their own opinions. Suggestions for further reading follow each chapter, providing guideposts for those interested in probing issues more deeply.

Many individuals helped in the preparation of this book. I am especially grateful to Thomas G. Paterson, General Editor of the series, for first suggesting this project to me, and for his valuable suggestions at every stage. For general advice, specific recommendations, and constructive criticism on the first edition, I thank Edward P. Crapol, William J. Duiker, George C. Herring, Gary R. Hess, Richard H. Immerman, John Israel, Melvyn P. Leffler, Gary May, Kell Mitchell, Samuel L. Popkin, Donald W. Rogers, Sandra C. Taylor, and William S. Turley. I acknowledge Ted Snow's help in locating certain materials for the first edition and the expert assistance of the secretarial staff at the University of Florida's History Department. For their written reviews and helpful recommendations during the preparation of this second edition of the book, I am extremely grateful to James A. Banks, Cuyahoga Community College; David Castle, Muskingum College; John F. Guilmartin, Jr., Ohio State University; Richard H. Immerman, Temple University; Gerald Newman, Kent State University; James R. Rush, Arizona State University; David F. Schmitz, Whitman College; Robert D. Schulzinger, University of Colorado, Boulder; and Robert Weisbrot, Colby College.

For their written reviews and helpful recommendations during the preparation of this third edition of the book, I am extremely grateful to Michael W. Flamm, Ohio Wesleyan University; Howard Jones, University of Alabama; Charles E. Neu, Brown University; and Sayuri Shimizu, Michigan State University. I am also indebted to Jean Woy and Fran Gay, my wonderfully supportive, enthusiastic, and efficient editors at Houghton Mifflin and, once again, to series editor Tom Paterson for his critical eye, shrewd suggestions, unfailing enthusiasm, and, most of all, for his enduring friendship.

My family has, as always, offered indispensable support, understanding, and encouragement. I will never be able to thank my wife Alison enough for all that she has done, and my sons Tom and Mike have provided a great reservoir of love and humor—mixed with youthful energy and the occasional dose of healthy skepticism.

I have taught courses on the Vietnam War at the University of Florida nearly every year since the late 1980s. I also offered a Vietnam War course at University College Dublin in 1999–2000, where I taught as the visiting Mary Ball Washington Professor of U.S. History. My students in each of those courses have invariably brought fresh questions and perspectives to the study of an event that, for most, occurred before they were born. They have shaped my own thinking about the Vietnam War and its impact, and hence the contours of this volume, in countless ways. For all those reasons, this volume is dedicated to my students.

R. J. M.

Commonly Used Acronyms

ARVN	Army of the Republic of Vietnam
CIA	Central Intelligence Agency
CINCPAC	U.S. Commander in Chief, Pacific
COSVN	Central Office for South Vietnam of the Communist Party
DMZ	Demilitarized Zone
DRV	Democratic Republic of Vietnam (North Vietnam)
GVN	Government of Vietnam (South Vietnam)
ICP	Indochinese Communist Party
JCS	Joint Chiefs of Staff
MAAG	U.S. Military Assistance Advisory Group
MACV	U.S. Military Assistance Command, Vietnam
MR	Military Region
NLF	National Liberation Front
NSC	National Security Council
NVA	North Vietnamese Army
NVN	North Vietnam
PAVN	Peoples' Army of Vietnam (regular army of North Vietnam)
PLAF	Peoples' Liberation Armed Forces (regular army of the NLF, then PRG)
PRG	Provisional Revolutionary Government
RVN	Republic of Vietnam (South Vietnam)
RVNAF	Republic of Vietnam Armed Forces
SEA	Southeast Asia
SEATO	Southeast Asia Treaty Organization
SVN	South Vietnam
VC	Vietcong

Southeast Asia

■ Major U.S. Bases during the Vietnam War

BURMA

Lao Cai
Cao Bang
Red R.
Thai Nguyen
Loc Binh
Dien Bien Phu
Black R.
Hanoi
Haiphong
Zhanjiang
(Harbor mined, 1972)
Nam Dinh
Gulf of Tonkin
NORTH
Thanh Hoa
("Maddox" attacked, 1964)
VIETNAM
Vinh
U.S. SEVENTH FLEET
Luang Prabang
Plain of Jars
Chiang Mai
Nan
(Pathet Lao Victory, 1975)
Vientiane
MU GIA PASS
Demarcation Line, July 1954
17°
Rangoon
Udon Thani
Nakhon Phanom
Sépone
Khe Sanh
DEMILITARIZED ZONE
Hué
Phitsanulok
THAILAND
Khon Kaen
Da Nang
My Lai
Chu Lai
Quang Ngai
Ubon Ratchathani
Ta Khli
Rachasima
Dak To
Kontum
Ban San Keo
Pleiku
An Khe
Qui Nhon
Duc Co
CENTRAL
Don Muang
Bangkok
Vietnamese Invasion, 1978
KAMPUCHEA (CAMBODIA)
SOUTH HIGHLANDS
VIETNAM
Nha Trang
Sattahip
Tonle Sap
Pursat
U.S. Invasion, 1970
Dalat
Cam Ranh Bay
ANDAMAN SEA
Kompong Cham
Bu Dop
Bien Hoa
Long Binh
Gulf of Siam
Phnom Penh
(Khmer Rouge Victory, 1975)
Cholon
Tan Son Nhut
Saigon
Vung Tau
Wai Is.
("Mayagues" Incident, 1975)
My Tho
Vinh Long
Ben Tre
Ca Mau Peninsula
Can Tho
U.S. Withdrawal, 1975
Mekong Delta
"Boat People" Refugees after 1975

SOUTH CHINA SEA

0   100   200   300
Miles

The Tet Offensive
January–February, 1968

THAILAND
LAOS
Khe Sanh
Lang Vei
Quang Tri
Hué
A Chau
Da Nang
Hoian
Mekong R.
Kham Duc
Dak To
Quang Ngai
Kontum
Pleiku
Qui Nhon
KAMPUCHEA
Tonle Sap
(CAMBODIA)
SOUTH
Ben Ma Thuot
Tuy Hoa
VIETNAM
Nha Trang
Dalat
Chau Duc
Cholon
Bien Hoa
My Tho
Saigon
Vinh Long
Ben Tre
Can Tho
Ca Mau

☆ Major Battles

MALAYSIA

From Thomas G. Paterson, *American Foreign Policy: A History, Since 1900,* 3rd ed. (Heath, 1988), p. 559.

CHAPTER
1

Vietnam and America:

An Introduction

✗

America's longest war, the Vietnam conflict also was one of its most divisive. As U.S. troop levels swelled to more than half a million by the late 1960s, American society split sharply over the morality and efficacy of the war effort. The war's inconclusiveness and unpopularity spawned not only a broad-based antiwar movement but also a reexamination of America's purpose as wrenching and far-reaching as any other since the Civil War. Neither President Richard M. Nixon's decision in 1969 to begin withdrawing U.S. troops nor the fall of Saigon to the communists in April 1975 did much to resolve the debate or to ease the traumas that it unleashed.

The selections in this opening chapter explore the larger boundaries of that debate by focusing on the following questions: Why did the United States intervene in Vietnam: to defend freedom and liberty or to protect imperial interests dictated by America's world position and economic needs? What did the United States seek to accomplish in Vietnam? Were its goals attainable? Who were its enemies? its allies? Can U.S. actions there be characterized as moral—or immoral? In the larger scope of U.S., Asian, and world history, how should the Vietnam War be interpreted and judged?

✗ *E S S A Y*

In the opening essay, Michael H. Hunt, a professor of history at the University of North Carolina, Chapel Hill, emphasizes the crippling costs that the Vietnam War exacted on both Vietnamese and Americans. He suggests that American leaders bear an especially heavy responsibility for the war's enormous human toll and for its unsettling consequences within Indochina and within the United States because they blindly plunged into an unnecessary conflict for wider Cold War considerations.

Author and journalist Michael Lind, the Washington editor of *Harper's Magazine*, offers a different perspective. He argues in the next selection that American intervention in Vietnam was both necessary and justifiable, characterizing the conflict as a limited war fought to defend South Vietnam and its neighbors against communist aggression. The United States also intervened in Indochina, and appropriately so, Lind asserts, to

1

demonstrate its credibility as a military power and its reliability as an ally, each a critical consideration in the context of the Cold War.

In the final essay, Robert Mann depicts the Vietnam War as a calamity for the United States that has exerted a negative impact on American society, politics, and diplomacy ever since. A former U.S. Senate aide and reporter, Mann contends that the war constituted "a grand and very tragic delusion" for the United States that could, and should, have been avoided.

The Wages of War

MICHAEL H. HUNT

William Shakespeare's *Henry V* has an English soldier about to face a superior French force remark grimly on the mayhem to come and the responsibility borne by leaders whose embrace of war produces that mayhem:

> [I]f the cause be not good, the King himself hath a heavy reckoning to make, when all those legs and arms and heads, chopped off in a battle, shall join together at the latter day and cry all, "We died at such a place"; some swearing, some crying for a surgeon, some upon their wives left poor behind them, some upon the debts they owe, some upon their children rawly left. I am afeard there are few die well that die in a battle.

This eloquent call from the ranks directs our attention to the "heavy reckoning" to which leaders, foremost Lyndon Johnson in this case, must submit.

In Vietnam an estimated 1.4 million—civilians as well as combatants on one side or the other—died during the U.S. combat phase of the war (1965 through 1972), and another 300,000 fell in the subsequent period down to April 1975. (Of these deaths perhaps only about 50,000 were the result of the controversial bombing of the North.) Saigon's forces alone suffered a total of 220,000 killed. By 1972 South Vietnam, with a population short of eighteen million, may have had a total of over ten million refugees. By the war's end a united Vietnam had 300,000 combatants lost without trace, some 1.4 million disabled and half a million orphans to care for, and schools, hospitals, and other public facilities to rebuild. The environment, especially in the South, had suffered long-term damage from the concentrated, even stupefying, application of U.S. ordnance (some fifteen million tons down to 1972) and from extensive spraying of herbicides (nineteen million gallons, well over half deadly dioxins). Unexploded bombs and shells seeded the soil both north and south.

While postwar Vietnam escaped the bloodbath that some had predicted, unification still proved a rocky road for a leadership good at struggle but less skillful at managing the politics of peace and development. Hanoi moved quickly to clap some 100,000 of those prominent in the old regime into "reeducation camps." It followed in the late 1970s by imposing roughshod a program of integrating the south (with its distinct style and strong French and American imprint) into the existing northern system of centralized political control and economic planning. Joblessness, already high because of the large numbers of demobilized soldiers, climbed still higher. A newly collectivized agricultural sector suffered an immediate fall in rice output. The resulting economic crisis together with persecution of ethnic Chinese produced a second round of refugees, the "boat people."

These domestic difficulties were intensified by conflict within the region. Relations with Cambodia deteriorated following border skirmishes provoked by the new Pol Pot regime and climaxing in 1979 with the Vietnamese invasion and occupation of a country gripped by a frenzy of self-destruction. An already suspicious Beijing at once responded by sending a punitive expedition against the upstart Vietnamese. With few friends and with influential Chinese and American enemies, Vietnam became heavily dependent on the Soviet Union both strategically and economically. An annual Soviet subsidy of $1–$2 billion kept a struggling Vietnam afloat through the 1980s.

Hanoi fundamentally revised its course in December 1986 following the death of the dominant figure in the Workers' Party, Le Duan. His replacement, Nguyen Van Linh, was a northerner who had served in the south between 1945 and 1975 and thereafter established a reputation as a maverick reformer. Linh implemented a new economic policy that returned land to peasants, stimulated free markets, encouraged foreign investment, promoted production for export, and tapped the agricultural and commercial expertise of the south. His foreign policy, geared to resolving outstanding conflicts, helped open foreign markets and attract foreign capital, both critical to developing one of the poorest countries in the world. Détente with China followed in 1991 and with the United States in 1995. Returning Americans were astonished by the lack of animosity and bitterness they encountered. Vietnamese had seemingly submerged the trauma of the war in the old and deep tradition of resistance and patriotism. They had played by a familiar national script, and, despite the high price, the promise of victory had been realized.

Cambodia, though it sought to remain a bystander to the conflict in Vietnam, may have suffered even more death and destruction. Incursions by NLF, DRV, Saigon, and American forces, together with devastating and repeated U.S. bombing raids, intensified the havoc already created by civil war and radicalized Cambodia's own revolutionary forces, the Khmer Rouge. Following [Prime Minister Norodom] Sihanouk's overthrow in 1970, this multifaceted conflict cost the lives of approximately a half million (mostly noncombatants), and roughly half the rural population (more than two million) became refugees, straining the cities and reducing agricultural production. Just as the war in Vietnam died out in April 1975, the Khmer Rouge came to power in what would turn into a reign of terror, starvation, and death. Pol Pot emptied the cities in his quest to purify his country of class enemies, those urbanites tainted by privilege and foreign influence. While some 300,000 of the elite fled into exile, perhaps 20 percent (roughly 1.5 million) of the remaining population died between 1975 and 1979 from revolutionary violence or deprivation. Vietnam's intervention in 1979 toppled the genocidal Khmer Rouge but also set off another cycle of civil conflict. Only in the early 1990s did the turmoil begin to ease.

In comparative terms, it is fair to say that the United States suffered only a flesh wound, although this estimate of the price Americans paid may be particularly difficult to accept for those whose lives were disrupted or whose loved ones were lost in the war. American soldiers killed in action, numbering slightly over 58,000, were but a quarter of the losses suffered by the despised Saigon forces and less than a twentieth of all the Vietnamese lives lost during the U.S. phase of the war. The treasure spent in waging the distant war came to but a small proportion of total national wealth, although a look at the actual numbers can be disconcerting. Military outlays between 1961 and 1975 totaled $141 billion. Long-term obligations such as care for veterans push the figure (by one rough estimate) into the range of $350 billion.

The American wound has been slow to heal, perhaps because the damage was more deeply psychic than physical. Involvement in Vietnam created bitter, deep, and lasting divisions within the country and left painful memories for many who served there (in all, some 2.7 million). So central has Vietnam become as a point of political and cultural reference that it invites comparison to the commanding place of Munich in the mind of an earlier generation. But while Munich and the broader experience of World War II gave rise to the crystalline certainties of the Cold War, Vietnam has assumed a far more ambiguous status that has made it a source of confusion and contention.

The willed amnesia that set in as the war drew to a close was broken by veterans. They began writing and talking as a form of therapy for what seemed to many troubling, wasted sacrifice. Their personal need to remember and understand forced the Vietnam experience back into the national consciousness. The rediscovery of Vietnam gave rise to acts of homage to those who served, nowhere more dramatically than at the Vietnam Veterans Memorial, built in 1982 in the heart of the capital, hardly a stone's throw from the White House, where the decisions for war had been made. Americans flocked to visit the low, stark black stone slab covered with the names of those who did not return.

The rediscovery of Vietnam also gave rise to disputes over what went wrong and what lessons to draw. Politicians, pundits, and the entertainment industry were soon in full cry. They generally agreed that Vietnam represented a national fall from grace, but differed fundamentally over whether the war was the best and the protest the worst or whether the war itself reflected the worst in the country and the protest the best.

Descendants of the wartime hawks took as their task expunging the blot on U.S. history and character. They placed blame for the first decisive American military defeat and the humiliation of a superpower at the apogee of its strength on Lyndon Johnson's poor leadership, irresponsible guidance by his team of advisers, and a national decline that had eroded patriotism and given rise to a radical antiwar movement. Ronald Reagan's estimate that the Vietnam War was a justified effort to stop the fall of dominoes and "counter the master plan of the communists for world conquest" and that, once America was committed, victory was the only acceptable goal expressed this influential "revisionist" point of view. The triumphant Grenada and Panama interventions and the Gulf War reflected the determination of Reagan as well as his successor, George Bush, to disprove what many feared Vietnam had shown—that the United States had become a pitiful, helpless giant.

The descendants of the doves traced the origins of Vietnam back to a lamentable Cold War arrogance. The United States had taken upon itself the role of world policeman without knowing the neighborhoods it presumed to patrol and without the informed consent of the American people. The practical conclusion drawn by latter-day doves and shared by much of the public was to approach intervention warily, a viewpoint that put a brake on the foreign-policy activism which was so marked a feature of the Cold War. As a result, Reagan had to reverse course following his intervention in Lebanon, and his involvement in Nicaragua and El Salvador encountered public and congressional opposition so strong that he had to pursue his goals covertly (resulting in the Iran-Contra affair).

The U.S. military drew its own lessons from Vietnam. Commentators took due note of the public impatience with an inconclusive war, the dangers of civilian interference in the conduct of war, and the risks inherent in free media access to the combat zone. The conclusion—applied in Grenada, Panama, and the Persian Gulf—was to fight only where U.S. goals were clear, public support assured, power overwhelming, and thus victory certain. How cautious Vietnam had left the U.S. military became dramatically evident in the Gulf War. The war did yield the quick military victory at a low cost in American lives, as it was designed to do. But it also ended inconclusively, with the agent of aggression, Saddam Hussein, still in power. This outcome did not so much kick as confirm the Vietnam syndrome. Americans nonetheless celebrated the triumph over Iraq as the surrogate for the victory that had eluded them in Vietnam.

Like any dramatic and controversial event, the Vietnam War was soon appropriated by Hollywood and conveyed to a fascinated public as a fantasy world where Americans tested their character, underwent youthful rites of passage, embarked on perilous rescues, suffered personal or national corruption, or replayed frontier dramas with the Vietnamese as the "wild Indians." Seldom in these re-creations did Vietnamese figure as anything more than two-dimensional stock figures. The war remained, as much as during the Cold War, an American drama in which the people of Vietnam played only minor parts.

The crosscurrents at work within the American mind were nowhere more evident than in the issue of normalizing relations with the former tormentor, the Communist leadership still in charge in Hanoi. Standing in the way of normalization were not only families of the missing-in-action but also the gnawing sense of humiliation over the war's outcome and the natural instinct to seek revenge rather than reconciliation. (Hanoi also threw up obstacles, none more troublesome than a 1977 demand for $3 billion in reparations.) But the 1986 changing of the guard in Hanoi led to greater cooperation in accounting for U.S. missing-in-action, thus removing one major obstacle. It also led to the opening of a new market attractive to U.S. corporations. By the early 1990s a majority of Americans supported normalization, and veterans groups were becoming vocal in support of reconciliation. President Bill Clinton, though embarrassed by his own avoidance of service in Vietnam, began the intricate process of rebuilding ties. Accounting for the missing-in-action (down to 1,621 by mid-1995) was the first serious step; removing the travel and trade embargoes was the next; establishing diplomatic relations in 1995 became the last.

The American wound is healing, but a scar remains. The small and distant country of Vietnam is intrinsically hardly more important today than it was when Franklin Roosevelt casually contemplated its future in 1943 or when [Harry] Truman fatefully placed it within the containment framework in 1950. Vietnam figured, above all else, at each of these and other critical turning points as a test—a test of American character and ideals. How Americans responded was a kind of referendum on their world leadership and the viability of their institutions and values.

But confident Americans with their globe-girdling organization and awesome technology did not prevail. Caught up in their Cold War crusade, U.S. leaders had plunged reluctantly and blindly into Vietnam. What they encountered was a people with a will and solidarity that far exceeded their own, with allies ready to take real risks, and, in the final analysis, with a capacity to absorb the blows of an uneven war undeterred until the enemy—demoralized in the field, divided at home—abandoned Vietnam to its stubborn people, just as the Chinese and the French had done. Americans are likely to continue to examine the war with its unsettling outcome as they might look into a mirror, the better to reflect on not just their recent tumultuous Cold War past but also their long-held claim as a special people.

The Necessary War

MICHAEL LIND

The U.S. wars in the Balkan and Indochinese peninsulas differed in one fundamental respect. The Yugoslav War [of 1999] was not a proxy war among great powers. Although Russia protested the NATO war against the Serbs and supplied some limited assistance to the [Slobodan] Milosevic regime, postcommunist Russia, truncated, impoverished, and weak in the aftermath of the Soviet collapse, did not commit itself to defeating American policy in the Balkans. The situation was radically different in the 1960s. The Vietnam War was a proxy war between the United States, the Soviet Union—then growing rapidly in military power, confidence, and prestige—and communist China. Despite their rivalry for leadership of the communist bloc of nations, the Soviets and the Chinese collaborated to support North Vietnam's effort to destroy South Vietnam, to promote communist revolutions in Indochina and, if possible, Thailand, and to humiliate the United States. In the 1990s, Serbia was a third-rate military power lacking great-power patrons. In the 1960s, North Vietnam was protected from an American invasion, and equipped with state-of-the-art weapons and air defenses, by the Soviet Union and China, the latter of which sent hundreds of thousands of troops to support Ho Chi Minh's war effort between 1965 and 1968. By the late 1970s, the Vietnamese communists, after annexing South Vietnam, occupying Cambodia, and breaking with and defeating China in a border war, possessed the third largest army in the world and ruled the most important satellite region of the Soviet empire outside Eastern Europe. At the time of the Vietnam War, the United States was engaged in a desperate worldwide struggle with two of the three most powerful and murderous totalitarian states in history; in 1999, the United States faced no significant challenge to its global primacy by another great power or coalition.

The American wars in defense of Kosovo and South Vietnam, then, differed chiefly in this respect: More—far more—was at stake in Vietnam.

As a result of the U.S. intervention in the Balkans, the assumption that America's intervention in Vietnam was an aberration, an assumption shared by many critics

Reprinted and edited with the permission of The Free Press, an imprint of Simon & Schuster Adult Publishing Group, from *Vietnam: The Necessary War: A Reinterpretation of America's Most Disastrous Military Conflict* by Michael Lind. Copyright © 1999 by Michael Lind.

across the political spectrum, is no longer plausible. Twice in thirty-five years, American armed forces have engaged in massive military intervention in a civil war in a peripheral region in order to demonstrate the credibility of the United States as a military power and an alliance leader. When the Korean War is taken into account, the Vietnam War looks less like an exception and more like one member of a series of similar American limited wars (as of 1999, the Gulf War looks like the exception to the norm established by the Korean, Vietnam, and Yugoslav wars). Whether or not the American intervention in Kosovo ultimately achieves its goals, one thing is certain—the debate about the Vietnam War in the United States will never again be the same.

After the Vietnam War ended in 1975, it took on a second life as a symbol in American politics. For the radical left, the war was a symbol of the depravity of the United States and the evils of "capitalist imperialism." For the neoisolationists and "realists" of the liberal left, the U.S. war in Indochina was a tragic and unnecessary mistake, brought about by American arrogance and an exaggerated fear of the threat posed to U.S. interests by the Soviet Union and communist China. Conservatives, too, had their orthodox view of the conflict. Conservatives joined many military officers in arguing that the United States could have achieved a quick and decisive victory in Indochina, if only the pusillanimous civilian policymakers of the Kennedy and Johnson administrations had not "tied the hands" of the U.S. military and "denied it permission to win."

One point of view has been missing from the debate over the Vietnam War. The political faction known as liberal anticommunists or Cold War liberals, identified with the Truman, Kennedy, and Johnson administrations, ceased to exist as a force in American politics in the 1970s, more as a result of partisan realignment than of the Vietnam War. One group of former Cold War liberal policymakers and thinkers sought to ingratiate themselves with the antiwar leftists and liberals who were ascendant in the Democratic party after 1968. Among these were the late McGeorge Bundy and his brother William (who, as part of his campaign to rehabilitate himself, recently wrote a harsh and unfair book criticizing Nixon's and Kissinger's handling of the war that the Bundys had helped to begin). Former defense secretary Robert McNamara not only recanted his support for the war in his book *In Retrospect* but endured the abuse of functionaries of the Vietnamese dictatorship during a humiliating pilgrimage to Vietnam in 1997. Another group of former Cold War liberals joined forces with anti-Soviet conservatives, maintaining their support for the Cold War while jettisoning their prolabor liberalism in domestic politics. The number of unreconstructed Cold War liberals thus dwindled in the 1970s and 1980s, making it easy for radical leftists, left-liberals, and conservatives, in their discussions of the Vietnam War and U.S. foreign policy in the 1960s, to caricature and vilify Presidents Kennedy and Johnson and their advisers with no fear of rebuttal.

Almost everything written by Americans about the Vietnam War in the past quarter century has conformed to one of the three scripts of radical leftism, anti–Cold War liberalism, or conservatism. Each of these three partisan schools has drawn attention to evidence that appeared to support its preconceptions, while ignoring evidence that contradicted them. These ritualized debates might have continued for another generation or two. But two historic developments have now made it possible to transcend the thirty-year-old debates about the Vietnam War.

The first development is the end of the Cold War and its aftermath, including the global collapse of communism and the realignment of world politics around the United States as the hegemonic military power. Only now is it possible to view the Cold War as a whole and to evaluate the U.S. strategy of global containment that led to the U.S. wars in defense of South Korea and South Vietnam, as well as the U.S. protectorate over Taiwan—"the three fronts," according to Mao Zedong, where the communist bloc met the American bloc in East Asia.

The second development is the demise of the radical left in North America and Western Europe as a political force (leftism survives only in pockets in the academy and the press). In the 1960s and 1970s, the ascendancy of the radical left in the liberal and social democratic parties of the West—the Democrats in the United States, the British Labor Party, and the German Social Democrats—caused western electorates to turn to conservative, anticommunist parties under the leadership of Ronald Reagan, Margaret Thatcher, and Helmut Kohl. The economic difficulties of Swedish social democracy, coming soon after the collapse of the Soviet Union, have discredited western as well as eastern Marxism and permitted the emergence of a new, more moderate center-left, variously described as "the Third Way" or "the New Center" and symbolized by President Bill Clinton and British prime minister Tony Blair. As recently as the Gulf War, which the overwhelming majority of Democrats in Congress voted against, foreign policy debates in the United States pitted anti-American leftists and isolationist liberals against interventionist conservatives. But the subsequent U.S.-led NATO war in the Balkans, supported by many liberals and opposed by a number of conservatives, has helped to rehabilitate the legitimacy of military intervention for many left-of-center Americans.

These developments in global politics and western politics have made it possible to write this book, which could not have been written in the 1970s or 1980s. In this book, I examine the Vietnam War in light of the end of the Cold War, from a centrist perspective more sympathetic to American Cold War policymakers than that of their critics on the left and the right.

The United States fought the war in Vietnam because of geopolitics, and forfeited the war because of domestic politics. This being the case, I make two major arguments in this [essay], one about the geopolitics, and one about the American domestic politics, of the Cold War. The argument about geopolitics is that in the circumstances of the Cold War, and particularly in the circumstances of the 1960s, the United States was justified in waging a limited war to defend South Vietnam and its neighbors against the communist bloc. The argument about U.S. domestic politics is that the Vietnam War was not uniquely divisive. Rather, this particular Cold War proxy conflict exposed preexisting regional, ethnic, and racial divisions in American attitudes about foreign policy—divisions familiar from previous American wars in the nineteenth and twentieth centuries.

The two subjects of geopolitics and domestic politics are connected by the issue of the costs, in treasure and blood, of American Cold War policy. In both the Korean and Vietnam wars, the balance of power between interventionists and isolationists in the U.S. Congress and the public at large was held by a "swing vote" sensitive to casualties. In the 1960s and 1970s, the United States could not afford to do too little in Indochina, for fear of a disastrous setback in the Cold War—a struggle that was as much a test of nerve as a test of strength. At the same time, the United States could not afford to do too much in Indochina, for fear of undermining American public support, first for the defense of the Indochina front, and then for U.S. Cold War strategy in general. The choice between global credibility and domestic consensus was forced on American leaders in the late 1960s and early 1970s by the costs of the war in Vietnam—chiefly, the costs in American lives, though the costs in Indochinese lives and the costs to America's global military infrastructure and its financial hegemony were also important factors.

This, then, is the story I have to tell about the Vietnam War. It was necessary for the United States to escalate the war in the mid-1960s in order to defend the credibility of the United States as a superpower, but it was necessary for the United States to forfeit the war after 1968, in order to preserve the American domestic political consensus in favor of the Cold War on other fronts. Indochina was worth a war, but only a limited war—and not the limited war that the United States actually fought.

The argument set forth here differs fundamentally from a new and misguided consensus on the subject of the Vietnam War that has become influential in recent years. That argument holds that it was a mistake to intervene in Indochina at all, but that once the United States had intervened, it should have used unlimited force to quickly win an unqualified victory. The political appeal of this emerging consensus is obvious. While it offers nothing to the radical left, it makes concessions to "realist" left-liberals (who are acknowledged to have been right about U.S. strategy) and to promilitary conservatives (who are acknowledged to have been right about U.S. tactics). As a rhetorical formula that can "heal the wounds of Vietnam," this emergent synthesis has much to recommend it. Unfortunately, as an assessment of the Vietnam War it is wrong, and to the extent that it influences U.S. foreign policy it is dangerous. . . .

The Cold War was the third world war of the twentieth century. It was a contest for global military and diplomatic primacy between the United States and the Soviet Union, which had emerged as the two strongest military powers after World War II. Because the threat of nuclear escalation prevented all-out conventional war between the two superpowers, the Soviet-American contest was fought in the form of arms races, covert action, ideological campaigns, economic embargoes, and proxy wars in peripheral areas. In three of these—Korea, Indochina, and Afghanistan—one of the two superpowers sent hundreds of thousands of its own troops into battle against clients of the other side.

In the third world war, Indochina was the most fought over territory on earth. The region owed this undesirable honor not to its intrinsic importance but to the fact that in other places where the two superpowers confronted one another they were frozen in a stalemate that could not be broken without the risk of general war. The Soviet Union and the United States fought proxy wars in Indochina because they dared not engage in major tests of strength in Central Europe or Northeast Asia (after 1953) or even the Middle East. Indochina was strategic *because* it was peripheral.

Throughout the Cold War, the bloody military struggles in the Indochina theater were shaped indirectly by the tense but bloodless diplomatic struggles in the European theater. By going to war in Korea and simultaneously extending an American military protectorate over Taiwan and French Indochina, the Truman administration signaled its resolve to defend its European allies. American officials swallowed their misgivings about French colonialism and paid for France's effort in its on-going war in Indochina from 1950 until 1954, in the hope of winning French support for the rearmament of Germany. Khrushchev's humiliation of the United States in the Berlin crisis of 1961 persuaded the Kennedy administration that a show of American resolve on the Indochina front was all the more important. In 1968, concern by members of the U.S. foreign policy elite that further escalation in Indochina would endanger America's other commitments, particularly in the European theater, was one of the factors that led the Johnson administration to begin the process of disengagement from the Vietnam War. The Eastern European revolutions of 1989, which led to the collapse of the Soviet Union itself in 1991, deprived communist Vietnam of its superpower protector and ideological model. . . .

Who won and who lost in the Vietnam War?

The only complete losers were the officials of South Vietnam, whose state was erased from the map. The North Vietnamese communists won, but at the cost of bankruptcy and isolation when their sponsor the Soviet Union collapsed.

The Vietnamese people as a whole were losers. The loss of around two million Vietnamese on both sides, and the devastation of much of the landscape, was followed by extension of the brutal and irrational Stalinist system of North Vietnam throughout the entire country in 1975. All Vietnamese suffered from the communist victory—those who stayed, and the nearly two million who fled. The Laotian people suffered similarly. The greatest agony befell the Cambodian people, who endured mass murder and large-scale starvation under the rule of the Cambodian communists.

Among the major powers that intervened in Indochina during the Cold War, France, China, and the United States were all losers. France sacrificed nearly one hundred thousand troops and still lost its Southeast Asian empire, upon which its claim to great power status after World War II was partly based. China discovered too late that by helping Hanoi it had created an ally for the hated Soviet Union on its border.

For its part, the United States suffered a devastating defeat. In the zero-sum reputational game of the bipolar world order, Washington's defeat was Moscow's gain. At the same time, the cost in American dead and wounded temporarily destroyed the domestic consensus in favor of the Cold War. The United States negotiated an unfavorable armistice with the Soviet empire and gave up the policy of global containment for the better part of a decade, returning to a militant anti-Soviet policy only in the late 1970s. The Vietnam War, then, was the second greatest defeat suffered by the United States in the Cold War. (The greatest defeat of American Cold War policy, though not of arms, was the victory of the Soviet-sponsored Chinese communists in 1949—a victory without which neither the Korean nor the Indochinese wars would have taken place in the form in which they did, if they had taken place at all.)

It is often said that the United States, an arrogant superpower, was defeated by the heroic efforts of a small, weak nation in Asia. It is not true. The deterrent provided by the Soviet Union and China—particularly the threat that China would intervene with combat troops, as it had in Korea—prevented the United States from invading or engaging in all-out war against North Vietnam. And the Soviet and Chinese military-industrial complexes kept the North Vietnamese effort going until its successful conclusion in 1975, after which even higher levels of Soviet aid made possible Vietnam's empire in Laos and Cambodia. Hanoi's success was inconceivable without the support of two of the three most powerful and murderous totalitarian states in history.

The Vietnam War inaugurated the era of the greatest Soviet successes in the Cold War. If the impositions of communist regimes by the Red Army and Soviet agents in Eastern Europe are not counted as genuine revolutions, then the greatest triumphs of the Soviet Union in sponsoring Marxist-Leninist regimes around the world came in the 1970s, when the United States, bloodied in Indochina, temporarily abandoned the containment strategy and began retreating into isolationism. By supporting Stalin's disciple, Ho Chi Minh, and his successors in a proxy war, the Soviet leaders, at a relatively small cost to themselves, regained world revolutionary leadership from Mao's China, pinned down China on its southern border, and humiliated and temporarily paralyzed the United States.

The only clear winner of the Vietnam War, then, was the Soviet Union. . . .

While the U.S. intervention in Vietnam served a number of complementary purposes, there was a hierarchy among U.S. goals. The administrations of Kennedy, Johnson, and Nixon may not have made that hierarchy as clear as intellectuals would like. Nevertheless, in hindsight it is possible to identify the place assigned to different goals in the hierarchy of purposes by these three presidents and their aides. The chief purpose of the United States in Vietnam was to demonstrate America's credibility as a military power and a reliable ally to its enemies and its allies around the world. The danger was that if the United States were perceived to be lacking in military capacity, political resolve, or both, the Soviet Union and/or China and their proxies would act more aggressively, while U.S. allies, including important industrial democracies such as West Germany and Japan, would be inclined to appease the communist great powers. It was in this global geopolitical context that preventing "falling dominoes"—whether in Southeast Asia proper, or in Third World countries far from Vietnam—was important. Least important of all the U.S. purposes in intervening in Vietnam was promoting liberty, democracy, and prosperity in South Vietnam itself. The defeat of the attempted takeover of South Vietnam by North Vietnam was a necessary, but not sufficient, condition for the evolution of the authoritarian government of South Vietnam toward liberalism and democracy. But America's political goals in South Vietnam were appropriately incidental and subordinate to America's goals in Southeast Asian power politics, which, in turn, were incidental and subordinate to America's global strategy in the third world war.

A Grand Delusion

ROBERT MANN

More than a quarter century after the last American combat troops left Southeast Asia, the social and political fires of the Vietnam War continue to burn throughout the United States and Vietnam. Millions of citizens in both countries bear the deep, painful scars of a twenty-five-year conflict that wreaked havoc on the political and

---

social landscapes of the United States and Vietnam. Even today, legions of war veterans endure the physical and emotional wounds inflicted during their tours of duty, while the 3 million people who perished on all sides are only memories to millions of husbands, wives, children, grandchildren, parents, siblings, and friends.

In the United States, the nation's ill-advised military foray into Vietnam continues to impact our political institutions. The war has emerged as an issue in virtually every presidential election, and many congressional elections, since it ended. Lately, those candidates who avoided service must, decades after the fact, defend impetuous—and sometimes calculating—decisions made in their teens.

More significant for Americans, however, may be the war's lasting impact on the country's government and its foreign and defense policies. The ghosts of Vietnam, former combat journalist Ward Just has observed, will not leave us, "rising whenever Washington contemplates a military adventure." In the years since the war's end, every American military action has been influenced by the experience of Vietnam. "For American statecraft," Just argues, "the legacy is as profound as that of World War II." Journalist Myra MacPherson's astute observations about the war, from her 1984 book, *Long Time Passing: Vietnam & the Haunted Generation,* remain timely: Vietnam's "consequences are still being felt in our foreign policy . . . in a haunted generation, in the new generation faced with possible new Vietnams, and in our hearts and minds."

The Vietnam War also profoundly altered Americans' view of their public institutions. While polls suggest that public confidence in the federal government has not declined significantly in more than thirty years, Vietnam did awaken millions of Americans to the fact that their presidents had routinely lied to them—about the American military role in Southeast Asia, about Watergate, and about a host of other issues.

Vietnam was, indeed, a turning point in American political history. The war destroyed the New Deal political coalition that dominated American politics for nearly four decades, opening the door to new and equally potent political forces that lasted into the twenty-first century. Vietnam unleashed a level and variety of public dissent never before seen in American politics, but one that profoundly altered the ways that the American people communicate with their elected leaders.

Before the war, and the Watergate scandal it helped to spawn, news reporters, the public, and even members of Congress generally accepted information supplied from presidents and their advisors. In the wake of the war and the Watergate scandal, the press and the American people grew, if not less trustful, more apathetic about government and doubtful of its ability to positively impact their lives. Congress, in turn, grew more adversarial in its relationship with the executive branch and—beginning with the War Powers Act in 1973—more zealous of its own constitutional prerogatives. Without a war in Vietnam and the political turmoil it sparked, it is unlikely that Richard Nixon, and perhaps even Ronald Reagan, would have been elected president.

The Vietnam War, a renowned sociologist has observed, actually divided America's historical view of itself: "On one side of that history," Todd Gitlin wrote, "America, whatever its rights and its wrongs, stands triumphant, its glorious destiny manifest. On the other, America knows defeat, even shame."

The tragedy of Vietnam, however, cannot be measured only by the conflict's dead-and-wounded statistics or by its impact on American society, politics, or diplomacy. Compounding the calamity is the simple fact that millions of deaths might have been averted had the American people and their leaders opened their eyes to the delusions leading them progressively deeper into the morass of Southeast Asia in the 1950s and 1960s—a national crusade undertaken to defeat an enemy that had once been our ally and that had originally wanted nothing more than independence from brutal colonial rule.

From beginning to end, America's political, military, and diplomatic leaders deluded themselves, accepting a series of myths and illusions about Vietnam that exacerbated and deepened the ultimate catastrophe.

• Most Americans and their leaders were deluded about the nature of the threat to freedom in Indochina, concluding that it was only "international" communism and not French colonialism. They also believed that the communist-supported nationalistic movement in Indochina was not indigenous, but directed from Moscow and Peking.

• President Eisenhower and his advisors were deluded about the success of their policies in Indochina and wrongly concluded that the armed struggle against the Vietminh guerrillas in the mid- and late-1950s was being won.

• American leaders in the 1950s were deluded about South Vietnamese Prime Minister Ngo Dinh Diem, wrongly concluding that he was a reformer dedicated to democratic ideals.

• President John F. Kennedy was deluded about the course of the conflict during his administration. With disastrous results, he disregarded the young reporters in South Vietnam who alerted him and their readers to the serious deficiencies of the American-backed South Vietnamese government and its military forces. Relying on advisors like Vice President Lyndon Johnson, Defense Secretary Robert McNamara, Secretary of State Dean Rusk, and National Security Advisor McGeorge Bundy, Kennedy rejected a fundamental reappraisal of U.S. policy in Vietnam that might have halted or slowed the nation's descent into the quagmire of Southeast Asia.

• Throughout the 1960s, Kennedy, Johnson, and other American political leaders were deluded about the true nature of the conflict. They wrongly assumed that the war was primarily a military, not a political struggle and that the application of military might was a legitimate substitute for an educated program to help the South Vietnamese regime win the "hearts and minds" of its people.

• American voters in 1964 were innocently deluded about Johnson's intentions in Vietnam, believing his promises of "no wider war."

• Leaders in Congress were deluded and misled about the nature of the incidents in the Gulf of Tonkin in August 1964, which resulted in a breathtaking grant of war-making power to Johnson from Congress in days following the incidents.

• Like Kennedy, President Johnson and his advisors were deluded by the prospects of military might—particularly bombing—and believed that a military solution, short of destroying North Vietnam, was possible.

• Both Johnson and his successor, Richard Nixon, successfully deluded American voters about the steps they were willing to take to achieve peace. In the 1968 election, American voters were again deluded by a winning presidential candidate when Nixon suggested that he possessed a plan to end the war with "honor." During the early months of Nixon's presidency, opponents of the war in Congress were also deluded into believing that Nixon planned to move quickly to end the fighting.

For the United States, Vietnam itself was a grand and very tragic delusion—a country that the American people and their leaders believed could be "saved" from what they believed was a Soviet-controlled communist regime that threatened to consume all of Southeast Asia. Indeed, for almost two decades, American leaders mistakenly concluded that the United States had the power, the will, and the means to win the war—if a definition of victory could ever be universally accepted. . . .

During the Vietnam era, had our presidents been honest with Congress and the American people, had members of Congress more closely guarded their constitutional war-making prerogatives, and had the American people and their leaders been better informed about Vietnam and the American policy there, millions of lives might have been spared and untold misery avoided.

✗ *F U R T H E R   R E A D I N G*

Addington, Larry H. *America's War in Vietnam* (2000).
Anderson, David L., ed. *Shadow on the White House: Presidents and the Vietnam War, 1945–1975* (1993).
———, ed. *The Columbia Guide to the Vietnam War* (2002).
Baritz, Loren. *Backfire* (1985).
Braestrup, Peter, ed. *Vietnam as History* (1984).
Brodie, Bernard. *War and Politics* (1973).
Charlton, Michael, and Anthony Moncrief. *Many Reasons Why* (1978).
Cooper, Chester A. *The Lost Crusade* (1970).
Davidson, Phillip B. *Vietnam at War* (1988).
DeGrout, Gerard J. *A Noble Cause?* (2000).
Edelman, Bernard, ed. *Dear America: Letters Home from Vietnam* (1985).
Ellsberg, Daniel. *Papers on the War* (1972).
Emerson, Gloria. *Winners and Losers* (1976).
Errington, Elizabeth Jane, and B. J. C. McKercher, eds. *The Vietnam War as History* (1990).
FitzGerald, Frances. *Fire in the Lake* (1972).
Gelb, Leslie H., and Richard K. Betts. *The Irony of Vietnam: The System Worked* (1979).
Gibbons, William C. *The U.S. Government and the Vietnam War* (1985–1995).
Gibson, James William. *The Perfect War* (1986).
Halberstam, David. *The Best and the Brightest* (1972).
Harrison, James Pinckney. *The Endless War* (1982).
Hearden, Patrick J. *The Tragedy of Vietnam* (1991).
———, ed. *Vietnam: Four American Perspectives* (1990).
Herring, George C. *America's Longest War* (1996).
Hess, Gary R. *Vietnam and the United States* (1990).
Higgins, Hugh. *Vietnam* (1982).
Joes, Anthony James. *The War for South Vietnam* (1990).
Joseph, Paul. *Cracks in the Empire: State Politics in the Vietnam War* (1981).
Kahin, George McT. *Intervention* (1986).
Kahin, George McT., and John W. Lewis. *The United States in Vietnam* (1969).
Kattenburg, Paul M. *The Vietnam Trauma in American Foreign Policy, 1945–1975* (1980).
Kolko, Gabriel. *Anatomy of a War* (1985).
Kutler, Stanley I., ed. *Encyclopedia of the Vietnam War* (1996).
Langguth, A. J. *Our Vietnam* (2000).
Lewy, Guenther. *America in Vietnam* (1978).
Lomperis, Timothy J. *The War Everyone Lost—and Won* (1984).
Maclear, Michael. *The Ten Thousand Day War* (1981).

McMahon, Robert J. *The Limits of Empire: The United States and Southeast Asia Since World War II* (1999).
McNamara, Robert S., et al. *Argument Without End* (1999).
Moss, George Donelson. *Vietnam* (1998).
Olson, James S., and Randy Roberts. *Where the Domino Fell* (1999).
Osborn, George K., et al., eds. *Democracy, Strategy, and Vietnam* (1987).
Podhoretz, Norman. *Why We Were in Vietnam* (1982).
Pratt, John Clark. *Vietnam Voices* (1984).
Schlesinger, Arthur M., Jr. *The Bitter Heritage* (1966).
Schulzinger, Robert D. *A Time for War* (1997).
Short, Anthony. *The Origins of the Vietnam War* (1989).
Thomson, James. "How Could Vietnam Happen? An Autopsy," *Atlantic Monthly,* 221 (1968), 47–53.
Tucker, Spencer C., ed. *The Encyclopedia of the Vietnam War* (1998).
Turley, William S. *The Second Indochina War* (1986).
Young, Marilyn B. *The Vietnam Wars, 1945–1990* (1991).

CHAPTER
2

The Development of Vietnamese Nationalism

✕

History, culture, and geography exert powerful influences on all peoples and nations. Vietnam is no exception. American officials were often accused of approaching Vietnam with little understanding of its culture and language, and even less appreciation of its rich history—forces that, specialists now agree, contributed mightily to the war's outcome.

One of the ironic effects of the war is that it generated an explosion of new scholarship on Vietnamese history, especially in the United States. Recent historical literature has paid particular attention to the genesis of modern Vietnamese nationalism, which is the focus of the selections in this chapter. In their endeavors, scholars have sought to account for elements of continuity and discontinuity in Vietnam's long history; tried to assess the impact of French colonial rule on the social structure, economic life, and intellectual outlook within the country; and struggled to explain the emergence of a strong Communist party within the larger nationalist movement.

✕ *D O C U M E N T S*

Document 1 is a selection from the prison notes of Phan Boi Chau, still revered as one of Vietnam's great nationalists. These reflections were written in 1914 while Chau was imprisoned in China, at the request of the French, for nationalist activities. From his release in 1917 until his death in 1941, he continued to agitate for Vietnamese independence. Document 2 contains comments made by Nguyen Ai Quoc (more commonly known by his adopted name, Ho Chi Minh) at a National Congress of the French Socialist party, held at Tours in December 1920. After denouncing French imperialism in his native land, he approved the resolution to found the French Communist party and to join the Third International. On February 3, 1930, Ho helped to establish the Communist party of Indochina. In Document 3, he exhorts his countrymen to join the party and to forge a revolution against French rule.

During the closing months of World War II, a terrible feminine that ultimately would claim between 1 and 2 million lives swept across northern Vietnam. The tragedy, which most Vietnamese blamed on the callousness of French and Japanese policies,

16

dramatically increased the appeal of the Vietnamese communist movement throughout the country. Document 4 is a selection from a book by Vietnamese writer Tran Van Mai, written at the time, and offers a firsthand account of the desperate conditions brought on by the famine. On September 2, 1945, Ho proclaimed an independent Democratic Republic of Vietnam; the declaration, which borrowed deliberately from the American Declaration of Independence, appears in Document 5.

1. Phan Boi Chau's Prison Reflections, 1914

The great victory of Japan in the Russo-Japanese war [1904–05] had a tremendous impact upon us. For it was like a new and strange world opening up.

Before the time of the French Protectorate, Vietnam only knew a world with China. And when the French arrived we only knew a world with France. But the world had changed. A strange new wave as yet undreamed of had arrived.

We had been caught up in our internal affairs for so long that even if our heads were cut off and our bodies lost we still had no fear. We were that way only because we cared for our country and our conscience forced us to be so. As for a way to build independence, at that time we were still dreaming in a very thick fog.

Alas! In the middle of the nineteenth century, even though the universe was shaken by American winds and European rains, our country was still in a period of dreaming in a deep sleep. Our people were still blind and resigned to their lot. We cannot blame them, for even well-known people from the higher classes like myself were like frogs in the bottom of a well or ants at the bottom of their hole. We knew nothing about life. I think that there must be no more tragic-comic people in the world than our people.

It is only because in former times we shut our doors and stayed at home, going round and round in circles of literary knowledge, examinations and Chinese studies. To say frankly that our people were deaf and blind is no exaggeration.

Even after the French invasion our people were still deaf and blind. If we had not been awakened by the violent sound of the guns at Port Arthur, perhaps we should not yet know that there were other foreign countries besides France.

After the beginning of the Russo-Japanese hostilities, during the years of the Dragon [1904] and the Serpent [1905], the competition and struggle between the Europeans and the Asians, between the white-skinned people and the yellow-skinned people, forced us to wake up with a start. We became increasingly enthusiastic and intense in our commitment to our ideals. The only problem we still sought to overcome was that of obtaining weapons. . . .

When in jail, it is of course no use to lament one's pain. But there is the sorrowful fact that I have had to be separated from my brothers, without any news, with only myself to speak Vietnamese for myself to hear, thinking only of my sad destiny. I think of my failures and weep, my tears falling like torrents of rain. Truly, from the day I was born until now I have never known the taste of suffering as I know it now.

But I have arrived at this suffering because of the ambition that I have held for these last thirty years. And what has this ambition been?

From Phan Boi Chau and Ho Chi Minh, *Reflections from Captivity,* David G. Marr. ed., pp. 22–23, 55–56, Ohio University Press, 1978. Reprinted by permission of the author.

It has been but a yearning to purchase my freedom even at the cost of spilling my blood, to exchange my fate of slavery for the right of self-determination.

Ah! With such an ambition I took in my own hands the supreme responsibility of speaking on behalf of my people. Is there anyone who dares say I should not have done this? Yet if such an ambition is to achieve anything great, we must rely on the toughness of our muscles, the excellence of our learning, the skill of our planning, and the careful manipulation of conditions. Instead, I wondered if at best I wasn't just a blind man leading the blind. Now I have failed simply because I am unskilled. I need complain no more.

However, I think that in this world there is no reason why a stream of water once it has flowed downward can never come up again, or why a life once set on its course cannot change. Who knows but that my failure today will not be good fortune for my people tomorrow? . . .

Let the thousands, ten thousands, even hundreds of thousands of my people who bear an ambition such as mine take heed from my failure. Let them become people who can take care of themselves. We must not wait until our finger has been cut the ninth time before we find the bandage.

I realize that I am a man who has not obtained steel weaponry worth holding on to, that on this earth I have laid down no strategy worth standing on. At most I am an empty-handed rogue with nothing to my name, weak in force and feeble in ability. Yet I am ready still to fight long-toothed tigers and sharp-clawed panthers. Those who understand my inner soul might console me by saying:

"What a brave man!"

Those who wish to look at my mistakes might well look down and say:

"What a stupid man!"

To sum up, in this world there is truly no one as stupid as I. If this be the last day of my life and if, upon my death, I still be called by such a forbidden name as "the most stupid," then this is very correct. It is impossible to call me anything else. But if I have the good fortune to survive and if, afterwards, I see tigers and panthers, then surely I will fight. May my people learn their lesson from my example.

2. Ho Chi Minh Deplores "Imperialist Crimes," 1920

Chairman: Comrade Indochinese Delegate, you have the floor.

Indochinese Delegate [Nguyen Ai Quoc]: Today, instead of contributing, together with you, to world revolution, I come here with deep sadness to speak as a member of the Socialist Party, against the imperialists who have committed abhorrent crimes on my native land. You all have known that French imperialism entered Indochina half a century ago. In its selfish interests, it conquered our country with bayonets. Since then we have not only been oppressed and exploited shamelessly, but also tortured and poisoned pitilessly. Plainly speaking, we have been poisoned with opium, alcohol, etc. I cannot, in some minutes, reveal all the atrocities that the predatory capitalists have inflicted on Indochina. Prisons outnumber schools and are

Ho Chi Minh speech at Tours Socialist Congress, December 1920, in Ho Chi Minh, *Selected Writings (1920–1969)* (Hanoi: Foreign Language Publishing House, 1973), pp. 15–17.

always overcrowded with detainees. Any natives having socialist ideas are arrested and sometimes murdered without trial. Such is the so-called justice in Indochina. In that country, the Vietnamese are discriminated against, they do not enjoy safety like Europeans or those having European citizenship. We have neither freedom of press nor freedom of speech. Even freedom of assembly and freedom of association do not exist. We have no right to live in other countries or to go abroad as tourists. We are forced to live in utter ignorance and obscurity because we have no right to study. In Indochina the colonialists find all ways and means to force us to smoke opium and drink alcohol to poison and beset us. Thousands of Vietnamese have been led to a slow death or massacred to protect other people's interests.

Comrades, such is the treatment inflicted upon more than 20 million Vietnamese, that is more than half the population of France. And they are said to be under French protection! The Socialist Party must act practically to support the oppressed natives. . . .

Indochinese Delegate: On behalf of the whole of mankind, on behalf of all the Socialist Party's members, both left and right wings, we call on you! Comrades, save us!

Chairman: Through the applause of approval, the Indochinese Delegate can realize that the whole of the Socialist Party sides with you to oppose the crimes committed by the bourgeois class.

3. Ho's Appeal at the Founding of the Communist Party of Indochina, 1930

Workers, peasants, soldiers, youth, and pupils!

Oppressed and exploited compatriots!

Sisters and brothers! Comrades!

Imperialist contradictions were the cause of the 1914–18 World War. After this horrible slaughter, the world was divided into two camps: One is the revolutionary camp including the oppressed colonies and the exploited working class throughout the world. The vanguard force of this camp is the Soviet Union. The other is the counterrevolutionary camp of international capitalism and imperialism whose general staff is the League of Nations.

During this World War, various nations suffered untold losses in property and human lives. The French imperialists were the hardest hit. Therefore, in order to restore the capitalist forces in France, the French imperialists have resorted to every underhand scheme to intensify their capitalist exploitation in Indochina. They set up new factories to exploit the workers with low wages. They plundered the peasants' land to establish plantations and drive them to utter poverty. They levied many heavy taxes. They imposed public loans upon our people. In short, they reduced us to wretchedness. They increased their military forces, firstly to strangle the Vietnamese revolution, secondly to prepare for a new imperialist war in the Pacific aimed at capturing new colonies, thirdly to suppress the Chinese revolution, fourthly to attack

Ho Chi Minh speech, February 18, 1930, in *Selected Writings,* pp. 39–41.

the Soviet Union because the latter helps the revolution of the oppressed nations and the exploited working class. World War II will break out. When it breaks, the French imperialists will certainly drive our people to a more horrible slaughter. If we give them a free hand to prepare for this war, suppress the Chinese revolution, and attack the Soviet Union, if we give them a free hand to stifle the Vietnamese revolution, it is tantamount to giving them a free hand to wipe our race off the earth and drown our nation in the Pacific.

However the French imperialists' barbarous oppression and ruthless exploitation have awakened our compatriots, who have all realized that revolution is the only road to life, without it they will die out piecemeal. This is the reason why the Vietnamese revolutionary movement has grown even stronger with each passing day. The workers refuse to work, the peasants demand land, the pupils strike, the traders boycott. Everywhere the masses have risen to oppose the French imperialists.

The Vietnamese revolution has made the French imperialists tremble with fear. On the one hand, they utilize the feudalists and comprador bourgeois in our country to oppress and exploit our people. On the other, they terrorize, arrest, jail, deport, and kill a great number of Vietnamese revolutionaries. If the French imperialists think that they can suppress the Vietnamese revolution by means of terrorist acts, they are utterly mistaken. Firstly, it is because the Vietnamese revolution is not isolated but enjoys the assistance of the world proletarian class in general and of the French working class in particular. Secondly, while the French imperialists are frenziedly carrying out terrorist acts, the Vietnamese Communists, formerly working separately, have now united into a single party, the Communist Party of Indochina, to lead our entire people in their revolution.

Workers, peasants, soldiers, youth, pupils!

Oppressed and exploited compatriots!

The Communist Party of Indochina is founded. It is the party of the working class. It will help the proletarian class to lead the revolution in order to struggle for all the oppressed and exploited people. From now on we must join the Party, help it and follow it in order to implement the following slogans:

1. To overthrow French imperialism, feudalism, and the reactionary Vietnamese capitalist class.
2. To make Indochina completely independent.
3. To establish a worker-peasant and soldier government.
4. To confiscate the banks and other enterprises belonging to the imperialists and put them under the control of the worker-peasant and soldier government.
5. To confiscate the whole of the plantations and property belonging to the imperialists and the Vietnamese Reactionary capitalist class and distribute them to poor peasants.
6. To implement the eight-hour working day.
7. To abolish public loans and poll tax. To waive unjust taxes hitting the poor people.
8. To bring back all freedoms to the masses.
9. To carry out universal education.
10. To implement equality between man and woman.

4. A Vietnamese Writer Recalls
the 1944–1945 Famine, 1956

Holding on to one another, crying, waiting for death

The Vietnamese people are accustomed to leading a hard working, frugal, and patient life. They believe that if they eat less, save some money, and work hard, then no matter how difficult life is for them, they can still "patch things up" and somehow manage to have at least one meal of greens and one meal of rice gruel each day. The changes in the economy of Vietnam between 1940 and 1945, however, greatly disrupted the people's livelihood, worst of all in the countryside.

In 1943 a ten-kilogram can of rice sold for only 1.00 piaster. A dozen eggs sold for only eight cents. In 1944 one had to pay 2.00 piasters a dozen.

The speculators hoarded, took advantage of their situation and their powerful influence, and very rapidly became rich. Prices of goods soared upward. Wages for labor, however, were raised very little and very slowly.

During the seasonal harvest of 1944 the wage for a harvester or a rice grinder was two meals of rice and salted cucumbers, an extra bowl of rice, and one piaster per day. A very strong laborer could earn only enough to feed himself, to say nothing of the taxes he had to pay or provision for his parents, wife, and children.

From May through September 1944 there were three typhoons in the coastal areas of Bac Viet [northern Vietnam]. In normal times this kind of catastrophe would be enough to put the population in an impossible situation. But now the disaster fell upon them during wartime and during a time of economic disorder. Worst of all, the French colonizers were plotting to destroy the very vitality of the population, to increase starvation in every possible way so as to be able to neutralize the traditional unyielding spirit of the Vietnamese people, and thus to rule them easily. For this reason, from September and October of 1944 onward, everybody realized that the tragedy of all times could not be avoided.

In normal times harvest season in the countryside was bustling with the activities of rice pounding and grinding. But during the seasonal harvest of the year 1944 things were completely different. The farmers went out into the fields, cried to the heavens, and moaned. People looked at each other with all hope drained from their eyes and uttered words that made it seem that they were saying farewells to one another: "There is no knowing whether we will still be alive to see each other by the time the next *chiem* harvest comes around."

The starvation began in early October. Earlier than any other year the weather was cuttingly cold. The north wind howled, and it pierced through the rags worn by the hungry and the poor. It penetrated their flesh and their bones and their weak insides. In the gray sky overhead there hung a damp layer of clouds that enveloped the hamlets and the villages. It rained continuously, day and night, and the dampness seeped into the very marrow of the hungry.

From *Before the Revolution: The Vietnamese Peasants Under the French* by Ngo Vinh Long, pp. 227–229. Copyright © 1973, 1991 Columbia University Press, New York. Reprinted with permission of the publisher.

All through October and on through December the sun kept itself hidden behind the thick clouds, with but feeble rays making their way through to the tops of the drooping bamboo groves. The days and months dragged by slowly. Rain, wind, hunger, and cold seemed to slow down the wheels of time. It was so cold that people would lie in haystacks, covering themselves up with banana leaves. They were so hungry that they had to eat marsh pennywort, potato leaves, bran, banana roots, and the bark of trees. The villagers—fathers and sons, brothers and sisters, husbands and wives, all of them alike—could no longer save one another. Regardless of the time of day or night, the hungry people, over and over again, would hug each other and would moan tragically.

5. The Vietnamese Declaration of Independence, 1945

All men are created equal; they are endowed by their Creator with certain unalienable Rights; among these are Life, Liberty, and the pursuit of Happiness.

This immortal statement was made in the Declaration of Independence of the United States of America in 1776. In a broader sense, this means: All the peoples on the earth are equal from birth, all the peoples have a right to live, to be happy and free.

The Declaration of the French Revolution made in 1791 on the Rights of Man and the Citizen also states: "All men are born free and with equal rights, and must always remain free and have equal rights."

Those are undeniable truths.

Nevertheless, for more than eighty years, the French imperialists, abusing the standard of Liberty, Equality, and Fraternity, have violated our Fatherland and oppressed our fellow citizens. They have acted contrary to the ideals of humanity and justice.

In the field of politics, they have deprived our people of every democratic liberty.

They have enforced inhuman laws; they have set up three distinct political regimes in the North, the Center, and the South of Viet-Nam in order to wreck our national unity and prevent our people from being united.

They have built more prisons than schools. They have mercilessly slain our patriots; they have drowned our uprisings in rivers of blood.

They have fettered public opinion; they have practiced obscurantism against our people.

To weaken our race they have forced us to use opium and alcohol.

In the field of economics, they have fleeced us to the backbone, impoverished our people and devastated our land.

They have robbed us of our rice fields, our mines, our forests, and our raw materials. They have monopolized the issuing of bank notes and the export trade.

They have invented numerous unjustifiable taxes and reduced our people, especially our peasantry, to a state of extreme poverty.

Ho Chi Minh speech, September 2, 1945, in *Selected Writings,* pp. 53–56.

They have hampered the prospering of our national bourgeoisie; they have mercilessly exploited our workers.

In the autumn of 1940, when the Japanese fascists violated Indochina's territory to establish new bases in their fight against the Allies, the French imperialists went down on their bended knees and handed over our country to them.

Thus, from that date, our people were subjected to the double yoke of the French and the Japanese. Their sufferings and miseries increased. The result was that, from the end of last year to the beginning of this year, from Quang Tri Province to the North of Viet-Nam, more than two million of our fellow citizens died from starvation. On March 9 [1945], the French troops were disarmed by the Japanese. The French colonialists either fled or surrendered, showing that not only were they incapable of "protecting" us, but that, in the span of five years, they had twice sold our country to the Japanese.

On several occasions before March 9, the Viet Minh League urged the French to ally themselves with it against the Japanese. Instead of agreeing to this proposal, the French colonialists so intensified their terrorist activities against the Viet Minh members that before fleeing they massacred a great number of our political prisoners detained at Yen Bay and Cao Bang.

Notwithstanding all this, our fellow citizens have always manifested toward the French a tolerant and humane attitude. Even after the Japanese *Putsch* of March, 1945, the Viet Minh League helped many Frenchmen to cross the frontier, rescued some of them from Japanese jails, and protected French lives and property.

From the autumn of 1940, our country had in fact ceased to be a French colony and had become a Japanese possession.

After the Japanese had surrendered to the Allies, our whole people rose to regain our national sovereignty and to found the Democratic Republic of Viet-Nam.

The truth is that we have wrested our independence from the Japanese and not from the French.

The French have fled, the Japanese have capitulated, Emperor Bao Dai has abdicated. Our people have broken the chains which for nearly a century have fettered them and have won independence for the Fatherland. Our people at the same time have overthrown the monarchic regime that has reigned supreme for dozens of centuries. In its place has been established the present Democratic Republic.

For these reasons, we, members of the Provisional Government, representing the whole Vietnamese people, declare that from now on we break off all relations of a colonial character with France; we repeal all the international obligation that France has so far subscribed to on behalf of Viet-Nam, and we abolish all the special rights the French have unlawfully acquired in our Fatherland.

The whole Vietnamese people, animated by a common purpose, are determined to fight to the bitter end against any attempt by the French colonialists to reconquer their country.

We are convinced that the Allied nations, which at Teheran and San Francisco have acknowledged the principles of self-determination and equality of nations, will not refuse to acknowledge the independence of Viet-Nam.

A people who have courageously opposed French domination for more than eighty years, a people who have fought side by side with the Allies against the fascists during these last years, such a people must be free and independent.

For these reasons, we, members of the Provisional Government of the Democratic Republic of Viet-Nam, solemnly declare to the world that Viet-Nam has the right to be a free and independent country—and in fact it is so already. The entire Vietnamese people are determined to mobilize all their physical and mental strength, to sacrifice their lives and property in order to safeguard their independence and liberty.

✗ *E S S A Y S*

In the opening essay, David G. Marr of Australian National University states that the Vietnamese revolution of 1945 cannot be understood without reference to prior changes in Vietnam's social structure and intellectual outlook. Particularly significant to alter developments were ideological transformations within the intelligentsia—shifts that preceded and ultimately contributed to the success of the Vietminh. Mark Philip Bradley, a specialist in Vietnamese and American history at the University of Wisconsin, Milwaukee, emphasizes in the second selection the important, if largely symbolic, influence of the United States upon the ideas and politics of Vietnamese nationalists. An imagined America, he contends, helped shape the Vietnamese intelligentsia's vision of social transformation and political independence.

The Colonial Impact

DAVID G. MARR

In 1938 at least eighteen million Vietnamese were being kept in check by a mere 27,000 colonial troops. Yet a scant sixteen years later, colonial forces totaling 450,000 were unable to avoid tactical disaster at Dien Bien Phu and compulsory strategic evacuation south of the seventeenth parallel. Finally, in the years 1965–1975, various combinations of American, Republic of Vietnam, South Korean, and other allied armed forces totaling up to 1.2 million men were outfoxed, stalemated, and eventually vanquished by the National Liberation Front and the People's Army of Vietnam.

A host of explanations have been offered for this dramatic transformation in the capabilities of both sides. French and American generals have argued that massive attacks in the early stages of Vietnamese revolutionary activity could have nipped resistance in the bud. Possibly. Nevertheless, those same generals discovered that political and economic realities at home, first in Paris, then in Washington, ruled out such a Draconian solution. Other participants or observers have variously stressed the strength of primordial Vietnamese patriotism, the fury of any oppressed people lashing out at its oppressors, sophisticated communist organizing techniques, an increased Vietnamese capability to assimilate and employ modern technology, substantial international support, French and American ignorance of Vietnamese conditions, and the mass media explosion, which may have heightened revulsion in the "home" country.

From David Marr, *Vietnamese Tradition on Trial, 1920–1945,* pp. 1–13, 413–416. Copyright © 1981 The Regents of the University of California. Reprinted by permission of University of California Press.

None of these answers should be ignored by serious students of the struggle in Vietnam. Yet none really succeeds in explaining how, in a matter of a few years, hundreds of thousands of Vietnamese changed from seemingly docile French colonial subjects to experienced political cadres, pith-helmeted soldiers (*bo-doi*), literacy instructors, hygienists or soil technicians—all dedicated to driving out the foreigner and establishing an independent, strong, egalitarian nation. Patriotism and angry reactions to oppression may well have provided the emotional foundations, yet neither could tell Vietnamese how, when, or where to act. Organization and modern technology were certainly important, but to employ both effectively demanded some degree of conceptual transformation. Although international support was valuable, psychologically as well as materially, ultimately it was what the Vietnamese did with this backing that made the difference. As for weaknesses in enemy ranks, Vietnamese revolutionaries tried to comprehend and to exploit these wherever possible. However, they also learned from painful experience that simply to wait for enemy contradictions to manifest themselves was often to leave the initiative in the hands of others.

. . . All such developments in the twentieth-century history of Vietnam must be understood within the context of fundamental changes in political and social consciousness among a significant segment of the Vietnamese populace in the period 1920–45. These changes, while not necessarily decisive, were at least one precondition for mass mobilization and successful people's war strategies from 1945 onward. To cite only one example, there was the growing conviction that one's life was not preordained, that one need not eat dirt forever, that one could join with others to force change. Victory would not occur in a blinding flash, as assumed by many earlier Vietnamese political and social movements. Yet victory was inevitable, the fruit of millions of Vietnamese perceiving their self-interests and uniting against the common enemy, foreign and domestic.

Such ideas were only the beginning of a new consciousness. What was to be the nature of that victory? Certainly it was not seen by most to be the transferring of a heavenly mandate from one ruler to another. Nor was it to be simply destruction of the colonial system. Often the objective was said to be transforming Vietnam into a "civilized" (*van minh*) nation. Although this concept meant different things to different people, it generally encompassed mastery over nature, a spirit of civic responsibility, full development of the individual's mental, physical, and moral faculties, and the ability of Vietnamese to stand proud among other peoples of the world.

These were not tasks to be accomplished overnight. Indeed, much time was spent in the early stages questioning Vietnamese capacities to do much of anything except obey fate, squabble incessantly, and scramble for petty personal gains. Beneath this severe self-criticism, even psychological flagellation, however, lurked the belief that people could change dramatically. Otherwise, why bother to publish hundreds of pamphlets and articles challenging readers to renovate themselves? At any rate, by the late 1920s both the mood of self-disparagement and the emphasis on moral rearmament were being replaced by the belief that history was moving in Vietnam's direction, and that social forces would accomplish what individual regeneration could not.

This new faith was badly shaken by the French colonial repression of 1929–32. It recovered in the Popular Front period of 1936–39. It suffered again in the Japanese-Vichy crackdowns of 1940–44. And then it burst forth as never before in the August 1945 Revolution. Through all these ups and downs a growing number of Vietnamese were learning to combine optimism and patience, moral suasion and social mobilization, theory and practice. The intelligentsia also rediscovered pride in Vietnamese culture—on a selective basis.

Without a variety of economic and social changes from precolonial to colonial times in Vietnam there would probably not have been major changes in consciousness, or, if such changes had occurred, they would have been limited to a much smaller group of people, perhaps "enlightened" members of the royal family, trusted mandarins, and a handful of foreign language interpreters, merchants, and literate Catholics. To carry this speculation a bit further, such men might have employed their newly acquired knowledge to engineer and to justify a range of institutional reforms. They might even have ended up sharing power with small new military and business elites, as happened in Thailand. But, just as in Thailand, the depth and breadth of intellectual transformation would have been far less substantial.

Vietnam never had that choice. From the 1850s Vietnam was under severe military threat. It was dismembered in the 1860s and 1870s, then swallowed completely by the French in the 1880s. By 1897 all armed resistance had been quelled. During the next five years Governor General Paul Doumer laid down the foundations and framework which were to characterize Indochina (Cambodia and Laos included) for the next four decades. These included a centralized and rather top-heavy administration, an expanded and greatly reinforced tax and corvée system, continued growth of the primary export sector by means of large land grants (often disregarding prior ownership or occupancy), near-monopoly status for French finance capital and product imports, and the construction of an impressive if not always economically viable network of railroads, roads, and canals.

Already before World War I three major changes were apparent in the lives of ordinary Vietnamese. First, the French had capacities to control and to coerce never dreamed of by previous rulers. For this reason less attention was devoted to the conciliatory political arts, to understanding local grievances, compromising, or sharing power with subordinates. It also meant that traditional village obligations to the ruler, in particular, taxes, corvée service, and military service, were no longer the subject of discreet negotiations, but could now be enforced with unprecedented efficiency. Nor was there still an open frontier beyond reach of the system, where aggrieved families could flee. It followed, too, that those Vietnamese who attached themselves to the new rulers and quickly grasped alien procedures could advance to positions of considerable wealth and self-esteem (but little real authority), without having to trouble themselves much about popular anger or any ethic of responsible government. In short, the French can be said to have strengthened some aspects of the traditional hierarchical structure to the detriment of the majority of Vietnamese, while allowing a new indigenous minority to share in the returns as long as they remained obedient and necessarily insensitive to popular grievances.

Secondly, through a policy of granting large land concessions to French companies and Vietnamese collaborators, together with the introduction of French concepts of private property and individual legal responsibility, the colonial government stimulated fundamental changes in village economic and social relations. Phrased most simply, there were now unprecedented pressures toward concentrated wealth, land alienation, and the growth of a class of landless and land-poor Vietnamese. For example, peasant families who had devoted one or more generations to clearing, tilling, and improving land now found themselves being evicted or converted into tenants, perhaps simply because they had not learned the new administrative rules as quickly as others. Small proprietors, who thought they had protected themselves legally, could still be outmaneuvered by means of usurious loans, cadastral manipulations, seizure for back taxes, or simply the duplicity of corrupt local officials. To cry out for redress in such situations was usually hopeless, and sometimes dangerous, since colonial retaliatory power was normally at the disposal of any landlord or official who kept in the good graces of his superiors.

As a corollary of this economic process, the corporate character of Vietnamese villages was gradually eroded. Communal lands—traditionally the basis of village social welfare palliatives, as well as providing modest support for local temples, schools, and routine administrative tasks—now increasingly became the private property of several well-placed families, or even came under the control of non-village members. As disparities in wealth increased, the selection of village notables, the observance of village festivals, the organizing of weddings, funerals, ceremonies to honor returning scholars and the like, became ever more the sources of contention and conspicuous consumption (both of which had always been present to some degree), and ever less the vital ritual reinforcements of community self-consciousness and solidarity. Simultaneously, richer and poorer members of clans and extended families drew further apart, the former mostly interested in special status to reflect their new wealth, the latter trying to borrow money cheaply and loosely according to outmoded lineage rationales. The ultimate breakdown of corporate ties often occurred, as one might expect, in those areas where individuals amassed enough land to leave the villages entirely. Such absentee landlords, particularly prevalent in south Vietnam, controlled the fates of hundreds or thousands of local people without ever having to meet them face to face, or, perhaps even more upsetting, showing up only at rent- or loan-collection times.

Finally, it may well be that the most important transformation of all had to do with the penetration of a cash economy into even the most isolated hamlets of Vietnam. While the implications of this change took several decades to become apparent, there is no doubt that from the turn of the century (earlier in Cochinchina) traditional multiple and personal forms of socio-economic interaction were being replaced by the single, essentially impersonal commercial exchange system. Central taxes were the cutting edge in most cases, levied on individuals rather than corporate villages as before. While several Vietnamese dynasties had experimented with taxes in cash, particularly portions of the land tax, payment in kind had always remained dominant. Now the French ordered that both the entire land tax and the even more onerous head tax be paid in silver—not the copper, zinc, or paper money recognized for other transactions, but solid silver piasters, which peasants often had to acquire solely for this purpose at marked-up rates of exchange from the money lenders or landlords. Corvée obligations could also be rendered in cash, for those who had it. On top of these payments there were diverse indirect taxes (marketing, stamp, consumer goods, transit, entrepot, navigation, etc.) as well as the government-controlled salt and liquor monopolies—all being more rigorously enforced than any comparable taxes of precolonial days. Even if a peasant continued to think of himself as essentially a subsistence farmer, he was being drawn further into the money economy by the tax system.

The preeminent economic objective of the French was to develop a modern export sector. They focused particularly on rice and mining, then later rubber as well. Taxation, monopoly, and market mechanisms soon worked relentlessly against the interests of peasants whose output had previously met the more diverse needs of an autonomous economy, but who were now non-competitive in an imperial operation controlled from Paris. Vietnamese might still need to eat something other than rice, but there were now financial disincentives in many regions to specializing in non-rice production. The same process hit traditional artisans hard, indeed wiping them out entirely if their specialty happened to compete with French imports. Peasants who derived some off-season income from making handicrafts, tools, or other simple essentials also found such opportunities drying up. Rice was now king—not just any rice, but rice in quantities and qualities suitable for export, and sent through channels dominated by non-local interests. A modicum of capital and contacts with officialdom were the two essential ingredients to success. Those who failed became part of the cheap labor pool, another essential ingredient if any company or family wished to set up a new plantation or start a new mining project.

With the outbreak of war in Europe in 1914 investments terminated abruptly. Vietnamese were pressed to help defeat the "Huns." As many as 100,000 peasants and artisans were rounded up and shipped to France to serve in labor battalions, and provided a source of some worry to the colonial authorities when they returned. Meanwhile, in Vietnam during the war, people were strongly "encouraged" to buy war bonds, in effect yet another tax. Rice exports increased. Locally produced goods were allowed temporarily to substitute for normal French imports. Larger numbers of Vietnamese were permitted to enter the bottom rungs of the colonial bureaucracy, and a modest expansion of the public school system was ordered. With that special French penchant for idealistic overstatement, Governor-General Albert Sarraut spun all of these changes into a vision of Franco-Vietnamese collaboration, complete with references to Liberty, Equality, and Fraternity. France, he said, was ready to act as "elder brother" in transmitting the full benefits of modern civilization, and to consider the possibility of native self-rule at some unspecified point in the future. After Germany was defeated, the French Government conveniently ignored these grandiloquent promises. But for many educated Vietnamese the cat had been let out of the bag. If the French needed reminding, they would be the ones to do it. If that did not work, they would try pursuing the ideal of "civilization" on their own.

In 1922, as France itself was slowly managing to pull out of a postwar depression, the Ministry of Colonies organized a grand exposition in Marseilles to try to revitalize in people's minds the French "mission" overseas and to attract new investment capital. Looked at in terms of overall twentieth-century historical trends, France had been permanently weakened by the Great War. The French people were probably more divided than ever on the colonial question. Nevertheless, viewed from the perspective of the 1920s, the response to the Marseilles exposition and other forms of colonial propaganda was nothing short of spectacular. While thousands of ordinary French citizens amused themselves by tasting strange foreign dishes, ogling native dancers, and laughing at the clothing and manners of diverse oriental potentates, potential capital investors concentrated their attention on government promises of monopoly privileges, tax shelters, cheap labor, and solid social order.

Close to three billion francs was invested in Indochina between 1924 and 1930, almost sixty per cent of the total since French arrival. Rubber cultivation, begun very modestly before the war, now was seen by investors as the new bonanza, some 700 million francs being advanced between 1925 and 1929. To provide the physical labor, somewhere between 100,000 and 200,000 Vietnamese were deceived or dragooned into the "red earth" rubber-growing region of Cochinchina during the boom years of the 1920s. Conditions were abysmal, including endemic malaria, contaminated or insufficient food and water, long hours, the docking of wages, and vicious punishments. Consequently the turnover rate due to death, escape, and nonrenewal of contracts was extraordinarily high, as indicated by the fact that the rubber plantation work force never exceeded 41,000 in any one year.

Conditions were only slightly better for the miners, of whom there were at least 50,000 during peak years, mostly in the Hon Gay pits of north Vietnam. Here the formula for profit-making included dirt-cheap labor, company stores, 12- to 14-hour shifts, physical brutality, and the absence of safety precautions. Yet French economists still complained that it was "carelessness," "lack of conscientiousness," and "delicate constitution(s)" that caused Vietnamese miners to produce at only one-quarter the rate of their French or Japanese counterparts. New coffee and tea plantations were established in the same way, and more land was cleared and drained so that more Vietnamese tenants and wage laborers could produce more rice for export. Significant expansion occurred in rice milling, distilling, sugar refining, and the production of cement, textiles, and timber. On top of this economic pyramid sat a handful of directors of prestigious French financial institutions. As of 1924, Paris and Saigon were linked by direct transoceanic cable for the first time. Direct airmail service soon followed. Indochina was now a classic colony, her economic fibers attuned to the demands of the "mother country" and the international marketplace.

With the advent of the Great Depression the bottom fell out of the rubber and rice markets. By early 1931 the Indochina economy was in serious trouble—landowners defaulting on bank loans, companies going into bankruptcy, *colons* banging on government doors demanding assistance, and uncounted thousands of Vietnamese tenants, agricultural laborers, plantation hands, miners, and factory workers thrown out of employment, roaming to and fro in search of survival. Not until 1936 did the economy begin to pick up again. Then, a mere four years later, Nazi Germany occupied France, the Vichy-sympathizing authorities in Indochina subordinated themselves to the Japanese, and the economy underwent dislocation once again. By the winter of 1944/45, a tragic but quite predictable situation had developed, whereby hundreds of thousands of tons of rice remained in warehouses in the south (or was converted to alcohol to propel motor vehicles), while somewhere between one and two million Vietnamese people died of starvation in the north.

Looked at from the perspective of eighty years of French colonial activity, the only period when truly favorable conditions existed for full-scale capitalist economic exploitation of Indochina was from 1922 to 1929—a mere eight years. Economic fragility combined with administrative uncertainty underlay the entire colonial operation. No governor-general ever spent a term of more than five and one-half years in Indochina, and the average tenure was a scant two years and eight months.

Conservative politicians spoke grandly about colonial restoration while socialists talked vaguely of provisional tutelage. Projects were begun and left uncompleted, or altered in such a way that profits survived but not the ameliorative social trimmings. This fundamental weakness of French colonialism, hardly sensed previously by even the most astute Vietnamese observers, was to become a subject of serious analysis among the new generation of intellectuals.

Vietnam has had three generations of intellectuals since 1900. Scholar gentry or literati (*si phu*) intellectuals realized during the first decade of the twentieth century that Vietnam was being transformed whether it liked it or not. They tried desperately with whatever weapons, physical or mental, that came to hand to face up to altered conditions. By the end of World War I, however, it was obvious that they were unable to formulate either a penetrating new view of the world or a realistic program of action. Even the most sophisticated and experienced scholar-gentry members remained suspended between the Neo-Confucian classics, which they knew intimately but had come to doubt, and the ideas of Montesquieu, Rousseau, Smith, and Spencer, which they understood only vaguely but assumed to be essential to Vietnam's future. What they did manage to convey to the next generation, nevertheless, was a sense of historical crisis, a profound respect for knowledge, a commitment to action, and faith in the perfectibility of humankind.

The intelligentsia (*gioi tri thuc*) that emerged during the 1920s faced many of the same problems as the scholar-gentry, but in yet another social and economic context and with very different intellectual equipment. While not divorced from the villages and the lives of the literati, small farmers, and handicraft workers, the intelligentsia was indubitably a product of the colonial system, just as were the big landlords, tenants, miners, and plantation laborers. Young intelligentsia graduating from French and Franco-Vietnamese schools in increasing numbers generally sought employment as clerks, interpreters, primary teachers, or journalists. As career aspirations exceeded colonial possibilities, there was considerable disenchantment and unrest. To assume a correlation between job frustration and anticolonial attitudes among the intelligentsia would be risky, however. There were well-employed Vietnamese who ended up opposing the French, just as there were thwarted journalists who joined the colonial police or signed on as overseers for landlords, mine supervisors, and plantation administrators.

Unlike the scholar-gentry, the intelligentsia understood the neoConfucian classics only vaguely but were impatient to digest two millennia of European learning in a matter of a few years. The great advantage, and simultaneously the primary weakness, of these young men and women was that they stood unsteadily between two worlds and tried hard to envisage a third. Most of them had either grown up in villages or had meaningful rural kinship ties. Their parents still believed in ghosts, arranged marriages, and strict social harmony. However, in school, and increasingly through extracurricular means, they learned of cameras, germs, atoms, galaxies, free love, class struggle, and biological evolution. Many found the advice of their elders to ignore the obvious contradictions between old and new and to concentrate on passing examinations and securing a clerkship morally and intellectually repulsive. They wanted to look further, to explain the contradictions, and to fashion a new consciousness for themselves and for the Vietnamese people at large. Often they used the image of discovering a conceptual "lodestone" (*kim chi nam*) that would guide everyone to a brighter future. Although the enthusiasm, aggressive curiosity, and iconoclasm of the intelligentsia were themselves repulsive to many other Vietnamese, social and economic changes were so profound that the latter often felt impotent, incapable of reasserting authority. Youth seized the day.

This was only the beginning, however. One of the most difficult tasks facing the intelligentsia was to distinguish universal insights from the particularities of either European or Vietnamese experience. The traditional Vietnamese preference had been to draw a line between cultured East Asians and the many barbarian peoples, Europeans included, who did not comprehend the way of the universe and hence behaved improperly. Well into the twentieth century some Vietnamese continued to seek comfort in this model of reality, even while being forced to admit that "Eastern spirit" no longer had any claim to universality. At the other extreme, many early products of French colonial schools tended to assume that to be European was civilized and to be Asian barbarian. Yet those who tried simply to imitate Europeans found that they were neither accepted as such by French *colons* nor emulated by the mass of Vietnamese.

The spectacle of China disintegrating into warlordism, of Japan trying to outfox the Western imperialists at their own game, and of the Vietnamese "emperor" on annual salary from the French, made Neo-Confucianism look pathetic. Buddhism and Taoism were seen to be more attractive in such chaotic times, yet only a small minority of the intelligentsia went beyond general knowledge of these philosophies to firm, sustained adherence. On the other side of the world, the spectacle of Europe tearing itself to pieces in World War I undercut those Vietnamese who advocated radical Westernization. If Verdun and the Somme lay at the end of the path of assimilation, then better not try.

During the 1920s Vietnamese writers started to reach beyond the East-versus-West paradigm. They eagerly sought information from anywhere, in the hope that it would help to explain and resolve their own dilemmas. Of particular interest were social upheavals in China, postwar unrest in Europe, the ongoing revolution in Russia, and non-violent resistance in India. Increasingly writers became convinced that there was no qualitative distinction between Europeans and Vietnamese. A vast reservoir of knowledge and techniques was available to anyone in the world. It might often appear to bear a particular national stamp, but that was superficial, capable of being isolated and eliminated. In place of idealized philosophical and cultural systems, Vietnamese writers moved increasingly to historical process as a central explanation of reality. The key question then became one of assessing Vietnam's place in this universal process, and determining how to improve it.

In politics this same historical quest led many Vietnamese writers to conclude that it was not enough to simply exhort people to be patriotic, to unite, and to help save the country. Writers were now poignantly aware of other peoples in the world who presumably loved their homeland and their mother tongue as deeply as did the Vietnamese their own, who even possessed a similar tradition of resisting foreign domination, yet ultimately were completely vanquished and absorbed. Clearly some ethnic groups survived and others did not. Understanding why and how became a major preoccupation. Again, Vietnamese came to the conclusion that much knowledge in the world bore no moral stamp but was available to the evil as well as the good, to colonials and anticolonials, to reactionaries, conservatives, liberals, and radical revolutionaries alike.

The next step was to relate new knowledge and techniques to specific Vietnamese conditions. This proved to be more difficult. First of all, the intelligentsia had to learn a great deal about Vietnam, past and present, that was either unavailable in the colonial schools or had previously been considered irrelevant by young men and women trying first to understand the outside world. Nor was it easy for members of the intelligentsia to move around the country collecting information. The colonial authorities imposed physical restrictions. And a young intellectual in Western dress, speaking with a different accent and having no local relatives, might have to spend months simply gaining the confidence of a few people. When it came time to publish, writers discovered a curious fact about colonial censorship: the authorities were often more charitable toward the printing of esoteric foreign information and theories than they were toward independent data on the Vietnamese experience. Many an article was blanked out precisely at the point where it shifted from foreign generalities to Vietnamese colonial particulars.

Vietnamese intellectuals overseas took the lead in discussing specific political and social developments inside the colony. Ho Chi Minh was the most notable example, but he was followed by scores of other Vietnamese residing for one period of time or another in France, the Soviet Union, and China. While they obviously could not conduct on-the-spot investigations, they did talk intensively with overseas Vietnamese from other provinces and social backgrounds. Publishing was less of a problem than smuggling copies home. Ironically, while most writers in Saigon, Hanoi, or Hue were still grappling with universals, whether in history, philosophy, the social sciences, medicine, or mathematics, writers in Paris, Moscow, or Canton were trying to analyze the Bank of Indochina, the conditions of Vietnamese peasants, miners, and plantation workers, or the causes of high infant mortality. Distance from events provided the perspective for sorting the momentous from the trivial, the politically relevant from the intellectually curious.

Eventually, however, this work would have to be carried on inside the country. In the late 1920s a few authors in Saigon and Hue were able to append a bit of specific Vietnamese data to otherwise general discussions of historical evolution, religion, nationalism, and imperialism. In the early 1930s novelists and short-story writers took the lead, describing the lives of Vietnamese functionaries, landlords, intellectuals, shopkeepers, and peasants according to conceptual and stylistic criteria that had not existed in the country several decades earlier. By the late 1930s they had been joined by critical essayists, and the emphasis increasingly was on the lives of poor peasants, tenants, proletarians, beggars, and prostitutes. Collectively these publications amounted to a penetrating indictment of both Vietnamese traditional society and the colonial system.

Preoccupation with the negative could prove self-defeating, however. By the early 1940s many discussions of current conditions were naturalistic caricatures rather than realistic exposes. Sensing an impasse, other writers shifted to selective revitalization of the Vietnamese past and to assertions of a bright future. Vietnam was now seen by even the most radical intelligentsia to possess a history to some degree unique, incapable of being understood simply by reference to universal laws. As might be expected, particular attention was given to military heroes, administrative innovators, and literary giants. Popular culture was mined for evidence of an underlying strength and wisdom among the Vietnamese masses transcending the historical dialectic.

These changes coincided with momentous political developments, including the collapse of the Popular Front (1939), the establishment of the Japanese-Vichy alliance (1940), and the formation of the Communist-led Viet Minh (1941). As a group, the Vietnamese intelligentsia was badly divided on how to respond to these events. Some saw the Japanese as liberators; others hoped for Vietnamese self-rule within a French Union; still others joined the Viet Minh and worked for an allied victory and international recognition of Vietnam's independence. Probably the only thing the intelligentsia shared by 1942–44 was a feeling that the urban milieu of office bureaus, elite societies, coffee shops, and amusement parlors was very constraining, perhaps unreal. The new focus was the Vietnamese village, whether for purposes of preserving its alleged communal character, for suggesting institutional reforms, or for convincing the peasants to seize control of their own destiny.

In 1944–45 members of the intelligentsia joined the Viet Minh by the thousands. Their skills as writers, speakers, teachers, and administrators proved extremely valuable, perhaps essential. They were also competent to ferret out information and to digest and distill it for broad political and military intelligence purposes. The same ability was put to use when learning how to utilize captured materiel, or when devising new equipment and techniques appropriate to primitive conditions. However, intelligentsia linking up with the Viet Minh soon discovered that they were regarded as neither the political nor the intellectual vanguard of society. Those roles were held by the Indochinese Communist Party. Although in 1944 most members of the ICP were probably still of intelligentsia background, the Party took its worker-peasant vision very seriously. The upheavals of 1945 provided a perfect opportunity to identify and enroll thousands of suitable members from these classes.

Members of the ICP, intellectuals or otherwise, had already learned through bitter experience that to will victory, or to analyze the road to victory, was not the same as to achieve victory. They had been forced into agonizing personal choices, endured considerable deprivation, tested a variety of concepts in practice, and tried to reformulate everything in terms meaningful to the majority of their unlettered (but not necessarily ignorant) countrymen. What they wanted from any intelligentsia recruit of 1945 was a willingness to accept group discipline, to concern himself more with means than with ends, and to help the Viet Minh to establish a common frame of reference between the elite and the masses, modernity and tradition, universal and particular. The era of the educated cadre, as distinct from the alienated explorer, had begun.

In the early 1920s Vietnam's young intelligentsia had had a talismanic approach to knowledge. It was to be their invincible weapon to gain independence, freedom, and "civilization." Twenty years later, however, many intelligentsia realized that new ideas might promote or impede change; they might produce unintended as well as intended and dysfunctional as well as functional consequences. Few ideas were inherently good or bad, and even fewer remained as originally conceived. To try to force the "right" ideas in the wrong historical conditions might prove disastrous, yet to wait for the right conditions might be equally dangerous. What was needed was a complex interweaving of ends and means, strategy and circumstance, conscious formulation and spontaneous action. . . .

Between that day in 1925, when several hundred spectators heard a French judge sentence Phan Boi Chau to life imprisonment, and the day in 1945, when a huge crowd listened to Ho Chi Minh proclaim independence, Vietnam underwent a profound transformation. In the mid-1920s, the colonial government had reason to believe that it had found a viable formula for the long-term, peaceful exploitation of Indochina. Only a smattering of Vietnamese dared to disagree openly. The vast majority accepted that change would have to come either by French fiat or by heavenly intervention, not by the actions of ordinary subjects.

Twenty years later, conditions were dramatically different. The French had been forced to drown several Vietnamese uprisings in blood. They had seen the colonial economy completely disrupted. They had been humiliated by the Germans in Europe and incarcerated by the Japanese in Indochina. Even to begin to reassert sovereignty in Indochina, the French were forced to go hat in hand to the Americans, British, and Chinese. Determined to regain pride in themselves, preoccupied by intra-Allied diplomacy, they failed to take accurate measure of Ho Chi Minh, of the new Democratic Republic of Vietnam, or—most importantly—of the political and social revolution sweeping the country. General Leclerc sensed a difficult struggle when he ordered his armored columns to push Vietnamese forces out of Saigon in October 1945. He had no inkling, however, that the end of the road lay at Dien Bien Phu, the ultimate French humiliation. Vietnamese had proven themselves energetic citizens rather than passive subjects.

Neither the August 1945 Revolution nor Dien Bien Phu can be understood without reference to prior changes in social structure and intellectual outlook. The traditional Vietnamese elite had become a pathetic shadow of its former self. Rural life had been altered fundamentally by the decline of the subsistence farmer, the spread of landlordism, the gutting of customary welfare palliatives, and the necessity for ever more family members to seek employment far beyond village boundaries. More than ever before, the tax system took from the poor and gave to the rich. . . .

Fortune favored the ICP in several respects. Most notably, the Tokyo-Vichy détente seriously weakened those Vietnamese groups which looked to either the Japanese or the French for political advancement. By the same token, it allowed the ICP to mount violent attacks against French colonial rule without being accused of unfaithfulness to the Allied cause. Communist parties in Malaya, Indonesia, and the Philippines were not so lucky. Important, too, was that Ho Chi Minh returned to Vietnam after thirty years, bringing with him impeccable credentials as an international revolutionary, unrivaled knowledge of world affairs, and a first-hand assessment of national united-front efforts in China.

Neither good fortune nor wise leadership would have counted for much, however, without the ideological transformations that preceded the formation of the Viet Minh and helped the ICP to take the historical initiative. Members of the intelligentsia had long before rejected the mood of bewilderment and pessimism which had characterized their elders. Instead, they possessed an infectious spirit of optimism and cultural pride. From an earlier naive acceptance of all things Western, they moved on to critical investigation and attempts at selective acculturation. Intelligentsia concepts of struggle and progress reached Vietnamese villagers in the 1930s, leading some to look at current conditions in a very different light. The fact that the colonial economy was in turmoil and rural society severely disrupted facilitated this process. When Vietnamese intellectuals and peasants came together in 1945 to uphold national independence and create a new society, there remained significant areas of misunderstanding and disagreement. Yet, there was sufficient consensus to mobilize millions to defeat the French.

Except for Ho Chi Minh, all ranking ICP leaders of the early 1940s had been members of the new intelligentsia. Many took prominent roles in the animated debates of the 1930s and drew heavily on the rhetoric of the Popular Front period in persuading people to join the Viet Minh. They defended the rights of the poor, encouraged women to participate in political struggle, stressed the importance of mass literacy, promised democratic freedoms, and portrayed the contemporary world in terms of a decisive confrontation between good and evil. To these themes were now added selective glorification of the Vietnamese past, praise of particular Vietnamese customs, and the claim that nothing could stand in the way of Vietnamese willpower asserted collectively.

The August 1945 Revolution was the sort of mass voluntarist surge of power that anticolonialists had dreamt of for decades. Even today, participants become excited as they recall the mood and events of 1945. For those who were in their teens or early twenties, it represented the formative experience of their lives, fostering a deep sense of solidarity and readiness to sacrifice; older Vietnamese saw the August Revolution as justification for previous agonies, capping three generations of struggle against unbelievable odds. Nothing that occurred subsequently, not even Dien Bien Phu or the rout of Republic of Vietnam forces in 1975, managed to capture the popular imagination in this way.

Vietnamese Nationalists and the United States

MARK PHILIP BRADLEY

In the winter and spring of 1919, as the Paris Peace Conference deliberated over the postwar peace settlement for Europe, members of the Vietnamese expatriate association known as the Groupe des Patriotes Annamites often gathered in a small Parisian apartment in the thirteenth arrondissement. Inspired by the Wilsonian rhetoric of self-determination, the focus of their meetings was to draft a proposal for the gradual emancipation of Vietnam from French colonial rule to present to the leaders of the Great Powers in Paris. The final document, titled "Revendications du Peuple Annamite," set forth an eight-point program that included calls for a general amnesty for political prisoners, equality of legal rights between French and Vietnamese, freedom of the press, the right to form political associations, and permanent Vietnamese representation in the French parliament.

Although the drafting of the proposal had been a collective effort that included the participation of Phan Chu Trinh, among the most famous and influential of

Vietnamese anticolonial leaders, the "Revendications" bore the signature of a relative unknown, Nguyen Ai Quoc, or Nguyen the Patriot. Shortly before the deliberations in Paris came to a close, the Groupe des Patriotes Annamites submitted its "Revendications" to the heads of various national delegations, including President Woodrow Wilson, asking that their proposals be added to the conference agenda. Their request was ignored.

Some twenty-five years later, Nguyen Ai Quoc, who reemerged on the Vietnamese political stage as Ho Chi Minh, would again pursue American support, this time as the leader of the communist-led Viet Minh movement that sought independence from the French during World War II. The passage of a quarter-century, however, fundamentally transformed the nature and aims of Vietnamese anticolonialism. The refusal of the Paris conference to consider the relatively modest demands of the Groupe des Patriotes Annamites marked the eclipse of a generation of scholar-gentry patriots, such as Phan Chu Trinh, who had embraced Social Darwinism and new currents of neo-Confucian thought to apprehend the humiliation of French conquest and chart a path of indigenous societal reform and anticolonial resistance. In their place arose a younger generation of anticolonial activists in the 1920s who conceived a more radical critique of Vietnamese society and French colonialism. By the 1930s, Marxist-Leninist internationalism had become the driving force in Vietnamese anticolonialism.

Just as the spirit of Wilsonianism hovered over the drafting of the "Revendications" by the Groupe des Patriotes Annamites in 1919, the United States occupied a persistent though often elliptical role in the transformation and radicalization of Vietnamese anticolonial thought and politics. Although Ho Chi Minh visited New York City in 1912, rarely, if ever, did most Vietnamese political elites encounter America or Americans directly. Reflecting the importance of East Asia and Europe as the primary source of foreign influence on Vietnam under French colonial rule, Vietnamese perceptions of the United States were refracted through Chinese, Japanese, French, and Russian commentaries on American history and society. Viewed at such a distance, an imagined America came to represent the shifting currents and tensions in Vietnamese anticolonial thought. As Ho Chi Minh and the leaders of the Viet Minh embarked on their path to power and Vietnamese independence in the 1940s, the legacies of the anticolonial political discourse under French colonial rule, and the place of America in it, would frame their vision of national liberation and the nature of their diplomacy with the United States.

Vietnamese images of the United States first emerged through the Reform Movement, which dominated anticolonialism in Vietnam during the early decades of the twentieth century. Members of the generation of elites that led the Reform Movement were born in the 1860s and early 1870s into scholar-gentry families often from north and north-central Vietnam. Like their fathers and grandfathers before them, they had studied Chinese classical texts in preparation for the imperial examinations that would enable them to enter government service and symbolically mark their right to rule as virtuous Confucian "superior men" (*quantu*). The examination system, reflecting centuries of cultural borrowing from the Chinese, inculcated Confucian values into the political culture of Vietnamese elites and served as the foundation of the administrative structure through which the Nguyen emperors had ruled Vietnam since 1802. Prizing stability over change and viewing the wider non-Confucian world beyond East Asia with suspicion and derision, it was a profoundly conservative political and social order that proved unable to withstand the French colonial challenge in the late nineteenth century.

Members of the reform generation, who came of age in the 1880s at the time of the French conquest of northern Vietnam, watched as the slow French enervation of Vietnamese political, economic, and social life undermined the neo-Confucian premises that had shaped their view of the world. For these young men, the failure of scholar-gentry resistance to French conquest, like the Aid the King (Can Vuong) Movement in which many of their fathers had played a leading role, demonstrated that Confucian principles alone provided an inadequate response to French rule and heightened the urgency of reversing what they termed "the loss of country" or "national extinction" (*mat nuoc; vong quoc*). As the author of one reform poem asked of the situation Vietnam faced under the onslaught of French colonialism,

> Why is the roof over the Western universe the broad lands and skies,
> While we cower and confine ourselves to a cranny in our house?
> Why can they run straight, leap far,
> While we shrink back and cling to each other?
> Why do they rule the world,
> While we bow our heads as slaves?

To explain Vietnam's predicament and formulate a new vision for the reconstruction and transformation of Vietnamese society, the reform generation increasingly looked outside their own tradition. For the first time, the European and American historical experience became a major part of Vietnamese political discourse. Reformers were captivated by the philosophical writings of Jean-Jacques Rousseau and Montesquieu; the nation-building efforts of Peter the Great, Giuseppe Garibaldi, and Otto von Bismarck; and the inventiveness of James Watt. Americans, including figures such as George Washington, Patrick Henry, and Thomas Edison, were also widely celebrated as deserving emulation by the Vietnamese. Among the most compelling Western thinkers for the Reform Movement was Herbert Spencer. To Vietnamese reformers, Social Darwinism offered a powerful explanation for the weaknesses in traditional society that had led to Vietnam's domination by the French. It also pointed to the strengths of the West that offered a potential path for Vietnam's future.

Significantly, Social Darwinism, or what reformers more broadly termed the "European wind and American rain" (*gio Au mua My*), entered Vietnam indirectly. Unable to read European or American texts themselves, Vietnamese reformers encountered Western thought and experiences in the writings of Liang Ch'i-ch'ao and K'ang Yu-wei, the leading intellectual advocates of self-strengthening reforms in China, and through what they came to know about the reform of Japanese society under the Meiji restoration. Discussions of the West in works by Chinese self-strengtheners in particular were a revelation to Vietnamese reformers whose training in the Chinese classics was bounded by the conservative curriculum of the Nguyen imperial examinations that favored the study of Sung neo-Confucianism and ignored contemporary intellectual innovations in the Sinic tradition.

But viewed within the interpretative veil of Chinese and Japanese informants, the revolutionary new currents of Western thought that animated the discourse of reform in early twentieth-century Vietnam were refracted through the persisting neo-Confucian sensibilities of the East Asian classical world. While the reformers in Vietnam were remarkably open to European and American ideas, they continued to see themselves as Confucian superior men and mediated Western thought through Confucian norms and values. As one reform text argued, "Among these European winds and American rains, who knows but what there may be men who on behalf of their country will sweep away the fog, lift up the clouds, and create a radiant and expansive horizon for us all." By emulating the achievements of the West, the leaders of the Reform Movement believed they could transcend French colonialism and regain their rightful place as the leaders of a newly strengthened Vietnam. Poised between neo-Confucianism and Social Darwinism, the articulation of this reformist vision would produce the earliest enduring Vietnamese images of America.

The Reform Movement was launched in 1904 with the publication of an anonymous tract titled *The Civilization of New Learning* [*Van Minh Tan Hoc Sach*]. Infused with the Social Darwinian themes that had characterized the writings of Chinese reformers, the manifesto offered a wide-ranging critique of Vietnamese society and a prescription for the future. It argued that Vietnamese civilization was "static" (*tinh*) and Western civilization was "dynamic" (*dong*). Using Spencerian rhetoric, the manifesto suggested that ceaseless change produced a strong civil society: "The more ideas, the more competition; the more competition, the more ideas." Appreciation for the importance of Darwinian intellectual competition in Europe and America, it continued, produced innovations in political thought, education, commerce, and industry. In Vietnam, by contrast, the rigid adherence to classical Chinese learning and suspicion of foreign ideas had foreclosed dynamic change.

Despite this grim Spencerian critique of traditional society, Vietnamese reformers were not without hope for the future. Because Chinese interpretations of Spencer's thought downplayed its relentless determinism in favor of a more optimistic voluntarism, Social Darwinism as it was received by the Vietnamese also presented a path to national revival. Much of *The Civilization of New Learning* was devoted to outlining a program of Vietnamese self-strengthening patterned on Western models that included plans for educational reform and the development of indigenous industry and commerce. Sharing the neo-Confucian perspective of Chinese interpreters of Social Darwinism, the manifesto insisted these projects were to be led by and directed to Vietnamese elites, arguing one could not "open up" the intellects of the masses until elite attitudes had been changed.

The critique of Vietnamese society and reform proposals contained in *The Civilization of New Learning,* aimed at bringing the dynamism of the West to Vietnam, would underlie much of the Reform Movement's activities. An Eastern Study (Dong Du) movement brought Vietnamese students to Japan, where they not only came in closer contact with the works of Chinese reformers such as Liang Ch'i-ch'ao, who was living in Yokohama, but also with the ideas of Japanese thinkers who had guided the country's rapid economic modernization and bid for Great Power status under the Meiji restoration. In Vietnam itself, reformers organized the Dong Kinh Free School (Dong Kinh Nghia Thuc) and the publication of a newspaper, *Old Lantern Miscellany* [*Dang Co Tung Bao*], which served as critical forums for the introduction of new currents of thought. They also worked to establish indigenous commercial enterprises and agricultural societies to reverse the traditional scholar-gentry disdain for commerce and to emulate what reformers perceived as the sources of Western wealth and power. Reinforcing their optimism that these projects could successfully bring about the transformation of Vietnamese society was the Japanese victory in the Russo-Japanese war of 1905. As the *Asia* ballad [*A-te-a*] that was popularized by the Dong Kinh Free School suggested, the Japanese experience confirmed that Asian peoples could match and even exceed the achievements of the West.

Within the broader consensus of the need to reform Vietnamese society along Western lines, substantial differences existed on the ultimate aims of the Reform Movement, illustrated by the careers of the two leading reformers, Phan Boi Chau and Phan Chu Trinh. Like others in the movement's leadership, both men were classically educated sons of scholar-gentry families who embraced reform after the failure of the Aid the King Movement. Phan Boi Chau, born in 1867 in Nghe An province in north central Vietnam, passed the regional imperial examination with the highest honors in 1900. Phan Chu Trinh, born in 1872 in Quang Nam province, passed both the regional and metropolitan imperial exams by 1900. Coming to reformist ideas through the medium of Chinese writers and short sojourns in Japan after 1900, both men played critical roles in establishing the Vietnamese movement for reform. Phan Boi Chau organized the Eastern Study Movement in Japan, and his writings were among the most important and influential reform works, forming the basis for much of the curriculum at the Dong Kinh Free School. Phan Chu Trinh, second only to Phan Boi Chau in the Reform Movement, became a widely read essayist, a particularly influential figure in the Dong Kinh Free School, and a strong advocate of scholar-gentry involvement in commerce and industry. But while Phan Boi Chau saw reform as part of a larger effort to organize effective anticolonial opposition against the French, Phan Chu Trinh believed political change should come to Vietnam only after a long process of social and cultural transformation.

Phan Boi Chau's calls for reform in Vietnam were accompanied by sustained efforts at political organization, including the development of the Reformation Society (Duy Tan Hoi) and the League for the Restoration of Vietnam (Viet-Nam Quang Phuc Hoi). The Reformation Society, active in the first decade of the twentieth century, aimed at Vietnamese independence under a constitutional monarch. The league, inspired by the Chinese revolution of 1911, sought to put into place a democratic republic. Little came of these ambitious goals, but both organizations reflected Phan Boi Chau's willingness to use political violence to bring about anticolonial ends. Members of the Reformation Society were instrumental in the wave of anticolonial demonstrations that erupted in 1908, including tax protests in central Vietnam and a plot to poison the food of the French colonial garrison in Hanoi. The league, too, was involved in a series of terrorist incidents that eventually brought Phan Boi Chau's imprisonment in 1914.

For Phan Chu Trinh, a lifelong opponent of violence whose father had been assassinated when Phan Chu Trinh was in his late teens, the educational and cultural projects of the Reform Movement were ends in themselves. Phan Chu Trinh uncompromisingly opposed the old order in Vietnam. In his best-known work, a letter to French governor general Paul Beau in 1906 seeking French support for institutional reform in Vietnam, Phan Chu Trinh was intensely critical of French colonial rule. But he reserved his harshest scorn for the traditional mandarinate whose obscurantism and petty jealousies, he believed, had prevented the emergence of reforms necessary for the transformation of Vietnam into a dynamic society. Because the indigenous barriers to reform were so great and the gap between Vietnam and the West was so vast, Phan Chu Trinh argued, independence could only follow an extended period of internal reform. Despite Phan's gradualist tone and repeated denouncements of anti-colonial violence, French colonial officials found his vision of radical enough that he was sentenced to life imprisonment on the penal island of Con Son in the wake of the anticolonial protests of 1908, a sentence later commuted to fourteen years of exile in Paris. In the prison poetry he composed on Con Son and in essays written from Paris, he continued to criticize the traditional elite and call for the social and cultural trans-formation of Vietnamese society.

Although important differences divided them, both Phan Boi Chau and Phan Chu Trinh shared and advanced the Social Darwinist critique that informed the Reform Movement. In their writings and those of other Vietnamese reformers, the European wind and American rain, filtered through the East Asian cultural prism, was essen-tial to the discourse of reform. For Vietnamese reformers, as for the Chinese and Japanese reform movements, Europe was without question the dominant influence in shaping their broader agenda. American models were often undifferentiated from those of the other Western powers that, with the United States, provided reformers with an essential rhetorical trope for Vietnam's failure to keep pace with the world struggle for national survival and served as an idealized representation of the salutary benefits of Darwinian competition that awaited Vietnam under the reformist vision. Reflecting the Vietnamese reform generation's embrace of the meanings Chinese and Japanese reformers ascribed to Social Darwinism, a poem written for the Dong Kinh Free School sharply delineated the Vietnamese and Western experiences and warned of the need to shift Vietnamese sensibilities:

> Our country from a very old time
> Always diligently and uninterruptedly followed Chinese learning.
> Aping old-fashioned and narrow-minded skills,
> We are paralyzed in a state of near-exhaustion.
> What do we know from the outside? From America? From Europe?

Similarly, American and European models infused prescriptions for the future offered by the reform generation in Vietnam. Chastising the traditional elite for "following the old ways" and blocking the development of modern industry in Vietnam, *The Civilization of New Learning* asked, "Has anyone shown the skill or the talent . . . of a Watt or an Edison?" The "talents of men like these," it argued, "truly merit awe." In using the word "talent" to describe Edison and Watt, the man-ifesto not only reflected the popular Vietnamese belief that talent (*tai*) could allow individuals to exert control over their destiny (*mang*) but revealed the Reform Movement's insistence that Western thought and experience was a more reliable and powerful weapon than the traditional repertoire of talents Vietnamese had used to shape their future. America and Europe were also an inspiration for the publication of the *Old Lantern Miscellany* in Hanoi. Pointing in wonder to the fact that "the United States had more than 14,150 newspapers" and noting the vitality of the European press, *The Civilization of New Learning* advocated the immediate estab-lishment of a Vietnamese newspaper to provide information about foreign innova-tions and local news so that the competition of ideas that had stimulated the rise of American and European power could be replicated in Vietnam.

The place of the United States in the exhortative essays and poetry of Vietnamese reformers, however, did depart from contemporary discursive practices elsewhere in East Asia. Significantly, the unwavering praise lavished on the United States in the writings of the Vietnamese reform generation far exceeded that of Chinese and Japanese reformers. While respectful of American power and political culture, leading reformers in China such as Liang Ch'i-ch'ao came to be wary of the United States, unsure of how its imperialist aspirations in the Pacific might affect China, and critical of the deleterious role big business played in American life. In Japan, too, appreciation for American models was tempered by the threat the United States posed to its own imperialist ambitions. For Vietnamese reformers, the European wind carried some of these ambivalent connotations as French colonial power threatened Vietnam's survival while European models offered a path to national reform. But Vietnamese depictions of the American rain raised none of the qualms that troubled many Chinese and Japanese reformers.

If the Social Darwinian sensibilities of reformers in China and Japan shaped the purposes to which Vietnamese writers put their images of the United States, the images themselves more closely resembled the admiring portrait of America and its political leaders that emerged in the first sustained Chinese writings on the United States in the mid-nineteenth century. Constructed in the wake of the Opium War, images of a powerful but benign America underlay Chinese hopes at mid-century that the United States might serve as a counterweight to the continuing European demands for expanded diplomatic and commercial intercourse. The terms the Vietnamese reform generation employed to refer to the United States and the meanings they conveyed were borrowed from Chinese usage that became common in this period. Vietnamese reform authors used "Beautiful" (*My;* Chinese *Mei-kuo*) to mean "America" or "Americans" and "Flowery Flag" (*Hoa Ky;* Chinese *Hua-ch'i-kuo*) for "the United States" to reflect their admiration of American models.

These earlier Chinese images of the United States also presaged the celebration of America's benign wealth and power by the Vietnamese reform generation. In a poem titled "Telling the Stories of the Five Continents" ["Ke Chuyen Nam Chau"], written by Phan Boi Chau in 1905 to introduce Vietnamese youth to developments in Europe, America, and Japan, Phan Boi Chau began his flattering description of the United States by drawing attention to American wealth, one of the critical factors mid-nineteenth-century Chinese had ascribed to American dynamism and power. . . .

The most sustained representations of American experiences by the Vietnamese reformers, utopian narratives of the life of George Washington and the American revolution, borrowed from admiring mid-nineteenth-century Chinese images as well. . . .

. . . [F]or Phan Boi Chau, who was organizing anticolonial resistance through the Reformation Society at the time, the experiences of Washington's career and the shared colonial heritage of the United States and Vietnam also offered very specific weapons for anticolonial political agitation in Vietnam. Phan Boi Chau's narrative concentrates on Washington's decision to become a soldier in the British army to acquire the skills necessary to undertake a successful military campaign against British colonialists. The intended lesson Phan Boi Chau offered to his readers was that Vietnamese revolutionaries should emulate Washington's efforts by infiltrating the French colonial militia and winning over to the anticolonial cause the

Vietnamese serving the French. Another poem written at the same time for the Dong Kinh Free School, titled "Advice for Fellow Sisters," urged Vietnamese women "to be worthy of marriage" to young Vietnamese who emulated heroes like George Washington.

The United States also played a hortatory role in the tracts that marked Phan Boi Chau's establishment of the League for the Restoration of Vietnam in 1912. In a manifesto that was distributed throughout Vietnam, the now familiar reformist image of America was put to use to support the league's aim of independence:

> While we have servilely imitated the Chinese,
> The people of America and the people of Europe have been their own masters.
> Knowing the power of these nations
> Lets us know that the strength of the people can transform our country.

Another proclamation took the image of the European wind and American rain to underlie its call for the establishment of an army to fight against the French. . . .

Phan Chu Trinh's rendering of the American revolution in part reflects his differences with Phan Boi Chau over the ultimate aims of the Reform Movement. Unlike Phan Boi Chau's use of American models as a call to immediate anticolonial action against the French, Phan Chu Trinh's more deliberate depiction of the sacrifices and hard-won victory of American revolutionaries aimed to evoke the rewards that awaited unwavering disciples of the arduous and protracted process of reform. In Phan Chu Trinh's account, military victory over the British was inseparable from the Americans' development of educational and commercial skills that allowed them to "build a rich and powerful country." By Social Darwinian criteria, the Americans were a "civilized race" and a "commendable" model for the Vietnamese reformers. . . .

Most substantively, Phan Chu Trinh's use of Confucian imagery betrayed the enduring elitism that infused reform thought. Like George Washington, in whose teeth he places a mandarin's badge of office for the commander's fateful trip across the Delaware, the leaders of the American revolution in Phan's poem displayed all of the virtues that Vietnamese elites commonly ascribed to Confucian superior men: righteousness, self-sacrifice, courage, and devotion to their country. His emphasis on the role of properly cultivated heroes in the American struggle reflected the broader reformist sentiment that politics and social change remained an elite domain. Given his disdain for the contemporary practices of much of the Vietnamese elite, Phan Chu Trinh's idealized portrait of American patriots as virtuous Confucian heroes offered a model for what a reformed and revitalized elite could accomplish in Vietnam. . . .

The reform generation's admiration for America cannot be understood without reference to these larger forces that shaped its critiques of Vietnamese society and prescriptions for reform, This imagined America, with its Confucian heroes who knew the path of social evolution led to a glorious future and used their conscious will to guide society toward it, was a central theme in works by Phan Chu Trinh, Phan Boi Chau, and other Vietnamese reformers, It reflected their own idealized self-image and articulated their aspirations for the movement they led. The reform generation passed from the Vietnamese political stage in the 1920s, as did the centrality of Social Darwinism for Vietnamese anticolonial thought. But the images of America that emerged in the radicalized political discourse of the next generation of Vietnamese anticolonialists betrayed the echoes and lingering potency of the neo-Confucian and Social Darwinian voluntarism that animated the reform generation's vision for Vietnam.

The political and intellectual upheavals of the 1920s in Vietnam set the stage for a reconsideration of the place of America in indigenous political discourse. Student demonstrations in Hanoi to protest the French decision in 1925 to sentence Phan Boi Chau to life imprisonment for his anticolonial activities and the public funerals organized by students throughout Vietnam to observe and commemorate the death of Phan Chu Trinh in 1926 marked the symbolic passage of leadership in Vietnamese anticolonial politics. These events ushered in a new generation of young nationalists whose embrace of more radical paths to Vietnam's social transformation and political independence would dominate indigenous political life in the interwar period. Among them were many of the future leaders of Vietnamese communism, including individuals who would guide Vietnam to independence in the 1940s and shape Vietnam's postcolonial diplomacy toward the United States.

Despite the homage this younger generation paid to the two leaders of the reform generation, students—along with clerks, interpreters, primary teachers, and journalists recently graduated from school or expelled for their anticolonial activities—who made up the radicalized "new intelligentsia" (*gioi tri thuc*) that emerged in the 1920s were dissatisfied and impatient with the scope and pace of the reform generation's prescriptions for Vietnamese society. But the student-led mass demonstrations and strikes of 1925–26 were not only an expression of a revitalized and radicalized patriotic anticolonialism. Viewed within the continuing social dislocations of French colonial rule, they also provided a vehicle for students to challenge the traditional authority of their parents and older teachers. The United States would play a critical symbolic role in the struggle of young radicals to redefine the relationship between the individual and society and articulate a new revolutionary anticolonial vision.

The sons, and sometimes the daughters, of mandarin families who formed the new intelligentsia of the 1920s were products of the French-controlled educational system that superseded the traditional academies that had taught the Chinese classics and Confucian morality. For their secondary education, many of these students attended French lycées and Franco-Annamite schools concentrated in urban centers. Some also undertook advanced study at the University of Hanoi, founded by the French to offer training in medicine, law, and teaching. A few, usually the children of wealthy southerners, were sent to France for university training, a practice that accelerated in the wake of the expulsions that followed the student protests of 1925–26.

The French and French-trained indigenous teachers at the secondary and university levels provided students with a Western-oriented curriculum that differed sharply from the Confucian examination system that had shaped the worldview of their fathers and grandfathers. The experience of French education, particularly its veneration of Western ideas and values, had a corrosive effect on the relationship between student radicals and their families as it accelerated the fraying of Confucian familial and social bonds under French colonialism. As one young radical of the period wrote, "Vietnamese youth is caught as if in whirling waters, not knowing where to swim for. Faced with a moral choice, it does not know on which morality to base its actions and its judgments."

Reflecting these profound differences in generational sensibilities, student activists aimed to address the dilemmas of youthful alienation with calls for the recreation rather than reform of the moral and social order in Vietnam. Indeed, the political discourse of the new intelligentsia, and its increasingly radical critique of Vietnamese society, was initially driven by individual and familial concerns as many students came to perceive disturbing links between what they saw as the confining boundaries of traditional family life and the burdens of colonialism. Young radicals sought to break with the Confucian past and the colonial present by investigating and internalizing new, often Western, ideas and values. . . .

Within this radical intellectual milieu, with its calls for individual and social transformation and embrace of revolutionary heroism, Ho Chi Minh founded the Vietnamese Revolutionary Youth League (Viet Nam Thanh Nien Kach Menh Hoi) in the spring of 1925. The Youth League, one of several radical Vietnamese anticolonial associations that emerged in the late 1920s, proved no more effective than the others at drawing on the voluntarist ethos expressed in biographies like that of Lincoln to restructure Vietnamese society and bring an end to French colonial rule. But while the lasting significance of most radical anticolonial groups proved ephemeral, the Youth League served as the forerunner of the Vietnamese communist movement, providing much of the latter's leadership and ideological orientation.

The Youth League's membership of young radicals included Pham Van Dong and Truong Chinh, whose importance for Vietnamese communism and its diplomacy in the 1940s was second only to Ho Chi Minh's. Pham Van Dong, born in 1906 to a mandarin family in Quang Ngai and active in the student protests at the prestigious Lycée Albert Sarraut in Hanoi, joined the league in 1925. Truong Chinh (a pseudonym he adopted in the 1930s meaning "Long March") was born Dang Xuan Khu to an impoverished scholar-gentry family in Nam Dinh province in 1907. A leader in student efforts to commemorate Phan Chu Trinh's death at the Franco-Annamite School of Nam Dinh, Truong Chinh became a Youth League member in 1927. Only Vo Nguyen Giap, who formed the third member of the leadership troika under Ho Chi Minh in the 1940s, was not a member of the league. He was, however, an active participant in the radicalizing events that shaped his generation. The youngest of his future compatriots, he was born in 1911 to a scholar-gentry family in Quang Binh province. As a student at the Imperial Academy in Hue, he was active in the student protest movement there. He also became a member of the New Vietnam Revolutionary Party (Tan Viet Cach Mang Dang), which had close links with the Youth League and eventually became a part of the Vietnamese Communist Party.

Central to the establishment of the Youth League and its revolutionary ideology was Ho Chi Minh. Several decades older than the students who made up the membership of the league, Ho Chi Minh was born sometime between 1890 and 1894 in Nghe An province to a poor scholar-gentry family. Through his father, a minor scholar official closely involved in anticolonial activities, he came to know many of the leaders of the reform generation, including Phan Boi Chau and Phan Chu Trinh. As a student at the National Academy in Hue, he joined in the anticolonial agitation organized under the auspices of the Reform Movement in 1908 and later taught briefly in one of the movement's schools. He left Vietnam for Europe in the summer of 1911, embarking on an intellectual and political odyssey that prefigured the experiences of many of the new intelligentsia in the 1920s. After traveling to southern France, northern Africa, New York City, and London, Ho Chi Minh eventually settled in Paris, where he worked with Phan Chu Trinh to draft the petition he presented to the peace conference at Paris in 1919. In the wake of the conference's unwillingness to consider these demands for greater Vietnamese political rights and responsibilities under French colonial rule, he turned from the more gradualist anticolonial ideas and strategies of the reform generation to Marxism. He became a founding member of the French Communist Party in 1920, a student at the University of the Toilers of the East in Moscow in 1923, and a leading spokesman for the anticolonial cause at the Fifth Congress of the Communist International in 1924. Sent to China as a Comintern agent in 1925, he began organizational work that resulted in the establishment of the Youth League.

The ideology of the Youth League was most fully expressed in *The Road to Revolution* [*Duong Cach Menh*], prepared by Ho Chi Minh in 1927 as a training manual for the organization's members. Marxism, particularly its Leninist formulations, occupied a dominant place in the analysis Ho presented in *Road to Revolution*. It provided an overarching framework to universalize the Vietnamese colonial experience and an organizational path to realize anticolonial aspirations and the transformation of Vietnamese society. But Ho emphasized the immediate imperative of the "national question" rather than "social revolution" or class issues and employed conceptual language that borrowed as much from indigenous political discourse as it did from Marx and Lenin. While the determinism of Marxism-Leninism injected a compelling note of historical inevitability into his consideration of Vietnamese national liberation, Ho devoted particular attention to the voluntarist dimension of revolutionary struggle. In discussions shaped by both Leninist themes and the voluntarist modes more familiar to his radical student readers, Ho drew not only from the Russian revolution and Marxism-Leninism as guides for the Vietnamese struggle for national liberation but also from the French and American revolutionary experiences and the ideas of Jefferson, Gandhi, and Sun Yat-sen. He also freely mixed neo-Confucian maxims with Leninist rhetoric from *What Is to Be Done?* to explicate the virtues necessary for young revolutionaries to bring about Vietnamese independence.

These diverse Marxist and indigenous intellectual legacies informed Ho's sustained discussion of the American revolution that, with analyses of the French and Russian revolutions, formed a substantial component of *Road to Revolution*. He opened his consideration of the American experience with a brief review of the European settlement of North America that foreshadowed both the materialist thrust of his analysis and its more traditional emphasis on the threats colonial rule posed to colonized peoples. Next, Ho turned to a consideration of the causes of the American revolution. At one level, the materialist emphasis of Ho's analysis of the reasons for the revolution substantially departed from the neo-Confucian renderings of the reform generation that attributed the success of American patriots to the emergence of virtuous elites:

> America is very rich in agricultural land, iron, coal, cotton, rice, cattle, and other resources as well. The English secretly wanted it all for themselves, so they promulgated the following three rules of behavior: 1) the Americans must always grant their resources to the English; they were not allowed to sell them to other nations; 2) the Americans were not permitted to set up factories or trading associations; 3) other countries were not allowed to trade with America; only the English could trade. These three laws, which also added heavy taxes and duties, made the American economy extremely poverty stricken.

But his analysis of revolution itself also reflected the persisting radical appreciation for the wealth and power of American society and its admiration for the voluntarist capacities of the Americans to exert their will to overcome historical circumstances:

> Angered, the Americans decided to "boycott" the English in 1770. The boycott against the English royal government lasted for five years. The English brought soldiers to suppress it and imposed their own officials. Every time they imposed one of their own officials, all the people felt more angry. In 1775, when the English army imposed a number of their own officials as well, the people pulled together to fight, and the English army killed nine people. This event, like adding fire to gunpowder, prompted the angry Americans to explode. In this life and death matter, they resolved to expel the new English government. After a year, on 4 July 1776, the revolution took place, and America declared itself independent and became a republic. Now, the United States has 48 states and 110 million people.

Finally, Ho combined aspects of Marxist-Leninist analysis with more traditional neo-Confucian formulations to present three lessons his Vietnamese readers should learn from the American revolution. The first lesson suggested in part that the shared experiences of imperialism and colonial rule made the United States a valuable model for Vietnamese to study. But Ho's efforts to differentiate aspects of the Vietnamese and American experiences drew less on Marxist-Leninist categories than on the familial images of reformist and radical rhetoric, reflecting the persistence of indigenous fears that colonialism threatened the very spirit and existence of the Vietnamese people:

> French policy toward Vietnam today is more shameful than English policy was toward America because the French put their grip on everything belonging to our people, hindering our people's labor and other affairs. They also forced us to smoke opium and drink liquor. The English were only fond of American money; the French want money but they also want to do away with our race, leaving Vietnam bereft of its children. Nonetheless, the Vietnamese people should still continue to study the American revolution!

A second lesson focused on the gap between American rhetoric and contemporary reality. It also expressed an admiration for American ideals one might not expect to find in a Marxist-Leninist analysis. But its emphasis on the collective rather than the individual nature of the rights ascribed to Americans fit both Confucian and Marxist conceptions of the subservient relationship of the individual to the state:

> In America's declaration of independence, there are these lines: "Under heaven all people have the right to liberty, the right to defend their lives, and the right to earn their living happily. If any government injures its people, they must bring down that government and build up another one. . . ." But now the American government does not want anyone to speak about revolution or attack the government!

Significantly, Ho's concern with collective rights and responsibilities prefigured the movement away from the individualistic concerns of many student radicals in the 1920s toward a focus on mass politics in subsequent decades.

In a final lesson that expressed an even more emphatic assertion of the importance of collective rights and responsibilities, Ho warned of the limitations of the American experience:

> Although the American revolution was successful more than 150 years ago, American workers and peasants are still extremely poor and carefully organize for the second

revolution. The American revolution then is a capitalist revolution. but a capitalist revolution is not a complete or world revolution. We lay down our lives for revolution, but
to make a complete or world revolution we must work in such a way to deliver rights
for all the masses rather than for a few people. Only by struggling many times over can
all the people have happiness.

But if America proved an imperfect guide to realizing Vietnam's revolutionary
aspirations, Ho's larger vision of a complete or world revolution was not rendered
in conventional Marxist terms as a dictatorship of the proletariat in *Road to Revolution.* While Ho offered the "courage," "spirit of sacrifice," and "unity" of workers
and peasants in the Russian revolution as models that came much closer to a world
revolution than the American or French experiences did, he used a Confucian rather
than a Bolshevik idiom to articulate the ultimate aims of the Vietnamese revolution.
Ho suggested "the great unity under heaven—that is, world revolution" (*thien ha dai
dong—ay la the gioi cach menh),* a characterization that both recalled the reform
generation's use of the Confucian utopian peace to denote Vietnam's idealized
postcolonial future and revealed radical efforts to recast and transform traditional
categories of analysis for revolutionary purposes.

Ho Chi Minh's account of the American revolution and other radical commentaries on America from the 1920s reflected the experimental, iconoclastic, and fluid
nature of the new intelligentsia's search for a new political and social order in Vietnam. As it had for the reform generation, America remained an important source of
inspiration for the celebration of voluntarism, which continued to infuse radical
political thought. The radical embrace of American figures such as Washington and
Lincoln shared aspects of the reformist concern with the cultivation of individual
neo-Confucian virtue and its respect for the wealth and power of the United States.
The new intelligentsia's training in French schools, its superior command of a wider
range of Western ideas, and its probing curiosity about the material sources of the
ideals that animated the European and American collective wills, however, served to
recast indigenous understandings of how revolutionary voluntarism could be exercised in Vietnam. For Ho Chi Minh and the radical students such as Pham Van Dong,
Truong Chinh, and Vo Nguyen Giap who were attracted to the ideas of the Youth
League and the universalism of Marxism-Leninism, the American experience was no
longer rendered as the ultimate objective of anticolonial politics but, rather, as one
stage in Vietnamese revolutionary development. But even in this case, indigenous
categories of analysis drawn from neo-Confucian, reformist, and radical discourse
shaped the articulation of Marxist-Leninist thought in Vietnam and the place of
America in it.

At the close of the decade, much of the radical agenda remained unrealized.
With the rise of the mass politics of the 1930s and its focus on collective rather
than individual interests, the radical effort to redefine the role of the individual
in Vietnamese society was forestalled. The symbolic space occupied by the United
States in the political discourse of the 1920s, like the broader eclectic contours of
radical thought itself, would continue to frame the Vietnamese intelligentsia's ongoing search for social transformation and political independence and shape the
Vietnamese encounter with the United States during and after World War II. . . .

In many ways, Vietnamese communists were no closer to transforming indigenous society and achieving independence at the end of the 1930s than the leaders

of the Reform Movement had been in the early decades of the century. With the fall of the Popular Front government in France in 1939 and the onset of renewed and more vigorous anticolonial repression in Vietnam, the prospects for their success grew even dimmer. But as the revolutionary situation became more favorable in the 1940s, the shifting contours of indigenous political thought under French rule that characterized the efforts of Vietnamese anticolonialists to understand and overcome the threatening forces that surrounded them had an enduring impact on Vietnamese communism and the future course of its diplomacy.

The movement from the neo-Confucianism and Social Darwinism of scholar-gentry reformers to the radicalism and internationalism of the new intelligentsia was less an evolutionary line than a continuing dialogue across generations that lacked a fixed or final synthesis. From this dialogue emerged a diverse repertoire of symbolic language and perceptual experiences that reflected not only an appreciation for Maoist internationalism and Leninist voluntarism but also an embrace of revolutionary heroism and Confucian moral virtue. As Ho Chi Minh, Pham Van Dong, Truong Chinh, and Vo Nguyen Giap organized the struggle for national liberation during World War II and turned to a largely imagined America for support, they relied on these powerful, if sometimes contradictory, legacies.

✕ *F U R T H E R   R E A D I N G*

Buttinger, Joseph. *The Smaller Dragon: A Political History of Vietnam* (1958).
————. *Vietnam: A Dragon Embattled* (1967).
Cady, John. *The Roots of French Imperialism in Asia* (1954).
Chailland, Gerard. *The Peasants of North Vietnam* (1970).
Chi, Hoang Van. *From Colonialism to Communism* (1971).
Duiker, William J. *The Communist Road to Power in Vietnam* (1981).
————. *The Comintern and Vietnamese Communism* (1975).
————. *Ho Chi Minh* (2000).
————. *Sacred War* (1995).
————. *Vietnam: Nation in Revolution* (1983).
Ennis, Thomas E. *French Policy and Developments in Indochina* (1956).
Hodgkin, Thomas L. *Vietnam: The Revolutionary Path* (1981).
Jamieson, Neil. *Understanding Vietnam* (1993).
Khanh, Huynh Kim. "The Vietnamese August Revolution Reinterpreted," *Journal of Asian Studies,* 30 (1971), 761–82.
Lacouture, Jean. *Ho Chi Minh* (1968).
Long, Ngo Vinh. *Before the Revolution: The Vietnamese Peasants Under the French* (1973).
McAlister, John T. *Viet Nam: The Origins of Revolution* (1969).
McAlister, John T., and Paul Mus. *The Vietnamese and Their Revolution* (1970).
Marr, David G. *Vietnamese Anti-Colonialism* (1971).
Murray, Martin. *The Development of Capitalism in Colonial Indochina* (1980).
Post, Ken. *Revolution, Socialism and Nationalism in Viet Nam* (vols. 1–3) (1989).
Robequain, Charles. *The Economic Development of French Indochina* (1944).
Tai, Hue-Tam Ho. *Radicalism and the Origins of the Vietnamese Revolution* (1992).
Thompson, Virginia. *French Indochina* (1937).
Tonnesson, Stein. *The Vietnamese Revolution of 1945* (1991).
Turner, Robert F. *Vietnamese Communism* (1975).
Vella, Walter F., ed. *Aspects of Vietnamese History* (1973).
Vien, Nguyen Khac, ed. *Tradition and Revolution in Vietnam* (1974).

CHAPTER
3

The Roots of the American

Commitment

✕

During World War II, President Franklin D. Roosevelt advanced a series of proposals aimed at liberalizing colonial rule and preparing dependent peoples for self-government. He often singled out French rule in Indochina as a particularly grievous example of colonial exploitation, and he advocated a trusteeship system for the postwar period. Yet shortly before his death in April 1945, Roosevelt had begun to retreat from his anticolonial stance. The determination of France and other imperial powers to retain their overseas possessions, and America's need to work with its European allies on a broad range of postwar diplomatic initiatives, forced a modification in the president's plans. FDR consequently did not challenge France's initial efforts to regain sovereignty in Indochina.

The establishment of the independent Republic of Vietnam in the wake of the Japanese surrender, and the subsequent outbreak of hostilities between French and Vietminh forces in November 1946, posed daunting policy dilemmas for the administration of Harry S Truman. Initially reluctant to support either side in the colonial struggle openly, the United States maintained a policy of official neutrality throughout the late 1940s. Washington finally abandoned that policy in 1950 and began to supply the French with substantial military and economic assistance.

Most scholars agree that the decision to aid the French in 1950 marks the initial U.S. commitment in Vietnam. But they have offered widely divergent explanations for that decision. Was the American commitment prompted by a growing appreciation of the economic importance of Southeast Asia to the United States? Or were strategic considerations stemming from America's perceived national security needs a more significant influence on American policymakers? To what extent might political, ideological, bureaucratic, or psychological factors have also played a role in the Truman administration's decision to support the French? Historians have agreed that broad global forces—and especially the intensifying Cold War between the United States and the Soviet Union—exerted a powerful pull on the U.S. gravitation toward the French in Indochina. They continue to disagree, however about the precise nature of that impact. This chapter explores these issues.

✗ D O C U M E N T S

Document 1 presents Secretary of State George C. Marshall's cable of May 1947 to the U.S. embassy in France, in which Marshall expresses American frustration with French policy in Indochina. In Document 2, the State Department reviews and evaluates U.S. policy toward Indochina, emphasizing the need to strike a balance between Vietnamese aspirations and French interests. On March 8, 1949, the Elysée Agreement established the State of Vietnam and the kingdoms of Laos and Cambodia as associated states within the French union. Document 3 is a public statement of American support for that agreement.

Documents 4 and 5 comprise the State Department's recommendation of February 1, 1950, to provide military aid to the French in Indochina and the recommendation of the National Security Council in its Policy Paper No. 64. Secretary of State Dean Acheson's announcement that American assistance would be forthcoming is featured in Document 6. In Document 7, taken from a press interview, Ho Chi Minh angrily denounces that decision and calls U.S. assistance imperialist intervention.

1. George C. Marshall on the
Indochina Dispute, 1947

We becoming increasingly concerned by slow progress toward settlement Indochina dispute. We fully appreciate French are making effort reach satisfactory settlement and hope visit Commissioner Bollaert to Indochina will produce concrete results. The following considerations, however, are submitted for your use any conversations you may have with French authorities at appropriate time this subject. We recognize it might not be desirable make such approach to newly constituted government in first days its reorganization, but nevertheless feel early appropriate opportunity might be found inform French Gov of our concern in this matter.

Key our position is our awareness that in respect developments affecting position Western democratic powers in southern Asia, we essentially in same boat as French, also as British and Dutch. We cannot conceive setbacks to long-range interests France which would not also be setbacks our own. Conversely we should regard close association France and members French Union as not only to advantage peoples concerned, but indirectly our own.

In our view, southern Asia in critical phase its history with seven new nations in process achieving or struggling independence or autonomy. These nations include quarter inhabitants world and their future course, owing sheer weight populations, resources they command, and strategic location, will be momentous factor world stability. Following relaxation European controls, internal racial, religious and national differences could plunge new nations into violent discord, or already apparent anti-Western Pan-Asiatic tendencies could become dominant political force, or Communists could capture control. We consider as best safeguard against these eventualities a continued close association between newly-autonomous peoples

Telegram from Marshall to Ambassador Jefferson Caffery in France, May 13, 1947, *Foreign Relations of the United States*, 1947, VI, 95–97.

and powers which have long been responsible their welfare. In particular we recognize Vietnamese will for indefinite period require French material and technical assistance and enlightened political guidance which can be provided only by nation steeped like France in democratic tradition and confirmed in respect human liberties and worth individual.

We equally convinced, however, such association must be voluntary to be lasting and achieve results, and that protraction present situation Indochina can only destroy basis voluntary cooperation, leave legacy permanent bitterness, and irrevocably alienate Vietnamese from France and those values represented by France and other Western democracies.

While fully appreciating difficulties French position this conflict, we feel there is danger in any arrangement which might provide Vietnamese opportunity compare unfavorably their own position and that of other peoples southern Asia who have made tremendous strides toward autonomy since war.

While we are still ready and willing to do anything we can which might be considered helpful, French will understand we not attempting come forward with any solution our own or intervene in situation. However, they will also understand we inescapably concerned with situation Far East generally, upon which developments Indochina likely have profound effect.

Plain fact is that Western democratic system is on defensive in almost all emergent nations southern Asia and, because identified by peoples these nations with what they have considered former denial their rights, is particularly vulnerable to attacks by demagogic leaders political movements of either ultra-nationalist or Communist nature which promise redress and revenge past so-called wrongs and inequalities. Signs development anti-Western Asiatic consciousness already multiplying, of which Inter-Asian Conf an example. Unanimity support for Vietnamese among other Asiatic countries very striking, even leading to moves Burma, India, and Malaya send volunteer forces their assistance. Vietnam cause proving rallying-cry for all anti-Western forces and playing in hands Communists all areas. We fear continuation conflict may jeopardize position all Western democratic powers in southern Asia and lead to very eventualities of which we most apprehensive.

We confident French fully aware dangers inherent in situation and therefore venture express renewed hope they will be most generous attempt find early solution which, by recognizing legitimate desires Vietnamese, will restore peace and deprive anti-democratic forces of powerful weapon.

For your info, evidence that French Communists are being directed accelerate their agitation French colonies even extent lose much popular support France may be indication Kremlin prepared sacrifice temporary gains with 40 million French to long range colonial strategy with 600 million dependent people, which lends great urgency foregoing views. . . . Dept much concerned lest French efforts find "true representatives Vietnam" with whom negotiate result creation impotent puppet Govt along lines Cochinchina regime, or that restoration Baodai may be attempted, implying democracies reduced resort monarchy as weapon against Communism. You may refer these further views if nature your conversations French appears warrant.

2. Statement of U.S. Policy Toward Indochina, 1948

Objectives

The immediate objective of US policy in Indochina is to assist in a solution of the present impasse which will be mutually satisfactory to the French and the Vietnamese peoples, which will result in the termination of the present hostilities, and which will be within the framework of US security.

Our long-term objectives are: (1) to eliminate so far as possible Communist influence in Indochina and to see installed a self-governing nationalist state which will be friendly to the US and which, commensurate with the capacity of the peoples involved, will be patterned upon our conception of a democratic state as opposed to the totalitarian state which would evolve inevitably from Communist domination; (2) to foster the association of the peoples of Indochina with the western powers, particularly with France with whose customs, language, and laws they are familiar, to the end that those peoples will prefer freely to cooperate with the western powers culturally, economically and politically; (3) to raise the standard of living so that the peoples of Indochina will be less receptive to totalitarian influences and will have an incentive to work productively and thus contribute to a better balanced world economy; and (4) to prevent undue Chinese penetration and subsequent influence in Indochina so that the peoples of Indochina will not be hampered in their natural developments by the pressure of an alien people and alien interests.

Policy Issues

To attain our immediate objective, we should continue to press the French to accommodate the basic aspirations of the Vietnamese: (1) unity of Cochinchina, Annam, and Tonkin, (2) complete internal autonomy, and (3) the right to choose freely regarding participation in the French Union. We have recognized French sovereignty over Indochina but have maintained that such recognition does not imply any commitment on our part to assist France to exert its authority over the Indochinese peoples. Since V-J day, the majority people of the area, the Vietnamese, have stubbornly resisted the reestablishment of French authority, a struggle in which we have tried to maintain insofar as possible a position of non-support of either party.

While the nationalist movement in Vietnam (Cochinchina, Annam, and Tonkin) is strong, and though the great majority of the Vietnamese are not fundamentally Communist, the most active element in the resistance of the local peoples to the French has been a Communist group headed by Ho Chi Minh. This group has successfully extended its influence to include practically all armed forces now fighting the French, thus in effect capturing control of the nationalist movement.

The French on two occasions during 1946 attempted to resolve the problem by negotiation with the government established and dominated by Ho Chi Minh. The general agreements reached were not, however, successfully implemented and widescale fighting subsequently broke out. Since early in 1947, the French have employed about 115,000 troops in Indochina, with little result, since the country-side except in Laos and Cambodia remains under the firm control of the Ho Chi Minh government. A series of French-established puppet governments have tended to enhance the prestige of Ho's government and to call into question, on the part of the Vietnamese, the sincerity of French intentions to accord an independent status to Vietnam.

Political.   We have regarded these hostilities in a colonial area as detrimental not only to our own long-term interests which require as a minimum a stable Southeast Asia but also detrimental to the interests of France, since the hatred engendered by continuing hostilities may render impossible peaceful collaboration and coopera-tion of the French and the Vietnamese peoples. This hatred of the Vietnamese people toward the French is keeping alive anti-western feeling among oriental peoples, to the advantage of the USSR and the detriment of the US.

We have not urged the French to negotiate with Ho Chi Minh, even though he probably is now supported by a considerable majority of the Vietnamese people, because of his record as a Communist and the Communist background of many of the influential figures in and about his government.

Postwar French governments have never understood, or have chosen to under-estimate, the strength of the nationalist movement with which they must deal in Indochina. It remains possible that the nationalist movement can be subverted from Communist control but this will require granting to a non-Communist group of na-tionalists at least the same concessions demanded by Ho Chi Minh. The failure of French governments to deal successfully with the Indochinese question has been due, in large measure, to the overwhelming internal issues facing France and the French Union, and to foreign policy considerations in Europe. These factors have combined with the slim parliamentary majorities of postwar governments in France to militate against the bold moves necessary to divert allegiance of the Vietnamese nationalists to non-Communist leadership.

In accord with our policy of regarding with favor the efforts of dependent peoples to attain their legitimate political aspirations, we have been anxious to see the French accord to the Vietnamese the largest possible degree of political and economic independence consistent with legitimate French interests. We have there-fore declined to permit the export to the French in Indochina of arms and munitions for the prosecution of the war against the Vietnamese. This policy has been limited in its effect as we have allowed the free export of arms to France, such exports thereby being available for re-shipment to Indochina or for releasing stocks from reserves to be forwarded to Indochina. . . .

Policy Evaluation

The objectives of US policy towards Indochina have not been realized. Three years after the termination of war a friendly ally, France, is fighting a desperate and appar-ently losing struggle in Indochina. The economic drain of this warfare on French recovery, while difficult to estimate, is unquestionably large. The Communist control in the nationalist movement has been increased during this period. US influence in Indochina and Southeast Asia has suffered as a result.

The objectives of US policy can only be attained by such French action as will satisfy the nationalist aspirations of the peoples of Indochina. We have repeatedly pointed out to the French the desirability of their giving such satisfaction and thus terminating the present open conflict. Our greatest difficulty in talking with the French and in stressing what should and what should not be done has been our inability to suggest any practicable solution of the Indochina problem, as we are all too well aware of the unpleasant fact that Communist Ho Chi Minh is the strongest and perhaps the ablest figure in Indochina and that any suggested solution which excludes him is an expedient of uncertain outcome. We are naturally hesitant to press the French too strongly or to become deeply involved so long as we are not in a position to suggest a solution or until we are prepared to accept the onus of intervention. The above considerations are further complicated by the fact that we have an immediate interest in maintaining in power a friendly French government, to assist in the furtherance of our aims in Europe. This immediate and vital interest has in consequence taken precedence over active steps looking toward the realization of our objectives in Indochina.

We are prepared, however, to support the French in every way possible in the establishment of a truly nationalist government in Indochina which, by giving satisfaction to the aspirations of the peoples of Indochina, will serve as a rallying point for the nationalists and will weaken the Communist elements. By such support and by active participation in a peaceful and constructive solution in Indochina we stand to regain influence and prestige.

Some solution must be found which will strike a balance between the aspirations of the peoples of Indochina and the interests to the French. Solution by French military reconquest of Indochina is not desirable. Neither would the complete withdrawal of the French from Indochina effect a solution. The first alternative would delay indefinitely the attainment of our objectives, as we would share inevitably in the hatred engendered by an attempted military reconquest and the denial of aspirations for self-government. The second solution would be equally unfortunate as in all likelihood Indochina would then be taken over by the militant Communist group. At best, there might follow a transition period, marked by chaos and terroristic activities, creating a political vacuum into which the Chinese inevitably would be drawn or would push. The absence of stabilization in China will continue to have an important influence upon the objective of a permanent and peaceable solution in Indochina.

We have not been particularly successful in our information and education program in orienting the Vietnamese toward the western democracies and the US. The program has been hampered by the failure of the French to understand that such informational activities as we conduct in Indochina are not inimical to their own long-term interests and by administrative and financial considerations which have prevented the development to the maximum extent of contacts with the Vietnamese. An increased effort should be made to explain democratic institutions, especially American institutions and American policy, to the Indochinese by direct personal contact, by the distribution of information about the US, and the encouraging of educational exchange.

3. The United States Praises the Elysée Agreements, 1949

The formation of the new unified state of Vietnam and the recent announcement by Bao Dai that the future constitution will be decided by the Vietnamese people are welcome developments which should serve to hasten the reestablishment of peace in that country and the attainment of Vietnam's rightful place in the family of nations.

The United States Government hopes that the agreements of March 8 between President Auriol and Bao Dai, who is making sincere efforts to unite all truly nationalist elements within Vietnam, will form the basis for the progressive realization of the legitimate aspirations of the Vietnamese people.

4. The State Department Recommends Military Aid to the French, 1950

The Problem

Should the United States provide military aid in Indochina and, if so, how much and in what way.

Assumption

A. There will not be an effective split between the USSR and Communist China within the next three years.

B. The USSR will not declare war on any Southeast Asian country within the next three years.

C. Communist China will not declare war on any Southeast Asian country within the next three years.

D. The USSR will endeavor to bring about the fall of Southeast Asian governments which are opposed to Communism by using all devices short of war, making use of Communist China and indigenous communists in this endeavor.

Facts Bearing on the Problem

1. When the Mutual Defense Assistance Act of 1949 was being written, the question of providing military aid to Southeast Asia was examined and it was decided not to include specific countries in that area, other than the Republic of the Philippines.

2. The attitude of the Congress toward the provision of military and economic aid to foreign countries recently has stiffened due to both economy and to policy considerations.

Department of State *Bulletin,* 21 (July 18, 1949), 75.

Foreign Relations of the United States, 1950, VI, 711–715.

3. At the same time, the Congress has shown considerable dissatisfaction with policies which are alleged to have contributed to the Communist success in China and which are involved in the current United States approach toward the question of Formosa.

4. Section 303 of the Mutual Defense Assistance Act of 1949 makes available to the President the sum of $75 million for use, at the President's discretion, in the general area of China to advance the purposes and policies of the United Nations.

5. Section 303 funds are unrestricted in their use.

6. The British Commonwealth Conference recently held at Colombo recognized that no SEA [Southeast Asia] regional military pact now exists due to divergent interest and that such an arrangement was now unlikely.

7. Communism has made important advances in the Far East during the past year.

8. Opposition to Communism in Indochina is actively being carried on by the three legally-constituted governments of Vietnam, Cambodia and Laos.

9. Communist-oriented forces in Indochina are being aided by Red China and the USSR. . . .

Conclusions

A. Significant developments have taken place in Indochina since the Mutual Defense Assistance Act of 1949 was drawn up, these changes warranting a reexamination of the question of military aid.

B. The whole of Southeast Asia is in danger of falling under Communist domination.

C. The countries and areas of Southeast Asia are not at present in a position to form a regional organization for self-defense nor are they capable of defending themselves against military aggressive Communism, without the aid of the great powers. Despite their lack of military strength, however, there is a will on the part of the legal governments of Indochina toward nationalism and a will to resist whatever aims at destroying that nationalism.

D. The French native and colonial troops presently in Indochina are engaged in military operations aimed at denying the expansion southward of Communism from Red China and of destroying its power in Indochina.

E. In the critical areas of Indochina France needs aid in its support of the legally-constituted anti-Communist states.

Recommendations

1. The United States should furnish military aid in support of the anti-Communist nationalist governments of Indochina, this aid to be tailored to meet deficiencies toward which the United States can make a unique contribution, not including United States troops.

2. This aid should be financed out of funds made available by Section 303 of the Mutual Defense Assistance Act of 1949.

5. National Security Council Paper No. 64, 1950

The Position of the United States with Respect to Indochina

The Problem

1. To undertake a determination of all practicable United States measures to protect its security in Indochina and to prevent the expansion of communist aggression in that area.

Analysis

2. It is recognized that the threat of communist aggression against Indochina is only one phase of anticipated communist plans to seize all of Southeast Asia. It is understood that Burma is weak internally and could be invaded without strong opposition or even that the Government of Burma could be subverted. However, Indochina is the area most immediately threatened. It is also the only area adjacent to communist China which contains a large European army, which along with native troops is now in armed conflict with the forces of communist aggression. A decision to contain communist expansion at the border of Indochina must be considered as a part of a wider study to prevent communist aggression into other parts of Southeast Asia.

3. A large segment of the Indochinese nationalist movement was seized in 1945 by Ho Chi Minh, a Vietnamese who under various aliases has served as a communist agent for thirty years. He has attracted non-communist as well as communist elements to his support. In 1946, he attempted, but failed to secure French agreement to his recognition as the head of a government of Vietnam. Since then he has directed a guerrilla army in raids against French installations and lines of communication. French forces which have been attempting to restore law and order found themselves pitted against a determined adversary who manufactures effective arms locally, who received supplies of arms from outside sources, who maintained no capital or permanent headquarters and who was, and is able, to disrupt and harass almost any area within Vietnam (Tonkin, Annam and Cochinchina) at will.

4. The United States has, since the Japanese surrender, pointed out to the French Government that the legitimate nationalist aspirations of the people of Indochina must be satisfied, and that a return to the prewar colonial rule is not possible. The Department of State has pointed out to the French Government that it was and is necessary to establish and support governments in Indochina particularly in Vietnam, under leaders who are capable of attracting to their causes the non-communist nationalist followers who had drifted to the Ho Chi Minh communist movement in the absence of any non-communist nationalist movement around which to plan their aspirations.

National Security Council 64, February 27, 1950, *Foreign Relations of the United States,* 1950, VI, 744–747.

5. In an effort to establish stability by political means, where military measures had been unsuccessful, i.e., by attracting non-communist nationalists, now followers of Ho Chi Minh, to the support of anti-communist nationalist leaders, the French Government entered into agreements with the governments of the Kingdoms of Laos and Cambodia to elevate their status from protectorates to that of independent states within the French Union. The State of Vietnam was formed, with similar status, out of the former French protectorates of Tonkin, Annam and the former French Colony of Cochinchina. Each state received an increased degree of autonomy and sovereignty. Further steps towards independence were indicated by the French. The agreements were ratified by the French Government on 2 February 1950.

6. The Governments of Vietnam, Laos and Cambodia were officially recognized by the United States and the United Kingdom on February 7, 1950. Other Western powers have, or are committed to do likewise. The United States has consistently brought to the attention of non-communist Asian countries the danger of communist aggression which threatens them if communist expansion in Indochina is unchecked. As this danger becomes more evident it is expected to overcome the reluctance that they have had to recognize and support the three new states. We are therefore continuing to press those countries to recognize the new states. On January 18, 1950, the Chinese Communist Government announced its recognition of the Ho Chi Minh movement as the legal Government of Vietnam, while on January 30, 1950, the Soviet Government, while maintaining diplomatic relations with France, similarly announced its recognition.

7. The newly formed States of Vietnam, Laos and Cambodia do not as yet have sufficient political stability nor military power to prevent the infiltration into their areas of Ho Chi Minh's forces. The French Armed Forces, while apparently effectively utilized at the present time, can do little more than to maintain the *status quo*. Their strength of some 140,000 does, however, represent an army in being and the only military bulwark in that area against the further expansion of communist aggression from either internal or external forces.

8. The presence of Chinese Communist troops along the border of Indochina makes it possible for arms, material and troops to move freely from Communist China to the northern Tonkin area now controlled by Ho Chi Minh. There is already evidence of movement of arms.

9. In the present state of affairs, it is doubtful that the combined native Indochinese and French troops can successfully contain Ho's forces should they be strengthened by either Chinese Communist troops crossing the border, or Communist-supplied arms and material in quantity from outside Indochina strengthening Ho's forces.

Conclusions

10. It is important to United States security interests that all practicable measures be taken to prevent further communist expansion in Southeast Asia. Indochina is a key area of Southeast Asia and is under immediate threat.

11. The neighboring countries of Thailand and Burma could be expected to fall under Communist domination if Indochina were controlled by a Communist-dominated government. The balance of Southeast Asia would then be in grave hazard.

12. Accordingly, the Departments of State and Defense should prepare as a matter of priority a program of all practicable measures designed to protect United States security interests in Indochina.

6. Dean Acheson Urges Aid for Indochina, 1950

The [French] Foreign Minister [Robert Schuman] and I have just had an exchange of views on the situation in Indochina and are in general agreement both as to the urgency of the situation in that area and as to the necessity for remedial action. We have noted the fact that the problem of meeting the threat to the security of Viet Nam, Cambodia, and Laos which now enjoy independence within the French union is primarily the responsibility of France and the Governments and peoples of Indochina. The United States recognizes that the solution of the Indochina problem depends both upon the restoration of security and upon the development of genuine nationalism and that United States assistance can and should contribute to these major objectives.

The United States Government, convinced that neither national independence nor democratic evolution exist[s] in any area dominated by Soviet imperialism, considers the situation to be such as to warrant its according economic aid and military equipment to the associated states of Indochina and to France in order to assist them in restoring stability and permitting these states to pursue their peaceful and democratic development.

7. Answers to Questions Put by the Press Regarding U.S. Intervention in Indochina, July 25, 1950

Question: What is, Mr. President, the present situation of the U.S. imperialists' interventionist policy in Indochina?

Answer: The U.S. imperialists have of late openly interfered in Indochina's affairs. It is with their money and weapons and their instructions that the French colonialists have been waging war in Viet-Nam, Cambodia, and Laos.

However, the U.S. imperialists are intensifying their plot to discard the French colonialists so as to gain complete control over Indochina. That is why they do their utmost to redouble their direct intervention in every field—military, political, and economic. It is also for this reason that the contradictions between them and the French colonialists become sharper and sharper.

Question: What influence does this intervention exert on the Indochinese people?

Answer: The U.S. imperialists supply their henchmen with armaments to massacre the Indochinese people. They dump their goods in Indochina to prevent the development of local handicrafts. Their pornographic culture contaminates the youth in areas placed under their control. They follow the policy of buying up, deluding,

U.S. Department of State *Bulletin,* 22 (May 22, 1950), 821.

From *Ho Chi Minh On Revolution: Selected Writings, 1920–1966,* Bernard B. Fall, editor, 1967, pp. 199–200. Reprinted with permission.

and dividing our people. They drag some bad elements into becoming their tools and use them to invade our country.

Question: What measure shall we take against them?

Answer: To gain independence, we, the Indochinese people, must defeat the French colonialists, our number-one enemy. At the same time, we will struggle against the U.S. interventionists. The deeper their interference, the more powerful are our solidarity and our struggle. We will expose their maneuvers before all our people, especially those living in areas under their control. We will expose all those who serve as lackeys for the U.S. imperialists to coerce, deceive, and divide our people.

The close solidarity between the peoples of Viet-Nam, Cambodia, and Laos constitutes a force capable of defeating the French colonialists and the U.S. interventionists. The U.S. imperialists failed in China, they will fail in Indochina.

We are still laboring under great difficulties but victory will certainly be ours.

✗ E S S A Y S

In the first essay, Patrick J. Hearden of Purdue University links U.S. involvement in Indochina to America's larger economic goals for the postwar world. Those goals encompassed, in his view, not just narrow U.S. commercial ambitions in Southeast Asia but the much broader needs of the world capitalist system as a whole. Hearden argues that the Truman administration's preoccupation with the economic revival of Japan played a decisive role in the U.S. commitment to the French.

Robert J. McMahon of the University of Florida also emphasizes the economic factors that tied Indochina to broader U.S. foreign-policy objectives. But material considerations cannot be viewed in isolation from strategic imperatives, McMahon emphasizes. He contends that it is the combination of economic calculations and national security fears, in conjunction with a set of powerful political and psychological pressures, that best explains the initial U.S. commitment to the French.

An Economic Perspective on U.S. Involvement

PATRICK J. HEARDEN

Even before the United States formally entered World War II, American leaders began making plans for the creation of a peaceful and prosperous international order after hostilities ceased. President Franklin D. Roosevelt and his State Department advisers hoped to establish a liberal capitalist world system based upon the principle of equal commercial opportunity. Confident that the United States would emerge from the conflict with a preponderance of military and economic power, they aimed to promote an open door policy that would give all industrial countries equal access to raw materials and commodity markets around the globe. American leaders realized that Great Britain would no longer be able to rule the world in the interest of free trade, and they believed that the United States should be prepared to fill the

---

power vacuum. They hoped that, just as the last century had belonged to England, an Allied victory over the Axis would mark the dawn of an American century. In short, they envisioned the establishment of a Pax Americana that would replace the Pax Britannica and thereby sustain the capitalist epoch.

But the nightmare of a depression haunted American leaders when they contemplated the nature of the postwar world. Following the stock market crash on Wall Street in 1929, the United States had plunged into a decade of depression. Businessmen shut down plants and laid off workers because of a lack of demand for consumer goods, and as unemployment increased and household spending declined, more companies closed their doors. President Roosevelt launched his New Deal program to counteract the vicious circle, but economic recovery did not come until the onset of World War II. When the shooting started in Europe in 1939, American factories began receiving orders for a vast array of weapons and munitions from both the United States government and the Allied nations. The stimulus of military spending continued turning the wheels of industry and creating jobs for those without work, and in 1942 Roosevelt boasted that "Dr. Win-the-War" had replaced "Dr. New Deal." Though pleased about the wartime prosperity, Roosevelt and his advisers realized that the New Deal had failed to overcome the Great Depression. Thus they feared that, when the demand for military hardware declined at the end of the war, the twin problems of overproduction and unemployment would return to plague the United States.

Top government officials and corporate executives who participated in the decision-making process understood that there were two different ways of avoiding a postwar depression in the United States. Either they could plan the American economy so that domestic production would match the requirements of the home market, or they could obtain foreign markets to absorb the surplus output of the farms and factories in the United States. American policy makers rejected the option of centralized economic planning to create an internal balance between supply and demand because they believed that excessive governmental controls would destroy the essentials of free enterprise. Fearing that an extension of New Deal regulations would undermine entrepreneurial freedom by taking management decisions out of private hands, American leaders chose the alternative of overseas commercial expansion to solve the problem of domestic overproduction. In other words, they looked to new frontiers in the markets of the world in hopes of preserving capitalism in the United States.

President Roosevelt and his State Department advisers also hoped to promote world peace by liberalizing international commerce. During the Great Depression, many manufacturing nations had erected high tariff walls around both their internal and colonial markets. The consequent decline in the volume of world trade had a particularly harmful impact on countries that did not have enough natural resources to sustain themselves in economic isolation. Germany and Japan, after being denied access to essential foodstuffs and raw materials, led a group of these "have-not-nations" in an attempt to redivide the world in order to satisfy their material needs. Although American policymakers assumed that the Allies would defeat the Axis drive to partition the planet into exclusive spheres of influences, they feared that a resumption of economic nationalism in the postwar era would sow the seeds for yet another global conflict. They were therefore intent on establishing a liberal international trading system after the war so that "have-not nations" like Germany and Japan could achieve prosperity by engaging in peaceful commerce rather than military conquest.

During their postwar planning sessions between 1941 and 1945, State Department officials drafted blueprints for the creation of a peaceful and prosperous international capitalist utopia. They carefully advanced a multidimensional economic program embracing the following five key points: (1) the extension of American loans to underwrite the economic reconstruction of industrial countries that had been devastated by the long military ordeal; (2) the reintegration of Germany into the global economy; (3) the limitation of armaments to permit small countries to devote their sparse resources to economic rehabilitation rather than military preparation; (4) the reduction of American tariffs to allow foreign countries to increase their exports to the United States and thereby earn dollars that they could use to purchase American products; and (5) the modification of the European imperial preference systems to give all nations equal access to raw materials and commodity markets in colonial areas such as British Malaya, Dutch Indonesia, and French Indochina.

The architects of the new world order spent much of their time in the State Department discussing the dangers of colonialism. Adolf Berle, Leo Pasvolsky, and others pointed out that the continuation of colonial monopolies in the postwar period would not only undermine American economic interests but that imperial preferences might even provoke dynamic "have-not nations" into taking aggressive actions that would culminate in World War III. These State Department experts also noted that continued colonial exploitation might stimulate a wave of revolutionary upheavals throughout the Third World. They were particularly worried that the imperial policies of the British, Dutch, and French in the Far East would give rise to a strong anticolonial movement under the banner of Asia for the Asians. Many Oriental nationalists, noncommunist as well as communist, were talking about the need for a united Asian crusade to end European rule in the Far East. American diplomats feared that such a Pan Asiatic movement would threaten the economic interests of the United States along with the other industrial countries around the world.

Disturbed by such dismal prospects, the postwar planners in the Department of State sponsored an ambitious trusteeship scheme to solve the troublesome problem of colonialism. They proposed that all dependent areas should be administered by either a single trustee country or a group of trustees acting under the auspices of the United Nations. These trustees would be responsible for helping the colonial peoples under their guardianship attain political maturity. By progressively introducing measures of self-government in dependent regions, the trustees were to prepare their wards for eventual independence. The State Department plan also called upon the trustee nations to promote economic development in colonial areas for the benefit of both the native populations and the rest of the world. The trustees would therefore be required to open the territories under their tutelage to the trade and investments of all countries regardless of their size. Under Secretary Sumner Welles stressed this point when he told his subordinates in the State Department that the issue of equal access to natural resources and commodity markets was "the keystone of the whole structure of trusteeship for dependent areas."

President Roosevelt gave the trusteeship proposal strong support. He liked to point out that during the last four decades the United States had been preparing the

Philippine Islands for self-government, and he frequently suggested that the American treatment of the Philippines should serve as a model for the European powers to emulate. Roosevelt believed that colonial peoples should go through an interim period of international guardianship until they were ready for independence. He thought that the training period might be as short as a decade or so for advanced areas like Indochina and as long as a century or more for backward regions like Borneo. Although he was a gradualist with regard to the decolonization question, Roosevelt emphasized the need for the European powers to fix definite timetables for granting independence to their wards. He insisted that dependent peoples should not be held in tutelage after they were able to stand on their own feet. In a nutshell, Roosevelt regarded the trusteeship interval as a transitional stage along the road from the colonialism of the past to the self-determinism of the future. . . .

. . . [N]either President Roosevelt nor his State Department advisers thought that the French had any claim to regain their Indochina empire. It is true that in an effort to encourage the French to resist their Nazi oppressors, American officials made public pronouncements favoring the return of all French colonies in the postwar period. In their private conversations, however, they made it quite clear that French Indochina should be administered by an international trusteeship. Sumner Welles lectured his colleagues in August 1942 that France had no inherent right to exploit Indochina. "There is a great moral question involved here," he observed, "and it is a question that will shape and color the history of the world after this war is over." President Roosevelt agreed. He told Secretary of State Cordell Hull in January 1944 that Indochina should not go back to France after the war. "France has had the country—thirty million inhabitants—for nearly one hundred years, and the people are worse off than they were at the beginning," Roosevelt complained. "France has milked it for one hundred years. The people of Indochina are entitled to something better than that."

American leaders hoped that their Russian allies would support their plans for the postwar era. After crossing through Eastern Europe, the German Wehrmacht had penetrated deep into the Soviet Union. Millions of Russians were dying in defense of their homeland, and the Nazi armies were destroying thousands of Soviet factories. Seeking to reduce Russian fears about a future German invasion, American officials indicated that the United States would participate in policing the postwar world. They also thought that they might be able to win Soviet cooperation in Eastern Europe by offering American loans for Russian economic reconstruction. But the apprehension grew in Washington that the Russians would attempt to dominate the countries of Eastern Europe in order to satisfy their security needs. As they became increasingly concerned about the likelihood of Soviet expansion on the European continent if both Germany and France were disarmed, American leaders began thinking that France should resume her traditional position as a principal European power. By November 1944, they concluded that it would be necessary to rearm France with American weapons.

After reversing himself with regard to the issue of French militarism, President Roosevelt also began changing his mind about the question of French colonialism. Roosevelt wanted to postpone making a final decision concerning Indochina until the peace settlement following the war, but after the Yalta Conference in February 1945, there was growing evidence that the Soviet Union aimed to dominate Poland

and other countries in Eastern Europe. In a discussion with the American ambassador in Paris on March 13, General Charles de Gaulle pointed to the Russian menace to Europe in an attempt to blackmail the United States into supporting the restoration of the French empire in Indochina. "The Russians are advancing apace," de Gaulle warned. "When Germany falls they will be upon us. If the public here comes to realize that you are against us in Indochina there will be terrific disappointment and nobody knows to what that will lead. We do not want to become Communist; we do not want to fall into the Russian orbit, but I hope that you do not push us into it." On the next day, Roosevelt told one of his close advisers that he would agree to let the French retain their colonies in Indochina with the proviso that independence would be the ultimate goal.

Although Roosevelt died a month later and Harry S Truman entered the White House, there was no sharp break in American policy toward Indochina. The State Department assumed the difficult task of attempting to reconcile American objectives in Europe and Asia. On the one hand, American diplomats thought that the United States should allow the French to keep their Indochina empire in order to maintain France as a military ally in the event of future Russian aggression in Europe. On the other hand, they believed that the United States should urge the French to grant local autonomy in their Southeast Asian possessions in order to prevent bloodshed in Vietnam. The State Department adopted these views on April 30 in a key policy paper that held that the United States should not oppose the restoration of French authority in Vietnam, Laos, and Cambodia but that American officials should seek assurance of French intentions to establish self-government in Indochina. A few days later, at the first meeting in San Francisco to create the United Nations, Secretary of State Edward R. Stettinius told the French ambassador that the United States had never questioned the sovereignty of his country in Indochina.

The French were eager to reestablish control over their Indochina colonies. Although Germany had delivered a sharp blow to their national pride by defeating and occupying their country, the French did not simply want to reassert their imperial authority because of a psychological need to compensate for the humiliation they had suffered at the hands of Hitler. Cosmopolitan French leaders were prompted by rational calculations rather than emotional feelings. The influential directors of the Bank of Indochina, hoping to safeguard their huge investments, demanded protection for French economic interests in the Orient. Concerned about maintaining the cohesion of their overseas empire as a whole, policymakers in Paris subscribed to the "tenpin theory," which held that if one French colony won its independence nationalism would be encouraged elsewhere in the French empire. If the first tenpin tumbled, it would strike others, and they in turn could bring down the whole stand. More specifically, should Vietnam fall to the forces of nationalism, the French might lose not only their economically less important colonies in Southeast Asia (Cambodia and Laos) but also their more valuable possessions in North Africa (Morocco, Tunisia, and Algeria).

The French received quiet assistance from the United States when they decided to send an expeditionary force to Vietnam. Two weeks after Japan surrendered in August 1945, the State Department informed the American embassy in India that the United States had no thought of opposing the reestablishment of French control over Indochina. But the American government did not merely acquiesce in the French effort to reconquer Vietnam. Although the State Department published a statement declaring that the United States would not participate in the forceful imposition of French authority in Indochina, American policymakers acted in ways that ran counter to their public posture of neutrality. The United States permitted the French to keep without payment the Lend-Lease equipment that had been given to General de Gaulle before Japan capitulated and to use these military supplies in Indochina after removing all the American insignia. The United States also provided a large number of ships for the transportation of French troops and American weapons to Vietnam.

While the American government attempted to conceal these actions, Great Britain openly supported the French campaign to recolonize Indochina. The Allied powers had agreed, at the Potsdam Conference in July 1945, that after the war the responsibility for disarming and repatriating the Japanese troops in French Indochina would go to the British in the region south of the sixteenth parallel and to the Chinese in the area north of that parallel. The first British troops arrived in Saigon on September 12, and a small detachment of French soldiers accompanied them. General Douglas D. Gracey, the commander of the British forces, promptly ordered the Vietnamese inhabitants of Saigon to turn over their weapons. When the Vietminh called a general strike in protest on September 17, General Gracey responded by proclaiming martial law, suspending all Vietnamese newspapers, and banning demonstrations of any kind. Gracey also released from prison and armed 1,400 French soldiers who had been interned by the Japanese after their March coup. The French troops immediately took over the public buildings in Saigon and stormed down the streets looking for Vietnamese to beat.

The brutal French rampage set the stage in southern Vietnam for the outbreak of a war for national liberation. The Vietminh called a general strike on September 24, and it was soon difficult to get food and supplies into Saigon. With insufficient British and French troops to restore order and expand his control beyond Saigon, General Gracey decided to use the Japanese soldiers he had been sent to disarm. Gracey threatened to treat Japanese officers as war criminals if they refused to order their men to help subdue the Vietminh. When the first military units arrived from France on October 5, they joined with the British and Japanese in cracking the blockade around Saigon and then in driving through the Mekong delta. The Vietminh retreated into the highlands and resorted to guerrilla tactics. The Japanese, after suffering heavy casualties in the intense fighting, were gradually disarmed and replaced by reinforcements from France. As their numbers grew, the French were able to administer the larger cities and provincial towns in southern Vietnam. But they could not prevent the Vietminh guerrillas from controlling the surrounding countryside.

In northern Vietnam, by contrast, the Vietminh exercised firm control of urban as well as rural areas. The government established by Ho Chi Minh in Hanoi following the revolution in August 1945 enjoyed widespread public support. Even Catholic priests backed the Vietminh regime after Ho initiated a reformist rather than a communist program. Besides allowing native landlords who had not collaborated with the foreign enemies to keep their large holdings, the Vietminh wiped out the salt monopoly, abolished the forced labor system, reduced land taxes, legalized unions, and instituted an eight-hour day. Gambling and prostitution were banned, the use of opium and alcohol was prohibited, and free classes were set up to teach the illiterate masses how to read and write. In addition to introducing these social and economic reforms, the Vietminh established a system of universal suffrage to bring more people into the political process. All men and women over eighteen years of age were given the right to vote on both the local and national level.

However, Vietminh efforts to implement this liberal program in northern Vietnam were suddenly disrupted on September 9 when the first Chinese forces arrived in Hanoi to disarm the Japanese. General Lu Han, a warlord from southern China, led between 125,000 and 150,000 troops into famine-stricken Tonkin. Swarming down from China like a ravenous horde of human locusts, these soldiers plundered and looted everything in their path. Their officers were even more destructive. Establishing a new exchange rate between the Chinese dollar and the Vietnamese piaster, General Lu Han made Chinese money worth three times more in Hanoi than at home. The Chinese then began using their overvalued currency to buy local businesses and property at little cost to themselves. Unlike the British in the south, Lu Han had no intention of helping the French regain control of northern Vietnam. Instead, he was willing to let the Vietminh govern Tonkin while his army gouged the whole region. Lu Han and his cohorts in southern China viewed the occupation of northern Vietnam as an opportunity to impose their own long-range program of economic exploitation in Indochina.

But the Nationalist government in China, headed by Generalissimo Chiang Kai-shek, had different ideas. Uninterested in controlling any part of Indochina on a permanent basis, Chiang viewed the Chinese occupation of northern Vietnam as a chance to extract political concessions from France. The Generalissimo succeeded in working out a deal with the French on the last day of February 1946. The French agreed to relinquish their old imperial right of extraterritoriality in China, and in return Chiang agreed to allow French troops to replace Chinese forces in Tonkin. A week later, on March 6, Ho Chi Minh signed an ambiguous treaty with the French. Ho agreed to permit 15,000 French soldiers to land peaceably in northern Vietnam but with the understanding that they would be gradually withdrawn during the next five years. The French agreed to recognize the Democratic Republic of Vietnam as a free state but only on the condition that it would remain part of the French Union. Finally, both parties agreed that there would be a referendum in Cochinchina to determine whether it would be reunited with the rest of Vietnam or remain a separate state in the French Union.

Ho Chi Minh signed this unpalatable treaty because he feared the Chinese more than the French. Chiang was determined to make his own agreement with France operative, and he therefore pressured Ho to allow the return of French troops into northern Vietnam. Not wanting to risk war with both France and China at the same time, Ho decided to compromise with the French in order to get the Chinese out of his country. Many of his colleagues charged him with making a bad deal, but Ho answered his critics with a lesson in geopolitics. "You fools!" he lectured. "Don't you realize what it means if the Chinese remain? Don't you remember your history? The last time the Chinese came, they stayed a thousand years. The French are foreigners. They are weak. Colonialism is dying. The white man is finished in Asia. But if the Chinese stay now, they will never go. As for me, I prefer to sniff French shit for five years than eat Chinese shit for the rest of my life."

But the French had no intention of abiding by the provisions of their treaty with Ho Chi Minh. The French refused to hold a plebiscite in Cochinchina because they realized that the vast majority of the peasants would vote for reunification with the rest of Vietnam. The French also rejected a Vietminh request for a cease-fire in southern Vietnam. In the spring of 1946, therefore, Ho traveled to France to try to work out a permanent settlement. But he could not find a middle ground. The French were not interested in making peace if it meant that they would lose any part of their Indochina empire, and Ho was not willing to make peace if it meant that he would have to sacrifice the independence of his country. Ho left France empty-handed after months of fruitless negotiations, and when he arrived home in the autumn of 1946 he found both sides preparing for a military showdown. While the French were building up their troop strength in Vietnam, General Vo Nguyen Giap had increased the size of his regular army from 30,000 to 60,000 men. The clash soon came. Using heavy naval guns, the French shelled Vietminh forces in the port of Haiphong on November 23, and when the Vietminh attacked French troops in Hanoi on December 19, a general war erupted.

After he had ignored repeated pleas from Ho Chi Minh for American support for Vietnamese independence, President Truman decided to assist France as full-scale fighting commenced in Tonkin. He and his advisers in the State Department chose not to exert pressure on Paris to make concessions that might end the bloodletting in Indochina for fear that France would refuse to help check the spread of Russian influence in Europe. Their Europe-first mentality was reinforced by their increasing concern about the communist leadership of the Vietminh. But while American policy-makers preferred French colonialism over Vietnamese communism, they did not want to be charged with sponsoring Western imperialism in the Far East. Thus they tried to camouflage American aid for the French military campaign in Vietnam by channeling most of it indirectly through metropolitan France. The United States sent France huge amounts of money and large quantities of weapons ostensibly for French economic reconstruction and European strategic protection. But American officials realized that the French were using a considerable portion of this military and financial assistance to sustain their war effort in Indochina.

Yet the French, even with the aid they were receiving from the United States, still could not defeat the Vietminh. . . .

. . . In October 1947, they mounted a major offensive against the Vietminh base area in the mountains north of Hanoi. The French captured large stores of Vietminh food and ammunition, yet they could not destroy their elusive foe. The guerrillas easily disappeared into the jungle when they heard the distant roar of French tanks and trucks rumbling along the narrow roads. Not only were the gains minimal, but the costs were prohibitive. The Vietminh staged ambush after ambush as the overextended French soldiers retreated slowly down the roads winding through the jungle-covered mountains of northern Tonkin. The French suffered heavy casualties: over 1,000 killed and over 3,000 wounded. The Vietminh were encouraged by their success, and early in 1948 they increased their attacks on iso-lated French outposts and exposed French convoys.

Unable to win a decisive battlefield victory, the French soon began to search for a political solution for their troubles in Indochina. They ultimately decided to install a puppet government in Vietnam under former Emperor Bao Dai with the hope of uniting all noncommunist nationalists behind the new regime. Bao Dai had fled to Hong Kong after the establishment of the Democratic Republic of Vietnam, but the French succeeded in persuading him to return home and assume the appearance of power. In an agreement with Bao Dai in June 1948, the French declared their recognition of Vietnamese independence within the framework of the French Union. Yet the status of Cochinchina remained unsettled, and Vietnamese nationalists were skeptical about French intentions. In a second agreement with Bao Dai in March 1949, the French promised that Cochinchina would be reunited with Annam and Tonkin, but they stipulated that both the military affairs and foreign relations of Vietnam must remain in their hands. Because the French were not willing to grant Bao Dai real independence, most noncommunist nationalists refused to back his regime. And since many of these conservatives concluded that they had no alternative but to follow Ho Chi Minh, the Vietminh achieved complete control of the Vietnamese resistance movement.

Despite the fact that Bao Dai lacked popular support, however, the Truman administration decided to back him. Red China and Soviet Russia opened diplomatic relations with the Democratic Republic of Vietnam in late January 1950, and a week later the United States formally recognized the Bao Dai puppet government. Still not satisfied, the French asked the United States for more aid for their military operations in Indochina. Secretary of State Dean G. Acheson worried that every franc that the French spent in Vietnam was one less franc they could use for the defense of Europe. Besides their desire to provide financial relief for France, Acheson and his colleagues in the State Department hoped to use American aid as a lever to compel the French not only to agree to the rearmament of West Germany but also to grant independence to the Bao Dai regime. But the French responded to American pressure by warning that without more support from the United States they might have to withdraw from Vietnam. Although the French remained intransigent, President Truman approved a $15 million aid package on March 10 to underwrite the French war effort in Indochina. With that seemingly small step, taken just a few months before the outbreak of the Korean War, the United States significantly moved from affording indirect to direct support for French colonialism in Indochina.

The American decision to cross that bridge grew out of concerns over a profound dislocation in the international economic system following World War II. The United States had enormously expanded its industrial capacity during the war, and American leaders realized the need for an enlarged export trade to avoid falling back into the depths of a depression. They also understood that the industrial countries of Europe needed to import capital goods from the United States to get their devastated factories running once again. But the European nations, victors and vanquished alike, did not have enough dollars to pay for the vital products that they needed to buy from the United States. American leaders referred to this global economic disequilibrium as the "dollar gap" in world trade. The United States was exporting far more than it was importing, and as the American export surplus grew the dollar gap widened. In fact, the trade imbalance ballooned from $7.8 billion in 1946 to $11.6 billion a year later.

European countries responded to their shortage of dollars by resorting to a wide range of controls over their international economic transactions. They aimed to conserve their dollars by using them only for essential capital goods and not on less important products. European nations not only limited the amount of their currency that could be converted into dollars for the purchase of American merchandise, but they also erected high tariffs to protect their domestic industries from American competition. Besides impeding the flow of trade across the Atlantic with monetary restrictions and customs barriers, Europeans entered into bilateral barter arrangements that closed more doors against American commerce. Government officials and business leaders in the United States feared that if the dollar gap problem remained unsolved, these measures of economic nationalism would become permanent and the European countries would turn toward either state capitalism or socialism. In other words, they worried that the European governments would manage their economies and isolate their countries from world markets and thereby shatter the American dream of a liberal capitalist international community.

The Marshall Plan, formally called the European Recovery Program (ERP), was the major American response to the crisis in world capitalism. Between 1948 and 1952, the United States provided $17 billion for European economic recovery. This huge sum was a gift rather than a loan to the nations of Western Europe. The United States government decided against lending the money because when the time arrived for the European countries to service their debts they would have fewer dollars available to buy surplus American commodities. By giving the money without demanding repayment, the United States government aimed to reduce the European dollar deficit and thereby sustain a high level of American exports. The basic goal of the Marshall Plan was to reconstruct the industries of Western Europe and make them competitive in the markets of the world. If the European countries became strong enough to sell abroad, they could earn foreign exchange needed to buy goods from the United States. American leaders hoped to make European manufacturers lean and mean by insisting that they cut wages and pay less in taxes. They also demanded that European governments reduce social welfare spending and deflate their currencies in order to lower the price of their industrial products. . . .

Before the dollar gap had created a crisis in American diplomacy, many government officials and business leaders hoped that China would become a golden market for the United States. They were captivated by the vision of a New China, containing 400 million customers, emerging from the ashes of World War II as a modern nation under the conservative leadership of Chiang Kai-shek. El Dorado beckoned from across the Pacific. But to keep the potentially vast China market free from the danger of foreign domination, the United States needed to declaw the Japanese dragon. General Douglas MacArthur was therefore commissioned to occupy Japan as soon as the war came to a close. Between 1945 and 1947, the American occupational authorities disarmed Japan and purged the military caste to prevent the old warlords from ever again threatening the peace of the Far East. The American authorities also aimed during the first two years of the military occupation to destroy the zaibatsu system of family capitalism in Japan and thereby render the interlocking monopolies less capable of manufacturing the sinews of war.

But the United States quickly reversed the course of its occupational policy in Japan when it became evident that Mao Tse-tung and his communist followers would emerge triumphant in China. Beginning in 1947, American administrators in Japan shifted their emphasis away from political reform and toward economic recovery. Policymakers in Washington decided that the Japanese industrial structure should be rebuilt so that Japan could replace China as a large market for American products. They wanted Japan to be part of the trilateral core in a new liberal capitalist world system: the United States would be the major workshop in the Western Hemisphere; Western Europe would be a regional workshop centered around West Germany; and Japan would be the industrial workshop in the Far East. American policymakers also decided that the Japanese should be rearmed so that Japan could replace China as an important military ally of the United States. They wanted Japan to serve as the sheet anchor in an island chain of American military bases around the Asian rim. In short, Japan was to play a key role as a junior economic and strategic partner in the evolving Pax Americana.

The United States implemented the so-called Dodge Plan in 1949 in an effort to promote the postwar reconstruction of Japan. Like the Marshall Plan for Western Europe, the basic goal of the Dodge Plan was to revive industrial production in Japan and to make Japanese goods competitive in world markets. The United States did not, however, funnel billions of dollars into Japan for industrial renovation. Unlike the Europeans, therefore, the Japanese were forced to finance their own economic rehabilitation. The Dodge Plan required severe cuts in wages and social welfare services and the reinvestment of profits in plant modernization. In addition, it demanded a balanced budget as well as the suppression of labor strikes to keep inflation down and prices low. But the Dodge Plan failed for the very same reason that the Marshall Plan proved inadequate. Although their industrial output increased, the Japanese lacked export outlets where they could acquire foreign exchange needed to purchase American goods. Thus Japan, like the countries of Western Europe, continued to suffer from a large dollar deficit.

The State Department advocated a huge rearmament program as a short-run solution to the global dollar gap problem. American companies would be less dependent upon foreign markets for civilian commodities if they received large military orders from the armed forces of the United States. Massive military spending would compensate both for the lack of foreign demand for American products and for the tariff wall that prevented foreign countries from obtaining a sufficient outlet for civilian goods in the United States. European countries and Japan could earn dollars if the armed forces of the United States purchased military hardware from overseas sources. In short, the offshore procurement of military equipment would replace foreign economic aid as a way of getting dollars to Europe and Japan. The State Department succeeded in persuading Congress to appropriate funds for a vast military buildup by playing upon fears of an international communist conspiracy to dominate the whole world. But the Mutual Security Program, conceived prior to the Korean War, was intended more as an interim solvent for the international economic crisis than as a check against Soviet expansion.

The State Department simultaneously called for the reintegration of colonial areas into a liberal international trading system as the long-run solution to the dollar gap problem. Before World War II, an important triangular trade pattern had evolved: the United States used dollars to buy raw materials from colonial areas; they in turn used these dollars to purchase industrial goods from European countries; and then they used the same dollars to pay for American products. For example, the United States purchased large quantities of rubber and tin from British Malaya with dollars, and British Malaya bought manufactured articles from Great Britain with these dollars, and finally the United Kingdom paid for American commodities with the same dollars. State Department officials hoped to reestablish this kind of triangular trade flow in order to restore international economic equilibrium, and they succeeded in getting federal funds earmarked for increasing the production of foodstuffs and raw materials in colonial areas. The precedent for this form of economic assistance was set in February 1950 when the Export-Import Bank received authorization to lend Indonesia $100 million to buy American equipment needed for the development of natural resources.

American policymakers believed that the expansion of primary commodity production in Southeast Asia was particularly important for the restoration of Japanese prosperity. They hoped that Japan would be able not only to obtain food-stuffs and raw materials in Southeast Asia without paying dollars for these essential imports but also to earn dollars by exporting manufactured goods to Southeast Asia. American leaders thought that in some parts of Southeast Asia the introduction of more irrigation would allow for the cultivation of two rice crops per year instead of the prevailing single crop. If these areas doubled their rice yield, they might also double their purchases of industrial products from Japan. Aiming to stimulate mineral and agricultural production throughout Southeast Asia, American economic experts estimated that by 1955 the region could absorb more than 50 percent of Japan's total exports. China had been Japan's most important market in the Far East before World War II, but after China fell to communism in 1949, American diplomats feared that Japan, if denied access to noncommunist markets in Southeast Asia, might become economically dependent upon Red China and be lured into making a political accommodation with the communist bloc. Thus they hoped that Southeast Asia would become Japan's major market in the Orient.

But Southeast Asia lacked political stability. Although the economic task of increasing the production of primary commodities in that part of the world would not require a large amount of American capital, the United States faced a difficult political problem there. Communist rebels and conservative nationalists were challenging colonial rule in French Indochina, British Malaya, and the Dutch East Indies. Regarding the military pacification of the region as a prerequisite for the economic revival of Japan, American policymakers concluded that the United States would have to help contain the rising tide of revolution in Southeast Asia. Before the Japanese or anyone else could walk the commercial streets of Southeast Asia, they repeatedly argued, those streets would have to be made safe from communism. A joint report, made by the Departments of State and Defense in January 1950, went to the heart of the matter: "Continuing, or even maintaining, Japan's economic recovery depends upon keeping Communism out of Southeast Asia, promoting economic recovery there and in further developing those countries, together with Indonesia, the Philippines, Southern Korea and India as the principal trading areas for Japan."

Concerned about Japan's need for noncommunist markets in Southeast Asia, officials in both the State Department and the Pentagon regarded French Indochina as vitally important to the political stability of the entire region. They realized that Vietnam, Cambodia, and Laos could absorb only a small amount of Japanese goods, but they perceived these French colonies as the linchpin in the long crescent that stretched from Japan all the way to India. French Indochina, while possessing little intrinsic commercial value for Japan, occupied a key strategic position between Red China to the north and the vast Malaya Archipelago to the south. Following the fall of China to communism in 1949, American policymakers subscribed to what came to be called the "domino theory," which held that if the Vietminh defeated the French in Indochina the cancer of communism would spread throughout the whole region. Guerrilla forces in other parts of Southeast Asia would not only be encouraged by the success of their neighbors in overcoming European colonialism, but they would also be able to obtain weapons from nearby communist countries. American leaders therefore feared that if the Vietnam domino fell to communism, it would tip over others until finally the whole row would be knocked down.

Such dire prospects generated a debate in the State Department over the wisdom of supplying direct American aid for the French military campaign in Indochina. A few State Department officials were pessimistic about the chances for a French victory because the Vietminh had widespread backing. Noting that the French were fighting against a large portion of the Vietnamese population, these skeptics concluded that the French would ultimately lose even if they received a massive dose of American financial and technical assistance. But Secretary of State Acheson and most of his top aides argued that the United States should back the French and Bao Dai even if the odds were heavily against them. While acknowledging that Bao Dai lacked popular support, they assumed that he was the only alternative to Ho Chi Minh. Acheson and his followers noted that Ho aimed to establish a communist government in Vietnam after he achieved his nationalist aspirations. They feared that if the French were driven out of Vietnam the rest of Southeast Asia would be in grave danger of succumbing to the forces of communism. They also worried that the French would object to American plans to include West Germany in a multilateral European military force if the United States refused to subsidize their war effort in Indochina.

Secretary Acheson and his colleagues in the State Department were determined to resist not only the expansion of Russian influence in Europe but also the spread of indigenous communism in Southeast Asia. They understood that communism was not monolithic and that all communist leaders did not take orders from Moscow. Marshal Tito, for example, had established an independent communist regime in Yugoslavia that remained free from Soviet domination. Acheson admitted in May 1949 that Vietnam might in fact develop as a "National Communist State on the pattern of Yugoslavia," but he thought that the United States should explore that possibility "only if every other avenue closed." While clearly preferring the puppet Bao Dai to a Titoist Ho Chi Minh, Acheson envisioned three different scenarios for the Indochina War: the Vietminh might defeat the French and become tools of the Kremlin; the Vietminh might win and establish an independent communist government in Vietnam that would remain free from Russian control; or the French might emerge victorious and stamp out the germ of communism before it infected the whole region. Given these choices, Acheson and his associates favored French colonialism rather than either international or indigenous communism.

The State Department believed that it was imperative for economic reasons to prevent any kind of communism from sweeping across Southeast Asia. American diplomats feared that even if Asian communists steered clear of Soviet political influence, they would follow the Russian model for economic growth. By emphasizing industrial development rather than the production of primary commodities, communist countries in Southeast Asia would become more self-sufficient and less dependent upon foreign commerce. Thus the spread of economic nationalism along with indigenous communism would restrict the opportunity for Japan and the capitalist countries of Western Europe to exchange manufactured goods for foodstuffs and raw materials produced in Southeast Asia. Prompted by such thoughts, the State Department decided in February 1950 to recommend direct American financial support for the French war effort in Indochina. Acheson and his colleagues urged that the United States should furnish money but not soldiers so that the war could be fought with American equipment and French troops. As already noted, President Truman gave his approval on March 10 to the proposal to provide the French with $15 million for their military operations in Indochina.

The Korean War, which began three months later, reinforced the American determination to draw the line against the advance of communism in Southeast Asia. Although the conflict in Korea took American policymakers by surprise, it actually helped them accomplish their basic objectives in the Far East. The hostilities in Korea made it easier for the Truman administration to get Congress to appropriate larger and larger sums of money to fund the French struggle against the Vietminh. They also provided the United States with the opportunity to purchase more and more military equipment from Japan. But while the Japanese were temporarily able to earn dollars by selling military supplies to the American army fighting in Korea, President Truman and his advisers continued to regard Japanese economic integration with Southeast Asia as the permanent solution to the dollar gap problem in Japan. They likewise continued to worry that the Japanese would be pulled into the communist political and economic orbit if they were denied access to noncommunist markets in Southeast Asia. "Communist control of all Southeast Asia," a State Department memorandum warned in March 1952, "would remove the chief potential area for Japanese commercial development, and would so add to the already powerful mainland pulls upon Japan as to make it dubious that Japan could refrain from reaching an accommodation with the Communist bloc."

A Strategic Perspective on U.S. Involvement

ROBERT J. MCMAHON

Indochina became crucial to Truman administration planners by the late 1940s because of a perceived relationship between stability in Southeast Asia and economic recovery in Western Europe and Japan. U.S. intervention in Indochina formed part of a carefully conceived, if ultimately flawed, effort to preserve the economic resources of Southeast Asia for the West while denying them to the communist powers. It grew, in short, from America's overall Cold War strategy for containing Soviet power and influence, a strategy that led to a blurring of distinctions between core and periphery and elevated Southeast Asia into a national security concern of the first order. . . .

The future of French Indochina was but one of a bewildering galaxy of problems that required an early decision by the new president [Harry S Truman]. At first

From Robert J. McMahon, "Harry S Truman and the Roots of U.S. Involvement in Indochina, 1945–1953," in David L. Anderson, ed., pp. 21–38 in *Shadow on the White House: Presidents and The Vietnam War, 1945–1975,* 1993 by the University Press of Kansas. Used by permission of the publisher.

glance, this particular problem appeared a good deal less complex than most. During his last months in office, Franklin D. Roosevelt had assured French authorities, as he had their British and Dutch counterparts, that Washington would not oppose the reimposition of European control over colonial territories occupied by Japan during the war. Certain that he was simply following a well-established policy for the Japanese-occupied areas of Southeast Asia, Truman quickly conveyed the same message to French, British, and Dutch officials.

Truman's reassurances were entirely consistent with those given earlier by Roosevelt; they were meant to signal continuity, not change. Nonetheless, Truman's straightforward recognition of the colonial powers' claims to territorial sovereignty in Southeast Asia obscured the more complex reality surrounding the U.S. stance toward colonialism. Roosevelt's various wartime plans and pronouncements regarding European colonies in general, and French Indochina in particular, were sufficiently contradictory that Truman actually inherited a much more ambiguous legacy than he could possibly have realized. The emergence in September 1945 of an independent Vietnamese nationalist regime, demanding international recognition and framing its case in terms of American wartime statements and promises, drove home the complexities and contradictions of the Roosevelt legacy.

During the early years of World War II, Roosevelt and other top officials declared with some regularity that the United States supported the principle of self-determination for all peoples. The president, who took the lead on this issue, often prodded European officials about the need to commit themselves to a timetable for eventual colonial independence. Much to the discomfiture of America's European allies, Roosevelt and Secretary of State Cordell Hull proposed that a trusteeship system be established in the post-war period through which different developed nations, acting as trustees, would prepare local elites to assume the responsibilities of self-government. Trusteeship represented a compromise solution to Roosevelt; he believed that it would guarantee future independence while avoiding the danger of a premature transfer of power to inexperienced indigenous rulers.

Roosevelt's plans for the colonial world represented a nearly indistinguishable blend of American ideals and American interests. The president found the conditions under which so many subject peoples lived appallingly primitive. After passing through the British colony of Gambia in early 1942, for example, he railed against the poverty and disease he had witnessed everywhere, referring to the dependency as a "hellhole" and calling the experience "the most horrible thing I have ever seen in my life." Although Roosevelt never visited Indochina, the lack of personal contact did not prevent the president from berating the colony's French overlords in equally harsh terms. In fact, he considered the French the least enlightened of all the colonial powers and often singled out for particular censure their sorry record in Indochina. Despite "nearly one hundred years" of French rule in Indochina, he complained on one occasion, "the people are worse off than they were at the beginning."

Roosevelt's genuine humanitarian impulses coexisted with a more practical strain. The preservation of the colonial system stood as an impediment to the kind of world order most conducive to U.S. interests. Roosevelt was convinced that the imperial order, with its restrictive trading practices, economic exploitation, and political repression, would simply sow the seeds for future instability within the colonies and future conflicts among the great powers. The United States sought a more open world, one characterized by free trade and democratic principles. Only such a world, according to the president and his chief advisers, would ensure the peace, prosperity, stability, and security that the United States sought. Roosevelt's proselytizing on behalf of a more liberal approach to dependent areas thus bespoke an unsentimental calculation of national interests as much as it did a revulsion against imperialism's excesses.

Before his death, Roosevelt significantly modified his approach to colonial questions. Late in 1944 he jettisoned trusteeship planning for Indochina and other areas, offering instead a promise not to interfere with the reimposition of colonial rule in Southeast Asia. This policy shift reflected the president's essential pragmatism in the face of a series of complex, cross-cutting interests. From its inception, his trusteeship formula had generated heated rebukes from the colonial powers. British Prime Minister Winston Churchill, Roosevelt's most important ally, made clear on numerous occasions his unbending opposition to U.S. tampering with European colonies. Free French leader General Charles de Gaulle was no less adamant in opposing U.S. plans. The Roosevelt administration feared that an aggressive advocacy of trusteeship, in the face of such angry and unified opposition, might create intolerable strains within the wartime alliance and might jeopardize postwar cooperation in Western Europe, the most vital region of all to the United States. Defense needs also militated against persisting in an anticolonial campaign. Planners in the War and Navy Departments insisted that U.S. national security required exclusive control over the Japanese-mandated islands in the Pacific. With the president's concurrence, they intended to establish a permanent U.S. military presence throughout the Pacific in order to add depth and flexibility to the nation's air and naval capability. That high-priority goal, according to military experts, could not be compromised by trusteeship principles that could easily be applied to strategic U.S.-occupied territory as well as to European colonies. Broader political, strategic, and military concerns, in short, necessitated a tactical retreat from earlier anticolonial pronouncements and plans.

Ho Chi Minh's declaration of an independent Vietnamese state on September 2, 1945, brought to a head many of the contradictions embedded in the Roosevelt administration's colonial policy. Quoting liberally from the American Declaration of Independence in his own independence proclamation, the veteran nationalist leader was in effect offering the opening bid in what would prove to be a concerted, if ill-fated, campaign for U.S. backing. Later that day, a Vietnamese band joined the independence-day festivities in Hanoi with a rendition of the "Star-Spangled Banner." U.S. Army officers listened from the reviewing stand as a series of Vietnamese nationalists echoed Ho with their own glowing tributes to the United States' anticolonial heritage. The previous evening Ho had invited two members of the Office of Strategic Services (OSS) for dinner. After thanking them for the valuable material assistance rendered by the United States to his guerrilla movement during the war, he appealed for "fraternal collaboration" in the future.

A shrewd tactician with the instincts of a born politician, the man previously known as Nguyen Ai Quoc was a communist, a revolutionary, but above all a Vietnamese nationalist. He sensed that the momentous events set in motion by the Japanese occupation of Indochina and the Nazi conquest of France had created a historic opportunity for the realization of his lifelong dream: independence from

French rule. From the outset Ho calculated that the United States, if it remained true to its wartime statements, could become his most useful ally. That view was not born of naiveté. It grew, instead, from the mutually beneficial collaboration between U.S. military and intelligence officers and Vietminh guerrillas that had taken place in the jungles of northern Tonkin during the struggle against Japan. It was nourished by the Vietnamese leader's belief that the United States' global interests would compel it to oppose the reestablishment of French colonialism.

Ho's assessment was not an unrealistic one. After all, Roosevelt had calculated that U.S. interests would best be served by the progressive evolution of colonial dependencies into self-governing states; the president's revulsion against French misrule in Indochina ran especially deep. Ho can hardly be faulted for failing to anticipate the shift in U.S. policy that occurred shortly before Roosevelt's death. Unaware that first Roosevelt and then Truman had reassured European allies that the United States would not block the reestablishment of the status quo antebellum, Ho appealed to Truman for recognition in a series of personal letters. "The carrying out of the Atlantic Charter and San Francisco Charter," he declared hopefully in one message, "implies the eradication of imperialism and all forms of colonial oppression."

Truman never responded to Ho's appeals. Neither he nor any of his top advisers ever seriously contemplated direct support for or diplomatic recognition of the Democratic Republic of Vietnam. To do so would have represented a sharp break with the policy Truman had inherited from Roosevelt in an area that ranked relatively low on the overall scale of U.S. priorities. Such a course must have seemed inconceivable to a president still overwhelmed by the myriad responsibilities of his new office. On August 29, during a White House meeting with de Gaulle, Truman signaled that there would be no such break. He reassured France's provisional president that the United States recognized the right of French authorities to reestablish sovereignty in Indochina. Ho's declaration of independence just three days later did not occasion a searching reexamination of that stance. Despite widespread respect for Ho's nationalist credentials and leadership abilities among U.S. intelligence and military personnel serving in Indochina, top U.S. policymakers were far more concerned with the needs and viewpoints of France. To alienate France, a country whose active support in Europe was crucial, would have undermined the overall foreign policy goals of the Truman administration. To do so on behalf of a national independence movement in remote Southeast Asia would have represented the height of diplomatic folly.

The United States instead pursued a policy of neutrality toward the colonial rebellion in Indochina, much as it did toward a contemporaneous colonial revolt in the Dutch East Indies. The Truman administration never questioned the legal right of the European sovereigns to reestablish control in Vietnam and Indonesia. At the same time, it realized that sheer pragmatism necessitated some concessions to indigenous nationalist movements. A harsh policy of political and military repression by the colonial powers would probably endanger not only the peace and order that the United States sought in Southeast Asia but the economic recovery and political stability that it sought in Western Europe.

Throughout 1945 and 1946, U.S. diplomats consequently urged their French counterparts to negotiate in good faith with Ho and his chief lieutenants in order to avert an outright conflict that would serve the interests of neither party. Washington applauded the conclusion of a preliminary Franco-Vietnamese accord on March 6, 1946, since it seemed to open the way for an amicable political compromise. Like

Roosevelt administration planners before them, Truman administration analysts believed that only a more liberal approach to colonial issues, one pointing toward eventual self-government, could establish the essential preconditions for order, stability, and prosperity in the developing world.

Those broad principles served as a general guidepost for U.S. policymakers during the four years following Vietnam's proclamation of independence. Although the principles were certainly sound, they produced little more than frustration for the Truman administration in a period punctuated by false hopes, failed negotiations, and savage fighting. The promise of the March 6 accord soon gave way to stalemated negotiations at Dalat and Paris. Although he was willing to accept less than immediate independence for all of Vietnam, Ho could not condone the retention of French supremacy in the southern province of Cochinchina. To this ardent patriot, Tonkin, Annam, and Cochinchina formed one unified country; he would rather fight than accept division. And fight he did. Following abortive talks at Fontainebleau in the summer of 1946, the imperatives of diplomacy yielded inevitably to preparations for war. In November, hostilities erupted with shattering suddenness. Following a vicious French naval bombardment of Haiphong that claimed more than 6,000 Vietnamese lives, Ho Chi Minh and his supporters fled Hanoi. The French moved quickly to establish their administrative control in the north, and the Vietminh mobilized for another guerrilla struggle. Conflict soon engulfed much of Vietnam. No one at the time could have imagined how many years would pass before peace returned to that embittered land.

U.S. analysts privately expressed dismay with France's resort to the use of force. A colonial war of reconquest represented a regrettable return to the discredited methods of the past. Even worse, the French seemed to lack the military power necessary to accomplish their goals. John Carter Vincent, director of the State Department's Office of Far Eastern Affairs, offered a pessimistic appraisal of French prospects to Under Secretary of State Dean Acheson in a memorandum of December 23. "The French themselves admit that they lack the military strength to reconquer the country," he observed. Possessing "inadequate forces, with public opinion sharply at odds, [and] with a government rendered largely ineffective through internal division," the French were embarking on a most unpromising course. "Given the present elements in the situation," Vincent predicted, "guerilla warfare may continue indefinitely."

For all of its misgivings about French policy in Indochina, the State Department carefully avoided open criticism of its European partner. On December 23, Acheson told French Ambassador Henri Bonnet of Washington's deep concern about "the unhappy situation in which the French find themselves." Calling existing conditions in Indochina "highly inflammatory," the under secretary stressed the importance of reaching a settlement as soon as possible. Only the most sensitive of diplomats could have read even an implied criticism into Acheson's mild remarks. Indeed, he made it clear that even though the United States had no wish to offer its services as a mediator, it did want the French government "to know that we are ready and willing to do anything which it might consider helpful in the circumstances."

Nineteen forty-seven brought no respite to the fighting in Indochina—and no essential change in U.S. policy toward the conflict. The Truman administration continued to view French military exertions as a misguided effort to turn back the clock. In a February 3 cable to the U.S. Embassy in Paris, Secretary of State

George C. Marshall expressed "increasing concern" with the stalemate in Indochina. He deplored both the "lack [of] French understanding [for] the other side" and their "dangerously outmoded colonial outlook and methods." At the same time, Washington displayed no inclination to intervene directly in yet another nettlesome regional conflict and even less interest in exerting unwanted pressure on an invaluable ally. "We have only [the] very friendliest feelings toward France," Marshall noted, "and we are anxious in every way we can to support France in her fight to regain her economic, political and military strength and to restore herself as in fact one of [the] major powers of [the] world." The enunciation in mid-1947 of the containment strategy and the Marshall Plan just underscored France's indispensability to the broader foreign policy aims of the Truman administration. Both initiatives were conceived as part of the administration's overall strategy for containing Soviet influence and power by fostering the economic recovery and political stability of Western Europe. In the intensifying Cold War struggle between the United States and the Soviet Union, no area was more vital than Western Europe and no country more crucial than France.

In view of its transcendent importance to the United States, France's persistence in a colonial conflict that most U.S. experts believed would leave it drained and weakened posed a fundamental dilemma to Truman and his senior advisers, one that they never adequately resolved. Precisely how could the United States help France recognize that its own self-interest required a nonmilitary solution in Indochina? And what specific course of action should the United States urge France to pursue? The dilemma was posed far more easily than it could be resolved. "Frankly we have no solution of [the] problem to suggest," Marshall conceded. "It is basically [a] matter for [the] two parties to work out [for] themselves."

The communist character of the Vietnamese independence movement and the absence of viable noncommunist alternatives further clouded an already murky picture. U.S. officials were keenly aware that the movement's outstanding figure had a long record as a loyal communist. Not only had Ho Chi Minh received political training in Moscow, but he had served for decades as a dedicated Comintern agent outside Indochina. Most U.S. diplomatic and defense officials worried that if Ho prevailed over the French, it would lead to "an independent Vietnam State which would be run by orders from Moscow." A handful of junior State Department officials dissented from that analysis, advancing the argument that Ho's ardent nationalism transcended any fraternal links to the Kremlin's rulers; they speculated that he might even emerge as an Asian Tito. Such unorthodox views never permeated the upper reaches of the Truman administration, however. Most senior policymakers calculated that, regardless of Ho's undeniably powerful credentials as a Vietnamese nationalist, the establishment of a Vietminh-dominated regime would benefit the Soviet Union. Moreover, other nations would almost certainly view the emergence of such a regime as a defeat for the West.

Yet, as the State Department acknowledged in September 1948, "we are all too well aware of the unpleasant fact that Communist Ho Chi Minh is the strongest and perhaps the ablest figure in Indochina and that any suggested solution which excludes him is an expedient of uncertain outcome." Much to Washington's consternation, the French search for an alternative figure with whom to negotiate produced only the weak and vacillating former emperor Bao Dai. Charles Reed, the U.S. consul in

Saigon, reminded Washington that "the reputed playboy of Hong Kong" commanded little support. Bao Dai counted among his followers only "those whose pockets will be benefited if he should return." Notwithstanding U.S. reservations and objections, the French promoted the pliant Bao Dai as their answer to Ho Chi Minh. Most U.S. analysts viewed France's "Bao Dai solution" as a transparent effort to retain colonial control; they saw it as confirmation of the bankruptcy of French policy. The restoration of Bao Dai as titular head of an "impotent puppet Gov[ernmen]t" prompted concern within the State Department that the democracies might be forced to "resort [to] monarchy as [a] weapon against Communism."

In September 1948 the State Department offered an internal assessment of U.S. policy vis-à-vis the Indochina dispute, remarkable both for its candor and for its self-critical tone. "The objectives of US policy towards Indochina have not been realized," it admitted flatly. "Three years after the termination of war a friendly ally, France, is fighting a desperate and apparently losing struggle in Indochina. The economic drain of this warfare on French recovery, while difficult to estimate, is unquestionably large. The Communist control in the nationalist movement has been increased during this period. US influence in Indochina and Asia has suffered as a result." U.S. objectives could be attained only if France satisfied "the nationalist aspirations of the peoples of Indochina." Yet a series of fundamental impediments bedeviled all U.S. efforts to nudge the French in that direction: the communist coloration of the nationalist movement; the seeming dearth of popular noncommunist alternatives; the unwillingness of the Truman administration to offer unsolicited advice to an ally on such an emotional issue; Washington's "immediate interest in maintaining in power a friendly French government, to assist in the furtherance of our aims in Europe"; and, perhaps most basic of all, the administration's "inability to suggest any practicable solution of the Indochina problem."

Over the next year and a half, the Truman administration engaged in a wide-ranging reexamination of U.S. policy toward Southeast Asia. A series of unsettling global developments, which deepened the administration's appreciation for Southeast Asia's strategic and economic salience, lent urgency to the internal debate. As a result of its reassessment, the Truman administration abandoned its quasi-neutral approach to the Indochina dispute in favor of a policy of open support for the French. On February 7, 1950, Secretary of State Acheson formally announced U.S. recognition of the Bao Dai regime, the nominally independent entity established by France the previous year, and its sister regimes in Cambodia and Laos. Emphasizing U.S. concern that neither security, democracy, nor independence could exist "in any area dominated by Soviet imperialism," he promised economic aid and military equipment for France and the Associated States of Vietnam, Cambodia, and Laos.

The decision to lend U.S. money, equipment, and prestige to France's struggle against the Vietminh cannot be understood without reference to the wider forces shaping the foreign policy of the Truman administration in late 1949 and early 1950. Those forces led both to a searching reevaluation of the world situation and to a fundamental reassessment of U.S. tactics and strategy. In the six months preceding its commitment to the French, the Truman administration came face to face with probably the gravest global crisis of the entire postwar era. In the summer of 1949 the Soviet Union exploded its first atomic device, putting an end to the United States' brief atomic monopoly and posing a host of unprecedented challenges to

U.S. national security. Truman and other leading officials feared that possession of the bomb might incline the Kremlin to take greater risks in an effort to extend its global reach and power. The collapse of the U.S.-backed Kuomintang regime in China and the establishment of a communist government in its stead provoked additional fears in U.S. policy circles. Events in China also gave rise to a round of nasty finger-pointing at home; a swelling chorus of Republican critics blamed the president personally for China's fate. Events outside the communist bloc appeared even more ominous to America's Cold Warriors. By the end of the year it was increasingly evident that the economic recoveries of Western Europe and Japan had stalled badly. U.S. decision makers feared that continued economic stagnation in those lands would generate social unrest and political instability, conditions that might prove a fertile breeding ground for communism.

Taken together, those developments portended a potentially catastrophic threat to U.S. national security. As the communist world gained strength and self-confidence, the United States and its allies seemed poised to lose theirs. To Truman and his senior strategists, the stakes in this global struggle for power were extraordinarily high, involving nothing less than the physical safety and economic health of the United States. "The loss of Western Europe or of important parts of Asia or the Middle East," wrote Acheson, "would be a transfer of potential from West to East, which, depending on the area, might have the gravest consequences in the long run." By early 1950, top U.S. diplomatic and defense officials concentrated much of their energy on defusing this hydra-headed crisis by resuscitating the economies of Western Europe and Japan and regaining the West's political and psychological momentum in the Cold War.

U.S. policymakers recognized that a multiplicity of links tied developments in Indochina to this daunting string of global crises. In Asia, the administration's overriding objective was to orient a politically stable and economically prosperous Japan toward the West. "Were Japan added to the Communist bloc," Acheson warned, "the Soviets would acquire skilled manpower and industrial potential capable of significantly altering the balance of world power." The secretary of state and other leading officials were convinced that Japan needed the markets and raw materials of Southeast Asia in order to spark its industrial recovery. The revitalization of Asia's powerhouse economy would create the conditions necessary for stability and prosperity within both Japan and Southeast Asia. U.S. geopolitical and economic interests in this regard formed a seamless web. Truman administration planners envisioned a revitalized Japan emerging once again as the dynamic hub of commercial activity throughout Asia. Achievement of this objective would give a much-needed boost to the regional and global economic systems, thwart communism's military threat and ideological appeal, and ensure Tokyo's loyalty to the West. According to the logic subscribed to by nearly all top U.S. strategists, Japan's economic health demanded that peace and stability prevail throughout Southeast Asia. Consequently, the Vietminh insurgency in Indochina, which posed the most serious threat to regional peace and stability, had to be vanquished with the greatest possible dispatch.

For a somewhat different set of reasons, U.S. strategic and economic interests in Europe pointed in the same direction. By the end of 1949, the optimism generated by the Marshall Plan on both sides of the Atlantic had long since dissolved. The unprecedented commitment of U.S. resources to the economic rehabilitation of Western Europe had not yet brought the dramatic transformation that the Truman administration so desperately sought. Instead, the United States' most important allies found themselves facing a frightening panoply of economic and political difficulties. The increasingly costly war in Indochina stretched France's resources to the breaking point, severely hampering its contribution to the European recovery program. Although West Germany's economic performance was not quite so dismal, U.S. officials continued to fret about the fragility of Bonn's commitment to the West. Certain that the ultimate success of the Marshall Plan required the reintegration of Germany into Europe, U.S. planners agonized about how to ease France's understandable fears about a resurgent Germany.

The enormous trade and currency imbalance between the United States and its European economic partners posed an even more immediate threat to U.S. interests. This so-called dollar gap continued to grow, reaching over $3.5 billion by the middle of 1949, and posed a particularly painful problem for Great Britain. "Unless firm action is taken," British Foreign Secretary Ernest Bevin implored Acheson in July 1949, "I fear much of our work on Western Union and the Atlantic pact will be undermined and our progress in the Cold War will be halted." Experts in Washington shared Bevin's fears. Former Assistant Secretary of State William Clayton spoke for many when he conjured up the image of "the patient little man in the Kremlin [who] sits rubbing his hands and waiting for the free world to collapse in a sea of economic chaos."

By early 1950, the Truman administration's senior planners were convinced that Western Europe's troubles, like Japan's, could be aided by the stabilization and pacification of Southeast Asia. France, Great Britain, and Holland had avoided a dollar gap problem during the prewar years through the establishment of triangular trading patterns in which their colonial dependencies in Southeast Asia earned dollars through the sale of raw materials to the United States. The health of the British sterling bloc had grown unusually dependent on American purchases of rubber and tin from Malaya. The disruption of traditional trading patterns as a result of raging colonial conflicts—an insurgency erupted in Malaya in 1948, joining those that already wracked Indochina and the East Indies—thus compounded the already desperate fiscal conditions plaguing Western Europe. The Truman administration's initial commitment to Southeast Asia, then, must also be placed within this context. U.S. officials believed that financial and material assistance to the French in Indochina would abet military pacification and political stabilization in Southeast Asia. At the same time, it would permit a more active French contribution to European recovery.

Political pressures reinforced Truman's inclination to link Southeast Asian developments to larger issues. The ferocity of the partisan assaults on Truman in the wake of Chiang Kai-shek's (Jaing Jieshi's) collapse increased the political pressure on the president to show greater resolution vis-à-vis the communist challenge in Asia. Aid to the French in Indochina enabled the beleaguered Truman to answer his critics' charges by demonstrating a determination to hold the line against further communist advances *somewhere*. It is of no small significance that the initial U.S. dollar commitment of February 1950 was drawn from funds earmarked by the president's congressional critics for the containment of communism within "the general area of China."

More diffuse psychological considerations also shaped the U.S. commitment to Southeast Asia. Administration analysts were convinced that the belief in many corners of the world was that historical momentum lay with communism and not with the West. U.S. strategists feared that such a perception, whether rooted in fact or fantasy, might take on a life of its own, producing a bandwagon effect that would have an extremely pernicious impact on U.S. global interests. In the words of NSC-68, an April 1950 administration document providing a comprehensive reappraisal of U.S. national security, the Soviet Union sought "to demonstrate that force and the will to use it are on the side of the Kremlin [and] that those who lack it are decadent and doomed." Because the fighting in Indochina was widely viewed as a contest between East and West, however erroneous that view might have been, the challenge it posed to Washington was almost as much psychological as it was geostrategic. State Department and Pentagon officials agreed that the U.S. commitment in Indochina helped meet that psychological challenge by demonstrating to adversaries and allies alike Washington's strength, resolution, and determination. The Truman administration's concern with such intangible matters as the United States' prestige, image, and reputation—in a word, its credibility—thus also entered into the complex policy calculus that made U.S. intervention in Southeast Asia seem as logical as it was unavoidable.

With the outbreak of the Korean War in June 1950, the strategic, economic, political, and psychological fears undergirding that initial commitment intensified. Convinced that Moscow and Beijing had become even more dangerously opportunistic foes, Truman and his senior advisers redoubled their efforts to contain the communist threat on every front. At the same time, they pursued with even greater vigor initiatives designed to strengthen the U.S. sphere of influence. Those vital global priorities demanded nothing less than an all-out effort to contain the communist threat to Southeast Asia, a threat manifested most immediately and most seriously by the Vietminh insurgency. Virtually all national security planners in the Truman administration agreed that Indochina was the key to Southeast Asia. If the Vietminh succeeded in routing the French, according to an analysis prepared by the Joint Strategic Survey Committee in November, "this would bring about almost immediately a dangerous condition with respect to the internal security of all of the other countries of Southeast Asia, as well as the Philippines and Indonesia, and would contribute to their probable eventual fall to communism." With uncommon unanimity, U.S. civilian and military policymakers agreed that a communist triumph in Indochina would represent a strategic nightmare for the United States. It would probably destabilize the entire region, disrupt important trading ties to Japan and Western Europe, deny to the West and make available to the communist powers important raw materials, endanger vital transportation and communication routes between the Pacific Ocean and the Middle East, and render vulnerable the United States' chain of off-shore military bases in the Pacific. "In addition, this loss would have widespread political and psychological repercussions upon other non-communist states throughout the world."

If the intersection of geostrategic, economic, political, and psychological imperatives helped crystallize U.S. policy objectives in Indochina, they did little to clarify the means necessary for the attainment of those objectives. By the autumn of 1950, the Vietminh had achieved a string of stunning military successes; the French, increasingly demoralized and immobilized, appeared on the verge of defeat. U.S. intelligence experts feared that open intervention by Chinese communist units, which were already providing material along with technical and training assistance to the Vietminh, might precipitate a complete French collapse. State Department consultant John Foster Dulles called attention in November 1950 to "what might be a hopeless military situation." A month later an interagency intelligence assessment, coordinated by the CIA, offered an equally grim prognosis. "If this [Chinese communist] aid continues and French strength and military resources are not substantially increased above those presently programmed," it forecast, "the Viet Minh probably can drive the French out of North Viet Nam (Tonkin) within six to nine months." The French position in the rest of Indochina would soon become untenable, leading eventually to "the transformation of Indochina into a Communist satellite."

Determined to help prevent such a calamitous occurrence, the Truman administration steadily accelerated its military and economic aid commitments to the French. By the end of 1950, Washington had committed over $133 million in aid to Indochina. By fiscal year 1951, the total value of U.S. military supplies earmarked for the Indochina war had swelled to approximately $316.5 million. Indochina ranked second by then, behind only Korea, as a recipient of U.S. military aid. That aid helped reinvigorate a faltering French military effort. Together with the appointment of the flamboyant and self-assured General Jean de Lattre de Tassigny as the commander of French forces in Indochina, it led to a substantial—albeit short-lived—improvement in French military fortunes throughout 1951. U.S. observers exulted, hoping that the most acute phase of the crisis might be behind them.

Still, realism tempered the Truman administration's appreciation of the de Lattre-inspired turnaround. Too much hinged on one man, an individual "not always concerned about how many eggs he breaks for his omelette." Furthermore, no matter how vigorous a military campaign the French waged, and no matter how much aid the United States pumped into Indochina, U.S. analysts understood that those factors could not by themselves resolve the Indochina crisis and secure Southeast Asia for the West. Reflecting a view widely shared within the Truman administration, the Joint Chiefs of Staff noted that "without popular support of the Indochinese people, the French will never achieve a favorable long-range military settlement of the security problem of Indochina."

U.S. officials in Washington, Saigon, and Paris were keenly aware that the political and military challenges of Indochina were inseparable. The more astute among them recognized as well that U.S. support for the French pacification effort might work at cross-purposes with U.S. encouragement of Vietnam's noncommunist elites. As early as May 1950, U.S. Ambassador to France David K. E. Bruce shrewdly put his finger on the core problem. The ultimate success of U.S. policy, he observed, "depends upon encouragement and support of both local nationalism and [the] French effort in Indochina. . . . Yet these two forces, brought together only by common danger of Communist imperialism, are inherently antagonistic and gains of one will be to some extent at expense of other." Much to the dismay of U.S. officials, the military dynamism of de Lattre found no political counterpart. The French, who remained extremely unpopular among the Indochinese, simply refused to transfer any genuine power to Bao Dai and his associates. The independence of the Associated States remained a sham; the peoples of Indochina accordingly viewed with disdain the coterie of local leaders serving as little more than French puppets. Lamented U.S. minister in Saigon Donald R. Heath, the "fact is that Ho Chi Minh is [the] only Viet[namese] who enjoys any measure of national prestige."

Notwithstanding its deep and well-founded misgivings about the direction of French policy, the United States carefully avoided open criticism of its European partner. Washington was footing a substantial portion of the bill for the Indochina war. Such a financial commitment would ordinarily bring a commensurate degree of leverage, but the Indochina conflict was anything but ordinary. The French military effort in Southeast Asia served U.S. interests at least as much as it served French interests, a point understood equally well in Paris and Washington. For all its dependence on the United States, France retained the ultimate leverage in the relationship. If U.S. advice became too meddlesome, or if the United States sought to tie strings to its aid, the French could simply withdraw from Indochina entirely. That threat, repeatedly made by French leaders, frightened U.S. decision makers, who worried that they might by default inherit direct responsibility for the Indochina morass.

From the outset of U.S. involvement in Indochina, the Joint Chiefs of Staff had insisted upon, and Truman had accepted, a critical limitation on available U.S. options: Namely, under no circumstances could U.S. troops be deployed in Southeast Asia. With U.S. resources already stretched to the breaking point by the nation's ever-expanding global commitments, the military establishment worried constantly about an increasingly dangerous over extension of U.S. power. Threats to U.S. interests may have been multiplying, but resources remained finite. John Ohly, deputy director of the Mutual Defense Assistance Program in the State Department, articulated the fundamental dilemma faced by U.S. planners. As he reminded Secretary of State Acheson: "We have reached a point where the United States, because of limitations in resources, can no longer simultaneously pursue all its objectives in all parts of the world and must realistically face the fact that certain objectives, even though they may be extremely valuable and important ones, may have to be abandoned if others of even greater value and importance are to be attained." Ohly's argument applied with especial force to Indochina, an area where U.S. interests had escalated far more rapidly than had the resources available to military planners. State Department and White House officials were convinced, as were their counterparts in the Pentagon, that the United States must contain the communist threat in Southeast Asia without using U.S. ground forces. That consensus also pointed to an unresolved—and perhaps unresolvable—contradiction at the root of U.S. policy toward Indochina. If Southeast Asia was so vital that its loss to communism would deal a severe blow to U.S. national security, how could the United States accept *any* limits on its actions?

Throughout 1952, in the course of an extended reexamination of U.S. policy toward Southeast Asia, the Truman administration struggled in vain to resolve that contradiction. Its efforts were carried out against the backdrop of a deteriorating French military position (made more ominous by the death of de Lattre in January of that year), renewed fears about the possibility of direct Chinese communist intervention, and growing concern that domestic political pressures might lead to a French withdrawal from Indochina. The numerous reappraisals prepared by the State Department, the Defense Department, and the National Security Council emphasized once again the critical importance of Southeast Asia to the United States. During a meeting of the National Security Council in March 1952, Secretary of Defense Robert A. Lovett referred to "the grave danger to U.S. security interests" that would occur "should Southeast Asia pass into the Communist orbit." Likewise, Acheson candidly informed British Foreign Secretary Anthony Eden several months later that "we are lost if we lose Southeast Asia without a fight," and thus "we must do what we can to save Southeast Asia."

According to NSC-124/2, a new statement of policy approved by Truman on June 25, 1952, "Communist domination, by whatever means, of all Southeast Asia would seriously endanger in the short term, and critically endanger in the longer term, United States security interests." The possibility of "overt or covert" aggression by Beijing posed the most immediate threat. If a single Southeast Asian nation succumbed as a result of Chinese intervention, it "would have critical psychological, political and economic consequences. In the absence of effective and timely counteraction, the loss of any single country would probably lead to relatively swift submission to or an alignment with communism by the remaining countries of the group." The long-term alignment of India and the nations of the Middle East with the communist bloc, the report noted, would almost certainly follow. "Such widespread alignment would endanger the stability of Europe." Further, a communist Southeast Asia would deprive the West of a range of strategic commodities, thus exerting even greater economic and political pressure on nations allied with the United States and probably impelling "Japan's eventual accommodation to communism."

It was a nightmarish—if familiar—scenario. The president and his top civilian and military advisers were agreed that a set of interdependent global interests made the preservation of a noncommunist Southeast Asia vital to U.S. security. Developing a consensus within the administration on the steps essential to secure that critical objective, however, proved more elusive. Certain that French resistance would crumble rapidly if Communist Chinese divisions entered the fray, military and civilian analysts agonized over how the United States might respond to such a move. Some Pentagon officials believed that only military action against China itself, or the threat of such action, could deter Beijing, raising the frightening question of whether preserving a noncommunist Indochina might necessitate another Sino-American conflict. The pragmatic Lovett suggested that the United States should be prepared instead to spend more money—"perhaps at the rate of a billion or a billion and a half dollars a year"—to support the French; "this would be very much cheaper," he argued, "than an all-out war against Communist China, which would certainly cost us fifty billion dollars."

Neither Truman, Acheson, Lovett, the service chiefs, nor any other senior administration official developed a satisfactory response to the multiple challenges posed by the Indochina conflict. In the end, the Truman administration had to content itself with an ever-deepening monetary commitment to the French. By the end of 1952, the United States was underwriting approximately 40 percent of the cost of the Indochina war. Obviously, as the formulators of U.S. policy themselves were quick to admit, it was an imperfect solution. "More and more dollars [are] being poured into an uninspired program of wait and see," acknowledged the service chiefs. At best, the United States' swelling financial commitment simply postponed the inevitable reckoning. Even if the much-discussed Chinese intervention never materialized, the United States could expect little more than a continuation of the present stalemate; and in the absence of meaningful French political concessions to noncommunist Vietnamese leaders, such a stalemate would simply play into the hands of the Vietminh. The blunt Army Chief of Staff General J. Lawton Collins doubtless spoke for many when he predicted in March 1952 that "the French will be driven out—it is just a question of time."

The Truman administration, which had done so much to elevate Southeast Asia to a diplomatic prize of the greatest importance, failed to develop the means necessary to secure that prize. It never reconciled strategy with tactics. Nor did the administration ever decide on an appropriate U.S. response should the French position suddenly collapse. Truman simply passed those daunting issues, along with an increasingly perilous U.S. commitment to Southeast Asia, on to his successor. It was a legacy fully as problematic and as wracked with contradictory currents as the one he had inherited from Roosevelt.

✗ *F U R T H E R   R E A D I N G*

Blum, Robert M. *Drawing the Line: The Origin of the American Containment Policy in East Asia* (1982).
Bodard, Lucien. *The Quicksand War* (1967).
Borden, William. *The Pacific Alliance* (1984).
Borg, Dorothy and Waldo Heinrichs. *Uncertain Years: Chinese-American Relations, 1947–1950* (1980).
Chen, King C. *Vietnam and China* (1969).
Colbert, Evelyn. *International Politics in Southeast Asia, 1941–1956* (1977).
Drachman, Edward. *United States Policy Toward Vietnam, 1940–1945* (1970).
Dunn, Peter M. *The First Vietnam War* (1985).
Fifield, Russell H. *Americans in Southeast Asia: The Roots of Commitment* (1973).
Gaddis, John Lewis. *Strategies of Containment* (1982).
Gardner, Lloyd C. *Approaching Vietnam* (1988).
Herring, George C. "The Truman Administration and the Restoration of French Sovereignty in Indochina," *Diplomatic History,* 1 (1977), 97–117.
Hess, Gary R. "Franklin D. Roosevelt and Indochina," *Journal of American History,* 59 (1972), 353–368.
———. *The United States' Emergence as a Southeast Asian Power* (1987).
———. "United States Policy and the Origins of the French-Vietminh War, 1945–1946," *Peace and Change,* 3 (1975), 21–33.
Iriye, Akira. *The Cold War in Asia* (1974).
Iriye, Akira and Yonosuke Nagai, eds. *The Origins of the Cold War in Asia* (1977).
McT. Kahin, George. *Intervention* (1986).
Lee, Steven Hugh. *Outposts of Empire* (1995).
Leffler, Melvyn P. *A Preponderance of Power* (1992).
Marr, David G. *Vietnam 1945: The Quest for Power* (1995).
McMahon, Robert J. "The Cold War in Asia: Toward a New Synthesis?" *Diplomatic History,* 12 (1988), 307–27.
———. "Toward a Post-Colonial Order: Truman Administration Policies in South and Southeast Asia," in Michael J. Lacey, ed., *The Truman Presidency* (1989).
O'Ballance, Edgar. *The Indochina War, 1945–1954* (1964).
Ovendale, Ritchie. "Britain, the United States, and the Cold War in Southeast Asia, 1949–1950," *International Affairs,* 63 (1982), 447–64.
Patti, Archimedes L. *Why Vietnam?* (1981).
Rose, Lisle A. *Roots of Tragedy* (1976).
Rotter, Andrew J. *The Path to Vietnam* (1987).
Schaller, Michael. *The American Occupation of Japan: The Origins of the Cold War in Asia* (1985).
Spector, Ronald H. *Advice and Support* (1983).
Sullivan, Marianne P. *France's Vietnam Policy* (1978).
Thorne, Christopher. *Allies of a Kind* (1978).
Tonnesson, Stein. *The Vietnamese Revolution of 1945* (1991).

CHAPTER 4

Dwight D. Eisenhower
and Vietnam:
Deepening the Commitment

✕

When Dwight D. Eisenhower assumed the presidency in January 1953, no resolution of the Indochina conflict appeared in sight. Despite the considerable material investment in the French military effort that it had made, the Truman administration bequeathed to its successor a much more serious and complex problem. The American stake in the war had grown almost as quickly as the French position had deteriorated. The United States, which was then bearing nearly 40 percent of the cost of the conflict, watched with dismay as French territorial control was reduced to a series of small enclaves around Hanoi, Haiphong, and Saigon and a narrow strip along the Cambodian border; while the Vietminh, bolstered by Chinese aid, grew bolder and stronger. Faced with the unsettling prospect of a French collapse and a communist victory in Vietnam, Eisenhower made a number of momentous decisions that transformed the nature of the American commitment to Vietnam.

First, Eisenhower chose not to attempt a rescue of the trapped French garrison at Dienbienphu with direct U.S. military intervention. When the remnants of the French defending force at that remote outpost surrendered to their Vietminh attackers on May 7, 1954, the battle served as a potent symbol of France's imminent defeat. The president next opted to participate in the Geneva Conference on Indochina— and to acquiesce in its results. The Geneva Accords of July 21, 1954, provided for the cessation of hostilities in Indochina, established independent states in Laos and Cambodia, demarcated a temporary division of Vietnam at the seventeenth parallel, and stipulated procedures that would lead to the eventual unification of the country. Following the Geneva Conference, the Eisenhower administration constructed the Southeast Asia Treaty Organization (SEATO) in order to defend the region against possible communist aggression, and moved to assist in creating a viable, noncommunist regime in southern Vietnam under the leadership of Prime Minister Ngo Dinh Diem. The all-Vietnam elections called for in the Geneva Accords were never held; soon the temporary geographical division came to appear permanent. During the Eisenhower years, the United States made a vigorous commitment to the Diem regime, providing it with massive amounts of aid. Nevertheless, by 1960, the prime minister faced growing internal opposition from the reborn Vietminh (or "Vietcong") guerrillas, a movement supported by the communist-dominated regime of Ho Chi Minh in the north.

In recent years, a vigorous scholarly debate about Eisenhower's foreign policy has emerged, and it has had a marked impact on historical assessments of the president's Vietnam policy. The following questions have proved especially controversial. Why did the president choose not to intervene at Dienbienphu? Did the United States violate the Geneva Accords? How should Eisenhower's ambitious nation-building program in South Vietnam be judged: as a partial success, or as an abject failure? Did Washington commit itself to too fragile a leader in Diem? Were there alternatives? What were the principal strengths and weaknesses of Diem's rule? How is the rebirth of a guerrilla movement in the south in the late 1950s best explained? And, in a broader sense, what were the domestic and international forces during the 1950s that catapulted Vietnam to such a position of prominence for the United States?

✗ D O C U M E N T S

In Document 1, President Eisenhower appeals to British Prime Minister Winston S. Churchill for "united action" to help save the French garrison at Dienbienphu. Document 2 is an excerpt from Eisenhower's press conference of April 7, 1954, in which he spells out what he means by the "domino theory" and its relationship to Indochina. Vo Nguyen Giap, the victorious Vietnamese commander at Dienbienphu, assesses the significance of that battle in Document 3. The final declaration of the Geneva Conference, July 21, 1954, established a temporary division between northern and southern Vietnam and set forth procedures for eventual unification. It is reprinted here as Document 4.

The remaining documents in this chapter focus on the regime of Ngo Dinh Diem in South Vietnam. In an April 28, 1955, National Security Council discussion of the sect crisis that nearly toppled Diem from power, sharp differences among top U.S. officials on Diem's abilities come to light. Document 6 is a declaration by the government of Vietnam, issued on August 9, 1955, renouncing any negotiations with the communist regime in the north. On January 1, 1957, U.S. Ambassador Elbridge Durbrow alerted Washington to a series of difficulties that plagued Diem's regime. In Document 8, a National Security Council discussion of May 9, 1960, Eisenhower and other leading officials ponder South Vietnam's deepening problems.

1. Dwight D. Eisenhower Appeals for British Help, 1954

Dear Winston:

I am sure that like me you are following with the deepest interest and anxiety the daily reports of the gallant fight being put up by the French at Dien Bien Phu. Today, the situation there does not seem hopeless.

But regardless of the outcome of this particular battle, I fear that the French cannot alone see the thing through, this despite the very substantial assistance in

Foreign Relations of the United States, 1952–1954, XIII, pt. 2, 1239–1241.

money and matériel that we are giving them. It is no solution simply to urge the French to intensify their efforts, and if they do not see it through, and Indochina passes into the hands of the Communists, the ultimate effect on our and your global strategic position with the consequent shift in the power ratio throughout Asia and the Pacific could be disastrous and, I know, unacceptable to you and me. It is difficult to see how Thailand, Burma and Indonesia could be kept out of Communist hands. This we cannot afford. The threat to Malaya, Australia and New Zealand would be direct. The offshore island chain would be broken. The economic pressures on Japan which would be deprived of non-Communist markets and sources of food and raw materials would be such, over a period of time, that it is difficult to see how Japan could be prevented from reaching an accommodation with the Communist world which would combine the manpower and natural resources of Asia with the industrial potential of Japan. This has led us to the hard conclusion that the situation in Southeast Asia requires us urgently to take serious and far-reaching decisions.

Geneva is less than four weeks away. There the possibility of the Communists driving a wedge between us will, given the state of mind in France, be infinitely greater than at Berlin. I can understand the very natural desire of the French to seek an end to this war which has been bleeding them for eight years. But our painstaking search for a way out of the impasse has reluctantly forced us to the conclusion that there is no negotiated solution of the Indochina problem which in its essence would not be either a face-saving device to cover a French surrender or a face-saving device to cover a Communist retirement. The first alternative is too serious in its broad strategic implications for us and for you to be acceptable. Apart from its effects in Southeast Asia itself, where you and the Commonwealth have direct and vital interests, it would have the most serious repercussions in North Africa, in Europe and elsewhere. Here at home it would cause a widespread loss of confidence in the cooperative system. I think it is not too much to say that the future of France as a great power would be fatally affected. Perhaps France will never again be the great power it was, but a sudden vacuum wherever French power is, would be difficult for us to cope with.

Somehow we must contrive to bring about the second alternative. The preliminary lines of our thinking were sketched out by Foster [Dulles] in his speech last Monday night when he said that under the conditions of today the imposition on Southeast Asia of the political system of Communist Russia and its Chinese Communist ally, by whatever means, would be a grave threat to the whole free community, and that in our view this possibility should now be met by united action and not passively accepted. He has also talked intimately with [British ambassador] Roger Makins.

I believe that the best way to put teeth in this concept and to bring greater moral and material resources to the support of the French effort is through the establishment of a new, *ad hoc* grouping or coalition composed of nations which have a vital concern in the checking of Communist expansion in the area. I have in mind in addition to our two countries, France, the Associated States, Australia, New Zealand, Thailand and the Philippines. The United States Government would expect to play its full part in such a coalition. The coalition we have in mind would not be directed against Communist China. But if, contrary to our belief, our efforts to save Indochina and the British Commonwealth position to the south should in any way increase the jeopardy to Hong Kong, we would expect to be with you there. I suppose that the United Nations should somewhere be recognized, but I am not confident that, given the Soviet veto, it could act with needed speed and vigor.

I would contemplate no role for Formosa or the Republic of Korea in the political construction of this coalition.

The important thing is that the coalition must be strong and it must be willing to join the fight if necessary. I do not envisage the need of any appreciable ground forces on your or our part. If the members of the alliance are sufficiently resolute it should be able to make clear to the Chinese Communists that the continuation of their material support to the Viet Minh will inevitably lead to the growing power of the forces arrayed against them.

My colleagues and I are deeply aware of the risks which this proposal may involve but in the situation which confronts us there is no course of action or inaction devoid of dangers and I know no man who has firmly grasped more nettles than you. If we grasp this one together I believe that we will enormously increase our chances of bringing the Chinese to believe that their interests lie in the direction of a discreet disengagement. In such a contingency we could approach the Geneva conference with the position of the free world not only unimpaired but strengthened.

Today we face the hard situation of contemplating a disaster brought on by French weakness and the necessity of dealing with it before it develops. This means frank talk with the French. In many ways the situation corresponds to that which you describe so brilliantly in the second chapter of "Their Finest Hour," when history made clear that the French strategy and dispositions before the 1940 breakthrough should have been challenged before the blow fell.

I regret adding to your problems. But in fact it is not I, but our enemies who add to them. I have faith that by another act of fellowship in the face of peril we shall find a spiritual vigor which will prevent our slipping into the quagmire of distrust.

If I may refer again to history, we failed to halt Hirohito, Mussolini and Hitler by not acting in unity and in time. That marked the beginning of many years of stark tragedy and desperate peril. May it not be that our nations have learned something from that lesson?

So profoundly do I believe that the effectiveness of the coalition principle is at stake that I am prepared to send Foster or [Under Secretary of State Walter] Bedell [Smith] to visit you this week, at the earliest date convenient to you. Whoever comes would spend a day in Paris to avoid French pique, the cover would be preparation for Geneva.

2. Eisenhower Explains the Domino Theory, 1954

Q. Robert Richards, Copley Press: Mr. President, would you mind commenting on the strategic importance of Indochina to the free world? I think there has been, across the country, some lack of understanding on just what it means to us.

The President: You have, of course, both the specific and the general when you talk about such things.

Public Papers of the Presidents: Dwight D. Eisenhower, 1954 (Washington: U.S. Government Printing Office, 1958), pp. 381–390.

First of all, you have the specific value of a locality in its production of materials that the world needs.

Then you have the possibility that many human beings pass under a dictatorship that is inimical to the free world.

Finally, you have broader considerations that might follow what you would call the "falling domino" principle. You have a row of dominoes set up, you knock over the first one, and what will happen to the last one is the certainty that it will go over very quickly. So you could have a beginning of a disintegration that would have the most profound influences.

Now, with respect to the first one, two of the items from this particular area that the world uses are tin and tungsten. They are very important. There are others, of course, the rubber plantations and so on.

Then with respect to more people passing under this domination, Asia, after all, has already lost some 450 million of its peoples to the Communist dictatorship, and we simply can't afford greater losses.

But when we come to the possible sequence of events, the loss of Indochina, of Burma, of Thailand, of the Peninsula, and Indonesia following, now you begin to talk about areas that not only multiply the disadvantages that you would suffer through loss of materials, sources of materials, but now you are talking about millions and millions and millions of people.

Finally, the geographical position achieved thereby does many things. It turns the so-called island defensive chain of Japan, Formosa, of the Philippines and to the southward; it moves in to threaten Australia and New Zealand.

It takes away, in its economic aspects, that region that Japan must have as a trading area or Japan, in turn, will have only one place in the world to go—that is, toward the Communist areas in order to live.

So, the possible consequences of the loss are just incalculable to the free world.

3. Vo Nguyen Giap on Dienbienphu (1954), 1964

Paramount Significance of the Great Dien Bien Phu Victory and of the Winter–Spring Victories

The historic Dien Bien Phu campaign and in general the Winter 1953–Spring 1954 campaign were the greatest victories ever won by our army and people up to the present time. These great victories marked a giant progress, *a momentous change in the evolution of the Resistance War for national salvation put up by our people against the aggressive French imperialists propped up by U.S. interventionists. . . .*

The great Dien Bien Phu victory and the Winter-Spring victories as a whole had a far-reaching influence in the world.

While the bellicose imperialists were confused and discouraged, the news of the victories won by our army and people on the battlefronts throughout the country especially the Dien Bien Phu victory, have greatly inspired the progressive people the world over.

Vo Nguyen Giap, *Dien Bien Phu* (Hanoi: Foreign Languages Publishing House, 1964), pp. 137, 145–146, 160–161.

The Dien Bien Phu victory was not only a great victory of our people but was regarded by the socialist countries as their own victory. It was regarded as a great victory of the weak and small nations now fighting against imperialism and old and new-colonialism for freedom and independence. Dien Bien Phu has become a pride of the oppressed peoples, a great contribution of our people to the high movement for national liberation which has been surging up powerfully since the end of World War II, and heralded the collapse of the colonial system of imperialism.

Dien Bien Phu was also a great victory of the forces of peace in the world. Without this victory, certainly the Geneva Conference would not be successful and peace could not be re-established in Indo-China. This substantiates all the more clearly that the victory won at Dien Bien Phu and in general the Resistance War put up by our people, and the victorious struggle for liberation waged by the oppressed people against imperialism and colonialism under all forms, played a role of paramount importance in weakening imperialism, thwarting the scheme of aggression and war of the enemy and contributing greatly to the defense of world peace. . . .

The aggressive war unleashed by the French imperialists in Indo-China dragged on for eight or nine years. Though they did their best to increase their force to nearly half a million men, sacrificed hundreds of thousands of soldiers, spent in this dirty war 2,688 billion French francs, squandered a great amount of resources, shed a great deal of blood of the French people, changed 20 cabinets in France, 7 high commissars and 8 commanders-in-chief in Indo-China, their aggressive war grew from bad to worse, met defeat after defeat, went from one strategic mistake to another, to end in the great Dien Bien Phu disaster. This is because the war made by the French colonialists was an unjust war. In this war the enemy met with the indomitable spirit of an entire people and therefore, no skillful general—be he Leclerc, De Tassigny, Navarre or any other general—could save the French Expeditionary Corps from defeat. Neither there would be a mighty weapon—cannon, tank or heavy bomber and even U.S. atomic bomb—which could retrieve the situation. On the upshot, if in autumn 1953 and winter 1954, the enemy did not occupy Dien Bien Phu by paratroopers or if he occupied it and withdrew later without choosing it as the site of a do-or-die battle, sooner or later a Dien Bien Phu would come up, though the time and place might change; and in the end the French and U.S. imperialists would certainly meet with a bitter failure.

4. Final Declaration of the Geneva Conference on Indochina, 1954

1. The Conference takes note of the agreements ending hostilities in Cambodia, Laos, and Vietnam and organizing international control and the supervision of the execution of the provisions of these agreements.

2. The Conference expresses satisfaction at the end of hostilities in Cambodia, Laos, and Vietnam; the Conference expresses its conviction that the execution of the provisions set out in the present declaration and in the agreements of the cessation of

American Foreign Policy: Basic Documents, 1950–1955, I, (Washington: U.S. Government Printing Office), pp. 785–787.

hostilities will permit Cambodia, Laos, and Vietnam henceforth to play their part, in full independence and sovereignty, in the peaceful community of nations.

3. The Conference takes note of the declarations made by the Governments of Cambodia and Laos of their intention to adopt measures permitting all citizens to take their place in the national community, in particular by participating in the next general elections, which, in conformity with the constitution of each of these countries, shall take place in the course of the year 1955, by secret ballot and in conditions of respect for fundamental freedoms.

4. The Conference takes note of the clauses in the agreement on the cessation of hostilities in Vietnam prohibiting the introduction into Vietnam of foreign troops and military personnel as well as of all kinds of arms and munitions. The Conference also takes note of the declarations made by the Governments of Cambodia and Laos of their resolution not to request foreign aid, whether in war material, in personnel, or in instructors except for the purpose of the effective defense of their territory and, in the case of Laos, to the extent defined by the agreements of the cessation of hostilities in Laos.

5. The Conference takes note of the clauses in the agreement on the cessation of hostilities in Vietnam to the effect that no military base under the control of a foreign State may be established in the regrouping zones of the two parties, the latter having the obligation to see that the zones allotted to them shall not constitute part of any military alliance and shall not be utilized for the resumption of hostilities or in the service of an aggressive policy. The Conference also takes note of the declarations of the Governments of Cambodia and Laos to the effect that they will not join in any agreement with other States if this agreement includes the obligation to participate in a military alliance not in conformity with the principles of the Charter of the United Nations or, in the case of Laos, with the principles of the agreement on the cessation of hostilities in Laos or, so long as their security is not threatened, the obligation to establish bases on Cambodian or Laotian territory for the military forces of foreign powers.

6. The Conference recognizes that the essential purpose of the agreement relating to Vietnam is to settle military questions with a view to ending hostilities and that the military demarcation line is provisional and should not in any way be interpreted as constituting a political or territorial boundary. The Conference expresses its conviction that the execution of the provisions set out in the present declaration and in the agreement on the cessation of hostilities creates the necessary basis for the achievement in the near future of a political settlement in Vietnam.

7. The Conference declares that, so far as Vietnam is concerned, the settlement of political problems, effected on the basis of respect for the principles of independence, unity, and territorial integrity, shall permit the Vietnamese people to enjoy the fundamental freedoms, guaranteed by democratic institutions established as a result of free general elections by secret ballot. In order to ensure that sufficient progress in the restoration of peace has been made, and that all the necessary conditions obtain for free expression of the national will, general elections shall be held in July 1956 under the supervision of an international commission composed of representatives of the Member States of the International Supervisory Commission, referred to in the agreement on the cessation of hostilities. Consultations will be held on this subject between the competent representative authorities of the two zones from July 20, 1955, onward.

8. The provisions of the agreements on the cessation of hostilities intended to ensure the protection of individuals and of property must be most strictly applied and must, in particular, allow everyone in Vietnam to decide freely in which zone he wishes to live.

9. The competent representative authorities of the North and South zones of Vietnam, as well as the authorities of Laos and Cambodia, must not permit any individual or collective reprisals against persons who had collaborated in any way with one of the parties during the war, or against members of such persons' families.

10. The Conference takes note of the declaration of the Government of the French Republic to the effect that it is ready to withdraw its troops from the territory of Cambodia, Laos, and Vietnam, at the request of the Governments concerned and within periods which shall be fixed by agreement between the parties except in the cases where, by agreement between the two parties, a certain number of French troops shall remain at specified points and for a specified time.

11. The Conference takes note of the declaration of the French Government to the effect that for the settlement of all the problems connected with the re-establishment and consolidation of peace in Cambodia, Laos, and Vietnam, the French Government will proceed from the principle of respect for the independence and sovereignty, unity and territorial integrity of Cambodia, Laos, and Vietnam.

12. In their relations with Cambodia, Laos, and Vietnam, each member of the Geneva Conference undertakes to respect the sovereignty, the independence, the unity, and the territorial integrity of the above-mentioned States, and to refrain from any interference in their internal affairs.

13. The members of the Conference agree to consult one another on any question which may be referred to them by the International Supervisory Commission, in order to study such measures as may prove necessary to ensure that the agreements on the cessation of hostilities in Cambodia, Laos, and Vietnam are respected.

5. National Security Council Discussion of the Sect Crisis, 1955

General Collins, accompanied by Mr. Paul J. Sturm of the State Department, entered the Cabinet Room when Item 5 came up for discussion. Mr. Allen Dulles also asked permission for Mr. Kermit Roosevelt of the Central Intelligence Agency to be present while Mr. Dulles briefed the Council on the latest developments in Saigon.

Mr. Dulles explained that last night serious street fighting had broken out in the city of Saigon. A mortar shell had landed on the Presidential Palace, the residence of Prime Minister Diem, at 1:15 P.M. After two further shells had landed in the Palace grounds, Diem had telephoned General Ely and stated that he was ordering counterfire by the Vietnamese national forces. Eleven rounds of such counterfire had been counted by three o'clock in the afternoon. While there had since been rumors that a ceasefire had been arranged, Mr. Dulles doubted the validity of these reports, and said it seemed that Prime Minister Diem had ordered all-out action

National Security Council Memo of Discussion, *Foreign Relations of the United States, 1955–1957*, I, 307–311.

against the Binh Xuyen. In other words, Diem was proposing to force a showdown. It was not easy, continued Mr. Dulles, to say which side had actually been responsible for precipitating last night's events, but the real trouble had begun on April 26, when Prime Minister Diem had ordered the removal of the Chief of Police of Saigon, who was a member of the Binh Xuyen gangster group.

In a showdown fight, continued Mr. Dulles, and if the Vietnamese National Army remains loyal to the Prime Minister, there was little doubt that the Army could drive the Binh Xuyen forces out of Saigon. The difficulty was that such an attempt would almost certainly result in disturbances and civil war throughout South Vietnam. In addition, the street fighting might very well result in atrocities against French civilians living in Saigon. Finally, said Mr. Dulles, Diem has advised that he now intends to form a complete new Cabinet, and that he will announce its members tonight. . . .

Secretary Dulles said that he would like to comment in general on the situation in which we found ourselves respecting South Vietnam. In his view, the present difficulties had two fundamental causes. First, the limitations of Prime Minister Diem as the head of a government. While Diem's good qualities were well known and need not be elaborated, it was a fact that he came from the northern part of the country and was not very trustful of other people, perhaps for good reason. Furthermore, he was not very good at delegating authority. Despite these shortcomings, Diem might have proved adequate to the situation if it had not been for the second fundamental limitation—namely, the lack of solid support from the French. While the top leaders of the French Government, such as Mendes-France, Faure and General Ely, have gone along with Diem reluctantly, French colonial officials on the scene in Vietnam have done their best to sabotage him. These two fundamental limitations in conjunction have brought about a situation that has finally induced General Collins to conclude that we must now look for a replacement for Diem.

As a matter of fact, continued Secretary Dulles, we have been telling the French for a considerable period that we would be prepared to consider an alternative to Diem if they could come up with one. They haven't as yet done so. Moreover, the mechanics of effecting a change at this time would be very difficult. A change of Premier would necessarily involve recourse to Bao Dai, and we have always felt that Bao Dai's influence would be invariably exerted in favor of the Binh Xuyen, which supplies his ample funds. We haven't therefore, been inclined to look with very much favor on a new South Vietnam government appointed by Bao Dai. On the contrary, we have felt that it was really essential that a showdown occur between Bao Dai and the rebellious sects. Such a showdown both Bao Dai and the French have consistently tried to avoid.

Late yesterday afternoon, however, we in the State Department dispatched a complicated series of cables to Saigon outlining ways and means of replacing Diem and his government. However, in view of the developments and the outbreak of last night, we have instructed our people in Saigon to hold up action on our plan for replacing Diem. The developments of last night could either lead to Diem's utter overthrow or to his emergence from the disorder as a major hero. Accordingly, we are pausing to await the results before trying to settle on [Pham Huy] Quat or Defense Minister [*sic*] Do as possible replacements. Secretary Dulles confessed that he was not much impressed with the Defense Minister. On the other hand, unless something occurs in the Saigon disorders out of which Diem will emerge as the hero, we will have to have a change. This is the view both of General Collins and General Ely, and Ely has played an honest game with us in this whole affair.

Secretary Dulles then pointed out that Bao Dai had actually threatened to take the matter in his own hands and establish a new government himself. Indeed, we are not absolutely sure that we can restrain him from so doing, since he so to speak represents the only existing source of legitimate governmental authority. Thus we find ourselves obliged to work with him and through him to some extent, until we are in a position to devise some alternative source of authority.

At the conclusion of his statement, Secretary Dulles asked General Collins to present his views. General Collins began by reminding the National Security Council of his earlier appearance before it prior to his departure for Saigon, and of the position he had taken at that time—namely, that there were five major factors on which the future of Free Vietnam would depend. He said that he would briefly run over these same five factors now.

1. The possibility of an overt attack on Free Vietnam by the Vietminh. Of this General Collins stated there was very little danger at the present time.

2. The loyalty of the Vietnamese National Army to Diem. General Collins emphasized that to date the Vietnamese National Army had been loyal to Diem, but that loyalty would almost certainly not extend to supporting the Prime Minister in a civil war. The Army violently disliked the Binh Xuyen, but it also disliked the prospect of engaging in a civil war in South Vietnam which would also include the Hoa Hao and the Cao Dai sects, which were quite strong in the southern portions of Free Vietnam. The great danger of trying to drive the Binh Xuyen from their strongholds in Saigon, said General Collins, was precisely the danger that such an attempt would end in widespread civil war.

3. The problem of the sects. General Collins pointed out that we have feared all along that efforts to cut down the size of the private armies of the sects and to dry up their financial resources would cause trouble. This was probably inevitable, whether Diem or anyone else made the effort. On the other hand, General Collins insisted that Diem's handling of the problem of the sects had been anything but astute.

4. The attitude of the French. General Collins said that since this had been thoroughly covered by Secretary Dulles, he would add no more except to point out that there could be no doubt of the loyal role played with him by General Ely.

5. The personality of Diem. On this point General Collins said that as early as the end of his first week in Saigon he had come to entertain very serious doubts as to Diem's ability to govern. Diem betrayed no political knack whatsoever in his handling of men. His ineptitude in this respect was responsible for the series of resignations from his Cabinet. It was no mere matter of rats quitting a sinking ship. General Collins felt that it was a particular misfortune to lose Minh, the young Secretary of Defense, and Do, the older Secretary of Foreign Affairs, whom General Collins considered to be a man of very good judgment. If, said General Collins, Diem makes good on his statement that he would name a new Cabinet, this Cabinet would almost certainly consist of unknown individuals who had no public standing.

All this induced General Collins to conclude that Prime Minister Diem's number was up. Nor had he ever felt that Diem was the indispensable man. Accordingly, even without Diem the program adopted by the Council for South Vietnam could and should go forward without interruption, even though its estimated costs would be $40 million more this year than previously estimated. General Collins emphasized that he still felt that this U.S. policy and program was a gamble worth taking, although certainly a gamble. A long-term solution of the sect problem was vital to the success of the program. It was likewise vital to take control of the police away from the Binh Xuyen. Finally, it was essential to get genuine French support for the policy and program, no matter who was the Vietnamese Prime Minister.

The President commented that it was an absolute sine qua non of success that the Vietnamese National Army destroy the power of the Binh Xuyen. Otherwise any new government was bound to fail. To this General Collins replied that the attempt to destroy the Binh Xuyen by military action would almost certainly produce civil war in Vietnam. The Binh Xuyen, if removed from Saigon, would take to the MaQuis and raise hell for years to come. Accordingly, General Collins said he personally preferred a political solution. He had wished Diem to form a genuine coalition government. He doubted very much whether Diem could be prevailed upon to try it, but such a political solution seemed most likely to bring success.

Secretary [of the Treasury George] Humphrey inquired how far the Communists were behind the disorders and outbreaks in Saigon. General Collins replied that there could be no doubt that they were stimulating and exploiting the disorders that existed.

At this point Mr. Anderson read the proposed record of action. The President inquired if there were any objections. There being none, the President observed that the proposed action sounded all right to him, and that he could not see what else we could do at this time.

At the close of the discussion, Mr. Allen Dulles commented that if it were any comfort to the Council, there was quite a good deal of evidence that the Vietminh were encountering considerable difficulty in their part of Vietnam.

6. South Vietnamese Statement on Reunification, 1955

In the last July 1955 broadcast, the Vietnamese national Government has made it clear its position towards the problem of territorial unity.

The Government does not consider itself bound in any respect by the Geneva Agreements which it did not sign.

Once more, the Government reasserts that in any circumstance, it places national interests above all, being resolved to achieve at all cost the obvious aim it is pursuing and eventually to achieve national unity, peace and freedom.

The Viet-Minh leaders have had a note dated July 19 transmitted to the Government, in which they asked for the convening of a consultative conference on general elections. This is just a propaganda move aimed at making the people believe that they are the champions of our territorial unity. Everyone still remembers that

---

Gareth Porter, ed., *Vietnam: The Definitive Documentation of Human Decisions* (Stanfordville, NY: Earle M. Coleman, 1979), II, 1–2.

last year at Geneva, the Vietnamese Communists boisterously advocated the partition of our territory and asked for an economically self-sufficient area whereas the delegation of the State of Viet-nam proposed an armistice without any partition, not even provisional, with a view to safeguarding the sacred rights of the Vietnamese national and territorial unity, national independence and individual freedom. As the Vietnamese delegation states, the Vietnamese Government then stood for the fulfillment of national aspirations by the means which have been given back to Viet-nam by the French solemn recognition of the independence and sovereignty of Viet-nam, as a legal, independent state.

The policy of the Government remains unchanged. Confronted with the partition of the country, which is contrary to the will of the entire people, the Government will see to it that everybody throughout the country may live free from fear, and completely free from all totalitarian oppression. As a champion of justice, of genuine democracy, the Government always holds that the principle of free general election is a peaceful and democratic means only if, first of all, the freedom to live and freedom of vote is sufficiently guaranteed.

In this connection, nothing constructive can be contemplated in the present situation in the North where, under the rule of the Vietnamese Communists, the citizens do not enjoy democratic freedoms and fundamental human rights.

7. Elbridge Durbrow Assesses the Diem Regime, 1957

Certain problems now discernible have given us a warning which, if disregarded, might lead to a deteriorating situation in Viet Nam within a few years.

Diem achieved notable successes in the first two years of his regime and remains the only man of stature so far in evidence to guide this country. He has unified free Viet Nam, brought it relative security and stability, and firmly maintains a pro-West, anti-communist position.

In the last year, however, Diem has avoided making decisions required to build the economic and social foundations necessary to secure Viet Nam's future independence and strength. He has made it clear that he would give first priority to the build-up of his armed forces regardless of the country's requirements for economic and social development. Events abroad which increase the danger of communist infiltration and subversion, and which threaten Viet Nam with possible isolation in this area have contributed to his concern and to his determination to strengthen his armed forces.

Certain characteristics of Diem—his suspiciousness and authoritarianism—have also reduced the Government's limited administrative capabilities. He assumes responsibility for the smallest details of Government and grants his Ministers little real authority.

Durbrow to the State Department, December 5, 1957, *Foreign Relations of the United States,* 1955–1957, I, 869–884.

At the same time, discontent is felt in different segments of the population for varied reasons. The base of the regime's popular support remains narrow. The regime might overcome such discontent and finally win over the loyalty of a majority of Vietnamese both in the North and South if it could show its ability to give the country stronger protection and create sound economic and social bases for progress. Progress, which is demanded in Viet Nam as throughout Asia, is perhaps the touchstone of the regime's enduring viability. Yet precisely because Diem is now procrastinating in making decisions affecting fundamental problems of his country's development, the lag between the people's expectations and the Government's ability to show results will grow.

We consider it therefore of importance that we bring strong pressure on the President to reach certain decisions basically in the economic and social fields which have been before him for some months but on which he has not acted. He has resented this and may resent it more, but in ours and his long range interests we must do our utmost to cause him to move forward in these fields.

The purpose of this evaluation of the present situation in Viet Nam is to examine the elements giving rise to some concern regarding certain developments in Viet Nam, to provide the Department [of State] and interested agencies salient background and to set forth conclusions and recommend certain broad courses of action. We feel that a frank discussion of the solution as we see it may be helpful to all concerned.

8. National Security Council Discussion of Diem's Growing Problems, 1960

Mr. [Robert] Amory [of the CIA] then reported that increasing troubles in South Vietnam were confronting Diem. For months Diem had been facing increased insurgent activity in the countryside similar to that which characterized the last days of the French regime. Moreover, Diem's own ranks had been crumbling. Critics of his one-man rule were becoming more vocal at all levels of government. This criticism asserted that Diem's administration had fostered corruption, condoned maladministration, and permitted dictatorial practices with the result that communism in South Vietnam was being promoted. Criticism of Diem was so far uncoordinated outside government circles but was becoming stronger, as indicated by a recent manifesto made public in Saigon by a group of former officials who called for extensive political reforms.

The President said he had received a stream of reports about South Vietnam. Heretofore we have been proud of Diem and had thought he was doing a good job. Apparently he was now becoming arbitrary and blind to the situation. Mr. Amory said one danger lay in the fact that Diem was not in direct touch with the people since he seldom went out into the countryside to see the people and talk with provincial leaders. He is inclined to leave this kind of activity, as well as the details

---

National Security Council Memo of discussion, May 9, 1960, *Foreign Relations of the United States, 1958–1960*, I, 446–447.

of administration, to his brothers, who have all the evils and none of the assets needed to do a good job. The President wondered whether we were doing anything to try to persuade Diem to remain in closer touch with the people. Mr. Amory said our Ambassador to South Vietnam and General [Samuel T.] Williams [chief of the Military Assistance Advisory Group in Vietnam] were constantly advising Diem to keep in touch with the people.

Mr. [Livingston] Merchant [under secretary of state for political affairs] said Diem was more and more coming to be surrounded by a small group. He was leaving administration to his two brothers and was losing touch with the grass roots. However, Ambassador Durbrow was keeping in close touch with Diem. Mr. Merchant hoped that what happened to Syngman Rhee in Korea would give Diem pause.

The President said Diem seemed to be calm and quiet and to have an attractive personality unlike Rhee. The President then asked Mr. Merchant to consider whether the situation might be improved by a letter from him (the President) to Diem.

Mr. [Thomas S.] Gates [secretary of defense] remarked that South Vietnam internal security forces were not well equipped to handle insurgent forces in the swampy areas where most of the trouble occurred.

The President said the U.S. ought to do everything possible to prevent the deterioration of the situation in South Vietnam. We had rescued this country from a fate worse than death and it would be bad to lose it at this stage. Mr. Merchant believed that South Vietnam was getting as much economic assistance as it could effectively absorb. The President recalled that when Diem had first been attempting to acquire power in South Vietnam, a recommendation had been made to the Council that the U.S. should oppose him. The President said he hoped the Departments of State and Defense and CIA would consult together to see what could be done about the situation in South Vietnam.

✗ E S S A Y S

In the opening essay, David L. Anderson of the University of Indianapolis offers a critical summary of Eisenhower's Vietnam policy. He contends that while Eisenhower may deserve high marks for choosing not to rescue the beleaguered French garrison at Dienbienphu, his administration's subsequent commitment to the Diem regime represented a massive intervention in Vietnamese affairs. Anderson says that the Eisenhower administration's generous economic, military, and political support for the Saigon government that it helped to establish never proved sufficient to create a viable nation. Instead, the United States became tied to a corrupt, inefficient, and unrepresentative regime in South Vietnam that never commanded popular support. In the process, it sowed the seeds for future troubles.

In the next selection, Ronald H. Spector, a leading U.S. military historian and professor of history at George Washington University, analyzes the shortcomings of the first American military advisory mission in Vietnam. He depicts the growth of the Vietcong insurgency in the late 1950s as an ominous threat to the South Vietnamese regime, one that American military advisers had not adequately prepared South Vietnam's armed forces to meet.

The Tragedy of U.S. Intervention

DAVID L. ANDERSON

"The loss of South Vietnam would set in motion a crumbling process that could, as it progressed, have grave consequences for us and for freedom," President Dwight D. Eisenhower declared in an April 1959 speech. This statement reaffirmed the famous "falling domino" analogy that he had used five years earlier to explain the strategic importance of Indochina. If the states of Southeast Asia fell under "the Communist dictatorship," he asserted in April 1954, the result would be a "disintegration" with the "most profound influence" for "millions and millions and millions of people." Throughout his eight years as president, Eisenhower never wavered in his conviction that the survival of an independent, noncommunist government in southern Vietnam was a vital strategic imperative for the United States. This objective, which Eisenhower's successors in the White House would also support, was the cornerstone of his policies in Southeast Asia, but it left open the question of the means of achieving that goal.

Eisenhower and his foreign policy advisers went through two stages in attempting to devise a successful method of securing U.S. interests in Vietnam. The first approach, which lasted through 1954 and into 1955, was to continue the Truman tactic of working with and through the French and other Western allies to contain communism in Southeast Asia. During this early phase, Eisenhower showed remarkable restraint considering the administration's Cold War rhetoric about the global danger of communist expansionism. He managed to avoid involving the United States militarily in Indochina as France suffered a humiliating defeat at Dienbienphu at the hands of the communist-led Vietminh army. After the French surrender at Dienbienphu, an international conference at Geneva, Switzerland, arranged a Franco-Vietminh cease-fire in July 1954. In the following months, the Eisenhower administration tried to maintain an allied strategy in Indochina. It established the Southeast Asia Treaty Organization (SEATO) and sent a special mission to Vietnam headed by General J. Lawton Collins to attempt, among other things, to continue a joint U.S.-French program in the region.

By the spring of 1955, however, the administration had begun a second, essentially unilateral approach in which the United States sought to protect its strategic interests in Southeast Asia by building a new Vietnamese nation around a reclusive autocrat named Ngo Dinh Diem. For the remainder of the Eisenhower presidency, the United States pegged its Vietnam policy on the questionable ability of Diem. In contrast to the cautious good judgment of the first phase that limited U.S. risks in Southeast Asia, the second phase exhibited a tragic irresponsibility by enmeshing the United States in the tangled web of Vietnamese politics and exposing Americans and American interests to considerable danger.

Eisenhower brought with him to the White House the conviction that the areas of the world "in which freedom flourishes" were under assault from a "Communist-regimented unity." In his first State of the Union address in February 1953, he described France's struggle against the Vietminh as holding "the line of freedom" against "Communist aggression throughout the world." As he prepared to leave office eight years later, his bipolar perception of the world divided between freedom and tyranny—with Southeast Asia at the center of that conflict—had not altered. Eisenhower's farewell address to the nation is remembered primarily for its warning against the dangerous influence of the military-industrial complex in America, but the speech opened with the stern reminder that the nation had faced and would continue to confront "a hostile ideology—global in scope, atheistic in character, ruthless in purpose, and insidious in method." The next day, on January 19, 1961, he warned president-elect John Kennedy that the civil war then raging in Laos threatened to spread communism throughout the entire region.

Besides his commitment to no compromise with world communism, the other hallmark of Eisenhower's policies in Indochina and elsewhere was cost reduction. In a strategy labeled the New Look, his administration sought the most economical ways to protect U.S. security. Commonly associated with the threat to use nuclear force for "massive retaliation," the New Look also called for a greater reliance on military alliances and covert operations.

The New Look was apparent during the initial phase of the administration's Indochina policies in the effort to work with France to defeat the Vietnamese communists. Although they shared the Truman administration's displeasure at the French intent to recolonize Indochina, the Republicans decided that the Cold War required them to stand with their North Atlantic Treaty Organization (NATO) ally. Secretary of State John Foster Dulles candidly admitted to the Senate Foreign Relations Committee that U.S. choices in this situation were distasteful, but in "the divided spirit" of the world today, the United States would have to tolerate the colonialists a bit longer to help block Soviet and Chinese infiltration of Southeast Asia. Dulles also felt compelled to cooperate with France in Indochina because he wanted French officials to accept a rearmed West Germany (a frightening prospect for many in France) as part of a U.S.-backed plan for NATO called the European Defense Community. To bolster French resolve in both Indochina and Europe, the Eisenhower administration increased U.S. aid to the point that it accounted for almost 80 percent of France's military expenditures in Southeast Asia by January 1954.

As the Eisenhower administration observed its first anniversary in office, however, Paris's perseverance was waning. The French public and politicians were tiring of the seven-year burden of the Indochina war. The resilient Vietminh, under the charismatic leadership of Ho Chi Minh, continued to exact a heavy price in blood and treasure from their would-be masters. To the regret of Washington, French leaders accepted a Soviet proposal for a multinational conference at Geneva, set to begin in April, that would attempt to structure a diplomatic settlement in Indochina. Then, in March, the Vietminh assaulted an entrenched French garrison at Dienbienphu with such overwhelming force that a French military disaster appeared possible on the eve of the truce talks. The French might decide at Geneva to capitulate to their communist foes.

The prospect of a socialist ally of the Soviet Union and the People's Republic of China (PRC) emerging triumphant over a member of NATO that had been openly aided by the United States deeply troubled U.S. leaders, who began serious consideration of the New Look's trump card—massive retaliation. Although this option implied the possibility of using nuclear weapons, few U.S. planners believed that the atomic bomb was necessary to balance the military scales at Dienbienphu. In this case, the proposal involved a staggering conventional bombardment of the attacking force using as many as 350 planes from U.S. aircraft carriers and from bases in Okinawa and the Philippines.

Throughout March and April, Eisenhower, Dulles, and other top administration officials weighed the air strike idea but never used it. In early May, the French garrison surrendered after sustaining heavy losses, and this outcome set the stage for the signing of a cease-fire agreement between France and the Vietminh at Geneva. This turn of events has long fascinated observers of Eisenhower's foreign policies. The president and his secretary of state encouraged the image that their hands were tied by congressional and allied reluctance to countenance a risky and perhaps unwarranted rescue of France's failed ambitions. Although this characterization made the White House appear passive, it paid excellent political dividends. It helped shield Eisenhower from personal attacks that he had "lost" something in Vietnam, as Truman had been excoriated for allegedly losing China.

While in office, Eisenhower was beloved by many Americans who admired his leadership of the Allied forces that defeated Nazi tyranny during World War II and who appreciated his humble demeanor and engaging grin. At the same time, however, he seemed to be a rather lackadaisical chief executive who presided over but did not propel his administration. The later declassification of confidential White House files reversed this picture dramatically. The record revealed Eisenhower to be directly and often decisively involved in key decisions such as those on Indochina in 1954. His management of the Dienbienphu crisis has become something of a centerpiece of the rehabilitation of his presidential image in recent years. He utilized the skills of talented subordinates such as Dulles and let them absorb some of the public pressure produced by controversial actions, but the president kept a firm, if hidden, hand on the administration's helm.

The origin of Eisenhower's leadership ability is clear. His rise to the pinnacle of the nation's military structure as a five-star general provided him with a wealth of experience that prepared him to be president. The military had been his leadership laboratory, and his advancement up the ranks in competition with other extremely able officers revealed that he was an adept student of management theory. His method of handling subordinates, for example, was carefully considered. During World War II, he delegated extensive responsibility to such forceful commanders as George Patton and Omar Bradley, but he retained the authority to call them to account when necessary. Similarly, his approach to public relations, contingency planning, and other areas of executive responsibility demonstrated active leadership and effective management style.

The details of the Dienbienphu decision have especially enhanced Eisenhower's reputation. Confronted with a military-diplomatic problem that corresponded to his personal experience, he confidently shaped the policy deliberations. Neither Dulles nor Vice-President Richard M. Nixon, both of whom often spoke out publicly and stridently on foreign policy, fashioned the administration's actions. The president made the decisions that kept U.S. ground and air forces out of combat. "It would be a great mistake for the United States to enter the fray in partnership only with France," Eisenhower believed; "united action by the free world was necessary, and in such action the U.S. role would not require use of its ground troops." The prudence of his course appears statesmanlike in contrast to the steps of later presidents who plunged U.S. forces into hostile action in Southeast Asia.

Yet praise for the decision can easily be overdrawn. Eisenhower's restraint had more to do with the immediate predicament of the French and the perception that Paris had lost the will to fight than with any careful reassessment of U.S. purposes in Vietnam. He was willing to accept a tactical setback in the Cold War at Dienbienphu but was not prepared to question the proclaimed importance of Indochina in the global balance of power. Also, it is a mistake to conclude that Eisenhower was an energetic leader just because the career soldier chose to involve himself personally in a national security issue. A few days after the French garrison surrendered, for example, the U.S. Supreme Court issued its momentous school desegregation decision, *Brown v. the Board of Education of Topeka*. On the matter of racial injustice, which burdened millions of American citizens every day, the president chose to stay uninvolved, declaring that he would express neither "approbation nor disapproval" of the Court's action.

When the Court ruled on the *Brown* case, U.S. delegates were sitting at the Geneva Conference deliberating the fate of Vietnam. The Vietminh victory at Dienbienphu made it likely that the French would accept a compromise with the communists. The Eisenhower administration took a largely passive role in the proceedings to avoid any responsibility for the outcome, but the United States maintained a presence there because the president and his advisers were not willing to embark on a separate, solitary course in the region. With Britain, the USSR, and the PRC mediating, the French and Vietminh reached a cease-fire agreement that temporarily partitioned the country at the 17th parallel. The communist-led Democratic Republic of Vietnam (DRV) would control the North, and France would regroup its military forces in the South. An all-Vietnam election was to be held in two years to determine the future political structure of the nation. The U.S. delegation publicly acknowledged these terms but did not sign or verbally endorse any of them.

Determined to salvage the southern part of Vietnam from communist domination and to do so by collective defense if possible, the Eisenhower administration championed the creation of SEATO in September 1954. Comprising the United States, France, Britain, Australia, New Zealand, the Philippines, Thailand, and Pakistan, this alliance was not a binding security pact like NATO, but it did provide a mechanism for possible joint action in future crises like Dienbienphu and especially in the event of overt aggression by the DRV or PRC. Under the terms of the Geneva Accords, Vietnam and neighboring Laos and Cambodia could not enter into military agreements, but the SEATO pact extended a vague commitment to their security in an attached protocol. Despite the treaty's weaknesses, Dulles hailed it as a "no trespassing" sign to warn away potential communist aggressors, and Eisenhower and his successors in the White House cited SEATO as the authority for U.S. intervention in the region's affairs.

Eisenhower's handling of Dienbienphu, Geneva, and SEATO, taken together, highlighted the strengths and weaknesses of his leadership style. He was managing the Vietnam issue politically but not solving it substantively. Using Dulles as his primary spokesman, Eisenhower had urged "united action" during the siege of Dienbienphu to counter the communist threat in Southeast Asia. With the formation of SEATO, such allied unity seemed possible. Opinion polls indicated that the American public favored this kind of multilateral approach over unilateral action. Similarly, Eisenhower's decision to maintain a discreet distance from the negotiations and final settlement at Geneva avoided a charge that he had accepted a compromise with communists—an allegation that critics had made against Franklin Roosevelt after the Yalta Conference of 1945. The American people wanted toughness in U.S. policy without the risk of war, and the administration's coolness toward the Geneva Accords and its creation of SEATO suited this public mood. In terms of policy, however, toughness alone was not a solution. The true alternatives were either to use force to break DRV power or to accept DRV success. The administration would do neither and hence only deepened the U.S. commitment in Southeast Asia with no realistic prospect for resolving the dilemma of how to protect U.S. interests without war.

Although France entered SEATO, U.S.-French cooperation in Southeast Asia after the Geneva Conference was strained almost to the breaking point. Eisenhower and many of his aides believed that Paris had essentially forfeited its influence on Western policies in Indochina with its weak performance against the Vietminh. The president complained that he was "weary" of the French and their "seemingly hysterical desire to be thought such a 'great power.'" Still, many of the French had strong economic and personal ties with Indochina and were loath to surrender what remained of their position.

In an effort to reestablish a working relationship with French officials in South Vietnam, Eisenhower sent General J. Lawton Collins, a trusted World War II colleague and former army chief of staff, to Saigon in November 1954 as his personal representative. "Lightning Joe" Collins was also to formulate "a crash program to sustain the Diem government and establish security in Free Vietnam." The president thought that French officials in Saigon would cooperate, but, if not, "we ought to lay down the law to the French," he told the National Security Council. "It is true that we have to cajole the French with regard to the European area," Eisenhower added, "but we certainly didn't have to in Indochina."

Collins had some success with military training programs and bureaucratic changes, but eventually his mission and U.S. policy in general reached an impasse with the French over the internal political structure of the South. At issue was the leadership of Ngo Dinh Diem. While the Geneva Conference was under way, Emperor Bao Dai had made Diem prime minister of the State of Vietnam, the vacuous regime that French officials had created as a Vietnamese nationalist alternative to the Vietminh and their alien Marxist ideology. It was this government, currently under the protection of the French in their regroupment zone south of the 17th parallel, that would face the DRV and its president Ho Chi Minh in the Geneva-mandated elections. Not all Vietnamese approved of the Vietminh, who had often ruthlessly silenced their political rivals, but the leaders of the DRV enjoyed the advantage of having forced the capitulation of the colonialists. Diem's regime would have to prove its ability and its patriotism if it was going to shake the appearance of dependence on the Westerners. Some Americans thought Diem might be able to meet this challenge, but only if the French allowed him the true independence to do so.

Diem himself was a complex individual. He was personally honest and coura-geous and had a well-established record of resistance to French domination of his homeland. These qualities were assets for a Vietnamese politician. He had genuine liabilities, though, that the French were quick to emphasize. He had no political base except his own large family, which had a well-earned reputation for clannish self-interest. His Catholic religion may have pleased the French but only served to isolate him from his predominantly Buddhist countrymen. His personality was aloof, even monkish—the opposite of the modern politician. In addition, he had lived briefly in the United States and knew some influential American politicians and church leaders, such as Senator Mike Mansfield (D-Mont.) and Francis Cardinal Spellman. In fact, it may have been Diem's ties to the United States that prompted Bao Dai to name him prime minister, in a move to court official U.S. support as French power waned in Vietnam.

How Bao Dai came to appoint Diem, a man whom he disliked immensely, is not known with certainty. Some accounts have speculated that the CIA or some other secret U.S. influence was behind the selection. There is no particular evidence available for this scenario, however, and Bao Dai may well have had his own rea-sons. Clandestine American contact with Diem after he became prime minister has become well known. Covert initiatives were an explicit element of the New Look, and CIA Director Allen W. Dulles (the secretary of state's brother) sent a special agent to Saigon at the same time that Diem assumed office. Allen Dulles's choice was Air Force Colonel Edward G. Lansdale, an unconventional warfare officer who had aided the Philippine government's successful resistance of a communist rebel-lion. Lansdale quickly became Diem's confidant and an ardent advocate for firm U.S. support of the prime minister.

Despite endorsement of Diem from Lansdale and others, Eisenhower had given explicit instructions to Collins to evaluate Diem's leadership qualities. After five months of close observation, Collins reported that he judged Diem incapable of providing South Vietnam with the dynamic leadership it needed. Diem and his brothers were running a "practically one-man government," the general informed Washington, and they were stubbornly resistant to helpful advice. Collins recom-mended other Vietnamese officials whom he thought could better organize a broad-based coalition to compete with the communists. Collins's report shocked Secretary of State Dulles. Although initially dubious of Diem's prospects, the secretary had come to accept the argument of Diem's American friends that the prime minister was the best hope for a nationalist alternative to Ho and that all Diem needed was the confidence that he had the "*wholehearted* backing" of the United States.

Unlike the Dienbienphu discussions of the previous year, debate on the Diem issue in the spring of 1955 did not directly engage the president. Eisenhower chose to stand aside and let Secretary Dulles and General Collins reach a conclusion. The president was preoccupied with the Taiwan Straits crisis and the approach of his first summit conference with Soviet leaders. Meeting with Dulles and other State Department officials in Washington on April 25, Collins maintained his position that Diem was not indispensable, and the secretary reluctantly agreed. Literally at the moment these decisions were being made, street fighting erupted in Saigon. Probably instigated by Diem himself in a desperate demonstration to Washington, the violence enabled the prime minister to obtain enough backing from the fledgling

South Vietnamese armed forces to quell the unrest. As Collins rushed back to Saigon to oversee U.S. interests in the unstable situation, Dulles's Asian advisers convinced him to reverse himself and to make wholehearted support of Diem the basis of U.S. policy. The aides argued that the violent outbreak proved that it was an inopportune time to tamper with Saigon's internal politics.

Once the Eisenhower administration had determined that it would stick with Diem, the task remained to convince the French to accept this course. In early May, exactly a year after the surrender of Dienbienphu, Dulles met several times with French premier Edgar Faure. The sessions were stormy, but Faure finally acquiesced to Dulles's insistence on Diem. It was clear that Paris no longer wished to contest Washington over the direction of Western policy in Vietnam. Through the rest of 1955, the French rapidly withdrew the remainder of their forces in South Vietnam and left the fate of the would-be nation to the Americans and their client Diem.

In the long-term history of U.S. involvement in Southeast Asia, Washington had turned an important corner. SEATO had provided a semblance of collective sanction to the U.S. intent to bolster South Vietnam, but the departure of the French demonstrated that the effort actually would be a unilateral U.S. program. The feasibility of the plan hinged on the questionable judgment that Diem could make it work. The administration entered a new and perilous policy phase.

With the basic decision having been made to build a nation around Diem, the implementation now fell to the foreign policy bureaucracy with little additional input from the president or Dulles. After Eisenhower suffered a heart attack in September 1955, many issues that his staff deemed routine, such as Vietnam, were kept from his schedule. The following year, Dulles developed abdominal cancer, and although he remained in office almost until his death in 1959, his personal agenda too became more restricted. Yet the course that Eisenhower and Dulles had set in Vietnam remained the administration's policy until the end of Eisenhower's presidency, and occasionally the two men would publicly reaffirm the concept of wholehearted support for Diem.

The task of nation building loomed large before the administration. The legitimacy of Diem's regime rested only on his appointment by the heir of Vietnam's last royal dynasty, and Sa Majesté Bao Dai had taken up permanent residence on the French Riviera. The State of Vietnam had a small army of 150,000 led by an inexperienced officer corps that, under the French, had never been allowed to have any command or staff authority. The civil bureaucracy consisted only of *fonctionnaires* trained to take orders, not to solve problems. Industry was virtually nonexistent in South Vietnam, and the agricultural base of rice and rubber, although potentially valuable, had been wrecked by exploitative landlords who had impoverished much of the peasantry. Diem himself had no political following that could compete with the regimented and motivated cadre in the DRV.

Diem's political weakness seemed especially important because of the national reunification elections that were supposed to occur in 1956. Although many observers of all ideological perspectives believed that Ho Chi Minh would win any truly free countrywide election, the chances of a referendum occurring were slim from the beginning. The Geneva conferees had drafted a vague proposal for elections because they could not fashion any workable political formula themselves. How the Vietnamese were to vote and on what was never specified. No official in North or

South Vietnam had ever organized or conducted a free election, and there was no reason to expect that the Vietnamese would do so now under these strained circumstances. In the months following the Geneva Conference, it was clear that Diem and his American patrons had no enthusiasm for an election, but there was also no pressure for a vote from China, the Soviet Union, Britain, or France. None of these governments was inclined to assume any risk to itself to champion elections in Vietnam for the benefit of the DRV. The Eisenhower administration can be given little credit or blame for the failure of the election provisions of the Geneva agreements.

Even without the serious possibility of a reunification vote, Diem's specious political legitimacy posed grave difficulties for U.S. objectives. Kenneth T. Young, the State Department officer in charge of Southeast Asian affairs, saw the problem as a paradox. He believed that if South Vietnam did not become a republic the anachronistic State of Vietnam would be easy prey for the revolutionary line of the DRV. At the same time, though, he feared that voting for a representative assembly in the South might open the door to political anarchy. While Young and other Americans worried, Diem acted. He staged a lopsided referendum in October 1955 to depose Bao Dai and to make himself president of a newly created Republic of Vietnam (RVN). In March 1956, Diem organized an election of a constituent assembly, heavily stacked in his favor, to draft a constitution. The voting was not an exercise in democracy, but it was impressive evidence of the ability of the Ngo family, especially Diem's brothers Ngo Dinh Nhu and Ngo Dinh Can, to manipulate ballots. The RVN provided a facade of popular government for an ambitious family aspiring to centralized authority.

Evidence of the emerging Ngo family dictatorship mounted. Nhu and Can operated a secret organization, the Can Lao, that used bribery and intimidation to garner personal support for Diem from key members of the military and bureaucracy. Vietminh "suspects," that is, persons thought disloyal to the regime, were arrested and sent to "reeducation camps." An RVN ordinance abolished elected village councils and substituted government appointees to run local affairs. Some U.S. officials, including Secretary Dulles, excused this authoritarianism as typical of Asia and even saw it as prudent because it provided a measure of stability in a nation still developing its institutional structure. Among his criticisms of Diem, Collins had warned that the Ngos' penchant for self-protection would only isolate Diem from the people and weaken the regime. That caution had been rejected, however, in favor of wholehearted support for Diem. As Collins had predicted, the Ngos increasingly behaved as if they could take U.S. aid for granted regardless of how they acted.

The level of U.S. assistance to South Vietnam was high, almost $250 million annually through the end of the Eisenhower years. Some of these funds were designated for economic development. Very little aid went to the agricultural sector, but after U.S. urging, the Diem government announced some rent controls and land transfer plans, which went largely unimplemented. In the urban areas, a U.S.-designed Commercial Import Program made U.S. dollars available to subsidize imports. Rather than stimulate economic activity, however, the plan produced an influx of consumer goods, such as refrigerators and motorbikes, that created an appearance of prosperity but masked the lack of real economic growth.

The bulk of U.S. aid, about 80 percent of it, went directly to the South Vietnamese armed forces. During the Eisenhower presidency, the number of U.S. military personnel in the RVN never exceeded 700, but the large percentage of U.S. aid that went for military purposes revealed the high priority placed on the military security of the new nation. Eighty-five percent of the funds for paying, equipping, and training the RVN's 150,000-man force came from the U.S. Treasury.

Eisenhower and his advisers chose to declare Diem's leadership of South Vietnam a grand success, despite the repressive nature of the Saigon regime and its heavy dependency on aid. On May 8, 1957, the president himself stood on the hot parking apron at Washington National Airport to greet Diem as the RVN leader arrived for a highly publicized state visit. During the next four days, among lavish receptions and private meetings, Diem conferred with Eisenhower, Dulles, and other officials and addressed a joint session of Congress. This pageantry was part of a series of such events hosted by the administration for a number of Asian and African dignitaries. The purpose was to improve U.S. relations with the Third World, which, as Washington had learned during the Suez Canal crisis of 1956, could be vitally important. Diem was a beneficiary of this administration initiative in personal diplomacy.

Eisenhower and other American speakers hailed Diem as a "tough miracle man" and the "savior" of South Vietnam. The administration congratulated Diem and itself on his survival since 1954 and characterized the RVN as a stalwart ally in the struggle against world communism. Behind closed doors the rhetoric was friendly but somewhat more restrained. When Diem asked for an increase in U.S. aid, for example, Eisenhower rebuffed him with the explanation that U.S. global aid commitments prevented greater assistance. The Eisenhower-Diem summit reconfirmed the administration's earlier decisions to treat South Vietnam as strategically important and to give wholehearted endorsement to Diem's regime. It also showed that, even in a region of vital interest, the New Look principle of fiscal restraint still applied.

In the late 1950s, Congress too was determined both to contain foreign aid budgets and to continue assistance to the Diem regime. Only once during the decade did congressional committees hold hearings specifically on Indochina, and that occasion was an investigation of alleged corruption in the management of the aid program in Saigon. Although both Democratic and Republican members questioned the amounts and uses of some funds, the probe uncovered no serious misconduct. At no time during the Eisenhower presidency did Congress as a body challenge the goals of the administration's policies in Vietnam. During the Dienbienphu crisis, some congressional leaders, including Senator Lyndon B. Johnson (D-Tex.), urged the White House to avoid a unilateral U.S. intervention in the French war, but that position was already preferred by the president. Later, as the U.S. commitment to Diem grew, a bipartisan alignment of lawmakers—many of them in an interest group called the American Friends of Vietnam that included Senator John F. Kennedy (D-Mass.)—staunchly defended U.S. involvement in the region.

During Eisenhower's second term, two pressures largely shaped the conduct of U.S. policy in Southeast Asia: (1) the proclaimed value of South Vietnam to U.S. security and (2) the need to manage economically the United States' global obligations. These twin concerns often exasperated the diplomats and military officers charged with devising and implementing appropriate actions. The problem was how to do more with less. With his attention on Sputnik, Cuba, and elsewhere, the president provided no additional direction to U.S. policymakers as conditions within Vietnam worsened.

By 1957 and 1958, terrorism and armed insurrection were on the rise in South Vietnam. This violence often represented retaliation and resistance to Diem's increasingly repressive regime. Most of these incidents occurred without the instigation of Hanoi. The DRV had not given up its objective of reuniting Vietnam under its rule, but its leaders had ordered their southern cadres to be patient. Hanoi preferred to try propaganda and other destabilizing techniques first rather than to plunge into an armed conflict that could prompt a U.S. military attack on the North. Southern resistance leaders, who faced being jailed and even executed, refused to wait, however, and began acting on their own with assassinations, firebombings, and small attacks on RVN military units and outposts.

Both Vietnamese and American officials in Saigon shared a mounting feeling of crisis, but the instructions from Washington remained clear that the nation-building program would have to make do with what it was already receiving, or likely even less, as the total foreign aid budget shrank. The result was a bitter and debilitating battle between American diplomats and the Ngo family and among the Americans themselves over how to utilize the available resources. The issue was whether to increase the already high percentage of U.S. funds that went to military use or to place more emphasis on economic development and political reform.

U.S. Ambassador in Saigon Elbridge Durbrow took the lead in arguing that the RVN government would remain under attack from within as a neo-colonialist dependent as long as it failed to take genuine steps toward improving the economic and social welfare of its citizens. He even went so far as to suggest to Washington that helicopters and other military items that Diem desired be withheld until the RVN president demonstrated progress on land reform, civil rights, and other abuses—urgent problems that were fueling the hostility toward his regime. Meanwhile, Diem and Nhu vehemently demanded more military aid of all types with which to increase the size and armament of their forces.

Lieutenant General Samuel T. Williams, the chief of the U.S. Military Assistance Advisory Group in Vietnam, took sharp exception to Durbrow's views and sided with the Ngos. He argued that economic and political reforms remained impossible until the partisan violence had been crushed militarily. He also considered it deplorable that Durbrow would propose threatening to deny matériel to Diem at a time when the RVN government was under attack by armed and ruthless opponents. The general complained privately that the ambassador was better suited to be a salesman in a ladies' shoe store than a diplomat in Asia. Williams got support from Lansdale, now a brigadier general in the Pentagon, who advised his Defense Department superiors that Durbrow was "insulting, misinformed, and unfriendly" toward Diem.

Lansdale's and Williams's personal attacks on the ambassador demonstrated that there was more to the policy debate than just the merits of military versus economic aid. In question was the long-standing Eisenhower administration commitment to wholehearted support of Diem. The generals contended that rather than criticism and pressure, Diem needed Washington's acceptance and reassurance. With the backing of the State Department's Southeast Asia specialists, Durbrow maintained that no one, including Diem, was indispensable. In a pointed comment to his diplomatic colleagues, the ambassador recalled his Pentagon critic's past association with Diem: "We have to recognize that we are dealing with a somewhat more complicated situation in the case of the GVN [Government of Vietnam]," Durbrow declared, "and that we have left the 'Lansdale days' behind." The intensity with which both sides argued revealed how important these officials considered Vietnam to be to the United States. The debate also gave no indication that any of these policymakers thought of doing nothing and simply leaving the outcome in Vietnam up to the Vietnamese.

In January 1961, a few days before John Kennedy took the oath of office as Eisenhower's successor, Lansdale returned from an inspection visit to South Vietnam with a dire report. The RVN was in "critical condition," he declared, and the Vietcong (Washington's new term for Vietnamese communists) "have started to steal the country and expect to be done in 1961." His urgent tone may have derived in part from his ongoing debate over tactics with State Department officers, but it also revealed that the time had come for either reaffirmation or reassessment of the United States' wholehearted support of Diem and the RVN.

As Lansdale delivered his evaluation to the Pentagon, Eisenhower was briefing the president-elect on current world conditions. With a civil war underway in Laos in which the United States and the Soviet Union were supplying weapons to the contending sides, their discussion turned to Southeast Asia. The retiring chief executive claimed that the SEATO treaty obligated the United States to defend the region from communist encroachment. The United States should protect the area's security in cooperation with the SEATO allies if possible, but if not, Eisenhower advised, "then we must go it alone." The next day, January 20, Eisenhower's constitutional authority over the direction of U.S. foreign policy expired, but the course that he had charted in Vietnam would continue.

A review of the long-term significance of the two phases of Eisenhower's Vietnam policies reveals that the second or post-1955 stage with its unilateral and assertive commitment to South Vietnam prevailed over the original multilateral and cautious approach. The goal during both periods was the same: to deny Vietnam or as much of it as possible to the Vietnamese communists. Phase one was a setback to this objective because it ended with de facto acceptance of communist control of the northern half of the country. Eisenhower's negative decision—to avoid taking overt action to resist this outcome—appears as a wise, statesmanlike acceptance of the reality of the Vietminh's success in resisting French colonialism. It was a caution dictated by the immediate circumstances, however. The second phase was also based upon a negative decision—to avoid acceptance of an internal Vietnamese resolution of political authority in the country. This decision was far from statesmanlike. It failed to acknowledge Diem's neo-colonial dependence on U.S. support. It placed U.S. actions in conflict with the manifest Vietnamese desire for national independence. Yet Washington's wholehearted support of Diem continued. By the time Eisenhower left office in 1961, the goal of a noncommunist South Vietnam and the means of obtaining that objective—nation building premised on the survival of the Diem regime—were so deeply embedded in U.S. global strategy as to be virtually unassailable.

Eisenhower's personal strengths served him well during the first phase. His knowledge of military affairs and the politics of war enabled him to perceive clearly the military and political costs inherent in U.S. intervention in the French war. His talent for utilizing a good staff organization also enhanced his analysis of policy options and enabled him to present the outcome as a bureaucratic decision. This maneuvering mitigated potential criticism about being pusillanimous in Vietnam. During the second phase, these same strengths failed him. Once the Geneva ceasefire took effect, the issue in Vietnam was not one of military strategy but of the internal political and economic development of a new nation. Although his experience on General Douglas MacArthur's staff in the Philippines in the 1930s made Eisenhower sensitive to the aspirations of Asian nationalists and familiar with the frustrations of dealing with them, he had no personal acquaintance with any Vietnamese leaders and little grasp of the complex sociopolitical realities of the Asian communism that Diem faced. His one meeting with Diem was largely ceremonial. Similarly, his system of having his staff sift through options did not help alleviate this problem of comprehending complexity. Indeed, the key staff member upon whom he relied for foreign policy advice, Secretary Dulles, generally accepted the single-minded fixation on Diem. It could be argued that Eisenhower's 1955 heart attack made him excessively dependent on his staff, but even after his recovery and return to a rather heavy work load, he gave little personal attention to the details of Vietnam, which his staff presented to him as an issue that was being managed well. He accepted their optimistic assessments and, during Diem's 1957 visit, lent his voice to the chorus of praise for the RVN's achievements. Beneath the miracle facade, however, were serious problems: Diem's narrow political base, his regime's weak military structure, South Vietnam's weak economy, and the growing insurgency. When Eisenhower yielded the White House to Kennedy, the policy of wholehearted support of Diem remained in place not because it was achieving U.S. objectives but because to waver even slightly could risk collapse of the administration's eight-year effort to keep the dominoes from falling. Eisenhower's accomplishments in Vietnam were negative: no war, but no peace. It was a record of nonsolution and ever-narrowing options.

The Failure of Vietnamization

RONALD H. SPECTOR

By 1957 the United States appeared well on the way to achieving its aims in South Vietnam. The government of Ngo Dinh Diem had vanquished the armies of the sects and the Binh Xuyen and had successfully defied North Vietnam on the issue of national elections. In July 1955 Diem had refused even to consult with the Democratic Republic of Vietnam on the subject. The Republic of Vietnam, said Diem, was in no way bound by the Geneva Agreements. His government had declined to adhere to them and, while eager for a "reunification in freedom," would consider no proposals from a regime which subordinated the national interest to the interests of communism.

The United States had never had much enthusiasm for the elections, believing that North Vietnam would never permit a really free expression of political views. Privately, many American officials also acknowledged that even a relatively "fair" election would almost certainly result in a lopsided victory for North Vietnam. Its larger population and superior political organization and control would weigh heavily in favor of the North, as would the personal prestige of Ho Chi Minh and a continuing popular identification of the Viet Minh with nationalism. As a State Department expert on Vietnam observed, the Diem government would "be campaigning against the massive fact of Viet Minh victory, against ubiquitous Viet Minh infiltration, and against the knowledge, shared even by illiterate coolies, that there would be no such independence as now exists had it not been for the Viet Minh." Nevertheless, the United States could hardly oppose or openly obstruct the holding of nationwide elections. To do so would contradict the traditional American stand that nations divided against their will, such as Germany and Korea, should be reunited through free elections supervised by the United Nations. This position had been reiterated by the American representative at Geneva, Walter Bedell Smith. There was also the possibility that the Communists might again resort to arms if elections were denied or postponed.

Eisenhower and his advisers never adopted a firm policy on the question of elections. In general, Washington leaders saw them as something to be delayed rather than eliminated. They counseled Diem to consult about elections, as required by the Geneva Agreements, but then to stall by insisting that elections be held only when, as the agreements specified, "all necessary conditions obtain for a free expression of national will." In the meantime the Diem government would presumably build up the popular support necessary to win the elections, should they take place. When Diem instead opted simply to have nothing to do with elections, the United States, impressed with his recent successes, went along with little protest. Although the Democratic Republic of Vietnam appealed to the cochairmen of the Geneva Conference—Britain and the Soviet Union—and hinted at renewed military action if the elections were not held, the July 1956 deadline for opening consultations passed without incident.

Early in 1957 Diem came to the United States aboard President Eisenhower's personal plane to be hailed everywhere as the savior of Southeast Asia. The South Vietnamese president addressed a joint session of Congress and paid a ceremonial visit to New York, where Mayor Robert F. Wagner pronounced him "a man history may yet ajudge as one of the great figures of the twentieth century." Senator John F. Kennedy referred to South Vietnam as "the cornerstone of the Free World in Southeast Asia, the keystone to the arch, the finger in the dike." The *Saturday Evening Post* called Diem the "mandarin in a sharkskin suit who's upsetting the Red timetable."

Yet even while Diem was receiving those accolades in the United States, members of the country team in Saigon were reaching different conclusions about the achievements of the South Vietnamese government. During the fall of 1957 Ambassador Durbrow, U.S. Operations Mission Chief Leland Barrows, Embassy Counselor Thomas D. Bowie, and Economic Affairs Officer Wesley Haroldson prepared a report sharply critical of the character and policies of the Diem regime. They described Diem as a man unable to delegate responsibility: "He overrides most of his Ministers, reduces their authority, and assumes personal responsibility for the smallest details of government. He is inclined to be suspicious of others; he lacks an understanding of basic economic principles." Economic development and agrarian reform had been neglected while the president concentrated on pet projects related to security. In the countryside, discontent with the government was increasing, and internal security was expected to decline. In the more sophisticated urban areas, there was considerable resentment and fear of Diem's covert Can Lao Party, which, the officials noted, had managed to infiltrate almost all political, social welfare, journalistic, cultural, and other public activities.

Other members of the country team including the CIA station chief and the Army, Navy, and Air Force attaches endorsed the report in general, but [Lieutenant General Samuel T.] Williams [Chief of the U.S. Military Assistance Advisory Group in Vietnam] dissented. He believed that in order to retain Diem's confidence and cooperation it was imperative to avoid associating with his critics and enemies. "Otherwise we would go the way of the French." General Williams also doubted that the situation was as serious as the report indicated. "The receipt [in Washington] of the proposed dispatch," he warned Ambassador Durbrow, "would unquestionably cause alarm and unnecessary concern . . . the reports I have seen do not indicate a state of considerable concern regarding internal security, the economic situation, or the executive ability of the government of Viet Nam." In a lengthy and heated discussion with other members of the country team, Williams insisted that he was unable to "subscribe to the idea that the president was on the way to failure." Even after persuading the foreign service officers to moderate the tone of their report, he refused to concur in its conclusion.

The months to come were to show that the country team had been, if anything, too mild in its criticism of the Diem government. From observing Diem on numerous trips and inspection tours, General Williams had become convinced that the president was extraordinarily popular, but that popularity turned out to be largely a sham. The American consul at Hue, for example, observed, that the villagers who were often paraded out to participate in ceremonies honoring Diem and to make appropriate responses to slogans "have virtually no concept of what they are doing." As a British journalist noted, "Diem holds the fort through the Army and the police force provided by U.S. [money]. It is not that the communists have done nothing because Diem is in power, rather Diem has remained in power because the communists have done nothing." . . .

Although American civilian officials were critical of both the road-building and resettlement projects, they pointed with pride to another South Vietnamese program: land reform. In the summer of 1959, for example, Ambassador Durbrow told a U.S. Senate subcommittee that the South Vietnamese government was carrying out "the largest land reform program in Asia."

Land reform was clearly a subject of importance in a country where 75 to 80 percent of the population lived in rural areas and large landholdings by absentee landlords were commonplace. The problem was most acute in the Mekong Delta region, where a majority of the rural population owned no land and a small but extremely wealthy class of absentee landlords held much of the fertile land. Most peasants rented land on a sharecropping basis, with the drawbacks attendant to such a system. To a landlord who provided no credit, seed, or fertilizer, the peasant paid one-third to one-half of the expected yield; in the event of crop failure, the landlord still had the right to demand his share of the normal yield.

During the long war against the French, the Viet Minh had driven away or killed many landlords and turned over their land to the poorer peasants. Instead of accepting that situation, the Diem government restored land to the landlords and then tried to regulate the extent of their landholdings and the landlord-tenant relationship. In 1955 the Diem government passed an ordinance setting a maximum of 15 to 25 percent of a crop as the lawful rent, and the following year limited individual landholdings to 247 acres. Acreage exceeding that maximum was to be purchased by the government and sold in small parcels to tenants, laborers, and other landless persons. Whether or not this constituted "the largest land reform program in Asia," it was certainly one of the most conservative. Landlords were allowed to select the lands to be retained, and the 247-acre limit was far greater than that allowed in Japan or Korea. In many provinces peasants were granted the right to purchase land that they had already been given by the Viet Minh. Although the government established loans to enable penniless peasants to buy land, its rigorous enforcement of repayment provisions often resulted in hardship. In Kien Phong Province, for example, farmers were forced to sell their rice at slump prices to meet loan payments. One farmer was reportedly "placed in a cage too small to stand up in and had to remain there until his wife sold their oxen" to pay the loan.

The implementation of the land reform program was so ensnarled in red tape and legalisms that in many areas relatively little land actually changed hands. In one province in the Mekong Delta, the first land redistribution took place only in 1958, almost two years after the land reform law was established. A 1960 census showed that only 23 percent of the farmers in the Mekong Delta owned any land at all, and about 56 percent of those lived on two-acre farms, one acre of which was rented.

Aside from the government's failure in land reform, rural residents were also affected adversely by a strongly promoted "anti-Communist campaign" mounted during 1955 and 1956 against known and suspected members and ex-members of the Viet Minh. The Viet Minh leaders had left Geneva confident that Vietnam would soon be unified under their control either through the scheduled elections or through the precipitate collapse of the South Vietnamese government. Following the Geneva Conference the Communist leadership began actively to prepare for a campaign of political agitation and propagandizing in the South. They summoned many former Viet Minh soldiers and cadres to regroup in North Vietnam while those who remained behind, an estimated 10,000 active agents, began to agitate for elections and reunion with the North. Mass meetings in the villages were organized by Communist cadres who harangued the crowds about "the victory of Geneva." In many villages in the south and southwest, photos of Ho Chi Minh and copies of the Geneva Agreements appeared on the wall of every house. In Saigon and other large cities the insurgents made a determined effort to win over non-Communist leftists, students, and intellectuals through such ostensibly patriotic organizations as the Saigon-Cholon Peace Movement.

The Diem government responded with the Anti-Communist Denunciation Campaign and with armed action against Viet Minh–led organizations and demonstrations. Although the campaign did considerable damage to the Viet Minh's civilian infrastructure, it was conducted in such a brutal, corrupt, and capricious manner that it alienated large segments of the population. Even former members of the Communist Party who were inactive or no longer loyal to the Viet Minh and former Viet Minh who had never been Communists were harassed, arrested, and in some cases executed. In some areas, families with sons who had gone to North Vietnam following the Geneva Agreements or who had relatives involved in insurgent activities were also affected. "Not only were local officials and police agents frequently incompetent at singling out the active Viet Minh agents, but many were also arrogant and venal in the execution of their tasks and by their offensive behavior generated sympathy for the Viet Minh." In one province, villagers could be jailed simply for having been in a rebel district. The people especially resented a curfew, which hampered fishermen and farmers, and a compulsory unpaid labor program to improve roads and perform other public works.

Despite the disruption to Communist Party organizations in many hamlets and districts, party cadres and innocent victims of the purges could often make their way to jungle, swamp, or mountain areas where they easily evaded government forces. By alienating large numbers of non-Communist and neutral peasants, the heavy-handed campaign also made it easy for the Viet Minh to rebuild their organizations and recruit new members.

Nevertheless, the campaign's short-run impact on the Communist apparatus in South Vietnam was severe. By early 1955 most Viet Minh cadres who had escaped arrest had been driven underground, and Communist-organized demonstrations had become infrequent. With many of its military forces regrouped in the North the party was in a poor position to meet the vigorous onslaught of the South Vietnamese government.

Pressure from the Diem government, combined with disappointment at the cancellation of the hoped-for elections, probably led to a decline in membership and morale in the party. At a meeting of top party leaders in the South in March 1956 Le Duan, Secretary of the Central Committee's Directorate for South Vietnam, expressed strong dissatisfaction with the North Vietnamese government's policy, which emphasized political agitation in the South and diplomatic pressure on the former Geneva conferees. The only way to achieve reunification, said Le Duan, was to wage armed struggle against the Diem regime.

Yet in 1956 many North Vietnamese leaders were reluctant to become involved in a renewed war, wanting first to "build socialism" in North Vietnam. War would retard development and would carry with it a risk of American intervention. Communist leaders in South Vietnam continued to object to that policy, preferring to proceed with overthrowing the Diem regime before Diem became fully established.

Finally Le Duan offered a compromise. In a pamphlet entitled *On the Revolution in South Vietnam* he argued for a long-term approach to the problem of South Vietnam which, while continuing political agitation and subversion, would also lay the groundwork for a future armed uprising against Diem. Le Duan's arguments were favorably received at the Eleventh Plenum of the Central Committee in December 1956.

By 1957, when Le Duan was recalled to fill a senior party position in North Vietnam, a campaign of terrorism and subversion had begun in the South without direct support from the North. During much of this time, Communist units consciously avoided contact with government forces, concentrating instead upon *tru gian* ("the extermination of traitors"), a systematic program of assassination of government officials and anyone considered an obstacle to the movement. In some provinces special assassination squads of about half a dozen men were formed solely for this purpose. Any village official or government functionary was considered a legitimate target for *tru gian*. "In principle," explained a former party leader in Dinh Tuong Province, "the Party tried to kill any [government] official who enjoyed the people's sympathy and left the bad officials unharmed in order to wage propaganda and sow hatred against the government." At times the insurgents terrorized or executed even persons known to be innocent of any pro-government activity to encourage anxiety and distrust among the villages. . . .

Incidents involving insurgents increased throughout 1957 and into 1958. During January 1957, Communist guerrillas clashed with South Vietnamese Army troops seven times in the Mekong Delta provinces. The following month a Viet Cong force of about thirty men attacked a government civic action team in the village of Tri Binh, fifteen miles south of Tay Ninh; the entire team was killed or wounded, and the local government militia force took no action against the raiders. During a single month in the autumn of 1957, 22 village notables and other local government officials were killed or wounded by the Viet Cong, 6 village chiefs were killed, and 11 members of local militia were killed and 14 kidnapped. During the last quarter of 1957 some 140 armed attacks and terrorist acts were reported throughout the country in addition to more than 50 skirmishes initiated by government troops or security forces. Terrorists wounded, assassinated, or killed at least 74 persons, including 20 government officials and 31 police and security personnel.

The Communists concentrated their armed activities in the southern provinces, mainly in the more rugged and inaccessible region along the Cambodian border where the terrain favored concealment and ambush. Toward late 1957 and early 1958 an increasing number of incidents were also reported on the outskirts of medium-sized towns such as Tan An, Can Tho, My Tho, Soc Trang, Rach Gia, and Ca Mau. Although the insurgents were either new recruits to or veterans of the Viet Minh, the Diem government for propaganda purposes renamed them Viet Cong, a derogatory term meaning Vietnamese Communists. By mid-1957 the name had come into general use.

Despite those developments and other signs that the tempo of insurgent activity was quickening, General Williams saw no reason for alarm. "There are no indications of a resumption of large-scale guerrilla warfare at this date," he told Ambassador Durbrow at the end of 1957. "They [the Viet Cong] lack sufficient strength, do not have a popular base and are faced with a central government whose efficiency to deal with the subversion threat has gradually improved since its inception." He estimated the Viet Cong's combat strength in the central provinces at no more than 1,000 including sect forces, plus around 200 political and propaganda cadres. Williams made this assessment of the situation based on the limited information available to him. The Military Assistance Advisory Group had no intelligence unit, so that in the main General Williams had to depend on South Vietnamese sources for information about the insurgents. . . .

While Americans and Vietnamese in Saigon argued over the question of paramilitary forces, the security situation in the countryside continued to deteriorate. Because travel through most parts of South Vietnam was safe and because Viet Cong units continued to avoid South Vietnamese Army units and fortified government positions of any strength, American officials long failed to detect the full extent of the deterioration. Yet signs were there. Early in 1958 South Vietnamese officials notified the advisory group that there were extensive Viet Cong supply trails in the western parts of the northern provinces of Quang Nam and Thua Thien, and along the Laotian border. During a single week in February in An Xuyen Province at the southern tip of South Vietnam, a Viet Cong company of about a hundred men attacked a government post in the town of Thoi Binh; a force of equal size attacked the town of Hung My; and a small South Vietnamese Army patrol was wiped out in an ambush near the town of Ganh Hao. The American embassy observed that "in many remote areas the central government has no effective control."

The Viet Cong were reportedly most active in the region of the Plain of Reeds adjoining the Cambodian border, which included portions of Kien Phong and Kien Tuong Provinces; the old sect strongholds of Tay Ninh, Binh Long, Phuoc Long, Bien Hoa; Binh Duong, Long Khanh, and Phuoc Tuy Provinces; and the Ca Mau peninsula at the southern tip of the country. The CIA estimated that, together with the remnants of the sect forces, the Viet Cong by early 1958 had an armed strength of some 1,700 men. By the spring there were reports of Viet Cong units operating out of small posts in heavily wooded areas north of Saigon. In June a Viet Cong force of from twenty to fifty men attacked a government detention center at Pleiku in the Central Highlands, releasing some fifty prisoners, many of them "known communists," while incurring no casualties. Diem attributed the failure to the fact that many of the prison guards were Montagnard tribesmen.

Although General Williams could hardly have been unaware of increasing Viet Cong pressure, he remained convinced that countering insurgency was not the primary business of the South Vietnamese Army. "A division on pacification duty goes to pieces fast," he observed. "The guerrillas go underground and soon the troops start sitting around on bridges and in market places and go to pot." When Vice President Nguyen Ngoc Tho warned Diem that the wave of terrorism and assassination was demoralizing the country, Williams insisted that using army units for security operations "is exactly what the communists want us to do." With division maneuvers scheduled to begin in the early spring of 1958, he observed: "If I were Giap, the first thing I would try to do would be to try to prevent these division maneuvers."

Despite Williams' misgivings the South Vietnamese government responded to the increased Viet Cong activity with a major military effort. For the first time Vietnamese Army units penetrated traditional Communist base areas in the Plain of Reeds, in the Ca Mau peninsula, and in War Zone D, the area northeast of Saigon. Many of these operations were slow and ponderous. In the Ca Mau peninsula a battalion of Vietnamese marines was able to capture some Viet Cong suspects and locate hidden caches of food but soon discovered that the Viet Cong had withdrawn to a strongpoint in the vast swamp and salt marsh immediately behind the western tip of the peninsula. The attackers could approach the enemy strongpoint only by a water route that would lead them directly along the line of fire of the defending Viet Cong. At that point the operation ground to a halt while the battalion commander negotiated with the military region commander and the South Vietnamese Air Force for air strikes.

Although slow and indecisive, the government's operations certainly dealt a heavy blow to the Viet Cong. Party membership in the South, which had stood at some 5,000 in mid-1957, fell to about one-third that level by the end of the year. Official party histories refer to the period of late 1958–early 1959 as "the darkest period" of the struggle in the South, a period when "the enemy . . . truly and efficiently destroyed our Party. . . . The political struggle movement of the masses although not defeated was encountering increasing difficulty and increasing weakness, the party bases, although not completely destroyed, were significantly weakened and in some areas quite seriously." In Gia Dinh Province party membership declined from more than 1,000 in mid-1954, to 385 in mid-1957, to about 6 in mid-1959.

By the end of 1958 surviving party cadres in many parts of South Vietnam had apparently decided, on their own initiative, to escalate the struggle beyond armed propaganda and assassinations even though this violated the party line. Armed units were formed into companies or battalions usually numbering less than one hundred men, armed with rifles, grenades, light machine guns, and sometimes merely pikes.

The renewed Viet Cong activity was most intense in War Zone D, a heavily forested region about fifty kilometers northeast of Saigon. Here Viet Cong units no longer always retreated from South Vietnamese Army forces of equal or inferior strength. During March 1959 there were at least ten firefights between army troops and the Viet Cong in which thirteen government soldiers were killed, wounded, or reported missing; five rifles, two automatic weapons, and a jeep were destroyed. In May 1959 a Viet Cong force occupying high ground in War Zone D, northeast of the town of Bien Hoa, successfully stood off attacks by an entire army battalion, then disengaged before the government troops could bring up artillery.

The Party Central Committee had meanwhile convened its fifteenth plenum in January 1959. At the urging of Le Duan, who had just completed an inspection tour of the South, and of other southern Communist leaders, the Central Committee adopted a resolution endorsing the use of armed force to overthrow the Diem regime. By May 1959 new directives were on their way from Hanoi to party leaders in the South. Insurgents, specially trained in the North, were infiltrated back into South Vietnam. A new Central Committee Directorate for South Vietnam was established, and communication routes into the South through Laos were improved and expanded. A new stage in the long struggle for South Vietnam had begun. . . .

Many people have come to regard the French Indochina War (1946–1954) as a rehearsal for the Vietnam War (1965-1973). Similarly, the early advisory period (1955–1960) to a degree foreshadows the period of Vietnamization during the Nixon and Ford administrations. True, there were important differences. The Military Assistance Advisory Group under Generals O'Daniel and Williams labored under advantages and disadvantages unknown to its successors in the 1960s and 1970s. The advantages were relative peace and calm in the countryside, especially from 1956 to 1958, and a relatively strong, stable civil government in Saigon. The disadvantages were the restrictions imposed by the Geneva Agreements on the size and activities of the military advisory effort, the strong budgetary constraints of the Eisenhower era, and the lack of attention and interest on the part of Washington leaders to the problems of Vietnam between 1956 and 1960. Another important difference was that in the Vietnamization years the United States was phasing down its military and civilian involvement. During the late 1950s, the degree of American involvement was relatively stable.

Yet despite the differences the two periods share a common overriding theme. In both the early advisory stage and the later period of Vietnamization, American leaders, were attempting to help the Vietnamese armed forces attain an ability to hold their own against their enemies without the assistance of large numbers of U.S. or other allied ground forces. In the 1950s this policy was precipitated by the rapid withdrawal of French combat forces from Vietnam and the inability of American forces to replace them because of limitations imposed by the Geneva Agreements and the New Look defense policy of the Eisenhower administration.

In both cases the Vietnamization effort ended in failure. The reasons for the failure of the second Vietnamization are still be assessed; the reasons for the failure of the first are easier to delineate. In the 1950s American military aims in Vietnam were never clearly defined. Although many Washington leaders believed that Communist subversion was a greater threat to South Vietnam than an overt, large-scale invasion, U.S. contingency planned tended to emphasize the latter. The chiefs of the Military Assistance Advisory Group therefore understandably tended to concentrate on building an army geared to resist attack from the North. In doing so they were merely following contemporary thinking, for in the 1950s, in contrast to the 1960s, there was little interest in, or knowledge of, counterinsurgency warfare within the U.S. armed forces.

The need for a capable security force to deal with the threat of internal subversion was not ignored. Yet responsibility for the training and equipping of paramilitary forces such as the Civil Guard and the Self-Defense Corps was vested not in the advisory group but in other agencies of the U.S. country team, agencies which differed radically in their view of the proper mission, composition, and employment of these forces. This disagreement was further complicated by delays, bureaucratic infighting, and personality clashes. The result was that when insurgency once again became a serious threat in 1959, the paramilitary forces were still unprepared, untrained, and unequipped to cope with it.

Consequently, the Vietnamese Army had to be directly committed against the Communist insurgents. Its indifferent performance in combat against the Viet Cong even after four years of U.S. support and training can be attributed to two sets of factors. The first involved weaknesses inherent in the Vietnamese Army as an institution. The rampant politicization in the higher ranks of the officer corps had enabled incompetent but politically reliable officers to attain and retain positions of responsibility and high command. An absence of unifying national spirit, motivation, or patriotism on the part of most Vietnamese soldiers reflected the lack of any widespread popular support for the Diem regime. Another factor was the poor security system of the army and its penetration at all levels by Viet Cong agents. Still another important element was the system of divided authority, routine subordination, and overlapping responsibility deliberately fostered by Diem within the army's command system to ensure that no military leader became too powerful. Added to this pattern was the inadequate technical competence of the Vietnamese combat soldier, who was often a recent conscript whose training had been interrupted or never started. Contemporary critics also pointed to the lack of specific training for guerrilla warfare, yet the Vietnamese Army's level of proficiency in basic combat skills was often so low as to make the question of specialized training irrelevant.

At the same time, the very organization, composition, and outlook of the Military Assistance Advisory Group ensured that the American advisers would remain either unaware of these inherent deficiencies or powerless to change them. The so-called short tour limited most U.S. advisers to less than eleven months in which to win the confidence of their Vietnamese counterparts and influence them to take needed measures to increase the effectiveness of their units. A wide gap in customs and culture also separated the advisers from their counterparts, a gap made wider by the small number of American officers able to communicate in any language other than English.

The limited ability of U.S. advisers to influence their counterparts holds true even for General Williams. He enjoyed President Diem's trust and confidence to an extent probably equaled by few other Americans, yet Williams' remark that "I can't remember one time that President Diem ever did anything of importance concerning the military that I recommended against" is surely an exaggeration. General Williams was unable to induce Diem to abandon favoritism in the appointment of officers, to rationalize the chain of command, or to abandon the project to create ranger battalions out of existing army formations. Moreover, Williams' closeness to Diem inclined him, in the view of some observers, to identify so closely with the president that he resisted and attempted to blunt all criticism of Diem, whether well founded or otherwise.

The success of an adviser was measured by his ability to influence his Vietnamese counterpart. Few were willing to report forthrightly that they had been unable to bring about needed reforms and improvements in the units to which they were assigned. Since the whole system of rating the performance of the Vietnamese Army was built upon the subjective, nonstandardized evaluations made by the advisers and their superiors, Saigon and Washington were guaranteed a superficial assessment. The dogged "Can Do" attitude of most officers and noncommissioned officers who tended to see all faults in the army as correctable, all failures as temporary, only further contributed to overoptimistic reports.

Considering the small size of the Military Assistance Advisory Group and the many limitations imposed upon its activities, its accomplishments with the weak, demoralized, divided, and disorganized army it inherited in 1955 represent a remarkable achievement. The complete reorganization of the Vietnamese Army, the establishment of a well-conceived and comprehensive school and training system, and the introduction, at least on paper, of a rationalized chain of command were only a few of the advisory group's solid contributions. Yet the subsequent failure of the South Vietnamese Army as an effective fighting force can only underline the warning which the Joint Chiefs of Staff gave to Secretary of State Dulles in 1954: that strong and stable governments and societies are necessary to support the creation of strong armies. That the reverse is seldom true would be clearly and tragically demonstrated in the years to follow.

✗ *F U R T H E R   R E A D I N G*

Anderson, David L. *Trapped By Success: The Eisenhower Administration and Vietnam, 1953–1961* (1991).
Arnold, James R. *The First Domino* (1991).
Bator, Victor. *Vietnam: A Diplomatic Tragedy* (1965).
Billings-Yun, Melanie. *Decision Against War: Eisenhower and Dien Bien Phu, 1954* (1988).

Burke, John P., and Fred I. Greenstein. *How Presidents Test Reality: Decisions on Vietnam 1954 and 1965* (1991).

Cable, James. *The Geneva Conference of 1954 on Indochina* (1986).

Combs, Arthur. "The Path Not Taken: The British Alternative to U.S. Policy in Vietnam, 1954–1956," *Diplomatic History,* 19 (1995), 33–57.

Currey, Cecil B. *Edward Lansdale* (1988).

Devillers, Philippe, and Jean Lacouture. *End of a War: Indochina, 1954* (1969).

Divine, Robert A. *Eisenhower and the Cold War* (1981).

Fall, Bernard B. *Hell in a Very Small Place* (1966).

Fifield, Russell H. *Southeast Asia in United States Policy* (1963).

Gardner, Lloyd C. *Approaching Vietnam* (1988).

Gurtov, Melvin. *The First Vietnam Crisis* (1967).

Hammer, Ellen J. *The Struggle for Indochina* (1966).

Herring, George C., and Richard H. Immerman. "Eisenhower, Dulles, and Dienbienphu: 'The Day We Didn't Go to War' Revisited," *Journal of American History,* 71 (1984), 343–363.

Immerman, Richard H. "The United States and the Geneva Conference of 1954: A New Look," *Diplomatic History,* 14 (1990), 43–66.

———. *John Foster Dulles* (1999).

Kaplan, Lawrence S., et al., eds. *Dien Bien Phu and the Crisis of Franco-American Relations, 1954–1955* (1990).

Khong, Yuen Foong. *Analogies at War: Korea, Munich, Dien Bien Phu and the Vietnam Decisions of 1965* (1992).

Kolko, Gabriel. *Anatomy of a War* (1985).

Lansdale, Edward Geary. *In the Midst of Wars* (1972).

Lyon, Peter. *Eisenhower* (1974).

McMahon, Robert J. "Eisenhower and Third World Nationalism: A Critique of the Revisionists," *Political Science Quarterly,* 101 (1986), 453–73.

Marks III, Frederick W. "The Real Hawk at Dienbienphu: Dunes or Eisenhower?" *Pacific Historical Review,* 69 (1990), 297–322.

Melanson, Richard A. and David Mayers, eds. *Reevaluating Eisenhower* (1987).

Morgan, Joseph G. *The Vietnam Lobby* (1997).

Randle, Robert F. *Geneva 1954* (1969).

Roberts, Chalmers M. "The Day We Didn't Go to War," *Reporter* 11 (September 14, 1954), 31–35.

Roy, Jules. *The Battle of Dienbienphu* (1965).

Smith, R. B. *Revolution Versus Containment* (1983).

Spector, Ronald H. *Advice and Support* (1983).

CHAPTER
5

John F. Kennedy and Vietnam:
Incremental Escalation

✕

The administration of John F. Kennedy inherited an increasingly troublesome commitment in Vietnam, a land that the young president had once described as the "cornerstone of the Free World in Southeast Asia." Fearful that the United States had lost the global initiative to the Soviet Union and China, Kennedy pursued a more activist foreign policy than his Republican predecessors. He especially sought to avoid additional Cold War defeats. In the spring of 1961, JFK supported—with some reluctance—a negotiated settlement in Laos that would lead to communist participation in a coalition government. Eager to avoid a similar compromise in Vietnam, where he believed that the stakes were much greater, Kennedy gradually increased the American presence there. In November 1961 he ordered the dispatch of several thousand U.S. military advisers to help to avert the collapse of the Diem government. Their number would swell to more than 16,000 by the end of Kennedy's presidency in 1963. When Diem's regime tottered in late 1963 in the face of challenges from both Vietcong guerrillas and Buddhist protesters, American officials backed a coup led by a group of South Vietnamese military officers. In the wake of the coup, Diem was murdered. Within weeks Kennedy himself would fall victim to an assassin's bullet.

JFK's role in the growing U.S. involvement in Vietnam has sparked intense scholarly scrutiny. Most historians agree that his decisions brought incremental, not dramatic, escalation and that he left his successors with deeper but still limited ties to South Vietnam. They differ on almost all other critical questions, including the underlying rationale for Kennedy's decisions, the significance of Vietnam to overall American foreign-policy objectives, the nature and strength of both Diem's regime and the Vietcong insurgency, the precise role of the United States in the coup against Diem, and the broader impact of Diem's ouster on the stability of South Vietnam and the U.S.–Vietnamese relationship. In view of Kennedy's sudden and untimely death, specialists have also speculated about what the president might have done with regard to the Vietnam problem had he lived—and had he been elected to a second term.

Document 1 is a cable of November 1, 1961, sent to President Kennedy by his military adviser, General Maxwell Taylor, recommending the introduction of a U.S. military force into South Vietnam. In a November 11 memorandum to the president, Document 2, Secretary of State Dean Rusk and Secretary of Defense Robert S. McNamara also urge the commitment of U.S. troops. They call for the speedy dispatch of support and advisory troops and the development of plans for the possible later commitment of combat forces. In Document 3, Jan Barry, a U.S. Army radio technician who served in South Vietnam from December 1962 to October 1963, reflects on his experiences there.

A memorandum from Senator Mike Mansfield to Kennedy is featured in Document 4. Mansfield, an enthusiastic early supporter of Diem, questions the deepening American commitment in South Vietnam. On September 2, 1963, in a television interview with Walter Cronkite of CBS, Kennedy made a series of critical remarks about Diem's regime. One week later, he expressed similar dissatisfaction with Diem in another television interview while reiterating his belief in the domino theory. Kennedy's interviews are excerpted in Documents 5 and 6.

Document 7 is a cable of October 25, 1963, from Ambassador Henry Cabot Lodge in Saigon to national security adviser McGeorge Bundy, speculating on the prospects for a coup against Diem. The plotters included South Vietnamese General Tran Van Don and CIA agent Lucien Conein. In an October 30 cable to Lodge, Document 8, Bundy expresses ambivalence about a U.S. role in any coup. Document 9, a transcript of Diem's final telephone conversation with Lodge, records the prime minister's fears for his safety after the outbreak of the rebellion in Saigon.

1. Maxwell Taylor Recommends the Dispatch of U.S. Forces, 1961

This message is for the purpose of presenting my reasons for recommending the introduction of a U.S. military force into SVN. I have reached the conclusion that this is an essential action if we are to reverse the present downward trend of events in spite of a full recognition of the following disadvantages:

a. The strategic reserve of U.S. forces is presently so weak that we can ill afford any detachment of forces to a peripheral area of the Communist bloc where they will be pinned down for an uncertain duration.

b. Although U.S. prestige is already engaged in SVN, it will become more so by the sending of troops.

c. If the first contingent is not enough to accomplish the necessary results, it will be difficult to resist the pressure to reinforce. If the ultimate result sought is the closing of the frontiers and the clean-up of the insurgents within SVN, there is no limit to our possible commitment (unless we attack the source in Hanoi).

d. The introduction of U.S. forces may increase tensions and risk escalation into a major war in Asia.

Telegram from Taylor to Kennedy, November 1, 1961, *United States–Vietnam Relations, 1945–1947* (Washington: U.S. Government Printing Office, 1971), Book 11, 337–342.

On the other side of the argument, there can be no action so convincing of U.S. seriousness of purpose and hence so reassuring to the people and Government of SVN and to our other friends and allies in SEA as the introduction of U.S. forces into SVN. The views of indigenous and U.S. officials consulted on our trip were unanimous on this point. I have just seen Saigon [cable] 575 to State and suggest that it be read in connection with this message.

The size of the U.S. force introduced need not be great to provide the military presence necessary to produce the desired effect on national morale in SVN and on international opinion. A bare token, however, will not suffice; it must have a significant value. The kinds of tasks which it might undertake which would have a significant value are suggested in Baguio [cable] 0005. They are:

a. Provide a U.S. military presence capable of raising national morale and of showing to SEA the seriousness of the U.S. intent to resist a Communist takeover.

b. Conduct logistical operations in support of military and flood relief operations.

c. Conduct such combat operations as are necessary for self-defense and for the security of the area in which they are stationed.

d. Provide an emergency reserve to back up the Armed Forces of the GVN [Government of (South) Vietnam] in the case of a heightened military crisis.

e. Act as an advance party of such additional forces as may be introduced if CINCPAC [U.S. Commander in Chief, Pacific] or SEATO [Southeast Asia Treaty Organization] contingency plans are invoked.

It is noteworthy that this force is not proposed to clear the jungles and forests of VC guerrillas. That should be the primary task of the Armed Forces of Vietnam for which they should be specifically organized, trained and stiffened with ample U.S. advisors down to combat battalion levels. However, the U.S. troops may be called upon to engage in combat to protect themselves, their working parties, and the area in which they live. As a general reserve, they might be thrown into action (with U.S. agreement) against large, formed guerrilla bands which have abandoned the forests for attacks on major targets. But in general, our forces should not engage in small-scale guerrilla operations in the jungle.

As an area for the operations of U.S. troops, SVN is not an excessively difficult or unpleasant place to operate. While the border areas are rugged and heavily forested, the terrain is comparable to parts of Korea where U.S. troops learned to live and work without too much effort. However, these border areas, for reasons stated above, are not the places to engage our forces. In the High Plateau and in the coastal plain where U.S. troops would probably be stationed, these jungle-forest conditions do not exist to any great extent. The most unpleasant feature in the coastal areas would be the heat and, in the Delta, the mud left behind by the flood. The High Plateau offers no particular obstacle to the stationing of U.S. troops.

The extent to which the Task Force would engage in flood relief activities in the Delta will depend upon further study of the problem there. As reported in Saigon 537, I see considerable advantages in playing up this aspect of the TF mission. I am presently inclined to favor a dual mission, initially help to the flood area and subsequently use in any other area of SVN where its resources can be used effectively to give tangible support in the struggle against the VC. However, the possibility of emphasizing the humanitarian mission will wane if we wait long in

moving in our forces or in linking our stated purpose with the emergency conditions created by the flood.

The risks of backing into a major Asian war by way of SVN are present but are
not impressive. NVN is extremely vulnerable to conventional bombing, a weakness which should be exploited diplomatically in convincing Hanoi to lay off SVN.
Both the D.R.V. and the Chicoms [Chinese communists] would face severe logistical difficulties in trying to maintain strong forces in the field in SEA, difficulties
which we share but by no means to the same degree. There is no case for fearing a
mass onslaught of Communist manpower into SVN and its neighboring states, particularly if our airpower is allowed a free hand against logistical targets. Finally,
the starvation conditions in China should discourage Communist leaders there
from being militarily venturesome for some time to come.

By the foregoing line of reasoning, I have reached the conclusion that the introduction of [word illegible] military Task Force without delay offers definitely more
advantage than it creates risks and difficulties. In fact, I do not believe that our program to save SVN will succeed without it. If the concept is approved, the exact size
and composition of the force should be determined by Sec Def in consultation with
the JCS, the Chief MAAG [Military Assistance Advisory Group] and CINCPAC.
My own feeling is that the initial size should not exceed about 8000, of which a
preponderant number would be in logistical-type units. After acquiring experience
in operating in SVN, this initial force will require reorganization and adjustment to
the local scene.

As CINCPAC will point out, any forces committed to SVN will need to be replaced by additional forces to his area from the strategic reserve in the U.S. Also,
any troops to SVN are in addition to those which may be required to execute
SEATO Plan 5 in Laos. Both facts should be taken into account in current considerations of the FY [fiscal year] 1963 budget which bear upon the permanent increase
which should be made in the U.S. military establishment to maintain our strategic
position for the long pull.

2. Dean Rusk and Robert S. McNamara's Alternative Plan, 1961

1. United States National Interests in South Viet-Nam.

The deteriorating situation in South Viet-Nam requires attention to the nature
and scope of United States national interests in that country. The loss of South
Viet-Nam to Communism would involve the transfer of a nation of 20 million
people from the free world to the Communist bloc. The loss of South Viet-Nam
would make pointless any further discussion about the importance of Southeast
Asia to the free world; we would have to face the near certainty that the remainder of Southeast Asia and Indonesia would move to a complete accommodation
with Communism, if not formal incorporation with the Communist bloc. The

Memo from Rusk and McNamara, November 11, 1961, *United States-Vietnam Relations, 1945–1947*
Book 11, 359–369.

United States, as a member of SEATO, has commitments with respect to South Viet-Nam under the Protocol to the SEATO Treaty. Additionally, in a formal statement at the conclusion session of the 1954 Geneva Conference, the United States representative stated that the United States "would view any renewal of the aggression . . . with grave concern and seriously threatening international peace and security."

The loss of South Viet-Nam to Communism would not only destroy SEATO but would undermine the credibility of American commitments elsewhere. Further, loss of South Viet-Nam would stimulate bitter domestic controversies in the United States and would be seized upon by extreme elements to divide the country and harass the Administration. . . .

3. The United States' Objective in South Viet-Nam.

The United States should commit itself to the clear objective of preventing the fall of South Viet-Nam to Communist [sic]. The basic means for accomplishing this objective must be to put the Government of South Viet-Nam into a position to win its own war against the Guerrillas. We must insist that that Government itself take the measures necessary for that purpose in exchange for large-scale United States assistance in the military, economic and political fields. At the same time we must recognize that it will probably not be possible for the GVN to win this war as long as the flow of men and supplies from North Viet-Nam continues unchecked and the guerrillas enjoy a safe sanctuary in neighboring territory.

We should be prepared to introduce United States combat forces if that should become necessary for success. Dependent upon the circumstances, it may also be necessary for United States forces to strike at the source of the aggression in North Viet-Nam.

4. The Use of United States Forces in South Viet-Nam.

The commitment of United States forces to South Viet-Nam involves two different categories: (A) Units of modest size required for the direct support of South Viet-Namese military effort, such as communications, helicopter and other forms of airlift, reconnaissance aircraft, naval patrols, intelligence units, etc., and (B) larger organized units with actual or potential direct military mission. *Category (A) should be introduced as speedily as possible.* Category (B) units pose a more serious problem in that they are much more significant from the point of view of domestic and international political factors and greatly increase the probabilities of Communist bloc escalation. Further, the employment of United States combat forces (in the absence of Communist bloc escalation) involves a certain dilemma: if there is a strong South-Vietnamese effort, they may not be needed; if there is not such an effort, United States forces could not accomplish their mission in the midst of an apathetic or hostile population. Under present circumstances, therefore, the question of injecting United States and SEATO combat forces should in large part be considered as a contribution to the morale of the South Vietnamese in their own effort to do the principal job themselves.

5. Probable Extent of the Commitment of United States Forces.

If we commit Category (B) forces to South Viet-Nam, the ultimate possible extent of our military commitment in Southeast Asia must be faced. The struggle may be prolonged, and Hanoi and Peiping may overtly intervene. It is the view of the Secretary of Defense and the Joint Chiefs of Staff that, in the light of the logistic difficulties faced by the other side, we can assume that the maximum United States forces required on the ground in Southeast Asia would not exceed six divisions, or about 205,000 men (CINCPAC Plan 32/59 PHASE IV). This would be in addition to local forces and such SEATO forces as may be engaged. It is also the view of the Secretary of Defense and the Joint Chiefs of Staff that our military posture is, or, with the addition of more National Guard or regular Army divisions, can be made, adequate to furnish these forces and support them in action without serious interference with our present Berlin plans. . . .

In the light of the foregoing, the Secretary of State and the Secretary of Defense recommend that:

1. We now take the decision to commit ourselves to the objective of preventing the fall of South Viet-Nam to Communism and that, in doing so, we recognize that the introduction of United States and other SEATO forces may be necessary to achieve this objective. (However, if it is necessary to commit outside forces to achieve the foregoing objective our decision to introduce United States forces should not be contingent upon unanimous SEATO agreement thereto.)

2. The Department of Defense be prepared with plans for the use of United States forces in South Viet-Nam under one or more of the following purposes:

    a.   Use of a significant number of United States forces to signify United States determination to defend Viet-Nam and to boost South Viet-Nam morale.

    b.   Use of substantial United States forces to assist in suppressing Viet Cong insurgency short of engaging in detailed counter-guerrilla operations but including relevant operations in North Viet-Nam.

    c.   Use of United States forces to deal with the situation if there is organized Communist military intervention.

3. We immediately undertake the following actions in support of the GVN:

. . . c.   Provide the GVN with small craft, including such United States uniformed advisers and operating personnel as may be necessary for quick and effective operations in effecting surveillance and control over coastal waters and inland waterways. . . .

    e.   Provide such personnel and equipment as may be necessary to improve the military-political intelligence system beginning at the provincial level and extending upward through the Government and the armed forces to the Central Intelligence Organization.

    f.   Provide such new terms of reference, reorganization and additional personnel for United States military forces as are required for increased United States participation in the direction and control of GVN military operations and to carry out the other increased responsibilities which accrue to MAAG under these recommendations. . . .

    i.   Provide individual administrators and advisers for insertion into the Governmental machinery of South Viet-Nam in types and numbers to be agreed upon by the two Governments. . . .

3. An Early U.S. Army Adviser Remembers His Experiences (1962–1963), 1981

I was nineteen and turned twenty when I was there. I joined the Army in May of 1962 and was in Vietnam in December, just as I finished radio school. That was my first assignment. I could've had orders, as everyone else in the class did, to Germany. Two of us had orders to Vietnam. Before I even joined the Army I ran into a guy who'd graduated from high school a year or two ahead of me. He had just gotten out of the Army from Alaska. He said, "Wow, the place to go is Vietnam. You get combat pay in addition to overseas pay. You can really clean up." In the Army there was an undercurrent that there was someplace in the world where you could get combat pay. But there was no real discussion in the newspapers, as I can recall.

Some people in the unit had no conception where they were in the world, they didn't care. It wasn't Tennessee. It wasn't the state they came from. So therefore they had no interest in learning anything. Other people were very interested and learned Vietnamese and became very close with a number of Vietnamese people. At some point you began to realize that the people around the military base were clearly cooperating with the guerrillas because they were able to infiltrate the inside of our bases and we hadn't the faintest idea where the guerrillas were.

When the Buddhist demonstrations began against the Diem government [1963], it became very clear to most Americans there who probably hadn't been paying attention that we were supporting a police state which, against its own people who were peaceably having demonstrations, would turn loose tanks and machine guns and barbed wire all over the country. From May of '63 all through the summer we'd get caught up in them, just trying to walk around in civilian clothes to go to bars. . . .

The entire contingent of Americans in Vietnam was so thinly spread out that there probably weren't more than five hundred in any one place. Tan Son Nhut had the highest concentration. And it was becoming apparent that the ARVN [Army of the Republic of Vietnam] might turn on us. That became a real worry in the summer of 1963. It became rather apparent from discussion going on that there was going to be a coup. I recall going to Saigon several times and hearing this undercurrent in bars where Vietnamese officers would be.

I left Vietnam in mid-October 1963 and the coup happened two weeks later. One of the people who was still there said that the night before the coup took place they were told to get packed up, be ready to leave the country, be ready to blow up their equipment. At that point one of the options was to completely leave Vietnam. . . .

Almost no one in the Washington area knew we had anything like what was going on in Vietnam. Those of us who had been there wore our military patches on our right shoulders, which denoted that we had been in the war. Colonels would stop me and say, "What war have you been in, son? Where is that? We have people fighting over there?"

From *Everything We Had* by Al Santoli. Copyright © 1981 by Albert Santoli and Vietnam Veterans of America. Used by permission of Random House, Inc.

4. Mike Mansfield Questions
American Policy, 1962

Even assuming that aid over a prolonged period would be available, the question still remains as to the capacity of the present Saigon government to carry out the task of social engineering. Ngo Dinh Diem remains a dedicated, sincere, hardworking, incorruptible and patriotic leader. But he is older and the problems which confront him are more complex than those which he faced when he pitted his genuine nationalism against, first, the French and Bao Dai and then against the sects with such effectiveness. The energizing role which he played in the past appears to be passing to other members of his family, particularly Ngo Dinh Nhu. The latter is a person of great energy and intellect who is fascinated by the operations of political power and has consummate eagerness and ability in organizing and manipulating it. But it is Ngo Dinh Diem, not Ngo Dinh Nhu, who has such popular mandate to exercise power as there is in south Vietnam. In a situation of this kind there is a great danger of the corruption of unbridled power. This has implications far beyond the persistent reports and rumors of fiscal and similar irregularities which are, in any event, undocumented. More important is its effect on the organization of the machinery for carrying out the new concepts. The difficulties in Vietnam are not likely to be overcome by a handful of paid retainers and sycophants. The success of the new approach in Vietnam presupposes a great contribution of initiative and self-sacrifice from a substantial body of Vietnamese with capacities for leadership at all levels. Whether that contribution can be obtained remains to be seen. For in the last analysis it depends upon a diffusion of political power, essentially in a democratic pattern. The trends in the political life of Vietnam have not been until now in that direction despite lip service to the theory of developing democratic and popular institutions "from the bottom up" through the strategic hamlet program.

To summarize, our policies and activities are designed to meet an existing set of internal problems in south Vietnam. North Vietnam infiltrates some supplies and cadres into the south; together with the Vietnamese we are trying to shut off this flow. The Vietcong has had the offensive in guerrilla warfare in the countryside; we are attempting to aid the Vietnamese military in putting them on the defensive with the hope of eventually reducing them at least to ineffectiveness. Finally, the Vietnamese peasants have sustained the Vietcong guerrillas out of fear, indifference or blandishment and we are helping the Vietnamese in an effort to win the peasants away by offering them the security and other benefits which may be provided in the strategic hamlets.

That, in brief, is the present situation. As noted, there is optimism that success will be achieved quickly. My own view is that the problems can be made to yield to present remedies, *provided* the problems and their magnitude do not change significantly and *provided* that the remedies are pursued by both Vietnamese and Americans (and particularly the former) with great vigor and self-dedication.

Mansfield Report to Kennedy, December 18, 1962, reprinted in *Two Reports on Vietnam and Southeast Asia to the President of the United States by Senator Mike Mansfield,* U.S. Senate, Committee on Foreign Relations, April 1973.

Certainly, if these remedies do not work, it is difficult to conceive of alternatives, with the possible exception of a truly massive commitment of American military personnel and other resources—in short going to war fully ourselves against the guerrillas—and the establishment of some form of neocolonial rule in south Vietnam. That is an alternative which I most emphatically do not recommend. On the contrary, it seems to me most essential that we make crystal clear to the Vietnamese government and to our own people that while we will go to great lengths to help, the primary responsibility rests with the Vietnamese. Our role is and must remain secondary in present circumstances. It is their country, their future which is most at stake, not ours.

To ignore that reality will not only be immensely costly in terms of American lives and resources but it may also draw us inexorably into some variation of the unenviable position in Vietnam which was formerly occupied by the French. We are not, of course, at that point at this time. But the great increase in American military commitment this year has tended to point us in that general direction and we may well begin to slide rapidly toward it if any of the present remedies begin to falter in practice.

As indicated, our planning appears to be predicated on the assumption that existing internal problems in South Vietnam will remain about the same and can be overcome by greater effort and better techniques. But what if the problems do not remain the same? To all outward appearances, little if any thought has been given in Saigon at least, to the possibilities of a change in the nature of the problems themselves. Nevertheless, they are very real possibilities and the initiative for instituting change rests in enemy hands largely because of the weakness of the Saigon government. The range of possible change includes a step-up in the infiltration of cadres and supplies by land or sea. It includes the use of part or all of the regular armed forces of North Vietnam, reported to be about 300,000 strong, under Vo Nguyen Giap. It includes, in the last analysis, the possibility of a major increase in any of many possible forms of Chinese Communist support for the Vietcong.

None of these possibilities may materialize. It would be folly, however, not to recognize their existence and to have as much clarification in advance of what our response to them will be if they do.

This sort of anticipatory thinking cannot be undertaken with respect to the situation in Vietnam alone. The problem there can be grasped, it seems to me, only as we have clearly in mind our interests with respect to all of Southeast Asia. If it is essential in our own interests to maintain a quasi-permanent position of power on the Asian mainland as against the Chinese then we must be prepared to continue to pay the present cost in Vietnam indefinitely and to meet any escalation on the other side with at least a commensurate escalation of commitment of our own. This can go very far, indeed, in terms of lives and resources. Yet if it is essential to our interests then we would have no choice.

But if on the other hand it is, at best, only desirable rather than essential that a position of power be maintained on the mainland, then other courses are indicated. We would, then, properly view such improvement as may be obtained by the new approach in Vietnam primarily in terms of what it might contribute to strengthening our diplomatic hand in the Southeast Asian region. And we would use that hand as vigorously as possible and in every way possible not to deepen our costly involvement on the Asian mainland but to lighten it.

5. John F. Kennedy Criticizes the South Vietnamese Government, 1963

Mr. Cronkite: Mr. President, the only hot war we've got running at the moment is of course the one in Viet-Nam, and we have our difficulties there, quite obviously.

The President: I don't think that unless a greater effort is made by the Government to win popular support that the war can be won out there. In the final analysis, it is their war. They are the ones who have to win it or lose it. We can help them, we can give them equipment, we can send our men out there as advisers, but they have to win it, the people of Viet-Nam, against the Communists.

We are prepared to continue to assist them, but I don't think that the war can be won unless the people support the effort and, in my opinion, in the last 2 months, the government has gotten out of touch with the people.

The repressions against the Buddhists, we felt, were very unwise. Now all we can do is to make it very clear that we don't think this is the way to win. It is my hope that this will become increasingly obvious to the government, that they will take steps to try to bring back popular support for this very essential struggle.

Mr. Cronkite: Do you think this government still has time to regain the support of the people?

The President: I do. With changes in policy and perhaps with personnel I think it can. If it doesn't make those changes, I would think that the chances of winning it would not be very good.

Mr. Cronkite: Hasn't every indication from Saigon been that President Diem has no intention of changing his pattern?

The President: If he does not change it, of course, that is his decision. He has been there 10 years and, as I say, he has carried this burden when he has been counted out on a number of occasions.

Our best judgment is that he can't be successful on this basis. We hope that he comes to see that, but in the final analysis it is the people and the government itself who have to win or lose this struggle. All we can do is help, and we are making it very clear, but I don't agree with those who say we should withdraw. That would be a great mistake. I know people don't like Americans to be engaged in this kind of an effort. Forty-seven Americans have been killed in combat with the enemy, but this is a very important struggle even though it is far away.

We took all this—made this effort to defend Europe. Now Europe is quite secure. We also have to participate—we may not like it—in the defense of Asia.

6. Kennedy Reaffirms the Domino Theory, 1963

Mr. Huntley: Mr. President, in respect to our difficulties in South Viet-Nam, could it be that our Government tends occasionally to get locked into a policy or an attitude and then finds it difficult to alter or shift that policy?

The President: Yes, that is true. I think in the case of South Viet-Nam we have been dealing with a Government which is in control, has been in control for 10 years.

Public Papers of the Presidents: John F. Kennedy, 1963, 651–652 (September 2, 1963).

Public Papers of the Presidents: John F. Kennedy, 1963, 658–659 (September 9, 1963).

In addition, we have felt for the last 2 years that the struggle against the Communists was going better. Since June, however—the difficulties with the Buddhists—we have been concerned about a deterioration, particularly in the Saigon area, which hasn't been felt greatly in the outlying areas but may spread. So we are faced with the problem of wanting to protect the area against the Communists. On the other hand, we have to deal with the Government there. That produces a kind of ambivalence in our efforts which exposes us to some criticism. We are using our influence to persuade the Government there to take those steps which will win back support. That takes some time, and we must be patient, we must persist.

Mr. Huntley: Are we likely to reduce our aid to South Viet-Nam now?

The President: I don't think we think that would be helpful at this time. If you reduce your aid, it is possible you could have some effect upon the government structure there. On the other hand, you might have a situation which could bring about a collapse. Strongly in our mind is what happened in the case of China at the end of World War II, where China was lost—a weak government became increasingly unable to control events. We don't want that.

Mr. Brinkley: Mr. President, have you had any reason to doubt this so-called "domino theory," that if South Viet-Nam falls, the rest of Southeast Asia will go behind it?

The President: No, I believe it. I believe it. I think that the struggle is close enough. China is so large, looms so high just beyond the frontiers, that if South Viet-Nam went, it would not only give them an improved geographic position for a guerrilla assault on Malaya but would also give the impression that the wave of the future in Southeast Asia was China and the Communists. So I believe it.

Mr. Brinkley: In the last 48 hours there have been a great many conflicting reports from there about what the CIA [Central Intelligence Agency] was up to. Can you give us any enlightenment on it?

The President: No.

Mr. Huntley: Does the CIA tend to make its own policy? That seems to be the debate here.

The President: No, that is the frequent charge, but that isn't so. Mr. [John A.] McCone, head of the CIA, sits in the National Security Council. We have had a number of meetings in the past few days about events in South Viet-Nam. Mr. McCone participated in every one, and the CIA coordinates its efforts with the State Department and the Defense Department.

Mr. Brinkley: With so much of our prestige, money, so on, committed in South Viet-Nam, why can't we exercise a little more influence there, Mr. President?

The President: We have some influence. We have some influence and we are attempting to carry it out. I think we don't—we can't expect these countries to do everything the way we want to do them. They have their own interest, their own personalities, their own tradition. We can't make everyone in our image, and there are a good many people who don't want to go in our image. In addition, we have ancient struggles between countries. In the case of India and Pakistan, we would like to have them settle Kashmir. That is our view of the best way to defend the subcontinent against communism. But that struggle between India and Pakistan is more important to a good many people in that area than the struggle against the Communists. We would like to have Cambodia, Thailand, and South Viet-Nam all in harmony. but there are ancient differences there. We can't make the world over, but we can influence the world. The fact of the matter is that with the assistance of the United States and SEATO [Southeast Asia Treaty Organization], Southeast Asia and indeed all of Asia has been maintained independent against a powerful force, the Chinese Communists. What I am concerned about is that Americans will get impatient and say, because they don't like events in Southeast Asia or they don't like the Government in Saigon, that we should withdraw. That only makes it easy for the Communists. I think we should stay. We should use our influence in as effective a way as we can, but we should not withdraw.

7. Henry Cabot Lodge Discusses Coup Prospects, 1963

1. I appreciate the concern expressed by you [national security advisor McGeorge Bundy] in ref. a relative to the Gen. Don/Conein relationship, and also the present lack of firm intelligence on the details of the general's plot. I hope that ref. b will assist in clearing up some of the doubts relative to general's plans, and I am hopeful that the detailed plans promised for two days before the coup attempt will clear up any remaining doubts.

2. CAS [Classified American Source—reference to CIA] has been punctilious in carrying out my instructions. I have personally approved each meeting between Gen. Don and Conein who has carried out my orders in each instance explicitly. While I share your concern about the continued involvement of Conein in this matter, a suitable substitute for Conein as the principal contact is not presently available. Conein, as you know, is a friend of some eighteen years' standing with Gen. Don, and General Don has expressed extreme reluctance to deal with anyone else. I do not believe the involvement of another American in close contact with the generals would be productive. We are, however, considering the feasibility of a plan for the introduction of an additional officer as a cut-out between Conein and a designee of Gen. Don for communication purposes only. This officer is completely unwitting of any details of past or present coup activities and will remain so.

3. With reference to Gen [Paul D.] Harkins' [chief of MAAG] comment to Gen. Don which Don reports to have referred to a presidential directive and the proposal for a meeting with me, this may have served the useful purpose of allaying the General's fears as to our interest. If this were a provocation, the GVN could have assumed and manufactured any variations of the same theme. As a precautionary measure, however, I of course refused to see Gen. Don. As to the lack of information as to General Don's real backing, and the lack of evidence that any real capabilities for action have been developed, ref. b provides only part of the answer. I feel sure that the reluctance of the generals to provide the U.S. with full details of their plans at this time, is a reflection of their own sense of security and a lack of confidence that in the large American community present in Saigon their plans will not be prematurely revealed.

4. The best evidence available to the Embassy, which I grant you is not as complete as we would like it, is that Gen. Don and the other generals involved with him are seriously attempting to effect a change in the government. I do not believe that

Cable from Lodge to Bundy, October 25, 1963, *Foreign Relations of the United States,* 1961–1963, 4, 434–436.

this is a provocation by Ngo Dinh Nhu, although we shall continue to assess the planning as well as possible. In the event that the coup aborts, or in the event that Nhu has masterminded a provocation, I believe that our involvement to date through Conein is still within the realm of plausible denial. CAS is perfectly prepared to have me disavow Conein at any time it may serve the national interest.

5. I welcome your reaffirming instructions contained in CAS Washington [cable] 74228. It is vital that we neither thwart a coup nor that we are even in a position where we do not know what is going on.

6. We should not thwart a coup for two reasons. First, it seems at least an even bet that the next government would not bungle and stumble as much as the present one has. Secondly, it is extremely unwise in the long range for us to pour cold water on attempts at a coup, particularly when they are just in their beginning stages. We should remember that this is the only way in which the people in Vietnam can possibly get a change of government. Whenever we thwart attempts at a coup, as we have done in the past, we are incurring very long lasting resentments, we are assuming an undue responsibility for keeping the incumbents in office, and in general are setting ourselves in judgment over the affairs of Vietnam. Merely to keep in touch with this situation and a policy merely limited to "not thwarting" are courses both of which entail some risks but these are lesser risks than either thwarting all coups while they are stillborn or our not being informed of what is happening. All the above is totally distinct from not wanting U.S. military advisors to be distracted by matters which are not in their domain, with which I heartily agree. But obviously this does not conflict with a policy of not thwarting. In judging proposed coups, we must consider the effect on the war effort. Certainly a succession of fights for control of the Government of Vietnam would interfere with the war effort. It must also be said that the war effort has been interfered with already by the incompetence of the present government and the uproar which this has caused.

7. Gen. Don's intention to have no religious discrimination in a future government is commendable and I applaud his desire not to be "a vassal" of the U.S. But I do not think his promise of a democratic election is realistic. This country simply is not ready for that procedure. I would add two other requirements. First, that there be no wholesale purges of personnel in the government. Individuals who were particularly reprehensible could be dealt with later by the regular legal process. Then I would be impractical, but I am thinking of a government which might include Tri Quang and which certainly should include men of the stature of Mr. Buu, the labor leader.

8. Copy to Gen. Harkins.

8. McGeorge Bundy Expresses Reservations, 1963

1. Your [cables] 2023, 2040, 2041 and 2043 examined with care at highest levels here. You should promptly discuss this reply and associated messages with Harkins whose responsibilities toward any coup are very heavy especially after you leave (see para. 7 below). They give much clearer picture group's alleged plans and also indicate chances of action with or without our approval now so significant that we

Cable from Bundy to Lodge, October 29, 1963, *Foreign Relations of the United States,* 1961–1963, 4, 473–475.

should urgently consider our attitude and contingency plans. We note particularly Don's curiosity your departure and his insistence Conein be available from Wednesday night on, which suggests date might be as early as Thursday.

2. Believe our attitude to coup group can still have decisive effect on its decisions. We believe that what we say to coup group can produce delay of coup and that betrayal of coup plans to Diem is not repeat not our only way of stopping coup. We therefore need urgently your combined assessment with Harkins and CAS (including their separate comments if they desire). We concerned that our line-up of forces in Saigon (being cabled in next message) indicates approximately equal balance of forces, with substantial possibility serious and prolonged fighting or even defeat. Either of these could be serious or even disastrous for U.S. interests, so that we must have assurance balance of forces clearly favorable.

3. With your assessment in hand, we might feel that we should convey message to Don, whether or not he gives 4 or 48 hours notice that would (A) continue explicit hands-off policy, (B) positively encourage coup, or (C) discourage.

4. In any case, believe Conein should find earliest opportunity express to Don that we do not find presently revealed plans give clear prospect of quick results. This conversation should call attention important Saigon units still apparently loyal to Diem and raise serious issue as to what means coup group has to deal with them.

5. From operational standpoint, we also deeply concerned Don only spokesman for group and possibility cannot be discounted he may not be in good faith. We badly need some corroborative evidence whether Minh and others directly and completely involved. In view Don's claim he doesn't handle "military planning" could not Conein tell Don that we need better military picture and that Big Minh could communicate this most naturally and easily to [General Richard] Stilwell [Harkins's Chief of Staff]? We recognize desirability involving MACV [U.S. Military Assistance Command, Vietnam] to minimum, but believe Stilwell far more desirable this purpose than using Conein both ways.

6. Complexity above actions raises question whether you should adhere to present Thursday schedule. Concur you and other U.S. elements should take no action that could indicate U.S. awareness coup possibility. However, DOD [Department of Defense] is sending berth-equipped military aircraft that will arrive Saigon Thursday and could take you out thereafter as late as Saturday afternoon in time to meet your presently proposed arrival Washington Sunday. You could explain this being done as convenience and that your Washington arrival is same. A further advantage such aircraft is that it would permit your prompt return from any point en route if necessary. To reduce time in transit, you should use this plane, but we recognize delaying your departure may involve greater risk that you personally would appear involved if any action took place. However, advantages your having extra two days in Saigon may outweigh this and we leave timing of flight to your judgment.

7. Whether you leave Thursday or later, believe it essential that prior your departure there be fullest consultation Harkins and CAS and that there be clear arrangements for handling (A) normal activity, (B) continued coup contacts, (C) action in event a coup starts. We assume you will wish Truehart as charge to be head of country team in normal situation, but highest authority desires it clearly understood that after your departure Harkins should participate in supervision of all coup contacts and that in event a coup begins, he become head of country team and direct

representative of President, with [William] Truehart [Deputy Chief of Mission] in effect acting as POLAD [Political Adviser]. On coup contacts we will maintain continuous guidance and will expect equally continuous reporting with prompt account of any important divergences in assessments of Harkins and Smith.

8. If coup should start, question of protecting U.S. nationals at once arises. We can move Marine Battalion into Saigon by air from Okinawa within 24 hours—if available. We are sending instructions to CINCPAC to arrange orderly movement of seaborne Marine Battalion to waters adjacent to South Vietnam in position to close Saigon within approximately 24 hours.

9. We are now examining post-coup contingencies here and request your immediate recommendations on position to be adopted after coup begins, especially with respect to requests for assistance of different sorts from one side or the other also request you forward contingency recommendations for action if coup (A) succeeds, (B) fails, (C) is indecisive.

10. We reiterate burden of proof must be on coup group to show a substantial possibility of quick success; otherwise, we should discourage them from proceeding since a miscalculation could result in jeopardizing U.S. position in Southeast Asia.

9. Diem's Final Appeal for U.S. Help, 1963

Diem: Some units have made a rebellion and I want to know what is the attitude of the U.S.?

Lodge: I do not feel well enough informed to be able to tell you. I have heard the shooting, but am not acquainted with all the facts. Also it is 4:30 a.m. in Washington and the U.S. Government cannot possibly have a view.

Diem: But you must have some general ideas. After all, I am a Chief of State. I have tried to do my duty. I want to do now what duty and good sense require. I believe in duty above all.

Lodge: You have certainly done your duty. As I told you only this morning, I admire your courage and your great contributions to your country. No one can take away from you the credit for all you have done. Now I am worried about your physical safety. I have a report that those in charge of the current activity offer you and your brother safe conduct out of the country if you resign. Had you heard this?

Diem: No. (And then after a pause) You have my telephone number.

Lodge: Yes. If I can do anything for your physical safety, please call me.

Diem: I am trying to re-establish order.

✗ E S S A Y S

In the first essay, Michael H. Hunt of the University of North Carolina, Chapel Hill, observes that the Kennedy administration's unshakable anti-communist faith and cult of toughness led to a progressive expansion and deepening of the U.S. commitment to Vietnam. JFK and his chief advisers never gave any serious thought to a diplomatic

---

Telephone conversation between Diem and Lodge, November 1, 1963, *Foreign Relations of the United States,* 1961–1963, 4, 513.

solution, he laments. In the second essay, David Kaiser, a professor of history and strategy at the Army War College, offers a more favorable assessment of Kennedy's Vietnam policies and leadership style. JFK, he insists, always moved with caution and prudence in Vietnam, studiously avoiding an open-ended commitment of U.S. resources and troops. Right up until his death, the president believed that the South Vietnamese–U.S. military effort was going well.

The Perils of Interventionism

MICHAEL H. HUNT

The man who entered the White House [John F. Kennedy] had serious personal problems. Still emotionally immature, he continued to pursue a playboy lifestyle that left him subject to blackmail from jilted lovers and dubious friends and that put his entire administration at risk of serious scandal. His incessant affairs, together with his frequent indifference to his wife, strained what the public took to be an ideal marriage. Kennedy was, moreover, hobbled by continuing ill health. Medication helped to keep him going—painkillers for his back, cortisone for malfunctioning adrenal glands, and a New York doctor's home brew (including amphetamines and steroids) that served as an all-purpose pick-me-up. But these drugs entered his bloodstream without being medically coordinated—producing effects on judgment and emotional stability that are difficult to measure.

Kennedy shared with his advisers a shallow understanding of foreign policy, never tested against practical, nuts-and-bolts experience with decision-making. The most pronounced feature of his foreign-policy outlook was a simple, reflexive anticommunism that was a core principle for Kennedy senior and a prerequisite for political success in Cold War America. In fact, in the late 1940s Congressman Kennedy had played on the dangers of domestic subversion, and that most infamous of Red hunters, Senator Joseph McCarthy, had become not just a political ally but also a family friend.

Through the 1950s and down to the eve of his presidency, Kennedy had defined the national mission in terms of a muscular defense of liberal institutions and values against the latest challenge, that of communism: "The American purpose remains what it has been since the nation's founding: to demonstrate that the organization of man and societies on the basis of human freedom is not an absurdity but an enriching, ennobling, practical achievement." As the 1960 election approached, he blamed the Republican Eisenhower for having lost Cuba to communism, and promised that he would do better, giving the world strong American leadership and America a strong military. He called for sacrifice—in the words of the well-received inaugural address (as usual, a Sorensen product), to "pay any price, bear any burden, meet any hardship, support any friend" to stop communism and defend freedom around the world.

Vietnam had for a decade figured prominently in Kennedy's thinking. His tour of the region in 1951 revealed that "the fires of nationalism so long dormant have been kindled and are now ablaze." In Vietnam, as elsewhere, colonialism was doomed, and those committed to saving that country from communism, he warned the Senate in April 1954 (with the Dien Bien Phu battle in progress), would make no headway as long as their cause was tainted by colonial ambitions. With the French soon in retreat, he joined the circle of American Catholics promoting Ngo Dinh Diem to lead a free South Vietnam. In June 1956, before a meeting of Diem's U.S. support-ers, Kennedy called for creating in Vietnam a revolution "far more peaceful, far more democratic, and far more locally controlled" than the communists could offer. By supplying capital, technicians, political guidance, and military assistance, Ameri-cans could "offer" the Vietnamese "a revolution of their own making." (The paternal-ism inherent in his idea of *offering* a revolution escaped Kennedy.)

The eager Kennedy crew came into Washington in January 1961, already gripped by global Cold War imperatives. While standing up to Nikita Khrushchev, especially in a divided Berlin, took first priority, the newcomers did not neglect Southeast Asia. The new administration was soon humming with fresh activity and new ideas as task forces sprang into existence and inspection teams flew off for a firsthand look at that troubled region, above all, Diem's South Vietnam as well as neighbor-ing Laos. But despite the hustle and bustle, the torrent of words and paper offering solutions, Kennedy did not in fact prove a pushover for a dramatic new commitment. Rather he moved at a surprisingly slow, at times even hesitant, pace.

Already waiting on the president's desk his first day in the Oval Office was the Vietnam problem that would recur throughout the Kennedy years—whether Diem would serve (or how he could be made to serve) as an effective or at least adequate instrument of U.S. policy. American officials in Saigon had already raised warning flags. Ambassador Elbridge Durbrow, a confirmed critic of Diem's autocratic style and his government's corruption and inefficiency, had won over the head of the American military mission, Lieutenant General Lionel C. McGarr. Together they were now proposing more assistance to keep Diem afloat, but only on the condition that he reform his regime in order to win popular support and make more effective use of U.S. aid.

Edward Lansdale, the well-known Vietnam expert, offered an alternative ap-proach—treating Diem as a patient who would respond better to solicitude and good doctoring than to attempts at browbeating him into better health. A visit to Vietnam in early January 1961 had left Lansdale depressed. Diem seemed isolated and more dependent than ever on his brother and chief adviser, Ngo Dinh Nhu; the guerrillas were winning the countryside; and the U.S. military still acted as though it were facing a conventional war. In a report that made its way to Kennedy, Lans-dale warned that Vietnam was "in a critical condition" and required emergency treatment." The cure lay in a new team headed, Lansdale hinted none too subtly, by Lansdale himself. As he explained, what Vietnam required was "a hard core of experienced Americans who know and really like Asia and the Asians, dedicated people who are willing to risk their lives for the ideals of freedom, and who will try to influence and guide the Vietnamese towards U.S. policy objectives with the warm friendships and affection which our close alliance deserves."

Kennedy responded hesitantly. How could he figure out what Diem and South Vietnam needed when Durbrow, McGarr, and Lansdale saw the same evidence and visited the same sites and yet came to markedly different conclusions? What was he to conclude when American representatives came away from meetings with Diem—clad in his usual baggy, double-breasted white suit and given to extended monologues—convinced the Vietnamese leader was inscrutable? The available information on the conflict in the countryside and especially on the nature of the enemy was variously thin, confused, and compromised and thus no more helpful. Kennedy was discovering that Vietnam was, for Americans at least, like a house of mirrors.

Compounding Kennedy's problem were the unpredictable, potentially unpalatable implications of the policy choices facing him. The United States could demand that Diem improve his government's performance as a condition for continued support. But what if he refused? Should the United States then withdraw and risk losing the region, or perhaps pursue an only slightly more attractive option—an international agreement to create a nonaligned government in the south? Such a government was not likely to last long, and thus the option only barely disguised defeat. Or what about a coup? Some senior officials were already advocating such a step to replace Diem with an able leader. But changing horses in midstream could be tricky and might even yield a successor regime no better, possibly even worse. The United States might then face a stark choice between outright defeat and an American takeover of the conflict. Or, finally, should the United States simply bite the bullet, as other officials were advocating, and move at once toward a greater American role in the planning and fighting? In that case, a coup would only make the task more difficult by adding to the turmoil. Better to work with the Diem regime, whatever its defects, and get on with applying American guidance and goods to the task of turning back the communist challenge.

A crisis in neighboring Laos complicated the picture and added to Kennedy's early hesitations. That crisis had developed suddenly, just as the new president took over the helm, but it had been brewing for nearly a decade. Anti-French Laotian nationalists, organized as the Pathet Lao, had cooperated with the Viet Minh in the defeat of the French, and after 1954 controlled several provinces in the mountainous eastern section of the country. From those bases, the Pathet Lao engaged in a three-way rivalry with neutralists and rightists for a dominant position in the country. In November 1960 the rightist forces seized power with the backing of the CIA. The Pathet Lao countered with its own military drive toward the capital, Vientiane. By mid-December the fighting was heavy, and by early the next year the Pathet Lao was making substantial headway against a disorganized central government backed by U.S. money and advisers (including some seven hundred military). The Pathet Lao for its part had the blessings and assistance of Hanoi and Moscow (including about five hundred Russian military advisers).

Meeting with President Eisenhower and his counselors on 19 January, just the day before the inauguration, the Kennedy foreign-policy team was informed that Laos was in peril and that the loss of Laos would doom the rest of Southeast Asia (consistent with the widely accepted domino theory). Eisenhower told Kennedy of his alarm over the situation. The outgoing president was, however, not clear what he thought Kennedy should do to avert disaster. The Eisenhower team probably relished handing the newcomers, so full of themselves and so critical of the Republican administration, a tough policy nut to crack.

Laos preoccupied the new administration for five months. At the peak of the crisis in March, Rostow argued forcefully for U.S. military intervention, and the Joint Chiefs of Staff reported that they could marshal at short notice an American force of about 60,000 equipped with nuclear weapons. The gamble that this force would stop the Pathet Lao and intimidate its outside patrons held little appeal to Kennedy, and so in April and May he moved toward his only other option, a negotiated solution to the conflict. Nikita Khrushchev and Ho indicated their willingness to cooperate in putting Laos on ice.

Despite the Laos distraction and the confusion over conditions in Vietnam, Kennedy had by then begun piecemeal to decide Diem's future. The need for a prompt, concerted, imaginative U.S. effort had been highlighted by a Khrushchev speech endorsing wars of national liberation, delivered in January just as Kennedy was taking office. Agitated by what seemed to be a fresh challenge issuing from the Kremlin, Kennedy had circulated the text of the speech to his aides to underline the test of wills in the making in Southeast Asia no less than in the Congo, Cuba, and Berlin. Kennedy had, moreover, responded favorably (along with Rostow and McNamara) to Lansdale's January report and had accordingly appointed a new ambassador, Frederick Nolting, with instructions to stop badgering Diem and to cultivate him instead. Also consistent with Lansdale's approach, Kennedy had called for more attention to counterinsurgency measures.

In late April and early May, with the Laos crisis settling down, Kennedy revisited Vietnam policy. The Bay of Pigs snafu, a badly botched invasion intended to topple Cuba's Fidel Castro, and the resort to a compromise settlement in Laos seemed now to dictate a strong stand in Vietnam if Kennedy was to repair his reputation for resolve. Within the White House, Rostow pressed for action, warning the president of the "extreme urgency of getting our Viet-Nam program moving with new faces, enlarged resources, and renewed conviction."

In a burst of activity Kennedy and his advisers in effect confirmed the initial decision to stand firm in Vietnam and to work with Diem, Their main objective was now "to prevent Communist domination of South Viet-Nam." They would leave the issue of reform in abeyance (although Rostow reminded the president that the United States still needed to find a "technique" to get Diem and other clients "to do things they ought to do but don't want to do"). To dramatize his commitment to South Vietnam, Kennedy dispatched a high-profile mission to Southeast Asia led by Vice President Lyndon Johnson, one of the early flying-inspection tours that were becoming a hallmark of Washington decision-making.

In private, Kennedy authorized more resources for both the U.S. team and Diem. He agreed to an additional one hundred military advisers (to reach five hundred by August) and the dispatch of four hundred army special forces ("Green Berets"), thus breaching the limits on foreign forces agreed upon at Geneva in 1954. He also agreed to help raise Diem's army to 200,000 in order to improve its chances against regular insurgent forces, estimated at about 7,000 at the beginning of the year. Kennedy even entertained talk of sending additional U.S. troops to bolster Saigon's position, but he would go no further than approving study of the issue by the Joint Chiefs of Staff. At the same time, he authorized CIA preparations for a secret effort in Laos to cut the main supply line running from the DRV to the south and for the dispatch of teams of South Vietnamese into the north on sabotage missions.

With the administration having settled, temporarily at least, its commitment to Diem, Rostow publicly explained the administration's course in terms of the broad, abstract social-science concepts that had been his academic stock-in-trade. In a speech cleared with Kennedy before delivery at the U.S. Army's Special Warfare School in June 1961, Rostow contended that third-world countries such as Vietnam were moving through a "revolution of modernization." This inevitably unsettling process was marked by painful internal tensions and by a vulnerability to subversion, but it would prove ultimately beneficial as countries finally emerged "with increasing degrees of human freedom." To help new nations such as South Vietnam through their time of turmoil, the United States needed to promote social and political reforms, provide material assistance, and even send special forces and military advisers to block insurgencies led by communists, the "scavengers of the modernization process." The successes of counterinsurgent campaigns in Greece, the Philippines, and Malaya proved to Rostow's satisfaction that the communist "vandals," bearers of an "international disease," could be stopped.

The issue of support for Diem subsided only to revive in the fall, as the Saigon regime's hold over the countryside eroded. Diem himself underlined the seriousness of the situation when in early October he suddenly requested U.S. troops or a defense treaty. To help determine his response, Kennedy sent an inspection mission to Saigon headed by General Maxwell D. Taylor and seconded by Rostow and Lansdale. Taylor was a self-possessed, articulate officer with a scholarly bent, who had crowned a distinguished career by serving as army chief of staff between 1955 and 1959. His criticism of Eisenhower's reliance on massive nuclear retaliation to the neglect of preparation for limited wars had won Kennedy's attention and an appointment in mid-1961, in the wake of the Bay of Pigs disaster, as his personal adviser on military issues. Taylor brought to his Vietnam assignment some Asian experience—service in Japan and China in the late 1930s and in Korea during the last phase of the limited war there, as well as several visits to Saigon after the 1954 partition.

Taylor's survey led him to call for an ambitious program to save the situation. His most controversial recommendation was for the dispatch of 8,000 American troops to the embattled Mekong delta (to be justified, publicly at least, on the excuse of helping with flood relief). Taylor also proposed sharply increased levels of assistance and advice so that the U.S. Military Assistance Advisory Group (MAAG) could in effect function as "an operational headquarters in a theater of war." He wanted Americans to serve at all levels of the Saigon civil and military organization and assume the role of partner in running the country. Such a partnership would, he predicted, at once stiffen Saigon's backbone and gradually correct the serious flaws in its handling of military and administrative affairs. But, Taylor warned, redoubled U.S. support for Diem carried some risk of Soviet-bloc countermeasures, and Washington thus had to be ready to "cover action in Southeast Asia up to the nuclear threshold in that area."

The irrepressible Rostow lobbied now, as he had since July, for vigorous action. He shared with Taylor the desire to get American forces on the ground. But he was ready to go a good deal further—to bomb Hanoi, perhaps seize Haiphong, and otherwise use U.S. military might to make clear to the North Vietnamese leaders and their Sino-Soviet patrons that the United States would not acquiesce in their ill-concealed effort to take the south. He urged the president to shed "the sickly pallor" of appeasement evident earlier in Cuba and Laos and to act with vigor and confidence against "a form of international banditry."

Bundy lined up behind Rostow as Kennedy moved toward a final decision on the Taylor report. He was "troubled" that Kennedy seemed to be sidestepping the troop issue, which "has now become a sort of touchstone of our will." The communists, he assured the president, did not want a military test and thus would not respond by escalating the conflict. Later on, if U.S. forces did not do the job of securing South Vietnam, then Kennedy could consider applying pressure directly on the DRV.

These strong recommendations put forward by Taylor and Rostow and endorsed by Bundy at last drew McNamara firmly and definitively from the margins into the center of Vietnam policymaking. When he had arrived in Washington, he had known nothing about the Vietnam problem. But its difficulty and its intricate mix of military and political issues were now to prove an irresistible challenge, one he would daily grapple with as long as he remained secretary of defense. As with his other Pentagon projects, McNamara approached Vietnam with the confidence that a hard-nosed, systematic examination of the issues and close administrative monitoring of the solutions would prove a winning formula.

McNamara at first reacted to the Taylor proposals with a perfunctory approval, but then—recalling what had happened when he had agreed to the Cuban invasion casually and with little knowledge—he decided to give Vietnam a closer look. Dean Rusk, who was reluctant to send U.S. troops to Vietnam before Diem had done more to help himself, joined McNamara in this reappraisal. On 11 November they submitted recommendations to President Kennedy that confirmed the earlier goal of saving South Vietnam from communism. To that end they called, first of all, for supporting Diem with higher levels of aid. The South Vietnamese government, the two policymakers argued, needed help even though it faced, by their estimate, at most only 20,000 "active" guerrillas. With the government in Saigon ineffective and the Vietnamese people seemingly passive in the face of communist terrorists, the United States had little choice but to do more.

McNamara and Rusk also called for an expanded U.S. combat presence, a recommendation that marked a significant advance over the policy of the previous May. In the short run they wanted to keep that presence small and unobtrusive and limited to units devoted to giving Saigon's military direct help with air transport, naval patrolling, reconnaissance, and intelligence gathering. These units would push the American military presence away from a purely aid and advisory role.

But looking further into the future, Rusk and McNamara saw the potential need for a more substantial U.S. combat capability and recommended planning for that eventuality. They were also ready to entertain the possibility of using "United States forces to strike at the source of the aggression in North Viet-Nam." At the same time they were clear to stress, as Taylor had, that large-scale U.S. involvement carried substantial risks. It might trigger a response from the communist bloc, thus forcing the United States into a prolonged war and into the dispatch of as many as 205,000 men. Or American troops might have to fight "in the midst of an apathetic or hostile population," and possibly without meaningful support from Vietnamese forces.

Kennedy was unsettled by a war that offered no easy answers and seemed to require ever-higher levels of U.S. involvement. The prospects of making a dramatic troop commitment seemed particularly unattractive. When Taylor had delivered his recommendations on 3 November, the president indicated that he was "instinctively against the introduction of US forces." He declared to his advisers on 11 November, "Troops are a last resort." Attorney General Robert Kennedy, the president's brother and intimate adviser, chimed in even more categorically: "We are not sending combat troops. [We are] not committing ourselves to combat troops." To one of his White House aides the president explained, "The troops will march in; the bands will play; the crowds will cheer." But then, he added, "It's like taking a drink. The effect wears off, and you have to take another."

On 22 November the president swallowed hard and accepted the McNamara-Rusk recommendations for at once stepping up the level of advisory and matériel support for the Diem government and for sending some operational units, such as helicopters and other aircraft to be flown by Americans under U.S. command. In exchange for this additional assistance, Kennedy wanted Diem to broaden his base of political support and improve the efficiency of his government. But pressed once more by the U.S. embassy on these points, Diem once more balked, grumbling over the prospect of becoming "a protectorate," while the government-controlled press unleashed a sharp attack on meddling Americans (described by one paper as "Capitalist-Imperialists"). Kennedy quickly backpedaled and settled instead for a face-saving formula that provided for "full and frank prior consultation" on all security operations. Kennedy's formal public pledge of support to Diem on 14 December was free of any injunctions to reform, while praising South Vietnamese courage in the face of a "campaign of force and terror" directed by Hanoi. Early the next year Kennedy observed, with a mixture of frustration and resignation, "Diem is Diem and the best we've got."

President Kennedy was back where he had been on coming into office—tightly tied to the Diem regime. He had given no serious thought to a diplomatic settlement in south Vietnam, an approach he had used to extricate himself from Laos, and he had closed, if not locked, that exit by linking his name repeatedly in public statements and secret deliberations to the defense of that regime. He had set aside reform and instead decided to gamble that ample American aid and a robust American presence would carry Diem—whatever his defects—to victory. The establishment in February 1962 of a Military Assistance Command, Vietnam, under General Paul Harkins, a Taylor protégé, reflected the greater operational role Americans had begun to play and the need for in-country planning in case of a major U.S. combat commitment. Saigon got more sophisticated equipment, such as aircraft, armored troop carriers, napalm, and defoliants—all calculated to give an element of surprise and shock in battle. A genuine enthusiast for new counterinsurgency techniques and new equipment suited to tropical combat, the president assigned Robert Kennedy to join McNamara and Taylor in overcoming the resistance by the Joint Chiefs to this critical, if unconventional, style of warfare. As part of the counterinsurgency effort, Washington encouraged a campaign of rural pacification, the centerpiece of which—the strategic hamlets program launched in March 1962—was aimed at isolating the communists from rural support.

As Kennedy and his learned advisers devised a program in late 1961 and early 1962, the president formally gave its principal author the task of making it work. In December McNamara left for the first of a long string of high-level conferences held either in Honolulu or in Saigon to monitor the war's progress. He warned the attendees at this first conference that the war would have to be fought without clear political goals and with decided limits on military action. At the same time, the president moved Rostow—the enthusiastic advocate of escalation—a comfortable distance from the White House, to take charge of long-term planning in the State Department. Kennedy explained, "Walt is a fountain of ideas; perhaps one in ten of them is absolutely brilliant. Unfortunately, six or seven are not merely unsound, but dangerously so."

Through 1962 and well into 1963 the new level of U.S. effort seemed to pay off. McNamara was getting from Harkins increasingly upbeat reports, confirmed by the statistics flowing from the field into Pentagon computers. Kennedy was happy to see Vietnam on the back burner, seemingly the scene of quiet progress, while he turned to fight communism on other fronts, most dramatically over Soviet missiles in Cuba in October 1962. However, the impression that this multiprong program was working and would eventually bring victory would be gradually undermined through the first half of 1963.

Ap Bac offered a signal that military training, new equipment, and a closer U.S. advisory role had not effected a significant transformation in the South Vietnamese army. As we have seen, the outcome of that battle in January 1963 suggested that National Liberation Front forces were learning to cope with the larger, better-armed, and ostensibly better-trained Saigon forces. But those at the top of the military chain of command running from Saigon back to Washington minimized the importance of the encounter. They argued that military advisers such as John Paul Vann were overreacting to the travails of the South Vietnamese army and thus were misleading eager young journalists such as the *New York Times*'s David Halberstam, United Press International's Neil Sheehan, and Associated Press's Malcolm Browne. Critical press reports were simply missing the progress government forces were making. McNamara seconded this optimistic assessment after an April visit to Saigon: "Every quantitative measurement we have shows we are winning this war." (Rusk also professed optimism about political trends, announcing that same month that he saw a "steady movement toward a constitutional system resting upon popular consent.")

But, in fact, the struggle in the countryside was not going well, for reasons difficult for McNamara and other high-level American officials to grasp. Hard numbers fixed in charts and lined up on graphs on the rural struggle were especially misleading. Much of the raw information on key indices of progress, such as enemy killed, villages secured, and supplies captured, came from Vietnamese commanders less concerned with accuracy than with making themselves look good and keeping the Americans happy. But even accurate statistics could not adequately measure the relative morale and motivation of the two contending Vietnamese sides or the peasant attitudes toward them and their respective programs; and thus two critical elements—political will and appeal—got lost in the analysis.

While American leaders could misconstrue the military and political struggle in the countryside, they could not blink away the collision between Diem and Buddhist protesters. That collision erupted right before their eyes in South Vietnam's major cities, ostensibly the regime's strongholds. Diem's last crisis began with a clash on 8 May 1963 in Hue between government troops and those celebrating Buddha's birthday. The encounter proved deadly, and it set off protests that spread in June to

Saigon and other cities. Soon headlines in American dailies and pictures on the television registered sensational self-immolations by monks, dramatic government raids, and harsh language by Diem's sister-in-law about the barbecuing of religious opponents. At first, U.S. officials tried to put the blame for this public-relations embarrassment on irresponsible journalists, just as they had after Ap Bac. But longtime critics of Diem within the U.S. government felt vindicated, and even longtime supporters were deeply troubled by the way the crisis was further narrowing Diem's base of political support and distracting his government from the anti-communist struggle.

The most fervent of Diem's critics came together in a State Department cabal bent on stimulating a coup. At its heart was Roger Hilsman, Jr., an assertive Columbia University political scientist serving as assistant secretary for Far Eastern affairs. A champion of counterinsurgency, he strenuously argued that a government locked in conflict with its own people was already lost. Hilsman's determination to turn a new page in Vietnam enjoyed the backing of his immediate superior, W. Averell Harriman, as well as Under Secretary of State George Ball. They acquired in Henry Cabot Lodge, Jr., a critical recruit to their cause. Though humbled by Kennedy in the 1952 Senate contest and again in 1960 as Nixon's running mate, Lodge had nonetheless responded as a patriot to the president's request in June 1963 that he replace Nolting as ambassador to a troubled Saigon. The cautious, soft-spoken Nolting had failed to reform Diem; a firm, new hand was needed. Michael V. Forrestal—a young Wall Street lawyer taken under Harriman's wing after the suicide of his father (James Forrestal, the first secretary of defense)—served as the group's representative in the White House. Firmly convinced that Diem had to go, they moved with such unity and force that ultimately, if reluctantly, the entire administration was pulled along.

Diem gave them the ammunition they needed to act. Violating a pledge to Ambassador Nolting, Diem had had army units raid Buddhist pagodas in Saigon and Hue on 21 August 1963, arresting over fourteen hundred dissidents under cover of martial law. The U.S. reaction came swiftly. Within three days, on Saturday the twenty-fourth, Ball sent Lodge a cable responding to coup overtures made earlier by Diem's generals. Drafted by Hilsman and casually approved by Kennedy—then enjoying a weekend at the family retreat in Hyannis Port, Massachusetts—the cable indicated with marvelous bureaucratic indirection that if Diem did not replace his brother with better people, "then we must face the possibility that Diem himself cannot be preserved." Lodge, who had concluded after less than a week in Saigon that Diem could not win the war, responded on the twenty-ninth, "We are launched on a course from which there is no respectable turning back: The overthrow of the Diem government." The signals he had already sent through CIA contacts with restive South Vietnamese generals would in time produce the desired results.

In Washington the anti-Diem cabal's bureaucratic coup at once set off recriminations and an extended and at times heated debate over whether Diem was salvageable and what alternatives existed for saving South Vietnam. The coup opponents, including notably McNamara, Taylor, Rusk, and John A. McCone (the head of the CIA), conceded Diem's flaws and the damage he was doing the war effort, but they saw no one better to take his place. Their suggestion was to confront Diem with a stiff ultimatum before following through with more drastic measures. Diem proved obdurate, flatly rejecting on 11 September Lodge's demand for Nhu's removal. Then frustration over the lagging war effort changed to alarm as Nhu talked of cutting a deal with Hanoi. Both Ngo brothers had grown resentful of American pressure for a shake-up of the government and the army, and, as patriots in their own way, feared American assistance was leading to American control.

Through the entire Buddhist crisis Kennedy showed himself perplexed about what to do with Diem. He veered first this way and then that, reflecting genuine indecision. In mid-June he had let the Vietnamese leader know through the embassy that a failure to conciliate the Buddhists and end the crisis would put U.S. support in question, and to drive the point home, the embassy received permission to build contacts with the opposition. While the CIA talked to the plotters in the military, the only group capable of overthrowing Diem and quickly putting a new government in place, Kennedy publicly called for patience as a country at war for twenty years tried to solve its problems, including now the religious dispute.

Kennedy's perfunctory approval in late August of a coup seemed only to deepen his uncertainty. At first he was angry that a policy shift of some magnitude had slipped by him, agitated that some of his most senior advisers were opposed to the shift, and disturbed that Lodge lacked General Harkins's support. But no heads rolled, and the president issued no clear, definitive reversal on the coup initiative. To the contrary, he seemed at first intent on increasing the pressure, stressing in a 2 September interview that Diem's government "has gotten out of touch with the people" and that "in the final analysis it is the people and government itself who have to win or lose this struggle."

Kennedy attempted with Bundy's help to provide Lodge guidance on what to do with Diem, but in fact the secret cables he sent created a verbal fog. One, on 17 September, seemed to put Lodge on a leash. The time was not opportune for a coup; the ambassador should limit himself to a policy of pressure "to secure whatever modest improvements on the scene may be possible." Hoping for fresh insight, Kennedy sent new missions to Saigon. The first, led by junior representatives from the Joint Chiefs of Staff and the State Department, produced two diametrically opposed reports, prompting Kennedy to wonder if its members had visited the same country. He sent another team, this time led by heavyweights, McNamara and Taylor. They returned from Saigon in early October to report that reform was indeed an illusion. Kennedy then authorized a dramatic aid cutoff, intended to make Diem reform but also serving as an unmistakable signal to Diem's generals of deep U.S. discontent. At the same time, he told Lodge that he was not to give "any active covert encouragement" to a coup, only monitor the coup plotters. Then a cable a few days later further muddied matters by telling Lodge not to discourage fresh leadership "capable of increasing effectiveness of military effort, ensuring popular support to win war and improving working relations with U.S."

While his advisers debated and his options narrowed, Kennedy waited. Just as it took the State Department cabal to push him toward a coup, it now took South Vietnam's army to end the suspense. Conspirators led by General Duong Van Minh finally struck on 1 November. Diem's overthrow was followed at once by his and Nhu's cold-blooded murder in an armored vehicle after their being detained in a Catholic Church in the Chinese section of Saigon. The news left Kennedy pale, upset, depressed. He had toppled an ally. He had also lost control of events, with fatal consequences for a fellow Catholic whom Kennedy had once promoted as the best hope for South Vietnam. Three weeks later Kennedy himself lay dead in Dallas.

Diem's death merely served to accentuate rather than resolve the policy bind that Kennedy and his advisers had created for themselves by the fall of 1963. As deeply anticommunist as any of their predecessors, just as obtuse on conditions in Vietnam, and perhaps less prudent than the Eisenhower team, they had steadily deepened and expanded the American commitment. By 1963 some 25,000 Americans were in Vietnam. Some 16,732 of them were military "advisers," up from 685 in early 1961 when Kennedy took office. By the time of his assassination, 78 of those Americans had died in combat. Aid was now running at a $400-million annual clip. All this U.S. support had, however, not undercut the enemy, and Diem's collapse revealed that the policy of the best and the brightest had reached a dead end, forcing Kennedy to look for an alternative approach that would do no serious harm to his presidency.

The president had repeatedly heard from a variety of confidential sources of the increasingly grim prospects for the anticommunist cause. Those with some insight into Diem's sack of defects; if not Ho's bag of tricks, had warned that the formidable enemy would grind down the weak U.S. ally. Thus they had advised Kennedy to limit his commitment, even consider withdrawal. For example, in November 1961 in the immediate wake of the Taylor mission, Senator Mike Mansfield drew on his knowledge of Asia, where he had served as a marine in the 1920s, which he had studied as a history professor in the 1930s, and which he had thereafter followed as one of Congress's leading voices on foreign policy. He pointed out to Kennedy the multiple risks of putting American troops on the Asian mainland. Better not to militarize the struggle, he argued, but rather to insist that the leaders in Saigon embrace "the kind of political and economic[-]social changes that offer the best resistance to communism" and leave the main responsibility for preserving South Vietnam to the South Vietnamese.

In April 1962 John Kenneth Galbraith, a Harvard economist serving as ambassador to India, delivered an even more emphatic warning. A quick tour of Vietnam revealed to him that the Diem government was "weak," "ineffectual," and perhaps "beyond the point of no return." Pacification was doing more harm than good. Expanding the U.S. military presence would place Americans in a colonial role and lead to a drawn-out and indecisive military commitment. Galbraith's advice to Kennedy was to disengage by promoting a noncommunist, nonaligned government in Saigon acceptable to Washington as well as Hanoi and Moscow.

A skeptical intelligence community reenforced the position of dissidents such as Mansfield and Galbraith. From the fall of 1961 into early 1963, it handed down worrisomely negative appraisals at odds with the increasingly rosy picture drawn by the military. And while the government analysts turned positive in the spring of 1963, academic specialists and reporters were expressing an offsetting pessimism that intensified as Diem's political fortunes began their long, final slide. By the summer of 1963, once-apathetic members of Congress, newspaper editors, and other public voices were for the first time raising skeptical questions about the U.S. role in Vietnam.

Kennedy himself seems to have developed serious second thoughts about his Vietnam policy. In April 1962, with the war appearing to be developing favorably, he had casually expressed an interest in reducing the U.S. involvement, translated by McNamara in July into a clear order to plan for phasing out U.S. forces by 1965, though, to be sure, he made withdrawals contingent on continued progress in the war effort. Kennedy clung to the withdrawal option in 1963. On 6 May McNamara asked the military for plans for an accelerated U.S. phaseout, including preparations for removing the first thousand men. As late as October, with coup talk in the air, McNamara joined Taylor in affirming the thousand-man pullout, while professing hope that the war could be won by the end of 1965. On 2 October the White House made public the withdrawal (now scheduled for the end of the year) and indicated that most of the American military would be out by 1965. On 31 October Kennedy himself again referred to a limited, end-of-the-year reduction. Diem's death the next day seems to have intensified Kennedy's impulse to close out or at least downgrade the Vietnam commitment. On 12 November he conceded to Senator Wayne Morse, a critic of Vietnam policy, serious flaws in the U.S. approach, and followed two days later with a press-conference statement about wanting to bring Americans home. On 21 November, before leaving for Texas, a nervous Kennedy privately indicated a readiness to initiate in the new year a thorough, general review of the U.S. role in Southeast Asia.

There is, however, good reason for caution in interpreting this talk of troop reductions and a fundamental policy reappraisal. Kennedy's comments to this effect were intermittent, often couched in vague language, and frequently joined to calls to pursue, even intensify, the Vietnam struggle. For example, he vowed at a 17 July 1963 press conference, "We are not going to withdraw from that effort. In my opinion, for us to withdraw from that effort would mean a collapse not only of South Viet-Nam, but Southeast Asia." Even later in the Diem crisis (on 2 and 9 September), he publicly and emphatically affirmed his belief in the domino theory, his preoccupation with winning the war, and his fear of South Vietnam's fall unleashing a Chinese assault across Southeast Asia. When he talked about getting Americans out of Vietnam on 14 November, he also called in the same breath for intensifying the American effort there. Even the Dallas trip, made with the 1964 election in mind, was to have been the occasion for a speech heavy in its emphasis on global anticommunism and military preparedness that was vintage Kennedy and that was distinctly at odds with any softening on Vietnam.

Moreover, we have to keep in mind that an order to plan was not the same as a decision to execute those plans. The U.S. military ordinarily planned for a great variety of contingencies, including major troop deployments as well as reductions. Even if carried out, a thousand-man withdrawal might have amounted to little more than a token of Kennedy's desire to bring the boys home at some undetermined time in the future, and could in practical terms have meant nothing if quiet increases in some units were to be offset by highly publicized reductions in others.

But it is possible that Kennedy was serious in the withdrawal plan and that he felt rising doubts about the Cold War approach to Vietnam. He did have a striking range of good reasons for rethinking basic policy. Not only had policy critics, both in and outside the government, repeatedly raised the warning flag. But political calculations also called for caution. Kennedy would not want to enter the 1964 election season as a president leading the country into a war on the Asian mainland. With unpleasant Korean War memories still fresh, the U.S. electorate, however anticommunist in principle, was not likely to welcome the prospect of American troops fighting in Vietnam. Kennedy may, moreover, have been personally anguished by the rising level of destruction within Vietnam and its toll on civilians. These concerns were evident in his qualms about the use of defoliants, napalm, and free-fire zones (although in each case he had finally given at least limited approval). Finally, the president may have remembered men who had died in battle by his side and under his command as a lengthening list of soldiers killed in Vietnam reached their commander in chief. Saving that country might mean the sacrifice of many fine men.

Despite all this, an exit from Vietnam would have proved for Kennedy an arduous and dangerous task. Part of the struggle would have played out within Kennedy. Quitting Vietnam would give the lie to the toughness and determination that among the Kennedy clan were highly prized traits. Perhaps more serious was his own resolutely anticommunist record. Was he ready to abandon a free people whom he had sworn to defend? Was he ready to face all the consequences that he had earlier predicted would flow from defeat—freeing the Chinese Communists to dominate the region, emboldening the Soviets to adventurism in Europe, and betraying the American national mission and people all around the world looking to American leadership? Was he ready to put in question his reputation as an effective cold warrior finally secured by his handling of the Cuban missile crisis?

Even if Kennedy had managed to transcend his cult of toughness and his anticommunist faith, he would still have had to face the prospects of a political firestorm set off by a retreat from Vietnam. Just as Truman struggled against charges of having "lost" China, Kennedy would have to face accusations of being the second Democratic president who had squandered an important piece of Asian real estate. He understood the special danger of being impeached by his own words. He had promised to do better than Eisenhower, who had let the northern half of Vietnam go. Kennedy had claimed he was ready "to pay any price, bear any burden." A retreat from Vietnam would allow partisan critics to picture him a weak-kneed appeaser who should not be trusted with the national security and the national honor. They would ask him to explain the terrible waste in lives and resources already spent for a cause he now wished to repudiate.

Anything short of victory could also lead to withering criticism from foreign-policy insiders. Kennedy could expect to hear from the two living ex-presidents, whose bipartisan Vietnam policy he had repeatedly, publicly, and formally affirmed but was now abandoning. Still others within his own party, the veteran cold warriors whose guidance he had respectfully sought at the outset of his presidency, were equally unlikely to suffer in silence while the communist bloc pierced the containment line and put all Southeast Asia and free lands beyond in danger. A reversal on Vietnam would also create dissension within his own already-divided administration, set off leaks of confidential information sure to embarrass the president, and leads to possible loss of control over the national-security bureaucracy.

We will never know how Kennedy would have resolved an agonizing choice that carried costs and risks no matter which way he turned. The responsibility for choosing form an unpalatable set of options now fell to his successor, Lyndon Baines Johnson.

Kennedy's Prudent and Cautious Policy

DAVID KAISER

Two thousand four hundred years ago, Thucydides the Athenian first explored the distinction between the long-term and immediate causes of conflicts in his history of the Peloponnesian War. The long-term causes of the American involvement in Vietnam, it is now clear, go back to the middle years of the Eisenhower administration, which decided upon a militant response to any new Communist advances virtually anywhere on the globe. The Vietnam War occurred largely because of Cold War policies adopted by the State and Defense Departments in 1954–1956 and approved secretly by President Eisenhower—policies that called for a military response to Communist aggression almost anywhere that it might occur, and specifically in Southeast Asia. These policies ensured that when American clients came under attack from Communist and other forces in Laos and South Vietnam the Pentagon and the State Department would propose American military action. They also ensured that military planners would rely upon nuclear weapons to make such action effective, and some continued to do so well into the Kennedy and Johnson administrations. Ironically, while Eisenhower's supposedly cautious approach in foreign policy has frequently been contrasted with his successors' apparent aggressiveness, Kennedy actually spent much of his term resisting policies developed and approved under Eisenhower, both in Southeast Asia and elsewhere. He also had to deal with the legacy of the Eisenhower administration's disastrous attempts to create a pro-Western rather than a neutral government in Laos—a policy he quickly reversed, thereby avoiding the need for American military intervention there.

Following the lines of policy Eisenhower had laid down, middle- and lower-level State and Defense Department officials began submitting one proposal for military intervention after another as soon as crises in Laos and South Vietnam became serious in 1960–1961. But while the military continually laid plans for action in Indochina, American war plans took relatively little account of the actual strategic situation there or of the capacity of American conventional forces to affect it. War plans were consistently designed to deal with conventional Communist aggression, but the threats that developed in Laos and South Vietnam in 1960–1964 were political in Laos and largely unconventional within South Vietnam. The Pentagon's plans for Southeast Asia involved action against North Vietnam from the air, from the sea, and on land, and consistently foresaw Chinese intervention and escalation to general war as a possible result. When American advisers became actively involved in the Vietnam War in 1962, a few civilians, junior officers, and foreign observers raised basic questions about the nature of the war and American strategy, but the American military never changed its basic approach to the conflict.

The underlying causes of the Vietnam War, we shall find, were the growing Communist insurgency in South Vietnam, on the one hand, and the State and

---

Reprinted by permission of the publisher from *American Tragedy: Kennedy, Johnson, and the Origins of the Vietnam War* by David Kaiser, pp. 2–4, 275–280, 284–285, Cambridge, Mass.: The Belknap Press of Harvard University Press. Copyright © 2000 by David Kaiser.

Defense Departments' reflexive proposals for implementing the Eisenhower administration's policies on the other. The more immediate causes of the war, however, and specifically the American decision in late 1964 and early 1965 definitely to begin it after declining to do so in 1961–1962, show the influence of both personality and chance. The appointed senior foreign policy leadership of the Kennedy and Johnson administrations—Secretary of State Dean Rusk, Secretary of Defense Robert McNamara, National Security Adviser McGeorge Bundy, and most of the Joint Chiefs of Staff—never questioned the assumptions of the Pentagon and State Department, and supported intervention in Southeast Asia from 1961 on. But President Kennedy resisted the proposals for intervention in both Laos and South Vietnam that reached him, largely because of broader strategic and political questions that the bureaucracy and his cabinet seemed to ignore. The Kennedy administration did dramatically increase American involvement in South Vietnam, raising the American military presence from about 600 personnel in 1960 to 17,500 in 1963. That increase, however, which took the form of a larger advisory presence and the introduction of helicopter, tactical air, and other forms of combat support, represented a compromise between the President, who sincerely wanted to help the South Vietnamese government cope with the Viet Cong but rejected war as a way to do so, and his bureaucracy and cabinet members, who wanted the United States to intervene directly in 1961.

As Kennedy repeatedly explained, he doubted—rightly as it turned out—that American intervention in Southeast Asia would enjoy much support from the nation's most important allies, or from Congress, or from the American people. Again and again he questioned whether Indochina was an appropriate place for the United States to fight. While keenly interested in the problem of Communist insurgency, he believed that threatened nations themselves bore the principal responsibility for combating it, and he wanted to assist them by means other than direct American military intervention. And Kennedy also looked for ways to improve relations with the Soviet Union and America's image in the Third World—efforts which were slowly succeeding by the end of his last year in office, but which rapidly came to a halt thereafter as the United States began the war in Vietnam. We shall never know what Kennedy would have done with respect to Vietnam had he lived to serve a second term, but it is clear that the Vietnam War would have begun three or four years earlier than it did had he taken his subordinates' advice to send troops. . . .

The administration's attempts to help the South Vietnamese government cope with the emerging Viet Cong failed, largely because neither Saigon nor the American military knew how to deal with a guerrilla war. Nor, it is clear, was Diem an effective leader unwisely abandoned by his American patrons. A bipartisan consensus had adopted Diem as the preferred South Vietnamese leader under the Eisenhower administration, but he lacked the skills necessary to unite non-Communist South Vietnamese, and his support had already declined significantly by 1961. . . . [T]he counterinsurgency effort in South Vietnam was failing even before the Buddhist crisis of 1963, and [Ngo Dinh] Diem and his brother Ngo Dinh Nhu had themselves to blame for their overthrow. . . . Robert McNamara and the Pentagon helped hide the true situation from the President, the rest of the government, and the American people, thereby putting off the need to reevaluate American policy. Kennedy died believing, mistakenly, that the war was still going well. . . .

In subsequent decades some American policymakers and historians—including Eileen Hammer, William Colby, Frederick Nolting, and Lyndon Johnson and Richard Nixon—cited the coup against Diem as the American government's biggest mistake and, perhaps, the most important cause of full-scale American involvement in the war. Nixon went further during his presidency, undertaking unsuccessful attempts to prove—wrongly—that Kennedy had ordered Diem's assassination. Like other simplistic explanations for America's failure in Vietnam, this one substitutes facile, politicized, emotional rhetoric for real analysis in an effort to keep alive the myth—so dear to Nixon and Colby's GI generation—that every problem has a solution.

Without question, the two men most responsible for the overthrow of the Diem government were Ngo Dinh Diem and Ngo Dinh Nhu. Diem in 1954 took power with the financial and political backing of the government of the United States and the support of most of the active non-Communists in South Vietnam. During the next nine years he steadily reduced his domestic support until it scarcely extended beyond his own family. Despite his control of the American-provided military budget, he never established a relationship of confidence with most of his generals. He was nearly overthrown in 1960 and nearly assassinated in 1962. He dealt with all opposition—the sects in 1954–1955, the political parties in the late 1950s, and the Buddhists and students in 1963—by trying to crush it. He never allowed popular province chiefs to remain in office for too long, and he never trusted anyone outside his narrow circle. As late as September 1963 he might have bought some more time simply by taking some generals into the cabinet, but he refused to do so and lost the critical support of General Dinh in Saigon. And while his political support faded, the Viet Cong—frequently taking advantage of his mistakes—added non-Communist adherents to its cause. Lansdale, Diem's most fervent American supporter, had concluded by 1961 that Diem must allow the opposition to operate legally, but Diem refused. And by the fall of 1963 even Lansdale—like his protégé Rufus Phillips—had concluded that Diem could only survive without Nhu. Nothing ever suggested that Diem would take that step, or that Nhu—who controlled the regime's secret police and political machine—would agree to it either.

The Buddhist crisis, then, was merely the last and biggest of a series of challenges to Diem's authority and political skill that called the American policy of relying upon him into question. Two years earlier, at the time of the Taylor-Rostow mission, many responsible Americans had argued that Diem had to make significant political changes in order to survive, but Nolting and McNamara had persuaded Washington to push ahead without them. During the intervening two years the same two men—and McNamara in particular—had told Washington that American policy was working and South Vietnam was winning the war. As late as mid-September the Pentagon had tendentiously refuted [correspondent David] Halberstam's latest military analysis, and as the coup took place McNamara was pressuring Rusk to withdraw the INR challenge to the Pentagon's analysis. Not until December did McNamara inform a new President, in effect, that Halberstam and INR had been right. Had Washington not suspended aid to Diem and Nhu, further crises and coup attempts would undoubtedly have occurred in any case, and the Viet Cong would probably have continued to gain.

On November 4, 1963, President Kennedy sat down in the oval office and dictated his own reflections on the coup. Never before heard, they show his thoughts, his style, and his approach to government very clearly. The President spoke carefully, settling accounts for the benefit of future historians.

> One two three four five. Monday, November 4, 1963. Over the weekend, the coup in Saigon took place. It culminated three months of conversation about a coup, conversation which divided the government here and in Saigon. Opposed to a coup was General Taylor, the Attorney General, Secretary McNamara to a somewhat lesser degree, John McCone, partly because of an old hostility to Lodge which causes him to lack confidence in Lodge's judgment, partly as a result of a new hostility because Lodge shifted his Station Chief; in favor of the coup was State, led by Averell Harriman, George Ball, Roger Hilsman, supported by Mike Forrestal at the White House.

After impartially summarizing his subordinates' views with hardly a trace of emotion, the President turned to his own role. It is interesting that he failed to ascribe any view at all to Dean Rusk.

> I feel that we must bear a good deal of responsibility for it, beginning with our cable of early August *(sic)* in which we suggested the coup. In my judgment that wire was badly drafted, it should never have been sent on a Saturday, I should not have given my consent to it without a roundtable conference at which McNamara and Taylor could have presented their views. While we did redress that balance in later wires, that first wire encouraged Lodge along a course to which he was in any case inclined. Harkins continued to oppose the coup on the ground that the military effort was doing well. Sharp split between Saigon and the rest of the country. Politically the situation was deteriorating, militarily it had not had its effect. There was a feeling however that it would. For this reason, Secretary McNamara and General Taylor supported applying additional pressures to Diem and Nhu to move them. . . .

This is perhaps the most significant revelation on the tape: that Kennedy, even at this late date, believed the assurances of his trusted subordinates McNamara and Taylor that the military effort was going well. He never learned the truth.

At this moment the President's ruminations were interrupted by one of his children, probably his son John-John, who was nearly three. His father invited him to say something, and the words "Hello," and "naughty, naughty Daddy" are clearly heard. After giving his son an impromptu lesson on the four seasons, Kennedy continued in a more somber vein:

> I was shocked by the death of Diem and Nhu. I'd met Diem with Justice Douglas many years ago. He was an extraordinary character. While he became increasingly difficult in the last months, nonetheless over a ten-year period he'd held his country together, maintained its independence under very adverse conditions. The way he was killed made it particularly abhorrent. The question now is whether the generals can stay together and build a stable government or whether Saigon will begin—whether public opinion in Saigon, the intellectuals, students etc., will turn on this government as repressive and undemocratic in the not too distant future.

After a pause, the President suddenly continued more rapidly. "Also we have another test on Autobahn today," he said, referring to the latest Berlin incident. He quickly moved on to other events of the day.

In the end there is no great mystery about the coup, no mysterious assassination plot designed to forestall a premature peace agreement. Although he had long-standing affection for Diem, Kennedy had quickly concluded during the summer of 1963 that Diem could not continue on the course that he was on. If he refused to mend his ways, a change of government seemed almost inevitable. Having appointed Lodge to Saigon both to pressure Diem and to provide critical liberal Republican political cover should controversial events take place, Kennedy was not likely to overrule Lodge's opinion or to replace him, despite the Attorney General's subsequent remarks. At the last critical meeting on October 30, he heard new, pessimistic reports about Diem's performance and cited [reporter Joseph] Alsop's well-founded doubts about Nhu. That meeting reached its decision not to head off a coup on the basis of a realistic assessment of the future. Had Kennedy known the truth about the military situation he might have considered other options, but he did not.

Kennedy refused at any time during the fall of 1963 bluntly to decide that Diem must either stay or go. The policy embodied in the McNamara-Taylor report and Lodge's subsequent instructions—some of which were written by Bundy for Kennedy himself—reflected his views: that the United States should pressure Diem to change, that Washington should not actively promote a coup, but that it might accept or even encourage alternative leadership if and when it emerged. Lodge—of all Americans the most responsible for the coup—eagerly moved the process along, although he did not, and could not, initiate it, and remained ignorant of key aspects of the plan right up until the end. Meanwhile, the McNamara-Taylor report had a most ironic effect. McNamara and Taylor apparently insisted upon its prediction that the American effort might largely be finished by 1965 and its planned announcement of a 1,000-man withdrawal largely as confirmation that their existing policy was working. McNamara had laid down both deadlines in May 1963, and the report simply affirmed publicly what he had already decreed privately. Yet according to several South Vietnamese military leaders, the deadline—as well as the suspension of American aid—stimulated the coup plotters to move. Seeing no way that Diem could win the war by the end of 1965, they decided they had to take drastic action to get the situation back on track before the Americans departed.

In another irony, the general optimism among the President's advisers decisively militated against any discussion of radical alternatives such as negotiation or neutralization. Kennedy on August 29 asked the ExCom, in the midst of a discussion of pressuring Diem, "whether we would really pull out of Vietnam in any event," and apparently received no reply. When Paul Kattenburg on August 31 suggested that things might be much worse than anyone expected, he received a career-threatening response. In another meeting, . . . Kennedy expressed skepticism about de Gaulle's neutrality proposals, although Roger Hilsman had indicated to *Newsweek* that they might eventually have to be implemented. Kennedy in 1961 opted for neutralization in Laos because the pro-American position was so weak both politically and militarily. All through the fall of 1963 his advisers insisted that despite Diem's political problems the military situation was progressing. And no one seems to have realized that the Buddhists were skeptical about the war, as well as about Diem, and would soon form the nucleus of a neutralist movement in South Vietnam.

Kennedy, in any case, never made decisions until he had to, and for the moment circumstances inclined him to hope for the best and try to defuse controversy over South Vietnam. . . .

From the time of the Geneva conference of 1954 through the moment of the American decision to go to war in Vietnam in 1965, Indochina had figured as one of many battlegrounds in the Cold War. There as elsewhere, successive administrations tried to prevent the further spread of Communism, first economically and politically, then through an advisory role, and finally with direct military intervention. All these measures reflected the containment policy that the United States followed for more than four decades after the Second World War, and President Johnson therefore found it easy to claim, as he frequently did, that he was merely continuing his predecessors' policies. Yet the simple formula of "containment" could be applied in many different ways. Johnson's foreign policy differed in subtle but critical ways from Kennedy's, and therefore led him to take the steps that Kennedy had consistently rejected.

Despite the sweeping rhetoric of his inaugural address, Kennedy never regarded the Cold War as a simple matter of opposing Communism wherever it appeared. Certainly he built up the American military substantially and contemplated military intervention in certain key areas—most notably in Cuba—but we have seen that military moves were never more than one part of his strategy. Throughout his tenure, he paid at least as much attention to keeping in step with major European allies, improving America's reputation among emerging nations, and looking for areas of agreement with the Soviet Union. The recently released transcripts of the ExCom meetings during the Cuban missile crisis show how those particular considerations decisively inclined him against war even in October 1962, and led him to a peaceful solution of the crisis. Even then, faced with the opportunity to eliminate Fidel Castro with the initial support of the American people, the President concluded that the possibility of Soviet retaliation in Berlin and the likely negative reaction of European allies made the risk of war too great. Here, too, he found himself in opposition to many of his senior civilian and military advisers, but his approach prevailed and successfully removed Soviet missiles from Cuba while laying the foundation for improved relations with Moscow.

Similar considerations had played a critical role in Kennedy's 1961 decision to seek the neutralization of Laos. Confronted repeatedly with proposals for intervention, he had always referred to the opposition of the British and the French and the lack of enthusiasm among Congress and the American people for war in Southeast Asia. He had also kept the basic strategic facts of the situation firmly in mind: that North Vietnam and China could respond to any American intervention with the infusion of hundreds of thousands of men. The American involvement in South Vietnam grew dramatically under his Presidency, but he never regarded it as anything but a liability. We shall never know what he would have decided had he realized that the pro-Western position in South Vietnam was collapsing, but we do know how he had handled a similar situation in Laos, and that he rejected several proposals for American troops in South Vietnam.

We also know that Kennedy would never have made a decision to fight in Southeast Asia in isolation from his broader foreign policy goals. Such a decision would have divided him, as it divided Johnson, from many important American allies and neutrals, and would have temporarily destroyed the prospect of improving relations with the Soviets. While Johnson was aware of these problems, he never allowed them significantly to influence his policy. The record of Kennedy's term in office suggests that they would have influenced him very heavily indeed.

✗ *F U R T H E R   R E A D I N G*

Bird, Kai. *The Color of Truth* (on McGeorge and William Bundy) (1998).

Blair, Anne E. *Lodge in Vietnam* (1995).

Burner, David. *John F. Kennedy and a New Generation* (1988).

Buzzanco, Robert. *Masters of War* (1996).

Catton, Philip E. "Counter-Insurgency and Nation Building: The Strategic Hamlet Programme in South Vietnam, 1961–1963," *International History Review,* 21 (1989), 918–40.

Chomsky, Noam. *Rethinking Camelot: JFK, the Vietnam War, and U.S. Political Culture* (1993).

Freedman, Lawrence. *Kennedy's Wars* (2000).

Giglio, James N. *The Presidency of John F. Kennedy* (1991).

Halberstam, David. *The Making of a Quagmire* (1965).

Hammer, Ellen J. *A Death in November: America in Vietnam, 1963* (1987).

Heath, Jim F. *Decade of Disillusionment* (1975).

Hilsman, Roger. *To Move a Nation* (1967).

Kinnard, Douglas. *The Certain Trumpet* (1991) (on Maxwell Taylor).

Logevall, Fredrik. *Choosing War* (1999).

McNamara, Robert. *In Retrospect* (1995).

Mecklin, John. *Mission in Torment* (1965).

Newman, John M. *JFK and Vietnam* (1992).

Parmet, Herbert S. *JFK* (1983).

Paterson, Thomas G. "Bearing the Burden: A Critical Look at JFK's Foreign Policy," *Virginia Quarterly Review,* 54 (1978), 193–212.

———, ed., *Kennedy's Quest for Victory* (1989).

Pelz, Stephen E. "John F. Kennedy's 1961 Vietnam War Decisions," *Journal of Strategic Studies,* 4 (1981), 356–385.

Rostow, Walt W. *The Diffusion of Power* (1972).

Rusk, Dean. *As I Saw It* (1990).

Rust, William J. *Kennedy in Vietnam* (1985).

Schlesinger, Jr., Arthur M. *Robert Kennedy and His Times* (1978).

———. *A Thousand Days* (1965).

Schoenbaum, Thomas J. *Waging Peace and War* (1988) (on Dean Rusk).

Schwab, Orrin. *Defending the Free World* (1998).

Sheehan, Neil. *A Bright Shining Lie* (1988) (on John Paul Vann).

Smith, R. B. *The Kennedy Strategy* (1985).

Snyder, Richard J., ed. *John F. Kennedy* (1988).

Sorensen, Theodore C. *Kennedy* (1965).

Taylor, Maxwell D. *Swords and Ploughshares* (1972).

Tregaskis, Richard. *Vietnam Diary* (1963).

Walton, Richard J. *Cold War and Counter-Revolution: The Foreign Policy of John F. Kennedy* (1972).

Warner, Geoffrey. "The United States and the Fall of Diem," Part I: "The Coup that Never Was," *Australian Outlook,* 29 (1974), 245–58.

———. "The United States and the Fall of Diem," Part II: "The Death of Diem," *Australian Outlook,* 29 (1975), 3–17.

Winters, Francis X. *The Year of the Hare* (1997).

Zeiler, Thomas. *Dean Rusk* (2000).

CHAPTER 6

Lyndon B. Johnson's

Decisions for War

✕

In the months following the Diem and Kennedy assassinations, political chaos gripped South Vietnam. Combined with spreading guerrilla insurgency in the South, this turmoil made American officials worry that the survival of the Saigon government hung in the balance. In December 1963 Defense Secretary Robert S. McNamara warned President Lyndon B. Johnson that without a reversal of current trends within the next two or three months, the most likely result would be a communist-controlled state. Many of Johnson's advisers urged military escalation, recommending bombing reprisals against the North and the dispatch of U.S. combat forces to the South.

In August 1964, in response to alleged attacks against U.S. naval vessels by North Vietnamese warboats in the Gulf of Tonkin, Congress passed a resolution that granted the president sweeping powers. It authorized him to take "all necessary measures to repel any armed attacks against the forces of the United States and to prevent further aggression." Nevertheless, Johnson moved cautiously. In July 1965, fearing the imminence of Saigon's collapse, he acted. After a lengthy deliberative process, LBJ ordered a sustained bombing campaign against North Vietnam and authorized the introduction of combat forces to stem the insurgency in the South. Those decisions committed the United States to a major land war in Asia.

Because Johnson's escalation of U.S. involvement in Vietnam had such profound consequences, his decisions have understandably generated much heated public and scholarly debate. How were the decisions reached? Did Johnson dominate the deliberative process? Or did he simply follow the recommendations of his principal advisers? Why did LBJ and senior policymakers dismiss the doubts raised by Under Secretary of State George Ball? What specific goals did Johnson expect to achieve through the use of combat troops and the air offensive? Did he expect to defeat the communists? Or only to prevent the fall of the South Vietnamese regime? How did he view the stakes involved in Vietnam? Did his concern with the likely domestic political fallout from the loss of South Vietnam to the communists affect his thinking? Did he seek merely to buy time for his Great Society reform program? What did he believe would be the international ramifications for the United States if its South Vietnamese ally perished?

✗ *D O C U M E N T S*

Document 1 features excerpts from a March 16, 1964, memorandum from Secretary of
Defense Robert S. McNamara to President Johnson. It recommended a deepening of the
U.S. commitment to South Vietnam and was approved by Johnson the next day as National Security Action Memorandum 288. LBJ and Democratic Senator Richard Russell
discuss U.S. options in Vietnam in Document 2, a transcription of their tape-recorded
conversation of May 27, 1964. The Tonkin Gulf Resolution (Document 3), which passed
the Senate on August 10, 1964, with only two dissenting votes, authorized the president
to use whatever force he deemed necessary in Vietnam. In Document 4, a speech of
April 7, 1965, at Johns Hopkins University, President Johnson explains why the United
States is fighting in Vietnam.

Document 5, another memorandum to the president from McNamara, recommends
a substantial expansion of U.S. military pressure against the Vietcong in the South and
the North Vietnamese in the North. Under Secretary of State Ball offers contrary advice
to the president in a memorandum of July 1, Document 6. An excerpt from Johnson's
memoir *The Vantage Point,* in which he reflects on his decision to accept McNamara's
advice, is Document 7. The final selection gives a soldier's perspective on the war.
Reprinted from Philip Caputo's best-selling memoir *A Rumor of War,* it captures the
innocence and idealism that some American fighting men brought with them to Vietnam.

1. Reassessment of U.S. Policy
in South Vietnam, 1964

I. U.S. Objectives in South Vietnam

We seek an independent non-Communist South Vietnam. We do not require that it
serve as a Western base or as a member of a Western Alliance. South Vietnam must
be free, however, to accept outside assistance as required to maintain its security.
This assistance should be able to take the form not only of economic and social
measures but also police and military help to root out and control insurgent elements.

Unless we can achieve this objective in South Vietnam, almost all of Southeast Asia will probably fall under Communist dominance (all of Vietnam, Laos,
and Cambodia), accommodate to Communism so as to remove effective U.S. and
anti-Communist influence (Burma), or fall under the domination of forces not now
explicitly Communist but likely then to become so (Indonesia taking over Malaysia).
Thailand might hold for a period with our help, but would be under grave pressure.
Even the Philippines would become shaky, and the threat to India to the west,
Australia and New Zealand to the south, and Taiwan, Korea, and Japan to the north
and east would be greatly increased.

All of these consequences would probably have been true even if the U.S. had
not since 1954, and especially since 1961, become so heavily engaged in South
Vietnam. However, that fact accentuates the impact of a Communist South Vietnam not only in Asia, but in the rest of the world, where the South Vietnam conflict

---

Foreign Relations of the United States, 1964–1968, I, 154–156, 166–167.

is regarded as a test case of U.S. capacity to help a nation meet a Communist "war of liberation."

Thus, purely in terms of foreign policy, the stakes are high. They are increased by domestic factors.

II. Present U.S. Policy in South Vietnam

We are now trying to help South Vietnam defeat the Viet Cong, supported from the North, by means short of the unqualified use of U.S. combat forces. We are not acting against North Vietnam except by a very modest "covert" program operated by South Vietnamese (and a few Chinese Nationalists)—a program so limited that it is unlikely to have any significant effect. In Laos, we are still working largely within the framework of the 1962 Geneva Accords. In Cambodia we are still seeking to keep Sihanouk from abandoning whatever neutrality he may still have and fulfilling his threat of reaching an accommodation with Hanoi and Peking. As a consequence of these policies, we and the GVN have had to condone the extensive use of Cambodian and Laotian territory by the Viet Cong, both as a sanctuary and as infiltration routes.

III. The Present Situation in South Vietnam

The key elements in the present situation are as follows:

A. The military tools and concepts of the GVN/US effort are generally sound and adequate. Substantially more can be done in the effective employment of military forces and in the economic and civic action areas. These improvements may require some selective increases in the U.S. presence, but it does not appear likely that major equipment replacement and additions in U.S. personnel are indicated under current policy.

B. The U.S. policy of reducing existing personnel where South Vietnamese are in a position to assume the functions is still sound. Its application will not lead to any major reductions in the near future, but adherence to this policy as such has a sound effect in portraying to the U.S. and the world that we continue to regard the war as a conflict the South Vietnamese must win and take ultimate responsibility for. Substantial reductions in the numbers of U.S. military training personnel should be possible before the end of 1965. However, the U.S. should continue to reiterate that it will provide all the assistance and advice required to do the job regardless of how long it takes.

C. The situation has unquestionably been growing worse, at least since September:

1. In terms of government control of the countryside, about 40% of the territory is under Viet Cong control or predominant influence. In 22 of the 43 provinces, the Viet Cong control 50% or more of the land area, including 80% of Phuoc Tuy; 90% of Binh Duong; 75% of Hau Nghia; 90% of Long An; 90% of Kien Tuong; 90% of Dinh Tuong; 90% of Kien Hoa; and 85% of An Xuyen.

2. Large groups of the population are now showing signs of apathy and indifference, and there are some signs of frustration within the U.S. contingent:

a. The ARVN and paramilitary desertion rates, and particularly the latter, are high and increasing.
b. Draft dodging is high while the Viet Cong are recruiting energetically and effectively.
c. The morale of the hamlet militia and of the Self Defense Corps, on which the security of the hamlets depends, is poor and falling.

3. In the last 90 days the weakening of the government's position has been particularly noticeable. . . .

VII. Recommendations

I recommend that you instruct the appropriate agencies of the U.S. Government:

1. To make it clear that we are prepared to furnish assistance and support to South Vietnam for as long as it takes to bring the insurgency under control.
2. To make it clear that we fully support the Khanh government and are opposed to any further coups.
3. To support a Program for National Mobilization (including a national service law) to put South Vietnam on a war footing.
4. To assist the Vietnamese to increase the armed forces (regular plus paramilitary) by at least 50,000 men.
5. To assist the Vietnamese to create a greatly enlarged Civil Administrative Corps for work at province, district and hamlet levels.
6. To assist the Vietnamese to improve and reorganize the paramilitary forces and to increase their compensation.
7. To assist the Vietnamese to create an offensive guerrilla force.
8. To provide the Vietnamese Air Force 25 A–1H aircraft in exchange for the present T–28s.
9. To provide the Vietnamese Army additional M–113 armored personnel carriers (withdrawing the M–114s there), additional river boats, and approximately $5–10 million of other additional material.
10. To announce publicly the Fertilizer Program and to expand it with a view within two years to trebling the amount of fertilizer made available.
11. To authorize continued high-level U.S. overflights of South Vietnam's borders and to authorize "hot pursuit" and South Vietnamese ground operations over the Laotian line for the purpose of border control. More ambitious operations into Laos involving units beyond battalion size should be authorized only with the approval of Souvanna Phouma. Operations across the Cambodian border should depend on the state of relations with Cambodia.
12. To prepare immediately to be in a position on 72 hours' notice to initiate the full range of Laotain and Cambodian "Border Control" actions (beyond those authorized in paragraph 11 above) and the "Retaliatory Actions" against North Vietnam, and to be in a position on 30 days' notice to initiate the program of "Graduated Overt Military Pressure" against North Vietnam.

Robert S. McNamara

2. Lyndon Johnson and Richard Russell Ruminate about the U.S. Dilemma in Vietnam, 1964

LBJ: Got lots of troubles.

Russell: Well, we all have those.

LBJ: . . . What do you think of this Vietnam thing? I'd like to hear you talk a little bit.

Russell: Frankly, Mr. President, if you were to tell me that I was authorized to settle it as I saw fit, I would respectfully decline and not take it.

LBJ: [chuckles]

Russell: It's the damn worst mess I ever saw; and I don't like to brag. I never have been right many times in my life. But I knew that we were going to get into this sort of mess when we went in there. And I don't see how we're ever going to get out of it without fighting a major war with the Chinese and all of them down there in those rice paddies and jungles. . . . I just don't know what to do.

LBJ: That's the way that I've been feeling for six months.

Russell: It appears that our position is deteriorating. And it looks like the more we try to do for them, the less that they're willing to do for themselves. It's just a sad situation. There's no sense of responsibility there on the part of any of their leaders that are bearing it. It's all just through the generations, or even centuries, they've just thought about the individual and glorifying the individual and that the only utilization of power is to glorify the individual and not to save the state, or help other people. And they just can't shed themselves of that complex. It's a hell of a situation. It's a mess. And it's going to get worse. And I don't know what to do. I don't think that the American people are quite ready to send our troops in there to do the fighting. If it came down to an option for us of just sending the Americans in there to do the fighting, which will, of course, eventually lead into a ground war and a conventional war with China, we'd do them a favor every time we killed a coolie, whereas when one of our people got killed, it would be a loss to us. If it got down to . . . just pulling out, I'd get out. But then I don't know. There's undoubtedly some middle ground somewhere. If I was going to get out, I'd get the same crowd that got rid of old Diem to get rid of these people and get some fellow in there that said he wished to hell we *would* get out. That would give us a good excuse for getting out. . . .

LBJ: How important is it to us?

Russell: It isn't important a damn bit, with all these new missile systems.

LBJ: Well, I guess it's important to us—

Russell: From a psychological standpoint.

LBJ: I mean, yes, and from the standpoint that we are party to a treaty. And if we don't pay any attention to this treaty, why, I don't guess they think we pay attention to any of them.

Russell: Yeah, but we're the only ones paying any attention to it!

LBJ: Yeah, I think that's right. . . . I don't think the people of the country know much about Vietnam and I think they care a hell of a lot less.

Russell: Yeah, I know, but you go to send a whole lot of our boys out there—

LBJ: Yeah, that's right. That's exactly right. That's what I'm talking about. You get a few. We had thirty-five killed—and we got enough hell over thirty-five—this year.

Russell: More than that . . . in Atlanta, Georgia, have been killed this year in automobile accidents.

LBJ: That's right, and eighty-three went down in one crash on a 707 in one day, but that doesn't make any difference. . . . The Republicans are going to make a political issue out of it, every one of them, even [Senator Everett M.] Dirksen.

Russell: It's the only issue they got.

LBJ: . . . [Senator Bourke] Hickenlooper said that we just had to stand and show our force and put our men in there and let come what may come. And nobody disagreed with him. Now Mansfield, he just wants to pull up and get out. And [Senator Wayne] Morse wants to get out, and [Senator Ernest] Gruening wants to get out. And that's about where it stops. *I* don't know. . . .

Russell: It's a tragic situation. It's just one of those places where you can't win. Anything that you do is wrong. . . . I have thought about it. I have worried about it. I have prayed about it.

LBJ: I don't believe we can do anything—

Russell: It frightens me 'cause it's my country involved over there and if we get into there on any considerable scale, there's no doubt in my mind but that the Chinese will be in there and we'd be fighting a danged conventional war against our secondary potential threat and it'd be a Korea on a much bigger scale and a worse scale. . . . If you go from Laos and Cambodia and Vietnam and bring North Vietnam into it too, it's the damndest mess on earth. The French report that they lost 250,000 men and spent a couple billion of their money and two billion of ours down there and just got the hell whipped out of them. . . .

LBJ: You don't have any doubt but what if we go in there and get 'em up against the wall, the Chinese Communists are gonna come in?

Russell: No sir, no doubt about it.

LBJ: That's my judgment, and our people don't think so. . . .

LBJ: The whole question, as I see it, is, is it more dangerous for us to let things go as they're going now, deteriorating every day—

Russell: I don't think we can let it go, Mr. President, indefinitely.

LBJ: Than it would be for us to move in.

Russell: We either got to move in or move out.

LBJ: That's about what it is. . . .

LBJ: Well, they'd impeach a President though that would run out, wouldn't they? I just don't believe that—outside of Morse, everybody I talk to says you got to go in, including Hickenlooper, including all the Republicans. . . . And I don't know how in the hell you're gonna get out unless they tell you to get out.

Russell: If we had a man running the government over there that told us to get out, we could sure get out.

LBJ: That's right, but you can't do that. . . . Wouldn't that pretty well fix us in the eyes of the world though and make it look mighty bad?

Russell: I don't know. [chuckles] We don't look too good right now. You'd look pretty good, I guess, going in there with all the troops and sending them all in there, but I tell you it'll be the most expensive venture this country ever went into.

LBJ: I've got a little old sergeant that works for me over at the house and he's got six children and I just put him up as the United States Army, Air Force, and Navy every time I think about making this decision and think about sending that father of those six kids in there. And what the hell are we going to get out of his doing it? And it just makes the chills run up my back.

Russell: It does me. I just can't see it.

LBJ: I just haven't got the nerve to do it, and I don't see any other way out of it.

Russell: It's one of these things where "heads I win, tails you lose."

LBJ: Well, think about it and I'll talk to you again. I hate to bother you, but I just—

Russell: I wish I could help you. God knows I do 'cause it's a terrific quandary that we're in over there. We're just in the quicksands up to our very necks. And I just don't know what the hell is the best way to do about it.

LBJ: I love you and I'll be calling you.

3. The Tonkin Gulf Resolution, 1964

To promote the maintenance of international peace and security in southeast Asia.

Whereas naval units of the Communist regime in Vietnam, in violation of the principles of the Charter of the United Nations and of international law, have deliberately and repeatedly attacked United States naval vessels lawfully present in international waters, and have thereby created a serious threat to international peace; and

Whereas these attacks are part of a deliberate and systematic campaign of aggression that the Communist regime in North Vietnam has been waging against its neighbors and the nations joined with them in the collective defense of their freedom; and

Whereas the United States is assisting the peoples of southeast Asia to protect their freedom and has no territorial, military or political ambitions in that area, but desires only that these peoples should be left in peace to work out their own destinies in their own way: Now, therefore, be it *Resolved by the Senate and House of Representatives of the United States of America in Congress assembled,* That the Congress approves and supports the determination of the President, as Commander in Chief, to take all necessary measures to repel any armed attack against the forces of the United States and to prevent further aggression.

SEC. 2. The United States regards as vital to its national interest and to world peace the maintenance of international peace and security in southeast Asia. Consonant with the Constitution of the United States and the Charter of the United Nations and in accordance with its obligations under the Southeast Asia Collective Defense Treaty, the United States is, therefore, prepared, as the President determines, to take all necessary steps, including the use of armed force, to assist any member or protocol state of the Southeast Asia Collective Defense Treaty requesting assistance in defense of its freedom.

U.S. Department of State *Bulletin,* 51 (August 24, 1964), 268.

SEC. 3. This resolution shall expire when the President shall determine that the peace and security of the area is reasonably assured by international conditions created by action of the United Nations or otherwise, except that it may be terminated earlier by concurrent resolution of the Congress.

4. Lyndon B. Johnson Explains Why Americans Fight in Vietnam, 1965

Why must this nation hazard its ease, its interest, and its power for the sake of a people so far away?

We fight because we must fight if we are to live in a world where every country can shape its own destiny, and only in such a world will our own freedom be finally secure.

This kind of world will never be built by bombs or bullets. Yet the infirmities of man are such that force must often precede reason and the waste of war, the works of peace.

We wish that this were not so. But we must deal with the world as it is, if it is ever to be as we wish.

The world as it is in Asia is not a serene or peaceful place.

The first reality is that North Viet-Nam has attacked the independent nation of South Viet-Nam. Its object is total conquest.

Of course, some of the people of South Viet-Nam are participating in attack on their own government. But trained men and supplies, orders and arms, flow in a constant stream from North to South.

This support is the heartbeat of the war.

And it is a war of unparalleled brutality. Simple farmers are the targets of assassination and kidnapping. Women and children are strangled in the night because their men are loyal to their government. And helpless villages are ravaged by sneak attacks. Large-scale raids are conducted on towns, and terror strikes in the heart of cities.

The confused nature of this conflict cannot mask the fact that it is the new face of an old enemy.

Over this war—and all Asia—is another reality: the deepening shadow of Communist China. The rulers in Hanoi are urged on by Peking. This is a regime which has destroyed freedom in Tibet, which has attacked India and has been condemned by the United Nations for aggression in Korea. It is a nation which is helping the forces of violence in almost every continent. The contest in Viet-Nam is part of a wider pattern of aggressive purposes.

Why are these realities our concern? Why are we in South Viet-Nam?

We are there because we have a promise to keep. Since 1954 every American President has offered support to the people of South Viet-Nam. We have helped to build, and we have helped to defend. Thus, over many years, we have made a national pledge to help South Viet-Nam defend its independence.

Public Papers of the Presidents: Lyndon B. Johnson, 1965, pp. 394–399.

And I intend to keep that promise.

To dishonor that pledge, to abandon this small and brave nation to its enemies, and to the terror that must follow, would be an unforgivable wrong.

We are also there to strengthen world order. Around the globe from Berlin to Thailand are people whose well being rests in part on the belief that they can count on us if they are attacked. To leave Viet-Nam to its fate would shake the confidence of all these people in the value of an American commitment and in the value of America's word. The result would be increased unrest and instability, and even wider war.

We are also there because there are great stakes in the balance. Let no one think for a moment that retreat from Viet-Nam would bring an end to conflict. The battle would be renewed in one country and then another. The central lesson of our time is that the appetite of aggression is never satisfied. To withdraw from one battlefield means only to prepare for the next. We must say in Southeast Asia—as we did in Europe—in the words of the Bible: "Hitherto shalt thou come, but no further."

There are those who say that all our effort there will be futile—that China's power is such that it is bound to dominate all Southeast Asia. But there is no end to that argument until all of the nations of Asia are swallowed up.

There are those who wonder why we have a responsibility there. Well, we have it there for the same reason that we have a responsibility for the defense of Europe. World War II was fought in both Europe and Asia and when it ended we found ourselves with continued responsibility for the defense of freedom.

Our objective is the independence of South Viet-Nam and its freedom from attack. We want nothing for ourselves—only that the people of South Viet-Nam be allowed to guide their own country in their own way.

We will do everything necessary to reach that objective and we will do only what is absolutely necessary.

In recent months attacks on South Viet-Nam were stepped up. Thus, it became necessary for us to increase our response and to make attacks by air. This is not a change of purpose. It is a change in what we believe that purpose requires.

We do this in order to slow down aggression.

We do this to increase the confidence of the brave people of South Viet-Nam who have bravely borne this brutal battle for so many years with so many casualties.

And we do this to convince the leaders of North Viet-Nam—and all who seek to share their conquest—of a simple fact:

We will not be defeated.

We will not grow tired.

We will not withdraw, either openly or under the cloak of a meaningless agreement.

We know that air attacks alone will not accomplish all of these purposes. But it is our best and prayerful judgment that they are a necessary part of the surest road to peace.

We hope that peace will come swiftly. But that is in the hands of others besides ourselves. And we must be prepared for a long continued conflict. It will require patience as well as bravery—the will to endure as well as the will to resist.

I wish it were possible to convince others with words of what we now find it necessary to say with guns and planes: armed hostility is futile—our resources are equal to any challenge—because we fight for values and we fight for principle, rather than territory or colonies, our patience and our determination are unending.

Once this is clear, then it should also be clear that the only path for reasonable men is the path of peaceful settlement. . . .

These countries of Southeast Asia are homes for millions of impoverished people. Each day these people rise at dawn and struggle through until the night to wrestle existence from the soil. They are often wracked by diseases, plagued by hunger, and death comes at the early age of forty.

Stability and peace do not come easily in such a land. Neither independence nor human dignity will ever be won though by arms alone. It also requires the works of peace. The American people have helped generously in times past in these works, and now there must be a much more massive effort to improve the life of man in that conflict-torn corner of our world.

The first step is for the countries of Southeast Asia to associate themselves in a greatly expanded co-operative effort for development. We would hope that North Viet-Nam would take its place in the common effort just as soon as peaceful co-operation is possible.

The United Nations is already actively engaged in development in this area, and as far back as 1961 I conferred with our authorities in Viet-Nam in connection with their work there. And I would hope tonight that the Secretary General of the United Nations could use the prestige of his great office and his deep knowledge of Asia to initiate, as soon as possible, with the countries of that area, a plan for co-operation in increased development.

For our part I will ask the Congress to join in a billion dollar American investment in this effort as soon as it is underway.

And I would hope that all other industrialized countries, including the Soviet Union, will join in this effort to replace despair with hope and terror with progress.

The task is nothing less than to enrich the hopes and existence of more than a hundred million people. And there is much to be done.

The vast Mekong River can provide food and water and power on a scale to dwarf even our own T.V.A.

The wonders of modern medicine can be spread through villages where thousands die every year from lack of care.

Schools can be established to train people in the skills needed to manage the process of development.

And these objectives, and more, are within the reach of a cooperative and determined effort.

I also intend to expand and speed up a program to make available our farm surpluses to assist in feeding and clothing the needy in Asia. We should not allow people to go hungry and wear rags while our own warehouses overflow with an abundance of wheat and corn and rice and cotton.

So I will very shortly name a special team of outstanding, patriotic, and distinguished Americans to inaugurate our participation in these programs. This team will be headed by Mr. Eugene Black, the very able former president of the World Bank.

This will be a disorderly planet for a long time. In Asia, and elsewhere, the forces of the modern world are shaking old ways and uprooting ancient civilizations.

There will be turbulence and struggle and even violence. Great social change—as we see in our own country—does not always come without conflict.

We must also expect that nations will on occasion be in dispute with us. It may be because we are rich, or powerful, or because we have made some mistakes, or because they honestly fear our intentions. However, no nation need ever fear that we desire their land, or to impose our will, or to dictate their institutions.

But we will always oppose the effort of one nation to conquer another nation. We will do this because our own security is at stake.

But there is more to it than that. For our generation has a dream. It is a very old dream. But we have the power, and now we have the opportunity to make that dream come true.

For centuries nations have struggled among each other. But we dream of a world where disputes are settled by law and reason. And we will try to make it so.

For most of history men have hated and killed one another in battle. But we dream of an end to war. And we will try to make it so.

For all existence most men have lived in poverty, threatened by hunger. But we dream of a world where all are fed and charged with hope. And we will help to make it so.

5. Robert S. McNamara Recommends Escalation, 1965

Introduction

Our objective is to create conditions for a favorable settlement by demonstrating to the VC/DRV that the odds are against their winning. Under present conditions, however, the chances of achieving this objective are small—and the VC are winning now—largely because the ratio of guerrilla to anti-guerrilla forces is unfavorable to the government. With this in mind, we must choose among three courses of action with respect to South Vietnam: (1) Cut our losses and withdraw under the best conditions that can be arranged; (2) continue at about the present level, with US forces limited to, say, 75,000, holding on and playing for the breaks while recognizing that our position will probably grow weaker; or (3) expand substantially the US military pressure against the Viet Cong in the South and the North Vietnamese in the North and at the same time launch a vigorous effort on the political side to get negotiations started. An outline of the third of these approaches follows.

I. Expanded Military Moves

The following military moves should be taken together with the political initiatives in Part II below.

A. Inside South Vietnam. Increase US/SVN military strength in SVN enough to prove to the VC that they cannot win and thus to turn the tide of the war. . . .

McNamara Memo to Johnson, June 26, 1965, *Foreign Relations of the United States,* 1964–1968, III, 97–104.

B. Against North Vietnam. While avoiding striking population and industrial targets not closely related to the DRV's supply of war material to the VC, we should announce to Hanoi and carry out actions to destroy such supplies and to interdict their flow into and out of North Vietnam. . . .

II. Expanded Political Moves

Together with the above military moves, we should take the following political initiatives in order (a) to open a dialogue with Hanoi, Peking, and the VC looking toward a settlement in Vietnam, (b) to keep the Soviet Union from deepening its military involvement and support of North Vietnam until the time when settlement can be achieved, and (c) to cement the support for US policy by the US public, allies and friends, and to keep international opposition at a manageable level. While our approaches may be rebuffed until the tide begins to turn, they nevertheless should be made. . . .

III. Evaluation of the Above Program

A. Domestic US Reaction. Even though casualties will increase and the war will continue for some time, the United States public will support this course of action because it is a combined military-political program designed and likely to bring about a favorable solution to the Vietnam problem.

B. Communist Reaction to the Expanded Programs.

1. *Soviet.* The Soviets can be expected to continue to contribute material and advisors to the North Vietnamese. Increased US bombing of Vietnam, including targets in Hanoi and Haiphong, SAM [surface-to-air missile] sites and airfields, and mining of North Vietnamese harbors, might oblige the Soviet Union to enter the contest more actively with volunteers and aircraft. This might result in minor encounters between US and Soviet personnel.

2. *China.* So long as no US or GVN troops invade North Vietnam and so long as no US or GVN aircraft attack Chinese territory, the Chinese probably will not send regular ground forces or aircraft into the war. However, the possibility of a more active Soviet involvement in North Vietnam might precipitate a Chinese introduction of land forces, probably dubbed volunteers, to preclude the Soviets' taking a pre-eminent position in North Vietnam.

3. *North Vietnam.* North Vietnam will not move towards the negotiating table until the tide begins to turn in the south. When that happens, they may seek to counter it by sending large numbers of men into South Vietnam.

4. *Viet Cong.* The VC, especially if they continue to take high losses, can be expected to depend increasingly upon the PAVN [People's Army of Vietnam, regular forces of North Vietnam] forces as the war moves into a more conventional phase; but they may find ways of continuing almost indefinitely their present intensive military, guerrilla and terror activities, particularly if reinforced with some regular PAVN units. A key question on the military side is whether POL [petroleum-oil-lubricants], ammunition, and cadres can be cut off and if they are cut off whether

this really renders the Viet Cong impotent. A key question on the political side is whether any arrangement acceptable to us would be acceptable to the VC.

C. Estimate of Success.

1. *Militarily.* The success of the above program from a military point of view turns on whether the increased effort stems the tide in the South; that in turn depends on two things—on whether the South Vietnamese hold their own in terms of numbers and fighting spirit, and on whether the US forces can be effective in a quick-reaction reserve role, a role in which they have not been tested. The number of US troops is too small to make a significant difference in the traditional 10–1 government-guerrilla formula, but it is not too small to make a significant difference in the kind of war which seems to be evolving in Vietnam—a "Third Stage" or conventional war in which it is easier to identify, locate and attack the enemy. (South Vietnam has 141 battalions as compared with an estimated equivalent number of VC battalions. The 44 US/3d country battalions mentioned above are the equivalent of 100 South Vietnamese battalions.)

2. *Politically.* It is frequently alleged that such a large expansion of US military personnel, their expanded military role (which would put them in close contact and offer some degree of control over South Vietnamese citizens), and the inevitable expansion of US voice in the operation of the GVN economy and facilities, command and government services will be unpopular; it is said that they could lead to the rejection of the government which supported this American presence, to an irresistible pressure for expulsion of the Americans, and to the greatly increased saleability of Communist propaganda. Whether these allegations are true, we do not know.

The political initiatives are likely to be successful in the early stages only to demonstrate US good faith; they will pay off toward an actual settlement only after the tide begins to turn (unless we lower our sights substantially). The tide almost certainly cannot begin to turn in less than a few months, and may not for a year or more; the war is one of attrition and will be a long one. Since troops once committed as a practical matter cannot be removed, since US casualties will rise, since we should take call-up actions to support the additional forces in Vietnam, the test of endurance may be as much in the United States as in Vietnam.

3. *Generally (CIA estimate).* Over the longer term we doubt if the Communists are likely to change their basic strategy in Vietnam (i.e., aggressive and steadily mounting insurgency) unless and until two conditions prevail: (1) they are forced to accept a situation in the war in the South which offers them no prospect of an early victory and no grounds for hope that they can simply outlast the US and (2) North Vietnam itself is under continuing and increasingly damaging punitive attack. So long as the Communists think they scent the possibility of an early victory (which is probably now the case), we believe that they will persevere and accept extremely severe damage to the North. Conversely, if North Vietnam itself is not hurting, Hanoi's doctrinaire leaders will probably be ready to carry on the Southern struggle almost indefinitely. If, however, both of the conditions outlined above should be brought to pass, we believe Hanoi probably would, at least for a period of time, alter its basic strategy and course of action in South Vietnam.

Hanoi might do so in several ways. Going for a conference as a political way of gaining a respite from attack would be one. Alternatively it might reduce the level of insurgent activity in the hopes that this would force the US to stop its punishment of the North but not prevent the US and GVN from remaining subject to wearying harassment in the South. Or, Hanoi might order the VC to suspend operations in the hopes that in a period of temporary tranquillity, domestic and international opinion would force the US to disengage without destroying the VC apparatus or the roots of VC strength. Finally, Hanoi might decide that the US/GVN will to fight could still be broken and the tide of war turned back again in favor of the VC by launching a massive PAVN assault on the South. This is a less likely option in the circumstances we have posited, but still a contingency for which the US must be prepared.

6. George Ball Dissents, 1965

1. *A Losing War:* The South Vietnamese are losing the war to the Viet Cong. No one can assure you that we can beat the Viet Cong or even force them to the conference table on our terms, no matter how many hundred thousand *white, foreign* (U.S.) troops we deploy.

No one has demonstrated that a white ground force of whatever size can win a guerrilla war—which is at the same time a civil war between Asians—in jungle terrain in the midst of a population that refuses cooperation to the white forces (and the South Vietnamese) and thus provides a great intelligence advantage to the other side. Three recent incidents vividly illustrate this point: (a) the sneak attack on the Da Nang Air Base which involved penetration of a defense perimeter guarded by 9,000 Marines. This raid was possible only because of the cooperation of the local inhabitants; (b) the B-52 raid that failed to hit the Viet Cong who had obviously been tipped off; (c) the search and destroy mission of the 173rd Air Borne Brigade which spent three days looking for the Viet Cong, suffered 23 casualties, and never made contact with the enemy who had obviously gotten advance word of their assignment.

2. *The Question to Decide:* Should we limit our liabilities in South Vietnam and try to find a way out with minimal long-term costs? The alternative—no matter what we may wish it to be—is almost certainly a protracted war involving an open-ended commitment of U.S. forces, mounting U.S. casualties, no assurance of a satisfactory solution, and a serious danger of escalation at the end of the road.

3. *Need for a Decision Now:* So long as our forces are restricted to advising and assisting the South Vietnamese, the struggle will remain a civil war between Asian peoples. Once we deploy substantial numbers of troops in combat it will become a war between the U.S. and a large part of the population of South Vietnam, organized and directed from North Vietnam and backed by the resources of both Moscow and Peiping.

The decision you face now, therefore, is crucial. Once large numbers of U.S. troops are committed to direct combat, they will begin to take heavy casualties in a war they are ill-equipped to fight in a non-cooperative if not downright hostile countryside.

Ball memo, July 1, 1965, *Foreign Relations of the United States,* 1964–1968, III, 106–109.

Once we suffer large casualties, we will have started a well-nigh irreversible process. Our involvement will be so great that we cannot—without national humiliation—stop short of achieving our complete objectives. *Of the two possibilities I think humiliation would be more likely than the achievement of our objectives—even after we have paid terrible costs.*

4. *Compromise Solution:* Should we commit U.S. manpower and prestige to a terrain so unfavorable as to give a very large advantage to the enemy—or should we seek a compromise settlement which achieves less than our stated objectives and thus cut our losses while we still have the freedom of maneuver to do so.

5. *Costs of a Compromise Solution:* The answer involves a judgment as to the cost to the U.S. of such a compromise settlement in terms of our relations with the countries in the area of South Vietnam, the credibility of our commitments, and our prestige around the world. In my judgment, if we act before we commit substantial U.S. troops to combat in South Vietnam we can, by accepting some short-term costs, avoid what may well be a long-term catastrophe. I believe we tended grossly to exaggerate the costs involved in a compromise settlement. An appreciation of probable costs is contained in the attached memorandum.

6. With these considerations in mind, I strongly urge the following program:

a.   Military Program

1. Complete all deployment already announced—15 battalions—but decide not to go beyond a total of 72,000 men represented by this figure.
2. Restrict the combat role of the American forces to the June 19 announcement, making it clear to General Westmoreland that this announcement is to be strictly construed.
3. Continue bombing in the North but avoid the Hanoi-Haiphong area and any targets nearer to the Chinese border than those already struck.

b.   Political Program

1. In any political approaches so far, we have been the prisoners of whatever South Vietnamese government that was momentarily in power. If we are ever to move toward a settlement. it will probably be because the South Vietnamese government pulls the rug out from under us and makes its own deal *or* because we go forward quietly without advance prearrangement with Saigon.
2. So far we have not given the other side a reason to believe there is *any* flexibility in our negotiating approach. And the other side has been unwilling to accept what *in their terms* is complete capitulation.
3. Now is the time to start some serious diplomatic feelers looking toward a solution based on some application of a self-determination principle.
4. I would recommend approaching Hanoi rather than any of the other probable parties, the NLF, Moscow or Peiping. Hanoi is the only one that has given any signs of interest in discussion. Peiping has been rigidly opposed. Moscow has recommended that we negotiate with Hanoi. The NLF has been silent.
5. There are several channels to the North Vietnamese, but I think the best one is through their representative in Paris, Mai Van Bo. Initial feelers of Bo should be directed toward a discussion both of the four points we have put forward and the four points put forward by Hanoi as a basis for negotiation. We can accept

all but one of Hanoi's four points. and hopefully we should be able to agree on some ground rules for serious negotiations—including no preconditions.

6. If the initial feelers lead to further secret, exploratory talks, we can inject the concept of self-determination that would permit the Viet Cong some hope of achieving some of their political objectives through local elections or some other device.

7. The contact on our side should be handled through a non-governmental cutout (possibly a reliable newspaper man who can be repudiated).

8. If progress can be made at this level a basis can be laid for a multinational conference. At some point, obviously, the government of South Vietnam will have to be brought on board, but I would postpone this step until after a substantial feeling out of Hanoi.

9. Before moving to any formal conference we should be prepared to agree once the conference is started:

   a.   The U.S. will stand down its bombing of the North
   b.   The South Vietnamese will initiate no offensive operations in the South, and
   c.   The DRV will stop terrorism and other aggressive action against the South.

10. The negotiations at the conference should aim at incorporating our understanding with Hanoi in the form of a multinational agreement guaranteed by the U.S., the Soviet Union and possibly other parties, and providing for an international mechanism to supervise its execution.

7. Johnson Recalls His Decision to Commit Troops (1965), 1971

We discussed Ball's approach for a long time and in great detail. I think all of us felt the same concerns and anxieties that Ball had expressed, but most of these men in the Cabinet Room were more worried about the results, in our country and throughout the world, of our pulling out and coming home. I felt the Under Secretary had not produced a sufficiently convincing case or a viable alternative.

Dean Rusk expressed one worry that was much on my mind. It lay at the heart of our Vietnam policy. "If the Communist world finds out that we will not pursue our commitments to the end," he said, "I don't know where they will stay their hand."

I felt sure they would *not* stay their hand. If we ran out on Southeast Asia, I could see trouble ahead in every part of the globe—not just in Asia but in the Middle East and in Europe, in Africa and in Latin America. I was convinced that our retreat from this challenge would open the path to World War III.

Our consultations had only begun. I met the next day with the Joint Chiefs of Staff and the Secretaries of the military services. In the afternoon I met again for nearly an hour and a half with Rusk, McNamara, Ball, General Wheeler, Bundy, and several civilian advisers, including Clark Clifford, John McCloy, and Arthur Dean.

Later that day I went up to Camp David to reflect. I invited several advisers to join me there for further long discussions on Sunday, July 25.

Secretary McNamara, Ambassador to the United Nations Arthur Goldberg, and Clark Clifford, then Chairman of the President's Foreign Intelligence Advisory Board, joined me in the Aspen Lodge at Camp David in the afternoon. One of the things we wanted to discuss was whether we should take any action in the United Nations in connection with Vietnam. The weight of opinion was against a major effort to persuade the United Nations to act at that time. Most of my advisers felt that the leaders in Hanoi would turn down any UN proposal, because they had consistently declared that Vietnam was not a proper matter for UN involvement. Moreover, it was virtually certain that the Soviet Union would veto any proposal Hanoi might have trouble accepting.

At this session my old friend Clark Clifford was in a reflective and pessimistic mood. "1 don't believe we can win in South Vietnam," he said. "If we send in 100,000 more men, the North Vietnamese will meet us. If North Vietnam runs out of men, the Chinese will send in volunteers. Russia and China don't intend for us to win the war."

He urged that in the coming months we quietly probe possibilities with other countries for some way to get out honorably. "1 can't see anything but catastrophe for my country," he said.

I told Clifford that he was expressing worries that many Americans, including the President, were experiencing. No one was more concerned than I was, but we could not simply walk out. Nor was I prepared to accept just any settlement as a cover-up for surrender. What we needed was a way to start real negotiations and I intended to keep pressing our offer to talk peace.

We continued our review of the military situation and the requirement for additional forces. Our military commanders had refined their estimates and indicated they could meet the immediate demand with 50,000 men. I called a meeting of the National Security Council two days later, on July 27. I asked McNamara at that time to summarize again the current need as he saw it.

McNamara noted that the Viet Cong had increased in size through local recruitment and replacements from the North. Regular North Vietnamese army units had increased in number and strength. Communist control of the countryside was growing. A dozen provincial capitals were virtually isolated from surrounding rural areas. The South Vietnamese army was growing, but not nearly fast enough to keep pace with the expanding enemy forces. Without additional armed strength, South Vietnam would inevitably fall to Hanoi. I told the NSC there were five possible choices available to us.

"We can bring the enemy to his knees by using our Strategic Air Command," I said, describing our first option. "Another group thinks we ought to pack up and go home."

"Third, we could stay there as we are—and suffer the consequences, continue to lose territory and take casualties. You wouldn't want your own boy to be out there crying for help and not get it."

"Then, we could go to Congress and ask for great sums of money; we could call up the reserves and increase the draft; go on a war footing; declare a state of emergency. There is a good deal of feeling that ought to be done. We have considered this. But if we go into that kind of land war, then North Vietnam would go to its friends, China and Russia, and ask them to give help. They would be forced into increasing aid. For that reason I don't want to be overly dramatic and cause tensions. I think we can get our people to support us without having to be too provocative and warlike.

"Finally, we can give our commanders in the field the men and supplies they say they need."

I had concluded that the last course was the right one. I had listened to and weighed all the arguments and counterarguments for each of the possible lines of action. I believed that we should do what was necessary to resist aggression but that we should not be provoked into a major war. We would get the required appropriation in the new budget, and we would not boast about what we were doing, We would not make threatening noises to the Chinese or the Russians by calling up reserves in large numbers. At the same time, we would press hard on the diplomatic front to try to find some path to a peaceful settlement.

I asked if anyone objected to the course of action I had spelled out. I questioned each man in turn. Did he agree? Each nodded his approval or said "yes." . . .

There was more to it than listening to the arguments and dissents, the explanations and justifications of my wisest advisers in and out of government. When a President faces a decision involving war or peace, he draws back and thinks of the past and of the future in the widest possible terms. On his sworn oath, a President pledges he will protect the nation. The security of the whole country is the foremost responsibility of the Chief Executive. The most important question I had to face was: How will the decisions we make in Vietnam or elsewhere affect the security and the future of our nation?

A President searches his mind and his heart for the answers, so that when he decides on a course of action it is in the long-range best interests of the country, its people, and its security.

That is what I did—when I was alone and sleepless at night in the Executive Mansion, away from official cables and advisers; when I sat alone in the Aspen Lodge at Camp David; when I walked along the banks of the Pedernales River or looked out over the Texas hill country. In those lonely vigils I tried to think through what would happen to our nation and to the world if we did not act with courage and stamina—if we let South Vietnam fall to Hanoi.

This is what I could foresee: First, from all the evidence available to me it seemed likely that all of Southeast Asia would pass under Communist control, slowly or quickly, but inevitably, at least down to Singapore but almost certainly to Djakarta. I realize that some Americans believe they have, through talking with one another, repealed the domino theory. In 1965 there was no indication in Asia, or from Asians, that this was so. On both sides of the line between Communist and non-Communist Asia the struggle for Vietnam and Laos was regarded as a struggle for the fate of Southeast Asia. The evidence before me as President confirmed the previous assessments of President Eisenhower and of President Kennedy.

Second, I knew our people well enough to realize that if we walked away from Vietnam and let Southeast Asia fall, there would follow a divisive and destructive debate in our country. This had happened when the Communists took power in China. But that was very different from the Vietnam conflict. We had a solemn treaty commitment to Southeast Asia. We had an international agreement on Laos made as late as 1962 that was being violated flagrantly. We had the word of three Presidents that the United States would not permit this aggression to succeed. A divisive debate about "who lost Vietnam" would be, in my judgment, even more destructive to our national life than the argument over China had been. It would inevitably increase isolationist pressures from the right and the left and cause a pulling back from our commitments in Europe and the Middle East as well as in Asia.

Third, our allies not just in Asia but throughout the world would conclude that our word was worth little or nothing. Those who had counted so long for their security on American commitments would be deeply shaken and vulnerable.

Fourth, knowing what I did of the policies and actions of Moscow and Peking, I was as sure as a man could be that if we did not live up to our commitment in Southeast Asia and elsewhere, they would move to exploit the disarray in the United States and in the alliances of the Free World. They might move independently or they might move together. But move they would—whether through nuclear blackmail, through subversion, with regular armed forces, or in some other manner. As nearly as one can be certain of anything, I knew they could not resist the opportunity to expand their control into the vacuum of power we would leave behind us.

Finally, as we faced the implications of what we had done as a nation, I was sure the United States would not then passively submit to the consequences. With Moscow and Peking and perhaps others moving forward, we would return to a world role to prevent their full takeover of Europe, Asia, and the Middle East—*after* they had committed themselves.

8. Philip Caputo Remembers His Idealism (1965), 1977

On March 8, 1965, as a young infantry officer, I landed at Danang with a battalion of the 9th Marine Expeditionary Brigade, the first U.S. combat unit sent to Indochina.

For Americans who did not come of age in the early sixties, it may be hard to grasp what those years were like—the pride and overpowering self-assurance that prevailed. Most of the thirty-five hundred men in our brigade, born during or immediately after World War II, were shaped by that era, the age of Kennedy's Camelot. We went overseas full of illusions, for which the intoxicating atmosphere of those years was as much to blame as our youth.

War is always attractive to young men who know nothing about it, but we had also been seduced into uniform by Kennedy's challenge to "ask what you can do for your country" and by the missionary idealism he had awakened in us. America seemed omnipotent then: the country could still claim it had never lost a war, and we believed we were ordained to play cop to the Communists' robber and spread our own political faith around the world. Like the French soldiers of the late eighteenth century, we saw ourselves as the champions of "a cause that was destined to triumph." So, when we marched into the rice paddies on that damp March afternoon,

---

we carried, along with our packs and rifles, the implicit convictions that the Viet Cong would be quickly beaten and that we were doing something altogether noble and good. We kept the packs and rifles; the convictions, we lost.

The discovery that the men we had scorned as peasant guerrillas were, in fact, a lethal, determined enemy and the casualty lists that lengthened each week with nothing to show for the blood being spilled broke our early confidence. By autumn, what had begun as an adventurous expedition had turned into an exhausting, indecisive war of attrition in which we fought for no cause other than our own survival.

✗ *E S S A Y S*

In the opening essay, Robert Dallek, a professor of history at Boston University and author of an acclaimed two-volume biography of Johnson, traces the steps by which LBJ brought the United States into open conflict in Vietnam. A combination of international, domestic, and personal factors led Johnson to overcome his initial ambivalence about deeper U.S. involvement. The president worried, Dallek notes, that failure in Vietnam might derail his ambitious domestic reform agenda and even ruin his presidency. The intensely competitive Johnson's lifelong compulsion to dominate and to win also played an important role in his decision to inaugurate a sustained bombing campaign and to dispatch U.S. ground forces.

In the next selection, Fredrik Logevall of the University of California, Santa Barbara, argues that Johnson and his top advisers consciously *chose* war in early 1965 in the face of deep skepticism among key sectors of domestic opinion and leading allies. Logevall emphasizes that the marked fluidity in domestic and international opinion during the critical 1963–1965 period made the Americanization of the Vietnam War both unnecessary and avoidable. Johnson's refusal to consider seriously alternatives to war stemmed, he suggests, from the president's obsession with the nation's, and his own personal, credibility. This selection is drawn from Logevall's prize-winning book, *Choosing War.*

Fear, Ambition, and Politics

ROBERT DALLEK

The Gulf of Tonkin Resolution in August 1964 gave Johnson a temporary respite from unpleasant choices in Vietnam. Having hit back at the North Vietnamese and having rallied Congress and the country behind a promise not to abandon South Vietnam, he wished to mute discussion about Southeast Asia. But he knew the problem would not go away. On August 10, he told national security advisers that the next challenge from Hanoi, which he expected soon, would have to be met with firmness. He had no intention of escalating the conflict "just because the public liked what happened last week," he said. But he wanted planning that would allow us to choose the grounds for the next confrontation and get maximum results with minimum danger.

Still, he wanted no significant change in policy before the November election. Having "stood up" to Communist aggression, he now wished to sound a moderate note. In speeches during the campaign, he emphasized giving Vietnam limited help: He would "not permit the independent nations of the East to be swallowed up by Communist conquest," but it would not mean sending " American boys 9 or 10,000 miles away from home to do what Asian boys ought to be doing for themselves."

Coups and counter coups in Saigon during August and September made it difficult for Johnson to hold to his word. Under Secretary George Ball told James Reston on August 29 that things were "very serious" in Saigon, and substantial doubts existed about the future "authority and stability" of the central government. On the 31st, Mac Bundy advised Johnson that the situation in Saigon "could hardly be more serious."

Contingency plans for limited escalation—"naval harassments, air interdiction in the Laos panhandle, and possible U.S. fleet movements"—were being considered as ways "to heighten morale and to show our strength of purpose." Thoughts were also being given to setting up a U.S. naval base in South Vietnam or sending in a limited number of Marines to guard installations. Bundy himself proposed the "more drastic possibility which no one is discussing" of using "substantial U.S. armed forces in operations against the Viet Cong. . . . Before we let this country go we should have a hard look at this grim alternative, and I do not at all think that it is a repetition of Korea."

In early September, Pentagon and State Department planners settled on steps to bolster Saigon and deter Hanoi. They included additional U.S. naval patrols in international waters, South Vietnamese operations along the coast of North Vietnam and in the air over Laos, and responses to Communist attacks on U.S. forces and to "any special DRV/VC action against SVN." The planners also discussed deliberately provoking Hanoi into a clash that would allow the United States to relieve Communist pressure on Saigon.

At a meeting on September 9 with national security advisers, Johnson anguished over what to do. First, he wanted to discuss stronger actions than those proposed by the planners. Vietnam Ambassador Maxwell Taylor, CIA Chief John McCone, and Secretary of State Dean Rusk argued against doing more than recommended. "Rusk said that a major decision to go North could be taken at any time—'at 5 minutes' notice.'" Johnson agreed, saying that attacks against the North should wait until "our side could defend itself in the streets of Saigon." He didn't "wish to enter the patient in a 10-round bout, when he was in no shape to hold out for one round. We should get him ready to face 3 or 4 rounds at least."

Johnson then questioned the value of staying in Vietnam. Taylor, Rusk, McCone, and Chairman of the Joint Chiefs Earle C. Wheeler repeated the now familiar case for holding fast. A retreat would undermine our overall position in the area and the world. Losing South Vietnam would mean losing Southeast Asia. Communist China would dominate the region. In sum, retreat was unthinkable. Johnson concurred. He declared his readiness "to do more, when we had a base" or when Saigon was politically more stable.

Johnson was not happy about his choices in Vietnam. None of them seemed quite right. His only certainty in the summer of 1964 was that election politics dictated an image of himself as a firm but cautious defender of the national security. At a background meeting with the press in mid-September, he restated his determination to sustain the Eisenhower-Kennedy policies of providing measured support for Vietnam while avoiding another Korea. But privately he worried about involvement in an unpredictable struggle, a conflict that might require greater commitments than he wished to make. He had a sense of foreboding about Vietnam—a feeling that no matter what he did things might end badly. . . .

But Johnson still refused to commit himself. "I am not giving any orders at all in this message," he told Taylor. He was betwixt and between. He didn't really care much about Vietnam per se. To him, it was a remote, backward place dominated by squabbling factions unresponsive to political reason. Few there seemed to understand the great American traditions of compromise and consensus, of getting on with business by accommodating to political, economic, social, and military realities.

In December, Mike Mansfield wrote Johnson that we were on a course in Vietnam "which takes us further and further out on a sagging limb." In time, he predicted, we could find ourselves saddled with "enormous burdens in Cambodia, Laos, and elsewhere in Asia, along with those in Viet Nam." In reply, Johnson said: "I think we have the same basic view of this problem, and the same sense of its difficulties." He objected, however, to Mansfield's suggestion that "we are 'overcommitted' there. Given the size of the stake, it seems to me that we are doing only what we have to do."

During a conversation in December with columnist Walter Lippmann, who was advocating a negotiated U.S. withdrawal from an unwinnable struggle, Johnson complained that he was not eager for American involvement, "but this is a commitment I inherited. I don't like it, but how can I pull out?" Lippmann repeated what de Gaulle had told him; Even with a million Americans in Vietnam, a lasting military victory would be impossible.

De Gaulle's opinion carried little weight with LBJ. However strong his reservations about expanded U.S. involvement in Vietnam, French defeat and judgments did not add greatly to them. In Johnson's view, a powerful anti-imperialist America was not like a divided France, which had tried to preserve colonial rule in Saigon. America's involvement in Vietnam was a defense of the free world against Communist advance, not an exercise in outdated imperialism.

In the winter of 1964–65, Johnson felt pressured much more by hawks than doves. He complained to some liberals "that all the [military] chiefs did was come in every morning and tell him, 'Bomb, bomb, bomb,' and then come back in the afternoon and tell him again, 'Bomb, bomb, bomb.'" His principal advisers also favored using force to resist a Communist takeover in South Vietnam. To be sure, they argued about the means and timing of attacks on the North Vietnamese and Viet Cong, but they believed it had to be done. Moreover, though polls revealed no well-defined majority in favor of escalation, a substantial plurality supported military action against the Communists, with only between 26 percent and 30 percent opposed.

Joe Alsop and conservatives in Congress also urged stronger measures. In December 1964, Alsop staged a one-man campaign to force Johnson's hand. In a column on December 23, he described Americans in Saigon as convinced that the President was "consciously prepared to accept defeat here." And if it occurred, it would "be his defeat as well as a defeat for the American people." In another column on the 30th, Alsop compared LBJ to JFK in the Cuban missile crisis. "If Mr. Johnson ducks the challenge [in Vietnam] we shall learn by experience about what it would have been like if Kennedy had ducked the challenge in October 1962."

The suggestion that he lacked Kennedy's guts and strength enraged Johnson. He was also incensed at congressional conservatives, who saw a larger military effort in Vietnam as not only an essential response to the Communist threat but also a way to derail Great Society reforms. Or so Johnson believed. He said that conservatives intended "to use this war as a way of opposing my Great Society legislation. . . . They hate this stuff, they don't want to help the poor and the Negroes but they're afraid to be against it at a time like this when there's been all this prosperity. But the war, oh, they'll like the war."

Yet whatever his irritation with Alsop and conservatives, Johnson also shared their concern about not losing Vietnam. He was much a believer in the need to stand up to the Communist threat as anyone in America. Throughout the Cold War he had consistently backed strong Truman, Eisenhower, and Kennedy actions against Communism. Nor, as President, was he loath to follow in their footsteps. Remembering Munich, he saw weakness overseas as leading to World War III. Moreover, if he held his hand and South Vietnam fell, it could work havoc with his political influence and power to achieve domestic advance. A new Joe McCarthy might come on the scene to pose rhetorical questions about how Vietnam had been lost.

Still, in the closing days of 1964, despite his national security and domestic political concerns, Johnson had doubts that restrained him from more decisive action. Would the country be better served by throwing itself into a possibly unwinnable fight or by delaying defeat, holding back from full-scale involvement, and using our resources to meet the Communist threat on more manageable ground? John Corson, a Johnson friend from NYA [National Youth Administration] days and the head of a task force on income maintenance, remembers a White House meeting of task force chairmen at this time. "The most impressive thing of the evening" was the President's discussion of Vietnam, which lasted between one and two hours, "and his seeming involvement in Vietnam to the exclusion of almost everything else." Johnson said: "I've tried this to get out of Vietnam; I've tried that; I've tried everything I can think of. What can I do next?"

With still no clear answers to his question, Johnson followed his political instincts. When confronted by sharp divisions of opinion throughout his career, he had almost always adopted a moderate position, identifying himself as an accommodationist who reflected the national desire for compromise rather than ideological rigidity. Since abandoning Vietnam seemed unthinkable and since public and congressional support for a full-scale conflict seemed unlikely to outlast substantial human and material costs, he chose measured increases in U.S. military action with continuing efforts to negotiate a settlement.

Achieving his goals depended on unlikely developments: unity among the South Vietnamese, North Vietnamese acceptance of Saigon's autonomy, and American acceptance of an open-ended limited war. But Johnson prided himself on being a can-do leader, the man who had made extraordinary breakthroughs on civil rights, had won a landmark electoral victory, and now confidently expected to enact bold domestic reforms that had eluded predecessors, including FDR. Against this backdrop, compelling an acceptable settlement in Vietnam did not seem out of reach. . . .

He sent [McGeorge] Bundy to Vietnam to discuss ways to help stabilize South Vietnam. He also agreed to a resumption in early February of an American naval patrol in the Tonkin Gulf. It would demonstrate U.S. resolve and might provoke a

North Vietnamese attack, which could then become the basis for U.S. retaliation. After hearing the news, Taylor cabled Washington: A North Vietnamese attack "followed by immediate strong and effective U.S. retaliation would offer a priceless advantage to our cause here."

Johnson's commitment represented a striking shift in judgment. His concern about having a stable regime in the South before attacking the North gave way to the hope that increased pressure on Hanoi could somehow bolster Saigon. Johnson had no evidence to support his altered assumption. But fear that a pro-Western South Vietnam would become first a neutralist and then a Communist regime drove him to expand American efforts to defend Saigon.

After a three-day visit to South Vietnam at the beginning of February, Mac Bundy confirmed Johnson's belief that "without new U.S. action defeat appears inevitable." Bundy also told him that "there is still time to turn it around" and that U.S. action would have the effect of blunting "the charge that we did not do all that we could have done, and this charge will be important in many countries, including our own." By fighting in Vietnam, "it should . . . somewhat increase our ability to deter such adventures" elsewhere.

Bundy's views reflected prevailing ideas in Washington. On February 6, after the Viet Cong killed eight U.S. advisers and wounded dozens of others in an attack on an American base at Pleiku in the central highlands, Johnson decided to retaliate. In a National Security Council meeting that included congressional leaders, he announced plans for an air attack against army barracks in southern North Vietnam.

When he asked for judgments on his decision, only Mike Mansfield, urging negotiation, dissented. Johnson's reply, according to Bill Bundy, was "terse and quite biting." Johnson remembered himself saying: "They are killing our men while they sleep in the night. I can't ask our American soldiers out there to continue to fight with one hand tied behind their backs." He believed that the air strike would show North Vietnam that it "could not count on continued immunity if they persisted in aggression in the South." Johnson also asserted that neither the Soviets nor the Chinese "wanted directed involvement" in the fighting, and would not intervene.

This retaliatory attack did not signal the beginning of a sustained air war against North Vietnam. When McNamara reported that weather conditions had allowed only one of four targets to be hit and that we would not stage a new raid to take out the other three, George Ball endorsed McNamara's recommendation, saying that to do otherwise would signal that we were "launching an offensive." The President agreed to McNamara's recommendation.

But on February 8, after reading Mac Bundy's report on his visit to Vietnam, Johnson decided on systematic bombing of the North. He would now order continuing air attacks. He wasn't happy about it; he wasn't even sure it was the right decision. But since abandoning Vietnam was unacceptable, his only alternative seemed to be forceful action. But he didn't want to make this evident to the Congress or the press or the public. . . .

"Rolling Thunder," as the sustained bombing campaign was named, was initiated on February 13, after the Joint Chiefs had identified a series of targets to be attacked during the next eight weeks. "We will execute a program of measured and limited air action jointly with GVN against selected military targets in DRV," the White House cabled Taylor. "We will announce this policy of measured action in general terms."

In fact, no public statement was issued. As columnist James Reston described it in the *New York Times* the following day, the United States had entered "an undeclared and unexplained war in Vietnam."

Johnson's refusal to make the expanded air war clear to the public partly rested on a concern not to distract Congress and the country from his reform agenda. But ambivalence about the policy also motivated him. The possibility that this was the beginning of ever larger commitments troubled him. Was this the start of something that would take on a life of its own and ultimately overwhelm him? Not going public with the bombing campaign was a form of denial; no announcement was a way not only to mute the reality of the fighting but also to keep it from gaining an importance Johnson did not wish it to have.

"He had no stomach for it," Mrs. Johnson told me, "no heart for it; it wasn't the war he wanted. The one he wanted was on poverty and ignorance and disease and that was worth putting your life into. . . . And yet every time you took it to the people, every time you said anything in a speech about civil rights your audience would begin to shift their feet and be restive and silent and maybe hostile. But then the moment you said something about defending liberty around the world—bear any burden—everybody would go to cheering." . . .

Even before the crisis in Santo Domingo intensified Johnson's desire for a long-term solution to the problem of South Vietnam, he had begun moving toward the only means he saw for rescuing the country from Communist control—great numbers of American ground troops who could inflict substantial losses on the Viet Cong and North Vietnamese regulars. His agreement at the beginning of April to broaden the mission of the Marines from strictly defensive to offensive operations and to plan for the introduction of two additional divisions had opened the way to the escalation of the land war. Between April 12 and 14 he advised U.S. senators that the aggressive use of American Marines in Vietnam was producing three times as many Communist casualties as before. If we were to sustain this and bring peace to the South, he would need to send Army forces.

On the 15th, Johnson approved the deployment of two Army brigades to guard bases in Vietnam. When Ambassador Taylor, who believed U.S. troops would be bogged down in an unwinnable land war, challenged the decision, Johnson suspended his order until advisers could evaluate the deployment at a Honolulu conference on April 20. On the 21st, McNamara reported that the Honolulu conferees had agreed not only to the need for two Army brigades but also three more Marine battalions and logistical troops to prepare for the two divisions. By the middle of June, the total of U.S. ground forces in Vietnam was to be 82,000, a 150 percent increase.

Only George Ball took exception to the proposal, and Johnson, who was ready to sign on to the escalation, gave Ball until the following morning to come up with "a settlement plan. If you can pull a rabbit out of the hat, I'm all for it!" the President said. Ball had no such magic at his command, and Johnson approved the additional troops.

As concerned as ever not to stir public debate, which could distract Congress from Great Society bills, Johnson hid his decision, preferring "to announce individual deployments at appropriate times." Yet the escalation was an open secret. On April 21, Hanson Baldwin, the military correspondent of the *New York Times,* published an account of the Honolulu recommendations and reported that U.S.

ground forces were shifting from defensive to offensive operations. Dean Rusk had tried and failed to squelch the *Times* story. Johnson complained that Rusk had been "too gentle" in trying to kill it.

Yet the President had no intention of unilaterally escalating the American ground effort in Vietnam. He believed it essential to have congressional support, but he wanted no debate that might distract Congress from domestic business and allow the Communists to see emerging divisions over his policy. Consequently, on May 2, in the midst of the Dominican crisis, he told congressional leaders that "Congress ought to show the world that it really backs up his policies." Two days later, he told the six most important congressional committees that he wanted a supplemental $700 million appropriation for Vietnam and the Dominican Republic. This was "no . . . routine appropriation," he said. "For each member of Congress who supports this request is voting to continue our effort to try to halt Communist aggression." A failure to stop the Communists in Vietnam would "show that American commitment is worthless," and then "the road is open to expansion and to endless conquest."

A special message to Congress later that day emphasized that "this is not a routine appropriation." Moreover, he offered no "guarantee [that] this will be the last request." If ensuring the safety of South Vietnam required more of a commitment, he would "turn again to the Congress."

The Congress, where voices of dissent over the escalating war had been heard in greater numbers since March, was surprisingly pliant. In two days, with next to no debate and no amendments in either chamber, the House approved the request by a 408 to 7 vote and the Senate by a margin of 88 to 3. With U.S. forces already in the field, the congressmen and senators saw no way to deny them what Senator John Stennis of Mississippi described as "the tools with which to fight." Senator Mansfield, an unbending opponent of escalation, asked that "no one misunderstand this vote. . . . There is not a Senator who would not prefer, with the President, that a decent peace might be achieved quickly in Vietnam. But we will vote for this measure because there is not one member of this body who does not desire to uphold the president and those who are risking their lives."

During the rest of May, while the Dominican crisis played itself out, Johnson made no additional commitments to expand the war in Vietnam. This was in spite of growing concern about Saigon's capacity to survive. Political instability brought the collapse of a civilian government and the return in early June of military rule under Nguyen Van Thieu as Chief of State and Nguyen Cao Ky as Prime Minister. Ky, who declared he had only one hero, Adolph Hitler, "because he pulled his country together," made American rhetoric about preserving South Vietnamese freedom seem ridiculous.

At the same time, a Communist offensive beginning in mid-May inflicted a series of defeats on South Vietnamese forces and threatened a military collapse. By the beginning of June, Ambassador Taylor was reporting that the bombing offensive against North Vietnam was changing nothing in the South, where we faced an impending disaster. He now came to the reluctant conclusion that "it will probably be necessary to commit U.S. ground forces to action." Bill Bundy says: "Almost with the suddenness of a thunder clap, it sank in to American military men, and through them to Taylor and Washington, that ARVN, or at least much of it, was outclassed and in danger of collapse."

Johnson, who was now spending more and more of his time on Vietnam, intensified his efforts to find a workable formula. On June 3, he discussed a wider air
campaign with congressional leaders, but made clear that he opposed "an irreversible
extension of the war" through attacks on Hanoi and Haiphong.

A larger ground war in the South held more appeal. On the 5th, he joined Rusk,
McNamara, Ball, and the Bundys for lunch at the State Department. "Lady Bird is
away, I was all alone, and I heard you fellows were getting together, so I thought
I'd come over," he said.

Bill Bundy recalls that the meeting "developed into a reflective discussion of
where we were headed, with no attempt to decide anything, but with much light on
the basic approach." When the discussion turned to troops, "Johnson pitched in.
Would more Americans, he asked, mean that the Vietnamese would do less?
McNamara said there was no sign of this reaction now." Johnson then asked, "How
do we get what we want?" Rusk, McNamara, and Ball ventured answers that rested
on "the rational belief that a frustrated and pained Hanoi must in time call it off."

For the time being, however, the North Vietnamese and Viet Cong seemed more
likely than ever to sustain their war effort. On June 7, the U.S. military command in
Saigon reported the disintegration of ARVN and the likely collapse of the government
unless U.S. and third-country forces came to the rescue. General William Westmoreland asked for an increase of U.S. troops from 82,000 to 175,000—41,000 immediately and another 52,000 over the next several months, a total of forty-four battalions.
He wanted to abandon a "defensive posture" and "take the war to the enemy."

In three meetings over the next seventy-two hours, Johnson "struggled to define a response. He settled on the idea that an increase to about 100,000 men would
allow the South Vietnamese to hold the line through the summer without turning
the conflict into an American or, as George Ball put it, "a white man's war." Ball
emphasized that, once you got above 100 to 150,000, you would end up going to
300 to 400,000 men and a shift from South Vietnamese reliance on themselves to
dependence on America to fight and win the war.

"At the end of the meetings on both the 10th and the 11th," Bill Bundy recalls,
"the President made remarks suggesting strongly that he accepted the recommendation [of 100,000] but he obviously wished to mull it over further and to put it into
an overall plan that included congressional consultation, some careful explanation
to the country, and perhaps a renewed form of congressional authority."

Whatever Johnson's caution, he had already made up his mind. During a conversation with Henry Graff, a Columbia University historian writing an article for the
New York Times Magazine on how Johnson made foreign policy, LBJ described
himself as boxed in by unpalatable choices: between sending Americans to die in
Vietnam and giving in to the Communists. If he sent additional troops, he would be
attacked as "an interventionist," and if he didn't, he risked being "impeached."
Phrased in these terms, could anyone doubt what Johnson's decision would be? The
real choice he was making was between "What will be enough and not too much?"

This is not to suggest that Johnson did not anguish over the decision. A *New
York Times* reporter, who saw him privately on June 24, spent most of the session
on foreign policy. He got the "impression of [a] deeply frustrated man. [LBJ] says
he doesn't know what to do." The thought occurred to the reporter that this may
have been Johnson's way of creating sympathy for himself. But the "thought also

flashed through my mind the way he was twitching and fidgeting when he talked about Vietnam, maybe he wouldn't last. . . . Overall impression: The man is deeply worried about Vietnam and sees no way out. Desperate for workable plan. His wife is worried about him." . . .

During the next two weeks, the struggle over Vietnam policy raged more intensely than ever. McNamara, Rusk, Ball, both Bundys, and former President Eisenhower weighed in with a variety of proposals ranging from Ball's renewed emphasis on reaching a compromise solution to McNamara's recommendation for substantial expansion of the ground and air wars.

Except for Ball, all agreed on the necessity of preserving the independence of South Vietnam from a Communist takeover. At a meeting on July 2, Johnson made clear that he wanted to postpone final decisions until the end of the month. He ordered McNamara to go to Saigon in mid-July to discuss Westmoreland's military plans; he directed Averell Harriman to travel to Moscow to discuss a possible reconvening of the Geneva Conference; and he asked Ball to explore possible contacts with the North Vietnamese and Viet Cong as a prelude to negotiations. Johnson wanted bold actions on Vietnam to wait until the voting rights and Medicare bills had been passed.

As part of the delaying process and effort to build a broad consensus, Johnson asked the counsel of the "wise men"—ten prominent, former foreign policy officials, including Dean Acheson and Clark Clifford. On July 8, they advised Johnson that he had no choice but to expand the war to prevent a Communist victory that would jeopardize America's national security around the world. He also needed to create national backing for the war by publicly explaining his decisions.

When Johnson began lamenting his predicament, complaining "how mean everything and everybody was to him—Fate, the Press, the Congress, the Intellectuals & so on," Dean Acheson blew his top and told him that he had no choice but to press on. "With this lead my colleagues came thundering in like the charge of the Scots Greys at Waterloo," Bill Bundy says. The President "probably expected that *most* of the Panel would be *generally* in favor of a firm policy," Bundy adds. "What he found was that *almost all* were *solidly* of this view."

Bundy considered this "'quickie' consultation with outsiders" a poor way to proceed. These elder statesmen may have had the wisdom of their experience but they had done "very little in terms of a really hard look at the difficulties of the particular case." George Ball shared Bundy's reservations about the casualness with which these elders gave their judgment. "You goddamned old bastards," he told Acheson and one other member of the group after the meeting, "you remind me of nothing so much as a bunch of buzzards sitting on a fence and letting the young men die. You don't know a goddamned thing about what you're talking about. . . . You just sit there and say these irresponsible things!"

Though Ball's remarks "shook the hell" out of Acheson, they were not repeated to Johnson, who accepted the advice of the elders as a confirmation of his own views. At a news conference on July 9, he stated that casualties were increasing in Vietnam on all sides and that things were likely to get worse before they get better. "Our manpower needs there are increasing, and will continue to do so." Seventy-five thousand U.S. troops "will be there very shortly. There will be others that will be required. Whatever is required I am sure will be supplied." He predicted that "understanding and endurance and patriotism" would be needed in the future, but he had no "plan to let up until the aggression ceases." Four days later, in another press conference, he declared that increased aggression from the North may require a greater American response on the ground in the South. "So it is quite possible that new and serious decisions will be necessary in the near future."

At a Rose Garden gathering of Rural Electric Cooperative officials on the 14th, the President predicted that long debates and criticism of him were in the offing over Vietnam. But "our national honor is at stake in southeast Asia, and we are going to protect it, and you might just as well be prepared for it." Despite "some dark days" ahead, he expected the country to continue to live up to its responsibilities abroad.

The question he posed to himself in the second half of July was not whether to put in additional troops but how many and at what pace. He wished to send enough men initially to prevent a South Vietnamese collapse and then to change the course of the war. But he also intended to make a commitment that would be compatible with domestic goals. On July 16 he told Deputy Defense Secretary Cyrus Vance that he could not submit a supplementary budget request to Congress of more than $300 to 400 million before next January; he believed an earlier and "larger request . . . will kill [his] domestic legislative program." Johnson took comfort from Mac Bundy's advice on the 19th that no additional appropriation was needed now, because "there are other ways of financing our full effort in Vietnam for the rest of the calendar year, at least."

Johnson was reluctant to make new commitments without another review of his choices. At a White House meeting on July 21, he asked McNamara for his judgment. After McNamara urged an increase in troops to between 175,000 and 200,000 and a reserve callup of 235,000 men, Johnson warned against "snap judgments"; he wanted careful consideration of "all our options." Did we want simply to come home? Johnson thought not. "The negotiations . . . , the other approaches have all been explored," he said. "It makes us look weak—with cup in hand." He wanted this option and all others discussed nevertheless, "Is anyone of the opinion we should not do what the [McNamara] memo says—If so I'd like to hear from them."

It was an invitation to George Ball to restate his case for withdrawal. Ball did so guardedly, saying that "if the decision is to go ahead, I'm committed." Johnson pressed him to make his case anyway, though expressing the belief that there was "very little alternative to what we are doing. . . . I feel it would be more dangerous for us to lose this now, than endanger a greater number of troops." Still, he wanted another meeting that afternoon to consider Ball's alternative.

Joseph Califano explains that, even after Johnson had made up his mind on a major question, he "continued to consult and ferret out opposing views . . . because he didn't want to be surprised by any opposition, fail to muster all possible support, or miss any opportunity to overwhelm or undermine an opponent he could not persuade."

Ball obliged the President. "We can't win," he declared when the group reconvened. He anticipated a "long protracted" struggle with a "messy conclusion." The war would produce serious problems at home and abroad. As casualties mounted, Americans would demand a strike at North Vietnam's jugular. The war would also encourage the view that "a great power cannot beat guerrillas." Ball had serious doubts that "an army of westerners can fight orientals in [an] Asian jungle and succeed." Ball recommended abandoning South Vietnam to its fate.

Johnson objected that we would lose credibility; "it would seem to be an irreparable blow." Yet Johnson wondered whether "westerners can ever win in Asia," and he doubted the viability of fighting a war for a country "whose government changes every month." But McGeorge Bundy, McNamara, and Rusk countered that Ball was underestimating the consequences of an American withdrawal and making too little of North Vietnamese costs from a larger U.S. effort. The President needed to make clear to the public that America was being asked "to bet more to achieve less," Bundy said, and if that didn't pay off, there would be time to withdraw after we had "given it a good try."

At the end of the meeting, Johnson summed up: "Withdrawal would be a disaster, a harsh bombing program would not win and could easily bring a wider war, and standing pat with existing forces ('hunkering up'—as he called it) was only slow defeat. Only . . . doing what McNamara urged was left. . . . It was the end of debate on policy," Bill Bundy says, "and the beginning of a new debate on tactics and above all on presentation to the country. In his own favorite phrase, the President had decided to 'put in his stack.'" . . .

To mute his decision, Johnson announced the expansion of the war at a press conference rather than in a speech to a joint session of Congress. Moreover, all he would say was that troop commitments were going up from 75,000 to 125,000, with additional forces to be sent later when requested. Nor would he call up reserve units now, though he would give it careful consideration in the future. His decision did "not imply any change in policy whatever," he also told reporters. To further downplay the action, Johnson surrounded it with talk of his Great Society goals, which he would not allow to be "drowned in the wasteful ravages of cruel wars," and announcements of Abe Fortas's nomination to the Supreme Court and John Chancellor's appointment as director of the Voice of America.

"If you have a mother-in-law with only one eye and she has it in the center of her forehead," Johnson joked privately, "you don't keep her in the living room." Yet Johnson knew that he could only hide the full meaning of his larger military commitment for so long. For he had no illusion that his administration was undergoing a sea change resembling FDR's shift in the 1940s from Dr. New Deal to Dr. Win-the-War.

Johnson did not reach his decision casually to fight a land war in Asia. He and his advisers had made exhausting reviews of their options. The defeat of the French in a similar struggle, the difficulty of fighting a guerrilla war with conventional forces, the determination of the North Vietnamese to make it long and costly, the likely hesitation of the American public once the price in blood and treasure began to register, and the likelihood that a protracted conflict would divert resources from the Great Society all gave Johnson pause.

But the conviction that a Communist victory would have worldwide repercussions for America's national security, especially in Southeast Asia, and would provoke a right-wing reaction in the United States that would wreck Johnson's administration overwhelmed his doubts. Moreover, he and most of his advisers thought it unlikely that the Viet Cong and North Vietnamese would be able to hold out forever against America's massive air, land, and sea power. True, it was going to cost American lives to accomplish the goal, but the extent of that sacrifice was not assumed to be large or anything like the Korean losses, which ran to 30,000 men. Before any such development, the Communists would have to come out and fight, and when they did, American forces, in the words of one general, would "cream them."

Were these considerations enough to trigger Johnson's escalation of the war? Yes. But something else was at work here that helped clinch the decision: ego or personality or Johnson's lifelong compulsion to be the best, to dominate and win. It seems worth repeating that few people were more competitive than Johnson. He could not bear to lose or take a back seat to anyone. As senator, he had to be the leader; as Vice President, he was a miserable second fiddle. Once he held the presidency, it wasn't enough to be *the* Chief Executive; he needed to be the best or, at a minimum, one of the best Presidents in American history. In particular, he saw Franklin Roosevelt as the President to measure himself against. FDR, the winner of a historic landslide election in 1936 and the most successful reform leader and greatest war President of the century, was Johnson's model and target to surpass.

This was not some casual game Johnson played with himself. His competitiveness and need to be top dog were at the core of his being. It translated into wanting unsurpassed reform accomplishments. He wanted to improve "life for more people and in more ways than any other political leader, including FDR," he later told [author Doris] Kearns.

When the historian William E. Leuchtenburg interviewed him about the Great Society in September 1965, Johnson gave him a glimpse of his reach for presidential greatness. "'Mr. President,'" Leuchtenburg began, "'this has been a remarkable Congress. It is even arguable whether this isn't the most significant Congress ever.' . . . Before I could add one more sentence to frame a question, Johnson interjected, 'No, it isn't. It's not arguable.' I grinned, then realized he was dead serious—even a little angry. It was my first indication that he believed his accomplishments were the most important in all our history. 'Not if you can read,' he snapped. 'You can perform a great service,' the President continued, 'if you say that never before have the three independent branches been so productive. Never has the American system worked so effectively in producing quality legislation—and at a time when our system is under attack all over the world.'"

Johnson had few illusions about what escalation of the war would mean at home. He knew that wars had sidetracked Populism, Progressivism, and the New and Fair Deals. "Losing the Great Society was a terrible thought," Johnson later told Kearns, "but not so terrible as the thought of being responsible for America's losing a war to the Communists. Nothing could possibly be worse than that."

Yet at the time, Johnson had every hope that escalation would not mean the end of reform. On the contrary, by the time Johnson was "putting in his stack," his legislative program was largely in place. True, he would put additional reforms before the second session of the 89th Congress, but it did not match the proposals of the first in importance. Johnson's comments to Leuchtenburg in September 1965 about the unprecedented achievement of the government was a statement of his belief that, even if future reforms were sidetracked, he had already gained enough major legislation to put foreign affairs on an equal and possibly even higher footing than domestic ones.

Harry McPherson, one of LBJ's principal White House aides, says that "by the end of 1965 Johnson had passed almost everything that anyone had ever conceived of. It was hard to imagine any other federal program in any field." Johnson seemed to agree when he told McPherson: "You know, you only have one year. No matter what your mandate is you have one year, and you've got to get everything done in that year." Given Johnson's continuing domestic initiatives, there is some exaggeration in his statement about one year. Still, it seems fair to say that he was now ready to focus as much and, if necessary, even more on Vietnam as on domestic advance.

But if Johnson had largely created the legislative framework for his Great Society and was ready to devote himself to Vietnam, why was he so reluctant to speak more openly to the country about expansion of the war? Because until October 1965, Congress was still at work on his reforms. After that, however, he was ready to see the war come front and center. By then, the most important Great Society laws would be fixtures on the national scene. World War II had not destroyed the major elements of the New Deal, and Johnson expected it to be the same with the Great Society and Vietnam. True, some of the programs would not get the full financing they needed; but this would come in time, when the struggle in Vietnam ended. And so to Johnson, fighting in Vietnam meant not destroying the Great Society but delaying its full impact on American life.

Indeed, for all his anguish over Vietnam, Johnson saw positive developments flowing from the war: It was an opportunity to combat Communist hopes of advancing their cause through wars of national liberation. It was also another in a series of brave responses to Cold War challenges faced by America since 1945. It was one more opportunity to show the Chinese and the Soviets that we could not be intimidated. They would then be more receptive to detente or a peaceful standoff with the West.

As he saw matters in the summer and fall of 1965, he was meeting the challenge to presidential greatness at home and now he hoped to do the same abroad. For the war in Vietnam was a chance not only to promote long-term international stability but also to allow Johnson to make a great mark in foreign affairs. He had not gone looking for a fight. He was not contriving an international conflict for the sake of his historical reputation. But confronted by a foreign challenge that seemed to pose a major threat to the national well-being, Johnson intended to do his duty. If it added to his presidential greatness, all to the good. But it was no more than a secondary, comforting reason to fight.

Yet however many constructive reasons Johnson saw for fighting, he could not quiet a fear that the war might ultimately ruin his presidency. There were no guarantees that U.S. military pressure would bring the Communists to negotiate a settlement or that the American right wouldn't mount an effective attack against a political compromise in Vietnam or that the domestic left wouldn't be able to stir mass opposition to a long war.

Choosing War

FREDRIK LOGEVALL

When the first contingent of American marines waded ashore near Danang in South Vietnam in the early part of March 1965, it signaled the end of the most important period of policy deliberation in the history of American involvement in Vietnam. This period began some eighteen months earlier, in the late summer of

From Fredrik Logevall, *Choosing War: The Lost Chance for Peace and the Escalation of War in Vietnam*, pp. 375–392, 393–395, 400, 403–404, 411–412. Copyright © 1999 The Regents of the University of California. Reprinted by permission of University of California Press.

1963, and it was characterized by a marked deterioration in the politico-military position of the Saigon government and a concomitant dilemma for Washington officials: whether to escalate dramatically U.S. involvement in the war or get out of it altogether. The landing of the marines and the initiation of regular, sustained bombing of North Vietnam and Vietcong-controlled areas of South Vietnam were dramatic proof of which way they had gone.

That the significance of this development is clearer in hindsight than it was at the time cannot be doubted. The question is how much clearer. Neither senior officials nor anyone else could know in the late winter of 1965 how large the American commitment would eventually become, or how long the war would go on, or how much blood would be shed before it was over. But all informed observers knew that a key moment had come and a line had been crossed. Lyndon Johnson would publicly insist otherwise and would instruct aides into the summer to say that the policy had not changed, that the new measures were a substitute for escalation, rather than escalation itself. But he really believed otherwise, as indicated by his deepening hostility in these months to early negotiations and his instructing top U.S. military officials in March to go out and "kill Vietcong." Few knowledgeable people, whether inside or outside the U.S. government, would have disagreed with Walter Lippmann's assertion early in the spring: "It used to be a war of the South Vietnamese assisted by the Americans. It is now becoming an American war very inefficiently assisted by the South Vietnamese."

Nor is hindsight necessarily much of an advantage in understanding the nature of the escalate-or-withdraw choice that first John Kennedy and then Lyndon Johnson faced in Vietnam. Judging by the existing historical literature, indeed, contemporaneous observers generally had a surer sense of that choice than those who came later. For Lippmann as for others writing at the time, whatever their position on the war, the outcome of the policy process in late 1964–early 1965 was in no way preordained. They were certain that Lyndon Johnson faced a genuine dilemma—that is, a choice between two or more unpalatable alternatives—and they devoted considerable attention in their analyses to each of the options before him. Historians, on the other hand, writing after the fact, have generally given short shrift to the dilemma if they have examined it at all. Some authors have identified the president's choice as a legitimate one and spoken vaguely of "missed opportunities" for withdrawal in the period, but they have asserted rather than demonstrated the viability of these opportunities. More commonly, students of the war have rejected the notion that there existed a viable choice for the administration—for them, Johnson's dilemma was not much of a dilemma at all. They have described an escalation process that was essentially an inevitable outcome of the domestic and international political climate of the time. More than that, most of these authors have implied that the president was justified in believing that each escalation might provide the critical increment—after all, practically everyone else thought so. Writes one distinguished historian: "What was most remarkable about the Vietnam War was that, with the exception of Charles de Gaulle, George Ball, and a handful of others, so few challenged the fundamental assumptions of the American vision."

It would indeed be remarkable, if it were correct. Leaving aside for a moment the vexing issue of what exactly those "fundamental assumptions" were, in reality a veritable chorus of voices challenged the direction of American policy, albeit often in muted tones. In the executive branch of government, Ball's views were shared by a sizable number of midlevel bureaucrats in the State Department and the National Security Council, as well as by analysts in the CIA. In American elite opinion, views were divided on what to do in Vietnam should the Saigon regime move to the point of collapse, with powerful elements on record by February 1965 as opposing a major American escalation—the group included the bulk of the Senate Democratic leadership and many other lawmakers in the party; the vice president–elect; prominent commentators such as Lippmann, Drew Pearson, Arthur Krock, and Hans J. Morgenthau; and newspapers across the country, including the *New York Times,* the *Wall Street Journal,* and the *Washington Post.*

Some elites, of course, spoke out in *favor* of a stepped-up American military involvement, should that become necessary—notables included the columnist Joseph Alsop, who rivaled (but did not quite match) Lippmann in terms of national influence, and once-and-future GOP presidential candidate Richard Nixon. *Time* magazine generally struck a hawkish tone, as did the *Los Angeles Times* and several smaller regional papers. Famed Vietnam correspondents David Halberstam and Neil Sheehan, both of whom would later turn against the war, in late 1964 remained supportive of a strong U.S. commitment. In terms of staking out a firm position on what to do if a Saigon collapse threatened, however, the pro-escalation advocates were a small minority, especially on Capitol Hill—if there were "war hawks" in Congress at the end of 1964, they were a timid bunch indeed. For that matter, the existence of both points of view merely underscores a main theme in this book: the fluidity in establishment thinking about the war in the crucial months of decision.

Within the general public, too, it is very difficult to speak of any kind of meaningful "consensus" on the war in 1964; Americans, to the extent that they followed developments in Vietnam, tended to support the effort there, in large measure because they took candidate-for-president Johnson at his word when he said the nation's commitment would stay at about its current level and that South Vietnamese boys would have to fight their own war. When pressed on what should be done if defeat loomed, however, middle Americans were deeply ambivalent, with only a small minority favoring the use of U.S. ground troops. The common assertion, standard enough to be found in almost any textbook on recent U.S. history, that the war effort enjoyed broad popular support well into 1966 and 1967, is true enough but is fundamentally misleading: near-universal support for a full-scale military effort on behalf of the South Vietnamese was there *after* Americanization, courtesy of the rally-around-the-flag effect; it was not there before. As late as February 1965, polls of the public and Congress revealed widespread antipathy for the introduction of U.S. ground troops into the conflict, and broad support for some form of negotiations. More than that, surveys revealed a willingness on the part of lawmakers and their constituents to follow the administration's lead on the war, whichever way it chose to go.

With respect to the international arena, the judgment quoted above would be more accurate if it were changed to read precisely the opposite: what is remarkable is how few *embraced* the "fundamental assumptions of the American vision." By the start of 1965, the United States was in large measure isolated on the Vietnam War. The key allied governments were sympathetic to Washington's dilemma and were prepared to offer tepid rhetorical support for American aims in the conflict (many because they thought it would smooth dealings with Washington on other issues). But they withstood strong and continuous U.S. pressure to make even a token man-power contribution to the conflict, in large measure because they were highly dubious about U.S. claims regarding Vietnam's importance to western security, and about whether any kind of meaningful "victory" there was possible in any event. Most thought absurd the standard American public claim that this was a case of external aggression against a freedom-loving, independent South Vietnam, considering it in-stead a civil war (whether between factions of southerners or between the North and South) in which the side with the least political legitimacy was the Saigon regime. Though few leaders in the West were prepared to follow de Gaulle's lead and openly challenge American policy, the majority of them saw things much the way he did—at the start of 1965 the Johnson administration could count on the firm backing of only Australia, Thailand, the Philippines, and South Korea. Of these only Australia could be considered unreservedly supportive. Out of 126 nations in the world in 1965, the United States had the unequivocal support for its Vietnam policy of exactly one.

Nothing speaks to this general American isolation on Vietnam more forcefully than this: even many Asian allies registered opposition to, or at least nonsupport for, a larger American effort in Vietnam. Early in 1966 the Central Intelligence Agency would report that the countries of the region were "permeated" with the views of American dissidents, and Lyndon Johnson would complain that "the countries [in Southeast Asia] don't want the war to go on." The situation was not markedly differ-ent a year earlier. When in December 1964 the administration launched an intensified campaign for increased third-country assistance, as a corollary to the planned Amer-ican increase, it found almost no support, even among the governments in Asia. Only a handful of allies eventually contributed manpower to the war effort, and some demanded large payments for doing so, which is to say that they were not true allies.

The chief consideration for all of the skeptics of U.S. policy, whether domestic or foreign, whether in Asia or elsewhere, was the utterly dismal politico-military situation in South Vietnam. The essential prerequisite for any successful outcome to the struggle—a stable Saigon government enjoying reasonably broad-based popular support—was not merely absent but further away than ever from becoming reality. In such a situation, these critics believed, a stepped-up American military effort could probably help stabilize the situation on the battlefield but could not rectify the fundamental problem, the unwillingness of the mass of southerners to fight for the regime. If anything, a larger American presence in the South would exacerbate the problem by making the regime seem more like a puppet than ever before. Those resentful of the existing American involvement would become more resentful; those apathetic about the struggle would become more so, since they could now rely on Americans to do the job. Among Asians generally, sympathy for the Vietcong and its North Vietnamese allies would increase as they took on a very big, very white, western power, in the same way that the Vietminh before them had taken on the French.

Many allied governments might nevertheless have contributed to the war ef-fort, and many domestic American critics supported the Johnson administration's escalation, had they not possessed deep doubts that the outcome in South Vietnam really mattered to western security. None questioned the need to contain possible Chinese communist expansion in Asia, only whether it was necessary or wise to fight in Vietnam to do it. For some, historic Chinese-Vietnamese friction precluded the possibility of Indochina falling under Beijing's actual or de facto control, a reality that suggested Washington should seek, if anything, to make common cause with North Vietnam rather than fighting it. Others were inclined to downplay the Chinese threat, arguing that Mao Zedong's main concern was internal development, not external expansion, and that Beijing's belligerent public rhetoric vis-à-vis the West did not signify any actual intention of moving southward. Still others thought the best way to control or modify China's behavior was to engage the Mao government, as de Gaulle had done in extending recognition in January 1964, not to isolate it as the United States insisted on doing. For some observers, all these considerations pertained. Most critics of American policy also rejected the standard administration assertion that the outcome in Vietnam would have a direct bearing on developments elsewhere in the region, that a Saigon defeat would start the dominoes falling. What mattered, they were convinced, was the constellation of forces within each individual country, not what occurred in a civil war in Vietnam. When Walter Lippmann wrote that "revolution is a homegrown product," whether in Algeria, Northern Ireland, or Vietnam, he expressed a view widely held outside American officialdom.

The critics did not deny that the Johnson administration occupied a difficult situation in Vietnam at the start of 1965, the result of ten years of steadily increasing involvement in the affairs of the South and constant reaffirmations of America's determination to stand firm. The United States had staked a sizable chunk of its prestige on a successful outcome in the war, they agreed, and to abandon that goal would be a blow to American credibility on the world stage. But most of them did not think it would be a big blow, particularly if it happened before American troops were on the ground—once it became a full-fledged American war, all could see, withdrawal would be infinitely more difficult. Before then, the administration had a ready-made excuse for disengagement: the evident unwillingness of the South Vietnamese to live up to their end of the bargain. Who could blame the United States for pulling up stakes and getting out, given the chaos that prevailed in the South as the year turned? If a unilateral American withdrawal was too difficult for an American president to pursue, a fig-leaf extrication could in all likelihood be engineered, perhaps via a Geneva-type conference—so said not only de Gaulle's government in Paris, but Harold Wilson's in London, Lester Pearson's in Ottawa, and Eisaku Sato's in Tokyo; so said the UN's U Thant; so said leading lawmakers on Capitol Hill; so said numerous columnists and editorial writers in the United States. The fact that most of these voices failed to spell out in detail how this negotiated withdrawal would be secured (a subject we shall return to) should not obscure the fact that they believed that it could be. They believed North Vietnam, China, and especially, the Soviet Union were anxious to avoid a dramatically escalated war, which boded well for the prospects of getting the United States some kind of face-saving agreement.

Thus the irony of America's credibility dilemma: far from it being enhanced or preserved by the decision to wage large-scale war in Vietnam, it suffered as a result, much as these outside observers predicted. The core component of the credibility imperative was an assumption that a failure to stand firm in the war would cause allies around the world to question, and perhaps lose faith in, America's commitment to their defense, and would embolden adversaries to act aggressively. It was a kind of "psychological domino theory," as Jonathan Schell has put it, and there was but one thing wrong with it: it did not reflect the realities of the international system of late 1964–early 1965. Already then, in the months *before* the escalation, what allied and nonaligned governments questioned was not America's will but its judgment; already then, many wondered why, in the wake of Johnson's massive election victory over Barry Goldwater, he did not take the cover that this victory (and large Democratic majorities in Congress) provided him and opt for a de-escalation of American involvement. The attitudes of the USSR and China are harder to measure, but certainly the Soviets were no less desirous than the western allies of averting a major war. For that matter, it seems undeniable that George Ball and Mike Mansfield were correct in arguing in 1964 that U.S. credibility vis-à-vis these two powers would in the medium and long run suffer much less from a negotiated American withdrawal from South Vietnam, even if the deal led eventually to a reunified Vietnam under Hanoi's control, than from getting drawn into a deep and deadly morass.

American officials were well aware of these widespread and fundamental doubts about the direction of U.S. policy. Indeed, the best proof for the absence of support for a larger war is the phenomenal amount of energy American officials expended fretting about it. Beginning already in the early fall of 1963, they worried about the fluidity in domestic opinion generally, and about the growing antipathy among elite voices in the United States and among important actors abroad. Surveys showing broad support for the Vietnam commitment were scant comfort to them, because they knew the support was soft. This explains why, early in 1964, White House and State Department aides began speaking of the need for a "public information" campaign on the war (subsequently launched in late spring). And it explains why administration insiders paid so much attention to each *New York Times* editorial advocating neutralization for Vietnam, each new Lippmann column calling the war unwinnable in any meaningful sense, each new pronouncement from de Gaulle or U Thant suggesting the need for a negotiated solution. The extensive efforts begun in mid 1963 and expanded in 1964 to pressure these critics to change their position or at least keep their objections silent is testimony to these official fears.

The pressure campaign produced mixed results. On the one hand, the administration succeeded in persuading many domestic dissidents to keep their objections quiet, partly by playing to their patriotism (true Americans do not challenge the commander in chief on global issues in a time of Cold War) and partly by seducing them into thinking their ideas were taken seriously. On the other hand, none of those targeted were converted to the administration's point of view, at least not fully—a few appear to have been half-converted, such as the *New York Times*'s James Reston, who would suggest in one column that wider U.S. military involvement would be folly and in the next that there might be no alternative. With the notable exception of Lyndon Johnson, who seems to have been genuinely mystified that domestic critics in particular would cling so stubbornly to their positions, senior officials were not really surprised at this lack of success. They faced a formidable group of dissidents, they knew, one that would not be easily swayed. Charles de Gaulle, U Thant, Hans Morgenthau, Walter Lippmann, Mike Mansfield, Frank Church, J. William Fulbright—no foreign policy slouches these. In later years, supporters of the war would have considerable success dismissing leaders of the so-called antiwar movement as ignorant and naive, as innocent in the affairs of the world. They could not make that claim with these earlier critics, all of whom were acknowledged "realists" in world politics and almost all of whom fully embraced the need for a vigorous (if discriminating) western posture in the Cold War.

But the key point here is not that policymakers shared, in many cases, the same backgrounds and foreign-policy experience as their detractors; the key point is that they also shared many of the same judgments about the state of the war in Vietnam and the prospects for a turnaround. Lyndon Johnson and his chief lieutenants fully agreed that the military picture was grim and getting grimmer, and though they liked to say (even privately among themselves) that bombing North Vietnam would make a major difference to the situation in the South, deep down they suspected otherwise. Most were not optimistic that Hanoi would succumb to this form of coercion and cease its support of the insurgency, and they knew that, regardless, the keys to victory lay below the seventeenth parallel. Even as they dispatched the first contingent of U.S. troops to the war, the president and his men understood that it would bring resentment from many southerners, including leaders in Saigon, and generate charges of "colonialism" from elsewhere in Asia and around the world. As for the quality of government in South Vietnam, U.S. leaders were no more sanguine than their critics: they knew it was less capable and less popular than ever, permeated with dissension, and—in some quarters at least—not altogether unsympathetic to an early end to the war through a deal with the NLF or Hanoi.

Even in their estimations of the regional and global implications of a defeat in Vietnam, many senior policymakers did not differ all that much from most of the dissenters—especially if the defeat occurred because of the perceived ineptitude or apathy of the South Vietnamese themselves. Hence the difficulty of speaking of "fundamental assumptions" in the American vision. Officials certainly worried about possible Chinese expansion in the wake of such an eventuality, but they too understood that historic Sino-Vietnamese friction and very current Sino-Soviet friction militated against that possibility. They were concerned about the possible increase in the appeal of Maoist revolutions in other newly emerging nations should Ho Chi Minh's be allowed to succeed, but they knew that the internal conditions that made Vietnam so ripe for a communist takeover did not exist in many other nations in the region. With regard to the likely Soviet reaction to a withdrawal without victory, it cannot be considered a major concern in the upper levels of the administration. Senior strategists believed that Moscow would want to continue steps toward improved bilateral relations with the United States regardless of the outcome in Vietnam, and they do not appear to have worried much about increased Soviet penetration in other Third World areas.

Seen in this light, the Americanization of the war becomes difficult to understand. The isolation of the United States on the war among its international allies at the end of 1964; the thin nature of domestic American popular support for the Vietnam commitment; the downright opposition to a larger war among many elite American voices; the spreading war-weariness and anti-Americanism in urban and rural areas of South Vietnam; and the political chaos in Saigon—add all these elements together, along with the fact that senor officials in Washington knew of them and worried about them and you have a policy decision that is far less easily explained than many would suggest (and this author used to believe). This does not mean it is impossible to explain. If the war was not overdetermined, it was not "underdetermined" either. Major escalation was bound to be one of the options under consideration in the halls of power in Washington in the winter of 1964–1965. Ever since the initial decision to aid the French war effort some fifteen years earlier, U.S. policymakers had always, at points of decision, opted to expand the nation's involvement rather than decrease it, and it stands to reason that they would give serious thought to doing so again, even if this time the escalation would be of an entirely different magnitude. That Johnson and his aides operated without deep public support and isolated from most western governments is a significant consideration in our analysis, but it is not by itself decisive—they would hardly have been the first lonely warriors in history, or the first to press ahead despite long odds against success. They commanded the greatest military power in the history of the world, they knew, and it makes sense that they would be tempted therefore to forge ahead, despite their general lack of optimism about the prospects in the war.

The more discerning opponents of escalation understood this and were hardly surprised when they learned, at various points in 1964, that the administration had begun laying contingency plans for expanded military action against North Vietnam. Significantly, however, few of these critics appear to have believed that these contingency plans would actually be implemented in the end. Surely Lyndon Johnson would prevent such a thing from happening, most assumed, if not before the November election, then certainly after. He was too skillful a politician, and too committed to his ambitious domestic agenda, to allow himself to be thrust into a major war in an politico-military swamp like South Vietnam. Moreover, many of these critics took for granted that alongside the planning for wider military action there would be planning, of roughly equal scope and intensity, for disengagement from the war. In the crisis situation of late 1964, staffers at the British Foreign Office, for example, thought their counterparts in the State Department must be working day and night to come up with imaginative ways of getting the United States out of a disastrous situation with minimum loss to the nation's prestige. In reality, little such thinking was taking place. That part of Foggy Bottom dealing with diplomacy in Vietnam was a quiet place as the year drew to a close, whatever small staff might be on hand usually home in time for supper.

For by then, the issue had really been decided in the inner sanctum of power: the United States would pursue a military solution in Vietnam, through escalation if necessary. As early as the previous spring the top officials had reached that conclusions, and they had never deviated from it. The question is why. As should be obvious from the foregoing analysis . . . I attach more explanatory power to the short-term and personal factors in that decision than to long-term and impersonal ones. To be sure, the longer history of American involvement in Indochina, dating back to at least 1945, laid the necessary foundation for the policies that came later. John F. Kennedy inherited a difficult situation in Vietnam in January 1961, and the one he handed to his successor was more difficult still. Americans had already begun to perish in the war, and that fact, along with constant public reaffirmations in the late 1950s and early 1960s of South Vietnam's importance to U.S. security, complicated the situation that Kennedy and, especially, Lyndon Johnson confronted.

In the same way it would be foolish to deny that the decision to go to war in Vietnam was partly the product of long-term, subterranean currents in American ideology and culture. Michael H. Hunt has described an American foreign-policy ideology that took shape at the nation's founding and from the start contained three principal components: a vision of national greatness; a belief in a racial hierarchy, in which Native Americans, blacks, and Asians ranked below whites; and fear of revolution. That the men who took the nation to war adhered to this ideological triad, that it helped shape their approach to the Vietnam issue, cannot be doubted. They were also products of their past, a past that had witnessed a devastating world war, one seemingly the result of a failed appeasement of Hitler at Munich, and which had been followed by a postwar division of Europe, by a communist takeover in China, and by a major conflict against communist foes in Korea. Americans, never wholly comfortable in the murky world of European-style diplomacy, with its emphasis on pragmatic give and take leading to imperfect solutions, took these experiences in World War II and its aftermath as reasons to be doubly suspicious of compromising with adversaries.

Diplomacy indeed held almost no place in the containment policy that emerged after 1945. Since the Soviets were thought to be fanatics, foreign to western ideas and traditions, talking to them was essentially pointless. Since they also were bent on exporting their system and imposing it on unwilling peoples, the United States, as the leader of the free world, had a moral obligation to stop them. Perceptive observers like Walter Lippmann and George Kennan saw already in 1947, with the enunciation in that year of the Truman Doctrine, the possibility that there was but a short step between this containment policy and an indiscriminate globalism that could compel the Untied States to intervene militarily on behalf of weak puppet states in remote areas of the world—places, that is, like Vietnam. Both men understood that the mere possession of great national power, such as America enjoyed after 1945, would make it hard for leaders to resist projecting that power far and wide and intervening in the affairs of others.

It could be tempting, therefore, to draw a straight line between the Truman Doctrine and the landing of the marines at Danang. The temptation should be resisted. For one thing, containment did not turn out to be quite the undiscriminating policy that Lippmann and Kennan feared it would be, which was one reason both of them often ended up supporting it in practice (even as they continued to object to it in theory) in the two decades that followed. American policymakers, it turned out, did not challenge communist expansion at every point; when they did, they did not always use military means. Moreover, though the Cold War Consensus that emerged in the early postwar period had a powerful hold on American culture and society, it had begun to fracture by the early 1960s, in large measure because the Cold War itself had changed. By 1963, certainly, there was de facto recognition by both superpowers of the other's legitimacy and therefore reduced attachment to the notion of irreconcilable ideological differences. By then one could speak of mutually (if tacitly) agreed spheres of influence, and of a tacit agreement not to use nuclear weapons except as a last resort. This new atmosphere suggested an opportunity for at least a limited rapprochement, and Kennedy and Khrushchev initiated moves in that direction in the last year of JFK's life. In western capitals, including Washington, officials and informed outside observers by now understood that communism was not monolithic, that Moscow and Beijing often viewed each other with more suspicion than they viewed the United States. They understood, most of them, that in Vietnam Ho Chi Minh possessed nationalist credentials that his counterparts in Saigon lacked.

The problem with structural explanations for the American war in Vietnam is that they ultimately do not explain very much. The ideology that Hunt delineates must be taken into consideration, but it could be applied as easily to the opponents of large-scale war on behalf of South Vietnam as to those who supported it. The Western European leaders who advised against Americanization could be said to have operated within a roughly similar ideological triad. For virtually everyone in public life in the early 1960s the word *Munich* had bad connotations, but not everyone thought *appeasement* had applicability in Southeast Asia—hence the danger of speaking of a "Munich generation" that took the United States into Vietnam. The Korean War analogy meant different things to different people, even those at the highest levels of decision making. And although many Americans were inclined to doubt the relevance of the France-in-Indochina analogy, on the grounds that America's power was so much greater, its purposes so much more noble, a significant number thought it very important indeed. Leaders in the later antiwar movement would say it was the "establishment," the "ruling elite," that got the United States into war, but this, too, explains little—the *New York Times* was a pillar of that establishment, as were Lippmann and Mansfield and others of like mind. Long before there were college sit-ins and draft-card burnings they were advising against a deeper involvement in Vietnam.

The same lack of explanatory power attends interpretations that emphasize the role played by American economic imperatives. The most sophisticated exponents of the neocolonalist model avoid crude economic determinism in their analysis. They acknowledge that Vietnam itself was not economically valuable to the United States and indeed make an argument that is essentially unassailable: that policymakers sought, as one author has put it, "to create an integrated, essentially capitalist world framework out of the chaos of World War Two and the remnants of the colonial systems." Perfectly true, but not very helpful. Exactly how did this commitment to an integrated capitalist order require a military intervention in Vietnam? Presumably the same imperatives were there in 1973, when Richard Nixon *ended* U.S. military involvement; certainly they must have been there in the spring of 1961, when JFK chose to pursue neutralization in Laos (the Laos that Eisenhower had called "the cork in the bottle") rather than a military solution. In the high-level policy deliberations of 1964–1965 concerns for the fate of world capitalism appear to have been *entirely* absent, while the main worry about the American economy was that it would be harmed by a larger war. Corporate America appears to have felt likewise. On 11 February 1965 the U.S. stock market took its biggest plunge since the day of the Kennedy assassination. The reason: investor concerns, after the Pleiku attack and American retaliatory air strikes, that the United States was sliding into a major land war in Asia.

The best arguments for the primacy of long-term factors in the 1965 escalation are those that confine themselves to the conflict itself—that is, to the cumulative weight of fifteen-plus years of American involvement in Vietnamese affairs and the sheer momentum (or, some would say, inertia) this caused. This is the "phenomenon of escalation," in which an initial set of decisions starts a chain of processes, each more difficult to control than the predecessor, each widening the area of action. But the decisions and developments of these early years only serve to make the decision for war more likely; they by no means *ensure* it. . . .

A quarter of a century ago, two students of the events described in this [essay] rightly observed that it would be a mistake to look for a single cause of the Americanization of the Vietnam War. But it will not do merely to list *x* number of causes. It is the task of the historian to reduce a given list of causes to order by establishing a casual hierarchy, and to relate the items in this hierarchy to one another. For the leading causes of the 1965 escalation we must look to the short term, and especially to the year 1964 and to the interaction in that period of Lyndon Baines Johnson and his most senior advisers. Robert McNamara, McGeorge Bundy, and Dean Rusk. They constituted the "Inner War Cabinet," to use Rusk's apt phrase; they were the "Awesome Foursome," as a newspaper scribe dubbed them. To a large extent these four men made the Vietnam policy, made it with input from various assistant secretaries, to be sure, and from the Joint Chiefs of Staff and the various members of the National Security Council, and, especially, from ambassador to Saigon General Maxwell Taylor, but with decisive power preserved for themselves.

Why did they choose war? Publicly they insisted they did it principally to defend a free people from external aggression, but this was false. Though policymakers constantly proclaimed that all they wanted for the South Vietnamese was the right of self-determination, they worked to thwart that right whenever it appeared that southern leaders might seek to broaden their base of support by shifting the emphasis of the struggle from the military to the political plane—hence the turning against the Ngo brothers in the late summer of 1963 and the Minh junta in early 1964, and the determination in late 1964 to prevent any Saigon move to end the war through a deal with the National Liberation Front. "We will oppose any independent South Vietnamese move to negotiate," said the interdepartmental Working Group's final report in late November 1964. By the start of 1964, certainly, and probably long before, the wishes of the very people the United States claimed to be defending in Vietnam had essentially ceased to matter to senior American officials. No doubt they believed that what they were doing served the Vietnamese people's ultimate interests, and that the inhabitants of the South would be grateful in the end. No doubt this assumption made them sleep better at night. But it had little to do with why they acted.

For the key consideration behind the decision for war we must look to the other rationale articulated by policymakers: *credibility* and the need to preserve it by avoiding defeat in Vietnam. This was the explanation typically advanced by officials when they addressed knowledgeable audiences in off-the-record meetings—one finds scant references to "moral obligations" or "defending world freedom" in the records of their interaction with congressional committees, with foreign government leaders, with journalists in private sessions. In these settings, the emphasis was almost always on abstract (and closely related) notions of prestige, reputation, and credibility and how these were on the line in Vietnam. Even here, however, the picture that emerges is incomplete, inasmuch as the "credibility" referred to was always a purely national concept, having to do with the position of the United States on the world stage. That is, it was *American* credibility that was at stake in Southeast Asia, *American* prestige that needed to be upheld there. Though it can be right and proper to define the credibility imperative in exclusively national terms, it will not suffice as an explanation for policy making in Vietnam. For Vietnam a broader definition is essential, one that also includes domestic political credibility and even personal credibility. For it was not merely the United States that had a stake in the outcome in Vietnam; so did the Democratic Party (or at least so Kennedy and Johnson believed), and so did the individuals who had helped shape the earlier commitment and who were now charged with deciding the next move.

We may go further and argue that, within this three-part conception of the credibility imperative, the national part was the least important. Geo-strategic considerations were not the driving force in American Vietnam policy in The Long 1964, either before the election or after; partisan political considerations were; individual careerist considerations were. True, some officials did see Vietnam as a vital theater in the larger Cold War struggle against world communism, did see American credibility as very much on the line—Dean Rusk was one, Walt Rostow another. Most, however, were more dubious. William Bundy and John McNaughton, two of the key players in the policy deliberations in late 1964, not only shared much of George Ball's pessimism about the long-term prospects in the war but on several occasions endorsed his relatively benign view of the likely consequences of defeat in South Vietnam. (Ball's views were at once more widely shared in the government and less influential in decision making than is often assumed.) Robert McNamara and McGeorge Bundy worried about the implications for America's world position of a defeat in Vietnam and were highly effective exponents of a staunch U.S. commitment to the war— never more forthrightly than in their "Fork in the Y" memo of 27 January 1965. But they cannot be considered true believers on Vietnam, at least not after the latter part of 1964, in the sense of truly believing that the United States had a moral obligation to help the South Vietnamese or that American national interests were seriously threatened by events in Indochina. So why did they favor Americanization? Less out of concern for America's credibility, I believe, than out of fears for their own personal credibility. For more than three years, McNamara and Bundy had counseled the need to stand firm in the war (a relatively easy thing to do in, say, 1962, when the commitment was small and the Cold War situation considerably more tense), and to go against that now would be to expose themselves to potential humiliation and to threaten their careers. It is not difficult to imagine both men, and especially McNamara, arguing with equal effectiveness for the need to cut losses and get out of the conflict, had they served a president who sought such a result.

Even if we draw back from this conclusion, even if we assume that all of the principal advisers meant it when they said that America's global credibility was on the line in Vietnam, it would still not necessarily mean that we had arrived at the main motivation behind the decision for war. For it would not tell us anything about the position and role of the central figure in the policy making, the president of the United States. And on this there can be no doubt: Kennedy and Johnson were the key players in this policy process, not merely in the obvious sense that they had to give final approval to any and all policy decisions but in the sense of actively shaping the outcome of the deliberations. Because Johnson was fated to be president when the critical choices came, it is his imprint on the policy that is our central concern. . . .

. . . Johnson was always first among equals, as the internal record makes clear. If his top Vietnam aides intimidated him with their accomplishments and academic pedigrees, he also intimidated them with his forceful presence and his frequent resort to bullying tactics, and he established firm control of his administration from the start. Furthermore, no president is a prisoner to his advisers—Eisenhower and Kennedy had rejected policy recommendations on Vietnam, and Johnson might have done the same had he so desired. (He showed a capacity to do so on non-Vietnam issues.) He did not. What, then, drove Johnson's approach to the Vietnam issue? Chiefly its potential to do harm to his domestic political objectives and to his personal historical reputation. Both concerns were there from the start—he determined already in late 1963 that Vietnam would be kept on the back burner in 1964, so as to avoid giving Republicans an issue with which to beat up on Democrats in an election year, and he vowed only hours after the Dallas assassination that he would not be the president who lost Vietnam.

Understanding this duality in Johnson's thinking about the war, in which partisan calculations competed for supremacy with concerns for his personal reputation, is essential to understanding the outcome of the policy process in Washington in the fifteen months that followed his taking office as president. The former explains his determination to keep Vietnam from being lost in an election year, a year in which he also sought to pass major pieces of the Democratic Party's legislative agenda. But it cannot by itself explain his willingness to proceed with a major military intervention—whose importance and viability he himself doubted—after the glorious election results, which brought not only a smashing victory over Barry Goldwater but also huge Democratic majorities in both houses of Congress. It cannot explain Johnson's refusal to even consider possible alternatives to a military solution, never more resolutely than in those important weeks after the election.

For this reason it would be wrong to overemphasize the importance of the Great Society in the decision to escalate the conflict—that is, to give too much weight to the idea that LBJ took the nation to war because of fears that if he did not, Republicans and conservative Democrats would oppose and possibly scuttle his beloved domestic agenda. Concerns along these lines certainly existed within Johnson, and they directly influenced the *way* in which he expanded the war—in particular, they dictated that the escalation be as quiet as possible so as to avoid the need for choosing between the war and the programs, between guns and butter. But strategizing of this sort cannot be considered the primary *cause* of the decision for escalation. McGeorge Bundy spoke well to this point years later: "I think if [Johnson] had decided that the right thing to do was to cut our losses, he was quite sufficiently inventive to do that in a way that would not have destroyed the Great Society. It's not a dependent variable. It's an independent variable." In Bundy's view, Johnson saw achieving victory in Vietnam as important for its own sake, not merely as something necessary to ensure the survival of some domestic agenda. LBJ had vowed steadfastness in Vietnam in his very first foreign-policy meeting in November 1963 and had adhered to that line at all points thereafter.

A healthy dose of skepticism is always warranted when considering the recollections of former policymakers, especially when the subject is responsibility for policy mistakes. But here Bundy had it right. Lyndon Johnson was a hawk on Vietnam, and he was so for reasons that went beyond immediate domestic political or geostrategic advantage. For it was not merely his country's and his party's reputation that Johnson took to be on the line, but also his own. His tendency to personalize all issues relating to the war, so evident in the later years, in 1966 and 1967 and 1968, was there from the start, from the time he vowed to not be the first American president to lose a war. From the beginning, he viewed attacks on the policy as attacks on himself, saw American credibility and his own credibility as essentially synonymous. In so doing he diminished his capacity to render objective judgment, to retain the necessary level of detachment. He failed to see that the international and domestic political context gave him considerable freedom of maneuver, if not in the period before the November 1964 election then certainly in the weeks thereafter.

It would be difficult to exaggerate the importance of this conflation of the national interest and his own personal interest in Johnson's approach to Vietnam. . . .

The concern here went deeper than merely saving his political skin. In private LBJ would sometimes say that he could not withdraw from Vietnam because it would lead to his impeachment, but he was too smart a politician to really believe such a thing. What he really feared was the personal humiliation that he believed would come with failure in Vietnam. He saw the war as a test of his own manliness. Many have commented on the powerful element of *machismo* in Johnson's world view, rooted in his upbringing and fueled by his haunting fear that he would be judged insufficiently manly for the job, that he would lack courage when the chips were down. In his world there were weak and strong men; the weak men were the skeptics, who sat around contemplating, talking, criticizing; the strong men were the doers, the activists, the ones who were always tough and always refused to back down. Thus Mansfield could be dismissed as spineless, as "milquetoast"; thus Fulbright could be castigated as a "crybaby." Though Johnson on occasion showed himself quite capable of asking probing questions in policy meetings, he had little patience with those who tried to supply probing answers. His macho ethos extended to relations among states. "If you let a bully come into your front yard one day," he liked to say, in reference to the lesson of Munich, "the next day he will be up on your porch and the day after that he will rape your wife in your own bed." In such a situation, retreat was impossible, retreat was cowardly. Johnson's approach did not make him reckless on Vietnam—he was, in fact, exceedingly cautious—but it made him quite unable to contemplate extrication as anything but the equivalent of, as he might put it, "tucking tail and running."

This personal insecurity in Johnson, so much a feature of the recollections of those who knew him and worked with him, might have been less important in Vietnam policy if not for the way it reinforced his equally well documented intolerance of dissent. Even in the early months of his presidency he was incredulous to learn that some Americans might be opposed to his policy of fully supporting South Vietnam; it was un-American, he believed, to make an issue during the Cold War of national security matters. Throughout his career Johnson had made his way in politics by intimidation, by dominating those around him, and he did not change this modus operandi once he got into the White House. "I'm the only president you have," he told those who opposed his policies. His demand for consensus and loyalty extended to his inner circle of advisers, a reality that, when combined with his powerful personality, must have had a chilling effect on anyone inclined to try to build support for a contrary view. . . .

. . . At the top of the causal hierarchy for the Americanization of the Vietnam War in 1964–1965 must go Lyndon Johnson's conception of the conflict and what it meant for his domestic political and personal historical credibility, followed by the workings of the advisory system, and, in particular, the centrality within that system of Mssrs. McNamara, Bundy, and Rusk. The decision for major escalation grew out of two decades of American involvement in Indochina, and two decades of containing global communism, and it emerged out of still-older undercurrents in American culture and ideology, but it was crucially dependent on the active intervention of this small group of men. To a large extent they were responsible for the bloody war that followed.

But responsibility for war cannot be ascribed solely to the perceptions and actions of senior American officials; it must also be given to the shortcomings of those who *opposed* Americanization. . . .

. . . [T]he Americanization of the Vietnam War occurred in a permissive context. Influential observers, at home and abroad, could see the futility that lay ahead for any American military effort in South Vietnam but often were timid about saying so. Those who did speak up often gave few clues on how Washington could exit the morass. The posture of the British government and the Senate Democratic leadership, in particular, was crucial in allowing American policy to go forward, in allowing the Johnson administration to escalate by stealth. Harold Wilson and his colleagues in London were as anxious as the administration in Washington to avoid an Anglo-American rupture over Vietnam, and key Democrats shared LBJ's desire to avoid a full-fledged congressional debate on the conflict in the early weeks of 1965. If Lyndon Johnson faced a legitimate choice in the weeks after his 1964 election victory about which way to go on Vietnam, so did the London government and so did the leadership on Capitol Hill.

The permissive context extended to the general public as well, though here the problem was not timidity or vagueness but apathy. The vast majority of Americans during The Long 1964 knew little about Vietnam and cared less. The "public information campaign" launched by the administration in the late spring of 1964 to a large extent failed. Partly it failed because of the contradictions at the heart of the campaign itself—Johnson wanted to educate Americans about the importance of America's commitment to South Vietnam, but also to avoid giving them any sense that major war could be the result. (There were really two campaigns: a public information campaign and a public deception campaign.) But John Q. Citizen was also ignorant because he preferred it that way. Lyndon Johnson may have worked hard to avoid a national debate on the war in 1964–1965, but he had help from his constitutents. The public . . . could have forced a debate had it wanted to; enough information existed. (The strikingly knowledgeable letters to the editor that appeared regularly in America's newspapers during the period are one proof of that.) The public did not want a debate and therefore must accept some responsibility for the debacle that followed. . . .

[Political Scientist Hans] Morgenthau's argument, that any American war in Vietnam would be an unnecessary war, was a hopeful argument in the context of January 1965, before the carpet bombings had commenced, before U.S. fighting troops were on the scene, before the real bloodshed had started. But it is a profoundly troubling argument in hindsight (the comforting retrospective argument is the one that says it was all inevitable), less because the Johnson team failed to heed his advice than because they failed to even consider it. And there was every reason why they should have given it close consideration, given the realities of the situation in Vietnam and the realities of the domestic American and international political context. A move to extricate the United States from the war would have exacted a political price from Lyndon Johnson, but it would not have been an exorbitant price. ("Nineteen sixty-five is the year of minimum political risk for the Johnson administration," Hubert Humphrey had advised him.) It would have required moral courage, but no more of it than Americans should expect of their leaders. Moreover, the president and his team chose the war option not because of any tangible foreign-policy concerns or moral attachment to the South Vietnamese, but because of the threat of embarrassment—to the United States and the Democratic Party and, most of all, to themselves personally. They were willing to sacrifice virtually everything to avoid the stigma of failure. If the morality of a policy is determined in large part by the commensurateness of means to ends, that of the Johnson administration in Vietnam must be judged immoral.

The certainty that this was an unnecessary war, not merely in hindsight but in the context of the time, also makes the astronomical costs that resulted from it during 1965–1973 that much more difficult to contemplate. Foremost among these, of course, was the staggering number of deaths especially among Vietnamese, and the utter destruction of much of the country of Vietnam and large portions of Laos and Cambodia. The war also caused deep social divisions within American society, fostered a destructive cynicism about government claims and actions that persists to this day, and exacted staggering short- and long-term economic costs. (The diversion of hundreds of billions of dollars to the war could have been used to fund, for example, the total urban renewal of most large American cities.) Then there were the diplomatic costs. The administration's obsession with Vietnam after early 1965 caused it to neglect other vital foreign-policy issues, including relations with Latin America, Europe, and the Middle East, as well as the difficult frictions between rich and poor nations. Most important, the war was largely responsible for the lack of progress in East-West relations in the Johnson years. It is entirely reasonable to suggest, as long-time Soviet ambassador to Washington Anatoly Dobrynin has done, that had it not been for the Vietnam War, détente between the superpowers might have come in the mid 1960s, with potentially longer-lasting effects than the version that came later. The thawing in Moscow-Washington relations that occurred in the year after the Cuban Missile Crisis might well have continued, leading, if not to an outright end to the Soviet-American confrontation then at least to something that could no longer be called a Cold War.

✗ *F U R T H E R   R E A D I N G*

Austin, Anthony. *The President's War* (1971).
Ball, George W. *The Past Has Another Pattern* (1982).
Barrett, David M. *Uncertain Warriors: Lyndon Johnson and His Vietnam Advisers* (1993).
Berman, Larry. *Planning a Tragedy* (1982).
Bird, Kai. *The Color of Truth* (1998).
Bornet, Vaughan. *The Presidency of Lyndon B. Johnson* (1983).
Brands, H. W. *The Wages of Globalism* (1995).
Burke, John P., and Fred I. Greenstein. *How Presidents Test Reality* (1991).

Buzzanco, Robert. *Masters of War* (1996).

Clifford, Clark. *Counsel to the President* (1991).

Cohen, Warren I. *Dean Rusk* (1980).

———, and Nancy B. Tucker. *Lyndon B. Johnson Confronts the World* (1994).

Cooper, Chester L. *The Lost Crusade* (1972).

DiLeo, David L. *George Ball, Vietnam, and the Rethinking of Containment* (1991).

Fulbright, J. William. *The Price of Empire* (1989).

Galloway, John. *The Gulf of Tonkin Resolution* (1970).

Gardner, Lloyd C. *Pay Any Price* (1995).

Gardner Lloyd C., and Ted Gittinger, eds. *Vietnam: The Early Decisions* (1998).

Gelb Leslie H., and Richard K. Betts. *The Irony of Vietnam* (1979).

Geyelin, Philip. *Lyndon B. Johnson and the World* (1966).

Goulden, Joseph C. *Truth Is the First Casualty: The Gulf of Tonkin Affair* (1969).

Halberstam, David. *The Best and the Brightest* (1972).

Kaiser, David. *American Tragedy* (2000).

Kearns, Doris. *Lyndon Johnson and the American Dream* (1976).

Khong, Yuen Foong. *Analogies at War* (1992).

McMaster, H. R. *Dereliction of Duty* (1997).

McNamara, Robert S. *In Retrospect* (1995).

Moïse, Edwin E. *Tonkin Gulf and the Escalation of the Vietnam War* (1996).

Palmer, Gregory. *The McNamara Strategy and the Vietnam War* (1978).

Rusk, Dean. *As I Saw It* (1990).

Schwab, Orrin. *Defending the Free World* (1998).

Shapley, Deborah. *Promise and Power* (1993) (on Robert McNamara).

Short, Anthony. *The Origins of the Vietnam War* (1989).

VanDeMark, Brian. *Into the Quagmire* (1991).

Vandiver, Frank E. *Shadows of Vietnam: Lyndon Johnson's Wars* (1997).

Windchy, Eugene C. *Tonkin Gulf* (1971).

Zeiler, Thomas. *Dean Rusk* (2000).

U.S. Military Strategy

X

*From the introduction of U.S. ground forces in 1965, President Johnson, General
William C. Westmoreland, and other top civilian and military officials sought
to define a strategy appropriate to U.S. objectives in Vietnam. How could American
superiority in firepower and technology be brought to bear on an elusive enemy
in an inhospitable climate? Were America's goals primarily military or political?
What role, if any, should the United States play in the political stabilization of its
South Vietnamese ally? Those essential questions defied easy solutions for LBJ and
his successors.*

*American military strategy in Vietnam provoked an intense debate. among
scholars, military officers, and politicians. That debate, which began with the escalation of the American commitment in the mid-1960s, has raged unabated since
then; it remains nearly as lively today as at the height of the war. Certain issues
have proved especially troublesome. Was the attrition strategy wise? Might alternative military tactics have been more effective? Why did the United States adopt the
tactics and strategy that it did? To what extent did the United States understand
its foe—and its ally? How clear were the objectives for which it was fighting? Did
Hanoi and the National Liberation Front evolve tactics and strategy superior to
those of Washington? And, perhaps the most controversial question of all, could the
United States have won the war? If so, how?*

X *D O C U M E N T S*

In Document 1, a November 30, 1965, memorandum to President Johnson, Defense
Secretary Robert McNamara recommended additional American troop deployments
while admitting that even those deployments could not guarantee victory. George F.
Kennan, former U.S. ambassador to the Soviet Union and author of the containment
strategy that guided much of post–World War II American foreign policy, criticized
the U.S. military commitment to Vietnam in a publicized appearance before the Senate
Foreign Relations Committee. Excerpts from Kennan's statement are reprinted as
Document 2. A summary and review of U.S. military operations in South Vietnam, by
General William C. Westmoreland, follows. He sent it to President Johnson in August
1966. Document 4, a Central Intelligence Agency memorandum of May 12, 1967,
offers a candid assessment of the American bombing campaign against North Vietnam,

acknowledging its shortcomings. A public statement by McNamara on the improved military outlook for the United States in Vietnam follows. Ironically, at the same time he was issuing this optimistic public prognostication, his private doubts about the war effort were growing.

In Document 6, Westmoreland offers a retrospective justification of the attrition strategy.

1. Robert S. McNamara Urges Additional Troop Deployments, 1965

1. *Introductory comments.* Before giving my assessment of the situation and recommendations, I want to report that United States personnel in Vietnam are performing admirably. The massive Cam Ranh Bay complex has sprung into operation since our last visit in July; the troops that we visited (the 173d Airborne Brigade and the 1st Cavalry Division) have fought and are fighting well and their morale is high; and the team in Saigon is working harmoniously.

2. *The situation.* There has been no substantial change since my November 3 memorandum in the economic, political or pacification situation. There is a serious threat of inflation because of the mixture of US force build-up and GVN deficit on the one hand and the tightly stretched Vietnamese economy on the other; the [Nguyen Cao] Ky "government of generals" is surviving, but not acquiring wide support or generating actions; pacification is thoroughly stalled, with no guarantee that security anywhere is permanent and no indications that able and willing leadership will emerge in the absence of that permanent security. (Prime Minister Ky estimates his government controls only 25% of the population today and reports that his pacification chief hopes to increase that to 50% two years from now.)

The dramatic recent changes in the situation are on the military side. They are the increased infiltration from the North and the increased willingness of the Communist forces to stand and fight, even in large-scale engagements. The Ia Drang River Campaign of early November is an example. The Communists appear to have decided to increase their forces in South Vietnam both by heavy recruitment in the South (especially in the Delta) and by infiltration of regular North Vietnamese forces from the North. Nine regular North Vietnamese regiments (27 infantry battalions) have been infiltrated in the past year, joining the estimated 83 VC battalions in the South. The rate of infiltration has increased from three battalion equivalents a month in late 1964 to a high of 9 or 12 during one month this past fall. General Westmoreland estimates that through 1966 North Vietnam will have the capability to expand its armed forces in order to infiltrate three regiments (nine battalion equivalents, or 4500 men) a month, and that the VC in South Vietnam can train seven new battalion equivalents a month—together adding 16 battalion equivalents a month to the enemy forces. Communist casualties and desertions can be expected to go up if my recommendations for increased US, South Vietnamese and third country forces are accepted. Nevertheless, the enemy can be expected to enlarge his present strength of

Memo from McNamara to Johnson, November 30, 1965, *Foreign Relations in the United States, 1964–1963*, III, 591–593.

110 battalion equivalents to more than 150 battalion equivalents by the end of calendar 1966, when hopefully his losses can be made to equal his input.

As for the Communist ability to supply this force, it is estimated that, even taking account of interdiction of routes by air and sea, more than 200 tons of supplies a day can be infiltrated—more than enough, allowing for the extent to which the enemy lives off the land, to support the likely PAVN/VC force at the likely level of operations.

To meet this possible—and in my view likely—Communist build-up, the presently contemplated Phase I forces will not be enough. Phase I forces, almost all in place by the end of this year, involve 130 South Vietnamese, 9 Korean, 1 Australian and 34 US combat battalions (approximately 220,000 Americans). Bearing in mind the nature of the war, the expected weighted combat force ratio of less than 2-to-1 will not be good enough. Nor will the originally contemplated Phase II addition of 28 more US battalions (112,000 men) be enough; the combat force ratio, even with 32 new South Vietnamese battalions, would still be little better than 2-to-1 at the end of 1966. The initiative which we have held since August would pass to the enemy; we would fall far short of what we expected to achieve in terms of population control and disruption of enemy bases and lines of communications. Indeed, it is estimated that, with the contemplated Phase II addition of 28 US battalions, we would be able only to hold our present geographical positions.

3. *Military options and recommendations.* We have but two options, it seems to me. One is to go now for a compromise solution (something substantially less than the "favorable outcome" I described in my memorandum of November 3), and hold further deployments to a minimum. The other is to stick with our stated objectives and with the war, and provide what it takes in men and matériel. If it is decided not to move now toward a compromise, I recommend that the United States both send a substantial number of additional troops and very gradually intensify the bombing of North Vietnam. Ambassador Lodge, General Wheeler, Admiral Sharp and General Westmoreland concur in this pronged course of action, although General Wheeler and Admiral Sharp would intensify the bombing of the North more quickly.

a. *Troop deployments.* With respect to additional forces in South Vietnam to maintain the initiative against the growing Communist forces, I recommend:

1.   That the Republic of Korea be requested to increase their present deployment of nine combat battalions to 18 combat battalions (the addition of one division) before July 1966 and to 21 combat battalions (the addition of another brigade) before October 1966.
2.   That the Government of Australia be requested to increase their present deployment of one combat battalion to two combat battalions before October 1966.
3.   That the deployment of US ground troops be increased by the end of 1966 from 34 combat battalions to 74 combat battalions.
4.   That the FY '67 Budget for the Defense Department and the January Supplement to the FY '66 Budget be revised to reflect the expansion of US forces required to support the additional deployments.

The 74 US battalions—together with increases in air squadrons, naval units, air defense, combat support, construction units and miscellaneous logistic support and advisory personnel which I also recommend—would bring the total US personnel in Vietnam to approximately 400,000 by the end of 1966. And it should be understood that further deployments (perhaps exceeding 200,000) may be needed in 1967.

b. *Bombing of North Vietnam.* With respect to the program of bombing North Vietnam, I recommend that we maintain present levels of activity in the three quadrants west and south of Hanoi, but that over a period of the next six months we gradually enlarge the target system in the northeast (Hanoi-Haiphong) quadrant until, at the end of the period, it includes "controlled" armed reconnaissance of lines of communication throughout the area, bombing of petroleum storage facilities and power plants, and mining of the harbors. (Left unstruck would be population targets, industrial plants, locks and dams.)

2. George F. Kennan Criticizes the American Military Commitment, 1966

I have not been anxious to press my views on the public but I gladly give them to you for whatever they are worth, claiming no particular merit for them except perhaps that they flow from experience with Communist affairs that runs back now for some thirty-eight years, and also from the deepest and most troubled sort of concern that we should find the proper course, the right course, at this truly crucial moment.

The first point I would like to make is that if we were not already involved as we are today in Vietnam, I would know of no reason why we should wish to become so involved, and I could think of several reasons why we should wish not to. Vietnam is not a region of major military, industrial importance. It is difficult to believe that any decisive developments of the world situation would be determined in normal circumstances by what happens on that territory. If it were not for the considerations of prestige that arise precisely out of our present involvement, even a situation in which South Vietnam was controlled exclusively by the Viet Cong, while regrettable, and no doubt morally unwarranted, would not, in my opinion, present dangers great enough to justify our direct military intervention.

Given the situation that exists today in the relations among the leading Communist powers, and by that I have, of course, in mind primarily the Soviet-Chinese conflict, there is every likelihood that a Communist regime in South Vietnam would follow a fairly independent course. There is no reason to suspect that such a regime would find it either necessary or desirable in present circumstances to function simply as a passive puppet and instrument of Chinese power. And as for the danger that its establishment there would unleash similar tendencies in neighboring countries, this, I think, would depend largely on the manner in which it came into power.

In the light of what has recently happened in Indonesia, and on the Indian subcontinent, the danger of the so-called domino effect, that is the effect that would be produced by a limited Communist success in South Vietnam, seems to me to be considerably less than it was when the main decisions were taken that have led to our present involvement. Let me stress, I do not say that that danger does not exist.

U.S. Senate Committee on Foreign Relations, Hearings, 1966, reprinted in J. William Fulbright, ed., *The Vietnam Hearings* (New York: Random House, 1966), pp. 108–111.

I say that it is less than it was a year or two ago when we got into this involvement. From the long-term standpoint, therefore, and on principle, I think our military involvement in Vietnam has to be recognized as unfortunate, as something we would not choose deliberately, if the choice were ours to make all over again today, and by the same token, I think it should be our government's aim to liquidate this involvement just as soon as this can be done without inordinate damage to our own prestige or to the stability of conditions in that area.

It is obvious, on the other hand, that this involvement is today a fact. It creates a new situation. It raises new questions ulterior to the long-term problems which have to be taken into account; a precipitate and disorderly withdrawal could represent in present circumstances a disservice to our own interests and even to world peace greater than any that might have been involved by our failure to engage ourselves there in the first place. This is a reality which, if there is to be any peaceful resolution of this conflict, is going to have to be recognized both by the more critical of our friends and by our adversaries.

But at the same time, I have great misgivings about any deliberate expansion of hostilities on our part directed to the achievement of something called "victory," if by the use of that term we envisage the complete disappearance of the recalcitrance with which we are now faced, the formal submission by the adversary to our will, and the complete realization of our present stated political aims. I doubt that these things can be achieved even by the most formidable military successes.

There seems to be an impression that if we bring sufficient military pressure to bear, there will occur at some point something in the nature of a political capitulation on the other side. I think this is a most dangerous assumption. I don't say that it is absolutely impossible, but it is a dangerous assumption in the light of the experience we have had with Communist elements in the past. The North Vietnamese and the Viet Cong have, between them, a great deal of space and manpower to give up if they have to, and the Chinese can give them more if they need it. Fidelity to the Communist tradition would dictate that if really pressed to extremity on the military level, these people should disappear entirely from the open scene and fall back exclusively on an underground political and military existence rather than to accept terms that would be openly humiliating and would represent in their eyes the betrayal of the future political prospects of the cause to which they are dedicated.

Any total rooting-out of the Viet Cong from the territory of South Vietnam could be achieved, if it could be achieved at all, only at the cost of a degree of damage to civilian life and of civilian suffering, generally, for which I would not like to see this country responsible. And to attempt to crush North Vietnamese strength to a point where Hanoi could no longer give any support for Viet Cong political activity in the South would almost certainly, it seems to me, have the effect of bringing in Chinese forces at some point, whether formally or in the guise of volunteers, thus involving us in a military conflict with Communist China on one of the most unfavorable theaters of hostility that we could possibly choose.

This is not the only reason why I think we should do everything possible to avoid the escalation of this conflict. There is another one which is no less weighty, and this is the effect the conflict is already having on our policies and interests further afield. This involvement seems to me to represent a grievous misplacement of emphasis on our foreign policies as a whole. Not only are great and potentially more important questions of world affairs not receiving, as a consequence of our involvement in Vietnam, the attention they should be receiving, but in some instances assets we already enjoy and hopefully possibilities we should be developing, are being sacrificed to this unpromising involvement in a remote and secondary theater. Our relations with the Soviet Union have suffered grievously, as was to be expected, and this at a time when far more important things were involved in those relations than what is ultimately involved in Vietnam and when we had special reason, I think, to cultivate those relations. And more unfortunate still, in my opinion, is the damage being done to the feelings entertained for us by the Japanese people; the confidence and the good disposition of the Japanese is the greatest asset we have had and the greatest asset we could have in East Asia. As the greatest industrial complex in the entire Far East, and the only place where the sinews of modern war can be produced on a formidable scale there, Japan is of vital importance to us and indeed to the prospects generally of peace and stability in East Asia.

There is no success we could have in Vietnam that would conceivably warrant, in my opinion, the sacrifice by us of the confidence and good will of the Japanese people.

3. William C. Westmoreland Reviews Military Operations in South Vietnam, 1966

The enemy has launched a determined campaign to gain control of South Vietnam—its land, its people, and its government. There are no indications that the enemy has reduced his resolve. He has increased his rate of infiltration, formed divisions in South Vietnam, introduced new weapons, and maintained his lines of communications into South Vietnam in spite of our increased air efforts. He continues to use Laos and the border regions of Cambodia as sanctuaries and recently moved a division through the Demilitarized Zone (DMZ) into the First Corps Tactical Zone. His campaign of terror, assassination intimidation, sabotage, propaganda and guerilla warfare continues unabated. The enemy still holds sway over large segments of the land and population. Although thwarted in his overt large scale campaign, he is still determined.

As a companion of the foregoing appreciation of the present enemy situation, a review of our strategic concept for the past year would appear to be useful.

A. During the period 1 May 1965 to 1 November 1965, our task was to build up our combat and logistical forces; learn to employ them effectively; gain confidence in ourselves in fighting in the counterinsurgency and Southeast Asian environment; gain the trust of the Vietnamese in our military skills, courage and ability; and protect our installation and forces from distraction by the enemy.

B. During the period 1 November 1965 to 1 May 1966, our objectives were to extend our deployments toward the frontiers; exercise our logistics in furnishing support to troops in sustained combat; indoctrinate commanders on the techniques

Westmoreland telegram to Johnson, August 1966, *Foreign Relations of the United States,* 1964–1968, IV, 604–606.

of sustained ground combat; interdict intensively by air the lines of communications leading from North Vietnam to South Vietnam; disrupt enemy bases by B–52 strikes; deny the enemy rice by protecting harvests and capturing caches in storage areas; increase our surveillance along the coast; and initiate a program of patrolling certain vital inland waterways. In summary, our purpose was to disrupt the enemy's effort to prepare his battlefield, to throw his plans off balance by offensive operations, and to continue to gain experience and self-confidence in this environment.

C. During the period 1 May to 1 November 1966—the Southwest monsoon season—our strategy has been and is to contain the enemy through offensive tactical operations (referred to as "spoiling attacks" because they catch the enemy in the preparation phases of his offensives), force him to fight under conditions of our choosing, and deny him attainment of his own tactical objectives. At the same time we have utilized all forces that could be made available for area and population security in support of revolutionary development, rich harvests heretofore available to the enemy have been protected, lines of communication required by us have been opened, and some of the inland waterways used by the enemy have been interdicted to disrupt his communication and supply systems. The threat of the enemy main forces (Viet Cong and North Vietnamese Army) has been of such magnitude that fewer friendly troops could be devoted to general area security and support of revolutionary development than visualized at the time our plans were prepared for the period.

During the period 1 November 1966 to 1 May 1967—the Northeast monsoon season—we will maintain and increase the momentum of our operations. Our strategy will be one of a general offensive with maximum practical support to area and population security in further support of revolutionary development.

A. The essential tasks of revolutionary development and nation building cannot be accomplished if enemy main forces can gain access to the population centers and destroy our efforts. US/Free World forces, with their mobility and in coordination with Vietnamese Armed Forces, must take the fight to the enemy by attacking his main forces and invading his base areas. Our ability to do this is improving steadily. Maximum emphasis will be given to the use of long range patrols and other means to find the enemy and locate his bases. Forces and bases thus discovered will be subjected to either ground attack or quick reaction B–52 and tactical air strikes. When feasible, B–52 strikes will be followed by ground forces to search the area. Sustained ground combat operations will maintain pressure on the enemy.

The growing strength of US/Free World forces will provide the shield that will permit ARVN to shift its weight of effort to an extent not heretofore feasible to direct support of revolutionary development. Also, I visualize that a significant number of the US/Free World Maneuver Battalions will be committed to Tactical Areas of Responsibility (TOAR) missions. These missions encompass base security and at the same time support revolutionary development by spreading security radially from the bases to protect more of the population. Saturation patrolling, civic action, and close association with ARVN, regional and popular forces to bolster their combat effectiveness are among the tasks of the ground force elements. At the same time ARVN troops will be available if required to reinforce offensive operations and to serve as reaction forces for outlying security posts and government centers under attack. Our strategy will include opening, constructing and using roads, as well as a start toward opening and reconstructing the National Railroad. The priority effort of ARVN forces will be in direct support of the revolutionary development program; in many instances, the province chief will exercise operational control over these units. This fact notwithstanding, the ARVN division structure must be maintained and it is essential that the division commander enthusiastically support revolutionary development. Our highly capable US division commanders, who are closely associated with corresponding ARVN commanders, are in a position to influence them to do what is required.

C. We intend to employ all forces to get the best results, measured, among other things, in terms of population secured; territory cleared of enemy influence; Viet Cong/North Vietnamese Army bases eliminated; and enemy guerrillas, local forces, and main forces destroyed.

D. Barring unforeseen change in enemy strategy, I visualize that our strategy for South Vietnam will remain essentially the same throughout 1967.

In summation, the MACV mission, which is to assist the Government of Vietnam to defeat the Viet Cong/North Vietnamese Army forces and extend Government control throughout South Vietnam, prescribes our two principal tasks.

We must defeat the enemy through offensive operations against his main forces and bases.

We must assist the Government to gain control of the people by providing direct military support of revolutionary development in coordination with the other agencies of the U.S. Mission.

The simultaneous accomplishment of these tasks is required to allow the people of South Vietnam to get on with the job of nation building.

Ambassador Lodge concurs, with the following comment:

"I wish to stress my agreement with the attention paid in this message to the importance of military support for revolutionary development. After all, the main purpose of defeating the enemy through offensive operations against his main forces and bases must be to provide the opportunity through revolutionary development to get at the heart of the matter, which is the population of South Vietnam. If this goal is achieved, we will be denying manpower and other support to the Viet Cong."

4. The Central Intelligence Agency's Assessment of the Bombing Campaign, 1967

Through the end of April 1967 the US air campaign against North Vietnam— Rolling Thunder—had significantly eroded the capacities of North Vietnam's limited industrial and military base. These losses, however, have not meaningfully degraded North Vietnam's material ability to continue the war in South Vietnam.

Total damage through April 1967 was over $233 million, of which 70 percent was accounted for by damage to economic targets. The greatest amount of damage

---

CIA Intelligence Memo, May 12, 1967, declassified document reprinted in Porter, *Definitive Documentation*, II, 470–472.

was inflicted on the so-called logistics target system—transport equipment and lines of communication.

By the end of April 1967 the US air campaign had attacked 173 fixed targets, over 70 percent of the targets on the JCS list. This campaign included extensive attacks on almost every major target system in the country. The physical results have varied widely.

All of the 13 targeted petroleum storage facilities have been attacked, with an estimated loss of 85 percent of storage capacity. Attacks on 13 of the 20 targeted electric power facilities have neutralized 70 percent of North Vietnam's power-generating capacity. The major losses in the military establishment include the neutralization of 18 ammunition depots, with a loss capacity of 70 percent. Over three fourths of the 65 JCS-targeted barracks have been attacked, with a loss of about one fourth of national capacity. Attacks on 22 of the 29 targeted supply depots reduced capacity by 17 percent. Through the end of April 1967, five of North Vietnam's air-fields had been attacked, with a loss of about 20 percent of national capacity.

North Vietnam's ability to recuperate from the air attacks has been of a high order. The major exception has been the electric power industry. One small plant—Co Dinh—is beyond repair. Most of the other plants would require 3–4 months to be restored to partial operations, although two plants—Haiphong East and Uong Bi—would require one year. For complete restoration, all of the plants would require at least a year. Restoration of these plants would require foreign technical assistance and equipment.

The recuperability problem is not significant for the other target systems. The destroyed petroleum storage system has been replaced by an effective system of dispersed storage and distribution. The damaged military target systems—particularly barracks and storage depots—have simply been abandoned, and supplies and troops dispersed throughout the country. The inventories of transport and military equipment have been replaced by large infusions of military and economic aid from the USSR and Communist China. Damage to bridges and lines of communications is frequently repaired within a matter of days, if not hours, or the effects are countered by an elaborate system of multiple bypasses or pre-positioned spans.

5. McNamara on the Improved Military Outlook, 1967

On the military field, let me say to start with, the military commanders I met with—and I met with all of the senior military commanders in the field, all of the senior Vietnamese commanders, many of the Allied commanders, Korean, and New Zealanders, for example, and many of the middle-ranking and junior U.S. officers—all of the military commanders stated that the reports that they read in the press of military stalemate were, to use their words, the "most ridiculous statements that they had ever heard."

McNamara statement, July 12, 1967, U.S. Department of State *Bulletin* (57 July 1967), 168–169.

In their view military progress had occurred and was continuing. How did they measure this? They measured it in particular by the success of what they called the large-unit actions. These are battalion-sized and larger actions.

They felt that these actions that General [William C.] Westmoreland had organized and carried on over the past several months, particularly in II and III Corps, had a spoiling effect on the Viet Cong and North Vietnamese. Before they could concentrate their troops to launch an offensive, Westmoreland, through his intelligence sources, had obtained information about the intended enemy plans and had struck the troop concentrations as they were developing, spoiling the potential of the enemy for carrying out these offensive actions.

Moreover, as you know, it has been General Westmoreland's strategy over the past several months to attack the base areas, particularly those in the II and III Corps, using B-52 strikes in some cases but in particular using a coordinated ground and air attack against these base areas to destroy the facilities, the stocks—the recuperation areas that the Viet Cong and the North Vietnamese had used.

The military commanders felt, as a result of this combination of spoiling attacks and attacks on the base areas, the pressure had been so great on the North Viet Cong that they had tended to shift their area of activity. Whereas up until very recently, the activity had been concentrated primarily in the II and III Corps, the offensive activities more recently—they had moved their area of action to the I Corps.

This is understandable because in the II and III Corps—with the loss of their base areas—they were at the end of a very long line of communication over which their men and supplies moved from the supply centers in North Viet-Nam. This line of communications moved down the panhandle of North Viet-Nam across into Laos, down Laos to the Cambodian border, and across into South Viet-Nam—a very, very long line of communication that was under very intense air attack, as a matter of fact.

And because this was a handicap to them—particularly so in connection with the strategy that Westmoreland was carrying out against them—they shifted their area of activity to I Corps.

This accounts for their military actions there in the past several weeks. Now they have the advantage of short lines of communication extending down to the southern border of Viet-Nam, very close to the point where the troops are now very active.

Perhaps the most dramatic change that I saw that reflects the military situation was the opening of the roads.

Highway No. 1, which is the coastal route that runs from the 17th parallel—the line of demarcation between North Viet-Nam and South Viet-Nam—clear south to Saigon, has been broken for many, many months in literally hundreds of places, and traffic on the route has been minimal.

But within the past several months, as a result of these military actions—planned and carried out by the free-world forces—that route has gradually been reopened in large segments.

As a matter of fact, day before yesterday, the route from the southern border of the II Corps up to Dong Hai, which is very close to the DMZ—just a few miles south of the DMZ—was opened for traffic.

There will continue to be ambushes, I presume, and Viet Cong strikes against it, but as I flew over the road after this long stretch was opened, literally hundreds of bicycles and scores of cars and trucks—civilian cars and trucks—were using it.

The same thing is true of many of the feeder roads in III and IV Corps—roads that are of importance to move vegetables or rice to market or otherwise serving as an underpinning of the day-to-day life of the society.

I don't want to exaggerate this or imply all roads are open—far from it. I don't even want to suggest that many of the roads being used can be used freely night and day. They can't. But there has been a very, very noticeable—when I say "noticeable," I mean one flying over the area can notice a very substantial increase in the miles of roads that are open to traffic and the volume of traffic on the roads.

Perhaps a word about the air operations is in order.

We have suffered materially in air operations because of night vision—the difficulty of acquiring targets at night.

There have been some very significant changes in technology. I don't want to go into the details of them other than to say they have greatly increased the capability of our forces to carry on all-weather attacks on the lines of communication, both in South Viet-Nam and in North Viet-Nam.

These, in conjunction with new weapons, new types of ordnance, that have been designed and developed in recent years and brought into production in recent months in combination have increased the effectiveness of the airstrikes. As a matter of fact, they have reduced the losses of both planes and pilots. The losses of planes, for example, are rather significantly lower than we had previously estimated.

Now a word on the pacification program. You are all aware that within the past few weeks there has been a reorganization of the American effort in pacification, an integration of the civilian and military staffs.

The responsibility for pacification has been assigned to General Westmoreland, whose deputy, Mr. Robert Komer, has been placed in direct charge of it. I was very pleased with what I saw.

The frictions that I had read about in the paper perhaps existed at one time but certainly have been dampened down, if not completely eliminated. Both civilian and military officers that I visited at the sector level, the provinces, and the sub-sector levels of the villages and hamlets, were working effectively together and appeared to have benefited from this integration and reorganization of the pacification efforts.

However, having said that, I should state to you that to be candid I must report the progress in pacification has been very slow. I think that the momentum will increase as the new organization gains in experience, but what we are really trying to do here is engage in nation-building. It is an extraordinarily complex process. I would anticipate progress in what is really a very significant field would continue to be slow.

I am sure that the first question you would ask me, if I didn't anticipate it, would be about additional military personnel; so I will address myself to that. I think some more U.S. military personnel will be required. I am not sure how many. I am certain of one thing: that we must use more effectively the personnel that are presently there.

When I say that, I am speaking of all free-world personnel. As you know, the Vietnamese, the Koreans, the Australians, the New Zealanders, the Filipinos, as well as we, have all contributed forces to the support of the operations in Viet-Nam.

There has been a very rapid buildup of those forces. We now have in uniform of the free-world forces over 1,300,000 men. As you might expect in any organization that has expanded as fast as this one has, there are bound to be areas of waste and inefficiency that can be corrected and eliminated—that must be corrected when we are considering additional troop requirements.

6. Westmoreland Reflects on a War of Attrition, 1977

In response to changes in national policy, there were basically six strategies adopted between 1954 and 1969. The first involved bolstering the South Vietnamese by sending advisers and logistical and economic support in the hope that this could stop and reverse the subversive efforts of the Communists within South Vietnam. The second was an overall strategy of gradually escalating pressure against North Vietnam in the hope of convincing the North to halt its support of the insurgency in the South. This was essentially a strategy based on bombing. The third was a base-security strategy, which was an adjunct of the decision to bomb North Vietnam but which can be called a strategy in that it represented the first commitment of American ground troops to the fighting, albeit in a defensive role. The fourth was an enclave strategy, which assumed protection by American troops of five important areas of South Vietnam but still left most of the fighting to the South Vietnamese. The fifth involved a gradual buildup of forces in the South for purposes of putting maximum pressure on the Communist structure and forces in the South, emphasizing pacification and nation building, expanding control by the South Vietnamese Government over the population, and, at the same time, escalating pressure on the North with air and naval power. The political objective was to bring the enemy to the conference table. The final strategy comprised maximum expansion of the Vietnamese armed forces, increased efforts to pacify all of South Vietnam and to build a viable nation, coupled with gradual withdrawal with or without negotiations.

The decision to launch an air campaign of rising intensity against the North was made against a background of anguished concern over the threat of South Vietnam's imminent collapse. Although the basic objective was to try to convince the North to end its support of the insurgency, another objective was to bolster the morale and strengthen the resolve of the South Vietnamese, who had long been absorbing punishment while the supporters of the insurgency enjoyed impunity.

Two basic considerations lay behind the gradual escalation of the campaign. First, a modest bombing effort might be enough to convince the North of American resolve and, if negotiations developed, might compensate for some of the leverage the Viet Cong victories gave the other side. Secondly, the fear of Chinese Communist intervention was always of immense concern to American officials. Since the Chinese had responded to earlier bombings in muted tones, policy makers in Washington deduced that a gradually increasing campaign might ruffle the Chinese less than would a sudden massive onslaught. The Administration was faced with a dilemma—mobilizing too much support for the war might produce "war fever" and cause the American people to look upon the war as a "great crusade." Nevertheless, I believe a better job could have been done in explaining the nature of our objectives to the American people and the historical background of our involvement.

The strategy of gradually escalating pressure was a new concept; the Joint Chiefs of Staff disagreed with it. It was not, to them, an early "win" policy. Most military men are accustomed to thinking in terms of terminating a war in the shortest practical time and at least cost, following a decision to fight. It is perhaps unnecessary to make the point that there is a relationship between the length of a war and its cost.

By early April 1965, it had become apparent that the new strategy, even with its adjunct of base security, was having no visible effect on the will of the North Vietnamese to continue to support the insurgency. As someone has put it, the United States was signaling Hanoi with a new alphabet that Hanoi could not or would not read. The realization that the air war alone was not doing the job—or at least would take a long time to do it—led to a belief that some new step had to be taken directly against the insurgency in the South. So long as the Viet Cong—reinforced at that point by North Vietnamese troops—continued to win, the leaders in the North, in expectation of ultimate victory, probably would endure the punishment the limited bombing campaign was inflicting.

Taking a new step against the Viet Cong clearly meant actively involving American troops, yet President Johnson and most of his advisers still shied from such a fateful step. Once committed, planes and ships could be readily withdrawn; not so with ground troops. Furthermore, how well would American troops with their sophisticated equipment perform in an Asian insurgency environment? Better to devise some kind of strategy that stopped short of unrestricted commitment, one that would further signal American resolve yet at the same time provide escape valves.

That was the thinking behind the enclave strategy whereby American troops were to take full responsibility for defense of five coastal enclaves and to be prepared to go to the rescue of South Vietnamese forces within fifty miles of the enclaves. Yet, as I pointed out at the time, it put American troops in the unfortunate position of defending static defensive positions with their backs to the sea—in effect, holding five embattled beachheads. It also left the decision of ultimate success or failure in the hands of South Vietnamese troops whose demonstrated inability to defeat the Viet Cong was the reason for committing American troops.

In the face of continuing crisis, my view, and that of the Joint Chiefs of Staff, prevailed. President Johnson's decision of July 1965 carried the United States across the threshold in Vietnam. Before 1965 ended, the United States was to have 184,000 military personnel in Vietnam, including an Army air-mobile division and a Marine division.

Based on my personal experience with the problems on the ground in South Vietnam—political and military—and considering my perception of the aims of the enemy, I anticipated in 1965 that this nation was becoming involved in a protracted war of attrition in which our national will would be sorely tried. As a student of the history of war, and remembering the relatively recent Korean War experience, I was aware of the likelihood that a limited war, fought with limited means for limited objectives, would put special strain on the body politic of a system of government such as ours.

It was in such a context that I recommended continuation of the one year tour that had been set for advisers. It was my belief that lengthy involuntary tours would more likely bring about a hue and cry to "bring the boys home" than a tour in which the "boys would come home" after one year unless they volunteered to stay longer. Also, in anticipation of a long war, it seemed to me that the burden of service should be shared by a cross section of American youth. I did not anticipate that numbers of our young men would be allowed by national policy to defer service by going to a college campus.

I hoped, perhaps with folly, that an emerging sense of South Vietnamese nationalism and a revitalized national will in South Vietnam—manifested in a viable government and a proficient fighting force—would in the long run compensate for the inevitable waning of public support in the United States for a difficult war. . . .

From a military standpoint, it clearly would have been better to have moved much earlier against the enemy's sanctuaries in Laos and Cambodia and possibly even in the southern reaches of North Vietnam. Yet that is speaking without consideration for the political consequences. Further, if the military could have employed air and naval power in accordance with its best judgment, our strategy could have been accelerated. However, the same caution may not have been exercised and the dangers of provoking China to get more deeply involved could have been enhanced.

The Vietnam conflict was an undeclared and limited war, with a limited objective, fought with limited means against an unorthodox enemy, and with limited public support. The longest war in our history, it was the most reported and the most visible to the public—but the least understood. It was more than a military confrontation; ideological, economic, psychological, political, and nation-building problems were involved. Our national involvement in Southeast Asia became an emotional public controversy and hence a political issue. This new and traumatic experience by our nation should provide lessons for our people, our leadership, the news media, and our soldiers.

✗ *E S S A Y S*

Harry G. Summers, Jr., a U.S. army colonel who served as a battalion and corps operations officer in Vietnam, criticizes both military strategy and civilian leadership during the Vietnam War. He believes that a different strategy could have brought victory to the United States. A selection from his influential book *On Strategy* is the first essay. George C. Herring, a professor of history at the University of Kentucky and author of several acclaimed books on the Vietnam War, doubts that a different strategy could have brought victory for the United States. Yet he, too, is sharply critical of U.S. conduct of the war. Herring enumerates some of the major problems that plagued American military strategy during the Johnson years, emphasizing, in particular, the deficiencies of LBJ's military leadership and the inherent difficulties associated with fighting a limited war.

A Critical Appraisal of American Strategy

HARRY G. SUMMERS, JR.

One of the continuing arguments about the Vietnam war is whether or not a formal declaration of war would have made any difference. On the one hand there are those who see a declaration of war as a kind of magic talisman that would have eliminated all our difficulties. On the other hand there are those who see a declaration of war as a worthless anachronism. The truth is somewhere in between. A declaration of war is a clear statement of *initial* public support which focuses the nation's attention on the enemy. (Continuation of this initial public support is, of course, contingent on the successful prosecution of war aims.) As we will see, it was the lack of such focus on the enemy and on the political objectives to be obtained by the use of military force that was the crux of our strategic failure.

Further, a declaration of war makes the prosecution of the war a shared responsibility of both the government and the American people. . . . Without a declaration of war the Army was caught on the horns of a dilemma. It was ordered into battle by the Commander in Chief, the duly elected President of the United States. It was sustained in battle by appropriations by the Congress, the elected representatives of the American people. The legality of its commitment was not challenged by the Supreme Court of the United States. Yet, because there was no formal declaration of war, many vocal and influential members of the American public questioned (and continue to question) the legality and propriety of its actions.

This dilemma needs to be understood. It transcends the legal niceties over the utility of a declaration of war. It even transcends the strategic military value of such a declaration. It should not be dismissed as a kind of sophisticated "stab in the back" argument. As will be seen, the requirement for a declaration of war was rooted in the principle of civilian control of the military, and the failure to declare war in Vietnam drove a wedge between the Army and large segments of the American public.

It is not as if we did not know better. We knew perfectly well the importance of maintaining the bond between the American people and their soldiers in the field, and that this bond was the source of our moral strength. As early as the Revolutionary War this moral strength was a primary factor in our defeat of the British, then a major world power. As a result of this experience we wrote the rules for invoking the national will into our Constitution. Article 1, Section 8 states them clearly:

> The Congress shall have Power . . . To declare War . . . To raise and support Armies . . . To make Rules for the Government and Regulation of the land and naval forces . . .

Implicit in this rule was the rejection of an 18th century-type army answerable only to the Executive. The American Army would be a people's Army to be committed only by the will of the people. As Alexander Hamilton explained:

> The whole power of raising armies [is] lodged in the *Legislature*, not in the *Executive;* This Legislature [is] to be a popular body, consisting of the representatives of the people,

---

Reprinted with permission from the book *On Strategy* by Harry G. Summers, Jr., pp. 21–23, 120–124, 1982, as published by Presidio Press, 31 Pameron Way, Novato, CA 94949.

periodically elected . . . .a great and real security against the keeping of troops without evident necessity.

   . . . The power of the President would be inferior to that of the Monarch

   . . . That of the British King extends to the *Declaring* of war and to the Raising and Regulating of fleets and armies; All which by the Constitution . . . would appertain to the Legislature.

Hamilton's remarks highlight a critical distinction. In other nations a declaration of war by the chief executive alone (emperor, king, premier, party chairman) may or may not represent the *substance* of the will of his people. By requiring that a declaration of war be made by the representatives of the people (the Congress), rather than by the President alone, the Founding Fathers sought to guarantee this substance and insure that our armed forces would not be committed to battle without the support of the American people. Ironically, President Johnson seemed to know that. In a peculiar passage in light of what was to follow, he said:

> I believed that President Truman's one mistake in courageously going to the defense of South Korea in 1950 had been his failure to ask Congress for an expression of its backing. He could have had it easily, and it would have strengthened his hand. I made up my mind not to repeat that error. . . .

Like President Truman in 1950, President Johnson could probably have had a declaration of war in August 1964 after the Gulf of Tonkin incidents when two American destroyers were attacked by North Vietnamese patrol boats. Instead of asking for a declaration of war, however, President Johnson asked Congress for a resolution empowering him to "take all necessary measures to repel an armed attack against the forces of the United States and to prevent further aggression.". . .

Because they made the cardinal military error of underestimating the enemy, our military leaders failed in their role as "the principal military advisors to the President." There are some who have yielded to the temptation to blame everything on the Commander in Chief, President Johnson. But even his severest critics would have to admit that he certainly did not set out to put the nation in turmoil, ruin his political career, and lose the Vietnam war. It was the duty and responsibility of his military advisors to warn him of the likely consequences of his actions, to recommend alternatives, and, as Napoleon put it, to tender their resignations rather than be the instrument of their army's downfall. In failing to press their military advice they allowed the United States to pursue a strategic policy that was faulty from the start. Instead of deliberately adopting the *strategic defensive,* and tailoring our strategies and tactics to that posture, we slipped into it almost unaware and confused it with the *strategic offensive.* In so doing we lost sight of our strategic purpose and found the truth in the Clausewitzian observation: "Defense without an active purpose is self-contradictory both in strategy and in tactics." By their own failure to understand what we were about, our military leaders were not able to warn our civilian decision-makers that the strategy we were pursuing could never lead to conclusive results.

    Although from 1965 until 1975 (with the exception of Tet-68 and the ill-fated Eastertide Offensive of 1972) the North Vietnamese were also in a defensive posture, there was a critical difference. The North Vietnamese were on the tactical defensive as part of a strategic offensive to conquer South Vietnam. Our adoption of the strategic defensive was an end in itself and we had substituted the negative aim of counterinsurgency for the positive aim of isolation of the battlefield. This was a fatal flaw. As Clausewitz said, "A major victory can only be obtained by positive measures aimed at a *decision,* never by simply waiting on events. In short, even in the defense, a major stake alone can bring a major gain. The North Vietnamese had a major stake—the conquest of Indochina. It was the United States that was "simply waiting on events."

. . . Clausewitz defined critical analysis as "not just an evaluation of the means actually employed, but of *all possible means.* . . . One can, after all, not condemn a method without being able to suggest a better alternative." From a "purely military" standpoint it might appear that the better alternative would have been a strategic offensive against North Vietnamese armed forces and their will to fight. But, as Clausewitz warned, there is no such thing as a "purely military" strategy. Military strategy exists to serve political ends, and, . . . for a variety of very practical political reasons an invasion of North Vietnam was politically unacceptable.

We were faced with essentially the same dilemma we had faced in the Korean war. Our political policy was to contain the expansion of communist power, but we did not wish to risk a world war by using military means to destroy the source of that power. We solved that dilemma in Korea by limiting our political objectives to containing North Korean expansion and successfully applied our military means to achieve that end. In Vietnam we began with just such limited objectives. Our mistake was in failing to concentrate our military means on that task. It would appear that we sensed this deficiency, since the Korean war model was essentially the alternative that General Vien, General Westmoreland and the JCS recommended. It was not identified as such because it did not fit the frame of reference we had established for ourselves. For one thing, establishment of a Korean war-type objective in the mid-1960s would have branded Army leadership as hopelessly anachronistic. . . . From the perspective of our total victory in World War II, Korea still looked like a defeat and it is only from the perspective of our actual defeat in Vietnam that we can see that Korea was actually a victory. Further, there was the tyranny of fashion. Counterinsurgency, not conventional tactics, appeared to be the wave of the future. Finally, their plans hinged on the mobilization of the Reserves, a political price President Johnson was not prepared to pay.

Time and bitter experience has removed these distortions from our frame of reference. In 1977, General Bruce Palmer, Jr. (USA, Retired), former commander of U.S. Army Vietnam and former Vice Chief of Staff, U.S. Army, saw clearly what should have been done. In a seminar at the U.S. Army War College, he said that, together with an expanded Naval blockade, the Army should have taken the tactical offensive along the DMZ across Laos to the Thai border in order to isolate the battlefield and then *deliberately* assume the strategic and tactical defensive. While this strategy might have entailed some of the same long-term costs of our Korean strategy, it would (like that strategy) have furthered our political objective of containing communist expansion. He said that in his opinion this could have been accomplished *without reserve mobilization,* without invading North Vietnam and running the risk of Chinese intervention, and with substantially fewer combat forces than were actually deployed to Vietnam.

In brief, General Palmer's strategic concept called for a five-division force (two U.S., two ROK [Republic of Korea] and one ARVN along the DMZ with three more U.S. divisions deployed to extend the defensive line to the Lao-Thai border). An additional U.S. division would have been used to stabilize the situation in the central highlands and in the Saigon area. The Marine divisions would have been held in strategic reserve, to be available to reinforce the DMZ and to pose an amphibious threat, thereby tying down North Vietnamese forces in coastal defense.

General Palmer believed that the advantages of such a strategy would have been enormous. It would have required four fewer divisions than the ten and two-thirds divisions we actually deployed. "Moreover," he said, "the bulk of these forces would have fought on ground of their choosing which the enemy would be forced to attack if he wanted to invade South Vietnam. [This would have provided U.S. forces with a clear and understandable objective—a peace-keeping operation to separate the belligerents.] In defending well-prepared positions, U.S. casualties would have been much fewer. . . . The magnitude and likelihood and intensity of the so-called 'Big War,' involving heavy fire power, would have been lessened [one of the main causes of U.S. public disenchantment with the war]." He went on to say that a much smaller U.S. logistics effort would have been required and we would have avoided much of the base development that was of no real value to the South Vietnamese. "Cut off from substantial out-of-country support, the Viet Cong was bound to wither on the vine and gradually become easier for the South Vietnamese to defeat," he concluded. This conclusion was recently reinforced by statements of former South Vietnamese leaders who believed that by providing a military shield behind which South Vietnam could work out its own political, economic, and social problems, the United States could have provided a reasonable chance for South Vietnamese freedom and independence.

Writing after the U.S. withdrawal from Vietnam, Brigadier Shelford Bidwell, editor of *RUSI,* the distinguished British military journal of the Royal United Services Institute, commented on the view that the war in Vietnam was unwinnable. "This is rubbish," he said, blaming our failure on our election of a strategy which "not only conferred on the North Vietnamese the privilege of operating on safe exterior lines from secure bases but threw away the advantages of a tactical and strategic initiative." He went on to note that by "using firepower of crushing intensity" we succeeded in defeating both the insurgency and the 1972 North Vietnamese offensive but at the strategic price of "American society in turmoil. . . . All this . . . would have been avoided," he said, "by adopting the classical principles of war by cutting off the trouble at the root. . . . If this was not politically realistic, then the war should not have been fought at all."

Just as the North Koreans and their Chinese allies were the "root of the trouble" in the Korean war, so the root in the Vietnam war was North Vietnam (*not* the Viet Cong). In Vietnam as in Korea our political objectives dictated a strategic defensive posture. While this prevented us from destroying the "root" at the source through the strategic offensive, Korea proved that it was possible to achieve a favorable decision with the strategic defensive. It restored the status quo ante, prevented the enemy from achieving his goals with military means, and provided the foundation for a negotiated settlement. All of this was within our means in Vietnam.

A Different Kind of War

GEORGE C. HERRING

Of the two great questions concerning involvement in Vietnam—why did the United States intervene and why did it fail—the latter has provoked the most emotional controversy. Historically, as a nation, America has been uniquely successful, so much so that its people have come to take success for granted. When failure occurs, scapegoats are sought and myths concocted to explain what is otherwise inexplicable. In the case of Vietnam, many critics of America's conduct of the war have thus insisted that a different approach would have produced the "proper" results. Such arguments can never be proven, of course, and they are suspect in method. As Wayne Cole observed many years ago of a strikingly similar debate in the aftermath of World War II, the "most heated controversies . . . do not center on those matters for which the facts and truth can be determined with greatest certainty. The interpretive controversies, on the contrary, rage over questions about which the historian is least able to determine the truth."

By examining the Johnson administration's conduct of the war—without presuming that it should have been won—this [essay] seeks to help explain why the world's greatest power was unable to impose its will on a "backward" Third World country. The outcome of the war was not exclusively or even primarily the result of bad management. Still, by looking at the formulation and implementation of strategy, the organization of pacification programs, the handling of various peace initiatives, the perception and manipulation of public opinion, and the post-Tet strategy of fighting while negotiating, [one can see] . . . various flaws in the administration's running of the war.

The most glaring deficiency is that in an extraordinarily complex war there was no real strategy. President Johnson and Secretary of Defense Robert S. McNamara provided no firm strategic guidance to those military and civilian advisers who were running programs in the field. They set no clearcut limits on what could be done, what resources might be employed, and what funds expended. Without direction from the top, each service or agency did its own thing. Strategy emerged from the field on an improvised basis without careful calculation of the ends to be sought and the means used to attain them.

Perhaps equally important and less generally recognized, despite widespread and steadily growing dissatisfaction among the president's top advisers with the way the war was being fought and the results that were being obtained, there was no change of strategy or even systematic discussion of such a change. Not until the shock of the 1968 Tet offensive compelled it were the basic issues of how the war was being fought even raised. Even then, they were quickly dropped and left largely unresolved. Despite talk among the president's top advisers of borrowing a page from the communists' book and fighting while negotiating, the administration after Tet replaced one makeshift strategy with another, perpetuating and in some ways exacerbating the problems that had afflicted its management of the war from the beginning.

Closely related to and to some extent deriving from the absence of strategy was the lack of coordination of the numerous elements of what had become by 1966 a sprawling, multifarious war effort. Johnson steadfastly refused to assume overall direction of the war, and he would not create special machinery or designate someone else to run it. In Vietnam, therefore, each service or agency tended to go about its own business without much awareness of the impact of its actions in other areas or on other programs. The air war against North Vietnam operated separately from the ground war in South Vietnam (and the air war in Laos was run separately from both). Through the first years of the war the various civilian programs in South Vietnam competed with each other for resources. Even after the establishment of CORDS brought some order to pacification, village-level activities were not closely integrated as harmonized with military operations. [General Creighton] Abrams's "One-War" concept represented a serious attempt to coordinate pacification and military operations, but it was not entirely successful in changing deeply entrenched ways of doing things. In any event it was too little, and it came too late. [Peace initiatives] MARIGOLD and SUNFLOWER were only the most glaring examples where poor management and lack of coordination destroyed possibly promising peace initiatives or caused the United States serious public relations problems. Even the most modest and limited efforts to better coordinate the war . . . came to naught.

It is more difficult to determine why these problems existed. In part, no doubt, institutional imperatives were at fault. The rule in bureaucracy, as Robert Komer has pointed out, is that when an organization does not know what to do—or is not told what to do—it does what it knows how to do. Thus, in the absence of strong leadership from the top, the various services and agencies acted on the basis of their own standard operating procedures whether or not they were appropriate or compatible. CIA operative William Colby recalls warning McGeorge Bundy during the U.S. buildup in 1965 that the growing militarization of the war was diverting attention from the more urgent problems in the villages of South Vietnam. He pleaded with the presidential adviser to refocus the administration's attention toward the proper area. "You may be right, Bill," Colby remembered Bundy answering, "but the structure of the American government won't permit it." "What he meant," Colby concluded, "was that the Pentagon had to fight the only war it knew how to fight, and there was no American organization that could fight any other." This was most true of the army, air force, and navy, but it was also true of the civilian agencies.

Limited war theory also significantly influenced the way the war was fought. Korea and especially the Truman-MacArthur controversy stimulated a veritable cult of limited war in the 1950s and 1960s, the major conclusion of which was that in a nuclear age where total war was unthinkable limited war was essential. McNamara, William and McGeorge Bundy, Rusk, and indeed Lyndon Johnson were deeply imbued with limited war theory, and it determined in many crucial ways their handling of Vietnam. Coming of age in World War II, they were convinced of the essentiality of deterring aggression to avoid a major war. Veterans of the Cuban missile crisis, they lived with the awesome responsibility of preventing nuclear conflagration and they were thus committed to fighting in "cold blood" and maintaining tight operational control over the military. They also operated under the mistaken assumption that limited war was more an exercise in crisis management than the application of strategy, and they were thus persuaded that gradual escalation would achieve their limited goals without provoking the larger war they so feared. Many of their notions, of course, turned out to be badly flawed.

To an even greater extent, Lyndon Johnson's own highly personalized style indelibly marked the conduct of the war and contributed to its peculiar frustrations. LBJ was a "kind of whirlwind," David Lilienthal has observed, a man of seemingly boundless energy who attempted to put his personal brand on everything he dealt with. He dominated the presidency as few others have. He sought to run the war as he ran his household and ranch, his office and *his* government, with scrupulous attention to the most minute detail. As with every other personal and political crisis he faced he worked tirelessly at the job of commander in chief of a nation at war. His approach was best typified by his oft-quoted and characteristically hyperbolic boast that U.S. airmen could not bomb an outhouse in North Vietnam without his approval. In the case of Vietnam, however, the result was the worst of both worlds, a strategic vacuum and massive intrusion at the tactical level, micromanagement without real control. Whether he would admit it or not, moreover, LBJ quickly found in Vietnam a situation that eluded his grasp and dissipated even *his* seemingly inexhaustible storehouse of energy.

In so many ways, the conduct of the war reflected Johnson's modus operandi. The reluctance to provide precise direction and define a mission and explicit limits, the highly politicized, for Johnson characteristically middle-of-the-road approach that gave everybody something and nobody what they wanted, that emphasized consensus and internal harmony over results on the battlefield or at the negotiating table, all these were products of a thoroughly political and profoundly insecure man, a man especially ill at ease among military issues and military people.

Johnson's intolerance for any form of intragovernmental dissent and his unwillingness to permit, much less order, a much-needed debate on strategic issues deserve special note. It was not, as his most severe critics have argued, the result of his determination to impose a hermetically sealed system or his preference for working with sycophants, the so-called Caligula syndrome. LBJ was a domineering individual, to be sure, and he did have a strong distaste for conflict in his official family. As David Barrett and others have pointed out, however, he eagerly sought out and indeed opened himself to a wide diversity of viewpoints. Whatever their faults, the people that worked with him were anything but sycophants.

The problem went much deeper than that. In part, it reflected the peculiar mix of personalities involved, the rigorous standards of loyalty of a Rusk or McNamara, Harriman's determination to retain influence at the cost of principle and candor. From Johnson's standpoint, it was largely a matter of control. "He wanted to control everything," Joe Califano recalled. "His greatest outbursts of anger were triggered by people or situations that escaped his control." He therefore discouraged the sort of open exchange of ideas, free-wheeling discussion of alternatives, or ranging policy reviews that might in any way threaten his control. His admonition to McGeorge Bundy that his advisers must not "gang up" on him reflected his reluctance to permit them to engage in discussions except under his watchful eye.

Johnson's inability to deal effectively with his military advisers posed even more difficult problems. Under fire from the right wing in 1968 for not letting the military run the war, he vigorously and properly defended the principle of civilian control. The brass had been heard, he insisted, but not always heeded, and that was the way it should be. "People who fled to these shores from military atrocities did not want military leadership and rule by Kings." He went on to play down the differences between himself and his military advisers. Traditional military narrow-mindedness had been whittled away, and his own generals and admirals fully appreciated the complexity of military issues in the nuclear age. He conceded that at times they had wanted to do more faster. But, he concluded, "on diplomatic matters an Air Force General doesn't know more than a Johnson City General."

While defending his prerogatives, Johnson also went to great lengths to prove to skeptics his faith in and close consultation with his top military advisers. If he were to list his twenty-five best friends in Washington, he proclaimed to a *Los Angeles Times* reporter in 1968, "Bus" Wheeler and the Joint Chiefs would be on it. Praising his Joint Chiefs of Staff as "restraint" men, "opposite from [Gen. Curtis] LeMay in disposition and temperament," he went on to claim that he had not taken a single major military decision without first securing their assent. On another occasion, he expressed appreciation for his field commander's loyalty and praised his "Marshallesque" refusal to complain. "I like Westmoreland," he told Generals Wheeler and Abrams in February 1968. "Westmoreland has played on the team to help me."

Literally speaking, of course, Johnson was right. He had reason to appreciate Westmoreland's willingness to suppress his convictions about how the war should be fought in the larger interest of team play. He and McNamara had selected for the Joint Chiefs of Staff military officers who were not likely to rock the boat, and the president had taken great pains in the case of each major military decision to consult with the JCS and make sure they were on board.

Yet what Johnson extolled here as virtues were in both cases part of the problem. JCS acquiescence and Westmoreland's team play, however much appreciated by the commander in chief, came at the high cost of an open, candid discussion of fundamental strategic differences. Many of Johnson's aides have conceded that it was difficult, if not impossible, for him to reveal to anyone what he was really thinking, and they were thus forced to figure it out on the basis of what he was doing. LBJ seems to have found it particularly difficult to level with the Joint Chiefs. Indeed, William Bundy has noted, the president may have been at his worst in dealing with his top military advisers. Deferential to them on the surface, he kept them at arm's length and never gave them a real chance to express their views.

Yet as many critics have correctly pointed out, the Joint Chiefs could never really lay it on the line with the president either. Perhaps they were inhibited by their anomalous position in the chain of command, perhaps by a tradition that encouraged deference to civilian authority, perhaps by the "lessons" of Korea and the Truman-MacArthur controversy. Whatever the reason, early in the war they refused to forcefully articulate the advantages of their preferred approach. Had they done so, they might have persuaded LBJ of the virtue of their proposals. More likely, they would have deterred him from going into Vietnam in force. In any event, they did not, opting instead for Wheeler's foot-in-the-door approach, ensnaring themselves and the president in a gradualist approach that caused much grief to all concerned and inflicted enormous destruction on North and South Vietnam without ending the war.

There were other major problems with the Johnson style: the determination to dupe or co-opt advisers and the public rather than confront them candidly and forcefully; the obsessive secrecy; the tendency toward personalization of the domestic debate. The steadily widening credibility gap and the president's own image problems complicated an already impossible public relations problem. Johnson repeatedly denied that Vietnam was his war. It was "America's war," he insisted, and "if I drop dead tomorrow, this war will still be with you." In one sense, of course, he was right. But in terms of the way the war was fought and the agony it caused, Vietnam was far more his than he was prepared to admit or even recognize.

It would be a serious mistake to attribute America's failure in Vietnam solely or even largely to bureaucratic imperatives, the false dogmas of limited war theory, or the eccentricities of Johnson leadership style. Had the United States looked all over the world in 1965 it might not have been able to find a more difficult place to fight. The climate and terrain were singularly inhospitable. More important, perhaps, was the formless, yet lethal, nature of warfare in Vietnam, a conflict without distinct battlelines or fixed objectives where traditional concepts of victory and defeat were blurred. And from the outset, the balance of forces was stacked against the United States in the form of a weak, divided, and far too dependent client lacking in political legitimacy and a fanatically determined and resilient enemy that early on seized and refused to relinquish the banner of Vietnamese nationalism.

American military leaders have left ample testimony of the complex and often baffling challenge they faced in Vietnam and on the home front. Speaking of the "fog of war" in December 1967, Wheeler observed that Vietnam was the "foggiest war" in his memory and the first where the fog was "thicker away from the scene of the conflict than on the battlefield." Marine Gen. Lewis Walt concurred. "Soon after I arrived in Vietnam," he later admitted, "it became obvious to me that I had neither a real understanding of the nature of the war nor any clear idea how to win it." Abysmal ignorance of Vietnam and the Vietnamese on the part of Lyndon Johnson, his advisers, and the nation as a whole thickened the fog of war, contributing to a mistaken decision to intervene, mismanagement of the conflict, and ultimate failure.

A considerable part of the problem also lay in the inherent difficulty of waging limited war. Limited wars, as Stephen Peter Rosen has noted, are by their very nature *"strange* wars." They combine political, military, and diplomatic dimensions in the most complicated way. Conducting them effectively requires rare intellectual ability, political acumen, and moral courage.

Johnson and his advisers went into the conflict confident—probably overconfident—that they knew how to wage limited war, and only when the strategy of escalation proved bankrupt and the American people unwilling or unable to fight in cold blood did they confront their tragic and costly failure.

Deeply entangled in a war they did not understand and could find no way to win, they struggled merely to put a label on it. "All-out limited war," William Bundy called it; "a war that is not a war," some military officers complained. Harry McPherson phrased it in the form of a question. "What the hell do you say? How do you half-lead a country into war?" Westmoreland was prosaic if more explicit in describing Vietnam as a "limited war with limited objectives, fought with limited means and programmed for the utilization of limited resources."

The search for labels suggests the fundamental difficulties of limited war, and it must be conceded in retrospect that there are no easy answers to the problems

Johnson and his advisers confronted. The key military problem, Rosen contends, is "how to adapt, quickly and successfully, to the peculiar and unfamiliar *battlefield* conditions in which our armed forces are fighting." That this was not done in Vietnam may reflect the limited vision of the political and military leaders, but it will not be easily done elsewhere.

And the military challenge is by no means the most difficult. Managing peace proved every bit as frustrating for the Johnson administration. If it ignored any of the various peace initiatives launched by third countries or private individuals, it risked missing an opportunity to negotiate or losing a propaganda advantage. If, on the other hand, it responded too eagerly it risked sending the wrong signal to the enemy or to domestic critics. And once involved in the peace process it could not be sure of controlling the results. The management of peace initiatives already underway also posed difficult challenges. If too many people knew what was going on there was the risk of a leak that could blow the initiative or cause embarrassment. If, on the other hand, information was restricted to a handful of people, as in MARIGOLD, peace moves could not be effectively coordinated with military operations.

Nor is there any obvious solution to the dilemma of domestic opinion. Vietnam exposed the enormous difficulties of fighting in cold blood. Without arousing popular emotions and especially without measurable success on the battlefield it was impossible over a long period of time to sustain popular support. Frederick the Great's dictum that war could only be successful when people did not know about it could not possibly work in the age of instant communications and mass media, especially when, as in the case of Vietnam, the size of the U.S. commitment quickly outgrew the presumed parameters of limited war. On the other hand, trying to play down the war also caused major problems. The Johnson and Nixon administrations both went to considerable lengths to maintain the semblance of normality at home. Thus, as D. Michael Shafer has observed, "those fighting [in Vietnam] faced the bitter irony that back in 'The World' life went on as normal while they risked their lives in a war their government did not acknowledge and many fellow citizens considered unnecessary or even immoral."

Johnson's inability to wage war in cold blood produced what appears on the surface a great anomaly—one of the shrewdest politicians of the twentieth century committing a form of political suicide by taking the nation into a war he would have preferred not to fight. To some extent, of course, LBJ was the victim of his considerable political acumen. He took the nation to war so quietly, with such consummate skill (and without getting a popular mandate) that when things turned sour the anger was inevitably directed at him. His inability to manage effectively the war he got so skillfully is typical of his leadership record. He was also much more effective in getting domestic programs through Congress than in managing them once enacted. In the final analysis, however, Johnson's failure reflects more than anything else the enormity of the problem and the inadequacy of the means chosen to address it.

Partial mobilization or a declaration of war provides at best debatable alternatives. George Bush's apparent success in mobilizing support for the Persian Gulf War of 1991 confirmed in the eyes of some critics the deficiencies of Johnson's leadership in Vietnam. In fact, the remarkable popular support for the Gulf War and especially for the troops was in a very real sense an expiation of lingering guilt for nonsupport in Vietnam. It also owed a great deal to perceptions of military success and the rapidity with which the war ended. In any event, Johnson's and Rusk's reservations about the dangers of a declaration of war in the Cold War international system were well taken, and congressional sanction in the War of 1812 and the Mexican War did nothing to stop rampant and at times crippling domestic opposition.

However much we might deplore the limitations of Johnson's leadership and the folly of limited war theory, they alone are not responsible for America's failure in Vietnam. That conflict posed uniquely complex challenges for U.S. war managers both in terms of the conditions within Vietnam itself and the international context in which it was fought. American policymakers thus took on in Vietnam a problem that was in all likelihood beyond their control.

In the new world order of the post–Cold War era, the conditions that appeared to make limited war essential and that made the Vietnam War especially difficult to fight will probably not be replicated, and the "lessons" of Vietnam will have at best limited relevance. There are many different kinds of limited war, however. Korea, Vietnam, and Persian Gulf War (which was, after all, limited in both ends and means) were as different from each other as each was from World War II. What they shared was the complexity in establishing ends and formulating means that is inherent in the institution of limited war itself. Even in this new era, therefore, it would be well for us to remember Vietnam and to recall Lady Bird Johnson's 1967 lament: "It is unbearably hard to fight a limited war."

✗ *F U R T H E R   R E A D I N G*

Baritz, Loren. *Backfire* (1985).

Bergerud, Eric M. *Red Thunder, Tropic Lightning: The World of a Combat Division in Vietnam* (1993).

Berman, Larry. *Lyndon Johnson's War* (1989).

Blaufarb, Douglas S. *The Counterinsurgency Era* (1977).

Cable, Larry E. *Conflict of Myths* (1986) (on counterinsurgency).

———. *Unholy Grail: The US and the War in Vietnam, 1965–1968* (1991).

Cincinnatus. *Self-Destruction: The Disintegration and Decay of the United States Army During the Vietnam Era* (1978).

Clodfelter, Mark. *The Limits of Air Power: The American Bombing of North Vietnam* (1989).

Colby, William E. *Lost Victory* (1989).

Conboy, Kenneth, and Dale Andradé. *Spies and Commandos* (2000).

Davidson, Phillip B. *Secrets of the Vietnam War* (1990).

Downs, Frederick. *The Killing Zone* (1978).

Gallucci, Robert L. *Neither Peace nor Honor* (1975).

Gibson, James William. *The Perfect War* (1986).

Grant, Zalin. *Facing the Phoenix* (1991).

Grinter, Lawrence E. "South Vietnam: Pacification Denied," *Southeast Asia Spectrum,* 3 (1975), 49–78.

Hennessy, Michael A. *Strategy in Vietnam* (1997).

Herring, George C. "American Strategy in Vietnam: The Postwar Debate," *Military Affairs,* 46 (1982), 57–63.

Hess, Gary R. "The Military Perspective on Strategy in Vietnam," *Diplomatic History,* 10 (1986), 91–106.

Hixson, Walter L. "Containment on the Perimeter: George F. Kennan and Vietnam," *Diplomatic History,* 12 (1988), 149–163.

Hooper, Edwin, et al. *The United States Navy and the Vietnam Conflict* (1976).
Hunt, Richard A. *Pacification* (1995).
Hunt, Richard A., and Richard H. Shultz, Jr. *Lessons from an Unconventional War* (1981).
Kinnard, Douglas. *The War Managers* (1977).
Krepinevich, Jr., Andrew F. *The Army and Vietnam* (1986).
Lewy, Guenther. *America in Vietnam* (1978).
Littauer, Raphael, and Normal Uphoff, eds. *The Air War in Indochina* (1972).
Mason, Robert. *Chickenhawk* (1983).
Middleton, Drew. *Air War—Vietnam* (1978).
Moore, Harold G., and Joseph L. Galloway. *We Were Soldiers Once . . . And Young* (1992).
Mrozek, Donald J. *Air Power and the Ground War in Vietnam* (1989).
Mueller, John. "The Search for the Breaking Point in Vietnam," *Strategic Studies,* 24 (1980), 497–519.
Osgood, Robert E. *Limited War Revisited* (1979).
Palmer, Jr., Bruce. *The 25-Year War* (1984).
Palmer, Dave Richard. *Summons of the Trumpet* (1978).
Palmer, Gregory. *The McNamara Strategy and the Vietnam War* (1978).
Prados, John. *Hidden History of the Vietnam War* (1995).
Record, Jeffrey. *The Wrong War: Why We Lost in Vietnam* (1998).
Roger, Bernard. W. *Cedar Falls–Junction City: A Turning Point* (1974).
Schlight, John. *The United States Air Force in Southeast Asia* (1988).
Shapley, Deborah. *Promise and Power* (1993) (on Robert McNamara).
Sharp, U. S. Grant. *Strategy for Defeat* (1978).
Sorley, Lewis. *Thunderbolt: General Creighton Abrams and the Army of His Times* (1993).
Stanton, Shelby L. *The Rise and Fall of an American Army* (1985).
Thayer, Thomas C. *War Without Fronts* (1985).
Thompson, James C. *Rolling Thunder* (1980).
Tilford, Jr., Earl H. *Crosswinds: The Air Force's Setup in Vietnam* (1993).
Trewhitt, Henry L. *McNamara* (1971).
West, Francis J. *The Village* (1972).
Westmoreland, William C. *A Soldier Reports* (1976).
Whitlow, Robert H. *U.S. Marines in Vietnam* (1976).

C H A P T E R
8

Americans in Combat

✕

The approximately 2.5 million Americans who served in Vietnam between 1962 and 1975 faced daunting challenges: an inhospitable climate, demanding terrain, an elusive enemy, and the difficulty of distinguishing friend from foe chief among them. The frustrations associated with trying to chart progress in a war based on attrition rather than on taking and holding enemy territory added to their frustrations. They soon discovered that warfare in Vietnam was nothing like World War II or the Korean conflict.

In the early years of U.S. involvement, most career military personnel and draftees alike came to Vietnam convinced of the righteousness of their nation's purpose. They typically saw the struggle in Indochina as part of the nation's global effort to check communist expansion and defend freedom. Those certainties often faded, however, as individuals gained firsthand experience with the complexities of the war and the moral ambiguities inherent in the way they were being asked to fight it. Later in the war, when public opinion at home became more divided and troop withdrawals began, the morale of U.S. troops declined precipitously. By the early 1970s, insubordination, racial conflict, and drug use within the ranks had become problems of epidemic proportion.

The documents and essays in this chapter focus on the experience of ordinary American combat soldiers in Vietnam. Among the questions addressed are the following: What did American combat forces encounter in Vietnam, and how did they react to the conditions of warfare there? How, overall, did U.S. troops behave? Why did atrocities take place, and how common were they? How did the strategy and tactics employed by U.S. military commanders affect the servicemen who implemented them? And, finally, what was the nature, composition, and societal representativeness of the armed forces that served in Vietnam?

✕ D O C U M E N T S

This chapter's initial documents are two letters sent home by infantrymen early in their tours of duty. Document 1, by PFC George Robinson, who was subsequently wounded in Vietnam, was written to his mother on February 14, 1966; Document 2, from Sp/4 Salvador Gonzalez, was written to his sister on February 19, 1969. Each soldier discusses with candor the nature of combat in Vietnam. Document 3, drawn from

Philip Caputo's memoir, depicts some of the hardships that beset American soldiers as they sought to adapt to Vietnam's climate and terrain as well as to the demands of the guerrilla war of attrition that they were waging. Vietnam, Caputo argues, was a war of "absolute savagery."

War crimes took place in Vietnam—on all sides. Documents 4 and 5 feature testimony before the U.S. Army's Criminal Investigation Division by one soldier who witnessed and another who participated in the My Lai massacre of March 16, 1968. In that episode, the most notorious of the war, between 400 and 500 innocent civilians were murdered by U.S. forces under the command of Lt. William Calley and Captain Ernest L. Medina. Only Calley was ever convicted of this war crime.

A reflection by Colin Powell about his tours of duty in Vietnam in 1962 and in 1968–69 follows in Document 6. Powell, who subsequently became a general and chairman of the Joint Chiefs of Staff, has served, since 2001, as secretary of state. He recalls here his frustrations with official hypocrisy, inappropriate strategy, and poor troop morale. This excerpt is drawn from Powell's best-selling memoir, *An American Journey.* Document 7 contains extracts from Colonel Robert D. Heinl, Jr.s', internal lament about the sorry state of U.S. Armed Forces. It appeared in a June 7, 1971, article in the *Armed Forces Journal.* Finally, Robert Conner, who served with the 25th Infantry Division, reflects on his Vietnam experience.

1. "Dear Mom," 1966

Dear Mom,

. . . I've seen some things happen here lately that have moved me so much that I've changed my whole outlook on life. I'll be the same in actions I guess, but inside I'll be changed. I feel different now after seeing some horrible things, and I'll never forget them. It makes you glad you're just existing. I can't say what I mean, but some of the things you see here can really change a man or turn a boy into a man. Any combat GI that comes here doesn't leave the same. I don't mean the cooks, clerks or special service workers, but the fighting man. I doubt if anybody realizes what combat is really like. I *thought* I knew until a few days ago when I started facing harsh realities and forgetting TV and movie interpretations. I never had much respect for GIs even after I was in for a while, but since I've seen what his real job is, I have more respect for him than any man on earth. To shoot and kill somebody, turn your head and walk away isn't hard, it's watching him die that's hard, harder than you could imagine and even harder when it's one of your own men.

I've said enough about it. Don't ask any questions. When I come home, if I feel like talking about it I will, but otherwise don't ask. It may sound dramatic, and I'll tell you it is. It's just something you don't feel like discussing and can't begin to write about.

Well, Mom, I'll sign off. Be careful driving.

Love,
George

From *Dear America: Letters Home from Vietnam* edited by Bernard Edelman for The New York Vietnam Veterans Memorial Commission, originally published by W. W. Norton & Company in 1985 and reissued in 2002. Reprinted with permission of Bernard Edelman.

2. Infantryman Salvador Gonzalez's
Letter Home, 1969

Hi [Connie],

This is to let you know that I'm OK. I want to tell you about that 120-day mission so that you can keep Mom from worrying. Don't show her this letter because the following is what I'll be doing for the next 11 months.

First it rained for six days solid, I got muddy and wet. My hands are covered with cuts. The jungles have thousands of leeches and mosquitoes of which I think I have gotten bitten almost all over my body. I personally had to dig up two dead gooks. The smell was terrible. I just about got sick. About three or four guys got hurt through accidents. Only two got shot chasing a gook.

Actually the fighting is not heavy yet, but the rumor is we're moving south on the A Shau Valley. I walk up and down mountains with a heavy pack on my back. But if everyone else does it, so can I. It's not so hard, actually, but one thing is for certain: you surely learn to appreciate some of the finer things you once had. Don't get me wrong, I'm not complaining or expecting sympathy. All I want to do is lay the line on what I'm doing. . . . In return you must tell Mom that I'm probably out in the field doing hardly a damn thing at all.

3. A Soldier's Perspective on
Combat in Vietnam, 1977

Writing about this kind of warfare is not a simple task. Repeatedly, I have found myself wishing that I had been the veteran of a conventional war, with dramatic campaigns and historic battles for subject matter instead of a monotonous succession of ambushes and fire-fights. But there were no Normandies or Gettysburgs for us, no epic clashes that decided the fates of armies or nations. The war was mostly a matter of enduring weeks of expectant waiting and, at random intervals, of conducting vicious manhunts through jungles and swamps where snipers harassed us constantly and booby traps cut us down one by one.

The tedium was occasionally relieved by a large-scale search-and-destroy operation, but the exhilaration of riding the lead helicopter into a landing zone was usually followed by more of the same hot walking, with the mud sucking at our boots and the sun thudding against our helmets while an invisible enemy shot at us from distant tree lines. The rare instances when the VC chose to fight a set-piece battle provided the only excitement; not ordinary excitement, but the manic ecstasy of contact. Weeks of bottled-up tensions would be released in a few minutes of orgiastic violence, men screaming and shouting obscenities above the explosions of grenades and the rapid, rippling bursts of automatic rifles.

Beyond adding a few more corpses to the weekly body count, none of these encounters achieved anything; none will ever appear in military histories or be studied by cadets at West Point. Still, they changed us and taught us, the men who fought in them; in those obscure skirmishes we learned the old lessons about fear, cowardice, courage, suffering, cruelty, and comradeship. Most of all, we learned about death at an age when it is common to think of oneself as immortal. Everyone loses that illusion eventually, but in civilian life it is lost in installments over the years. We lost if all at once and, in the span of months, passed from boyhood through manhood to a premature middle age. The knowledge of death, of the implacable limits placed on a man's existence, severed us from our youth as irrevocably as a surgeon's scissors had once severed us from the womb. And yet, few of us were past twenty-five. We left Vietnam peculiar creatures, with young shoulders that bore rather old heads. . . .

There is also the aspect of the Vietnam War that distinguished it from other American conflicts—its absolute savagery. I mean the savagery that prompted so many American fighting men—the good, solid kids from Iowa farms—to kill civilians and prisoners. . . . War by its nature, can arouse a psychopathic violence in men of seemingly normal impulses.

There has been a good deal of exaggeration about U.S. atrocities in Vietnam, exaggeration not about their extent but about their causes. The two most popularly held explanations for outrages like My Lai have been the racist theory, which proposes that the American soldier found it easy to slaughter Asians because he did not regard them as human beings, and the frontier-heritage theory, which claims he was inherently violent and needed only the excuse of war to vent his homicidal instincts.

Like all generalizations, each contains an element of truth; yet both ignore the barbarous treatment the Viet Cong and ARVN often inflicted on their own people, and neither confront the crimes committed by the Korean division, probably the most bloody-minded in Vietnam, and by the French during the first Indochina war.

The evil was inherent not in the men—except in the sense that a devil dwells in us all—but in the circumstances under which they had to live and fight. The conflict in Vietnam combined the two most bitter forms of warfare, civil war and revolution, to which was added the ferocity of jungle war. Twenty years of terrorism and fratricide had obliterated most reference points from the country's moral map long before we arrived. Communists and government forces alike considered ruthlessness a necessity if not a virtue. Whether committed in the name of principles or out of vengeance, atrocities were as common to the Vietnamese battlefields as shell craters and barbed wire. The marines in our brigade were not innately cruel, but on landing in Danang they learned rather quickly that Vietnam was not a place where a man could expect much mercy if, say, he was taken prisoner. And men who do not expect to receive mercy eventually lose their inclination to grant it.

At times, the comradeship that was the war's only redeeming quality caused some of its worst crimes—acts of retribution for friends who had been killed. Some men could not withstand the stress of guerrilla-fighting: the hair-trigger alertness constantly demanded of them, the feeling that the enemy was everywhere, the inability to distinguish civilians from combatants created emotional pressures which built to such a point that a trivial provocation could make these men explode with the blind destructiveness of a mortar shell.

Others were made pitiless by an overpowering greed for survival. Self-preservation, that most basic and tyrannical of all instincts, can turn a man into a coward or, as was more often the case in Vietnam, into a creature who destroys without hesitation or remorse whatever poses even a potential threat to his life. A sergeant in my platoon, ordinarily a pleasant young man, told me once, "Lieutenant, I've got a wife and two kids at home and I'm going to see 'em again and don't care who I've got to kill or how many of 'em to do it."

General Westmoreland's strategy of attrition also had an important effect on our behavior. Our mission was not to win terrain or seize positions. but simply to kill: to kill Communists and to kill as many of them as possible. Stack 'em like cordwood. Victory was a high body count, defeat a low kill-ratio, war a matter of arithmetic. The pressure on unit commanders to produce enemy corpses was intense, and they in turn communicated it to their troops. This led to such practices as counting civilians as Viet Cong. "If it's dead and Vietnamese, it's VC," was a rule of thumb in the bush. It is not surprising, therefore, that some men acquired a contempt for human life and a predilection for taking it.

Finally, there were the conditions imposed by the climate and country. For weeks we had to live like primitive men on remote outposts rimmed by alien seas of rice paddies and rain forests. Malaria, blackwater fever, and dysentery, though not the killers they had been in past wars, took their toll. The sun scorched us in the dry season, and in the monsoon season we were pounded numb by ceaseless rain. Our days were spent hacking through mountainous jungles whose immensity reduced us to an antlike pettiness. At night we squatted in muddy holes, picked off the leeches that sucked on our veins, and waited for an attack to come rushing at us from the blackness beyond the perimeter wire.

The air-conditioned headquarters of Saigon and Danang seemed thousands of miles away. As for the United States, we did not call it "the World" for nothing; it might as well have been on another planet. There was nothing familiar out where we were, no churches, no police, no laws, no newspapers, or any of the restraining influences without which the earth's population of virtuous people would be reduced by ninety-five percent. It was the dawn of creation in the Indochina bush, an ethical as well as a geographical wilderness. Out there, lacking restraints, sanctioned to kill, confronted by a hostile country and a relentless enemy, we sank into a brutish state. The descent could be checked only by the net of a man's inner moral values, the attribute that is called character. There were a few—and I suspect Lieutenant [William] Calley [implicated in the My Lai atrocity] was one—who had no net and plunged all the way down, discovering in their bottommost depths a capacity for malice they probably never suspected was there.

Most American soldiers in Vietnam—at least the ones I knew—could not be divided into good men and bad. Each possessed roughly equal measures of both qualities. I saw men who behaved with great compassion toward the Vietnamese one day and then burned down a village the next. They were, as Kipling wrote of his Tommy Atkins, neither saints "nor blackguards too/But single men in barracks most remarkable like you." That may be why Americans reacted with such horror to the disclosures of U.S. atrocities while ignoring those of the other side: the American soldier was a reflection of themselves.

4. Herbert Carter Testifies about the My Lai Massacre, 1969

We were picked up by helicopters at LZ Dottie early in the morning and we were flown to My Lai (4). We landed outside the village in a dry rice paddy. There was no resistance from the village. There was no armed enemy in the village. We formed a line outside the village.

The first killing was an old man in a field outside the village who said some kind of greeting in Vietnamese and waved his arms at us. Someone—either Medina or Calley—said to kill him and a big heavy-set white fellow killed the man. I do not know the name of the man who shot this Vietnamese. This was the first murder.

Just after the man killed the Vietnamese, a woman came out of the village and someone knocked her down and Medina shot her with his M16 rifle. I was 50 or 60 feet from him and saw this. There was no reason to shoot this girl. Mitchell, Conti, Meadlo, Stanley, and the rest of the squad and the command group must have seen this. It was a pure out and out murder.

Then our squad started into the village. We were making sure no one escaped from the village. Seventy-five or a hundred yards inside the village we came to where the soldiers had collected 15 or more Vietnamese men, women, and children in a group. Medina said, "Kill everybody, leave no one standing. Wood was there with an M-60 machine gun and, at Medina's orders, he fired into the people. Sgt. Mitchell was there at this time and fired into the people with his M16 rifle, also. Widmer was there and fired into the group, and after they were down on the ground, Widmer passed among them and finished them off with his M16 rifle. Medina, himself, did not fire into this group.

Just after this shooting, Medina stopped a 17 or 18 year old man with a water buffalo. Medina said for the boy to make a run for it—he tried to get him to run—but the boy wouldn't run, so Medina shot him with his M16 rifle and killed him. The command group was there. I was 75 or 80 feet away at the time and saw it plainly. There were some demolition men there, too, and they would be able to testify about this. I don't know any other witnesses to this murder. Medina killed the buffalo, too.

Q: I want to warn you that these are very serious charges you are making. I want you to be very sure that you tell only the truth and that everything you say is the truth?

A: What I have said is the truth and I will face Medina in court and swear to it. This is the truth; this is what happened.

Q: What happened then?

A: We went on through the village. Meadlo shot a Vietnamese and asked me to help him throw the man in the well. I refused and Meadlo had Carney help him throw the man in the well. I saw this murder with my own eyes and know that there was no reason to shoot the man. I also know from the wounds that the man was dead.

From James S. Olson and Randy Roberts, *My Lai: A Brief History with Documents.* Bedford Books, 1998, pp. 79–82.

Also in the village the soldiers had rounded up a group of people. Meadlo was guarding them. There were some other soldiers with Meadlo. Calley came up and said that he wanted them all killed. I was right there within a few feet when he said this. There were about 25 people in this group. Calley said when I walk away, I want them all killed. Meadlo and Widmer fired into this group with his M16 on automatic fire. Cowan was there and fired into the people too, but I don't think he wanted to do it. There were others firing into this group, but I don't remember who. Calley had two Vietnamese with him at this time and he killed them, too, by shooting them with his M16 rifle on automatic fire. I didn't want to get involved and I walked away. There was no reason for this killing. These were mainly women and children and a few old men. They weren't trying to escape or attack or anything. It was murder.

A woman came out of a hut with a baby in her arms and she was crying. She was crying because her little boy had been in front of her hut and between the well and the hut and someone had killed the child by shooting it. She came out of the hut with her baby and Widmer shot her with an M16 and she fell. When she fell, she dropped the baby then Widmer opened up on the baby with his M16 and killed the baby, too.

I also saw another woman come out of a hut and Calley grabbed her by the hair and shot her with a caliber .45 pistol. He held her by the hair for a minute and then let go and she fell to the ground. Some enlisted man standing there said, "Well, she'll be in the big rice paddy in the sky."

Q: Do you know any witnesses to these incidents?

A: Stanley might have [seen] the one Calley killed. There were a lot of people around when Widmer shot the woman with the baby. I can't definitely state any one person was there, but there were a lot of people around.

I also saw a Vietnamese boy about 8 years old who had been wounded, I think in the leg. One of the photographers attached to the company patted the kid on the head and then Mitchell shot the kid right in front of the photographer and me. I am sure the boy died from the fire of Mitchell.

About that time I sat down by a stack of dying people and Widmer asked me if he could borrow my caliber .45 pistol and finish off the people. I gave him my pistol and he walked in among the people and would stand there and when one would move, he would shoot that person in the head with the pistol. He used three magazines of caliber .45 ammunition on these people. These were men, children, women, and babies. They had been shot by machinegunners and riflemen from Company C, 1/20th Infantry. This was at a T-junction of two trails on the outskirts of the village. I got my pistol back from Widmer and holstered it again.

Q: How many people do you figure Widmer finished off when he used your pistol?

A: I know he shot some twice, so I figure he shot fifteen or so with my pistol. I know he shot one guy in the head and I imagine that was where he was shooting them all.

Q: What happened then?

A: We went on through the village and there was killing and more killing. I was with Stanley, mainly. I sat down with Stanley and Widmer came up again and asked to borrow my pistol again. I gave it to him. I saw a little boy there—wounded, I believe in the arm—and Widmer walked up close to the kid and shot him with my pistol. Widmer said something like, "Did you see me shoot that son of a bitch," and Stanley said something about how it was wrong. My gun had jammed when Widmer shot the kid. As far as I could tell, the kid died as a result of this gunshot. Then Widmer gave me my pistol back and walked off. I was trying to clean it when it accident[al]ly went off and I was shot in the left foot. Stanley gave me medical aid and then the medics came. Medina and some of the command group came up and then I was flown out in a helicopter. The next day the medics brought Meadlo into the hospital. He had stepped on a booby-trap and had lost his foot. He said he thought God might be punishing him for what he had done in My Lai (4). . . .

Q: Did you murder anyone in Vietnam?

A: The only people I killed in Vietnam I killed in combat. I didn't kill any women or kids or unarmed persons at all, ever.

Q: How many people do you think were killed in My Lai (4)?

A: There were more than 100, but I couldn't tell you accurately how many people were killed. I don't believe there were any people left alive.

5. Varnado Simpson Testifies about the My Lai Massacre, 1969

I, Varnado Simpson want to make the following statement under oath:

The next day we went to MyLai (4). I was in the second or third lifts. Another Platoon, the First Platoon of Company C, went in ahead of us. I was with my unit, the Third Squad, 2d Platoon. My Platoon Leader was Lt Brooks. My Squad Leader was Sgt LaCroix. My Platoon Leader or rather Platoon Sergeant was Sgt Buchanon. . . .

After we landed we advanced by fire into the village. We started on the left, but during the advance through the village the troops were all mixed up. Some of the 1st Platoon got with the 2d Platoon and so forth.

Just after we got into the village, I came upon Wood and Stanley with four or five Vietnamese detainees. Stanley said they were going to take them to the Platoon Collection area. They were asking these people some questions in Vietnamese. Then Roschevitz, who had come up with me, said to kill all the people and told me to kill them. I hadn't killed anyone yet, so I said that I would not. Then Roschevitz grabbed my M16 away from me and put it on automatic fire and killed all of the Vietnamese who had been standing there. These people were not armed and were not trying to escape.

Q: What happened then?

A: I continued on into the village and found a place where a boy had been shot by a well near a hut. A woman, carrying a baby, came out of the hut crying and carrying

From James S. Olson and Randy Roberts, *My Lai: A Brief History with Documents.* Bedford Books, 1998, pp. 79–82.

on. Roschevitz, Lamartina, and LaCroix were there. Wright, Hutto, and Hudson were
there also. I think Brooks may have been around. Brooks told me to kill the woman,
and, acting on his orders, I shot her and her baby. I have been shown a group of
photographs and I identify the photograph of the woman and the baby as being the
ones I shot as related here. I remember shooting the baby in the face. . . .

Q: What happened then?

A: There were four or five people—mostly children—still in the hut. Hutto,
Wright, and Hudson went into the hut and Hudson fired the machinegun into the
children. I had gone into the hut at that time and saw that the bodies were all torn
up and I have no doubt they were all killed. There was a little old hole in the hut
where the people took shelter from attack, and Wright dropped a grenade into the
hole, in case someone was hiding there.

Q: What happened then?

A: As we moved into the village we heard a lot of firing and then came on an
area where the platoon ahead of us had rounded up 25 or 30 people and executed
them. We did not see the shooting, but it had just happened. Medina was there
when we got there, but I don't know if he had witnessed the killing while it was going on. I heard about another execution that day not far from this scene (but didn't
see it either during the killing of the people or afterwards), and also found a ditch
full of people at MyLai (4).

Q: What happened next?

A: We were on the left, moving ahead and burning huts and killing people. I
killed about 8 people that day. I shot a couple of old men who were running away.
I also shot some women and children. I would shoot them as they ran out of huts
or tried to hide.

Q: Did you see anyone else killed?

A: Yes. I saw Wright, Hutto, Hudson, Rucker (deceased), and Mower go into a
hut and rape a 17 or 18 year old girl. I watched from the door. When they all got
done, they all took their weapons, M-60, M16's, and caliber .45 pistols and fired into
the girl until she was dead. Her face was just blown away and her brains were just
everywhere. I didn't take part in the rape or the shooting.

Q: Did each of these men—Hutto, Wright, Hudson, Rucker, and Mower—
have sexual intercourse with that girl?

A: Yes they did.

Q: Did each of them—Wright, Hutto, Hudson, Rucker, and Mower—fire into
the girl after the act of intercourse was completed?

A: Yes they did.

Q: Did you see anyone else killed?

A: I witnessed a lot of people being killed, but there was a lot of confusion going
on and I can't relate details of every killing I saw. I estimate there were 400 people
killed in MyLai (4). I would like to stress that everyone was ordered by Medina to
kill these people: that the killing was done on his orders.

Q: You said you saw a ditch full of people. Please tell me about that?

A: The First Platoon had been there and gone when we arrived. We saw an irrigation ditch with 30–40 dead Vietnamese in it. They had all been just killed. Some
had been killed in the ditch and some had made it to the top of the ditch, but they
were all dead. I don't know who did this by name, but it was the First Platoon.

6. Colin Powell Remembers His Two Tours of Duty in Vietnam, 1995

The Saigon I had known in 1962 now looked as if it had been trampled by a giant. Where before the streets had been full of pedicabs, now they were jammed with jeeps, staff cars, and Army trucks. Where previously the U.S. presence had been muted, GIs now swarmed all over the place. Quiet bistros had been displaced by noisy bars populated by B-girls catering to our troops. The charming colonial capital was encircled by American barracks, headquarters, storage depots, airfields, hospitals, even military jails. Saigon now resembled an American garrison town more than the Paris of the Orient. I could not wait to go up-country.

I arrived at Duc Pho on July 27, 1968, assigned to the resurrected World War II 23d Infantry Division, known as the Americal. I was to serve as executive officer of the 3d Battalion, 1st Infantry, 11th Infantry Brigade. The Americal's headquarters was in Chu Lai on the northern coastal plain. Duc Pho was about a half-hour helicopter ride farther inland and to the south.

Most armies are a combination of fighting machine and bureaucratic beast, and our beast had a long tail. My job as exec was to make sure the battalion had all the support it required to remain in fighting trim, and my duties included everything from ordering up ammo, to making sure the helos had fuel, to getting mail out to the troops. As soon as I arrived, my new boss, the battalion commander, Lieutenant Colonel Hank Lowder, a compact, feisty scrapper, handed me another assignment. I was to prepare for the Annual General Inspection, a task better suited to peacetime at Fort Devens than Vietnam in the middle of a war. Still, the Army took its inspections seriously. Hank Lowder wanted me to handle the administrative headaches in preparing for the inspection so that he would be free to concentrate on fighting the war. Consequently, while he led the troops in the field, I was at Duc Pho making sure that the fumigation schedule, troop inoculation records, and other endless reels of red tape were inspection-ready. . . .

Besides getting Duc Pho in shape, I had to go out and make sure that field units were also ready for the annual inspection. We had several FSBs (fire support bases) and LZs (landing zones)—Dragon, Liz, Chevy—located throughout our area. Early in August, I got a helicopter and flew out to check out LZ Dragon. I had heard that its messing facilities were substandard. Bad chow proved to be the least of Dragon's problems. I had not expected to find stateside spit and polish. Still, what I discovered jolted me. As I stepped out of the helo, I practically stumbled over rusted ammo left lying around the landing site. Sanitation was nil, weapons dirty, equipment neglected, and the troops sloppy in appearance, bearing, and behavior. Seven years had passed since American advisors had first gone to Vietnam in force, and it was four years since the big buildup after the Tonkin Gulf Resolution. Still, the end was nowhere in sight, and deterioration of discipline and morale was obvious. I issued orders to get Dragon back into shape, told the officers I would be back to check on their compliance, and moved on to the next site.

These were good men, the same kind of young Americans who had fought, bled, and died winning victory after victory throughout our country's history. They were no less brave or skilled, but by this time in the war, they lacked inspiration and a sense of purpose. Back home, the administration was trying to conduct the war with as little inconvenience to the country as possible. The reserves had not been called up. Taxes to finance the war had not been raised. Better-off kids beat the draft with college deferments. The commander in chief, LBJ himself, was packing it in at the end of his term. Troops of the ally we had come to aid were deserting at a rate of over 100,000 a year. That flying statesman Nguyen Cao Ky had gone beyond air marshal to become South Vietnam's premier by age thirty-four, though by my second tour he had been reduced to vice president. Ky had married a young airline hostess who wore the same silk flying suit and trailing scarf as he did as they hopscotched around the country in his plane. Ky had said, "I have only one [hero]—Hitler. . . . But the situation here is so desperate now that one man would not be enough. We need four or five Hitlers in Vietnam." This was the man for whose regime three, four, even five hundred Americans were dying every week in 1968. They were dying with the same finality as at Valley Forge or Normandy, but with little of the nobility of purpose.

Our men in the field, trudging through elephant grass under hostile fire, did not have time to be hostile toward each other. But bases like Duc Pho were increasingly divided by the same racial polarization that had begun to plague America during the sixties. The base contained dozens of new men waiting to be sent out to the field and short-timers waiting to go home. For both groups, the unifying force of a shared mission and shared danger did not exist. Racial friction took its place. Young blacks, particularly draftees, saw the war, not surprisingly, as even less their fight than the whites did. They had less to go home to. This generation was more likely to be reached by the fireworks of an H. Rap Brown than the reasonableness of the late Martin Luther King, Jr. Both blacks and whites were increasingly resentful of the authority that kept them here for a dangerous and unclear purpose. The number one goal was to do your time and get home alive. I was living in a large tent and I moved my cot every night, partly to thwart Viet Cong informants who might be tracking me, but also because I did not rule out attacks on authority from within the battalion itself. . . .

My Lai was an appalling example of much that had gone wrong in Vietnam. Because the war had dragged on for so long, not everyone commissioned was really officer material. Just as critical, the corps of career noncommissioned officers was being gutted by casualties. Career noncoms form the backbone of any army, and producing them requires years of professional soldiering. In order to fight the war without calling up the reserves, the Army was creating instant noncoms. Shake-and-bake sergeants, we called them. Take a private, give him a little training, shake him once or twice, and pronounce him an NCO. It astonished me how well and heroically some of these green kids performed, assuming responsibility far beyond their years and experience. Still, the involvement of so many unprepared officers and noncoms led to breakdowns in morale, discipline, and professional judgment— and to horrors like My Lai—as the troops became numb to what appeared to be endless and mindless slaughter.

I recall a phrase we used in the field, MAM, for military-age male. If a helo spotted a peasant in black pajamas who looked remotely suspicious, a possible MAM, the pilot would circle and fire in front of him. If he moved, his movement was judged evidence of hostile intent, and the next burst was not in front, but at him. Brutal? Maybe so. But an able battalion commander with whom I had served at Gelnhausen [Germany,], Lieutenant Colonel Walter Pritchard, was killed by enemy sniper fire while observing MAMs from a helicopter. And Pritchard was only one of many. The kill-or-be-killed nature of combat tends to dull fine perceptions of right and wrong.

My tour was to end in July 1969. Judged solely in professional terms, it was a success. Holding down the G-3 spot for the largest division in Vietnam, as a major, was a rare credit. My efficiency reports continued highly favorable. I received the Legion of Merit, and General Gettys awarded me the Soldier's Medal for my role in the helicopter crash rescue. That was Vietnam as experienced by the career lobe of my brain. And, for a long time, I allowed myself to think only on that side, an officer answering the call, doing his best, "content to fill a soldier's grave."

But as time passed and my perspective enlarged, another part of my brain began examining the experience more penetratingly. I had gone off to Vietnam in 1962 standing on a bedrock of principle and conviction. And I had watched that foundation eroded by euphemisms, lies, and self-deception. The pernicious game-playing that I had first detected in Gelnhausen had been exported to Vietnam during my first tour and had reached its full flowering during my second tour. . . .

Readiness and training reports in the Vietnam era were routinely inflated to please and conceal rather than to evaluate and correct. Like the children of Lake Wobegon, everybody came out "above average." The powers that be seemed to believe that by manipulating words, we could change the truth. We had lost touch with reality. We were also deluded by technology. The enemy was primitive, and we were the most technologically advanced nation on earth. It therefore should be no contest. Thus, out of the McNamara shop came miracles like the "people sniffer," a device that could detect concentrations of urine on the ground from an airplane (brought to you by the same people who later came up with Agent Orange). If the urine was detected in likely enemy territory, we now had an artillery target. But woe to any innocent peasants or water buffalos that happened to relieve themselves in the wrong place. The people sniffer was of a piece with McNamara's Line, a series of electronic sensors strung across the country that were going to alert us whenever an enemy force began moving down the Ho Chi Minh Trail, an idea stillborn.

The Legion of Merit I received? It might have meant more to me in a war where medals were not distributed so indiscriminately. . . .

Dark episodes like My Lai resulted, in part, because of the military's obsession with another semifiction, the "body count," that grisly yardstick produced by the Vietnam War. The 11th Infantry Brigade had actually been awarded a Special Commendation for 128 "enemy" killed at My Lai, before the truth came out. The Army, under Pentagon pressure to justify the country's investment in lives and billions, desperately needed something to measure. What military objectives could we claim in this week's situation report? A hill? A valley? A hamlet? Rarely. Consequently, bodies became the measure. But body counts were tricky. The press knew precisely the casualties on our side. They simply counted the caskets going out. Twenty caskets, twenty KHAs in the latest firefight. What do we have to show for it? How many of the enemy fell? Finding out was not easy. The VC and NVA did not use caskets. They were also skilled at breaking off contact and taking their dead with them. We might have used weapons captured as a measure. But you have to produce the weapons, and reporters can count. Enemy bodies did not have to be brought back. Every night, the company would make a tally. "How many did your platoon get?" "I don't know. We saw two for sure." "Well, if you saw two, there were probably eight. So let's say ten." Counting bodies became a macabre statistical competition. Companies were measured against companies, battalions against battalions, brigades against brigades. Good commanders scored high body counts. And good commanders got promoted. If your competition was inflating the counts, could you afford not to?

The enemy actually was taking horrendous casualties. But it made little difference. As one military analyst put it, divide each side's casualties by the economic cost of producing them. Then multiply by the political cost of sustaining them. As long as your enemy was willing to pay that price, body counts meant nothing. This enemy was obviously prepared to pay, and unsportingly refused to play the game by our scorekeeping. We were forever trying to engage the NVA in a knockout battle—a Vietnamese Waterloo, an Iwo Jima, an Inchon—but the NVA refused to cooperate. No matter how hard we struck, NVA troops would melt into their sanctuaries in the highlands or into Laos, refit, regroup, and come out to fight again. We had our sanctuaries too, stretching from the South China Sea all the way back to the U.S.A. The two forces joined to kill each other between the mountains and coastal plains of Vietnam. Every Friday night, our side toted up the body count for the week, then we went to bed and started all over again the next day.

At the end of my first tour, I had guessed that finishing the job would take half a million men. Six years later, during my second tour, we reached the peak, 543,400, and it was still not enough. Given the terrain, the kind of war the NVA and VC were fighting, and the casualties they were willing to take, no defensible level of U.S. involvement would have been enough.

I remember a soldier, while I was still battalion exec, who had stepped on a mine. One leg hung by a shred, and his chest had been punctured. We loaded him onto a slick and headed for the nearest evac hospital at Duc Pho, about fifteen minutes away. He was just a kid, and I can never forget the expression on his face, a mixture of astonishment, fear, curiosity, and, most of all, incomprehension. He kept trying to speak, but the words would not come out. His eyes seemed to be saying, why? I did not have an answer, then or now. He died in my arms before we could reach Duc Pho.

7. Robert D. Heinl, Jr., Details Disarray Within U.S. Armed Forces, 1971

The morale discipline and battleworthiness of the U.S. Armed Forces are, with a few salient exceptions, lower and worse than at any time in this century and possibly in the history of the United States.

By every conceivable indicator, our army that now remains in Vietnam is in a state approaching collapse, with individual units avoiding or having refused combat, murdering their officers and noncommissioned officers, drug-ridden, and dispirited where not near-mutinous.

From Robert D. Heinl, Jr., "The Collapse of the Armed Forces," *Armed Forces Journal,* June 7, 1991, 30–37. Reprint permission granted by Armed Forces Journal Publishing Company.

Elsewhere than Vietnam, the situation is nearly as serious.

Intolerably clobbered and buffeted from without and within by social turbulence, pandemic drug addiction, race war, sedition, civilian scapegoatise, draftee recalcitrance and malevolence, barracks theft and common crime, unsupported in their travail by the general government, in Congress as well as the executive branch, distrusted, disliked, and often reviled by the public, the uniformed services today are places of agony for the loyal, silent professionals who doggedly hang on and try to keep the ship afloat.

The responses of the services [to] . . . these unheard-of conditions, forces and new public attitudes, are confused, resentful, occasionally pollyanna-ish, and in some cases even calculated to worsen the malaise that is wracking them.

While no senior officer (especially one on active duty) can openly voice any such assessment, the foregoing conclusions find virtually unanimous support in numerous non-attributable interviews with responsible senior and midlevel officers, as well as career noncommissioned officers and petty officers in all services.

Historical precedents do exist for some of the services' problems, such as desertion, mutiny, unpopularity, seditious attacks, and racial troubles. Others, such as drugs, pose difficulties that are wholly new. Nowhere, however, in the history of the Armed Forces have comparable past troubles presented themselves in such general magnitude, acuteness, or concentrated focus as today.

By several orders of magnitude, the Army seems to be in worst trouble. But the Navy has serious and unprecedented problems, while the Air Force, on the surface at least still clear of the quicksands in which the Army is sinking, is itself facing disquieting difficulties.

Only the Marines—who have made the news this year by their hard line against indiscipline and general permissiveness—seem, with their expected staunchness and tough tradition, to be weathering the storm.

To understand the military consequences of what is happening to the U.S. Armed Forces, Vietnam is a good place to start. It is in Vietnam that the rearguard of a 500,000-man army, in its day (and in the observation of the writer) the best army the United States ever put into the field, is numbly extricating itself from a nightmare war the Armed Forces feel they had foisted on them by bright civilians who are now back on campus writing books about the folly of it all.

"They have set up separate companies," writes an American soldier from Cu Chi, quoted in the *New York Times,* "for men who refuse to go out into the field." It is no big thing to refuse to go. If a man is ordered to go to such and such a place he no longer goes through the hassle of refusing; he just packs his shirt and goes to visit some buddies at another base camp. Operations have become incredibly ragtag. Many guys don't even put on their uniforms any more. . . .

"Frag incidents" or just "fragging" is current soldier slang in Vietnam for the murder or attempted murder of strict, unpopular, or just aggressive officers and NCOs. With extreme reluctant (after a young West Pointer from Senator Mike Mansfield's Montana was fragged in his sleep) the Pentagon has now disclosed that fraggings in 1970 (209) have more than doubled those of the previous year (96).

Word of the deaths of officers will bring cheers at troop movies or in bivouacs of certain units.

In one such division—the morale-plagued Americal—fraggings during 1971 have been authoritatively estimated to be running about one a week.

Yet fraggings, though hard to document, form part of the ugly lore of every war. The first such verified incident known to have taken place occurred 190 years ago when Pennsylvania soldiers in the Continental Army killed one of their captains during the night of 1 January 1781.

Bounties, raised by common subscription in amounts running anywhere from $50 to $1,000, have been widely reported put on the heads of leaders whom the privates and Sp4s want to rub out.

Shortly after the costly assault on Hamburger Hill in mid-1969, the GI underground newspaper in Vietnam, "GI Says," publicly offered a $10,000 bounty on LCol Weldon Honeycutt, the officer who ordered (and led) the attack. Despite several attempts, however, Honeycutt managed to live out his tour and return Stateside. . . .

The issue of "combat refusal," an official euphemism for disobedience of orders to fight—the soldier's gravest crime—has only recently been again precipitated on the frontier of Laos by Troop B, 1st Cavalry's mass refusal to recapture their captain's command vehicle containing communication gear, codes and other secret operation orders. . . .

"Search and evade" (meaning tacit avoidance of combat by units in the field) is now virtually a principle of war, vividly expressed by the GI phrase, "CYA (cover your ass) and get home!"

That "search-and-evade" has not gone unnoticed by the enemy is underscored by the Viet Cong delegation's recent statement at the Paris Peace Talks that communist units in Indochina have been ordered not to engage American units which do not molest them. The same statement boasted—not without foundation in fact— that American defectors are in the VC ranks.

Symbolic anti-war fasts (such as the one at Pleiku where an entire medical unit, led by its officers, refused Thanksgiving turkey), peace symbols, "V"-signs not for victory but for peace, booing and cursing of officers and even of hapless entertainers such as Bob Hope, are unhappily commonplace.

As for drugs and race, Vietnam's problems today not only reflect but reinforce those of the Armed Forces as a whole. In April, for example, members of a Congressional investigating subcommittee reported that 10 to 15% of our troops in Vietnam are now using high-grade heroin, and that drug addiction there is "of epidemic proportions."

Only last year an Air Force major and command pilot for Ambassador Bunker was apprehended at Tan Son Nhut air base outside Saigon with $8-million worth of heroin in his aircraft. This major is now in Leavenworth.

Early this year, an Air Force regular colonel was court-martialed and cashiered for leading his squadron in pot parties, while, at Cam Ranh Air Force Base, 43 members of the base security police squadron were recently swept up in dragnet narcotics raids.

All the foregoing facts—and many more dire indicators of the worst kind of military trouble—point to widespread conditions among American forces in Vietnam that have only been exceeded in this century by the French Army's Nivelle mutinies of 1917 and the collapse of the Tsarist armies in 1916 and 1917.

It is a truism that national armies closely reflect societies from which they have been raised. It would be strange indeed if the Armed Forces did not today mirror the agonizing divisions and social traumas of American society, and of course they do.

For this very reason, our Armed Forces outside Vietnam not only reflect these conditions but disclose the depths of their troubles in an awful litany of sedition, disaffection, desertion, race, drugs, breakdowns of authority, abandonment of discipline, and, as a cumulative result, the lowest state of military morale in the history of the country.

Sedition—coupled with disaffection within the ranks, and externally fomented with an audacity and intensity previously inconceivable—infests the Armed Services:

• At best count, there appear to be some 144 underground newspapers published on or aimed at U.S. military bases in this country and overseas. Since 1970 the number of such sheets has increased 40% (up from 103 last fall). These journals are not mere gripe-sheets that poke soldier fun in the "Beetle Bailey" tradition, at the brass and the sergeants. "In Vietnam," writes the Ft Lewis-McChord Free Press, "the Lifers, the Brass, are the true Enemy, not the enemy." Another West Coast sheet advises readers: "Don't desert. Go to Vietnam and kill your commanding officer."

• At least 14 GI dissent organizations (including two made up exclusively of officers) now operate more or less openly. Ancillary to these are at least six anti-war veterans' groups which strive to influence GIs. . . .

Racial conflicts (most but not all sparked by young black enlisted men) are erupting murderously in all services.

At a recent high commanders' conference, General Westmoreland and other senior generals heard the report from Germany that in many units white soldiers are now afraid to enter barracks alone at night for fear of "headhunting" ambushes by blacks.

In the quoted words of one soldier on duty in West Germany, "I'm much more afraid of getting mugged on the post than I am of getting attacked by the Russians."

Other reports tell of jail-delivery attacks on Army stockades and military police to release black prisoners, and of officers being struck in public by black soldiers. Augsburg, Krailsheim, and Hohenfels are said to be rife with racial trouble. Hohenfels was the scene of a racial fragging last year—one of the few so far recorded outside Vietnam.

In Ulm, last fall, a white noncommissioned officer killed a black soldier who was holding a loaded .45 on two unarmed white officers.

Elsewhere, according to *Fortune* magazine, junior officers are now being attacked at night when inspecting barracks containing numbers of black soldiers.

Kelley Hill, a Ft Benning, Ga., barracks area, has been the scene of repeated nighttime assaults on white soldiers. One such soldier bitterly remarked, "Kelley Hill may belong to the commander in the daytime but it belongs to the blacks after dark." . . .

The drug problem—like the civilian situation from which it directly derives—is running away with the services. In March, Navy Secretary John H. Chafee, speaking for the two sea services, said bluntly that drug abuse in both Navy and Marines is out of control.

In 1966, the Navy discharged 170 drug offenders. Three years later (1969), 3,800 were discharged. Last year in 1970, the total jumped to over 5,000.

Drug abuse in the Pacific Fleet—with Asia on one side, and kinky California on the other—gives the Navy its worst headaches. To cite one example, a destroyer due to sail from the West Coast last year for the Far East nearly had to postpone deployment when, five days before departure, a ring of some 30 drug users (over 10 percent of the crew) was uncovered.

Only last week, eight midshipmen were dismissed from the Naval Academy following disclosure of an alleged drug ring. While the Navy emphatically denies allegations in a copyrighted article by the *Annapolis Capitol* that up to 1,000 midshipmen now use marijuana, midshipman sources confirm that pot is anything but unknown at Annapolis.

Yet the Navy is somewhat ahead in the drug game because of the difficulty in concealing addiction at close quarters aboard ship, and because fixes are unobtainable during long deployments at sea.

The Air Force, despite 2,715 drug investigations in 1970, is in even better shape: its rate of 3 cases per thousand airmen is the lowest in the services.

By contrast, the Army had 17,742 drug investigations the same year. According to Col. Thomas B. Hauschild, of the Medical Command of our Army forces in Europe, some 46 percent of the roughly 200,000 soldiers there had used illegal drugs at least once. In one battalion surveyed in West Germany, over 50 percent of the men smoked marijuana regularly (some on duty), while roughly half of those were using hard drugs of some type.

What those statistics say is that the Armed Forces (like their parent society) are in the grip of a drug pandemic—a conclusion underscored by the one fact that, just since 1968, the total number of verified drug addiction cases throughout the Armed Forces has nearly doubled. One other yardstick: according to military medical sources, needle hepatitis now poses as great a problem among young soldiers as VD.

At Ft Bragg, the Army's third largest post, adjacent to Fayetteville, N.C. (a garrison town whose conditions one official likened to New York's "East Village" and San Francisco's "Haight-Ashbury") a recent survey disclosed that 4% (or over 1,400) of the 36,000 soldiers there are hard-drug (mainly heroin and LSD) addicts. In the 82nd Airborne Division, the strategic-reserve unit that boasts its title of "America's Honor Guard," approximately 450 soldier drug abusers were being treated when this reporter visited the post in April. About a hundred were under intensive treatment in special drug wards. . . .

In 1970, the Army had 65,643 deserters, or roughly the equivalent of four infantry divisions. This desertion rate (52.3 soldiers per thousand) is well over twice the peak rate for Korea (22.5 per thousand). It is more than quadruple the 1966 desertion-rate (14.7 per thousand) of the then well-trained, high-spirited professional Army.

If desertions continue to rise (as they are still doing this year), they will attain or surpass the WWII peak of 63 per thousand which, incidentally, occurred in the same year (1945) when more soldiers were actually being discharged from the Army for psychoneurosis than were drafted.

The Air Force—relatively uninvolved in the Vietnam war, all-volunteer, management-oriented rather than disciplinary and hierarchic—enjoys a numerical rate of less than one deserter per thousand men, but even this is double what it was three years ago.

The Marines in 1970 had the highest desertion index in the modern history of the Corps and, for that year at least, slightly higher than the Army's. As the Marines now phase out of Vietnam (and haven't taken a draftee in nearly two years), their desertions are expected to decrease sharply. Meanwhile, grimly remarked one officer, "Let the bastards go. We're all the better without them."

Letting the bastards go is something the Marines can probably afford. "The Marine Corps Isn't Looking for a Lot of Recruits," reads a current recruiting poster, "We Just Need a Few Good Men." This is the happy situation of a Corps slimming down to an elite force again composed of true volunteers who want to be professionals.

But letting the bastards go doesn't work at all for the Army and the Navy, who do need a lot of recruits and whose reenlistment problems are dire.

Admiral Elmo R. Zumwalt, Jr, Chief of Naval Operations, minces no words. "We have a personnel crisis," he recently said, "that borders on disaster."

The Navy's crisis, as Zumwalt accurately describes it, is that of a highly technical, material oriented service that finds itself unable to retain the expensively-trained technicians needed to operate warships, which are the largest, most complex items of machinery that man makes and uses. . . .

The trouble of the services—produced by and also in turn producing the dismaying conditions described in this article—is above all a crisis of soul and backbone. It entails—the word is not too strong—something very near a collapse of the command authority and leadership George Washington saw as the soul of military forces. This collapse results, at least in part, from a concurrent collapse of public confidence in the military establishment. . . .

But the fall in public esteem of all three major services—not just the Army—is exceeded by the fall or at least the enfeeblement of the hierarchic and disciplinary system by which they exist and, when ordered to do so, fight and sometimes die.

8. Robert Conner Reflects on His Vietnam Experience, 1993

I was eighteen years old. I should have been home getting ready to take a pretty girl to the prom. Getting my car cleaned up, getting on my tux, putting on some English Leather. Instead, for some reason, I didn't know why, I was in South Vietnam. We were supposed to be fighting communism, but I couldn't have told you exactly what communism was at the time. All I knew was that some little guy with a black hat was shooting at me. Looking back, I bet he didn't really know why he was shooting at me either. The whole period I was over there, all I saw was escalation. The more we'd fight, the worse it got.

We fought in a war that not too many people can explain. I have never heard a reason why we were actually over there, what we were supposed to accomplish over there. I was glad to see us out of Vietnam, but I didn't understand why we were out. Why we went over under one president, then another president pulls us out. Why? I believe one of these days, those generals, congressmen, and presidents are going to have to give an account to Almighty God for making that stupid mistake. I mean, it's the same Vietnam today as in 1965. Why aren't we still over there fighting?

From Robert Conner interview, in Eric M. Bergerud, *Red Thunder, Tropic Lightning: The World of a Combat Division in Vietnam,* pp. 319–320. Reprinted with permission of the author.

I read the book *Close Quarters* lately, and it brought back bad memories. In a way, I'm glad I did read it, but in a way, I wish I hadn't. It brought back memories I thought I had put out of my mind. It brought back those painful nights as I lay shivering on those ambush patrols, mosquitoes eating me up, praying to God that no Viet Cong would come along. Those hot summer days of walking through the jungle saying, "Please God, don't let us run into any Viet Cong today, don't let Charlie be out here today." But he would be there, and someone would get shot and killed. Some mother's son would have to be buried.

After I came home from Vietnam, I still had a year in the service. I was stationed in upstate New York. One of our duties was to be an honor guard for the dead. I probably went to ten funerals. We were the ones who would stand back and fire the salute. The MPs would fold up the flag and present it. The guy in the corner would blow taps. You'd hear the moaning and groaning of some mom or dad of some eighteen-, nineteen-, or twenty-year-old son, husband, or even daddy. And they had killed him. The Army had taken us up and mowed us down. There had to be a better reason than for a war that killed innocent people. I hope I never live to see another Vietnam or hear about another one.

✗ *E S S A Y S*

Christian Appy, who teaches at the Massachusetts Institute of Technology, explores the background and experiences of the mostly young Americans who served in Vietnam in the first essay. His central contention is that the 2.5 million Americans stationed in Vietnam were not representative of their generation as a whole. Roughly eighty percent of them came from working class or poor backgrounds, leading Appy to categorize Vietnam as more of a working-class war than perhaps any other conflict in the nation's history. His essay also emphasizes the demoralization felt by many U.S. troops as a result of the contradictions between official justifications for the war and the realities they experienced on the ground.

Next, Gerard J. deGroot, a professor of history at St. Andrews University (Scotland), examines the peculiar nature of combat operations in Vietnam. He also discusses the impact that the difficult conditions of warfare there had on ordinary American soldiers. DeGroot emphasizes that, by the late 1960s, the morale of U.S. troops had plummeted and racial tensions, insubordination, and drug use had become grave problems eroding the cohesion of U.S. armed forces.

A Working Class War

CHRISTIAN APPY

This [essay] explores the war-related experiences and attitudes of the 2.5 million young American enlisted men who served in Vietnam. Drawn from the largest generation in U.S. history, from the 27 million men who came of draft age during the war, American troops represented a distinct and relatively small subset of those born during the post–World War II baby boom. However, this subset was not representative of

From *Working Class War: American Combat Soldiers and Vietnam* by Christian G. Appy. Copyright © 1993 by the University of North Carolina Press. Used by permission of the publisher.

the generation as a whole. Roughly 80 percent came from working-class and poor backgrounds. Vietnam, more than any other American war in the twentieth century, perhaps in our history, was a working-class war. The institutions most responsible for channeling men into the military—the draft, the schools, and the job market—directed working-class children to the armed forces and their wealthier peers toward college. Most young men from prosperous families were able to avoid the draft, and very few volunteered. Thus, America's most unpopular war was fought primarily by the nineteen-year-old children of waitresses, factory workers, truck drivers, secretaries, firefighters, carpenters, custodians, police officers, salespeople, clerks, mechanics, miners, and farmworkers: people whose work lives are not only physically demanding but in many cases physically dangerous. From 1961 to 1972, an average of 14,000 American workers died every year from industrial accidents; the same number of soldiers died in Vietnam during 1968, the year of highest U.S. casualties. Throughout the war, moreover, at least 100,000 people died each year from work-related diseases. Combat may be more harrowing and dangerous than even the toughest civilian jobs, but in class terms there were important commonalities between the two. In both cases soldiers and workers did the nation's "dirty work"—one group abroad and the other at home—and did it under strict orders with little compensation. While working-class veterans have often found pride in their participation in America's tradition of military victory, Vietnam veterans lack even that reward and have had to draw what pride they can from other aspects of their experience. Soldiers in Vietnam, like workers at home, believed the nation as a whole had little, if any, appreciation for their sacrifices. If that perception was not always accurate, there is little doubt that many well-to-do Americans would have been more concerned about U.S. casualties had their own children been the ones doing the fighting.

In Vietnam, American soldiers encountered a reality utterly at odds with the official justifications of the war presented by American policymakers. Though many men arrived in Vietnam believing they had been sent to stop communism and to help the people of South Vietnam preserve democracy, their experience fundamentally contradicted those explanations. Told they were in Vietnam to help the people, soldiers found widespread antagonism to their presence. Told they were there to protect villagers from aggression, they carried out military orders that destroyed villages and brought terror to civilians. Told they were fighting to prevent the spread of communism, they discovered that support for revolution already flourished throughout the country and could not be contained behind fixed boundaries.

The demoralization caused by the contradictions in American policy was exacerbated by the fact that U.S. troops fought at a tactical and strategic disadvantage. Despite the much-vaunted superiority of American technology—our greater firepower and mobility—the Vietnamese opposition clearly established the terms of battle. American soldiers spent much of their time in fruitless searches for an enemy who almost always determined the time and place of battle. The majority of American infantrymen who lost their lives in Vietnam were killed by enemy ambushes, by enemy booby traps and mines, or by their own side's bombs, shells, or bullets ("friendly fire"). Pitted against such an elusive enemy, American search-and-destroy missions were essentially efforts to attract enemy fire. American soldiers were used as bait to draw the enemy into identifiable targets so the full weight of American firepower—bombs, rockets, napalm—could be dropped on the Vietnamese. As American troops soon learned, the central aim of U.S. policy in Vietnam was to maximize the enemy body count. In executing that policy, soldiers also learned that the high command was rarely particular about determining if dead Vietnamese were combatants or civilians.

In the face of this experience most soldiers came to perceive the war as meaningless, as a war for nothing, but they responded to that common perception in various ways. Some took the war on its own terms and found exhilaration in its danger and violence. Others thought of the war as a specialized job and blocked from their minds questions about the purpose or value of that job. Others gave as little of themselves to the war as possible by avoiding or resisting combat, shirking duties, or withdrawing into drugs or alcohol. . . .

Many veterans still struggle to free themselves from a paralyzing fixation on the history they lived so long ago, desperately wishing that somehow it might have turned out differently. That way of thinking often leads veterans to rage against the various people and groups they believe were responsible for sending them to fight an unwinnable war, for not finding a way to win, or for the deep divisions at home that widened as the war continued. . . .

"We all ended up going into the service about the same time—the whole crowd." I had asked Dan Shaw about himself, why *he* had joined the Marine Corps; but Dan ignored the personal thrust of the question. Military service seemed less an individual choice than a collective rite of passage, a natural phase of life for "the whole crowd" of boys in his neighborhood, so his response encompassed a circle of over twenty childhood friends who lived near the corner of Train and King streets in Dorchester, Massachusetts—a white, working-class section of Boston.

Thinking back to 1968 and his streetcorner buddies, Dan sorted them into groups, wanting to get the facts straight about each one. It did not take him long to come up with some figures. "Four of the guys didn't go into the military at all. Four got drafted by the army. Fourteen or fifteen of us went in the Marine Corps. Out of them fourteen or fifteen"—here he paused to count by naming—"Eddie, Brian, Tommy, Dennis, Steve: six of us went to Nam." They were all still teenagers. Three of the six were wounded in combat, including Dan.

His tone was calm, almost dismissive. The fact that nearly all his friends entered the military and half a dozen fought in Vietnam did not strike Dan as unusual or remarkable. In working-class neighborhoods like his, military service after high school was as commonplace among young men as college was for the youth of upper-middle-class suburbs—not welcomed by everyone but rarely questioned or avoided. In fact, when Dan thinks of the losses suffered in other parts of Dorchester, he regards his own streetcorner as relatively lucky. "Jeez, it wasn't bad. I mean some corners around here really got wiped out. Over off Norfolk street ten guys got blown away the same year."

Focusing on the world of working-class Boston, Dan has a quiet, low-key manner with few traces of bitterness. But when he speaks of the disparities in military service throughout American society, his voice fills with anger, scorn, and hurt. He compares the sacrifices of poor and working-class neighborhoods with the rarity of wartime casualties in the "fancy suburbs" beyond the city limits, in places such as Milton, Lexington, and Wellesley. If three wounded veterans "wasn't bad" for a streetcorner in Dorchester, such concentrated pain was, Dan insists, unimaginable in a wealthy subdivision. "You'd be lucky to find three Vietnam veterans in one of those rich neighborhoods, never mind three who got wounded."

Dan's point is indisputable: those who fought and died in Vietnam were overwhelmingly drawn from the bottom half of the American social structure. The comparison he suggests bears out the claim. The three affluent towns of Milton, Lexington, and Wellesley had a combined wartime population of about 100,000, roughly equal to that of Dorchester. However, while those suburbs suffered a total of eleven war deaths, Dorchester lost forty-two. There was almost exactly the same disparity in casualties between Dorchester and another sample of prosperous Massachusetts towns—Andover, Lincoln, Sudbury, Weston, Dover, Amherst, and Longmeadow. These towns lost ten men from a combined population of 100,000. In other words, boys who grew up in Dorchester were four times more likely to die in Vietnam than those raised in the fancy suburbs. An extensive study of wartime casualties from Illinois reached a similar conclusion. In that state, men from neighborhoods with median family incomes under $5,000 (about $15,000 in 1990 dollars) were four times more likely to die in Vietnam than men from places with median family incomes above $15,000 ($45,000 in 1990 dollars).

Dorchester, East Los Angeles, the South Side of Chicago—major urban centers such as these sent thousands of men to Vietnam. So, too, did lesser known, midsize industrial cities with large working-class populations, such as Saginaw, Michigan; Fort Wayne, Indiana; Stockton, California; Chattanooga, Tennessee; Youngstown, Ohio; Bethlehem, Pennsylvania; and Utica, New York. There was also an enormous rise in working-class suburbanization in the 1950s and 1960s. The post–World War II boom in modestly priced, uniformly designed, tract housing, along with the vast construction of new highways, allowed many workers their first opportunity to purchase homes and to live a considerable distance from their jobs. A a result, many new suburbs became predominantly working class.

Long Island, New York, became the site of numerous working-class suburbs, including the original Levittown, the first mass-produced town in American history. Built by the Levitt and Sons construction firm in the late 1940s, it was initially a middle-class town. By 1960, however, as in many other postwar suburbs, the first owners had moved on, often to larger homes in wealthier suburbs, and a majority of the newcomers were working class. Ron Kovic, author of one of the best-known Vietnam memoirs and films, *Born on the Fourth of July,* grew up near Levittown in Massapequa. His parents, like so many others in both towns, were working people willing to make great sacrifices to own a small home with a little land and to live in a town they regarded as a safe and decent place to raise their families, in hope that their children would enjoy greater opportunity. Many commentators viewed the suburbanization of blue-collar workers as a sign that the working class was vanishing and that almost everyone was becoming middle class. In fact, however, though many workers owned more than ever before, their relative social position remained largely unchanged. The Kovics, for example, lived in the suburbs but had to raise five children on the wages of a supermarket checker and clearly did not match middle-class levels in terms of economic security, education, or social status.

Ron Kovic volunteered for the marines after graduating from high school. He was paralyzed from the chest down in a 1968 firefight during his second tour of duty in Vietnam. Upon returning home, after treatment in a decrepit, rat-infested

VA hospital, Kovic was asked to be grand marshal in Massapequa's Memorial Day parade. His drivers were American Legion veterans of World War II who tried unsuccessfully to engage him in a conversation about the many local boys who had died in Vietnam:

> "Remember Clasternack? . . . They got a street over in the park named after him. . . . he was the first of you kids to get it. . . . There was the Peters family too. . . . both brothers. . . . Both of them killed in the same week. And Alan Grady. . . Did you know Alan Grady? . . .
>
> "We've lost a lot of good boys. . . . We've been hit pretty bad. The whole town's changed."

A community of only 27,000, Massapequa lost 14 men in Vietnam. In 1969, *Newsday* traced the family backgrounds of 400 men from Long Island who had been killed in Vietnam. "As a group," the newspaper concluded, "Long Island's war dead have been overwhelmingly white, working-class men. Their parents were typically blue collar or clerical workers, mailmen, factory workers, building tradesmen, and so on."

Rural and small-town America may have lost more men in Vietnam, proportionately, than did even central cities and working-class suburbs. You get a hint of this simply by flipping through the pages of the Vietnam Memorial directory. As thick as a big-city phone book, the directory lists the names and hometowns of Americans who died in Vietnam. An average page contains the names of five or six men from towns such as Alma, West Virginia (pop. 296), Lost Hills, California (pop. 200), Bryant Pond, Maine (pop. 350), Tonalea, Arizona (pop. 125), Storden, Minnesota (pop. 364), Pioneer, Louisiana (pop. 188), Wartburg, Tennessee (pop. 541), Hillisburg, Indiana (pop. 225), Boring, Oregon (pop. 150), Racine, Missouri (pop. 274), Hygiene, Colorado (pop. 400), Clayton, Kansas (pop. 127), and Almond, Wisconsin (pop. 440). In the 1960s only about 2 percent of Americans lived in towns with fewer than 1,000 people. Among those who died in Vietnam, however, roughly four times that portion, 8 percent, came from American hamlets of that size. It is not hard to find small towns that lost more than one man in Vietnam. Empire, Alabama, for example, had four men out of a population of only 400 die in Vietnam—four men from a town in which only a few dozen boys came of draft age during the entire war.

There were also soldiers who came from neither cities, suburbs, nor small towns but from the hundreds of places in between, average towns of 15,000 to 30,000 people whose economic life, however precarious, had local roots. Some of these towns paid a high cost in Vietnam. In the foothills of eastern Alabama, for example, is the town of Talladega, with a population of approximately 17,500 (about one-quarter black), a town of small farmers and textile workers. Only one-third of Talladega's men had completed high school. Fifteen of their children died in Vietnam, a death rate three times the national average. Compare Talladega to Mountain Brook, a rich suburb outside Birmingham. Mountain Brook's population was somewhat higher than Talladega's, about 19,500 (with no black residents of draft age). More than 90 percent of its men were high school graduates. No one from Mountain Brook is listed among the Vietnam War dead.

I have described a social map of American war casualties to suggest not simply the geographic origins of U.S. soldiers but their class origins—not simply where they came from but the kinds of places as well. Class, not geography, was the crucial factor in determining which Americans fought in Vietnam. Geography reveals discrepancies in military service primarily because it often reflects class distinctions. Many men went to Vietnam from places such as Dorchester, Massapequa, Empire, and Talladega because those were the sorts of places where most poor and working-class people lived. The wealthiest youth in those towns, like those in richer communities, were far less likely either to enlist or to be drafted.

Mike Clodfelter, for example, grew up in Plainville, Kansas. In 1964 he enlisted in the army, and the following year he was sent to Vietnam. In his 1976 memoir, Clodfelter recalled, "From my own small home town . . . all but two of a dozen high school buddies would eventually serve in Vietnam and all were of working class families, while I knew of not a single middle class son of the town's businessmen, lawyers, doctors, or ranchers from my high school graduating class who experienced the Armageddon of our generation."

However, even a sketchy map of American casualties must go farther afield, beyond the conventional boundaries of the United States. Although this fact is not well known, the military took draftees and volunteers from the American territories: Puerto Rico, Guam, the U.S. Virgin Islands, American Samoa, and the Canal Zone. These territories lost a total of 436 men in Vietnam, several dozen more than the state of Nebraska. . . .

. . . The forces that fought in Vietnam were drawn from the largest generation of young people in the nation's history. During the years 1964 to 1973, from the Gulf of Tonkin Resolution to the final withdrawal of American troops from Vietnam, 27 million men came of draft age. The 2.5 million men of that generation who went to Vietnam represent less than 10 percent of America's male baby boomers.

The parents of the Vietnam generation had an utterly different experience of war. During World War II virtually all young, able-bodied men entered the service—some 12 million. Personal connections to the military permeated society regardless of class, race, or gender. Almost every family had a close relative overseas—a husband fighting in France, a son in the South Pacific, or at least an uncle with the Seabees, a niece in the WAVES, or a cousin in the Air Corps. These connections continued well into the 1950s. Throughout the Korean War years and for several years after, roughly 70 percent of the draft-age population of men served in the military; but from the 1950s to the 1960s, military service became less and less universal. During the Vietnam years, the portion had dropped to 40 percent: 10 percent were in Vietnam, and 30 percent served in Germany, South Korea, and the dozens of other duty stations in the United States and abroad. What had been, in the 1940s, an experience shared by the vast majority gradually became the experience of a distinct minority.

What kind of minority was it? In modern American culture, *minority* usually serves as a code word for nonwhite races, especially African Americans. To speak of American forces in Vietnam as a minority invites the assumption that blacks, Hispanics, Asian Americans, and Native Americans fought and died in numbers grossly disproportionate to their percentage of the total U.S. population. It is a common assumption, but not one that has been sufficiently examined. For that matter, the whole experience of racial minorities in Vietnam has been woefully ignored by the media and academics. For Hispanics, Asian Americans, and Native Americans, even the most basic statistical information about their role in Vietnam remains either unknown or inadequately examined.

We know how many black soldiers served and died in Vietnam, but the more important task is to interpret those figures in historical context. Without that context, racial disproportions can be either exaggerated or denied. To simplify: At the beginning of the war blacks comprised more than 20 percent of American combat deaths, about twice their portion of the U.S. population. However, the portion of black casualties declined over time so that, for the war as a whole, black casualties were only slightly disproportionate (12.5 percent from a civilian population of 11 percent). The total percentage of blacks who served in Vietnam was roughly 10 percent throughout the war.

African Americans clearly faced more than their fair share of the risks in Vietnam from 1965 to 1967. That fact might well have failed to gain any public notice had the civil rights and antiwar movements not called attention to it. Martin Luther King was probably the most effective in generating concern about the number of black casualties in Vietnam. King had refrained from frequent public criticism of the war until 1967, persuaded by moderates that outspoken opposition to the war might divert energy from the cause of civil rights and alienate prowar politicians whose support the movement sought (President Johnson, for example). By early 1967, however, King believed the time had come to break his silence. As for diverting energy and resources from domestic social reform, King argued, the war itself had already done as much. More importantly, he could not in good conscience remain silent in the face of a war he believed unjust. . . .

While King focused attention on the economic condition of white and black soldiers, he emphasized the additional burden on blacks of fighting overseas in disproportionate numbers while being denied full citizenship at home. . . .

. . . In fact, had the civil rights movement not brought attention to racial disproportions in Vietnam casualties, those disproportions almost certainly would have continued. According to Commander George L. Jackson, "In response to this criticism the Department of Defense took steps to readjust force levels in order to achieve an equitable proportion and employment of Negroes in Vietnam." A detailed analysis of exactly what steps were taken has yet to be written. It is clear, however, that by late 1967, black casualties had fallen to 13 percent and then to below 10 percent in 1970–72. . . .

Though racial discrimination and racist attitudes surely persisted in the military, class was far more important than race in determining the overall social composition of American forces. Precisely when the enlisted ranks were becoming increasingly integrated by race, they were becoming ever more segregated by class. The military may never have been truly representative of the general male population, but in the 1960s it was overwhelmingly the domain of the working class.

No thorough statistical study has yet been conducted on the class origins of the men who served in Vietnam. Though the military made endless, mind-numbing efforts to quantify virtually every aspect of its venture in Vietnam, it did not make (so far as anyone has discovered) a single study of the social backgrounds of its fighting men. Quantitative evidence must be gathered from a variety of disparate studies. Probably the most ambitious effort to gather statistical information about the backgrounds of Vietnam-era soldiers was conducted just prior to the large-scale American escalation. In 1964 the National Opinion Research Center (NORC) surveyed 5 percent of all active-duty enlisted men.

According to NORC's occupational survey . . . roughly 20 percent of American enlisted men had fathers with white-collar jobs. Among the male population as a whole more than twice that portion, 44 percent, were white-collar workers. Of course, not all white-collar jobs are necessarily middle class in the income, power, and status they confer. Many low-paying clerical and sales jobs—typically listed as white collar—are more accurately understood as working-class occupations. While the white-collar label exaggerates the size of the middle class, it nonetheless encompasses almost all privileged Americans in the labor force. Thus, the fact that only 20 percent of U.S. soldiers came from white-collar families represents a striking class difference between the military and the general population.

The high portion of farmers in the sample is a further indication of the disproportionate number of soldiers from rural small towns. In the 1960s only about 5 percent of the American labor force was engaged in agriculture. In the NORC survey, more than twice as many, 12 percent, came from farm families. Though the survey does not reveal the economic standing of this group, we should avoid an American tendency to picture all farmers as independent proprietors. At the time of the survey about two-thirds of the workers engaged in agricultural labor were wage earners (farm laborers or migrant farmworkers) with family incomes less than $1,000 per year.

There is also good reason to believe that most of the men with absent fathers grew up in hard-pressed circumstances. In 1965, almost two-thirds of the children in female-headed families lived below the census bureau's low-income level. All told, the NORC survey suggests that on the brink of the Vietnam escalation at least three-quarters of American enlisted men were working class or poor.

Although this [essay] focuses on enlisted men, the inclusion of officers would not dramatically raise the overall class backgrounds of the Vietnam military. Officers comprised 11 percent of the total number of men in Vietnam, so even if many of them were from privileged families, the statistical impact would be limited. Furthermore, though we need further studies of the social backgrounds of the Vietnam-era officer corps, it may well have been the least privileged officer corps of the twentieth century. For example, in his study of the West Point class of 1966, Rick Atkinson found a striking historical decline in the class backgrounds of cadets. "Before World War I, the academy had drawn nearly a third of the corps from the families of doctors, lawyers, and other professionals. But by the mid 1950s, sons of professionals made up only 10 percent of the cadets, and links to the upper class had been almost severed. West Point increasingly attracted military brats and sons of the working class." Also, as the war dragged on, the officer corps was depleted of service school and ROTC graduates and had to rely increasingly on enlisted men who were given temporary field commissions or sent to officer candidate school. These officers, too, probably lowered the class background of the officer corps. . . .

. . . When measured against backgrounds of nonveterans of the same generation, Vietnam veterans came out on the bottom in income, occupation, and education.

The key here is disproportion. The point is not that *all* working-class men went to Vietnam while everyone better off stayed home. Given the enormous size of the generation, millions of working-class men simply were not needed by the military. Many were exempted because they failed to meet the minimum physical or mental standards of the armed forces. However, the odds of working-class men going into the military and on to Vietnam were far higher than they were for the middle class and the privileged. . . .

Education, along with occupation and income, is a key measure of class position. Eighty percent of the men who went to Vietnam had no more than a high school education (table 1). This figure would compare well to statistics of some previous wars. After all, at the time of the Civil War and well into the twentieth century, only a small minority of Americans had high school educations. However, if considered in historical context, the low portion of college educated among American soldiers is yet another indication of the disproportionately working-class composition of the military. The 1960s was a boomtime for American education, a time when opportunities for higher education were more widespread than ever before. By 1965, 45 percent of Americans between eighteen and twenty-one had some college education. By 1970 that figure was more than 50 percent. Compared with national standards, American forces were well below average in formal education. Studies matching school enrollments to age and class show that the educational levels of American soldiers in Vietnam correspond roughly to those of draft-age, blue collar males in the general population (table 2). Of course, many veterans took college courses after their military service. However, [one] . . . study found that by 1981 only 22 percent of veterans had completed college compared with 46 percent of nonveterans.

The portion of soldiers with at least some college education increased significantly in the late 1960s as draft calls increased and most graduate school deferments ended. By 1970 roughly 25 percent of American forces in Vietnam had some college education. Impressive as this increase was, it still fell well below the 50 percent for the age group as a whole, and it came as American troop levels in Vietnam were beginning to drop. Moreover, college education per se was no longer so clear a mark of privilege as it had been prior to World War II. Higher education in the post–World War II era expanded enormously, especially among junior and state colleges, the kinds of schools that enrolled the greatest number of working-class students. Between 1962 and 1972, enrollments in two-year colleges tripled. College students who went to Vietnam were far more likely to come from these institutions than

Table 1.   Educational Attainment of Vietnam Veterans at Time of Separation from the Armed Forces, 1966–1971 (Percent)

FISCAL YEAR	LESS THAN 12 YEARS OF SCHOOL	12 YEARS OF SCHOOL	1 TO 3 YEARS OF COLLEGE	4 OR MORE YEARS OF COLLEGE
1966	22.9	62.5	8.3	6.3
1967	23.6	61.8	9.0	5.6
1968	19.6	65.5	9.7	6.2
1969	18.3	60.0	15.9	5.8
1970	17.5	56.9	17.0	8.6
1971	14.7	55.4	19.4	10.5
Total, 1966–71	19.4	60.3	13.2	7.2

Source: Reports and Statistics Service, Office of Controller, Veterans' Administration, 11 April 1972, in Helmer, *Bringing the War Home,* p. 303.

Table 2.   Percentage of Males Enrolled in School, 1965–1970

AGE	BLUE-COLLAR	WHITE-COLLAR
16–17	80	92
18–19	49	73
20–24	20	43

Source: Levison, Working-Class Majority, p. 121.

from elite. four-year, private colleges. A survey of Harvard's class of 1970, for example, found only two men who served in Vietnam. College students who did go to Vietnam usually secured noncombat assignments. Among soldiers in Vietnam, high school dropouts were three times more likely to experience heavy combat than were college graduates.

Young men have fought in all wars, but U.S. forces in Vietnam were probably, on average, the youngest in our history. In previous wars many men in their twenties were drafted for military service, and men of that age and older often volunteered. During the Vietnam War most of the volunteers and draftees were teenagers; the average age was nineteen. In World War II, by contrast, the average American soldier was twenty-six years old. At age eighteen young men could join or be drafted into the army. At seventeen, with the consent of a guardian, boys could enlist in the Marine Corps. Early in the war, hundreds of seventeen-year-old marines served in Vietnam. In November 1965 the Pentagon ordered that all American troops must be eighteen before being deployed in the war zone. Even so, the average age remained low. Twenty-two-year-old soldiers were often kidded about their advanced age ("hey, old man") by the younger men in their units. Most American troops were not even old enough to vote. The voting age did not drop from twenty-one to eighteen until 1971. Thus, most of the Americans who fought in Vietnam were powerless, working-class teenagers sent to fight an undeclared war by presidents for whom they were not even eligible to vote.

No statistical profile can do justice to the complexity of individual experience, but without these broad outlines our understanding would be hopelessly fragmented. A class breakdown of American forces cannot be absolutely precise, but I believe the following is a reasonable estimate: enlisted ranks in Vietnam were comprised of about 25 percent poor, 55 percent working class, and 20 percent middle class, with a statistically negligible number of wealthy. Most Americans in Vietnam were nineteen-year-old high school graduates. They grew up in the white, working-class enclaves of South Boston and Cleveland's West Side; in the black ghettos of Detroit and Birmingham; in the small rural towns of Oklahoma and Iowa; and in the housing developments of working-class suburbs. They came by the thousands from every state and every U.S. territory, but few were from places of wealth and privilege.

The Selective Service System was the most important institutional mechanism in the creation of a working-class army. It directly inducted more than 2 million men into the military, and just as important, the threat or likelihood of the draft indirectly induced millions more to enlist. These "draft-motivated" volunteers enlisted because they had already received their induction notices or believed they soon would, and thus they enlisted in order, they hoped, to have more choice as to the nature and location of their service. Even studies conducted by the military suggest that as many as half of the men who enlisted were motivated primarily by the pressure of the draft. Draft pressure became the most important cause of enlistments as the war lengthened.

The soldiers sent to Vietnam can be divided into three categories of roughly equal size: one-third draftees, one-third draft-motivated volunteers, and one-third true volunteers. In the first years of the American buildup most of the fighting was done by men who volunteered for military service. That does not mean they volunteered to fight in Vietnam. Few did. Even among West Point's class of 1966 only one-sixth volunteered for service in Vietnam (though many more eventually ended up there). As the war continued, the number of volunteers steadily declined. From 1966 to 1969 the percentage of draftees who died in the war doubled from 21 to 40. Almost half of the army troops were draftees, and in combat units the portion was commonly as high as two-thirds; late in the war it was even higher. The overall number of draftees was lower because the Marine Corps—the other service branch that did the bulk of fighting in Vietnam—was ordinarily limited to volunteers (though it did draft about 20,000 men during the Vietnam War).

The draft determined the social character of the armed forces by whom it exempted from service as well as by whom it actually conscripted or induced to enlist. Because the generation that came of age during the 1960s was so large, the Selective Service exempted far more men than it drafted. From 1964 to 1973, 2.2 million men were drafted, 8.7 million enlisted, and 16 million did not serve. Of course, the millions of exemptions could have been granted in a manner designed to produce a military that mirrored the social composition of society at large. A step in that direction was made with the institution of a draft lottery in late 1969, a method that can produce a representative cross-section of draftees. However, this reform did little to democratize the forces that fought in Vietnam because student deferments were continued until 1971, troop withdrawals late in the war lowered draft calls, and physical exemptions remained relatively easy for the privileged to attain.

A Grunt's Life

GERARD J. DEGROOT

A generous Cold War budget produced a highly trained American military, albeit one prepared for war in Eastern Europe. Thomas Giltner's "training for combat in Vietnam was non-existent"; it was instead "conventional . . . Monte Casino, North Africa, the Battle of the Bulge." Within the military, the lack of counter-insurgency training was not a cause for concern. In 1962 the Army Chief of Staff, General George Decker, told Kennedy that "any good soldier can handle guerrillas." A common view among military professionals held that the war would be won with mobile tank warfare on South Vietnam's "savannah grasslands and open plains, just like in Europe or west Texas."

The American answer to guerrilla warfare was air mobility. Helicopters encouraged an unwarranted confidence:

> "Totally different war now." The lieutenant flipped his cigarette out to the dew-covered ground. "The French couldn't get around like we can." He patted the Huey's deck. "Machines like this make all the difference. How'd you like to be a guerrilla trying to fight an army that can be anywhere, anytime?"

The US put together the most lavish airmobile effort in history, at huge cost. The 1st Aviation Brigade, established in May 1966, eventually became one of the largest commands in Vietnam, with over 24,000 men and 4,230 aircraft. On an average day a utility helicopter consumed 4,000 pounds of fuel. Almost 5,000 helicopters, each with a price tag exceeding US$250,000, were lost. Nearly 6,000 pilots and crew were killed, one-tenth of war fatalities.

The attrition strategy began the search and destroy operation. If an enemy presence was suspected, a mission would be launched, its size determined by the anticipated enemy concentration. American units usually did not break down lower than company level, since smaller squads were easily ambushed. A landing zone (LZ) would be chosen by overflying the area. Artillery and air support would first "soften" the sector, whereupon troop helicopters, flying just above the jungle canopy and supported on the flanks by helicopter gunships, would hit the LZ, arriving within seconds of the last artillery round. Since the LZ was seldom more than 30 minutes from the base area, reinforcements could be ferried in quickly, and casualties removed. As additional ground units arrived, the target would be compressed, with air bombardment intensifying. Finally, infantry would sweep the area.

South Vietnam was divided into tactical areas of responsibility, usually covering several provinces. The division (or separate brigade) assigned an area would stay there unless pulled away to contribute to a major operation. For example, the 1st Cavalry Division had its headquarters, commanding general, and principal staff at Phuoc Vinh, north of Saigon. The rear headquarters, where most of the logistical and administrative support was located, was at Bien Hoa. The division's three brigades had separate bases 50 to 100 miles from each other. Division and brigade bases were semi-permanent. Battalions were dispersed to a number of strategically situated firebases, which could be activated or de-activated according to need.

The standard infantry weapon was the M-16 assault rifle. With a stock made of plastic, it was considerably lighter than previous rifles. It fired a .223 calibre bullet, the smallest ever used in war, at a prodigious rate of fire. The advantage of the weapon's lighter weight was lost by the necessity to carry huge supplies of ammunition. The standard load was 200 rounds per man, but many carried 600 rounds to keep the hungry weapon fed. The muzzle velocity (3,800 feet per second) and the tendency of the bullet to be easily deflected on impact meant that it could inflict horrific wounds.

The small bullet lacked range and stopping power and was not terribly accurate—small objects like twigs or leaves could deflect its flight. But the most serious problem with the M-16 was its tendency to jam. . . .

"They say if you kept the thing clean it worked just fine, which is great as long as you're operating on concrete. But out in the jungle, where it's nothing but dirt, it's totally impossible to keep them clean," one GI remarked. Most soldiers envied the enemy's AK-47. "You could drive a truck over them, and you couldn't hurt those damn things; you could pour sand down their barrels and they would still fire. Ours would jam if you looked at them wrong."

Troops were constantly on the move in search of the enemy. "You'd be surprised how similar killing is to hunting," a grunt wrote to his brother. "I get all excited when I see a VC, just like when I see a deer." Most engagements began as some form of ambush. "Sometimes we found Charlie, sometimes it was the other way."

> One night we wandered far and long
> To kill young men who, brave and strong
> And precious to their loved, their own,
> Were coming to kill us.
> Aching, filthy, weak, afraid,
> Creeping through the dripping shades,
> Searching forms through jungle haze,
> We stalked those men as prey.

A great deal of damage could be done in a few seconds of chaos. If ambushed troops called for artillery or air support, deadly moments would pass before help arrived. "Charlie played his game," one veteran remarked with grudging admiration. "By the time the mortar rounds got there, he was already gone."

Limitless weaponry and ammunition eroded combat prowess. Soldiers fired indiscriminately the second the enemy was engaged, often running out of ammunition in the middle of a firefight. Commanders called in artillery barrages and air support to silence the lightest opposition. Officers preferred to waste shells rather than men, thus giving the enemy ample warning of American intentions. "There developed . . . a great respect and affection for the men we commanded and a powerful reluctance to shed their blood. Our overall effectiveness as a fighting force was diminished," one officer felt. Huge logistical problems arose as support troops struggled to transport and protect the massive supplies needed for an operation. Firepower became the solution to every problem—an expression of power and of fear. The destruction was sometimes senseless, but criticism is easy in retrospect. "I didn't think of our targets as homes where exhausted and frightened people were praying for their lives," Tobias Wolff comments. "When you are afraid you will kill anything that might kill you. [When] the enemy had the town, the town was the enemy."

Often the only evidence of VC presence was the booby traps or mines which, between 1965 and 1970, caused 11 per cent of American combat deaths and 17 per cent of injuries. The simplest and most common was the punji stake trap, in which sharpened bamboo stakes spread with human excrement were planted in a camouflaged pit. The unsuspecting soldier who stepped on one was certain to suffer immense pain, often followed by infection or gangrene. Traps slowed patrols and eroded morale. [Veteran and novelist Tim] O'Brien described an all-pervasive fear:

> You hallucinate. You look ahead a few paces and what your legs will resemble if there is more to the earth in that spot than silicates and nitrogen. Will the pain be unbearable? Will you scream or fall silent? Will you be afraid to look at your own body, afraid of the sight of your own red flesh and white bone?

Primitive weapons were often constructed from material inadvertently supplied by Americans. A beer can, primed with explosive from a dud bomb, became a grenade or mine. The ability to recognize traps came with experience, which explains why green GIs were most vulnerable.

"When you are fighting a war like Vietnam, you have no idea if you're doing anything useful militarily or not," one soldier felt. Another admitted being troubled by "the knowledge that as soon as we left, they would be back, and most likely, so would we." O'Brien wrote of his fellow soldiers:

> They did not know even the simple things: a sense of victory, or satisfaction, or necessary sacrifice. They did not know the feeling of taking a place and keeping it, securing a village and then raising the flag and calling it a victory. No sense of order or momentum. No front, no rear, no trenches laid out in neat parallels. No Patton rushing from the Rhine, no beachheads to storm and win and hold for the duration. They did not have targets. They did not have a cause. They did not know if it was a war of ideology or economics or hegemony or spite.

The body count was an inadequate measure of progress:

> no contact was made, and the gunships got bored. So they made a gun run on a hooch with mini-guns and rockets. When they left the area we found one dead baby . . . in its mother's arms, and we found a baby girl about three years old, also dead. . . . When it was reported to battalion, the only reprimand was to put the two bodies on the body count board and just add them up with the rest of the dead people.

The best indicator of progress was, sadly, the way men changed from green recruit to tired, desensitized veteran in a matter of months:

> [We] watched the rest of Bravo Company come and go to the field—each time more scroungy and grungy and hangdog-looking than the time before. There were always fewer faces when they came humping those last three hundred meters up the hill . . . always newer faces, pale and astonished, when they left the camp again. . . . a month or six weeks later, when the company came back . . . those fucking new guys would be indistinguishable from the rest, except for the eyes. . . . the eyes took longer.

"His eyes were what I saw first," one veteran recalled. "What I saw in Lawrence's eyes was the horror, The Horror. What spooked me . . . was that I could tell immediately that he knew that everything was different now."

The vast majority of GIs were relatively safe, since most were not in combat. Even among combat units the risk varied according to the unit's area of operation and the year of the war. Perhaps as many as 1.6 million men either fought, provided close support, or were regularly exposed to danger between 1965 and 1973. Of those, 58,202 died and 303,704 were injured, roughly half requiring hospitalization. Small arms fire caused 51 per cent of the deaths and 16 per cent of the wounds, with artillery and mortars responsible for 36 per cent and 65 per cent, respectively. As in any war, venereal disease was rampant. Large numbers also fell victim to tropical diseases, insect and snake bites, and the bothersome ailments caused by a hostile climate and poor hygiene. "I had jungle rot so bad that the only way I could carry my rifle was to cradle it in the bend in my elbows with my hands in front of my face," one soldier recalled. "I couldn't hold on to it my hands were so sore and burning. My feet were like that too." The lack of clearly defined front lines meant a higher than normal number of friendly fire casualties. Over 1,000 died in vehicle crashes and an almost equal number drowned or were suffocated. One in five deaths were "non-hostile."

American forces were, perhaps to their detriment, deeply concerned about casualties. "I guess my standard of success was keeping my soldiers alive," one commander admitted. Troops often performed best when rescuing wounded comrades. The injured received the best medical care ever experienced in war. A soldier was usually rescued and under surgical care in less time than a civilian involved in a car accident on one of America's highways. But since care was better and quicker, more men survived who in earlier wars would have died, which in turn meant many more ended up severely disabled. Amputations and crippling wounds were 300 per cent higher proportionately than in the Second World War and 70 per cent higher than in Korea. Multiple amputations were over three times as high as in the Second World War.

> After our war, the dismembered bits
> —all those pierced eyes, ear slivers, jaw splinters,
> gouged lips, odd tibias, skin flaps, and toes—
> came squinting, wobbling, jabbering back.

At base hospitals, nurses and doctors worked under enormous strain. It was hard to watch young, healthy men being destroyed:

> A bullet went through the base of his skull and ricocheted inside his helmet until its momentum ran out. . . . He is fully alert but "locked in," paralyzed from the eyes down from a severed brain stem. He is able only to blink, move his eyes down, and cry, and there's no hope of his ever doing more than that.
>
> How long can he live this way? Ten years? Twenty years? Thirty or forty? What God would permit such a fate? None that I want to believe in.
>
> We print the alphabet on a piece of cardboard, so he can communicate more than yes or no. We run a finger along the letters, and he blinks out a message.
>
> Once in the middle of the night he blinks the message "L-E-T M-E D-I-E"

A stoical detachment was essential. "I don't want to get close to anybody," one nurse repeatedly reminded herself. "I don't want to get to know anything about them. Because if I do, I find myself getting drawn and attached to this person. I can't afford to lose more people like this because it will destroy me and I won't function."

"We didn't see much shell shock," Lily Adams recalled. Psychiatric casualties composed just 5 per cent of medical evacuations in 1965–66, falling to less than 3 per cent in 1967–68. This compares dramatically with 23 per cent during the Second World War. The explanation seems to be the absence of sustained combat, the one-year rotation and a greater awareness of war's psychiatric effects. There were two neuropsychiatric treatment centre teams, and psychiatrists attached to each division. Line officers were instructed to be sensitive to the mental torment of battle. One psychiatrist reasoned that, due to the one-year rotation, there was "not the sense of hopelessness that prevailed in previous conflicts where death, injury or peace became the only possible ways in which the soldier could find himself extricated from combat."

War destroys, but it also creates. Deep emotional bonds were formed between fellow soldiers. A West Point graduate remarked how the Army had taught him how to kill, but not how to handle the death of a comrade. "No one had ever said, 'Cadets, you're going to see a great deal of death and gore, and here are some possible ways to accommodate it.' That omission [seemed] . . . a serious oversight, almost like sending a man into combat without proper training in marksmanship."

The war has often been presented as a morality tale: the disintegration of the US Army, it is argued, demonstrates what happens when good men are used for corrupt purposes. Or a different version asserts that the war was lost because inadequate soldiers, polluted by Sixties hedonism, were sent to Vietnam. Ironically, both arguments rely upon a similarly distorted image of the American soldier. Drug-crazed sadists were either victims of a cruel government or symptoms of a sick society.

American soldiers went to war in 1965 firmly committed to their country's cause. From a very early age they underwent a comprehensive, if informal, indoctrination. For most, America was a "city on a hill"—not only wealthy and powerful, but morally righteous. W.D. Ehrhart

> believed sincerely that if we did not stop the communists in Vietnam, we would one day have to fight them in San Diego. I had no reason up to that point in my life to doubt either my government or my high school teachers or the *New York Times*. I believed in my country and in its God-given role as the leader of the Free World—that it was the finest nation on earth, that its political system and its leaders were essentially good, and that any nation or people who opposed us must be inherently bad. Furthermore, I valued my freedom, and took seriously the notion that I owed something to my country.

These men were the perfect raw material for an army preparing for war. But commitment to *this* war required an act of faith. "I figured that [the war] was more or less right," one soldier confessed, "because why would I be going if it wasn't right?" Potential soldiers were given very little formal indoctrination. In contrast, communist political cadres worked tirelessly to indoctrinate fellow soldiers about the righteousness of their war. Formalized propagandizing of this type is antithetic to a liberal democracy like the United States. But without it, American soldiers had difficulty understanding their mission. When they discovered the "real" war, they had few barriers to disillusionment:

> The American people had been told that we were defending a free democracy. What I found was a military dictatorship rife with corruption and venality and repression. The premier of South Vietnam openly admired Adolf Hitler. Buddhist priests who petitioned for peace were jailed or shot down in the streets. Officials at every level engaged in blatant black-marketeering . . . at the expense of their own people.

Chanting the Pledge of Allegiance or recalling amber waves of grain were weak defences against the creeping uncertainty which afflicted nearly every soldier.

The soldier's disillusionment mirrored a crisis of confidence within America as a whole, where the naive certainties of the 1950s gave way to 1970s self-doubt. The evaporation of support for the war at home undoubtedly exacerbated the unease experienced by soldiers. They did not need to be told that they were fighting an ignoble war, but telling them made them feel worse.

> A lot of guys would get newspapers from home and . . . we'd read about all the protesting and rioting back home about the war. We just couldn't understand it. Here we was,

over there humping ourselves to death and we were worried about what was going to happen next, and here these bunch of long-haired hippies back home protested on the streets and did what they wanted to do.

Innocent men became scapegoats for an unpopular war. Their sense of betrayal ran deep. Shocked by the outcry when four students were killed at Kent State in 1970, one soldier wrote: "So why don't your hearts cry out and shed a tear for the 40-plus thousand red-blooded Americans and brave, fearless, loyal men who have given their lives so a bunch of bloody bastard radicals can protest, dissent and generally bitch?"

Thus, by the late 1960s, the sense of purpose which the American soldier took to Vietnam had evaporated. A Marine corporal and Purple Heart winner, on his second tour of duty, wrote to his father after the battle of Hué:

15 months in the Nam and I'm still charging the lines with as much balls as any other stud I know because the adventure and pride . . . within me demands it. . . . And why? Suddenly I'm sitting in my vacuum wondering WHY? A nasty collision with reality and I damn well wouldn't give my life for any of this. You're damned straight. Not for any President who got into office by a fluke to begin with, and now continues to brainwash the troops, and the country, with phoney pretenses accounting for our participation in this cesspool. So, not me. No sir. Not this kid's life. Not even a limb and hopefully not even another goddamn drop of blood. Oh, I'll fight. I'll fight for the adventure and the preservation of my ass, when a damn zip tries to level it. But not for that man . . . No sir. I hate that man. I [also] hate these mustard, prideless, ambitionless, leeching bastards, whose government is merely an extension of our own government's corruption.

"I never felt I was fighting for any particular cause," David Parks commented. "I fought to stay alive and I killed to keep from being killed." Colonel Robert Heinl admitted in 1971 that "'Search and evade' . . . is now virtually a principle of war, vividly expressed by the GI phrase, 'CYA (cover your ass) and get home!'" Soldiers took to painting UUUU on their helmets: "the unwilling, led by the unqualified, doing the unnecessary, for the ungrateful."

Drugs became a serious problem. The RVN Navy kept the supply flowing, and top politicians (including Ky and Thieu) profited from the trade. NLF sympathizers also kept American soldiers well-stocked with all manner of mind-numbing drugs. According to one study, by 1971 marijuana use stood at 50.9 per cent of military personnel, heroin and other narcotics 28.5 per cent, and hallucinogenics 14 per cent. During one court-martial, the judge asked the accused how he had earned the Silver Star ribbon he was wearing. The latter replied that he could not remember since he was "strung out on heroin" at the time.

The decline in morale eroded the soldier's respect for authority. Officers became pariahs. Between 1969 and 1971 there were 730 recorded cases of fragging, with 83 officers killed. The figures for actual cases do not accurately convey the gravity of the problem, since fear of fragging intimidated officers, seriously undermining their ability to lead. Back at home, some 144 underground newspapers encouraged disobedience among personnel at military bases. "In Vietnam, the Lifers, the Brass are the true Enemy, not the enemy," a paper distributed at Fort Lewis argued. "Don't desert," another advised; "Go to Vietnam and kill your commanding officer." Problems of indiscipline were not confined to ground troops. In 1972 a House inquiry found "literally hundreds of instances of damage to naval property wherein sabotage is suspected." During the Chrismas bombing of 1972, some pilots refused to perform their assigned role of attacking AA batteries. One B-52 commander was tried for refusing to fly, and at one point a state of "near mutiny" existed. The precipitate troop withdrawals during the Nixon administration should be seen in this light—they were partly intended to save the military from itself.

Racial tension also increased. In 1968, 200 African-American prisoners rioted at Long Binh jail. Two years later, one of the worst race riots of the war occurred at Camp Baxter in Da Nang. Though statistics suggest otherwise, African-American soldiers felt they were bearing the brunt of the war.

> When you're on patrol and moving into an area, it's always the negro who's walking point. That means he is the first to get it if a mine explodes. That's the kind of harassment we get from the whites. . . . Look at the guys who go out on sweeps, who protect the hills. Brothers, as many brothers as they can find.

Some wrote on their helmets "NO GOOK EVER CALLED ME NIGGER." It is fair to assume that a significant proportion of fragging incidents were racially motivated, especially as the Army has traditionally had a high percentage of white southern officers and urban African-American enlisted men. African-Americans arriving in Vietnam were astonished to see Confederate flags attached to jeeps. "We are fighting and dying in a war that is not very popular in the first place and we still have some stupid people who are still fighting the Civil War," one commented.

Desertion was high, but not as high as might be expected for such an unpopular war. In 1965 the desertion rate stood at 15.7 per 1,000 soldiers, peaking at 73. 5 in 1971. This compares favourably with a peak rate of 63 in 1944. Rates for soldiers going absent without leave (AWOL) were higher in the Korean War than in Vietnam. A significant number deserted *after* they had served a full term and returned to the United States. The problem was kept in check by the fact that desertion in Vietnam was not easy, since there were few places to hide in the hostile countryside. Only a tiny percentage deserted within Vietnam, and an even smaller fraction from combat.

The disintegration of the American military can be measured by the escalating legal burden. In 1965 the US Army had four lawyers in Vietnam. By 1969, 135 attorneys were working ten to twelve hours per day, seven days a week, could not keep up with the case load. Around 25,000 courts-martial were tried by the US Army in Vietnam between 1965 and 1969, peaking in the latter year at 9,922. In the same year, 66,702 Article 15s were administered. Roughly 20 per cent of cases involved drug offences. Judges often faced a dilemma, since many combat soldiers preferred a spell in the stockade to a jungle patrol. Many cases involving rear echelon soldiers which ordinarily would have resulted in courts-martial were handled instead with Article 15 proceedings, with punishment taking the form of a combat assignment.

Combat is often a spur to morale. The survival instinct focuses the mind and distracts attention from corrosive anxieties. This explains why most problems of indiscipline occurred in the rear areas. Dissension on a patrol endangers the lives of everyone in the unit. The same holds true for drug abuse. "Nobody did drugs or alcohol in the field," one soldier claimed. "That was the wrong time and place. You needed everything you had to stay alive, and doing drugs wasn't one of them. . . . if you were doing drugs, you might get shot out in the field during a firefight. . . . maybe get the whole squad killed." Harry Bergson of the 25th Infantry confirmed this view: "I think that all of that crap took place in the base camp. That's where the drug problems and the black power groups and all of the rest of that junk was."

Battlefield morale survived much longer than political morale. Men who despised the war still fought like heroes. The glue that held them together was the duty felt to each other. O'Brien mourned the loss of Captain Johansen—"losing him was like the Trojans losing Hector":

> Vietnam was under siege in pursuit of a pretty, tantalizing, promiscuous, particularly American brand of government and style. And most of Alpha Company would have preferred a likeable whore to self-determination. So Captain Johansen helped to mitigate and melt the silliness, showing the grace and poise a man can have under the worst circumstances, a wrong war. We clung to him.

"Your family was your squad, and that's who you look after," one soldier commented. "Mom and apple pie and stuff, that was out the window. You were fighting for each other. You were trying to keep each other alive so you could make it home."

The military tried to boost morale by making available an endless supply of creature comforts. Soldiers returned from a firefight and within a half hour sat down to steaks, beer, french fries and ice cream. Helicopters brought cold beer to soldiers in the throes of battle. An American major commented wryly to Robert Shaplen in 1967, "One of these days they'll be pumping Muzak down to company level." When the Americans left, they abandoned 71 swimming pools, 90 service clubs, 159 basketball courts, 30 tennis courts, 55 softball diamonds, 85 volleyball pitches, 337 libraries and 2 bowling alleys. Prostitutes were cheap, readily available and generally tolerated by the military brass.

Davidson Loehr, trained as a forward artillery observer, "beat the game" when he landed a job as an entertainment officer:

> They gave me a secretary and an air-conditioned office in Saigon, and my job consisted of meeting movie stars and professional entertainers at the airport, taking them out to dinner on an expense account, and keeping their refrigerator stocked with beer and soft drinks. After work, I stopped . . . for steam bath, massage, and sex; or, less often spent the night with Thom, my favourite barmaid.

The comfortable existence enjoyed by REMFs ("rear echelon mother fuckers") eroded morale among combat soldiers. They complained about the arbitrary and corrupt process by which others were chosen for easy assignments, and concluded (with justification) that combat was a form of punishment. But the REMFs were sometimes tormented by a purposeless life. "I have had a shit existence on a bad army post in a deserted area," one soldier stuck at Long Binh base complained. "If I had really been in Vietnam, I might have seen some of the country, talked to its farmers, eaten its food, played with its children or killed some of its men."

Creature comforts, designed to boost morale, may in fact have eroded efficiency. General Hamilton Howze felt that "Our base camps became too elaborate, soaked up too much manpower, diverted our attention from the basic mission and lessened our operational flexibility." The war could seem unreal:

> It was weird, really; you'd be out in the bush for two or three weeks or longer and come in for a stand down. You could have a cookout, go to the PX, see movies at night. It was almost like being back in the world. I personally could never get used to that, and to

me, it was one of the problems. We were deceiving ourselves. If we were going to fight the war and win it, let's fight the war and win it and go home. But this artificial living . . . was beyond me. It may have kept the troops entertained, but it prevented them from focusing on what we were there for.

Some of war's sharp edges had been smoothed. "It was difficult for [the Americans] to suffer all the hardships of the Vietnamese battlefront," one PAVN veteran commented. "When we had no water to drink, they had water for showers! We could suffer the hardships much better than they could. That, probably, was the main reason we won."

In another misguided attempt to boost morale, more than 1.25 million bravery medals were awarded, compared to just 50,258 during the Korean War. The total exceeds even the most generous estimate of the number who actually faced danger. Rewards were not, however, distributed equally. During his first 26 weeks of command in Vietnam, Colonel John Donaldson received 27 medals. Perhaps not surprisingly, the number of citations increased as the American combat role decreased. There was little awareness that medals, like money, devalue with inflation.

Because the enemy seemed so alien, a brotherhood of arms did not develop between the two sides. Second World War films have encouraged the cliché of the GI who shares a cigarette with a captured enemy and then perhaps passes around photos of his family. As with all clichés, this one has some truth. But Vietnam was different:

> We did not speak their language, so we could not ask their names, their home villages, or even if they were the same age as us. We were ignorant of their history or culture, so we had no idea if they were even Vietnamese, Cambodian, or possibly Chinese. . . . [There was] tremendous group pressure not to feel any compassion. . . . Many times I saw individual acts of compassion that were immediately counteracted by cruelty and deliberate steps taken to show . . . that to be human had no place in war.

It was a short step from cruelty to atrocity. Lee Childress saw a fellow soldier shoot an old Vietnamese woman who tried to steal his chewing gum. "He shot her point blank through the chest and killed her." His crime went unpunished. "We got in more trouble for killing water buffalo than for killing people," Childress remarked. Norman Ryman collected ears cut from dead enemy soldiers and photographs of mutilated "gooks." He loved the war so much that he volunteered for two extra tours of duty. "I had an excuse to be hostile and aggressive and I also had a license to kill without prosecution which made my actions enjoyable and my insanity bearable."

On 16 March 1968 members of Company C, Task Force Barker, a battalion-sized unit of the American Division commanded by Lieutenant William Calley, murdered some 350 unarmed civilians in the village of My Lai. According to Calley,

> I was ordered to go in there and destroy the enemy. That was my job . . . That was the mission I was given. I did not sit down and think in terms of men, women and children. They were all classified the same . . . I felt then and I still do that I acted as I was directed, and I carried out the orders that I was given and I do not feel wrong in doing so. . . .
>
> We weren't in My Lai to kill human beings, really. We were there to kill an ideology that is carried by—I don't know. Pawns. Blobs. Pieces of flesh. And I wasn't in My Lai to destroy intelligent men. I was there to destroy an intangible idea. To destroy

communism . . . I looked at communism as a southerner looks at a Negro, supposedly. It's evil. It's bad.

The incident, the worst atrocity by American soldiers during the war, caused a huge outcry at home, though not everyone condemned Calley. Charges were subsequently brought against thirteen men, with Calley accused of 109 acts of murder. He was convicted and received life imprisonment, a sentence eventually reduced to ten years on the intervention of the Secretary of the Army. This made him eligible for parole after six months, which was granted. The other twelve were acquitted. A further twelve officers of the American division were accused of covering up the crime, but only two, Captain Ernest Medina and Colonel Oran Henderson, were court-martialled. Both were acquitted.

In 1970 six Rangers at base club boasted how, after ambushing and killing enemy soldiers, they had "cut open the bodies from throat to groin and stuffed them with rice." "Calling cards" of this type were designed to strike fear in enemy soldiers; a PLAF variant was to stuff an American soldier's genitalia into his mouth. The Rangers were reported, and charges brought. A mission was dispatched to search for evidence. Air Force jets and helicopter gunships prepped the area, whereupon a Huey carrying a rifle platoon and the defence lawyer arrived. The team found burlap rice sacks, lots of blood, but no bodies. Since there was no actual proof of the crime, the case was dismissed. It reveals the difficulties of investigating war crimes and of punishing the guilty. Prosecutors faced enormous practical difficulties collecting evidence and finding witnesses in a war zone. The dilemma of precisely defining criminal behaviour in this type of war made conviction even more complicated.

Between 1965 and 1973, around 250 cases of alleged war crimes by Americans came before military authorities. Further investigation revealed that 160 of these were unsubstantiated. Eventually, 36 resulted in trials by courts-martial. It is difficult to say whether these were just the tip of the iceberg. One officer felt that "My Lai represented to the average professional soldier nothing more than being caught in a cover-up of something which he knew had been going on for a long time on a smaller scale." Many incidents, especially early in the war, probably went unreported. Others fell into the grey area which exists between cruelty, carelessness and atrocity. Wantonly shooting at an individual running across a paddy attracted adverse attention only if it turned out afterwards that the individual was a fourteen-year-old girl. Death could be random, but cold-blooded murder was probably relatively rare. One must bear in mind the fact that Vietnam was a very public war; especially after 1969 reporters roamed the countryside in search of the genuine atrocity which would win them a Pulitzer Prize.

"War by its nature," writes Caputo, "can arouse a psychopathic violence in men of seemingly normal impulses." This war, in particular, did so. Many explanations are offered: the tension of guerrilla war, a futile attrition strategy, racist attitudes toward the enemy, poor quality officers, the shame of defeat, and drugs. As former marine W.D. Ehrhart put it:

> It's practically impossible
> to tell civilians
> from the Vietcong.

Nobody wears uniforms.
They all talk
the same language,
(and you couldn't understand them
even if they didn't).

They tape grenades
inside their clothes,
and carry satchel charges
in their market baskets.

Even their women fight,
and young boys,
and girls.

It's practically impossible
to tell civilians
from the Vietcong;
after awhile,
you quit trying.

Vietnam, according to Caputo, was "an ethical as well as a geographic wilderness where "lacking restraints, sanctioned to kill, confronted by a hostile country and a relentless enemy, we sank into a brutish state." So, too, did the enemy, who regularly mutilated corpses and executed prisoners. Hanoi decided early on that the "laws of war" did not apply to revolutionary struggle in South Vietnam. While some analysts find it possible to apply a different moral code to communist crimes, there is no doubt that there were Norman Rymans on both sides.

"Most American soldiers in Vietnam," writes Caputo, "could not be divided into good men and bad. Each possessed roughly equal measures of both qualities. I saw men who behaved with great compassion toward the Vietnamese one day and burned down a village the next." Norman Ryman, who should never have become a soldier, was not typical. The myth of an ignorant, psychotic, drug-crazed and murderous military has served as a convenient explanation for defeat. As hard as it might be to accept, good American soldiers got beaten in Vietnam. The defeat cannot be blamed on bad men. But defeat did make some men bad.

X *FURTHER READING*

Anderson, David L., ed. *Facing My Lai* (1998).
Baker, Mark. *Nam* (1981).
Ball, Phil. *Ghosts and Shadows: A Marine in Vietnam* (1998).
Bilton, Michael, and Kevin Sim. *Four Hours in My Lai* (1992).
Broyles, Jr., William. *Brother in Arms: A Journey from War to Peace* (1986).
Gwin, Larry. *Baptism: A Vietnam Memoir* (1999).
Herr, Michael. *Dispatches* (1997).
Herrington, Stuart A. *Silence Was a Weapon: The Vietnam War in the Villages* (1982).
Hersh, Seymour. *My Lai 4* (1970).

Humphries, James E. *Through the Valley: Vietnam, 1967–1968* (1999).

Kovic, Ron. *Born on the Fourth of July* (1976).

Krepenevich, Jr., Andrew F. *The Army and Vietnam* (1986).

Lehrack, Otto J. *No Shining Armor: The Marines at War in Vietnam* (1992).

Marshall, Kathryn. *In the Combat Zone: An Oral History of American Women in Vietnam* (1987).

Mason, Robert. *Chickenhawk* (1983).

Maurer, Harry. *Strange Ground: An Oral History of Americans in Vietnam* (1998).

Moore, Harold G., and Joseph L. Galloway. *We Were Soldiers Once . . . And Young* (1992).

Murray, Edward F. *Semper Fi–Vietnam* (1998).

Puller, Jr., Lewis. *Fortunate Son* (1991).

Santoli, Al, ed. *Everything We Had* (1984).

Spector, Ronald H. *After Tet* (1993).

Solis, Gary D. *Son Thang: An American War Crime* (1997).

Terry, Wallace, ed. *Bloods: An Oral History of the Vietnam War by Black Veterans* (1984).

Westheider, James E. *Fighting on Two Fronts: African Americans and the Vietnam War* (1997).

Wolff, Tobias. *In Pharaoh's Army* (1994).

CHAPTER
9

The Enemy: North Vietnam

and the

National Liberation Front

✕

Following the Geneva Conference of 1954, Ho Chi Minh and most of the former Vietminh leadership devoted their energies to the establishment of a socialist state in the territory north of the seventeenth parallel: the Democratic Republic of Vietnam. In the area south of the parallel, Ngo Dinh Diem, with strong American backing, attempted to consolidate his hold on power in the Republic of Vietnam. By 1956, any lingering hope that the all-Vietnam elections promised at Geneva would be held had been dashed, and the two "regroupment areas" increasingly resembled independent countries.

The northern leaders had not abandoned the goal of national unification. Opposition to Diem spread throughout the countryside during the late 1950s; a revolutionary guerrilla movement reemerged in the south at that time, composed in part of former Vietminh cadres. At least by 1960, Hanoi was giving active support to that movement, and in November of that year the National Liberation Front (NLF) was founded as a broad populist coalition that sought to appeal to all groups opposed to Diem's regime.

The nature and extent of Hanoi's involvement in the southern revolution stands as one of the most controversial aspects of the Vietnam War. The issue divided scholars, activists, and policymakers at the height of American involvement, and it continues to spark lively debate. The following questions rank among the most significant: Did North Vietnam orchestrate the revolution in the south from its inception? Were the "Vietcong" guerrillas and the NLF merely puppets of Hanoi? or did the southern revolution have important internal roots? How and why did the Vietcong gain such a strong foothold in the countryside so quickly? Did the communist program appeal to the peasants, and, if so, how? What role, if any, did the Soviet Union and China play in the deepening conflict in Vietnam? Finally, from the perspective of the United States, who were America's principal enemies in Vietnam?

After the conclusion of the Geneva Agreements, Ho Chi Minh urged all Vietnamese to comply with their provisions. His appeal of July 22, 1954, appears as Document 1. In Document 2, Troung Nhu Tang, an opponent of the Diem regime, recalls the events that led to the formation of the National Liberation Front. The NLF's manifesto of December 1960, Document 3, reflected the organization's interest in attracting the broadest possible coalition in opposition to the Diem government.

Documents 4 and 5 present personal testimony from peasants who were recruited by Vietcong cadres in the early 1960s. Nguyen Tan Thanh, who eventually rose to become a senior captain and deputy commander in the main forces of the Vietcong, explains how the land question prompted his decision to join the insurgency. Le Ly Hayslip, in an excerpt from her remarkable memoir *When Heaven and Earth Changed Places,* recounts how an innocent young girl metamorphosed into a dedicated Vietcong supporter.

In Document 6, dating from 1961, Vo Nguyen Giap spells out the essential strategy of what he called a "people's war," insisting that even an insufficiently equipped people's army, by devising right tactics and strategy, could defeat a modern army. Nguyen Chi Thanh, a South Vietnamese communist who would later command all communist forces in the south, offered a similarly optimistic perspective in an article published in July 1963, reproduced here as Document 7. He stressed that a powerful North Vietnam and an effective revolutionary movement in the south were mutually complementary and required careful coordination. Document 8 features an exhortation by Chinese leader Mao Zedong to a visiting North Vietnamese delegation, in Beijing, on October 20, 1965. In Document 9, a speech delivered over Radio Hanoi on July 17, 1966, Ho displays characteristic determination in the face of growing American military pressure.

1. Ho Chi Minh's Appeal After the Geneva Agreements, 1954

The Geneva Conference has come to an end. It is a great victory for our diplomacy.

On behalf of the Government, I cordially make the following appeal:

1. For the sake of peace, unity, independence, and democracy of the Fatherland, our people, armymen, cadres, and Government have, during these eight years or so, joined in a monolithic bloc, endured hardship, and resolutely overcome all difficulties to carry out the Resistance; we have won many brilliant victories. On this occasion, on behalf of the Government, I cordially congratulate you, from North to South. I respectfully bow to the memory of the armymen and people who have sacrificed their lives for the Fatherland, and send my homages of comfort to the wounded and sick armymen.

This great victory is also due to the support given us in our just struggle by the peoples of our brother countries, by the French people, and by the peace-loving people of the world.

Thanks to these victories and the efforts made by the delegation of the Soviet Union at the Berlin Conference, negotiations were opened between our country and

Ho Chi Minh's statement, July 22, 1954, in Ho Chi Minh, *On Revolution: Selected Writings,* Fall, ed. pp. 271–273.

France at the Geneva Conference. At this conference, the struggle of our delegation and the assistance given by the delegations of the Soviet Union and China have ended in a great victory for us: The French Government has recognized the independence, sovereignty, unity, and territorial integrity of our country; it has agreed to withdraw French troops from our country, etc.

From now on, we must make every effort to consolidate peace and achieve reunification, independence, and democracy throughout our country.

2. In order to re-establish peace, the first step to take is that the armed forces of both parties should cease fire.

The regroupment in two regions is a temporary measure; it is a transitional step for the implementation of the armistice and restoration of peace, and paves the way for national reunification through general elections. Regroupment in regions is in no way a partition of our country, neither is it an administrative division.

During the armistice, our army is regrouped in the North; the French troops are regrouped in the South, that is to say, there is a change of regions. A number of regions which were formerly occupied by the French now become our free zones. Vice versa, a number of regions formerly liberated by us will now be temporarily occupied by the French troops before they leave for France.

This is a necessity; North, Central, and South Viet-Nam are territories of ours. Our country will certainly be unified, our entire people will surely be liberated.

Our compatriots in the South were the first to wage the war of Resistance. They possess a high political consciousness. I am confident that they will place national interests above local interests, permanent interests above temporary interests, and join their efforts with the entire people in strengthening peace, achieving unity, independence, and democracy all over the country. The Party, Government, and I always follow the efforts of our people and we are sure that our compatriots will be victorious.

3. The struggle to consolidate peace and achieve reunification, independence, and democracy is also a long and hard struggle. In order to carry the day, our people, armymen, and cadres from North to South must unite closely. They must be at one in thought and deed.

We are resolved to abide by the agreements entered into with the French Government. At the same time, we demand that the French Government correctly implement the agreements they have signed with us.

We must do our utmost to strengthen peace and be vigilant to check the maneuvers of peace wreckers.

We must endeavor to struggle for the holding of free general elections throughout the country to reunify our territory.

We must exert all our efforts to restore, build, strengthen, and develop our forces in every field so as to attain complete independence.

We must do our utmost to carry out social reforms in order to improve our people's livelihood and realize genuine democracy.

We further tighten our fraternal relations with Cambodia and Laos.

We strengthen the great friendship between us and the Soviet Union, China, and other brother countries. To maintain peace, we enhance our solidarity with the French people, the Asian people, and people all over the world.

4. I call on all our compatriots, armymen, and cadres to follow strictly the lines and policies laid down by the Party and Government, to struggle for the consolidation

of peace and the achievement of national reunification, independence, and democracy throughout the country.

I eagerly appeal to all genuine patriots, irrespective of their social class, creed, political stand, and former affiliation, to cooperate sincerely with us and fight for the sake of our country and our people so as to bring about peace and achieve reunification, independence, and democracy for our beloved Viet-Nam.

If our people are as one, if thousands of men are like one, victory will certainly be ours.

Long live a peaceful, unified, independent, and democratic Viet-Nam.

2. Truong Nhu Tang on the Origins of the National Liberation Front (1957–1959), 1985

By the time 1957 merged into 1958, Ngo Dinh Diem had exhausted the patient hopefulness that had initially greeted his presidency. From the first he had moved ruthlessly to consolidate his personal power, crushing the private army of the Binh Xuyen,* then subduing the armed religious sects. From there he attacked those suspected of communist sympathies in what was called the To Cong ("Denounce the Communists") campaign, jailing and executing thousands who had fought against the French. Each of these moves was carried out with surprising energy, and in their own terms they succeeded. As he surveyed the political landscape three years after assuming power, Diem could see no well-organized centers of opposition to his rule. The National Assembly was wholly dominated by his brother's National Revolutionary Movement, the troublesome private armies had been severely handled, and the Communist-dominated resistance veterans were cowed and in disarray.

But Diem's successes had all been of a negative sort. Though he had asserted his authority and gained time, he had done nothing about establishing positive programs to meet the nation's economic and social needs. He had not used the time he had gained. After three years it was apparent that the new president was a power-monger, not a builder. For those who could see, the fatal narrowness of his political understanding was already evident.

In the first place, Diem's armed enemies had for the most part only been mauled, not destroyed. Elements of the defeated sect armies went underground, licking their wounds and looking for allies. Gradually they began to link up with groups of former Vietminh fighters fleeing from the To Cong suppression. The core of a guerrilla army was already in the making.

Even as old enemies regrouped, Diem was busy adding new ones. In the countryside he destroyed at a blow the dignity and livelihood of several hundred thousand peasants by canceling the land-redistribution arrangements instituted by the Vietminh in areas they had controlled prior to 1954. He might have attempted to use

---

*A tightly run organized crime syndicate that controlled underworld activities in Saigon and Cholon and was not adverse to injecting itself into politics.

Truong Nhu Tang was a founding central committee member of the National Liberation Front and minister of justice in the Provisional Revolutionary Government. Excerpt from Truong Nhu Tang, David Chanoff, and Doan Van Toai, *Vietcong Memoir,* Harcourt Brace, 1985. Reprinted with permission of David Chanoff.

American aid to compensate owners and capitalize on peasant goodwill; instead he courted the large landholders. Farmers who had been working land they considered theirs, often for years, now faced demands for back rent and exorbitant new rates. It was an economic disaster for them.

In 1957 Diem promulgated his own version of land reform, ostensibly making acreage available, though only to peasants who could pay for it. But even this reform was carried out primarily on paper. In the provinces it was sabotaged everywhere by landowners acting with official connivance. The result of all this was a frustrated and indignant peasantry, fertile ground for anti-Diem agitation.

Meanwhile, the city poor were tasting their own ration of misery. In Saigon the government pursued "urban development" with a vengeance, dispossessing whole neighborhoods in favor of modern commercial buildings and expensive apartments, which could only be utilized by Americans and the native upper classes. Not a few times, poorer quarters were completely razed by uncontrollable fires (Khanh Hoi and Phu Nuan were particularly calamitous examples). Few thought these fires were accidental; they were too closely followed by massive new construction. The displaced moved onto sampans on the river or to poorer, even more distant districts. In the slums and shanty villages resentment against the Americans mixed with a simmering anger toward the regime.

In the highland regions of the Montagnards too, Diem's policies were cold-blooded and destructive. Attempting to make the tribespeople more accessible to government control, troops and cadres forced village populations down out of the mountains and into the valleys—separating them from their ancestral lands and graves. In Ban Me Thuot and other areas, the ingrained routines of social life were profoundly disrupted by these forced relocations, which seemed to the tribespeople nothing more than inexplicable cruelty.

By the end of 1958, Diem had succeeded brilliantly in routing his enemies and arrogating power. But he had also alienated large segments of the South Vietnamese population, creating a swell of animosity throughout the country. Almost unknown at first, in a few short years he had made himself widely detested, a dictator who could look for support only to the Northern Catholic refugees and to those who made money from his schemes. Most damning of all, he had murdered many patriots who had fought in the struggle against France and had tied his existence to the patronage of the United States, France's successor. To many nationalist-minded Vietnamese, whose emotions were those of people just emerging from a hundred years of subjection to foreigners, Diem had forfeited all claims to loyalty.

In light of Diem's conduct of the presidency, two facts were clear: First, the country had settled into an all too familiar pattern of oligarchic rule and utter disregard for the welfare of the people. Second, subservience to foreigners was still the order of the day. We had a ruler whose overriding interest was power and who would use the Americans to prop himself up—even while the Americans were using him for their own strategic purposes.

As far as I was concerned, this situation was intolerable. Replacing the French despots with a Vietnamese one was not a significant advance. It would never lead to either the broad economic progress or the national dignity which I (along with many others) had been brooding about for years. Among my circle of friends there was anger and profound disappointment over this turn of events. We were living, we felt, in historic times. A shameful, century-long era had just been violently closed out, and a new nation was taking shape before our eyes. Many of us agreed that we could not acquiesce in the shape it was taking. If we were not to be allowed a say about it from within the government, we would have to speak from without.

By the end of 1958, those of us who felt this way decided to form an extralegal political organization, complete with a program and plan of action. We had not moved toward this decision quickly; it was an undertaking of immense magnitude, which would require years of effort before giving us the strength to challenge Diem's monopoly on power. To some, that prospect seemed quixotic at best. But most of us felt we had little choice.

From casual discussions, we began to meet in slightly more formal groups, sometimes only a few of us, sometimes eight or ten together. Two doctors, Duong Quynh Hoa and Phung Van Cung, took active roles, as did Nguyen Huu Khuong, a factory owner, Trinh Dinh Thao, a lawyer, and the architect Huynh Tan Phat. We were joined by Nguyen Van Hieu and Ung Ngoc Ky, who were lycee teachers, and other friends such as Nguyen Long and Tran Buu Kiem. Our first order of business was to identify and make contact with potential allies for what we knew would be a long and bitter struggle.

To do this we formed what we called the mobilization committee, whose members were myself, Hieu, Kiem, Ky, Long, Cung, and architect Phat. Through friends, relatives, business and political contacts we began to establish a network of people who felt as we did about Diem and his policies. Phat and a few of the others were old resisters and had kept their ties with fellow veterans of the French war, many of whom were hiding with friends and family from the To Cong hunters. They too were beginning to organize, and they had colleagues and sympathizers in every social stratum throughout the country. They were natural allies.

Among us we also had people with close ties to the sects, the legal political parties, the Buddhists. In each group we made overtures, and everywhere we discovered sympathy and backing. Sometimes individuals would indicate their desire to participate actively. More often we would receive assurances of quiet solidarity. At the same time, we sent Nguyen Van Hieu to Hanoi to begin working out a channel of support from our Northern compatriots.

At each stage we discussed carefully the ongoing search for allies, wary about how to gather support and still retain our own direction and freedom of action. It was a delicate and crucial problem, of the utmost complexity. The overwhelming strength of our enemy urged us to acquire whatever assistance we could, from whatever source. In addition, the anticolonial war had not simply ended in 1954; a residual Vietminh infrastructure was still in place and was beginning to come alive again. For better or worse, our endeavor was meshed into an ongoing historical movement for independence that had already developed its own philosophy and means of action. Of this movement, Ho Chi Minh was the spiritual father, in the South as well as the North, and we looked naturally to him and to his government for guidance and aid. . . . And yet, this struggle was also our own. Had Ngo Dinh Diem proved a man of breadth and vision, the core of people who filled the NLF and its sister organizations would have rallied to him. As it was, the South Vietnamese nationalists were driven to action by his contempt for the principles of independence and social progress in which they believed. In this sense, the Southern revolution was generated of itself, out of the emotions, conscience, and aspirations of the Southern people.

The complexity of the struggle was mirrored in the makeup of our group. Most were not Lao Dong ("Workers' Party"—the official name of the Vietnamese Communist Party) members; many scarcely thought of themselves as political, at least in any ideological way. Our allies among the resistance veterans were also largely nationalist rather than political (though they had certainly been led and monitored by the Party). But we also had Party activists among us, some open, some surreptitious. . . .

But I was not overly concerned at that point about potential conflicts between the Southern nationalists and the ideologues. We were allies in this fight, or so I believed. We needed each other, and the closest ties of background, family, and patriotism united us in respect for each other's purposes. This was my reading of the situation in 1959 as the yet-to-be-named National Liberation Front gathered momentum. I was not alone in drawing this conclusion. And I was not the only one whom time would disabuse.

3. Manifesto of the National Liberation Front, 1960

Compatriots in the country and abroad!

Over the past hundred years the Vietnamese people repeatedly rose up to fight against foreign aggression for the independence and freedom of their fatherland. In 1945, the people throughout the country surged up in an armed uprising, overthrew the Japanese and French domination and seized power. When the French colonialists invaded our country for the second time, our compatriots, determined not to be enslaved again, shed much blood and laid down many lives to defend their national sovereignty and independence. Their solidarity and heroic struggle during nine years led the resistance war to victory. The 1954 Geneva Agreements restored peace in our country and recognized "the sovereignty, independence, unity and territorial integrity of Viet Nam."

Our compatriots in South Viet Nam would have been able to live in peace, to earn their livelihood in security and to build a decent and happy life.

However, the American imperialists, who had in the past helped the French colonialists to massacre our people, have now replaced the French in enslaving the southern part of our country through a disguised colonial regime. They have been using their stooge—the Ngo Dinh Diem administration—in their downright repression and exploitation of our compatriots, in their maneuvres to permanently divide our country and to turn its southern part into a military base in preparation for war in Southeast Asia.

The aggressors and traitors, working hand in glove with each other, have set up an extremely cruel dictatorial rule. They persecute and massacre democratic and patriotic people, and abolish all human liberties. They ruthlessly exploit the workers, peasants and other labouring people, strangle the local industry and trade, poison the minds of our people with a depraved foreign culture, thus degrading our national culture, traditions and ethics. They feverishly increase their military forces,

December 1960, reprinted in Porter, *Definitive Documentation*, II, 86–89.

build military bases, use the army as an instrument for repressing the people and serving the US imperialists' scheme to prepare an aggressive war.

Never, over the past six years, have gun shots massacring our compatriots ceased to resound throughout South Viet Nam. Tens of thousands of patriots here have been murdered and hundreds of thousands thrown into jail. All sections of the people have been living in a stifling atmosphere under the iron heel of the US-Diem clique. Countless families have been torn away and scenes of mourning are seen everywhere as a result of unemployment, poverty, exacting taxes, terror, massacre, drafting of manpower and pressganging, usurpation of land, forcible house removal, and herding of the people into "prosperity zones," "resettlement centres" and other forms of concentration camps.

High anger with the present tyrannical regime is boiling among all strata of the people. Undaunted in the face of barbarous persecution, our compatriots are determined to unite and struggle unflaggingly against the US imperialists' policy of aggression and the dictatorial and nepotic regime of the Ngo Dinh Diem clique. Among workers, peasants and other toiling people, among intellectuals, students and pupils, industrialists and traders, religious sects and national minorities, patriotic activities are gaining in scope and strength, seriously shaking the US-Diem dictatorial regime.

The attempted coup d'etat of November 11, 1960 in Saigon in some respects reflected the seething anger among the people and armymen, and the rottenness and decline of the US-Diem regime. However, there were among the leaders of this coup political speculators who, misusing the patriotism of the armymen, preferred negotiation and compromise rather than to overthrow Ngo Dinh Diem. Like Ngo Dinh Diem, they persisted in following the pro-American and traitorous path, and also used the anti-communist signboard to oppose the people. That is why the coup was not supported by the people and large numbers of armymen and, consequently, ended in failure.

At present, our people are urgently demanding an end to the cruel dictatorial rule; they are demanding independence and democracy, enough food and clothing, and peaceful reunification of the country.

To meet the aspirations of our compatriots, the *South Viet Nam National Front for Liberation* came into being, pledging itself to shoulder the historic task of liberating our people from the present yoke of slavery.

The *South Viet Nam National Front for Liberation* undertakes to unite all sections of the people, all social classes, nationalities, political parties, organizations, religious communities and patriotic personalities, without distinction of their political tendencies in order to struggle for the overthrow of the rule of the US imperialists and their stooges—the Ngo Dinh Diem clique—and for the realization of independence, democracy, peace and neutrality pending the peaceful reunification of the fatherland.

The *South Viet Nam National Front for Liberation* calls on the entire people to unite and heroically rise up as one man to fight along the line of a program of action summarized as follows:

1. To overthrow the disguised colonial regime of the US imperialists and the dictatorial Ngo Dinh Diem administration—lackey of the United States—, and to form a national democratic coalition administration.

2. To bring into being a broad and progressive democracy, promulgate freedom of expression, of the press, of belief, of assembly, of association, of movement and other democratic freedoms. To grant general amnesty to all political detainees, dissolve all concentration camps dubbed "prosperity zones" and "resettlement centres," abolish the fascist 10–59 law and other anti-democratic laws.

3. To abolish the economic monopoly of the United States and its henchmen, to protect home-made products, encourage home industry and trade, expand agriculture and build an independent and sovereign economy. To provide jobs for the unemployed, increase wages for workers, armymen and office employees. To abolish arbitrary fines and apply an equitable and rational tax system. To help those who have gone South to return to their native places if they so desire, and to provide jobs for those among them who want to remain in the South.

4. To carry out land rent reduction, guarantee the peasants' right to till present plots of land, redistribute communal land and advance toward land reform.

5. To do away with enslaving and depraved US-style culture, build a national and progressive culture and education. To wipe out illiteracy, open more schools, carry out reforms in the educational and examination system.

6. To abolish the system of American military advisers, eliminate foreign military bases in Viet Nam and build a national army for the defence of the fatherland and the people.

7. To guarantee equality between men and women and among different nationalities, and the right to autonomy of the national minorities; to protect the legitimate interests of foreign residents in Viet Nam; to protect and take care of the interests of Vietnamese living abroad.

8. To carry out a foreign policy of peace and neutrality, to establish diplomatic relations with all countries which respect the independence and sovereignty of Viet Nam.

9. To re-establish normal relations between the two zones, pending the peaceful reunification of the fatherland.

10. To oppose aggressive war; to actively defend world peace.

Compatriots!

Ours are a heroic people with a tradition of unity and indomitable struggle. We cannot let our country be plunged into darkness and mourning. We are determined to shatter the fetters of slavery, and wrest back independence and freedom.

Let us all rise up and unite!

Let us close our ranks and fight under the banner of the *South Viet Nam National Front for Liberation* to overthrow the rule of the US imperialists and Ngo Dinh Diem—their henchmen.

Workers, peasants and other toiling people! The oppression and misery which are now heavily weighing on you must be ended. You have the strength of tens of millions of people. Stand up enthusiastically to save your families and our fatherland.

Intellectuals! The dictatorial rulers have stripped us of the most elementary human rights. You are living in humiliation and misery. For our great cause, stand up resolutely!

Industrialists and traders! A country under the sway of foreign sharks cannot have an independent and sovereign economy. You should join in the people's struggle.

Compatriots of all national minorities! Compatriots of all religious communities! Unity is life, disunity is death. Smash all US-Diem schemes of division. Side with the entire people in the struggle for independence, freedom and equality among all nationalities.

Notables! The interests of the nation are above all else. Support actively the struggle for the overthrow of the cruel aggressors and traitors.

Patriotic officers and soldiers! You have arms in your hands. Listen to the sacred call of the fatherland. Be definitely on the side of the people. Your compatriots have faith in your patriotism.

Young men and women! You are the future of the nation. You should devote your youthful ardour to serving the fatherland.

Compatriots living abroad! Turn your thoughts toward the beloved fatherland, contribute actively to the sacred struggle for national liberation.

At present the movement for peace, democracy and national independence is surging up throughout the world. Colonialism is irretrievably disintegrating. The time when the imperialists could plunder and subjugate the people at will is over. This situation is extremely favourable for the struggle to free South Viet Nam from the yoke of the US imperialists and their stooges. Peace-loving and progressive people in the world are supporting us. Justice is on our side, and we have the prodigious strength of the unity of our entire people. We will certainly win! The US imperialist aggressors and the Ngo Dinh Diem traitorous clique will certainly be defeated. The cause of liberation of South Viet Nam will certainly triumph.

Compatriots around the country!

Let us write and march forward confidently and valiantly to score brilliant victories for our people and our fatherland!

4. A Vietcong Recruit Explains Why He Joined the Revolution (1961), 1986

I joined the VC [Vietcong] when I was thirty-five years old. I was married and had four children. I was leasing farmland—one hectare [about 2.5 acres]—that was very poor in quality, almost sterile. That was why the owner rented it out to us. Despite working hard all year round, we got only about 100 *gia* of rice out of it. Of this amount, 40 *gia* went to the landlord. We borrowed money to buy ducks and geese. We lived a very hard life. But I cultivated the land carefully, and in time it became fertile. When it did, the owner took it back; my livelihood was gone. I had to go back to my parents, to raise ducks for my father.

I was poor. I had lost my land and I didn't have enough money to take care of my children. In 1961 propaganda cadres of the Front [National Liberation Front] contacted me. These guys had joined the resistance against the French, and after Geneva they had stayed underground in the South. They came to all the poor farmers and made an analysis of the poor and rich classes. They said that the rich people

From *Portrait of the Enemy* by David Chanoff and Doan Van Toai. Copyright © 1986 by David Chanoff and Doan Van Toai. Used by permission of Random House, Inc.

had always served the French and had used the authority of the French to oppress the poor. The majority of the people were poor, not because they wasted their money but because they had been exploited by the landlords who had worked with the French. In the past, the ancestors of the poor had broken ground for tillage. Then powerful people had seized their land. Without any other means to live, the poor had become slaves of the landlords. The cadres told us that if the poor people don't stand up the rich people, we would be dominated by them forever. The only way to ensure freedom and a sufficient life was to overthrow them.

When I heard the cadres, I thought that what they said was correct. In my village there were about forty-three hundred people. Of these, maybe ten were landlords. The richest owned five hundred hectares [1,236 acres], and the others had at least twenty hectares [49 acres] apiece. The rest of the people were tenants or honest poor farmers. I knew that the rich oppressed the poor. The poor had nothing to eat, and they also had no freedom. We had to get rid of the regime that allowed a few people to use their money and authority to oppress the others.

So I joined the Liberation Front. I followed the VC to fight for freedom and prosperity for the country. I felt that this was right.

5. A South Vietnamese Peasant Girl Becomes a Vietcong Supporter (c. 1961), 1989

Before I was twelve and knew better, I played war games with the children in my village. . . .

. . . When I played a Republican, I always imagined that the laughing face at the end of my stick-rifle was my brother Bon Nghe, who had gone to Hanoi and who might one day come back to fight around Ky La. When I played a Viet Cong, I could think only of my sister Ba in Danang, who, being married to a policeman, locked her door every night out of fear of "those terrorists" who blew up power stations and cars and took potshots at the officials for whom her husband worked. I could not accept the idea that either my brother or sister must somehow become my enemy.

In school, the pressure to make sides was enormous. Our teacher, a villager named Manh, who was paid by the government, asked us, "What will you do if you see a Viet Cong, or hear about someone who's helping them?" We answered in chorus, "Turn him in to the soldier!" Manh praised us for our answer and told us that the Republicans would pay our families big rewards for every Viet Cong we helped them capture. Still, when we played among ourselves, there was no shortage of Viet Cong fighters, and the children who pretended to be Republicans usually did so halfheartedly. . . .

The first time I saw a Viet Cong fighter close up it was just about dark and I was cleaning up our kitchen. I happened to gaze out the window to the house next door, which (although it was owned by Manh, who had been my teacher) was often used by villagers for gambling. Without a sound, a half-dozen strangers scampered into Manh's house and then shouted "Nobody move!" The oil lamp in Manh's window went out and people began running from the house. At first I thought it was Republican soldiers raiding the gamblers, as they had done several times before, but it soon became obvious that this was not that kind of raid.

Manh was the last one out, led at gunpoint with his hands atop his head. I could hear this familiar voice arguing with the strangers: "But—I don't know what you're talking about!" and "Why? Who told you that?" I leaned into the window to get a better view when I saw one of the strangers standing just outside. He wore black garments, like everyone else, and had on a conical sun hat, even though it was already dark. His sandals were made from old tires and his weapon had a queer, curved ammunition clip that jutted down from the stock like a banana. He seemed to be keeping an eye on the dusty road that ran by Manh's house and he was so close to me that I was afraid to run away or even duck down for fear that he would hear me.

Suddenly one of the strangers barked an order in an odd, clipped accent (I found out later this was how everyone talked in the North) and two of his *comrades* prodded Manh to the edge of the road. I could still hear Manh begging for his life when two rifle shots cut him short. The strangers then ran a Viet Cong flag up the pole that stood outside our schoolhouse and left as quickly as they had come. The leader shouted over his shoulder: "Anyone who touches that flag will get the same thing as that traitor!"

The guard who was standing by my window glanced over and gave me a wink, showing he knew I had been there all the time and had learned the lesson he had come to teach; he then followed his troop into the night. The handsome, cocky face beneath the sun hat reminded me of my brother Bon Nghe, but it stimulated me the way my thoughts of brother Bon never did.

By now all the villagers were out of their houses, staring curiously into the darkness and chattering wildly among themselves. Manh's wife ran with her relatives to the road and retrieved his body while his six children—two of whom had been my playmates—looked after them, too stunned to leave their house or even to cry. Finally, the youngest called out her father's name and ran off, just as my own father's hand fell upon my shoulder.

"Bay Ly," he said quietly—with none of the alarm I heard in the other voices. "Do you know what you've just seen?"

"My teacher—" I said, suddenly aware of the catch in my throat, "they killed him! The Viet Cong shot him! But he was nice to us! He never hurt anyone!"

"He was Catholic," my father said, sounding like a teacher himself. "And a follower of President Diem. He talked too much about how Buddhists were ruining the country."

"But we're Buddhists, Father! He never said bad things about us!"

"No." My father cradled my head against his chest. "But what he said endangered others—and some of those people lost their lives. I am sorry for Manh and his wife and children. But Manh's own careless words got him into trouble. We'll give him a decent burial, but you remember what you've seen—especially when you think about talking again to the soldiers."

On the very next day, the Republicans came back to Ky La—more than we'd ever seen—with trucks full of steel girders and cement and barbed wire. They chopped down the Viet Cong flag and told the farmers to build defenses around the village. The ditches left over from the French occupation, now overgrown with weeds, were made deeper and bamboo trees were cut down to make spikes and watchtowers. During the weeks of construction, the soldiers told us to stay indoors and keep our houses dark at night. As soon as the sun went down, the Republicans set up ambushes around the village and waited for the dogs to bark—a sure sign that intruders were lurking outside.

But nothing happened. After a while, the Republican troops pulled out and left us in the hands of the "Popular Force"—the *Dan De*—local villagers who had been given small arms and a little training in how to use them. Because the war seemed to leave with the soldiers, the PF officials declared peace and Ky La, despite its new necklace of stakes and barbed wire, tried very hard to believe them.

Unfortunately, the peace didn't last very long. A few days later, my father awakened me in the middle of the night and took us to the place where the Republicans had left their biggest cache of materials, including some long metal poles. Within a few minutes, we were joined by most of our neighbors. One PF officer said, "Here—take these poles and hide them so that the Republicans won't find them. Our fighters need them for protection against enemy tanks."

Without further discussion, we took as many poles as we could carry and hurried off to bury them outside our house. "Oh yes," the PF officer added. "If you have a watchdog, give him to a relative out of town or boil him up for supper. We can't have any dogs barking the next time our freedom fighters come to the village!"

Although I wanted badly to ask my father what was happening, I obediently helped him carry some twenty poles to our house. By the time we finished burying them, a huge bonfire had been started in a clearing behind our house, with most of the villagers—including the children—collected around it. In the light of the dancing flames, I recognized the handsome Viet Cong soldier who had winked at me on the night my teacher Manh was killed. He just strolled along, cradling his weapon, wearing the amused smile I'd seen many young men wear when they eyed pretty girls at the market. The Viet Cong cadre, and many of the villagers, piled onto the fire everything the Republicans had given them to defend the village—bamboo stakes, fence posts, and thatching from the watchtowers. The only thing that was spared was the material from our half-completed schoolhouse.

"Save the school!" the cadre leader told us in his funny Northern accent. "Your children need their education but we will teach them what they should know. The first thing they must learn is that on this night, Ky La was saved." He gestured to the black-uniformed troops around the fire, "We are the soldiers of liberation! That is how you will call us. We are here to fight for our land, and our country! Help us stop the foreign aggression and you will have peace. Help us win and you will keep your property and everything else you love. Ky La is *our* village now—and yours. We have given it back to you."

As he spoke, another soldier ran yet another Viet Cong flag up the pole beside the schoolhouse.

"Know where your bunkers are, comrades, and be ready to fill them soon! The battle is on its way!"

The Viet Cong soldiers who had up to this time been everywhere in the village—ripping down the Republican construction and prodding the villagers out to the meetings—now fell into ranks behind their leader. As they moved into the jungle, the leader turned and told us, "Down the road you will find two traitors. I trust they are the last we will see in Ky La. We must leave now, but you will see us again." . . .

When the Viet Cong could not be found (they spent most of their time, after all, hiding in caverns underground with entrances hidden by cookstoves, bushes, false floors, or even underwater by flowing rivers themselves), the Republican soldiers took out their frustration on us: arresting nearby farmers and beating or shooting them on the spot, or carting anyone who looked suspicious off to jail. As these actions drove even more villagers to the Viet Cong cause, more and more of our houses were modified for Viet Cong use. The cadremen told us that each family must have a place in which liberation troops could hide, so my father dug an underground tunnel beneath our heavy cookpot which could house half a dozen fighters. While my father and other villagers worked on their tunnels, we children were taken to a clearing beyond the village graveyard, on the threshold of the swamp, where we were taught revolutionary songs. One of the first we learned was in praise of Uncle Ho—Ho Chi Minh—who, we were told, awaited news of our heroism like a kindly grandfather:

> The full moon shines on our land,
> So that we can sing and dance
> And make wishes for Uncle Ho.
> Uncle Ho—we wish you a long life!
> We wish you a long beard that we can stroke
> While you hold us in your arms
> And tell us how much you love us and our country!

We were also taught what we were expected to do for our village, our families, and the revolution. If we were killed, we were told we would live on in history. We learned that, like the French, men of another race called *Americans* wanted to enslave us. "Their allies are the traitorous Republicans of Ngo Dinh Diem!" the Viet Cong shouted. "Just as our fathers fought against the French and their colonial administrators, so must we now fight against these new invaders and their running dogs!" We learned that cheating, stealing from, and lying to Republican soldiers and their allies were not crimes, and that failing to do these things, if the situation demanded it, was treason of the highest sort. Girls were shown the pattern of the Viet Cong flag—half blue (for the North—the direction of peace), half red (for the bloody South), with a yellow star (for the union of yellow-skinned people) in between—and told to sew as many as they could for use in demonstrations or whenever one was asked for by a fighter. Even when the hated Republicans were in our village and our flag could not be displayed, we were to fly it proudly in our hearts. We then sang songs to celebrate those brothers and fathers that went north to Hanoi in 1954. I sang loudly and thought of Bon Nghe and knew he would be proud.

Although it was nearly dawn when I got home from the first meeting, my parents were still awake. They asked what I'd been doing and I told them proudly that I was now part of the "political cadre"—although I had no idea what that meant. I told them we were to keep an eye on our neighbors and make sure the liberation leaders knew if anyone spoke to the hated Republicans. I told my mother to rejoice, that when her son—my beloved brother Bon—came back from Hanoi, he would be a leader in the South, just as the leaders of our own cadre had been trained in Hanoi and now were helping our village gain victory over the invaders.

Although my mother was not sure that my involvement with the cadre was a good idea, she seemed happy that through them, somehow, Bon's return might be hastened. My father, however, looked at me with an expression I had never seen before and said nothing. Although Ky La's first big battle had yet to be fought, it was as if he had seen, in my shining, excited, determined little face, the first casualty of our new war.

6. Vo Nguyen Giap on People's War, 1961

The Vietnamese people's war of liberation was a just war, aiming to win back the independence and unity of the country, to bring land to our peasants and guarantee them the right to it, and to defend the achievements of the August Revolution. That is why it was first and foremost a people's war. To educate, mobilise, organise and arm the whole people in order that they might take part in the Resistance was a crucial question.

The enemy of the Vietnamese nation was aggressive imperialism, which had to be overthrown. But the latter having long since joined up with the feudal landlords, the anti-imperialist struggle could definitely not be separated from anti-feudal action. On the other hand, in a backward colonial country such as ours where the peasants make up the majority of the population, a people's war is essentially a peasant's war under the leadership of the working class. Owing to this fact, a general mobilisation of the whole people is neither more nor less than the mobilisation of the rural masses. The problem of land is of decisive importance. From an exhaustive analysis, the Vietnamese people's war of liberation was essentially a people's national democratic revolution carried out under armed form and had a twofold fundamental task: the overthrowing of imperialism and the defeat of the feudal landlord class, the anti-imperialist struggle being the primary task.

A backward colonial country which had only just risen up to proclaim its independence and install people's power, Viet Nam only recently possessed armed forces, equipped with still very mediocre arms and having no combat experience. Her enemy, on the other hand, was an imperialist power [France] which has retained a fairly considerable economic and military potentiality despite the recent German occupation [during World War II] and benefited, furthermore, from the active support of the United States. The balance of forces decidedly showed up our weaknesses against the enemy's power. The Vietnamese people's war of liberation had, therefore, to be a hard and long-lasting war in order to succeed in creating conditions for victory. All the conceptions born of impatience and aimed at obtaining speedy victory could only be gross errors. It was necessary to firmly grasp the strategy of a long-term resistance, and to exalt the will to be self-supporting in order to maintain and gradually augment our forces, while nibbling at and progressively destroying those of the enemy; it was necessary to accumulate

Vo Nguyen Giap, *People's War, People's Army* (Hanoi: Foreign Language Publishing House, 1961), pp. 27–30.

thousands of small victories to turn them into a great success, thus gradually altering the balance of forces, in transforming our weakness into power and carrying off final victory.

At an early stage, our Party was able to discern the characteristics of this war: a people's war and a long-lasting war, and it was by proceeding from these premises that, during the whole of hostilities and in particularly difficult conditions, the Party solved all the problems of the Resistance. This judicious leadership by the Party led us to victory.

From the point of view of directing operations, our *strategy and tactics had to be those of a people's war and of a long-term resistance.*

Our strategy was, as we have stressed, to wage a long-lasting battle. A war of this nature in general entails several phases; in principle, starting from a stage of contention, it goes through a period of equilibrium before arriving at a general counter-offensive. In effect, the way in which it is carried on can be more subtle and more complex, depending on the particular conditions obtaining on both sides during the course of operations. Only a long-term war could enable us to utilise to the maximum our political trump cards, to overcome our material handicap and to transform our weakness into strength. To maintain and increase our forces, was the principle to which we adhered, contenting ourselves with attacking when success was certain, refusing to give battle likely to incur losses to us or to engage in hazardous actions. We had to apply the slogan: to build up our strength during the actual course of fighting.

The forms of fighting had to be completely adapted that is, to raise the fighting spirit to the maximum and rely on heroism of our troops to overcome the enemy's material superiority. In the main, especially at the outset of the war, we had recourse to guerrilla fighting. In the Vietnamese theatre of operations, this method carried off great victories: it could be used in the mountains as well as in the delta, it could be waged with good or mediocre material and even without arms, and was to enable us eventually to equip ourselves at the cost of the enemy. Wherever the Expeditionary Corps came, the entire population took part in the fighting; every commune had its fortified village, every district had its regional troops fighting under the command of the local branches of the Party and the people's administration, in liaison with the regular forces in order to wear down and annihilate the enemy forces.

Thereafter, with the development of our forces, guerilla warfare changed into a mobile warfare—a form of mobile warfare still strongly marked by guerilla warfare—which would afterwards become the essential form of operations on the main front, the northern front. In this process of development of guerilla warfare and of accentuation of the mobile warfare, our people's army constantly grew and passed from the stage of combats involving a section or company, to fairly large-scale campaigns bringing into action several divisions. Gradually, its equipment improved, mainly by the seizure of arms from the enemy—the material of the French and American imperialists.

From the military point of view, *the Vietnamese people's war of liberation proved that an insufficiently equipped people's army, but an army fighting for a just cause, can, with appropriate strategy and tactics, combine the conditions needed to conquer a modern army of aggressive imperialism.*

7. Nguyen Chi Thanh on Communist Strategy, 1963

In 1954, the U.S. imperialists, taking advantage of the French colonialists' defeat at Dien Bien Phu, drove the French out of south Viet Nam and set up a puppet regime headed by Ngo Dinh Diem. In essence, this meant that U.S. neocolonialism replaced French old colonialism and became dominant in south Viet Nam.

The United States thought that, with its numerous arms, dollars, rich political and military experience and a faithful lackey Ngo Dinh Diem, it could solve all the problems in south Viet Nam in a very short time. Events, however, have proved this to be sheer wishful thinking. . . .

It is true that U.S. neo-colonialism has scored certain successes in some parts of the world. In south Viet Nam, however, it is "born at the wrong time," or to borrow from business language, it will not "pay off." This is because the United States has overlooked a fundamental factor, that is, when U.S. neo-colonialism made its way to south Viet Nam, it ran into certain unexpected circumstances, which may be listed as follows:

• Great, sharp social contradictions exist between U.S. imperialism and north Viet Nam which is advancing towards socialism.

• With the restoring of peace, social contradictions in south Viet Nam, instead of being eased, have further sharpened and matured. These are contradictions between the south Vietnamese people on the one hand and the U.S. imperialists, the feudal landlord class and comprador capital represented by Ngo Dinh Diem on the other.

• The south Vietnamese people have learned much from their struggle and have been able to utilize correct methods to resolve the social contradictions in south Viet Nam. These methods have been crystallized in the clear-sighted programmes of the South Viet Nam National Liberation Front and of the People's Revolutionary Party of South Viet Nam.

• Generally speaking, the world situation is not favourable to U.S. imperialism. The socialist camp is mightier than the imperialist camp; the movements for democracy and national independence are gaining momentum. These are great and ever-sharpening contradictions, driving the U.S. imperialists into a situation in which they can no longer do as they please. . . .

When the U.S. imperialists dispatched ten thousand troops to south Viet Nam, they believed that the rebellious forces could be put down within eighteen months. Later they said it would probably take ten years. Now, some people in the United States are not at all sure if they could succeed in eighteen years.

U.S. imperialism is certainly not ready to reconcile itself to its defeat in south Viet Nam. But it is an indisputable fact that it is being confronted with a crisis in its political line, which has, in turn, given rise to crises in military strategy and tactics.

The causes of these crises lie in the following:

• The fundamental cause is that the U.S. imperialists are doing an unjust thing— invading another country—and therefore they meet with the firm resistance of the south Vietnamese people, are disapproved of by the American people, condemned by other peoples, and even disliked by some of their henchmen in the Ngo Dinh Diem administration.

July 1963, reprinted in Porter, *Definitive Documentation,* II, 183–187.

• Pursuing its aggressive aims, the United States egged Ngo Dinh Diem, on to adopt a number of stupid policies, which aggravated the contradictions within the Ngo Dinh Diem regime.

• The U.S.-Diem clique faces an opponent who, although lacking American dollars, arms and other material, is full of anti-imperialist spirit, full of patriotism and revolutionary courage, and experienced in political and military struggles.

Although ultimate conclusions cannot yet be reached insofar as the struggle is still going on in south Viet Nam, we may however put forth the following views:

1. The U.S. imperialists are not invincible. Compared with imperialists of other countries, they are mightier, but compared with the revolutionary forces and the forces of the people of the world, they are not at all strong. If the proletarian revolution and people of the world resolutely struggle against U.S. imperialism, they can surely repel it step by step and narrow down its domain.

We do not have any illusions about the United States. We do not underestimate our opponent—the strong and cunning U.S. imperialism. But we are not afraid of the United States. The strategic concept thoroughly pervades the revolutionary line of south Viet Nam and is the fundamental factor determining the success of the revolution. If, on the contrary, one is afraid of the United States and thinks that to offend it would court failure, and that firm opposition to U.S. imperialism would touch off a nuclear war, then the only course left would be to compromise with and surrender to U.S. imperialism.

2. A powerful north Viet Nam will be a decisive factor in the social development of our entire country. But this does not mean that simply because the north is strong, the revolutionary movement in the south will automatically succeed. The powerful north Viet Nam and the revolutionary movement of the south Vietnamese people are mutually complementary and must be closely coordinated; the building of the north itself cannot replace the resolution of the inherent social contradictions of south Viet Nam. Adhering to this correct view, we have avoided opportunistic mistakes. If, on the contrary, we had feared the United States and had no faith in the success of our struggles against it, we would have called on the people in south Viet Nam to "wait" and "coexist peacefully" with the U.S.-Diem clique, and committed an irreparable error. We have correctly handled the relations between north and south Viet Nam. This is a Marxist-Leninist strategic concept which is in conformity with the latest experience in the world developments and those in our own country.

8. Mao Zedong Exhorts His North Vietnamese Allies, 1965

You are fighting an excellent war. Both the South and the North are fighting well. The people of the whole world, including those who have already awakened and those who have not awakened, are supporting you. The current world is not a peaceful one. It is not you Vietnamese who are invading the United States, neither are the Chinese who are waging an aggressive war against the United States. . . .

From *Cold War International History Project Bulletin,* Issues 6/7, pp. 245–246, Winter 1995/1996. Reprinted with permission.

. . . In fact what will solve the problem is the war you are fighting. Of course you can conduct negotiations. In the past you held negotiations in Geneva. But the American did not honor their promise after the negotiations. . . .

You withdrew your armed forces from the South in accordance with the Geneva Accords. As a result, the enemy began to kill people in the South, and you revived armed struggle. At first you adopted political struggle as a priority supplemented by armed struggle. We supported you. In the second stage when you were carrying out political and armed struggles simultaneously, we again supported you. In the third stage when you are pursuing armed struggle as a priority supplemented by political struggle, we still support you. In my view, the enemy is gradually escalating the war; so are you. In the next two and three years you may encounter difficulties. But it is hard to say, and it may not be so. We need to take this possibility into consideration. So long as you have made all kinds of preparations, even if the most difficult situation emerges, you will not find it too far from your initial considerations. Isn't this a good argument? Therefore there are two essential points: the first is to strive for the most favorable situation, and the second to prepare for the worst. . . .

I have not noticed what issues you have negotiated with the United States. I only pay attention to how you fight the Americans and how you drive the Americans out. You can have negotiations at certain time[s], but you should not lower your tones. You should raise your tones a little higher. Be prepared that the enemy may deceive you.

We will support you until your final victory. The confidence in victory comes from the fighting you have done and from the struggle you have made. For instance, one experience we have is that the Americans can be fought. We obtained this experience only after fighting the Americans. The Americans can be fought and can be defeated. We should demolish the myth that the Americans cannot be fought and cannot be defeated. Both of our two parties have many experiences. Both of us have fought the Japanese. You have also fought the French. At the moment you are fighting the Americans.

The Americans have trained and educated the Vietnamese people. They have educated us and the people of the whole world. In my opinion it is not good without the Americans. Such an educator is indispensable. In order to defeat the Americans, we must learn from the Americans. Marx's works do not teach us how to fight the Americans. Nor do Lenin's books write about how to fight the Americans. We primarily learn from the Americans.

The Chinese people and the people of the whole world support you. The more friends you have, the better you are.

9. Ho Vows to "Fight Until Complete Victory," 1966

Compatriots and fighters throughout the country!

The barbarous U.S. imperialists have unleashed a war of aggression in an attempt to conquer our country, but they are sustaining big defeats.

They have rushed an expeditionary corps of about 300,000 men into the southern part of our country. They have used a puppet administration and a mercenary army

---

Ho Chi Minh speech, July 1, 1966, in Ho, *Selected Writings* (1920–1969) (Hanoi: Foreign Language Publishing House, 1973), pp. 307–310.

fostered by them as instruments of their aggressive policy. They have resorted to extremely savage means of warfare—toxic chemicals, napalm bombs, and so forth. With such crimes they hope to subdue our southern compatriots.

But under the firm and wise leadership of the NFLSV [National Front for the Liberation of South Vietnam, or NLF], the South Viet-Nam army and people, closely united and fighting heroically, have scored very glorious victories and are determined to struggle until complete victory with a view to liberating the South, defending the North, and subsequently achieving national reunification.

The U.S. aggressors have brazenly launched air attacks on North Viet-Nam in an attempt to get out of the quagmire in the South and to impose negotiations on us on their terms.

But North Viet-Nam will not falter. Our army and people have shown redoubled eagerness in the emulation to produce and fight heroically. So far we have blasted out of the skies more than 1,200 aircraft. We are determined to defeat the enemy's war of destruction and at the same time to extend all-out support to our dear compatriots in the South.

Of late the U.S. aggressors hysterically took a very serious step further in the escalation of the war: They launched air attacks on the suburbs of Hanoi and Haiphong. That was an act of desperation comparable to the agony convulsions of a grievously wounded wild beast.

Johnson and his clique should realize this: They may bring in 500,000 troops, 1 million, or even more to step up the war of aggression in South Viet-Nam. They may use thousands of aircraft for intensified attacks against North Viet-Nam. But never will they be able to break the iron will of the heroic Vietnamese people to fight against U.S. aggression, for national salvation. The more truculent they are, the further they will aggravate their crime. The war may still last ten, twenty years, or longer. Hanoi, Haiphong, and other cities and enterprises may be destroyed, but the Vietnamese people will not be intimidated! Nothing is more precious than independence and freedom. When victory day comes, our people will rebuild our country and endow it with bigger and more beautiful construction.

It is common knowledge that each time they are about to step up their criminal war, the U.S. aggressors always resort to their peace talks swindle in an attempt to fool world opinion and blame Viet-Nam for unwillingness to enter into peace talks!

President Johnson! Reply publicly to the American people and the peoples of the world: Who has sabotaged the Geneva Agreements which guarantee the sovereignty, independence, unity, and territorial integrity of Viet-Nam? Have Vietnamese troops invaded the United States and massacred Americans: Is it not the U.S. Government which has sent U.S. troops to invade Viet-Nam and massacre the Vietnamese?

Let the United States end its war of aggression in Viet-Nam, withdraw from this country all U.S. and satellite troops, and peace will return here at once. . . .

The Vietnamese people cherish peace, genuine peace, peace in independence and freedom, not sham peace, American peace.

For the defense of the independence of the fatherland and for the fulfillment of our obligation to the peoples struggling against U.S. imperialism, our people and army, united as one man, will resolutely fight until complete victory, whatever the sacrifices and hardships may be. In the past we defeated the Japanese fascists and the French colonialists in much more difficult junctures. Today the conditions at home and abroad are more favorable; our people's struggle against U.S. aggression for national salvation is sure to win a total victory.

✗ *E S S A Y S*

William Duiker, formerly of Pennsylvania State University, examines the evolution of North Vietnam's strategy for achieving its revolutionary goals in South Vietnam during the 1959–1965 period. An expert on modern Vietnamese history and author of a highly regarded biography of Ho Chi Minh, Duiker stresses that Ho and his associates never wavered in their commitment to the reunification of the country under communist rule. They were willing to use whatever means were necessary to secure that goal, however, and only reluctantly embarked on the road to revolutionary war in the south, initially preferring to utilize political tactics. Duiker's contribution forms this chapter's first essay selection.

In recent years, Vietnam War scholars have paid increasing attention to the importance of Chinese and Soviet diplomatic and material support to North Vietnam throughout the course of the conflict. The next selection features an extract from the work of Qiang Zhai, a professor of history at Auburn University, Montgomery, and one of the foremost experts on Chinese-North Vietnamese relations. In it, he contends that Beijing provided substantial and much-needed aid to Hanoi, especially between 1965 and 1968, but that distrust, suspicion, and conflicting priorities nonetheless plagued the relationship between the two communist powers from the outset of the Vietnam War, leading eventually to an acrimonious break.

Hanoi's Strategy in the South

WILLIAM DUIKER

Did the United States fight the wrong war in Vietnam? Did it adopt a counter-guerrilla strategy in a conflict that, from Hanoi's point of view, was essentially conventional in nature? That issue was debated actively by U.S. policymakers during the Vietnam War, notably during the Kennedy administration, when advocates of a primarily "political" or "military" approach competed briefly for control over U.S. strategy in South Vietnam. More recently, it has been the subject of lively interest among historians, journalists, and foreign policy analysts, with no signs of abatement or of any prospective consensus emerging on the subject for the foreseeable future.

This is not a topic of mere academic interest. In fact, it is one of the key bones of contention in the running debate over the "lessons of Vietnam," a debate that centers around the fundamental issue of how the United States can and should react to the rise of revolutionary insurgencies and other political and military disturbances in the post-Vietnam era. To some, the primary lesson of the Vietnam War was that the failure to apply the full weight of its military and technological superiority cost the United States victory in the war. Others counter that the salient lesson of Vietnam is that external power cannot overcome a revolutionary movement with a solid base of support among the mass of the population.

This is not the place to undertake a lengthy evaluation of U.S. war strategy in Vietnam. But the appearance of a number of new documentary sources on Hanoi's conduct of the war in South Vietnam does offer an opportunity to enhance our understanding of Communist war strategy and to determine whether, as some have alleged, Hanoi used guerrilla tactics as a stratagem to hoodwink the United States, while intending to win by conventional military means all along.

The tradition of combined political and military struggle has a long pedigree in Communist revolutionary strategy in Vietnam. The first explicit reference to the idea came shortly after the formation of the Viet Minh Front by the Indochinese Communist Party (ICP) at the beginning of World War II, when the party's founder and leader Ho Chi Minh called for an approach that would begin with political struggle and move gradually toward an emphasis on armed conflict as the revolution reached its height. Although party sources have not elaborated in detail on the reasons for Ho's choice of approach, it is clear from the context that he realized that the ICP would need time to build up its military forces for a major effort to seize power from the Japanese occupation forces and the returning French troops at the end of the war. In the meantime, the party, through the medium of the Viet Minh Front, would build up a mass base among the local population.

As it turned out, the August Revolution that brought the Viet Minh to power in North Vietnam in the late summer of 1945 was more political than military in nature, as the surrender of Japan left a military vacuum that Ho Chi Minh's small but well-trained revolutionary forces were able to fill with a minimum of violence. The August Revolution model, involving the seizure of power by means of a popular uprising supported by selected attacks on the part of armed revolutionary units, would later assume an almost sacred quality in the minds of party strategists, a Vietnamese equivalent of the model of the October Revolution of 1917 in Russia. Undoubtedly one reason for its appeal was the belief that, unlike the latter (when Lenin admitted that the Bolsheviks did not have widespread popular support), the August Revolution had triumphed precisely because the Viet Minh Front had already won wide acceptance as the legitimate representative of the great mass of the Vietnamese population.

Unfortunately for the party and its supporters, the course of events in the immediate postwar period would soon demonstrate that more than human spirit was required to triumph over the power of modern weaponry. When negotiations with the French broke down in the fall of 1946, Ho Chi Minh and his colleagues discarded the strategy applied during the August Revolution and adopted a revised version of the Chinese model of "people's war." This Maoist concept of three-stage warfare, beginning with a stage of retrenchment and culminating in a conventional assault on enemy forces in the major urban areas, does not entirely neglect the importance of political struggle, but the latter is clearly subordinated to the buildup of revolutionary armed forces for a final confrontation with the enemy on the battlefield.

During the opening years of the Franco–Viet Minh conflict, party strategists applied the three-stage concept in Indochina, with some variations to take into account local conditions and circumstances. By 1951, however, the disadvantages of the Maoist model became increasingly apparent, as least as applied in Vietnam,

where the revolutionary forces could not hope to achieve absolute military superiority over their adversary. In the last last years of the war, Viet Minh strategy
concentrated on achieving limited military victories on the battlefield that could
contribute to a satisfactory peace agreement at the conference table.

The Geneva Conference of 1954 resulted in a compromise settlement of the
Franco–Viet Minh conflict, dividing the country in half, with Ho Chi Minh's Democratic Republic of Vietnam (DRV) in the North and a non-Communist state in the
South. Party leaders were now faced with the new problem of achieving reunification
of their divided land. The Chinese model of people's war did not seem appropriate
for several reasons:

1. pressure from Hanoi's allies, China and the Soviet Union, who wished to
   avoid a resumption of the conflict in Indochina;
2. the expectation (or the hope) that reunification could take place through national
   elections, as called for by the political declaration at Geneva;
3. the conviction that, even in the absence of national elections, the new government of Ngo Dinh Diem in Saigon would gradually disintegrate under the
   pressure of the revolutionary movement in the South, leading eventually to a
   takeover on the model of the August Revolution by means of a general uprising
   supported by low-level paramilitary forces.

Under any of the above circumstances, an extensive role for the main force units of
the People's Army of Vietnam (PACVN) would probably not be necessary.

It was not long, however, before some leading party cadres operating in the
South began to argue that such expectations were overly optimistic. Not only had the
Diem regime refused to hold consultations on national elections with representatives
of the DRV, but Diem's control over the southern provinces was tightening, rather
than disintegrating. In 1956, the party's leading representative in South Vietnam,
Politburo member Le Duan, began to press for a more active approach to protect the
southern revolutionary movement from Diem's security forces. In a report that he
wrote to the central party leadership sometime in the late summer or fall, Le Duan
argued that a more aggressive combination of political and military struggle would
be needed to bring the Saigon regime to its knees.

Le Duan's report was approved at the Eleventh Plenum of the Party Central
Committee in December, which now adopted a new policy to strengthen the revolutionary movement in the South to enable it to defend itself against counterrevolutionary terror. In fact, party leaders in Hanoi had apparently already begun to
question the assumption that national reunification could be achieved by peaceful
means. At the Ninth Plenum in April 1956, Ho Chi Minh had argued that recent
Soviet speculation over the possibility of a "peaceful road to socialism" was irrelevant in countries like Vietnam where the aggressive nature of U.S. imperialism and
its ally in Saigon might compel the people to resort to armed struggle. At the Conference of Communist Parties of Socialist Countries held in Moscow in November
1957, he lobbied successfully for a statement to this effect to be included in the final
conference communique.

Still, although party leaders were aware of the possibility of a return to war,
most still assumed that the two zones could be reunified under Hanoi's authority
without a return to the primarily military approach that they had adopted in their

war against the French in 1946, and hoped that the Saigon regime would collapse as a result of a strategy relying principally on what was termed the "political force of the masses." Past U.S. behavior in China and Korea was cited as evidence that Washington would hesitate to become actively involved militarily in an area of clearly secondary importance to American national security.

But in early 1959, party leaders revised their views of the situation and decided that the basic road to a revolutionary victory in the South was by means of violent struggle, through a revolutionary war to achieve the reunification of the two zones. That decision, approved by the Fifteenth Plenum of the Central Committee in January and announced in May, was not specific on what strategy should be adopted, merely announcing that both political and military struggle would be required. According to a history of the war published recently in Hanoi, the plenum resolution merely stated that the "political force of the masses" would be the primary instrument of the revolutionary movement, supported by armed forces "to a greater or lesser degree, depending on the situation."

Why Hanoi decided to accelerate the revolutionary struggle in the South in early 1959 has been a matter of lively debate among scholars and other foreign policy analysts in the West. Some have maintained that party leaders in the North were belatedly and perhaps reluctantly reacting to pressure from their colleagues stationed in South Vietnam, who argued that the movement must either take up arms or be destroyed by the repressive efforts of the Diem regime.

There seems to be some merit to this argument. There is no doubt that some of the leading cadres in the South had been arguing for several years that a more active effort would be needed to bring the revolution there to a successful conclusion. But it is probably misleading to portray the debate in terms of a North–South confrontation, or to assert that the former preferred a political solution and were persuaded against their best judgment to accept a military one. As we have seen, a number of party leaders in the North (including Ho Chi Minh, Vo Nguyen Giap, and of course Le Duan himself) had been aware for years that armed struggle in some form might be required to bring about national reunification.

If there was a debate at the Fifteenth Plenum, then, it was probably more about timing and the proper balance of political and military struggle to be adopted than about whether to shift to a more active approach, although some might have been reluctant to return to a strategy of revolutionary war. Le Duan, now acting general secretary of the party and generally recognized as the party's leading expert on conditions in the South, probably argued for a variation of the August Revolution model, with partial insurrections in rural areas leading to the formation of liberated base areas and culminating in a general uprising in the cities. In this version, the main role would still be played by the political force of the masses, with assistance from armed revolutionary units to reduce the strength of Saigon's armed forces, formally known as the Army of the Republic of Vietnam (ARVN).

In the end, the Fifteenth Plenum approved a decision to return to the strategy of revolutionary war to achieve the liberation of the South, using an as yet undetermined combination of political and armed struggle. According to sources in Hanoi, it was seen at the time as a crucial moment in the Vietnamese revolution, and the leadership took time to evaluate the situation in the South and to seek support from its allies before issuing the final resolution in May.

For the next two years, the party attempted to increase the strength of the revolutionary armed forces by recruiting efforts within South Vietnam, supplemented by the limited infiltration of cadres and materiel from the North. As the level of violence escalated, the debate over strategy continued. Some leading southern cadres were critical of the alleged overemphasis on political struggle and apparently argued for more stress on military activities and a qualified return to the Maoist strategy of people's war that had been applied during the war against the French, with revolutionary forces in the rural areas surrounding and eventually attacking the enemy bastions in the cities.

Le Duan attempted to counter such views. in a letter to Nguyen Van Linh, his successor as the party's senior representative in South Vietnam, Le Duan pointed out that the revolutionary movement was still weak, while the Diem regime still retained the loyalty of the majority of the armed forces. The primary advantage of the revolution, he said, lay in its political superiority over its rival, and this must be used to the greatest advantage. Such a strategy would also serve to reduce the likelihood of direct U.S. intervention in the South.

The debate apparently was not fully resolved by the autumn of 1960, because the party's Third National Congress, meeting in September, did not make any significant decisions affecting the existing strategy, simply noting that the period of stability in the South was at an end and a period of disintegration under way. To take advantage of this favorable new stage of the revolution, the Third Congress decided to place military and political struggle on an equal footing in the South, while heightening the level of support from the North. It apparently did make one concrete decision, approving a plan to form a new united front to seek political support among the population in South Vietnam. This would become the famous National Liberation Front, formed in December.

The following January, the Politburo met, in the words of an official history of the war, to "concretize" the results of the Third Party Congress. The resolution issued at the end of the meeting was decidedly optimistic, echoing the views of the Party Congress by noting that the period of stability of the Saigon regime was at an end, and a period of continuous crisis was about to begin. In the North, the DRV was stronger and moving toward socialism. Based on that analysis, the Politburo called for an intensification of the military effort in the South aimed at final victory through a combined General Offensive and Uprising, with intensified military attacks in rural areas (now divided into two regions, the Central Highlands and the Mekong River Delta) coordinated with a mass popular insurrection in the major cities. To provide centralized direction for the effort, in September the Regional Committee for the South (*Uy ban Nam Bo*) was transformed into a Central Office for South Vietnam (*Trung uong cuc Mien Nam,* also known as COSVN) similar to the one that had existed in the South during the previous war against the French.

In letters written to Nguyen Van Linh, Le Duan—formally named general secretary at the Third Party Congress—described the recent decisions and added his own appraisal of the overall situation. The revolution in the South was progressing well, he said, but it was still in the "first stage" of the development, since enemy military strength was still substantially intact and many ARVN troops were still ambivalent about the revolution. Criticizing some southern leaders for their recent tendency to feel that the general uprising could be launched without extensive prior preparation (such as the formation of liberated base areas and the adoption of a strategy of protracted war), Le Duan warned Linh not to be impetuous, noting that a greater emphasis on military struggle might provoke an enemy reaction and make the party's legal activities more difficult to carry out. Citing the examples of the Bolshevik Uprising and the August Revolution, he pointed out that revolution could not succeed unless the enemy's armed forces had been militarily defeated or undermined by internal subversion.

During the remainder of 1961, the party's southern leadership carried out the joint politico-military strategy that had been devised at the Politburo meeting in January. Revolutionary forces, newly unified under the name of the People's Liberation Armed Forces (PLAF), began to increase in numbers, and the first main force units were organized in July. Liberated base areas under the control of the PLAF expanded while the political problems of the Diem regime intensified. Such harbingers of success, however, were counterbalanced by growing indications that the new Kennedy administration in Washington had decided to escalate U.S. involvement in the war. The number of American advisers began to increase well beyond the limits set by the Geneva Accords and Washington announced a new counterinsurgency strategy to cope with the increased threat from the insurgent forces. A key element in that strategy was the construction of so-called "strategic hamlets" (*ap chien luoc*) to protect the rural population from the revolution.

The decision by the Kennedy administration to escalate American involvement in the conflict complicated strategic planning in Hanoi. In February 1962 the Politburo met to evaluate the situation and concluded that the struggle in the South had now turned into a protracted war, but had not essentially changed the balance of forces between the revolution and the Saigon regime. The growing U.S. military role necessitated an increase in the military strength of the PLAF, with a particular emphasis on the buildup of guerrilla forces at the regional level. But political struggle continued to received close attention, and the COSVN leadership was criticized for an excessive emphasis on military struggle and an erroneous belief that a revolutionary "high tide" was just around the corner.

The importance of achieving a proper balance of political and military activity came into even sharper focus as a result of the negotiated settlement of the conflict in Laos reached in July, a settlement that raised hopes in Hanoi for the possibility of a similar agreement in South Vietnam. In a letter to Nguyen Van Linh that same month, Le Duan pointed out that a flexible use of political and military tactics had enabled the revolutionary forces in Laos to win a significant victory at the conference table. Without the battlefield successes achieved by Laotian guerrilla forces, the United States would not have been forced to agree to a settlement. But if those forces had realized even greater success, it might have provoked the United States into open intervention. How far we win, and how far they lose, he said, is very important.

The experience of Laos, Le Duan continued, provided a useful lesson on how to carry on the struggle in South Vietnam, where it was highly important to keep the United States in the stage of Special War (e.g., fighting the war with South Vietnamese troops rather than introducing U.S. combat forces). In fact, he warned, the danger of direct U.S. military intervention was even greater in South Vietnam than it was in Laos since the former, unlike the latter, does not have a direct border with China. As a result, if the war in the South was pushed "beyond reasonable limits," it could result in "some bad consequences."

The goal in South Vietnam, he concluded, was to win while at the same time preserving world peace, to make the United States lose, but up to a tolerable point where it would be willing to accept a negotiated settlement of the war. The enemy must thus be foiled rather than totally defeated, while at the same time the ground for a diplomatic settlement must be prepared by tightening links with progressive and neutralist elements in the South who might serve in a future coalition government in Saigon. Party leaders in Hanoi were wary that a negotiated settlement might arouse anger among party operatives in the South, and Le Duan attempted to reassure them that this was but a temporary "transitional step" to total victory in the South.

As it turned out, the Kennedy administration rejected Hanoi's overtures for a political settlement in South Vietnam, and party strategists were compelled to return to their earlier plans for a combined General Offensive and Uprising. A resolution issued by the Politburo after a meeting held in December called for intensified efforts to strengthen the revolutionary armed forces while expanding liberated areas and destroying the enemy's strategic hamlets. In a speech given the following March, Le Duan warned that because of imperialist aggression, the working class, while seeking to make revolution by peaceful means, had no alternative but to make preparations for a seizure of power by violence.

During the next several months, the party's southern leadership focused on the effort to destroy the strategic hamlet program and cope with increased enemy mobility brought about by the use of helicopters. Although histories of the war written by Vietnamese historians point to the battle of Ap Bac in January 1963 as a firm indication that the PLAF had mastered the challenge, Le Duan's assertion that the results of the battle aroused profound discouragement in Washington remains debatable, since most U.S. intelligence estimates published during the spring were guardedly optimistic about the military situation. As it turned out, it was Diem's political weakness rather than the situation on the battlefield that led to growing anxiety in Washington and the overthrow of his regime by a military junta in November.

At first Hanoi appeared uncertain how to react to the November coup, not only because party leaders were initially unclear over the attitude of the new leadership in Saigon, but also because of the uncertainty over the possible reaction in Washington. In December, Hanoi convened its Ninth Plenum to assess the situation. The Central Committee concluded that the United States could react to heightened revolutionary pressure in two possible ways: by maintaining the existing strategy of Special War, or by moving to a higher level of commitment, involving the introduction of U.S. combat troops. It was the consensus view that the Johnson administration would be most likely to escalate if it became convinced that the revolutionary forces would be unable to resist a growing U.S. presence. Such a development would be unacceptable to Hanoi, since it would make it significantly more difficult to maintain the momentum of the revolution.

The Ninth Plenum therefore approved a decision to strengthen the PLAF as rapidly as possible in order to realize a basic change in the balance of forces and achieve victory in a short time. In that process, the role of armed struggle was seen as "direct and decisive," since the most urgent task was to destroy the ARVN in preparation for a General Offensive and Uprising.

There have been persistent reports of disagreement within the party leadership over how to respond to the overthrow of Ngo Dinh Diem, and some may have called for the direct intervention of the PAVN in the struggle in the South. In the end, however, the introduction of large numbers of North Vietnamese main force units was rejected, probably out of the fear that such actions could trigger an escalation of the U.S. role in the war. The plenum did call for increased aid from the North to deal with the heightened U.S. military effort, but indicated that the roles of the two zones would continue to be different, thus implying that the PAVN would play, at most, a limited combat role in the South.

Party leaders were well aware that the decision to increase the level of violence in the South would strain relations with Moscow, and possibly with Beijing, and for that reason Hanoi sent out a circular letter to fraternal parties explaining the decision and promising that even if the United States should intervene directly in the South, the DRV would restrain Washington from extending the war to North Vietnam.

Over the course of the next twelve months, Hanoi's gamble proved to be, on most counts, a success. Bolstered by the modest infiltration of PAVN units from the North, the PLAF imposed severe losses on the armed forces of the Saigon regime, while the political situation in South Vietnam continued to deteriorate. By the fall of 1964 U.S. intelligence estimates were predicting a Communist victory within six months in the absence of a major U.S. response. On the international scene, Hanoi's bid to win Soviet support had no immediate effect in Moscow, but the fall of Nikita Khrushchev from power in October 1964 brought to office a new Soviet leadership somewhat more willing to follow the Vietnamese lead in Southeast Asia.

At a meeting of the Politburo in early 1965, Hanoi attempted to press its advantage, approving an accelerated effort to destroy the South Vietnamese armed forces and prepare conditions for a general uprising in the major cities. In a report on the results of the meeting to Nguyen Chi Thanh, the new COSVN chief in the South, Le Duan raised the fundamental question: could the PLAF defeat the ARVN before it had a chance to revive (as had taken place in Laos) or the United States decided to intervene? If so, Washington would have no choice but to negotiate a compromise settlement and withdraw.

Le Duan answered the question in the affirmative. He admitted that the balance of forces was not as favorable to the revolution as had been the case just before the Geneva Conference of 1954, but asserted that the guerrilla movement was stronger now and the overall political situation was more favorable. If several ARVN divisions could be disabled and others lured out of the cities through guerrilla attacks in rural areas, urban uprisings in major cities like Saigon, Da Nang, and Hue would have a good chance of success. Then politics would become a key factor, as a coalition of neutralist forces, secretly guided by the party, could form a government in Saigon and ask the United States to withdraw. Le Duan admitted that there was no guarantee of success, but quoted Lenin: let's act and then see. Even if we do not succeed, he said, we can always retire and try again.

But Hanoi once again miscalculated the U.S. reaction. Beginning in February, the Johnson administration announced a bombing campaign against the North and began to introduce U.S. combat troops into the South. A few days after the first troop announcement in Washington, the party Central Committee held its Eleventh Plenum in Hanoi. According to one source, some members wanted to avoid a direct confrontation with the United States and seek a negotiated settlement but, perhaps persuaded by Le Duan's confidence, the party ultimately opted to maintain the existing strategy to "win a decisive victory within a relatively short period of time" while preparing for the possibility of a large-scale introduction of U.S. combat troops.

But Lyndon Johnson's decision to add additional troops during April and May forced Hanoi to recognize that a basic change had taken place in the attitude in Washington. In a letter to Nguyen Chi Thanh in May, Le Duan conceded that if U.S. troop levels in South Vietnam reached 100,000 or even 200,000 the revolutionary forces would lack the military power to inflict "mortal blows" on the enemy. The large-scale introduction of U.S. troops would also reduce the rate of infiltration from the North and put pressure on revolutionary base areas. But Le Duan insisted that Washington was still afraid of a protracted war and hoped for a negotiated settlement, and he pressed his colleagues not to abandon the existing strategy. Even if the United States should move to a Limited War (*khang chien cuc bo*) with 250,000 to 300,000 troops, he said, we can return to a protracted war, which is their most vulnerable point, since history shows that they lack the patience to fight more than three or four years. If the Americans want a protracted war, he concluded, we will give it to them.

By the end of the summer, with the projected size of the American presence in South Vietnam nearing 200,000, it was clear that Le Duan's "worst case" scenario had become a reality. It was also painfully evident that Hanoi's allies were not prepared to respond actively to the U.S. escalation of the war. The Vietnamese had hoped that the People's Republic of China would keep the United States guessing as to its own intentions. But during the summer, Beijing signaled to Washington that it would not directly enter the war unless the United States attacked China.

In September, the Politburo met to consider its options. Party leaders now realized that they lacked the capacity to achieve a complete military victory in the South. But according to the report that Le Duan sent to COSVN a few weeks later, Hanoi was also convinced that the United States remained vulnerable. The Johnson administration dared not attack the North directly, for it would face the united strength of the entire socialist camp. At the same time the American people lacked the patience to fight and win a protracted war. So a "decisive victory" (here Le Duan distinguished the idea of a decisive victory, which he compared to the battle of Dien Bien Phu, from a total victory) was still possible through a coordinated General Offensive and Uprising, even if the United States should increase its presence to half a million troops. The key to success was to destroy the bulk of South Vietnamese troops while doing sufficient damage to American forces to compel the Johnson administration to withdraw.

The Politburo's decision was confirmed at the Twelfth Plenum in December. Hanoi would match the U.S. escalation and maintain an offensive strategy in the South. But the goal would not be a total military victory but rather to use a combination of political, military, and diplomatic techniques to force the United States to get bogged down in a protracted war and defeat it at that level.

In a letter to a colleague, Politoburo member Le Duc Tho explained the decision. Tho admitted that the situation had changed since the previous plenum in March with the addition of 200,000 U.S. troops, and that the opportunity to achieve a quick victory had passed. Sometimes, he noted, the revolution in the South has developed more rapidly than we expected. Such was the case in recent months, when the Saigon regime disintegrated so quickly that revolutionary forces did not have adequate time to complete the destruction of its armed forces.

Tho also admitted that the divisions within the socialist community were a distinct disadvantage. Previously, he said, we could rely on our socialist allies; now we must do it ourselves. But he reaffirmed the conclusion of the Twelfth Plenum that a flexible combination military and political struggle was the best strategy to pursue. Citing the examples of Laos, Algeria, and World War II, he said that history showed there were many ways to win.

What conclusions can be drawn from the above account? Perhaps the most salient point is that although party leaders moved steadily from a primarily political to a predominantly military approach between 1959 and 1965, even in the shadow of the U.S. escalation of the mid-1960s they viewed political struggle as a crucial component of their revolutionary strategy in the South. The validity of that assumption, of course, is dependent on acceptance of Hanoi's definition of "political struggle," which, in this context, means a primarily nonviolent but vigorous and sometimes extralegal effort to bring down a hostile regime.

Secondly, it seems clear that the party embarked on the road to revolutionary war in the South with some reluctance. This is not to say, as some have done, that the central leadership in the North was forced into the decision by pressure from comrades in the South. In fact, as we have seen, some leading party figures in Hanoi were probably convinced from the outset that the military option would be necessary. But most appeared to recognize the risks involved in a return to revolutionary war, not only in terms of the cost in human lives but even more in terms of the danger of a direct U.S. role in the war. Hanoi was willing to go to considerable lengths to prevent that from taking place.

One reason that Hanoi preferred the political option, of course, is that party leaders were convinced from the start that here they possessed a clear advantage over the enemy. We need not accept their assumption that this superiority necessarily had any moral basis to recognize the validity of their conviction that in the absence of foreign intervention, the revolutionary movement would have had little trouble in besting their rivals within the political arena. When they found themselves at a military disadvantage, they made use of their political advantage as a counterweight.

Finally, it is clear that party leaders, or at least the ruling group around Ho Chi Minh and Le Duan, were quite flexible in their approach to the problem, and were willing to use whatever means were necessary—political, military, diplomatic, or a combination of all three—in order to complete reunification with the South. If necessary, as had occurred in 1946 and again in 1954, they were prepared to go through a "transitional phase" (by which was meant a neutralist coalition government) in order to give the United States a face-saving way out of its predicament. Perhaps the most telling phrase in one of the documents cited here is Le Duan's simple statement that if U.S. leaders want a protracted war, we will give it to them. We will fight, he said, whatever way the United States wants.

In that sense, it can be said that the conflict became a predominantly military struggle with the characteristics of a conventional war not, as some have said, because Hanoi planned it that way but because the United States wanted it that way. Given Hanoi's political superiority over its rivals in the South and the ineluctable reality of U.S. technological superiority, it must have seemed in Washington the easier way out. The results have proven otherwise.

China's Crucial Role

QIANG ZHAI

During the Vietnam War, and especially between 1965 and 1968, Beijing invested substantial amounts of time, energy, and money in the Democratic Republic of Vietnam (DRV) to assist Hanoi in its struggle against the United States. But by the time the war ended in 1975, Sino-DRV ties were very much strained. Four years later, the two former allies went to war with each other. How did this happen?

A close examination of the Beijing-Hanoi interactions during the Vietnam War indicates that despite the common goal of resisting the United States, the two communist states differed in their approaches to the issues of waging war and pursuing peace and that despite the rhetoric of "comrades plus brothers," distrust and suspicion existed on both sides. This [essay] . . . will draw primarily on newly released Chinese materials to chart the course of the evolution of Chinese-DRV relations during the Vietnam War and will analyze the reasons for the fluctuations in the relationship. It argues that it was primarily China's insensitivity to the needs of the DRV and Mao's sense of superiority and arrogance that contributed to the final breakdown of the Sino-DRV friendship.

During the First Indochina War, China played an important role in Ho Chi Minh's victory over the French by providing military advisers and weapons to the Viet Minh. In the decade after the 1954 Geneva Conference, Beijing continued to assist the DRV in consolidating its power and reconstructing its economy. When the Sino-Soviet dispute emerged in the late 1950s, Ho tried to remain neutral for fear of losing support from either of the two Communist powers.

Between 1962 and October 1964, however, Hanoi looked primarily to Beijing for support in resisting the United States and carrying out its goal of unifying the South, given Khrushchev's indifference to the conflict in Indochina. During this period, Moscow remained primarily an onlooker regarding events in Southeast Asia. This role suited Khrushchev's purpose of seeking peaceful coexistence with the United States and avoiding clashes similar to the Cuban missile crisis of 1962. As the major provider of military hardware to the DRV during this period, China supplied Hanoi with 90,000 rifles and machine guns, 446 pieces of artillery, 21 million bullets, and 76,400 artillery shells.

During the first half of 1964, Washington's attention was increasingly focused on Hanoi. This trend reflected a mounting U.S. concern over the infiltration of men and supplies from the North and growing dissatisfaction with a policy that allowed Hanoi to encourage the insurgency without punishment. The Johnson administration expanded its covert operations against North Vietnam, including intelligence overflights, the dropping of propaganda leaflets, and OPLAN 34A commando raids along the North Vietnamese coast.

At the same time, tensions were also increasing in Laos. In April, a right-wing coup shook the Lao government, prompting Prime Minister Souvanna Phouma to

International Perspectives on Vietnam, by Lloyd C. Gardner and Ted Gittinger, eds., Texas A&M University Press, 2000.

reorganize the government by excluding the communists. Considering the 1962 Geneva Accords irrelevant, the Pathet Lao attacked the pro-government forces on the Plain of Jars in May. Souvanna permitted unarmed U.S. reconnaissance flights over the Plain of Jars. After communist antiaircraft guns shot one down on June 6, the United States retaliated three days later by using F-100s to strike the communist antiaircraft battery at Xieng Khouang. Apparently without U.S. authorization, Thai-piloted Royal Lao Air Force T-28s attached the Pathet Lao headquarters at Khang Khay and hit the Chinese Economic and Cultural Mission there, killing one Chinese and wounding five others.

Leaders in Beijing watched these developments closely and with apprehension. At a diplomatic reception hosted by a visiting Tanzanian delegation in Beijing on June 16, Chinese Premier Zhou Enlai condemned the U.S. bombing of the Pathet Lao headquarters and the Chinese Mission as a violation of the Geneva Accords and an escalation of the conflict in Indochina.

To confront the increasing American pressure in Indochina, the Chinese Communist Party (CCP) stepped up its coordination with the Vietnamese and Lao communists. On June 21 and 22, 1964, General Van Tien Dung, chief of staff of the People's Army of Vietnam (PAVN), visited Beijing, where he talked with Zhou Enlai about China's military aid to the DRV. Mao told Dung: "Our two parties and two countries must cooperate and fight the enemy together. Your business is my business and my business is your business. In other words, our two sides must deal with the enemy together without conditions."

During July 5–8, Zhou Enlai led a CCP delegation to Hanoi, where he discussed with representatives from the Vietnam Workers' Party (VWP) and the Pathet Lao the situations in South Vietnam and Laos. The Vietnamese and Lao leaders briefed the Chinese on how the United States was using South Vietnam as a base to attack socialism and as a test ground for its "special warfare." After noting that Southeast Asia was the area in the world where "contradictions are most concentrated, struggle most fierce, and revolutionary conditions most ripe," Zhou pointed out two possible military developments in the region: (1) the United States might intensify the "special warfare"; (2) it might turn the "special warfare" into a local war with a direct deployment of American troops in South Vietnam and Laos, or with bombing or invasion of the DRV. No matter what approach the United States adopted, Zhou said, China would surely intervene to support the struggle of the Southeast Asian people. As to concrete measures that the VWP and the Pathet Lao might take, Zhou suggested a combination of political and military struggles: on the political front, to adhere to the two Geneva Accords, exploit Franco-American contradictions, and organize a broad international united front to lay bare U.S. violations of both Geneva Accords; in the military area, to strengthen armed forces, consolidate base areas, and win battles of annihilation. "Our principle for the struggle," Zhou continued, was "to do everything we can to limit the war to the current scale while preparing for the second possibility" of American intervention. Should the second possibility occur, Zhou said, China would match American actions: if the United States sent troops, China would also send troops. Zhou confirmed the agreement made between China and the DRV in 1963 that Beijing would send combat soldiers into North Vietnam if the United States used ground troops to invade the DRV. Clearly Chinese leaders did not want war with the United States; at the same time they had to be prepared for the worst scenario.

Immediately after the Gulf of Tonkin incident, Zhou Enlai and Luo Ruiqing, chief of staff of the People's Liberation Army (PLA), cabled Ho Chi Minh, Pham Van Dong, and Van Tien Dung on August 5, asking them to "investigate the situation, work out countermeasures, and be prepared to fight." In the meantime, leaders in Beijing instructed the Kunming and Guangzhou Military Regions and the air force and naval units stationed in South and Southwest China to begin a state of combat readiness. Four air divisions and one antiaircraft division were dispatched into areas adjoining Vietnam and put on a heightened alert status. In August, China also sent approximately 15 MiG-15 and MiG-17 jets to Hanoi, agreed to train North Vietnamese pilots, and began to build new airfields near the Vietnamese border, which would serve as sanctuaries and provide repair and maintenance facilities for Hanoi's jet fighters. Beijing intended to deter the United States from expanding the war in South Vietnam and from attacking the DRV.

The first months of 1965 witnessed a significant escalation of the American war in Vietnam. On February 7, 9, and 11, U.S. aircraft struck North Vietnamese military installations just across the seventeenth parallel, ostensibly in retaliation for Viet Cong attacks on American barracks near Pleiku and in Qui Nhon. On March 1, the Johnson administration stopped claiming that its air attacks on North Vietnam were reprisals for specific communist assaults in South Vietnam and began continuous bombing of the DRV. On March 8, two battalions of marines armed with tanks and eight-inch howitzers landed at Danang.

Worried about the increasing U.S. involvement in Vietnam, Zhou Enlai during his visit to Pakistan on April 2 asked Pakistani President Ayub Khan, who was scheduled to visit the United States later in the month, to convey to President Johnson a four-point message:

> (1) China will not take the initiative to provoke a war with the United States. (2) The Chinese mean what they say. In other words, if any country in Asia, Africa, or elsewhere meets with aggression by the imperialists headed by the United States, the Chinese government and people will definitely give it support and assistance. Should such just action bring on American aggression against China, we will unhesitatingly rise in resistance and fight to the end. (3) China is prepared. Should the United States impose a war on China, it can be said with certainty that, once in China, the United States will not be able to pull out, however many men it may send over and whatever weapons it may use, nuclear weapons included. (4) Once the war breaks out, it will have no boundaries. If the United States bombards China, China will not sit there waiting to die. If they come from the sky, we will fight back on the ground. Bombing means war. The war cannot have boundaries.

Ayub Khan did not deliver the Chinese message. Just nine days before his arrival in the United States, President Johnson, dismayed by Ayub's flirtation with China, suddenly canceled his invitation. On June 8, Zhou Enlai asked President Julius Nyerere of Tanzania to forward the same four-point message to the United States. This was the most serious warning issued by the Chinese government to the United States, and given the caution exercised by Johnson in carrying out the "Rolling Thunder" operations against the DRV, it was one that Washington did not overlook.

Clearly, U.S. leaders had drawn a lesson from the Korean War, when the Truman administration's failure to heed Beijing's warning against crossing the thirty-eighth parallel led to a bloody confrontation between the United States and China.

The U.S. escalation in early 1965 made the DRV desperate for help. Le Duan and Vo Nguyen Giap rushed to Beijing in early April to ask China to increase its aid and send troops to the DRV. Duan told Chinese leaders that Hanoi needed "volunteer pilots, volunteer soldiers as well as other necessary personnel, including road and bridge engineers." The Vietnamese envoys expected Chinese volunteer pilots to perform four functions: to limit U.S. bombing to the southern part of the country, to defend Hanoi, to protect several major transportation lines, and to boost morale. On behalf of the Chinese leadership, Liu Shaoqui, vice chairman of the CCP Central Committee, replied to the Vietnamese visitors on April 8 that "it is the obligation of the Chinese people and party" to support the Vietnamese struggle against the United States. "Our principle is," Liu continued, "that we will do our best to provide you with whatever you need and whatever we have. If you do not invite us, we will not go to your place. We will send whatever part (of our troops) that you request. You have the complete initiative."

During April 21 and 22, Vo Nguyen Giap discussed with Luo Ruiqing and Yang Chengwu, first deputy chief of staff, the arrangements for sending Chinese troops to the DRV. In May, Ho Chi Minh met with Mao in China, where he asked the Chinese leader to help the DRV repair and build twelve roads in the area north of Hanoi. Mao accepted Ho's request and instructed Zhou Enlai to see to the matter.

In discussions with Luo Ruiqing and Yang Chengwu, Zhou said: "According to Pham Van Dong, U.S. blockade and bombing has reduced supplies to South Vietnam through sea shipment and road transportation. While trying to resume sea transportation, the DRV is also expanding the corridor in Lower Laos and roads in the south. Their troops would go to the south to build roads. Therefore they need our support to construct roads in the North." Yang suggested that because assistance to the DRV involved many military and government departments, a special leadership group should be created to coordinate the work of various agencies. Approving the proposal, Zhou immediately announced the establishment of the "Central Committee and State Council Aid Vietnam Group" with Yang as director.

In early June, Van Tien Dung held discussions with Luo Ruiqing in Beijing to flesh out the general Chinese plan to assist Vietnam. According to their agreement, if the war continued as it was, the DRV would fight by itself and China would provide various kinds of support as the Vietnamese needed it. If the United States used its navy and air force to support a South Vietnamese attack on the North, China would also provide naval and air force support to the DRV. If U.S. ground forces were directly used to attack the North, China would use its land forces as strategic reserves for the DRV and conduct military operations whenever necessary. As to the forms of Chinese-Vietnamese air force cooperation, Dung and Luo agreed that China could either send volunteer pilots to Vietnam to operate Vietnamese aircraft, station both pilots and aircraft in Vietnam airfields, or fly aircraft from bases in China to join combat in Vietnam and only land at Vietnamese bases temporarily for refueling. The third option was known as the "Andong model" (a reference to the pattern of Chinese air force operations during the Korean War). As to the methods of employing Chinese ground troops, the two military leaders agreed that Chinese forces would either help to strengthen the defensive position of the North Vietnamese troops while they prepared for a counteroffensive, or launch an offensive themselves to disrupt the enemy's deployment and win strategic initiatives.

But despite Liu Shaoqu's April promise to Le Duan and Luo Ruiqing's agreement with Van Tien Dung, China in the end failed to provide pilots to Hanoi. According to the Vietnamese "White Paper" of 1979, the Chinese General Staff on July 16, 1965, notified its Vietnamese counterpart that "the time was not appropriate" to send Chinese pilots to Vietnam. China's limited air power may have caused leaders in Beijing to have second thoughts. Beijing's hope to avoid a direct confrontation with the United States may also have played a role. Whatever the reasons for China's decision, the failure to satisfy Hanoi's demand must have greatly disappointed the Vietnamese and undoubtedly contributed to North Vietnam's decision to rely more on the Soviet Union for air defense.

Beginning in June, 1965, China sent ground-to-air missiles, antiaircraft artillery, railroad, engineering, mine-sweeping, and logistical units into North Vietnam. The total number of Chinese troops serving in North Vietnam between June, 1965, and March, 1968, amounted to over 320,000. Participation peaked in 1967, when 170,000 Chinese soldiers were present. They operated antiaircraft guns, built and repaired roads, bridges, and rail lines, and constructed factories. They enabled the PAVN to send large numbers of troops to South Vietnam for the fighting. When the last Chinese troops withdrew from Vietnam in August, 1973, 1,100 soldiers had lost their lives and 4,200 had been wounded.

Both Mao and Zhou Enlai followed events in Vietnam closely and issued directions regarding China's aid to the DRV. After reading a report by a group of Chinese journalists about the difficult living conditions of the Vietnamese Communist troops in the southern mountain regions, Mao announced in November, 1965, that China "must give mosquito nets, cloth, canned food, dried meats, medicine, water-proof cloth, hammocks and other materials in large quantities" to the Vietnamese. Zhou Enlai directed that Chinese equipment sent to South Vietnam should be designed so as to be "easy to use, easy to carry, and easy to hide." For this purpose, he demanded specifically that each piece of equipment should not weigh over thirty kilograms, so that Vietnamese women would have no difficulty in carrying it on head or shoulder.

To supervise the transport of materials to the DRV, Beijing in 1965 established a special leadership group. Luo Ruiqing was appointed director. Materials provided by China, the Soviet Union, and other socialist countries were shipped by rail to cities near the Vietnamese border, where they were transported into the DRV either by rail or by trucks. The North Vietnamese transport system was soon overwhelmed, and an overstocking of supplies occurred at Chinese railway stations and warehouses. Beginning in 1967, China employed over 500 trucks to help carry supplies into the DRV.

To facilitate the infiltration of supplies into South Vietnam, China created a secret coastal transportation line to ship goods to several islands off Central Vietnam for transit to the South. A secret harbor on China's Hainan Island was constructed to serve this transportation route. Beijing also operated a costly transportation line through Cambodia to send weapons, munitions, food, and medical supplies to the National Liberation Front (NLF) in South Vietnam. Between 1965 and 1967, Chinese weapons for 50,000 soldiers arrived by ship via Sihanoukville.

Why did Mao choose to commit China's resources to North Vietnam? Mao's decision to aid Hanoi involved his perception of U.S. threats to China's security, his commitment to national liberation movements, his criticism of Soviet revisionist foreign policy, and his determination to transform the Chinese state and society. These four factors are mutually related and reinforcing. . . .

The newly available Chinese documents clearly indicate that Beijing provided extensive support (short of volunteer pilots) for Hanoi during the Vietnam War and risked war with the United States in helping the Vietnamese. As Allen S. Whiting has perceptively observed, the Chinese did not take pains to conceal their deployment of troops in Vietnam. Chinese troops wore regular uniforms and did not disguise themselves as civilians. Their presence was easily confirmed by U.S. intelligence through aerial photography and electronic intercepts. This deployment, along with the large base complex that China built at Yen Bai in Northwest Vietnam, provided credible and successful deterrence against an American invasion of North Vietnam.

The specter of Chinese intervention in a manner similar to the Korean War was a major factor in shaping President Johnson's gradualist approach to the Vietnam War. Johnson wanted to forestall Chinese intervention by keeping the level of military actions against North Vietnam controlled, exact, and below the threshold that would provoke a direct Chinese entry. This China-induced U.S. strategy of gradual escalation was a great help for Hanoi, for it gave the Vietnamese Communists time to adjust to U.S. bombing and to develop strategies to frustrate U.S. moves. As John W. Garver has aptly noted, "By helping to induce Washington to adopt this particular strategy, Beijing contributed substantially to Hanoi's eventual victory over the United States."

Signs of Chinese-Vietnamese differences emerged even upon the beginning of China's intervention in the Vietnam conflict. Two major factors complicated Sino-Vietnamese relations. One was the historical pride and cultural sensitivity that the Vietnamese carried with them in dealing with the Chinese. The other was the effect of the Sino-Soviet split.

Throughout their history, the Vietnamese have had a love-hate attitude toward their big northern neighbor. On the one hand, they were eager to borrow advanced institutions and technologies from China; on the other, they wanted to preserve their independence and cultural heritage. When they were internally weak and facing external aggression, they sought China's help and intervention and downplayed their inherent differences with the Chinese. When they were unified and free from foreign threats, they tended to resent China's influence and paid more attention to problems in the bilateral relationship.

This pattern certainly applied during the 1950s and the first half of the 1960s. The Vietnamese Communists during this period confronted formidable enemies, the French and the Americans, in their quest for national unification. Ho Chi Minh avidly sought advice and weapons from China. But sentiments of distrust were never far below the surface. Friction emerged between Chinese military advisers and Vietnamese commanders during the First Indochina War. Vietnamese distrust of the Chinese manifested itself again when Chinese support troops entered Vietnam in the mid-1960s.

When Chinese troops went to the DRV in 1965, they found themselves in an awkward position. The Vietnamese leadership wanted their service in fighting U.S.

aircraft and in building and repairing roads, bridges, and rail lines. But the Vietnamese made a point of restricting the Chinese troops' contact with the local population. When a Chinese medical team offered treatment to save the life of a Vietnamese woman, Vietnamese officials blocked the effort. Informed of incidents like this, Mao urged the Chinese troops in Vietnam to "refrain from being too eager" to help the Vietnamese. While Chinese soldiers were in Vietnam, the Vietnamese media reminded the public that China had invaded Vietnam in the past. The journal *Historical Studies* published articles in 1965 describing the history of Vietnamese resistance against Chinese imperial dynasties.

Increasing animosity between Beijing and Moscow also hampered Sino-DRV cooperation. Chinese and Soviet efforts to win Hanoi's allegiance put the Vietnamese in a dilemma. On the one hand, the change of Soviet attitudes toward Vietnam from reluctant to active assistance in late 1964 and early 1965 made the Vietnamese less willing to echo Chinese criticisms of Soviet "revisionism." On the other hand, Hanoi still needed China's assistance and the deterrence it provided.

Meanwhile, Mao's rejection of the Soviet proposal for "united action" on Vietnam ruled out the possibility of a closer coordination within the international communist camp in support of the DRV. During Soviet Premier Alexei Kosygin's visit to Beijing in February, 1965, he proposed to Mao and Zhou Enlai that Beijing and Moscow end their mutual criticisms and cooperate on aid to Vietnam. Mao dismissed Kosygin's suggestion that polemics be suspended, asserting that China's argument with the Soviet Union would continue for another nine thousand years. The Chinese also rejected Soviet requests for an "air corridor" through which an airlift could be conducted and for the cession of a base in Yunnan where hundreds of Soviet military personnel could be stationed to assist Hanoi's war effort. Instead they accused the Russians of taking advantage of the war in Vietnam to violate Chinese sovereignty. While rejecting this kind of coordination, Beijing did allow the Soviet Union to transport its aid to the DRV through the Chinese rail corridor, which remained a major supply route for the Vietnamese war effort during 1965–68. . . .

The Beijing-Hanoi relationship included both converging and diverging interests. The two countries shared a common ideological outlook and a common concern over American intervention in Indochina, but leaders in Hanoi wanted to avoid the danger of submitting to a dependent relationship with China. As long as policymakers in Hanoi and Beijing shared the common goal of ending the U.S. presence in the region, such diverging interests could be subordinated to their points of agreement. But when the common fear of the United States that bound China and the DRV closely together disappeared, disagreement overweighed agreement in Sino-DRV relations. In the absence of a common threat, cordial relations soon gave way to tensions and division.

During the Vietnam War, the DRV was a small power caught in the fight of three giants. It had to confront not only the military might of the United States but also political and ideological pressure from China and the Soviet Union. While Washington wanted Hanoi to cease its effort to unify the South, the Chinese and the Russians pressed the Vietnamese Communists to follow their respective international lines. Both Beijing and Moscow approached the Vietnam conflict with their own self-interests in mind.

Glenn Snyder's description of the alliance security dilemma can be usefully applied to illuminate the problems in the alliance between China and the DRV. According to Snyder, the alliance security dilemma involves a choice between support or nonsupport of allies and tension between fears of entrapment and abandonment. In the late 1950s and early 1960s, Ho Chi Minh was afraid of being entrapped by China in the emerging Sino-Soviet dispute. He did not want to be dragged into a conflict over China's interests that he did not share. Therefore, he visited both Beijing and Moscow in 1960 in an attempt to mediate the difference between Mao and Khrushchev and to promote unity in the international communist movement. In the late 1960s and the early 1970s, the Vietnamese Communists began to fear that China would abandon the DRV in its search for rapprochement with the United States. Thus Pham Van Dong came to Beijing in November, 1971, asking Mao not to invite President Nixon to China.

While policymakers in Hanoi constantly feared betrayal by their big allies, they were not the submissive puppets of Beijing or Moscow. In fact, they were highly self-willed and independent actors, who were able to make their own strategic choices, often without consulting China or the Soviet Union. They were weak but not meek. They made the world, too.

Mao and his associates often ignored the interests, priorities, and needs of the VWP. Their advice to the DRV not to rely on Soviet support and their disapproval of Hanoi's strategy of fighting while talking clearly demonstrated this tendency. For the Hanoi leadership, the Russian connection was crucial. Moscow provided not only advanced weaponry but also international contact for the DRV. The Soviet Union was a member of the UN Security Council, maintained diplomatic relations with the United States, and enjoyed a wide contact with the global community. Especially in the early stage of the war between 1965 and 1967, the Soviet Union played the role of Hanoi's envoy in its dialogue with the West. Soviet officials and diplomats informed their counterparts in Washington, Paris, London, and other Western capitals of Hanoi's stance on various issues regarding the settlement of the war. They also supplied the North Vietnamese with information on Western views. Chinese leaders were jealous of this Soviet role in Vietnam.

Realizing that Vietnam was a small and underdeveloped country facing an industrialized foreign power and that the resistance could not end in a total military victory over the enemy, leaders in Hanoi finally had to accept negotiations with the enemy as a fact of life and an integral component of their struggle for national reunification. They needed a period of peace in which to consolidate military and political strength. To them, negotiations were an extension of warfare rather than an alternative to it. What they sought in direct negotiations with Washington was a way to improve their chance of winning the war, not a way of preventing or ending it. Negotiations served as a tactic of warfare. Hanoi often employed the lure of negotiations as a way to win friends in the international arena, to disrupt support for the war in the United States, and to drive a wedge between Washington and Saigon.

At times, especially before the launching of a major military operation, Hanoi would express an interest in conducting talks with the United States simply to trick Washington into halting its bombing and enmesh the United States in a negotiating trap. DRV Foreign Minister Nguyen Duy Trinh's declaration on the eve of the Tet Offensive of Hanoi's willingness to hold discussions with the Americans was a case in point. Officials in Beijing, however, often failed to appreciate the importance of negotiations in Hanoi's strategy. They kept urging the DRV to wage a protracted war against the United States.

Since the late 1950s when the Sino-Soviet dispute erupted, policymakers in Beijing had habitually judged the VWP in light of the doctrine of opposition to Soviet revisionism, which distorted far more that it illuminated. The tendency to evaluate fraternal parties through the prism of antirevisionism also manifested itself in China's relations with Cuba in the 1960s. Just like the later deterioration of Beijing-Hanoi relations, the worsening of Chinese-Cuban ties in the mid-1960s derived primarily from Mao's dissatisfaction with Castro's flirtations with Moscow. Mao and his lieutenants were too much prisoners of their competition with the Soviets.

In a deeper historical sense, the Sino-Vietnamese conflict was caused by the clash of the competing visions held by leaders in the two countries regarding their respective roles in Indochina. These visions or self-images were informed by historical memory as well as concerns for national prestige and destiny. What Mao and his comrades sought in their commitment to revolutionary struggle was not just the rescue of China from the clutches of perennial poverty, warlord rule, and imperialist penetration but also the rejuvenation of the Chinese nation and the restoration of its historical greatness in East Asia. Historically speaking, the Chinese held a Sinocentric view of the world, regarding other countries as inferior. The Celestial Emperor in the Forbidden City considered small nations on China's periphery, including Vietnam, as within the orbit of China's influence and kept those countries within the tributary system.

Despite his claims of adherence to Marxism and Leninism, Mao fully inherited China's historical legacy. His strong belief in the absolute correctness and universal relevance of his revolutionary practice and theory for the oppressed peoples of the world against colonialism and imperialism was reminiscent of the claims of Chinese imperial rulers about the superiority of Chinese models and institutions. He felt perplexed and indignant when the Vietnamese Communists refused to echo the Chinese line in the Sino-Soviet quarrel after 1965, and when Hanoi defied his wish in entering into negotiations with the United States in 1968.

Ho Chi Minh and his associates were also conscientious students of history. What they sought in their struggle against the French and the Americans was not just the end of Vietnam's suffering under colonialism but also the reconstruction of their motherland and the re-establishment of its leading role in Indochina. Since the restoration of independence from Chinese control in the tenth century, Vietnamese imperial rulers had created hegemony over their neighbors to the west and introduced a tributary system in mainland southeast Asia. After the establishment of the Indochinese Communist Party (ICP) in 1930, party strategists saw Indochina as a single strategic space and assumed a leading role for Vietnam in guiding the revolutionary struggle in Laos and Cambodia. Although the ICP was dissolved in 1951 and separate Communist organizations were established in Laos and Cambodia, Vietnamese strategic thinking remained unchanged.

The CCP's attempt to assert China's influence over Indochina was at longerheads with the VWP's effort to maintain its "special relationship" with Laos and Cambodia. At the 1954 Geneva Conference, Zhou Enlai, apprehensive about Vietnamese intentions to create a military bloc of all three Indochinese countries after the defeat of the French, criticized Hanoi's tendency to subordinate the interests of Laos and Cambodia to those of Vietnam. In the mid-1960s when Beijing dispatched an advisory team to Pathet Lao territory, the Vietnamese advisers there defended their superior position by minimizing the role of their Chinese competitors.

In the end, it was not just the United States who lost the Vietnam War. China also failed in Vietnam. It shed blood and spent enormous amounts of material resources in Vietnam but did not secure the gratitude and goodwill of the Vietnamese. The Chinese-Vietnamese contradiction was determined not only by contemporary conflicts between their national interests but also by historically rooted mutual distrust and suspicion.

✕ *F U R T H E R   R E A D I N G*

Andrews, William. *The Village War* (1973).
Bergerud, Eric M. *The Dynamics of Defeat* (1991).
Brigham, Robert K. *Guerrilla Diplomacy: The NLF's Foreign Relations and the Vietnam War* (1999).
Chen, King C. "Hanoi's Three Decisions and the Escalation of the Vietnam War," *Political Science Quarterly,* 90 (1975), 239–259.
Chi, Hoang Van. *From Colonialism to Communism* (1964).
Dinh, Nguyen Thi. *No Other Road to Take* (1976).
Duiker, William J. *The Communist Road to Power in Vietnam* (1981).
———. *Ho Chi Minh* (2000).
FitzGerald, Frances. *Fire in the Lake: The Vietnamese and the Americans in Vietnam* (1972).
Funnell, V. C. "Vietnam and the Sino-Soviet Conflict," *Studies in Comparative Communism,* 11 (1978), 142–199.
Gaiduk, Ilya V. *The Soviet Union and the Vietnam War* (1996).
Giap, Vo Nguyen. *Big Victory, Big Task* (1967).
———. *Unforgettable Days* (1978).
Gilbert, Marc Jason, ed. *How the North Won the Vietnam War* (2002).
Henderson, William Darryl. *Why the Vietcong Fought* (1979).
Hess, Martha. *Then the Americans Came: Voices from Vietnam* (1993).
Honey, P. J. *Communism in North Vietnam* (1963).
Jamieson, Neil L. *Understanding Vietnam* (1993).
Jian, Chen. *Mao's China and the Cold War* (2001).
Lacouture, Jean. *Ho Chi Minh: A Political Biography* (1968).
Lanning Michael Lee, and Dan Cragg. *Inside the VC and the NVA* (1992).
Lockhart, Greg. *Nation in Arms: The Origins of the People's Army of Vietnam* (1991).
Macdonald, Peter. *Giap: The Victor in Vietnam* (1993).
Moïse, Edwin E. *Land Reform in China and North Vietnam* (1983).
Papp, Daniel S. *Vietnam: The View from Moscow, Peking, Washington* (1978).
Pike, Douglas. *History of Vietnamese Communism* (1978).
———. *PAVN: People's Army of Vietnam* (1986).
———. *Viet Cong* (1966).
———. *Vietnam and the Soviet Union* (1987).
Popkin, Samuel L. *The Rational Peasant* (1979).
Post, Ken. *Revolution, Socialism and Nationalism in Viet Nam* (vols. 1–3) (1989).
Prados, John. *The Bood Road: The Ho Chi Minh Road and the Vietnam War* (1999).
Pribbenow, Merle L., transl. *Victory in Vietnam: The Official History of the People's Army of Vietnam, 1954–1975* (2002).
Tin, Bui. *Following Ho Chi Minh* (1995).

Race, Jeffrey. *War Comes to Long An* (1972).
Sansom, Robert L. *The Economics of Insurgency in the Mekong Delta of Vietnam* (1970).
Smyser, W. R. *The Independent Vietnamese: Vietnamese Communism Between Russia and China, 1956–1969* (1980).
Stettler, Russell, ed. *The Military Art of People's War* (1970).
Taylor, Sandra C. *Vietnamese Women at War* (1999).
Trullinger James. *Village at War* (1980).
Turner, Karen G. *Even the Women Must Fight* (1999).
Turner Robert F. *Vietnamese Communism: Its Origins and Development* (1975).
Woodside, Alexander B. *Communist and Revolution in Vietnam* (1976).
Zagoria, Donald, S. *Vietnam Triangle* (1967).
Zhai, Qiang. *China and the Vietnam Wars* (2000).

The Tet Offensive

✗

The Tet lunar holidays of 1968 broke across South Vietnam like a thunderclap as the North Vietnamese and Vietcong launched a series of well-coordinated attacks throughout the country. The offensive heralded a new, much bolder phase in communist military and political strategy. Although American and South Vietnamese forces ultimately repelled the attacks, inflicting heavy casualties on their adversary, the Tet offensive raised fundamental questions about the efficacy of American policy that reverberated throughout the United States. Most important, it forced a wrenching reexamination of Washington policy that culminated in President Lyndon B. Johnson's decisions in March 1968 to call for negotiations and to set a ceiling on U.S. troop levels.

Most analysts now agree that the communists suffered heavily for their boldness. They point especially to the devastating losses of Vietcong cadres in the fighting. Following Tet, North Vietnamese troops were compelled to play an increasingly heavy role in the struggle. Specialists agree as well that the offensive dealt the United States a powerful psychological blow, generating strong opposition to the war among elite groups and the general public. They differ, however, in their evaluation of Tet's precise military and political effects. Two questions predominate in recent studies: why was Tet such a turning point for the United States, and should it have been?

✗ D O C U M E N T S

Documents 1 and 2 reflect the immediate response to Tet. First is an excerpt from a February 4, 1968, joint television interview of Robert McNamara and Dean Rusk, in which they presented their assessment of the Tet offensive. Then on February 8, Senator Robert F. Kennedy called for a reevaluation of America's Vietnam policy, denouncing the illusions that had been guiding the U.S. war effort. On February 27, CBS television anchorman Walter Cronkite hosted a report from Vietnam; parts of it appear as Document 3. In the program, he characterized American policy as one "mired in stalemate." Document 4 contains extracts from a report of February 27 by General Earle G. Wheeler, chairman of the Joint Chiefs of Staff. Wheeler evaluated the military situation in the wake of the Tet attacks and repeated General William Westmoreland's request for more than 200,000 additional troops. In Document 5, written in March 1968, the southern branch of the Vietnamese communist party gives an early evaluation of the offensive's contributions and shortcomings.

The next three readings are personal reminiscences. In Document 6, Eunice Splawn, a U.S. Air Force nurse, recalls the fears and pressures brought on by the Tet attacks. Next, Robert Komer, head of the pacification program in South Vietnam, recollects Tet's impact on U.S. officials in Saigon and Washington. Finally in Document 8, Clark Clifford, who replaced McNamara as defense secretary on March 1, 1968, remembers the critical questions that he posed to top administration figures at that time.

Document 9 is Johnson's public address of March 31, in which he called for a bombing halt and the beginning of negotiations with North Vietnam—and then stunned his audience with the announcement of his withdrawal from the 1968 presidential race.

1. Robert McNamara and Dean Rusk Assess the Tet Offensive, 1968

Mr. Able: Secretary McNamara, it is 3 years this week since we started bombing North Viet-Nam. It was also in '65 that we started the big buildup on the ground. What happened this week? How do you relate the ability of the Viet Cong to stage as major an offensive as this one was to the efforts we have been making these past 3 years?

Secretary McNamara: Three years ago, or more exactly, 2 1/2 years ago, in July of 1965, President Johnson made the decision—announced to our people the decision to move significant numbers of combat troops into South Viet-Nam. At that time the North Vietnamese and their associates, the Viet Cong, were on the verge of cutting the country in half and of destroying the South Vietnamese Army. We said so at the time, and I think hindsight has proven that a correct appraisal. What has happened since that time, of course, is that they have suffered severe losses, they have failed in their objective to destroy the Government of South Viet-Nam, they have failed in their objective to take control of the country. They have continued to fight.

Just 4 days ago I remember reading in our press that I had presented a gloomy, pessimistic picture of activities in South Viet-Nam. I don't think it was gloomy or pessimistic; it was realistic. It said that while they had suffered severe penalties, they continued to have strength to carry out the attacks which we have seen in the last 2 or 3 days.

Mr. Able: Mr. Secretary, are you telling us the fact that the Viet Cong, after all these years, were able to, temporarily at least, grab control of some 20-odd Provincial capitals and the city of Saigon—are you telling us this has no military meaning at all?

Secretary McNamara: No; certainly not. I think South Viet-Nam is such a complex situation—one must always look at the pluses and the minuses, and I don't mean to say there haven't been any minuses for the South Vietnamese in the last several days. I think there have been, but there have been many, many pluses. The North Vietnamese and the Viet Cong have not accomplished either one of their major objectives: either to ignite a general uprising or to force a diversion of the troops which the South Vietnamese and the United States have moved into the northern areas of South Viet-Nam, anticipating a major Viet Cong and North Vietnamese offensive in that area.

News conference, February 4, 1968, U.S. Department of State *Bulletin,* 58 (February 26, 1968), 261–270.

And beyond that, the North Vietnamese and the Viet Cong have suffered very heavy penalties in terms of losses of weapons and losses of men in the past several days. They have, of course, dealt a very heavy blow to many of the cities of South Viet-Nam.

Mr. Frankel: Secretary Rusk, the administration has naturally been stressing the things that they think the Viet Cong did not achieve in this week of attacks—didn't cause an uprising, which you say may have been one of their goals, didn't seize cities for any permanent period. But yet we have also been given to understand that the real name of this game out there is "Who can provide safety for whom?" And haven't they in a very serious way humiliated our ability in major cities all up and down this country to provide the South Vietnamese population that is listed as clearly in our control with a degree of assurance and safety that South Vietnamese forces and American forces together could give them?

Secretary Rusk: There is almost no way to prevent the other side from making a try. There is a way to prevent them from having a success.

I said earlier that I thought there would be a number of South Vietnamese who would take a very grumpy view over the inability of the Government to protect them against some of the things that have happened in the last 3 or 4 days. But the net effect of the transaction is to make it clear that the Viet Cong are not able to come into these Provincial capitals and seize Provincial capitals and hold them; that they are not able to announce the formation of a new committee, or a coalition or a federation, and have it pick up any support in the country; that they are not able to undermine the solidarity of those who are supporting the Government.

No; I think there is a psychological factor here that we won't be able to assess until a week or two after the event, and I might say also that we know there is going to be some hard fighting ahead. We are not over this period at all. As a matter of fact, the major fighting up in the northern part of South Viet-Nam has not yet occurred, so there are some hard battles ahead. . . .

Mr. Frankel: Secretary McNamara, let me take advantage of your valedictory mood. Looking back over this long conflict and especially in this rather agonized week in Viet-Nam, if we had to do it all over again, would you make any major changes in our—

Secretary McNamara: This is not an appropriate time for me to be talking of changes, with hindsight. There is no question but what 5 or 10 or 20 years from now the historians will find actions that might have been done differently. I am sure they will. . . . I am learning more and more about Viet-Nam every day. There is no question I see better today than I did 3 years ago or 5 years ago what might have been done there.

On balance, I feel much the way the Asian leaders do. I think the action that this Government has followed, policies it has followed, the objectives it has had in Viet-Nam, are wise. I do not by any means suggest that we have not made mistakes over the many, many years that we have been pursuing those objectives.

Mr. Frankel: You seem to suggest that we really didn't—that none of us appreciated what we were really getting into.

Secretary McNamara: I don't think any of us predicted 7 years ago or 15 years ago the deployment of 500,000 men to Viet-Nam. I know I didn't.

2. Robert F. Kennedy Calls Vietnam an Unwinnable War, 1968

Our enemy, savagely striking at will across all of South Vietnam, has finally shattered the mask of official illusion with which we have concealed our true circumstances, even from ourselves. But a short time ago we were serene in our reports and predictions of progress.

The Vietcong will probably withdraw from the cities, as they were forced to withdraw from the American Embassy. Thousands of them will be dead.

But they will, nevertheless, have demonstrated that no part or person of South Vietnam is secure from their attacks: neither district capitals nor American bases, neither the peasant in his rice paddy nor the commanding general of our own great forces.

No one can predict the exact shape or outcome of the battles now in progress, in Saigon or at Khesanh. Let us pray that we will succeed at the lowest possible cost to our young men.

But whatever their outcome, the events of the last two weeks have taught us something. For the sake of those young Americans who are fighting today, if for no other reason, the time has come to take a new look at the war in Vietnam; not by cursing the past but by using it to illuminate the future.

And the first and necessary step is to face the facts. It is to seek out the austere and painful reality of Vietnam, freed from wishful thinking, false hopes and sentimental dreams. It is to rid ourselves of the "good company," of those illusions which have lured us into the deepening swamp of Vietnam.

We must, first of all, rid ourselves of the illusion that the events of the past two weeks represent some sort of victory. That is not so.

It is said the Vietcong will not be able to hold the cities. This is probably true. But they have demonstrated despite all our reports of progress, of government strength and enemy weakness, that half a million American soldiers with 700,000 Vietnamese allies, with total command of the air, total command of the sea, backed by huge resources and the most modern weapons, are unable to secure even a single city from the attacks of an enemy whose total strength is about 250,000. . . .

For years we have been told that the measure of our success and progress in Vietnam was increasing security and control for the population. Now we have seen that none of the population is secure and no area is under sure control.

Four years ago when we only had about 30,000 troops in Vietnam, the Vietcong were unable to mount the assaults on cities they have now conducted against our enormous forces. At one time a suggestion that we protect enclaves was derided. Now there are no protected enclaves.

This has not happened because our men are not brave or effective, because they are. It is because we have misconceived the nature of the war: It is because we have sought to resolve by military might a conflict whose issue depends upon the will and conviction of the South Vietnamese people. It is like sending a lion to halt an epidemic of jungle rot.

This misconception rests on a second illusion—the illusion that we can win a war which the South Vietnamese cannot win for themselves.

You cannot expect people to risk their lives and endure hardship unless they have a stake in their own society. They must have a clear sense of identification with their own government, a belief they are participating in a cause worth fighting for.

People will not fight to line the pockets of generals or swell the bank accounts of the wealthy. They are far more likely to close their eyes and shut their doors in the face of their government—even as they did last week.

More than any election, more than any proud boast, that single fact reveals the truth. We have an ally in name only. We support a government without supporters. Without the efforts of American arms that government would not last a day.

The third illusion is that the unswerving pursuit of military victory, whatever its cost, is in the interest of either ourselves or the people of Vietnam.

For the people of Vietnam, the last three years have meant little but horror. Their tiny land has been devastated by a weight of bombs and shells greater than Nazi Germany knew in the Second World War.

We have dropped 12 tons of bombs for every square mile in North and South Vietnam. Whole provinces have been substantially destroyed. More than two million South Vietnamese are now homeless refugees.

Imagine the impact in our own country if an equivalent number—over 25 million Americans—were wandering homeless or interned in refugee camps, and millions more refugees were being created as New York and Chicago, Washington and Boston, were being destroyed by a war raging in their streets.

Whatever the outcome of these battles, it is the people we seek to defend who are the greatest losers.

Nor does it serve the interests of America to fight this war as if moral standards could be subordinated to immediate necessities. Last week, a Vietcong suspect was turned over to the chief of the Vietnamese Security Services, who executed him on the spot—a flat violation of the Geneva Convention on the Rules of War.

The photograph of the execution was on front pages all around the world— leading our best and oldest friends to ask, more in sorrow than in anger, what has happened to America?

The fourth illusion is that the American national interest is identical with—or should be subordinated to—the selfish interest of an incompetent military regime.

We are told, of course, that the battle for South Vietnam is in reality a struggle for 250 million Asians—the beginning of a Great Society for all of Asia. But this is pretension.

We can and should offer reasonable assistance to Asia; but we cannot build a Great Society there if we cannot build one in our own country. We cannot speak extravagantly of a struggle for 250 million Asians, when a struggle for 15 million in one Asian country so strains our forces, that another Asian country, a fourth-rate power which we have already once defeated in battle, dares to seize an American ship and hold and humiliate her crew.

The fifth illusion is that this war can be settled in our own way and in our own time on our own terms. Such a settlement is the privilege of the triumphant: of those who crush their enemies in battle or wear away their will to fight.

We have not done this, nor is there any prospect we will achieve such a victory.

Unable to defeat our enemy or break his will—at least without a huge, long and ever more costly effort—we must actively seek a peaceful settlement. We can no longer harden our terms every time Hanoi indicates it may be prepared to negotiate; and we must be willing to foresee a settlement which will give the Vietcong a chance to participate in the political life of the country.

These are some of the illusions which may be discarded if the events of last week are to prove not simply a tragedy, but a lesson: a lesson which carries with it some basic truths.

First, that a total military victory is not within sight or around the corner; that, in fact, it is probably beyond our grasp; and that the effort to win such a victory will only result in the further slaughter of thousands of innocent and helpless people—a slaughter which will forever rest on our national conscience.

Second, that the pursuit of such a victory is not necessary to our national interest, and is even damaging that interest.

Third, that the progress we have claimed toward increasing our control over the country and the security of the population is largely illusory.

Fourth, that the central battle in this war cannot be measured by body counts or bomb damage, but by the extent to which the people of South Vietnam act on a sense of common purpose and hope with those that govern them.

Fifth, that the current regime in Saigon is unwilling or incapable of being an effective ally in the war against the Communists.

Sixth, that a political compromise is not just the best path to peace, but the only path, and we must show as much willingness to risk some of our prestige for peace as to risk the lives of young men in war.

Seventh, that the escalation policy in Vietnam, far from strengthening and consolidating international resistance to aggression, is injuring our country through the world, reducing the faith of other peoples in our wisdom and purpose and weakening the world's resolve to stand together for freedom and peace.

Eighth, that the best way to save our most precious stake in Vietnam—the lives of our soldiers—is to stop the enlargement of the war, and that the best way to end casualties is to end the war.

Ninth, that our nation must be told the truth about this war, in all its terrible reality, both because it is right—and because only in this way can any Administration rally the public confidence and unity for the shadowed days which lie ahead.

No war has ever demanded more bravery from our people and our Government—not just bravery under fire or the bravery to make sacrifices—but the bravery to discard the comfort of illusion—to do away with false hopes and alluring promises.

Reality is grim and painful. But it is only a remote echo of the anguish toward which a policy founded on illusion is surely taking us.

This is a great nation and a strong people. Any who seek to comfort rather than speak plainly, reassure rather than instruct, promise satisfaction rather than reveal frustration—they deny that greatness and drain that strength. For today as it was in the beginning, it is the truth that makes us free.

3. Walter Cronkite Criticizes a Policy
"Mired in Stalemate," 1968

Walter Cronkite: These ruins are in Saigon, capital and largest city of South Vietnam. They were left here by an act of war, Vietnamese against Vietnamese. Hundreds died here. Here in these ruins can be seen physical evidence of the Vietcong's Tet offensive, but far less tangible is what those ruins mean, and like everything else in this burned and blasted and weary land, they mean success or setback, victory or defeat, depending upon whom you talk to.

President Nguyen Van Thieu: I believe it gives to the VC, it shows first to the VC that the—the Vietnamese people from whom they hoped to have a general uprising, and to welcome the VC in the cities, this is a very bad test for them.

Nguyen Xuan Oanh (critic of government): I think the people have realized now that there [are] no secure areas. Your own home in the heart of the city is not secure. I am stunned myself when I see that the Vietcong can come to your door and open the door and just kill you instantly, without any warning, and without any protection from the government.

Cronkite: There are doubts about the measure of success or setback, but even more, there are doubts about the exact measure of the disaster itself. All that is known with certainty is that on the first two nights of the Tet Lunar New Year, the Vietcong and North Vietnamese Regular Forces, violating the truce agreed on for that holiday, struck across the entire length of South Vietnam, hitting the largest 35 cities, towns, and provincial capitals. How many died and how much damage was done, however, are still but approximations, despite the official figures.

The very preciseness of the figures brings them under suspicion. Anyone who has wandered through these ruins knows that an exact count is impossible. Why, just a short while ago a little old man came and told us that two VC were buried in a hastily dug grave up at the end of the block. Had they been counted? And what about these ruins? Have they gone through all of them for buried civilians and soldiers? And what about those 14 VC we found in the courtyard behind the post office at Hue? Had they been counted and tabulated? They certainly hadn't been buried.

We came to Vietnam to try to determine what all this means to the future of the war here. We talked to officials, top officials, civilian and military, Vietnamese and American. We toured damaged areas like this, and refugee centers. We paid a visit to the Battle at Hue, and to the men manning the northernmost provinces, where the next big communist offensive is expected. All of this is the subject of our report. . . .

We'd like to sum up our findings in Vietnam, an analysis that must be speculative, personal, subjective. Who won and who lost in the great Tet offensive against the cities? I'm not sure. The Vietcong did not win by a knockout, but neither did we. The referees of history may make it a draw. Another stand-off may be coming in the big battles expected south of the Demilitarized Zone. Khe Sanh could well fall, with a terrible loss in American lives, prestige, and morale, and this is a tragedy of our stubbornness there; but the bastion no longer is a key to the rest of

---

Text by Walter Cronkite found in Peter Braestrup, *Big Story: How the American Press and Television Reported and Interpreted the Crisis of Tet 1968 in Vietnam and Washington,* 1977, Vol. II.

the northern regions, and it is doubtful that the American forces can be defeated across the breadth of the DMZ with any substantial loss of ground. Another stand-off. On the political front, past performance gives no confidence that the Vietnamese government can cope with its problems, now compounded by the attack on the cities. It may not fall, it may hold on, but it probably won't show the dynamic qualities demanded of this young nation. Another stand-off.

We have been too often disappointed by the optimism of the American leaders, both in Vietnam and Washington, to have faith any longer in the silver linings they find in the darkest clouds. They may be right, that Hanoi's winter-spring offensive has been forced by the communist realization that they could not win the longer war of attrition, and that the communists hope that any success in the offensive will improve their position for eventual negotiations. It would improve their position, and it would also require our realization, that we should have had all along, that any negotiations must be that—negotiations, not the dictation of peace terms. For it seems now more certain than ever that the bloody experience of Vietnam is to end in a stalemate. This summer's almost certain stand-off will either end in real give-and-take negotiations or terrible escalation; and for every means we have to escalate, the enemy can match us, and that applies to invasion of the North, the use of nuclear weapons, or the mere commitment of 100-, or 200-, or 300,000 more American troops to the battle. And with each escalation, the world comes closer to the brink of cosmic disaster.

To say that we are closer to victory today is to believe, in the face of the evidence, the optimists who have been wrong in the past. To suggest we are on the edge of defeat is to yield to unreasonable pessimism. To say that we are mired in stalemate seems the only realistic, yet unsatisfactory, conclusion. On the off chance that military and political analysts are right, in the next few months we must test the enemy's intentions, in case this is indeed his last gasp before negotiations. But it is increasingly clear to this reporter that the only rational way out then will be to negotiate, not as victors, but as an honorable people who lived up to their pledge to defend democracy, and did the best they could.

4. Earle G. Wheeler's Report on Military Prospects After Tet, 1968

1. The Chairman, JCS and party visited SVN on 23, 24 and 25 February. This report summarizes the impressions and facts developed through conversations and briefings at MACV and with senor commanders throughout the country.

2. *Summary*
- The current situation in Vietnam is still developing and fraught with opportunities as well as dangers.
- There is no question in the mind of MACV that the enemy went all out for a general offensive and general uprising and apparently believed that he would succeed in bringing the war to an early successful conclusion.

Wheeler report, February 27, 1968, declassified document reprinted in Porter, ed., *Definitive Documentation,* II, 501–504.

- The enemy failed to achieve this initial objective but is continuing his effort. Although many of his units were badly hurt, the judgment is that he has the will and the capability to continue.
- Enemy losses have been heavy; he has failed to achieve his prime objectives of mass uprisings and capture of a large number of the capital cities and towns. Morale in enemy units which were badly mauled or where the men were oversold the idea of a decisive victory at TET probably has suffered severely. However, with replacements, his indoctrination system would seem capable of maintaining morale at a general adequate level. His determination appears to be unshaken.
- The enemy is operating with relative freedom in the countryside, probably recruiting heavily and no doubt infiltrating NVA units and personnel. His recovery is likely to be rapid; his supplies are adequate; and he is trying to maintain the momentum of his winter-spring offensive.
- The structure of the GVN held up but its effectiveness has suffered.
- The RVNAF held up against the initial assault with gratifying, and in a way, surprising strength and fortitude. However, ARVN is now in a defensive posture around towns and cities and there is concern about how well they will bear up under sustained pressure.
- The initial attack nearly succeeded in a dozen places, and defeat in those places was only averted by the timely reaction of US forces. In short, it was a very near thing.
- There is no doubt that the RD [rural development, or pacification] Program has suffered a severe set back.
- RVNAF was not badly hurt physically—they should recover strength and equipment rather quickly (equipment in 2–3 months—strength in 3–6 months). Their problems are more psychological than physical.
- US forces have lost none of their pre-TET capability.
- MACV has three principal problems. First, logistic support north of Danang is marginal owing to weather, enemy interdiction and harassment and the massive deployment of US forces into the DMZ/Hue area. Opening Route 1 will alleviate this problem but takes a substantial troop commitment. Second, the defensive posture of ARVN is permitting the VC to make rapid inroads in the formerly pacified countryside. ARVN, in its own words, is in a dilemma as it cannot afford another enemy thrust into the cities and towns and yet if it remains in a defensive posture against this contingency, the countryside goes by default. MACV is forced to devote much of its troop strength to this problem. Third, MACV has been forced to deploy 50% of all US maneuver battalions into I Corps, to meet the threat there, while stripping the rest of the country of adequate reserves. If the enemy synchronizes an attack against Khe Sanh/Hue-Quang Tri with an offensive in the Highlands and around Saigon while keeping the pressure on throughout the remainder of the country, MACV will be hard pressed to meet adequately all threats. Under these circumstances, we must be prepared to accept some reverses.
- For these reasons, General Westmoreland has asked for a 3 division-15 tactical fighter squadron force. This force would provide him with a theater reserve and an offensive capability which he does not now have.

3. The situation as it stands today:

    a.   Enemy capabilities

        (1) The enemy has been hurt badly in the populated lowlands, but is practically intact elsewhere. He committed over 67,000 combat maneuver forces plus perhaps 25% or 17,000 more impressed men and boys, for a total of about 84,000. He lost 40,000 killed, at least 3,000 captured, and perhaps 5,000 disabled or died of wounds. He had peaked his force total to about 240,000 just before TET, by hard recruiting, infiltration, civilian impressment, and draw-downs on service and guerrilla personnel. So he has lost about one-fifth of his total strength. About two-thirds of his trained, organized unit strength can continue offensive action. He is probably infiltrating and recruiting heavily in the countryside while allied forces are securing the urban areas. . . .

4. What does the future hold?

    a.   Probable enemy strategy. . . . We see the enemy pursuing a reinforced offensive to enlarge his control throughout the country and keep pressures on the government and allies. We expect him to maintain strong threats in the DMZ area, at Khe Sanh, in the highlands, and at Saigon, and to attack in force when conditions seem favorable. He is likely to try to gain control of the country's northern provinces. He will continue efforts to encircle cities and province capitals to isolate and disrupt normal activities, and infiltrate them to create chaos. He will seek maximum attrition of RVNAF elements. Against US forces, he will emphasize attacks by fire on airfields and installations, using assaults and ambushes selectively. His central objective continues to be the destruction of the Government of SVN and its armed forces. As a minimum he hopes to seize sufficient territory and gain control of enough people to support establishment of the groups and committees he proposes for participation in an NLF dominated government.

    b.   MACV Strategy:

        (1) MACV believes that the central thrust of our strategy now must be to defeat the enemy offensive and that if this is done well, the situation overall will be greatly improved over the pre-TET condition.

        (2) MACV accepts the fact that its first priority must be the security of Government of Vietnam in Saigon and provincial capitals. MACV describes its objectives as:

    •   First, to counter the enemy offensive and to destroy or eject the NVA invasion force in the north.

    •   Second, to restore security in the cities and towns.

    •   Third, to restore security in the heavily populated areas of the countryside.

    •   Fourth, to regain the initiative through offensive operations.

    c.   Tasks:

        (1) *Security of Cities and Government.* MACV recognizes that US forces will be required to reinforce and support RVNAF in the security of cities, towns and government structure. At this time, 10 US battalions are operating in the environs of Saigon. It is clear that this task will absorb a substantial portion of US forces.

(2) *Security in the Countryside.* To a large extent the VC now control the countryside. Most of the 54 battalions formerly providing security for pacification are now defending district or province towns. MACV estimates that US forces will be required in a number of places to assist and encourage the Vietnamese Army to leave the cities and towns and reenter the country. This is especially true in the Delta.

(3) *Defense of the borders, the DMZ and the northern provinces.* MACV considers that it must meet the enemy threat in I Corps Tactical Zone and has already deployed there slightly over 50% of all US maneuver battalions. US forces have been thinned out in the highlands, notwithstanding an expected enemy offensive in the early future.

(4) *Offensive Operations.* Coupling the increased requirement for the cities and subsequent reentry into the rural areas, and the heavy requirement for defense of the I Corps Zone, MACV does not have adequate forces at this time to resume the offensive in the remainder of the country, nor does it have adequate reserves against the contingency of simultaneous large-scale enemy offensive action throughout the country.

5. Force Requirements:

a.   Forces currently assigned to MACV, plus the residual Program Five forces yet to be delivered, are inadequate in numbers and balance to carry out the strategy and to accomplish the tasks described above in the proper priority. To contend with, and defeat, the new enemy threat, MACV has stated requirements for forces over the 525,000 ceiling imposed by Program Five.

5. A Communist Party Evaluation, 1968

I. *Great and unprecedented successes recorded in all fields during the first-month phase of the General Offensive and General Uprising.*

Since the beginning of Spring this year, the "Anti-U.S. National Salvation" resistance war of our people in the South has entered a new phase:

In this phase of General Offensive and General Uprising, after a month of continuous offensives and simultaneous uprisings conducted on all battlefields in the South, we have recorded great and unprecedented victories in all fields, inflicting on the enemy heavier losses than those he had suffered in any previous period.

1. We wore down, annihilated and disintegrated almost one-third of the puppet troops' strength, wore down and annihilated about one-fifth of U.S. combat forces, one-third of the total number of aircraft, one-third of the total number of mechanized vehicles, and an important part of U.S. and puppet material installations; destroyed and forced to surrender or withdraw one-third of the enemy military posts, driving the enemy into an unprecedentedly awkward situation: from the position of the aggressor striving to gain the initiative through a two-prong tactic [military action and rural pacification], the enemy has withdrawn into a purely passive and defensive

Lao Dong Party Training Document, March 1968, reprinted in Porter, ed. *Definitive Documentation,* II, 505–508.

position, with his forces dispersed on all battlefields in the South for the purpose of defending the towns, cities and the main lines of communications. The struggle potential and morale of U.S. and puppet troops have seriously weakened because our army and people have dealt thundering blows at them everywhere, even at their principal lairs, and because they are facing great difficulties in replenishing troops and replacing war facilities destroyed during the past month.

2. We attacked all U.S.-puppet nerve centers, occupied and exerted our control for a definite period and at varying degrees over almost all towns, cities and municipalities in the South, and destroyed and disintegrated an important part of puppet installations at all levels, seriously damaging the puppet administrative machinery.

3. We liberated additional wide areas in the countryside containing a population of 1.5 million inhabitants; consolidated and widened our rear areas, shifted immense resources of manpower and material, which had been previously robbed by the enemy in these areas, to the support of the front-line and of victory; encircled and isolated the enemy, and reduced the enemy's reserves of human and material resources, driving him into a very difficult economic and financial situation.

4. We have quantitatively and qualitatively improved our armed forces and political forces which have become outstandingly mature during the struggle in the past month. Our armed forces have progressed in many aspects, political organizations are being consolidated and have stepped forward, much progress has been realized in leadership activities and methods and we have gained richer experiences.

The above-mentioned great and unprecedented successes in all fields have strongly encouraged and motivated compatriots in towns and cities and areas under temporary enemy control to arise to seize the state power, have created a lively and enthusiastic atmosphere and inspired a strong confidence in final victory among compatriots in both the North and the South. These successes have moreover won the sympathy and support of the socialist countries and the world's progressive people (including the U.S. progressive people) for our people's revolutionary cause, seriously isolated the U.S. imperialists and their lackeys, deepened their internal contradictions and thereby weakened the U.S. will of aggression.

The above-mentioned great successes in all fields have been recorded thanks to the clear-sighted and correct policy, line and strategic determination of the Party, the wise and resolute leadership of the Party Central Committee, the correct implementation of the Party's policy and line by Nam Truong and Party committee echelons, the sacrifice and devotion of all Party cadres and members who have in an exemplary manner carried out the Party's strategic determination, the eagerness for independence and freedom of the people in the South who are ready to shed their blood in exchange for independence and freedom, the absolute loyalty to the Party's and masses' revolution of the People's armed forces who have fought with infinite courage, the great assistance from the northern rear area and brotherly socialist countries, and the sympathy and support from the world people.

We have won great successes but still have many deficiencies and weak points:

1. In the military field—From the beginning, we have not been able to annihilate much of the enemy's live force and much of the reactionary clique. Our armed forces have not fulfilled their role as "lever" and have not created favorable conditions for motivating the masses to arise in towns and cities.

2. In the political field—Organized popular forces were not broad and strong enough. We have not had specific plans for motivating the masses to the extent that they would indulge in violent armed uprisings in coordination with and supporting the military offensives.

3. The puppet troop proselyting failed to create a military revolt movement in which the troops would arise and return to the people's side. The enemy troop proselyting task to be carried out in coordination with the armed struggle and political struggle has not been performed, and inadequate attention had been paid to this in particular.

4. There has not been enough consciousness about specific plans for the widening and development of liberated rural areas and the appropriate mobilization of man-power, material resources and the great capabilities of the masses to support the front line.

5. The building of real strength and particularly the replenishment of troops and development of political forces of the infrastructure has been slow and has not met the requirements of continuous offensives and uprisings of the new phase.

6. In providing leadership and guidance to various echelons, we failed to give them a profound and thorough understanding of the Party's policy, line and strategic determination so that they have a correct and full realization of this phase of General Offensive and General Uprising. The implementation of our policies has not been sharply and closely conducted. We lacked concreteness, our plans were simple, our coordination poor, control and prodding were absent, reporting and requests for in-structions were much delayed.

The above-mentioned deficiencies and weak points have limited our successes and are, at the same time, difficulties which we must resolutely overcome.

6. A U.S. Air Force Nurse Remembers the Tet Offensive (1968), 1987

It was around that time that I Corps, up the road from us a small distance, was almost overrun. One of the guys from the ambulance group said to me, "Come on!" so I went. I remember going up to a place close to I Corps headquarters where they had a big cement landing strip. It was lined up, row after row, with Viet Cong people that had been killed the first night of Tet. How many I saw, I don't know. But I remember a Marine gunny [gunship] sergeant came in to see me and was extremely upset—he had realized that some of those bodies laying out there were women, and he was afraid he had possibly killed a woman. I explained to him that when someone has a gun and is shooting at you, you don't look to see if it's a man or a woman. This was very difficult for him to accept.

The first two days of the Tet offensive, we worked something like thirty hours without sleep.

I remember going down to the hospital. It was night, and the area was not secure at all—there were fires everywhere, and rockets and mortars were dropping all along

Excerpted from *In the Combat Zone: An Oral History of American Women in Vietnam* (Little, Brown), edited by Kathryn Marshall. Copyright © 1987 by Kathryn Marshall. Reprinted by permission of Mielanie Jackson Agency, L.L.C.

the runway. Some of the girls were running on ahead of me. When they passed the wing commander's trailer, a guy said, "Halt! Who goes there?" One of the girls said, "We're nurses. We're on our way to the hospital—" I distinctly heard her say that, but apparently he didn't. Well, I had just gotten past the guy when I heard the loudest sound of my life—even with all the rockets and sirens, I heard him move the safety catch of his M-16. I stopped dead still, right in my tracks. Very slowly I turned to him and said, "We are nurses. We are on our way to the hospital." And this little voice said, "OK, ma'am." I realized then how scared he was—how close we'd come to getting mowed down by one of our own guys.

That night at the hospital, the chaplain and I crawled around underneath beds with patients who were not able to go to the bunkers—you took as many as you could to the bunkers, and the ones who could not go to the bunkers, you put them on stretchers and got them underneath the bed. Some of them were mental patients, guys who had just broken under all the strain. Myself, I'm sure I felt some anxiety, but there was so much to be done I didn't have time to feel it. For one thing, I was in charge of the ward and had to set up the triage area. So you had to triage—you had to decide which ones were critical, which ones had to be treated first, which ones would make it and which ones wouldn't. And you had to get their medicines attended to, and get their dressings changed. You had to get them bedded down if they were going to spend the night or get them set up to go on the ambuses if they were going out on air evac—during Tet, we'd get three or four flights out before midnight, because somewhere near midnight was usually when Charlie would start hitting us.

So you constantly had something or other going—you didn't have time to stand around and worry about the next rocket attack. You just kept working as long as you could. At one point during those first thirty hours we were told to get a few moments' sleep, and some little guy said, "Here, ma'am, take part of my mattress." For ten or fifteen minutes I shared a mattress with someone, I don't know who he was. But there was no way I could get any sleep.

7. Robert Komer Recalls Tet's Impact (1968), 1987

What really surprised us about Tet—and boy it was a surprise, lemme tell you, I was there at Westy's [General Westmoreland] elbow—was that they abandoned the time-tested Mao rural strategy where the guerrillas slowly strangle the city, and only at the end do they attack the seat of imperial power directly. At Tet they infiltrated right through our porous lines and attacked some forty cities. They abandoned the countryside where they were doing very well, and boy did they get creamed in the cities. For once, the enemy, who we could not find out there in the triple canopy jungle, who could control his losses by deciding to cut and run every time we got after him, for once we could find him. He was right there shooting at us in our own headquarters, and the cost to him was enormous militarily.

I always felt that the Tet offensive was a desperate gamble on the part of Hanoi. They saw the American presence going up and up and up, they saw us beginning to

Kim Willenson, et al., *The Bad War: An Oral History of the Vietnam War;* pp. 95–97. Copyright © 1987, Newsweek, Inc. Reprinted with permission.

get a pacification program going, and they decided they better go for broke. And they did dislocate us. It cost them enormously. They had snuffed out the best of the southern cadre by sending them into the cities. We had a startling success in pacification after the Tet offensive because the enemy had sacrificed the core of his guerrilla movement. After Tet it really became an NVA war.

But he had also fatally weakened us at the center of our political structure. I mean Washington panicked. LBJ panicked. Bus Wheeler, Chairman of the Joint Chiefs, panicked. *We* [American officials in South Vietnam] didn't panic, mainly because we were too goddamn busy. But after the first day we knew we were back on top. The one place where after three days we were still out of control was Hue. Now that was two North Vietnamese divisions. And that was a big problem. They really had to be dug out, and we didn't finish it until February twenty-sixth [nearly a month after the offensive began].

It was the Tet shock to the American psyche that made me first think we might lose. And the shock in Washington was materially increased by the fact that the top command—Bunker and Westmoreland in particular—had come back in late November and reported confidently to the President that "Boss, finally all this stuff you have given us is beginning to pay off, and we look forward to 1968 as a big year of success for us." Westy has great plans for pushing back the NVA. Finally we have an elected government even though it's Thieu and not Ky, and so on.

We were not engaging in deception. We genuinely believed at the end of 1967 that we were getting on top. Hell, I was there in the top three or four Americans in Saigon. Westmoreland believed, Abrams believed, Bunker believed, and I believed that finally, with five hundred thousand goddamn troops and all that air, and pacification finally getting underway, with the Vietnamese having set up a constitution and elections, we really were winning. We couldn't quite see clearly how soon, but this wasn't public relations, this wasn't Lyndon Johnson telling us to put a face on it. We genuinely thought we were making it.

And then boom, forty towns get attacked, and they didn't believe us anymore. Bus Wheeler with his three dwarfs, [Phil] Habib, [George] Carver, and [Gen. William] DePuy, comes out about the twelfth of February. The Chiefs have decided, because they too panicked, that we're losing. Besides which, there's the *Pueblo* incident [the seizure by North Korea of an American naval vessel] in Korea, and maybe there's another Berlin crisis brewing. We have no strategic reserve; it's all either out in Vietnam or on the way. The Chiefs want to go to the President and say "We've got to call up the reserves, because if we get a second front in Korea there's not a goddamn thing we could do about it."

Wheeler comes out and asks Westmoreland "What do you need if we call up the reserves and the wraps are off." Westmoreland says "Look, if you call up the reserves and we've got five hundred thousand more men to play with, I would like two hundred thousand more." He pulls out of the drawer a request he had made in the spring of 1967, which was turned down, and has his guys burn a little midnight oil to update it. He gives it to Wheeler and he says "Look, this is to speed up the pace of victory. We think we have creamed them at Tet. They are on the run now. By God, if you'll give me the resources I'll chase them back into Cambodia, Laos and North Vietnam." He also has some plans that he tells Wheeler about: A hook around the DMZ at Cua Viet and go up there north of Dong Ha. Go into Laos. Go into Cambodia. He wants to hit the enemy in his sanctuaries. He says "We've got them on the run. They're going to retreat to the sanctuaries, and by God let's follow them in there and we'll win this war." Nothing big like taking Haiphong or anything like that. It's a conditional request. Westy is saying "If you're going to call up reserves and the other theater commanders are bidding, I too am going to put in a bid: two hundred thousand more men in two tranches, a hundred thousand in '68 and a hundred thousand in '69. I'll win your war for you in three or four years."

And then they decide not to do anything about the *Pueblo,* and the Berlin crisis proves evanescent. By the time Wheeler gets back, the whole case for calling up the reserves, which the JCS have argued for since the day we entered Vietnam, has disappeared—except the Vietnam case. But the fact that Westmoreland's conditional requisition, which is based on A. calling up the reserves and B. letting him use these troops to go into the sanctuaries, none of that is ever mentioned by Wheeler to either the President or to McNamara. By God they would have thrown him out on his ear. Can you imagine? So the perception in Washington is that we have just suffered a massive defeat and here's the commander saying "Boy, I've just won a massive victory. Give me some more guys and I'll clean this thing up fairly quickly."

So the three gnomes, Habib, Carver, and DePuy, go and talk to the President with Wheeler's patronage, and they say "Those guys in Saigon are smoking opium. We think the situation is much worse than they do. We have just been out there and we disagree with Komer's optimism, with Westmoreland's optimism, with Bunker's optimism and Thieu's optimism. Those guys just got surprised. Who wants to listen to them? We are in deep trouble, and that's why we need more men—not to insure victory but to stave off defeat." And of course this is leaked by some civilian who knows nothing of the conditionality of the request. The Chiefs never tell anybody anything. The goddamn Chiefs of Staff. Wheeler's the evil genius of the Vietnam war in my judgment.

8. Clark M. Clifford Remembers His Post-Tet Questions (1968), 1969

I took office on March 1, 1968. The enemy's Tet offensive of late January and early February had been beaten back at great cost. The confidence of the American people had been badly shaken. The ability of the South Vietnamese Government to restore order and morale in the populace, and discipline and esprit in the armed forces, was being questioned. At the President's direction, General Earle G. Wheeler, Chairman of the Joint Chiefs of Staff, had flown to Viet Nam in late February for an on-the-spot conference with General Westmoreland. He had just returned and presented the military's request that over 200,000 troops be prepared for deployment to Viet Nam. These troops would be in addition to the 525,000 previously authorized. I was directed, as my first assignment, to chair a task force named by the President to determine how this new requirement could be met. We were not

Clark M. Clifford, "A Vietnam Reappraisal: The Personal History of One Man's View and How It Evolved," *Foreign Affairs* (July 1969), pp. 609–612, 613. Reprinted by permission of *Foreign Affairs,* July 1969. Copyright © 1969 by the Council on Foreign Relations, Inc.

instructed to assess the need for substantial increases in men and matériel; we were to devise the means by which they could be provided.

My work was cut out. The task force included Secretary Rusk, Secretary Henry Fowler, Under Secretary of State Nicholas Katzenbach, Deputy Secretary of Defense Paul Nitze, General Wheeler, CIA Director Richard Helms, the President's Special Assistant, Walt Rostow, General Maxwell Taylor and other skilled and highly capable officials. All of them had had long and direct experience with Vietnamese problems. I had not. I had attended various meetings in the past several years and I had been to Viet Nam three times, but it was quickly apparent to me how little one knows if he has been on the periphery of a problem and not truly in it. Until the day-long sessions of early March, I had never had the opportunity of intensive analysis and fact-finding. Now I was thrust into a vigorous, ruthlessly frank assessment of our situation by the men who knew the most about it. Try though we would to stay with the assignment of devising means to meet the military's requests, fundamental questions began to recur over and over.

It is, of course, not possible to recall all the questions that were asked nor all of the answers that were given. Had a transcript of our discussions been made—one was not—it would have run to hundreds of closely printed pages. The documents brought to the table by participants would have totaled, if collected in one place—which they were not—many hundreds more. All that is pertinent to this essay are the impressions I formed, and the conclusions I ultimately reached in those days of exhausting scrutiny. In the colloquial style of those meetings, here are some of the principal issues raised and some of the answers as I understood them:

"Will 200,000 more men do the job?" I found no assurance that they would.

"If not, how many more might be needed—and when?" There was no way of knowing.

"What would be involved in committing 200,000 more men to Viet Nam?" A reserve call-up of approximately 280,000, an increased draft call and an extension of tours of duty of most men then in service,

"Can the enemy respond with a build-up of his own?" He could and he probably would.

"What are the estimated costs of the latest requests?" First calculations were on the order of $2 billion for the remaining four months of that fiscal year, and an increase of $10 to $12 billion for the year beginning July 1, 1968.

"What will be the impact on the economy?" So great that we would face the possibility of credit restrictions, a tax increase and even wage and price controls. The balance of payments would be worsened by at least half a billion dollars a year.

"Can bombing stop the war?" Never by itself. It was inflicting heavy personnel and matériel losses, but bombing by itself would not stop the war.

"Will stepping up the bombing decrease American casualties?" Very little, if at all. Our casualties were due to the intensity of the ground fighting in the South. We had already dropped a heavier tonnage of bombs than in all the theaters of World War II. During 1967, an estimated 90,000 North Vietnamese had infiltrated into South Viet Nam. In the opening weeks of 1968, infiltrators were coming in at three to four times the rate of a year earlier, despite the ferocity and intensity of our campaign of aerial interdiction.

"How long must we keep on sending our men and carrying the main burden of combat?" The South Vietnamese were doing better, but they were not ready yet to replace our troops and we did not know when they would be.

When I asked for a presentation of the military plan for attaining victory in Viet Nam, I was told that there was no plan for victory in the historic American sense. Why not? Because our forces were operating under three major political restrictions: The President had forbidden the invasion of North Viet Nam because this could trigger the mutual assistance pact between North Viet Nam and China; the President had forbidden the mining of the harbor at Haiphong, the principal port through which the North received military supplies, because a Soviet vessel might be sunk; the President had forbidden our forces to pursue the enemy into Laos and Cambodia, for to do so would spread the war, politically and geographically, with no discernible advantage. These and other restrictions which precluded an all-out, no-holds-barred military effort were wisely designed to prevent our being drawn into a larger war. We had no inclination to recommend to the President their cancellation.

"Given these circumstances, how can we win?" We would, I was told, continue to evidence our superiority over the enemy; we would continue to attack in the belief that he would reach the stage where he would find it inadvisable to go on with the war. He could not afford the attrition we were inflicting on him. And we were improving our posture all the time.

I then asked, "What is the best estimate as to how long this course of action will take? Six months? One year? Two years?" There was no agreement on an answer. Not only was there no agreement, I could find no one willing to express any confidence in his guesses. Certainly, none of us was willing to assert that he could see "light at the end of the tunnel" or that American troops would be coming home by the end of the year.

After days of this type of analysis, my concern had greatly deepened. I could not find out when the war was going to end; I could not find out the manner in which it was going to end; I could not find out whether the new requests for men and equipment were going to be enough, or whether it would take more and, if more, when and how much; I could not find out how soon the South Vietnamese forces would be ready to take over. All I had was the statement, given with too little self-assurance to be comforting, that if we persisted for an indeterminate length of time, the enemy would choose not to go on.

And so I asked, "Does anyone see any diminution in the will of the enemy after four years of our having been there, after enormous casualties and after massive destruction from our bombing?"

The answer was that there appeared to be no diminution in the will of the enemy. . . .

And so, after these exhausting days, I was convinced that the military course we were pursuing was not only endless, but hopeless. A further substantial increase in American forces could only increase the devastation and the Americanization of the war, and thus leave us even further from our goal of a peace that would permit the people of South Viet Nam to fashion their own political and economic institutions. Henceforth, I was also convinced, our primary goal should be to level off our involvement, and to work toward gradual disengagement.

9. Johnson Calls for Negotiations, 1968

Good evening, my fellow Americans. Tonight I want to speak to you of peace in Viet-Nam and Southeast Asia.

No other question so preoccupies our people. No other dream so absorbs the 250 million human beings who live in that part of the world. No other goal motivates American policy in Southeast Asia.

For years, representatives of our Government and others have traveled the world seeking to find a basis for peace talks.

Since last September, they have carried the offer that I made public at San Antonio.

That offer was this: that the United States would stop its bombardment of North Viet-Nam when that would lead promptly to productive discussions—and that we would assume that North Viet-Nam would not take military advantage of our restraint.

Hanoi denounced this offer, both privately and publicly. Even while the search for peace was going on, North Viet-Nam rushed their preparations for a savage assault on the people, the Government, and the allies of South Viet-Nam.

Their attack—during the Tet holidays—failed to achieve its principal objectives.

It did not collapse the elected government of South Viet-Nam or shatter its army, as the Communists had hoped.

It did not produce a "general uprising" among the people of the cities, as they had predicted.

The Communists were unable to maintain control of any of the more than 30 cities that they attacked. And they took very heavy casualties.

But they did compel the South Vietnamese and their allies to move certain forces from the countryside into the cities. They caused widespread disruption and suffering. Their attacks, and the battles that followed, made refugees of half a million human beings.

The Communists may renew their attack any day. They are, it appears, trying to make 1968 the year of decision in South Viet-Nam—the year that brings, if not final victory or defeat, at least a turning point in the struggle.

This much is clear: If they do mount another round of heavy attacks, they will not succeed in destroying the fighting power of South Viet-Nam and its allies.

But tragically, this is also clear: Many men—on both sides of the struggle— will be lost. A nation that has already suffered 20 years of warfare will suffer once again. Armies on both sides will take new casualties. And the war will go on.

There is no need for this to be so.

There is no need to delay the talks that could bring an end to this long and this bloody war.

Tonight I renew the offer I made last August—to stop the bombardment of North Viet-Nam. We ask that talks begin promptly, that they be serious talks on the substance of peace. We assume that during those talks Hanoi will not take advantage of our restraint.

Johnson speech, March 31, 1968, U.S. Department of State *Bulletin,* 58 (April 15, 1968), 481–486.

We are prepared to move immediately toward peace through negotiations. So tonight, in the hope that this action will lead to early talks, I am taking the first step to deescalate the conflict. We are reducing—substantially reducing—the present level of hostilities. And we are doing so unilaterally and at once.

Tonight I have ordered our aircraft and our naval vessels to make no attacks on North Viet-Nam, except in the area north of the demilitarized zone where the continuing enemy buildup directly threatens Allied forward positions and where the movements of their troops and supplies are clearly related to that threat.

The area in which we are stopping our attacks includes almost 90 percent of North Viet-Nam's population and most of its territory. Thus there will be no attacks around the principal populated areas or in the food-producing areas of North Viet-Nam.

Even this very limited bombing of the North could come to an early end if our restraint is matched by restraint in Hanoi. But I cannot in good conscience stop all bombing so long as to do so would immediately and directly endanger the lives of our men and our allies. Whether a complete bombing halt becomes possible in the future will be determined by events.

Our purpose in this action is to bring about a reduction in the level of violence that now exists.

It is to save the lives of brave men and to save the lives of innocent women and children. It is to permit the contending forces to move closer to a political settlement.

And tonight I call upon the United Kingdom and I call upon the Soviet Union, as cochairmen of the Geneva conferences and as permanent members of the United Nations Security Council, to do all they can to move from the unilateral act of deescalation that I have just announced toward genuine peace in Southeast Asia.

Now, as in the past, the United States is ready to send its representatives to any forum, at any time, to discuss the means of bringing this ugly war to an end.

I am designating one of our most distinguished Americans, Ambassador Averell Harriman, as my personal representative for such talks. In addition, I have asked Ambassador Llewellyn Thompson, who returned from Moscow for consultation, to be available to join Ambassador Harriman at Geneva or any other suitable place just as soon as Hanoi agrees to a conference.

I call upon President Ho Chi Minh to respond positively and favorably to this new step toward peace.

But if peace does not come now through negotiations, it will come when Hanoi understands that our common resolve is unshakable and our common strength is invincible. . . .

On many occasions I have pointed out that without a tax bill or decreased expenditures next year's deficit would again be around $20 billion. I have emphasized the need to set strict priorities in our spending. I have stressed that failure to act—and to act promptly and decisively—would raise very strong doubts throughout the world about America's willingness to keep its financial house in order.

Yet Congress has not acted. And tonight we face the sharpest financial threat in the post-war era—a threat to the dollar's role as the keystone of international trade and finance in the world. . . .

One day, my fellow citizens. there will be peace in Southeast Asia.

It will come because the people of Southeast Asia want it—those whose armies are at war tonight and those who, though threatened, have thus far been spared.

Peace will come because Asians were willing to work for it—and to sacrifice for it—and to die by the thousands for it.

But let it never be forgotten: Peace will come also because America sent her sons to help secure it.

It has not been easy—far from it. During the past 4-1/2 years, it has been my fate and my responsibility to be Commander in Chief. I lived daily and nightly with the cost of this war. I know the pain that it has inflicted. I know perhaps better than anyone the misgivings that it has aroused.

Throughout this entire long period, I have been sustained by a single principle: that what we are doing now in Viet-Nam is vital not only to the security of Southeast Asia, but it is vital to the security of every American.

Surely we have treaties which we must respect. Surely we have commitments that we are going to keep. Resolutions of the Congress testify to the need to resist aggression in the world and in Southeast Asia.

But the heart of our involvement in South Viet-Nam—under three different Presidents, three separate administrations—has always been America's own security.

And the larger purpose of our involvement has always been to help the nations of Southeast Asia become independent and stand alone, self-sustaining as members of a great world community—at peace with themselves and at peace with all others.

With such an Asia, our country—and the world—will be far more secure than it is tonight.

I believe that a peaceful Asia is far nearer to reality because of what America has done in Viet-Nam. I believe that the men who endure the dangers of battle—fighting there for us tonight—are helping the entire world avoid far greater conflicts, far wider wars, far more destruction, than this one.

The peace that will bring them home some day will come. Tonight I have offered the first in what I hope will be a series of mutual moves toward peace.

I pray that it will not be rejected by the leaders of North Viet-Nam. I pray that they will accept it as a means by which the sacrifices of their own people may be ended. And I ask your help and your support, my fellow citizens, for this effort to reach across the battlefield toward an early peace. . . .

Throughout my entire public career I have followed the personal philosophy that I am a free man, an American, a public servant, and a member of my party, in that order always and only.

For 37 years in the service of our nation, first as a Congressman, as a Senator and as Vice President and now as your President, I have put the unity of the people first. I have put it ahead of any divisive partisanship.

And in these times as in times before, it is true that a house divided against itself by the spirit of faction, of party, of region, of religion, of race, is a house that cannot stand.

There is division in the American house now. There is divisiveness among us all tonight. And holding the trust that is mine, as President of all the people, I cannot disregard the peril to the progress of the American people and the hope and the prospect of peace for all peoples.

So I would ask all Americans, whatever their personal interests or concern, to guard against divisiveness and all its ugly consequences.

Fifty-two months and 10 days ago, in a moment of tragedy and trauma, the duties of this Office fell upon me. I asked then for your help and God's, that we might continue America on its course, binding up our wounds, healing our history, moving forward in new unity, to clear the American agenda and to keep the American commitment for all of our people.

United we have kept that commitment. United we have enlarged that commitment.

Through all time to come, I think America will be a stronger nation, a more just society, and a land of greater opportunity and fulfillment because of what we have all done together in these years of unparalleled achievement.

Our reward will come in the life of freedom, peace, and hope that our children will enjoy through ages ahead.

What we won when all of our people united just must not now be lost in suspicion, distrust, selfishness, and politics among any of our people.

Believing this as I do, I have concluded that I should not permit the Presidency to become involved in the partisan divisions that are developing in this political year.

With America's sons in the fields far away, with America's future under challenge right here at home, with our hopes and the world's hopes for peace in the balance every day, I do not believe that I should devote an hour or a day of my time to any personal partisan causes or to any duties other than the awesome duties of this Office—the Presidency of your country.

Accordingly, I shall not seek, and I will not accept, the nomination of my party for another term as your President.

But let men everywhere know, however, that a strong, a confident, and a vigilant America stands ready tonight to seek an honorable peace—and stands ready tonight to defend an honored cause—whatever the price, whatever the burden, whatever the sacrifices that duty may require.

Thank you for listening.

Good night and God bless all of you.

✕ *E S S A Y S*

In the opening essay, drawn from his book, *Masters of War,* Robert Buzzanco of the University of Houston seeks to puncture what he calls "the myth of Tet." Rather than a severe military defeat for the North Vietnamese and Vietcong, as it is commonly portrayed, the Tet offensive in reality constituted a crippling strategic and political defeat for the United States and its South Vietnamese allies. The Pentagon, Buzzanco asserts, clearly understood at the time the catastrophic consequences of the Tet attacks for the United States.

William Hammond, a senior historian with the U.S. Army's Center of Military History, explores another aspect of this subject in the second selection: the nature and influence of the media's coverage of U.S. policy in the immediate aftermath of the offensive. The consistently gloomy reports emanating from the media about U.S. prospects in Vietnam following Tet, according to Hammond, helped shape American decision making. Negative stories in the press and on television reinforced doubts about U.S. policy within the Johnson administration itself, he asserts, and ultimately contributed to LBJ's decision in March 1968 to opt for a partial bombing halt and to pursue negotiations with North Vietnam.

A Crippling Defeat for the United States

ROBERT BUZZANCO

Less than two months after Westmoreland's [November 1967] tour of the White House, the halls of Congress, and the National Press Club, the MACV began to anticipate large-scale enemy action, and in late January the PAVN massed perhaps 40,000 troops for an attack on U.S. outposts at Khe Sanh, in the northwest RVN near the Laotian border, just below the seventeenth parallel. By late spring, it would become clear that Khe Sanh had been a DRVN ruse to draw U.S. troops from urban centers in anticipation of the Tet attacks. Nonetheless, Westmoreland—facing 20,000 PAVN forces with 6,000 U.S. soldiers—decided to make a stand at Khe Sanh, ultimately expending over 100,000 tons of munitions there. At the same time, he warned of the enemy's "threatening posture" in the north, and also anticipated further Communist initiatives, warning of a "country-wide show of strength just prior to Tet." Wheeler similarly warned that the MACV "is about to have the most vicious battle of the Vietnam War." And during a press briefing just days before the Tet attacks began, General Fred Weyand, one of Westmoreland's deputies, admitted that "there is no question about it, the South Vietnamese Army is outgunned by the Vietcong."

Wheeler and Weyand were right. Taking advantage of a Tet New Year cease-fire, roughly 60,000 PAVN and VC forces attacked virtually every military and political center of importance, even invading the U.S. embassy grounds. Initially Westmoreland, still focusing on the war in the northern provinces, argued that the attacks were a Communist diversion to move military emphasis from I Corps and Khe Sanh in particular, but he also claimed that the U.S. forces had the situation "well in hand" while President Johnson interpreted the attacks as a "complete failure" for the DRVN.

General Weyand, however, pointed out that the enemy had successfully concentrated on "remunerative" political and psychological objectives in its attacks. Wheeler likewise admitted that the Communist presence was expanding because "in a city like Saigon people can infiltrate easily. . . . This is about as tough to stop as it is to protect against an individual mugging in Washington, D.C." General Edward Lansdale, now serving as special assistant to Ambassador Ellsworth Bunker in Saigon, also lamented that Tet had practically "destroyed all faith in the effectiveness" of the government of the RVN, brought Vietnamese morale "dangerously low," and made southern villagers even more "vulnerable to further VC exploitation." Still worse, any possible American countermeasures appeared to Lansdale to be "rather shopworn and inadequate."

General [John] Chaisson elaborated on such problems. "We have been faced with a real battle," he admitted at a 3 February briefing in Saigon, "there is no sense in ducking it; there is no sense in hiding it." Because of its coordination, intensity, and audacity, Chaisson had to give the Communists "credit for having engineered and planned a very successful offensive in its initial phases." Moreover, the DRVN and

VC had withheld their main-force and PAVN units in many areas, with Westmoreland pointing out that the enemy "continues to maintain a strong capability to re-initiate attacks country-wide at the time and place of his choosing." Although Chaisson then concluded that the Communists' sizable casualties might eventually constitute a "great loss," his analysis had revealed the depth and nature of the MACV's dilemma as a result of the offensive.

The JCS in Washington also recognized the perilous situation, conceding that "the enemy has shown a major capability for waging war in the South." But on 3 February the brass requested an intensified bombing campaign against Hanoi, even though the scope of the Tet attacks had demonstrated the ineffectiveness of air power in preventing or containing enemy initiatives. Once more, the military's approach to deteriorating conditions in the south seemed like a non sequitur. Despite admitting that grave problems existed, the armed forces asked for bold but unsound responses that placed the burden for a decision firmly on the shoulders of civilian officials in Washington.

As Washington debated the bombing request and the full dimensions of Tet began to emerge, military officials remained worried. "From a realistic point of view," Westmoreland reported to Wheeler, "we must accept the fact that the enemy has dealt the GVN a severe blow. He has brought the war to the towns and cities and has inflicted damage and casualties on the population. . . . Distribution of the necessities has been interrupted . . . and the economy has been disrupted. . . . The people have felt directly the impact of the war." As a result, the RVN faced a "tremendous challenge" to restore stability and aid those who had suffered. But Westmoreland's report ended on an upbeat note. Because enemy losses were sizable and the VC had not gained political control in the south, he contended, the offensive had been a military failure.

Westmoreland then contradicted himself, making the crucial recognition that the enemy's objectives were finally clear and "they were primarily psychological and political." The Communists, he observed, sought to destroy southern faith in the government of the RVN, intimidate the population, and cause significant desertions among the ARVN. The DRVN's military objectives, Westmoreland admitted, may have been secondary to its political goals, and included diverting and dispersing U.S. forces throughout the south. The enemy, moreover, posed major threats at many areas, including Saigon, Khe Sanh, the DMZ, and at Hue, and more attacks were likely. Thus at the same time that Westmoreland claimed military success, he conceded that the Communists were engaged in psychological and political warfare. Throughout the next two months, his and other officers' reports would further reveal that the enemy criteria for success—undermining the southern government and military, prompting popular discontent, and destabilizing American policy—had indeed been accomplished throughout the RVN.

Such military concern was further evident when Westmoreland and the JCS, on 9 February, reported that the DRVN had added between 16,000 and 25,000 troops in the Khe Sanh area and continued to pose a threat of "major proportions." The enemy, Wheeler predicted, "is going to take his time and move when he has things under control as he would like them." To that end, PAVN infiltration had risen from 78 to 105 battalions and the ratio of U.S. and ARVN forces to Communist troops, which had been 1.7 to 1, was now at 1.4 to 1. The Communists were also applying heavy pressure in Hue and Da Nang, had cut off the much-traveled Hai Van pass, and threatened Highway 1—the major transportation route in southern Vietnam. In Quang Tri and Thua Thien, in northernmost I Corps, the controlling factor in America's performance would be logistics, which Westmoreland admitted were "now marginal at best" even though he had redirected the 101st Airborne Division and 1st Cavalry Division to the north. But further to the south, the MACV claimed, the enemy posed no serious threat. The ally, however, did.

Extensive damage to lines of communication and populated areas, heavy casualties—about 9,100 between 29 January and 10 February—and significant desertion rates had riddled the ARVN. Accordingly, Westmoreland urged RVN President Nguyen Van Thieu to lower the draft age to eighteen to increase the armed forces by at least 65,000 troops, the number depleted in the initial Tet attacks. "Realistically," the MACV commander lamented, "we must assume that it will take [the ARVN] at least six months to regain the military posture of several weeks ago." Consequently, Westmoreland, for the first time since Tet, asked for additional forces. Wheeler had encouraged the MACV commander to seek reinforcements, but admitted he could not guarantee them. "Our capabilities are limited," the JCS chair explained, with only the 82d Airborne Division and half of a Marine division available for deployment to Vietnam. Nonetheless, as Wheeler saw it, the "critical phase of the war is upon us" and the MACV should not "refrain in asking for what you believe is required under the circumstances." The JCS chair's timing in raising the reinforcement issue was appropriate, for Westmoreland had thinned out III Corps by transferring forces to the north after a PACVN strike at Lang Vei days earlier. That diversion had troubled the MACV because it needed those forces to fight the enemy's main-force units and support pacification, but the commander did not see it as an unacceptable risk.

It was "needless to say," however, that Westmoreland would welcome reinforcements to offset casualties and ARVN desertions, to react to the DRVN's replacement of southern forces, which was conditioning the MACV's own plans, and to put friendly forces in a better position to contain Communist attacks in the north and take the offensive if given an opportunity. Again Westmoreland finished an otherwise frank evaluation of the military situation in southern Vietnam with a non sequitur: high hopes that additional forces would facilitate greater U.S. success. Washington was not so enthusiastic. Having turned down the JCS's bombing request three days earlier, on 9 February the Pentagon directed the chiefs to furnish plans to provide for the emergency reinforcement of the MACV. The resulting back-channel memoranda between Westmoreland and Wheeler demonstrated that the military understood that its position in Vietnam was untenable.

Although the MACV publicly claimed that only pockets of resistance remained, Wheeler told the president that the JCS "feel that we have taken several hard knocks. The situation can get worse." In fact, at a 12 February meeting, White House officials found that Westmoreland's reports had raised as many questions and concerns as they had answered. The MACV reports from Vietnam had made the president and his advisors anxious and they had interpreted Westmoreland's messages and requests for reinforcements as indications of the ARVN's weaknesses and evidence that the troubled logistics and transport systems in the north had made deployment of additional forces imperative simply to maintain the American position.

Such candid reports continued to unnerve Johnson, who wondered "what has happened to change the situation between then [initial optimism] and now." Maxwell Taylor, the president's military advisor, also "found it hard to believe" that the bleak reports reaching Washington were "written by the same man," Westmoreland, as the earlier optimistic cables. Against the backdrop Washington began to discuss the reinforcements issue. The president and McNamara reiterated their reservations over additional deployments because of the impact of Tet and the spiraling financial burdens of the war. General Taylor, however, believed that the situation was urgent, interpreting Westmoreland's cables as proof that "the offensive in the north is against him."

Westmoreland told the White House that defeat was not imminent. Nonetheless, he admitted that he could not regain the initiative without additional forces, and he warned that "a setback is fully possible" without reinforcements, while it was "likely that we will lose ground in other areas" if the MACV had to continue diverting forces to I CTZ. But Westmoreland still maintained that the enemy's strong position at Khe Sanh and the DMZ, not the VC infrastructure in the cities, was the most serious threat, and if it was not contained the U.S. position in the northern RVN would be in jeopardy. The MACV commander also expected another Communist offensive in the north, which he pledged to contain either with *"reinforcements, which I desperately need,"* or at the risk of diverting even greater numbers of forces from other areas. Thus far, Westmoreland added, Vietnam had been a limited war with limited objectives and resources, but, as a result of Tet, "we are now in a new ballgame where we face a determined, highly disciplined enemy, full mobilized to achieve a quick victory."

Based on such communication with Westmoreland, the JCS developed its analysis for McNamara. As of 11 February, the chiefs noted, the PAVN and VC had attacked thirty-four provincial towns, sixty-four district towns, and all of the autonomous cities. Despite heavy losses, the enemy had yet to commit the vast proportion of its northern forces, while the PAVN had already replaced much of its losses and equaled U.S. troop levels in I Corps. Westmoreland and his deputy Creighton Abrams were moreover concerned that the ARVN was relying even more on American firepower to avoid combat and that widespread looting was alienating the population. The ARVN, additionally, had suffered its worst desertion rates to that point. Its average battalion was at 50 percent strength, its average Ranger Battalion was at 43 percent strength, and five of nine airborne battalions were not combat-effective, according to MACV standards.

Even when using questionable criteria such as enemy losses or inability to capture control of government as measures of military success, the MACV and JCS appraisals pointed out increasing problems. As a result, the chiefs had strong reservations about reinforcing the MACV. Admiral Sharp had urged the White House to meet Westmoreland's request, arguing that additional forces could exploit enemy weaknesses. If U.S. officials had underestimated Communist strength, he added, "we will need them even more." Nonetheless the JCS warned that transferring forces to Vietnam would drain the strategic reserve and exacerbate shortages of skilled personnel and essential equipment. Thus for the first time the chiefs rejected a MACV request for additional support. "At long last," the *Pentagon Papers* authors explained, "the resources were beginning to be drawn too thin, the assets became unavailable, the support base too small."

The JCS had rejected Westmoreland's plea for more troops principally to pressure the president to activate Reserves in the United States, or face responsibility for continued deterioration. . . .

Wheeler visited Westmoreland from 23 to 25 February and filed his report with the president on 27 February. The chair's appraisals contrasted sharply with public optimism about the war. As Westmoreland publicly continued to claim success—concluding that he did "not believe Hanoi can hold up under a long war"—Wheeler told reporters that he saw "no early end to this war," and cautioned that Americans "must expect hard fighting to continue." Privately, Wheeler was more pessimistic.

The JCS chair, a skilled veteran of Pentagon politics, was losing confidence in the MACV commander and, as Clark Clifford put it, "presented an even grimmer assessment of the Tet offensive than we had heard from Westmoreland and Bunker." There is no doubt that the enemy launched a major, powerful nationwide assault," Wheeler observed. "This offensive has by no means run its course. In fact, we must accept the possibility that he has already deployed additional elements of his home army." The JCS chair also admitted that American commanders in Vietnam agreed that the margin of success or survival had been "very small indeed" during the first weeks of Tet attacks. The enemy, with combat-available forces deployed in large numbers throughout the RVN, had "the will and capability to continue" and its "determination appears to be unshaken." Although the enemy's future plans were not clear, he warned, "the scope and severity of his attacks and the extent of his reinforcements are presenting us with serious and immediate problems." Several PAVN divisions remained untouched, and troops and supplies continued to move southward to supplement the 200,000 enemy forces available for hostilities. The MACV, however, still faced major logistics problems due to enemy harassment and interdiction and the massive redeployment of U.S. forces to the north. Westmoreland in fact had deployed half of all maneuver battalions to I Corps while stripping the rest of the RVN of adequate reserves.

Worse, Wheeler, though surprisingly pleased with the ARVN's performance, nonetheless questioned its ability to continue, pointing out that the army was on the defensive and had lost about one-quarter of its pre-Tet strength. Similarly, the government of the RVN had survived Tet, but with diminished effectiveness. Thieu and Ky faced "enormous" problems, with morale at the breaking point, 15,000 civilian casualties, and a flood of about 1 million additional refugees, one-third in the area of Saigon—all part of the huge task of reconstruction, which would require vast amounts of money and time. The offensive moreover had undermined pacification. Civic action programs, Wheeler admitted, had been "brought to a halt. . . . To a large extent, the VC now control the countryside." He added that the guerrillas, via recruiting and infiltration, were rebuilding their infrastructure and its overall recovery was "likely to be rapid." Clearly, then, the military had developed its analyses and policy recommendations in February 1968 from candid, at times desolate, views of the effects of Tet. Later claims of success aside, in February Wheeler at best found the situation "fraught with opportunities as well as dangers" and conceded that only the timely reaction of U.S. forces had prevented Communist control in a dozen or so places." Whereas Harold K. Johnson plainly admitted that "we suffered a loss," Wheeler, more euphemistically, admitted that "it was a very near thing."

Having been concerned up to Wheeler's visit with the shorter-term results of Tet, the military understood clearly throughout February 1968 that the enemy offensive had created dynamic new problems for its forces in Vietnam. Subsequently, Tet entered its "second phase" and the MACV and JCS began to discuss longer-term policy in the wake of the enemy's attacks. Yet, in doing so, service leaders continued to acknowledge problems in the RVN but still rejected developing new approaches to the war. Instead, they insisted that the MACV simply continue its war of attrition, but with a huge increase in American soldiers—206,000 troops and the activation of 280,000 reservists. With such a proposal, which "simply astonished Washington" and "affect[ed] the course of the war and American politics forever," in Clark Clifford's words, the brass had conceded that substantive success would not be forthcoming, but left it to the president to accept responsibility for subsequent military failures in Indochina. Wheeler's reports and request caused a political hurricane in Washington in February 1968 and, since then, have had central places in considerations of Tet. While scholars correctly point to Wheeler's candid assessments as proof of American problems in Vietnam, they tend to see the subsequent reinforcement request as a military response to the crisis: having failed to stem the enemy's advances with 525,000 forces, the military sought a 40 percent increase in troop strength to either stave off defeat or take the offensive, and also to replenish the strategic reserve at home. There was, however, an essentially political character to the proposal for additional troops. Even before the crises of February and March 1968, military and civilian leaders understood that the political environment in Washington had made reinforcement—especially in such vast numbers—impossible. . . .

Thus, by mid-February, as Clark Clifford has pointed out, "the President did not wish to receive a formal request from the military for reinforcements, for fear that if it leaked he would be under great pressure to respond immediately." More important, Clifford added that the military was conscious of the situation and so "a delicate minuet took place to create the fiction that no request was being made." Similarly, Philip Habib, a State Department specialist in East Asian affairs, reported that there was "serious disagreement in American circles in Saigon over the 205,000 request." White House aide John Roche elaborated that "Johnson hadn't under any circumstances considered 206,000 men. Wheeler figured this Tet offensive was going to be his handle for getting the shopping list okayed." Along those lines, Ambassador Bunker, in late February, had warned Westmoreland about asking for those troops, explaining, as Neil Sheehan reports, that such reinforcement was now "politically impossible" even if the president had wanted it, which was also more unlikely than ever. To say the least, the military's candid, bleak outlooks throughout the first month of Tet followed by the huge reinforcement request had badly unnerved the White House.

Even worse, the dollar–gold crisis was becoming more acutely dangerous in February and March 1968. In January, the president, alarmed by a $7 billion balance-of-payments deficit for the fourth quarter of 1967, proposed a tax surcharge to finance the war. Congress, no doubt annoyed by Johnson's repeated attempts to shift the burden for economic sacrifice onto it, stalled, thereby creating even greater anxiety among European bankers. At home, even before Tet, Gardner Ackley was warning of a "possible spiraling world depression" if the dollar and gold issues were not resolved, while Allan Sproul, past head of the New York Federal Reserve

Bank, lamented that the Vietnam War was "at the core" of America's "domestic and international political, social, and economic difficulties." By late February, as Senator Jacob Javits called for an end to the gold pool and another $118 million in bullion left the United States in just two days, "the specter of 1929 haunted [the president] daily."

By mid-March European banks had withdrawn another $1 billion in gold, and, on 14 March, the U.S. Treasury lost $372 million in bullion, and, fearing the possible loss of another billion the next day, closed the gold market. Administration officials then called an emergency meeting in Washington of European central bankers, who rejected an American request to give up their right to claim gold for dollars from the U.S. Treasury. The Europeans essentially told the president that they would restrain their gold purchases only if he put the defense of the dollar above all other economic considerations, including Vietnam. Given the confluence of military and economic calamities that had struck Washington in February and March 1968, the administration had to acknowledge that further troop increases in Indochina threatened not only the U.S. economy, but America's position in the world political economy as well. Tet, it is not an exaggeration to suggest, marked the end of America's postwar hegemony.

Accordingly, Johnson, already floored by the dollar–gold crisis and further alarmed by the Wheeler report and similar evaluations from the CIA and SA officials, directed incoming Secretary of Defense Clark Clifford to begin an "A to Z Reassessment" of the war. Johnson charged the Clifford group with reviewing current and alternative courses of action, with two questions central to its study: Should the United States stay the course in Vietnam? And could the MACV succeed even with 206,000 additional forces? . . .

Only months after Westmoreland had forecast America's bright prospects in Vietnam, the Communist Tet offensive had torpedoed U.S. efforts and shocked a hopeful nation. Yet in early 1968 and thereafter supporters of the war claimed that Tet was in fact a decisive American victory undermined at home by antiwar forces. Such claims, however, are disingenuous at best, for American military leaders themselves had consistently recognized that the enemy offensive was laying bare the contradictions inherent in the U.S. war in Indochina. Despite committing billions of dollars and 500,000 men, and inflicting huge casualties and massive hardship, the United States could neither contain the enemy nor protect its allies. Communist attacks had continued throughout 1968, and the DRVN retained the capacity to match American escalation of the war. American forces also suffered sizable losses of their own in early 1968. If, as Westmoreland and others contend, such conditions constituted a decisive military victory, then America had been waging war through the looking glass.

On a more salient level, the military also recognized that Tet had been a devastating political failure for the United States. Accusations of being "stabbed in the back" notwithstanding, the military realized that political factors in Vietnam, far more than in Washington, had doomed the American effort. Westmoreland and others had recognized the DRVN's conception of political warfare, understood the enemy's psychological goals, and lamented the RVN's instability. The military also understood that the already volatile domestic situation seemed ready to boil over. Media and public perceptions of Tet, as military leaders charged at the outset of the offensive and repeatedly since, had made any attempt to escalate the war politically risky. Most important, America's position in the world economy verged on collapse, in principal measure because of its vast commitment to Indochina. When considered in light of such factors and the president's, defense secretary's, and key political leaders' misgivings about, and opposition to, an increased commitment, reinforcement became politically impossible. Yet after the shock of Tet, Westmoreland and Wheeler chose to continue their war of attrition and asked for 206,000 more troops and 280,00 reservists. Why was American military thought so apparently barren in early 1968?

The military implicitly expected and understood the impact of its proposals. Operating from the recognition that the war had descended to its nadir and that reinforcement would not be forthcoming, U.S. officers made their immense request for troops in order to defer their share of responsibility for the American failure in Vietnam onto the White House. Although recognizing the American dilemma in Vietnam, Westmoreland and Wheeler discounted advice to change strategy and instead proposed a massive escalation of the war, which necessarily would have made the president accountable for the failed conduct of Vietnam policy. Bewildered by the enemy's initiative and under increasing fire at home, the military asked for more of the same and forced Johnson to choose between the Scylla of reinforcement and its attendant consequences or the Charybdis of staying the course and bearing responsibility for the continued stasis. More than simply conniving for troops, military leaders sought to immunize themselves from greater culpability for the U.S. failure in Indochina and in the process forced the president into an intractable political dilemma. By rejecting the military's request to escalate, Johnson provided the services with an alibi for future failures, as the emergence of postwar revisionism on the war attests.

U.S. forces continued to fight for nearly five years after the Tet Offensive, but America's fate was effectively sealed by mid-1968. Intervention in Vietnam, as so many officers had predicted for over a decade, had become a catastrophe. American soldiers kept pouring into Southeast Asia, pilots dropped millions of tons of bombs on Vietnam, north and south, and U.S. weapons killed untold numbers of enemy soldiers and civilians and ravaged a country. Yet William Westmoreland was no closer to being a victorious commander in the spring of 1968 than when he had arrived in Saigon in 1964. Tet, as it were, had become the U.S. obituary in Vietnam.

The MACV commander, Wheeler, Sharp, and others, however, conducted their political warfare more skillfully. The president who never seemed to determine clearly his own objectives and strategies for Vietnam, had simultaneously escalated the war to unexpected levels while trying to limit it because of the political implications of total war. Lyndon Johnson, his critics would later allege, had tied his commanders' hands throughout the war, especially in early 1968. By that time, civilian, and military, leaders had already established patterns of behavior that had more to do with avoiding blame for failure than finding a solution to the war. Under such circumstances, victory, no matter how defined, was not possible. Escalation and attrition, it was just as obvious, did not constitute a viable strategy. American forces, no matter the number deployed or tactics used, could not stop the enemy. Lyndon Johnson and Robert McNamara, for all their shortcomings, did not cause America's defeat. The Vietnamese Communists did.

Tet and the Media

WILLIAM HAMMOND

Westmoreland viewed the [Tet] offensive as a diversion in preparation for the long-awaited attack in the I Corps Tactical Zone. Confident in his ability to repel it, he told Wheeler that the enemy's concentration on high-visibility targets indicated a desire to have some sort of psychological effect on world public opinion. Hanson W. Baldwin made the same point in the *New York Times* the next morning.

If Westmoreland was composed and well collected, the Saigon correspondents were aghast. Unable to reach most of the fighting around the country, they centered their attention on Saigon and the target most accessible to them, the U.S. embassy. Hearing great volumes of fire coming from the building's direction, they took the word of officers and military policemen at the scene and concluded that Communist commandos had penetrated at least the lower floors of the facility. In contact with the embassy at all times and aware that it remained sealed to the enemy, the State Department attempted to correct the erroneous reports that followed. Westmoreland did the same at an impromptu press conference at the scene shortly after U.S. forces regained control of the compound. Coming in the wake of the president's optimism campaign, the offensive had nonetheless so wounded official credibility that some in the press continued to place their reliance in the word of their initial low-level sources, who in theory had nothing to sell. As a result, CBS played Westmoreland's comment on the 1 February edition of the morning news, but NBC anchorman Chet Huntley told his audience that enemy snipers in the embassy and on nearby rooftops had fired down on the rescuers in the courtyard—the exact opposite of what had happened. As late as 2 February, the *New York Times* was still willing to publish an article asserting that guerrillas had penetrated at least the first floor of the embassy. The newspaper added in an editorial that the success of the enemy's offensive threw both the administration's claims of progress and the competence of the South Vietnamese armed forces into serious doubt. Other journals were just as harsh.

A news conference Westmoreland held on 1 February did little to ease the reporters' concerns. Under instructions from President Johnson to provide a brief personal comment to the press each day in order to reassure the American public, the general claimed that MACV had foreseen attacks during the new year even though it had failed to predict an initiative during Tet itself. He then explained that the enemy was in the midst of a three-phase campaign. The first had been intended to bleed allied forces at Loc Ninh and Dak To. The second, in progress, targeted government facilities. The third would be an all-or-nothing effort in South Vietnam's northernmost regions. Overall, Westmoreland said, the enemy had lost fifty-eight hundred killed in the first days of the offensive alone—so many that it would take him weeks and months to recover. When Robert Schakne of CBS asked for an assessment of the situation, the general responded that the Viet Cong had exposed themselves to American firepower and had suffered a great defeat. He added that the attacks were only diversions from the enemy's main effort, which would come across the Demilitarized Zone and around Khe Sanh. To many reporters, Westmoreland seemed to be mouthing platitudes while the wolf was at the gate.

Gloom pervaded the news stories that followed. Orr Kelly of the *Washington Star* stressed that the United States had been caught off guard. Mike Wallace remarked on CBS that the offensive had "demolished the myth" that allied strength controlled South Vietnam. *New York Daily News* reporter Jerry Greene characterized the attack as a "potent propaganda victory" for the enemy that had clouded a steady stream of official American optimism. The *New York Times* observed, "These are not the deeds of an enemy whose fighting efficiency has 'progressively declined' and whose morale is 'sinking fast,' as United States military officials put it in November."

According to Westmoreland, the Johnson administration fell into "great consternation" at the news from Saigon. The U.S mission attempted to restore balance by assuring the president that the situation was under control, but as Westmoreland observed, the effort was more than offset by the "doom and gloom" emanating from South Vietnam. Adding to the effect was a chorus of alarmed comments from Congress, where supporters of the war sided with Westmoreland but numerous middle-of-the-road members expressed shock and dismay. Even the supporters were none too happy. "What happened?" one stalwart remarked. "I thought we were supposed to be winning this war."

Public affairs officers in Saigon could do little to counter the trend. With communications from the field lagging by as much as a day, they had only fragments to work with. On the morning of 1 February, as a result, they could announce only that there had been firing around Hue and that some portions of the city's northern sectors had been surrounded. They had little more to say that evening, by which time almost the entire city was in enemy hands.

MACV's information officers attempted to clarify the situation at Hue and elsewhere by having the director of the command's operations center, Brig. Gen. John Chaisson, USMC, brief reporters. Although predicting erroneously that Hue would be cleared in a few days, Chaisson admitted that U.S. intelligence had failed to predict the full dimensions of the attack. He then credited the enemy with "a very successful offensive, in its initial phases." The general's candor did not sit well with some. The next day, the chief of MACV intelligence, Brig. Gen. Phillip B. Davidson, Jr., attempted to explain away the general's admission that the breadth and violence of the offensive had been a surprise. American commanders had recognized the enemy's ability to attack at Tet, he declared, and had expected some sort of offensive all along. Chaisson, he said, had admitted only that he *personally* had been surprised.

President Johnson also spoke. At a White House ceremony on 1 February and at an impromptu news conference the next day, he asserted that the enemy would fail again and again because America would never yield. Indeed, he said, even if the enemy attempted to twist what had happened into some sort of psychological victory, Communist forces had lost 10,000 men, while at most 249 Americans and 500 South Vietnamese had fallen. Although time lines would have to be adjusted, he added, he saw no reason to revise his assertion that "we have made progress."

Comparing the various versions of what had happened, many in the press questioned the body counts Johnson had cited and proclaimed their suspicion that the attacks had hardly been as well anticipated as Davidson and others had said. Cynthia Parsons, for one, made it a point to remark in the *Christian Science Monitor* that although one general had admitted the attack had been a surprise, another had all but denied it. If MACV had been so certain that the enemy would attack, the *New Republic* added in an editorial entitled "Misled in Every Sense," why had U.S. and South Vietnamese forces been so ill prepared to repel the assault? "Or is forewarned," the magazine asked, "not forearmed in this weird war?" Quoting *New York Times* columnist James Reston, the magazine's editors went on to charge, "We are the flies that captured the flypaper."

General Westmoreland responded to the criticisms by instructing his public affairs officers to screen measures of progress carefully. Even so, he believed that Hanoi had exposed its forces to the full fury of American firepower and that MACV's body count was more than plausible. "We seldom know the number of killed . . . resulting from B-52, tactical air, and artillery strikes," he told reporters on 25 February, ". . . [or] how many die from their wounds. . . . These unknowns more than offset the relatively small inaccuracies of our accounting system."

Although time and events would ultimately convert many reporters to Westmoreland's point of view, for the enemy had indeed suffered grievous casualties during the offensive, there was little the general could do about another aspect of the offensive that drew the attention of the press—apparent violations of the laws of war. The issue arose on the morning of 2 February, when AP photographer Eddie Adams photographed Brig. Gen. Nguyen Ngoc Loan, the chief of South Vietnam's National Police, in the act of summarily executing a newly captured Viet Cong officer. The AP filed a brief story, quoting Loan, to accompany the picture. The Viet Cong had "killed many Americans," the general said, "and many of my people." A film of the incident by NBC News cameraman Vo Suu, slightly edited to eliminate the gore, played that evening on NBC's Huntley-Brinkley Report. Limited by time, correspondent Howard Tuckner contributed only the barest commentary. Noting little more than that the victim had been the commander of a Viet Cong commando unit and that he had been "roughed up," the reporter let the film speak for itself. The man approached. The general fired. The man fell.

Adams's picture appeared in virtually every important newspaper in the United States. Many of the journals that commented attempted to balance it with some allusion to enemy atrocities. The *New York Times,* for example, published it with a photograph of a South Vietnamese officer holding the body of his murdered child. Both the *New York Daily News* and the *Chicago Daily News* implied that Loan's act paled in the context of the violence occurring in South Vietnam on both sides. The *Chicago Tribune* charged that the antiwar movement was quick to exaggerate allied atrocities but said little when the Viet Cong obliterated whole villages.

These attempts at balance were lost in the reaction that set in almost immediately. A report by the AP led the way. If the enemy kept lists of men to be killed, it maintained, government troops also executed enemy prisoners, sometimes with the approval of their American advisers. To demonstrate the point, the story's author quoted an anonymous U.S. Army sergeant. "If I had my way," the man had said, "we would execute on the spot every Viet Cong and Viet Cong suspect we catch."

General Wheeler responded in a widely publicized letter to Congressman Henry S. Reuss of Wisconsin. Alluding to the picture of the officer holding his murdered child, he contended that the South Vietnamese army was far more scrupulous in its handling of civilians and prisoners than the Communists. The U.S. mission, meanwhile, warned the South Vietnamese on their treatment of prisoners and obtained the removal of several execution posts they had erected in Saigon's central market.

Despite these efforts, the issue of American and South Vietnamese atrocities gained rather than lost momentum. On 19 February, the *New York Times* and the *Washington Post,* along with a number of other papers, published an AP photograph of a South Vietnamese marine shooting an enemy captive. An accompanying article quoted an unnamed American adviser who had told newsmen. "We usually kill the seriously wounded Viet Cong. . . . The hospitals are so full . . . there is no room for the enemy . . . [and] when you've seen five-year-old girls with their eyes blind-folded . . . and bullets in their brains, you look for revenge. I saw two little girls that dead [*sic*] yesterday. One hour ago I shot a Viet Cong." The State and Defense Departments warned MACV that if the soldier was telling the truth rather than merely attempting to impress a gullible newsman, a serious violation had occurred that could implicate U.S. commanders if they failed to investigate. The command did what it could, but with eyewitnesses unwilling to come forward, legal action against offenders proved impossible.

In the end, the pictures of General Loan's atrocity probably had little effect on American public opinion. Twenty million people watched Huntley-Brinkley on the night Suu's film played, but NBC received only ninety letters on the subject. Fifty-six accused the network of bad taste. The rest complained that the film had appeared at a time when children could watch. Few alluded to the conflict in Vietnam. War, apparently, was war.

By the end of the first week in February, heavy fighting was continuing in Saigon's suburbs and other areas, and the enemy retained possession of much of Hue, but the Communists had failed to achieve their main military objectives. Although they had sought to spark a general uprising among South Vietnam's people, none had occurred. Instead, the bulk of the nation's armed forces had fought hard.

The offensive, however, had still done drastic damage to South Vietnam's economy and to many of its cities. South Vietnamese troops had looted parts of Can Tho, My Tho, and Chau Duc in the Mekong delta, and they and their American allies had brought so much gratuitous firepower to bear in rooting out the enemy that they had devastated towns such as Can Tho and Ben Tre. The net effect was that the inhabitants of many areas and the government functionaries who served them seemed immobilized by shock. General Westmoreland set up a special working group to speed recovery, but over the short term the going was difficult. Money ran out and red tape abounded.

The press covered it all, particularly the suffering both sides had imposed on innocent civilians. "At what point do you turn your heavy guns and fighter bombers on your own city?" Peter Arnett asked after visiting Ben Tre. "When does the infliction of civilian casualties become irrelevant as long as the enemy is destroyed?" Observing that the South Vietnamese command had declined to authorize air strikes and artillery fire at Ben Tre until the total destruction of their forces seemed imminent, the reporter answered the question with a comment by an unnamed U.S. adviser who had said, "It became necessary to destroy the town to save it." The *New York*

Times seized upon the remark as soon as it appeared. So did *Time.* From there it passed into the lore of the war, to become one of the most serviceable icons of the antiwar movement.

Reporters also began to evaluate the damage the offensive had caused to pacification. While some observed cautiously that the effects of the attack on the pacification effort had yet to be gauged because conditions in the countryside were still unclear. Lee Lescaze and Ward Just of the *Washington Post,* Charles Mohr of the *New York Times,* and the editors of *Newsweek,* to name just a few, all agreed that the program was a shambles. That the enemy had moved through the countryside without betrayal by the people, *Newsweek* claimed, made a mockery of Robert Komer's claim prior to the attack that 67 percent of South Vietnam's people lived in secure areas.

A report by the Office of the Assistant Secretary of Defense for Systems Analysis agreed with the reporters' analysis, noting that the enemy largely controlled South Vietnam's countryside and that pacification "as currently conceived" was dead. The U.S. mission was of a different mind. If pacification teams had withdrawn from the countryside to fight in the cities during Tet, Ambassador Bunker observed on the 18 February edition of the CBS News program *Face the Nation,* so had enemy forces. Tet was a revered tradition among the Vietnamese people, Bunker added, and had not been violated in over a thousand years. In that sense, by breaking with custom, the enemy had forfeited the respect of many South Vietnamese.

Robert Komer attempted to give reporters a framework for judging the program at a 24 February news conference. Conceding that pacification had been damaged, he noted nevertheless that the enemy had bypassed secure areas in order to ensure that his plans remained secret. By so doing, he had left up to 80 percent of all pacification teams undisturbed. Komer claimed that the main effects of the offensive in the countryside were psychological, with many people living in fear that the Communists would come back. Although six months might elapse before the situation returned to normal, he added, pacification would recover.

Komer's message was lost on the press. Concentrating on the negatives the administrator had admitted to, the *New York Times,* for one, headlined its account of the session "U.S. Admits Blow to Pacification." In all fairness, Komer's points were difficult to see at the time. Although the Office of Systems Analysis ultimately retracted its conclusion that pacification was dead, for example, it refused to relinquish the idea until well into September.

Circumstances in the northern portion of South Vietnam tended to confirm the opinion of many journalists that the war was going sour. Reporters had only to look toward the old imperial capital at Hue and toward the marine base at Khe Sanh to its west for evidence that seemed to confirm that conclusion. For if MACV continued to issue optimistic bulletins on Hue until as late as 8 February, every reporter knew that the enemy held most of the city and that the fighting there had been bitter.

Involving the sort of house-to-house fighting that had occurred during World War II, the battle for Hue, was in fact, relatively easy for the press to cover. Although the South Vietnamese did most of the fighting and suffered four times more casualties than the U.S. Marines at the scene, reporters found the easiest going with the Americans, where they at least knew the language and where the American public expected them to be. As a result, with a few exceptions, most exaggerated the marines' role in the battle, describing how the Americans were fighting "foot by blood soaked foot" while saying little about the South Vietnamese and their efforts. In the end, nonetheless, the circumstances may have worked to the benefit of the South Vietnamese. For if many of their units did well in the battle, others did so poorly that, at one point, three battalions of South Vietnamese marines—the strongest force in Hue's Citadel—took three days to advance less than half a city block. The Saigon correspondents never noted that failure and others like it because they were preoccupied with the American effort.

As the fighting continued, Hue's Communist captors began to execute government officials, student leaders, priests, bonzes, ministers, and anyone else who might ultimately question their aims, consigning, in all, as many as four thousand noncombatants to mass graves. Informed by the city's mayor that executions were occurring, the AP carried the story on 11 February along with the *Washington Post* and the *New York Times,* but the rest of the press was slow to follow. On a slow news day the story might have received more of a hearing, but the mayor was well known as an incompetent, and reporters already had more than enough to do. Even MACV hesitated when it heard the word. Unable, at first, to confirm the mayor's account, it waited until 9 March, two weeks after the fighting in Hue had ended, before issuing a communique on what had happened. By then the story was out of date, and MACV's statement seemed just another attempt by U.S. spokesmen to publicize enemy atrocities.

If the battle for Hue received heavy coverage, the press paid far more attention to events at Khe Sanh. Westmoreland had predicted that the main enemy threat would come from the north. Looking in that direction, the Saigon correspondents recognized that the enemy was on the defensive at Hue but saw as well that his forces surrounded some six thousand marines at Khe Sanh. They assumed that a climactic battle was in the making similar to the one that had occurred during the French Indochina War in which Communist forces had trapped a large French force at Dien Bien Phu. President Johnson was thinking the same thought and becoming increasingly disturbed. With criticism of the war rising in the United States and with his own political fortunes at stake, he could ill afford the bad publicity that would accompany the annihilation of a major American force.

Westmoreland and Wheeler attempted to reassure the president. In fact, they noted, the situation at Khe Sanh was hardly as dire as the one at Dien Bien Phu. The United States could reinforce and resupply the base by air, and B-52 bombers could pound the enemy's positions at will. Johnson was unimpressed. Aware that Westmoreland was preparing contingency plans for the employment of nuclear weapons, he told Wheeler he had no wish to use them to save the base. Westmoreland responded by telling the president that ample nonnuclear means existed to protect the base. He told Wheeler privately, however, that he was unprepared to rule out the option if the enemy launched a major invasion across South Vietnam's northern border. His troops were stretched too thin.

For that reason, Westmoreland continued planning for the possible use of nuclear weapons, but by then too many knew what he was doing. On 5 February, an anonymous telephone caller informed the Senate Committee on Foreign Relations that one of the foremost experts on nuclear weapons in the United States had recently traveled to South Vietnam with several other scientists. Suspicious, the committee took up the issue in closed session, where several senators expressed concern that the president might feel compelled to use an atomic bomb if Khe Sanh were in danger of falling. Shortly after the meeting, the antiwar candidate for the Democratic presidential nomination, Senator Eugene J. McCarthy of Minnesota, brought the issue into the open at a news conference.

With the press playing the story in full and with a crescendo of criticism developing around the world, the Johnson administration labeled McCarthy's allegation false and unfair speculation. The president himself told newsmen that the secretaries of state and defense had never "considered or made a recommendation in any respect to the employment of nuclear weapons." Meanwhile, Admiral Sharp quietly instructed Westmoreland to discontinue planning and to lock up all written materials generated by the project.

While the controversy over nuclear weapons played itself out, the situation at Khe Sanh grew ominous. Early on the morning of 7 February, Communist forces employing tanks for the first time in the war attacked the Lang Vei Special Forces camp, eight kilometers southwest of the base. Two hundred of the facility's five hundred South Vietnamese defenders went down, along with ten of their twenty-four American advisers. Artillery and rocket fire pounded Khe Sanh itself, and the enemy launched a series of bitter assaults against marine outposts on nearby hills. Although the marines defending the base were never in danger of annihilation, they were well within range of the enemy's artillery, which cost them 125 killed and 812 wounded between 1 January and 25 February.

The situation proved irresistible to the American news media, particularly after 24 February, when the enemy's withdrawal from Hue left Khe Sanh the only major combat story in South Vietnam for reporters to cover. Like the president, the Saigon correspondents were particularly interested in the similarities between the battle and the siege at Dien Bien Phu. MACV attempted to put the issue to rest by adopting the same line with them that Westmoreland had taken with Johnson, but reporters found the topic too compelling to drop as long as a chance existed that an attack would occur. As late as 8 March, when it was becoming clear that no enemy attack on the base would materialize, reporter Charles Mohr felt justified in observing that U.S. firepower had yet to silence the enemy's artillery and that the Communists' delay in attacking resembled the slow strangulation that had befallen the French force at Dien Bien Phu fourteen years earlier.

Although the battle figured in 38 percent of all stories on Vietnam filed by the AP from outside of Saigon during February and March and played heavily in newspapers across the United States, television news far outstripped the print media in the prominence it gave the subject. CBS, for example, devoted 28 percent of its filmed reports from Vietnam during the period to the battle. Constrained by the nature of television to show action but unable to feature combat because none occurred within camera range, many of these reports featured the damage the enemy was causing to the marines while neglecting the havoc American artillery and B-52s were inflicting on the besiegers. "Here the North Vietnamese decide who lives and who dies," CBS correspondent Murray Fromson intoned solemnly from the base on 14 February, ". . . and sooner or later they will make the move that will seal the fate of Khe Sanh."

Television correspondents also exaggerated aircraft losses at the base. . . .

. . . [B]y the end of February 1968, pessimism pervaded the American news media. Cataloging an accumulation of woes from high crime rates to a "looming bloodbath" at Khe Sanh, a *Life* headline on 23 February avowed "Wherever We Look, Something's Wrong." Shortly after that, following a two-week fact-finding trip to South Vietnam, CBS anchorman Walter Cronkite aired his own misgivings in a widely discussed television documentary. "To say we are closer to victory today," he said, "is to believe . . . optimists who have been wrong in the past. To suggest we are on the edge of defeat is to yield to unreasonable pessimists. To say we are mired in stalemate seems the only realistic yet unsatisfactory conclusion. . . . It is increasingly clear . . . that the only rational way out would be to negotiate—not as victims, but as an honorable people who . . . did the best they could."

Newsman Howard K. Smith provided one of the few counterpoints to the mood. Charging that the press was "contributing to the confusion and frustration now damaging the American spirit," he resigned his position at ABC News because he felt he was no longer participating in an age of great journalism. Press coverage of Eddie Adams's picture of General Loan executing the Viet Cong was an example of what he meant, he said. No one had made "even a perfunctory acknowledgment . . . of the fact that such executions, en masse, are the Viet Cong way of war."

Whatever the pessimism of the press, however, the majority of Americans went their own way. Queried by the Gallup Poll on whether they considered the war a mistake, 45 percent responded "yes," the same percentage as in December 1965; 43 percent said "no," a drop of 3 points; and 12 percent had no opinion. Even more telling, the number of those who considered themselves "hawks" on the war rose 4 percentage points between December and February, while those who saw themselves as "doves" fell by the same percentage. The number of those expressing confidence in the government's military policies in South Vietnam rose from 61 to 74 percent. Queried by Louis Harris on whether a bombing halt would hasten the chances for peace, 71 percent of respondents favored continuing the bombing, a rise of 8 points over the previous October, while the number of those favoring a halt fell from 26 to 15 percent.

If Americans were unwilling to repudiate the war, they nonetheless appeared increasingly dissatisfied with their president. Willing to back any decision he made, they saw little forward motion on his part. Instead, after making a few public comments after the start of the offensive, he left all efforts to marshal public opinion to his staff and aides. The air of indecision that hung about his policies as a result took a toll on his standing in the polls, where disapproval of his handling of the war rose from 47 to 63 percent by the end of February. By the end of March, the figures were even worse. The number of those expressing confidence in U.S. military policies in South Vietnam dropped from 74 to 54 percent, while the number of those who deemed the war a stalemate rose from 38 to 42 percent.

If the gloomy reporting of the press had little effect on American public opinion, it nonetheless reinforced doubts already circulating within the Johnson administration. Presidential speechwriter Harry McPherson described his own feelings:

> I was extremely disturbed. I would go in two or three mornings a week and study the cable book and talk to Rostow . . . and get from him what almost seemed hallucinatory from the point of view of what I had seen on television the night before. . . . Well, I must say that I mistrusted what he said. . . . I put aside my own interior access to

confidential information and was more persuaded by what I saw on the tube and in the newspapers. . . . I was fed up with . . . the optimism that seemed to flow without stopping from Saigon.

The military recognized what was happening but had no answers. They were convinced that while the allies had suffered losses, the enemy was on the verge of a catastrophic defeat. All that was needed, the chief of staff of the army, Gen. Harold K. Johnson, told Westmoreland, was "a little bit of a push from us." Johnson added, however, that a revival of confidence in Washington would be necessary before that could happen, and that it would be "an uphill fight all the way."

General Johnson expected no help from the press, and little was forthcoming. Instead, throughout March and April, American newspapers ran articles on Westmoreland's alleged lack of confidence in the marine units fighting in South Vietnam's northernmost regions. During the Battle of Hue, *Los Angeles Times* correspondent William Tuohy wrote, marine battalions had been understrength and poorly supplied; the marine chain of command had been confused; and little coordination had existed between marine and South Vietnamese units. Thoroughly dissatisfied, Tuohy said, Westmoreland had put his deputy, Gen. Creighton Abrams, in charge to remedy the situation.

All the more annoying because it was painfully close to the facts, the article galled Wheeler, who labeled it "unfounded and deleterious speculation." Westmoreland agreed. Failing to refer to a 22 January message he had sent to Wheeler in which he had questioned the marines' professionalism and their ability to defend Quang Tri Province in an emergency, he dismissed the report as just another attempt by the press to manufacture news.

General Sidle managed to divert a number of negative stories by convincing the reporters involved that interservice rivalry was a problem only at the lowest levels and that relationships at command levels were completely harmonious. Even so, the *Washington Star* published a story titled "The Army-Marine Feud" in Vietnam on 14 March. In April, George Wilson of the *Washington Post* reported that U.S. Army officers at Khe Sanh had alleged that the marines there were so psychologically defeated that "they were seeing shadows outside [the] . . . wire and wouldn't go out to pick up their dead." Westmoreland considered disaccrediting Wilson because the article had also revealed the general's desire to use Khe Sanh as a springboard for future operations into Laos, but he reconsidered when he learned that Gen. Robert E. Cushman, Jr., the marine commander in South Vietnam, had revealed those plans in an on-the-record briefing—an indiscretion on the part of the general, not the reporter.

As the controversy over the marines ran its course, a more damaging subject caught the eye of the press. Early in the offensive, at Wheeler's prompting, Westmoreland had requested the deployment of an additional army division and half of a marine division. He did so not because he feared defeat but because he believed he needed the troops to seize the initiative from the enemy and to ensure that he would have ample resources to repel the enemy offensive he expected from the north. Wheeler, however, had larger stakes in mind. Since the buildup for the Vietnam War had sapped the ability of U.S. forces to respond to potential crises elsewhere in the world, he intended to use the offensive as an excuse to reconstitute the U.S. strategic reserve. To that end, in passing Westmoreland's request along, he replaced the general's rationale with a more forceful one that stressed the uncertainties confronting U.S. forces in South Vietnam. He then appended a request for the call-up of enough reservists to provide for the increased requirements of all the services.

Unwilling to take any action that would spark a public outcry or require congressional approval, President Johnson dispatched only a portion of the force Westmoreland had requested, a single brigade from the army's Eighty-second Airborne Division and a marine regimental landing team, about 10,500 men. A short while later, Wheeler visited South Vietnam to confer with Westmoreland. The two decided that 205,000 men could be deployed in three stages over the next year. Of these, 108,000 would go to South Vietnam, while the rest would become part of the strategic reserve. Reporting to the president upon returning to Washington, Wheeler again neglected to mention that Westmoreland felt no immediate need for a deployment of the size requested and painted the situation in South Vietnam in the starkest terms. If the enemy synchronized the coming offensive in the north with attacks around the country, he said, Westmoreland's margins would be "paper thin."

Far from making a case for more troops, Wheeler's report drew out the many doubts that had haunted the Johnson administration over the previous year. At a meeting to discuss Westmoreland's request, Rostow and Rusk supported the dispatch of at least some reinforcements, but former secretary of defense McNamara questioned the economic, political, diplomatic, and moral consequences of a larger American buildup. Ambassador Bunker observed that a large increase in troops might destroy what was left of South Vietnamese initiative, and Clifford avowed that the move would leave an inevitable impression that Johnson was "pouring troops down a rat hole." It was time, Clifford said, for the United States to reevaluate its entire position in Southeast Asia.

Taking Clifford at his word, Johnson asked him to chair a study to determine the least objectionable course in South Vietnam. Clifford made his report on 4 March. "We can no longer rely just on the field commander," he said. "He can want troops and want troops. . . . We must look at . . . our other problems in the world . . . ; we must consider whether or not this thing is tying us down so that we cannot do some of the other things we should be doing." Clifford recommended the dispatch of no more than twenty-two thousand men, just enough to cover problems that might arise over the next four months.

Aware that his administration was divided on the issue and concerned as well that the dispatch of 205,000 troops would be politically difficult, Johnson held back. While he was still deliberating, on the morning of 10 March, Hedrick Smith and Neil Sheehan revealed Westmoreland's request in the *New York Times*. Basing the story on a number of sources rather than on a single massive leak, they detailed the discussions under way within the administration and the doubts that accompanied them. The story went around the world.

Shortly after it appeared, opponents of the War in Congress seized upon it. Senator Mike Mansfield asserted, "We are in the wrong place and we are fighting the wrong kind of war." Senator Robert Kennedy warned that it would be a mistake to commit more troops without the support and understanding of Congress and the American people. Senator Frank Church told reporters dramatically that the president seemed "poised to plunge still deeper into Asia, where huge populations wait to engulf us and legions of young Americans are being beckoned to their graves."

Senator Fulbright held a nationally televised hearing to grill Secretary Rusk. Pressed on whether the administration was considering escalation, Rusk responded that the president was considering his options but would consult with Congress before sending additional troops to South Vietnam.

Obliged to make a decision but under the lash, Johnson quietly authorized a limited call-up of reserves and the deployment of some 35,000 men. Shortly afterward, however, he reevaluated his decision. When Westmoreland revealed a plan for a major offensive to relieve Khe Sanh using only the troops at hand, he decided that additional deployments were hardly as necessary as Wheeler had said and sent only 13,500 support troops.

On 12 March, the day Fulbright's hearing ended, Eugene McCarthy came within a few hundred votes of defeating Johnson in the New Hampshire Democratic primary election. Although pollster Louis Harris and others warned that the vote represented popular dissatisfaction with more than Johnson's stand on the war and more than half of those who voted against the president considered themselves hawks, the election seemed to signify a swing in popular opinion toward McCarthy's antiwar position. A Gallup Poll released on the day after the election reinforced that conclusion. It revealed that 69 percent of all Americans favored a phased withdrawal of American troops as soon as the Untied States could train and equip enough South Vietnamese to take over.

Viewing it all from a distance, General Westmoreland was amazed. As far as he was concerned, the troop request had been an academic exercise. That the three troop increments he and Wheeler had discussed totaled 205,000 men, he later related in his memoirs, had never even crossed his mind.

By the end of March, the president and his advisers were urgently seeking some way to regain the political initiative. A bombing halt seemed the best approach, but President Johnson hesitated. Since the weather in North Vietnam during April was usually too poor to make air attacks profitable, he was concerned that the North Vietnamese would view the move only as an empty gesture. By 31 March, however, he had made up his mind. As General Wheeler explained to Westmoreland at that time, public and congressional support for the war had decreased at an alarming rate over the preceding weeks, while many of the strongest proponents of forceful action in Vietnam had begun either to waver or to head for neutral ground. Johnson hoped a unilateral move toward peace would reverse the trend, the general said, and, as a result, would probably announce a halt during a speech he had slated for that evening.

Although Wheeler considered the speech a public relations ploy, Johnson had other ideas. As the general had predicted, Johnson announced a partial bombing halt in his speech that evening, but then he emphasized his hope that it would lead to early negotiations. Adding that there would be no time limits and no conditions for the North Vietnamese to fulfill, he spent the rest of the speech describing the accomplishments of his administration and pleading for national unity. At its conclusion, he then electrified the world by declaring that he would neither seek nor accept nomination for a second term as president in order to spend the rest of his time in office in the pursuit of peace.

Confronted by Johnson's move and having little to lose, the North Vietnamese went along. Three days later they announced their readiness to talk, engendering hopes around the world that the war would soon end. No one realized at the time that four more years would elapse and tens of thousands of additional casualties would occur before the promise of the moment would find fulfillment.

✗ F U R T H E R   R E A D I N G

Berman, Larry. *Lyndon Johnson's War* (1989).

Braestrup, Peter. *Big Story* (1977).

Brodie, Bernard. "The Tet Offensive," in Noble Frankland and Christopher Dowling, eds. *Decisive Battles of the Twentieth Century* (1976), 321–34.

Clifford, Clark. *Counsel to the President* (1991).

DeForest, Orrin, and David Chanoff. *Slow Burn: The Rise and Fall of American Intelligence in Vietnam* (1990).

Duiker, William J. *The Communist Road to Power in Vietnam* (1981).

Ford, Ronnie E. *Tet 1968: Understanding the Surprise* (1995).

Gelb, Leslie H., and Richard K. Betts. *The Irony of Vietnam* (1979).

Gilbert, Marc, and William Head, eds. *The Tet Offensive* (1996).

Hallin, Daniel C. *The "Uncensored War": The Media and Vietnam* (1986).

Hoopes, Townsend. *The Limits of Intervention* (1970).

Johnson, Lyndon B. *The Vantage Point* (1971).

Lewy, Guenther. *America in Vietnam* (1978).

Oberdorfer, Don. *Tet* (1971).

Palmer, Jr., Bruce. *The 25-Year War* (1984).

Pisor, Robert. *The End of the Line: The Siege of Khe Sanh* (1982).

Prados, John, and Ray Stubble. *Valley of Decision: The Siege of Khe Sanh* (1991).

Schandler, Herbert Y. *The Unmaking of a President* (1977).

Spector, Ronald H. *After Tet* (1993).

Summers, Jr., Harry G. *On Strategy: A Critical Analysis of the Vietnam War* (1982).

Westmoreland, William C. *A Soldier Reports* (1976).

Wiltz, John L. *The Tet Offensive: Intelligence Failure in War* (1991).

C H A P T E R
11

The Ally: South Vietnam

X

A consistent aim of American policy from the late 1940s was the creation of an alternative to communist rule in Vietnam. After the defeat of the French, that objective centered on the establishment of an independent regime in the south that would prove capable of resisting both internal and external military threats. It also encompassed the development of effective political, economic, and social institutions, a process often referred to by American officials as nation building. As the American military presence in Vietnam ballooned during the 1960s, America's fate increasingly became tied to the fortunes of its Saigon ally. Washington's military objective in Vietnam—the defeat of the communists—could not easily be dissociated from its political goal—the establishment of a viable state in South Vietnam.

Although the nature of the South Vietnamese regime inspired a flood of polemical tracts in the United States during the 1960s and early 1970s, relatively few scholars have probed deeply into the underlying structure of the government in Saigon. The most basic questions can be posed simply: Did South Vietnam have the potential to emerge as a viable, independent state? or were its inherent weaknesses so great that it can only be characterized as a doomed dependency?

X *D O C U M E N T S*

In Document 1, a conversation between Presidents Diem and Eisenhower, the South Vietnamese ruler discusses his country's pressing defense needs and requests additional aid from the United States. The discussion took place at the White House on March 9, 1957. Tran Van Don, one of the leaders in the coup against Diem, reflects in Document 2 on South Vietnam's need for political and economic reforms following Diem's ouster. Document 3, excerpted from the memoirs of former South Vietnamese president Nguyen Cao Ky, reiterates a complaint that South Vietnamese leaders often made of their American allies: that they were insensitive, patronizing, and arrogant. On April 7, 1969, Ky's successor, Nguyen Van Thieu, announced his position on a negotiated settlement to the National Assembly; it appears here as Document 4. The speech, issued on the eve of the Paris peace talks, left little room for compromise with the communists. In Document 5, American serviceman Bobby Muller bitterly recalls his experience with South Vietnamese troops. His blunt disparagement of their fighting ability and commitment to the struggle reflects a viewpoint that many other U.S. soldiers shared.

1. Ngo Dinh Diem Requests
Additional U.S. Aid, 1957

After introductory remarks by the President praising President Diem for the excellent achievements he has brought about in the last three years in stabilizing the situation in Viet-Nam, President Eisenhower asked President Diem to outline the principal problems he is facing today.

President Diem replied that his country has gone through a very grave and serious crisis and has been able to hold on despite strong pressures from all sides. The principal problem of establishing internal security and building up their defense posture has been achieved to a considerable extent. The principal reason Viet-Nam has been able to hold out against these pressures has been because of the sympathy and encouragement given by the United States despite the fact that for a time even some people in the United States did not think that the Diem government could maintain itself.

At the present time Viet-Nam is faced with the possibility of a strong Communist offensive from the Vietminh who have 400 thousand men under arms. Fortunately, however, the Vietminh are faced with serious problems such as high taxes needed to maintain this large force and must have other controls which have caused discontent among the population in the North. Diem feels that Red China is faced with the same problems. They are maintaining a large army which requires heavy taxes and controls over the people, which Diem hopes in the long run will force the Chinese Government to demobilize a considerable portion of their forces and treat the people in a more liberal manner. There is, nevertheless, the possibility that the Vietminh with their large army might try to attack now while they have a superiority in numbers. The Vietminh during the first year after the Geneva Conference did not think it would be necessary to use armed force to take over the South; they thought the government in the South would crumble and they could take over without difficulty. With internal stability in Free Viet-Nam and the build-up of their own armed forces, they have now the possibility of holding out for a few years more during which time Diem reiterated the strain and drain on the economy of the Vietminh may cause them to demobilize some of their forces and adopt a more liberal attitude toward the population. . . .

Diem [stated] that Viet-Nam has attained stability due primarily to the volume of American aid. He pointed out that the magnitude of American aid permitted the US Government to have a large number of advisers and consultants in Viet-Nam who not only can assist Viet-Nam with its problems but also follow closely developments and the use to which aid is placed. In contrast, the small amounts of aid given to other countries, such as 20/30 million dollars, does not permit the US Government to maintain such close control over developments in other countries as is the case in Viet-Nam. Diem pleaded for the maintenance of the present aid level of 250 million dollars a year of which 170 million dollars is allocated for defense purposes. This aid has permitted Viet-Nam to build up its armed strength and thus play an important role in Southeast Asia. If this aid should be cut both the military and economic

---

Memo of conversation, May 9, 1957, *Foreign Relations of the United States, 1955–1957*, I, 794–799.

progress would have to be reduced. This would cause serious repercussions not only in Viet-Nam but among neighboring countries in Southeast Asia who look on Viet-Nam as an example of the good US aid can bring. Any cut would also bring serious political repercussions in Viet-Nam.

2. Tran Van Don on the Need for Reforms After the Coup Against Diem (1963), 1978

Immediately after the success of the coup d'etat [against Diem], a provisional constitutional charter was proclaimed. It provided for General Big Minh to be the chairman of the MRC [Military Revolutionary Council], which was composed of twelve generals, and for a civilian cabinet of fifteen ministers to be headed by a prime minister who would be responsible to the MRC and to Minh as head of state. This was appropriate because Minh was our leader and known by all as the hero of the coup. Mr. Nguyen Ngoc Tho, former vice president of the republic under the Diem regime was appointed prime minister. He was chosen because of his long administrative experience which would help to smooth this transition phase. In addition, he was a long-time friend of Big Minh and we felt we could trust him.

Having promoted the coup, we were well aware of the difficulties that always follow a sudden change of regime. We understood that this provisional government structure should be replaced as soon as a definitive constitution could be promulgated. Another closely related problem involved our decision to purge the administration and the army of elements we knew to be inept, despotic, or corrupt. We expected a certain breakdown in the functioning of the administration because of this, but thought that the good psychological effect on the people and the purifying influence of new officials would more than overcome any disruptions.

Students, priests, and those politically opposed to the previous government were immediately released from prison and instructions were issued prohibiting arbitrary arrest and confinement. Freedom of the press and of religious belief were solemnly proclaimed and welcomed with enthusiasm. Hard labor in the rural areas was abolished in connection with the strategic hamlet program, and we attempted to obtain support for our new government from the religious sects Hoa Hao and Cao Dai.

The economic and financial situation was disturbing, however, because American aid had been temporarily suspended during the months preceding the coup. Further, the Tho cabinet was having difficulty since its members could not agree with each other. Part of the problem was that Tho, the former vice president under Diem, was inflexible and narrow in his policies. . . .

Toward the end of January, after a series of contacts with many political, religious, and military leaders, I had been able to plan out the main orientation of our revolutionary program. On January 27, I gave my reform program to Big Minh and [General] Khiem for further submission to the government. It suggested many radical changes, political, economic, social, and cultural, and handed power over to a

---

Reprinted with permission from the book *Our Endless War* by Tran Van Don, pp. 115, 116–118. © by Presidio Press, 31 Pamaron Way, Novato, CA 94949.

new revolutionary cabinet under a different prime minister. Especially important were the roles to be entrusted to the youth of the nation for the realization of our revolutionary goals.

I knew that if the war were to be won against the Communists, military measures alone would not suffice. Our struggle against the NLF had to be waged with political, economic, cultural, and social considerations as well. The NLF strategy had been to occupy and control the countryside and turn it into a springboard for advancing to the cities. We, therefore, had to make our presence felt in the same rural areas, winning the people's support, seducing them away from Communist influences, and enlisting their participation in a full-scale struggle. My concept was that the war in Vietnam was between two factions of Vietnamese, so it should have been settled between ourselves by all means available. Aid obtained from our Free World friends should have been confined to moral, technical, and material support. Our national policy should have been geared toward solving simultaneously the two overall goals of winning the support of the population and then annihilating the enemy's armed forces.

We also wanted to show the people that we meant what we said, that we truly intended to do away with graft and corruption and special privileges for the governors. I proposed to my colleagues that we lead austere lives, turn in the official limousines so prized by the Diem administration, and sell off the luxurious homes maintained at the expense of the common people. We had to get ourselves used to the idea that we had to get closer to the people, living our lives more like them.

In our military mission we needed to destroy the enemy's secret bases, prevent infiltration of men, weapons, equipment, and supplies, and neutralize his units. Local organizations such as the civil guard and the police were to be responsible for law and order within the local areas. Their purpose was to protect the villages and the people living in them from the political and military cadres of the NLF. In areas that were so rugged that our troops would have unusual difficulty conducting normal military operations, we might have had to request air support such as helicopter transport from our allies.

In winning the support of the populace, we had to remove the insidious influence of the NLF from the villages. This had to be the principal object of the war, with all necessary resources utilized for this purpose. We had to help the people develop their individual capabilities and get them to understand their political rights and enjoy them. To achieve this they needed a great number of well-trained and sympathetic local officials capable of replacing the Communist cadres who had been working with them. Once the people in the countryside, who were 80 percent of our overall population, were won over to the national cause, the NLF could no longer be sustained because it would have lost its main source of support.

I still believe that these objectives were obtainable because the NLF had not yet achieved such power in the countryside as to deny us access to the populace. It is good to remember that no large-scale infiltration of North Vietnamese regular units had yet occurred so that we were faced only by the irregular cadres. The principle we wanted to follow in pacifying the countryside was that of an "oil spot" spreading out from a safe area, making it larger and larger as we gradually made whole provinces secure. Eventually these spots would meet and after a certain time full sections of the country would be thoroughly under government control. Then we would go on to destroy enemy secret bases that had been set up and interrupt the infiltration routes, such as the Ho Chi Minh trail. After all this had been accomplished, we might feel secure enough to contemplate active operations against the North in order to try to unify the national territory.

These plans would, I believe, have permitted our government to secure the countryside and make South Vietnam a safer and better place to live. We had our chance. We had seized power and had the overwhelming mass of the people with us. We were inexperienced, but this probably was in itself something of an advantage. We certainly did not want to continue the sins of the past.

But, our hopes and aspirations were not to be realized.

3. Nguyen Cao Ky on the Battle for Hearts and Minds, 1976

Alongside the military war, fought with bombs and bullets, we had to fight another war—one to convince our own people that South Vietnam offered a way of life superior to that of the Communists. It was a war for the hearts and minds of the people.

It was not, as some thought, a matter of simple materialism, a philosophy that started with filling bellies. Ambassador Ellsworth Bunker was hopelessly wrong when he told me on one occasion, "People are drifting toward Communism because they are poor. If you give the people everything they want—television sets, automobiles, and so on—none of them will go over to Communism."

Poor Bunker! He was trying to impose American standards of life on people he did not understand, people who basically had no desire for the so-called good things of the American way of life.

Like so many well-meaning Americans, Bunker, when he came to Vietnam, was unable to grasp the fact that he had made an excursion into a culture as different from America's as an African Negro's is different from that of an Eskimo. No man could hope to span the differences in American and Vietnamese culture and heritage in the short time of his appointment in our land. How could I explain to Bunker's Western mind, for example, that while an American would be lost without a future to conquer, a Vietnamese is lost without the refuge of the past.

"Material goods are not the answer," I replied. "It's much more important to win the hearts and minds of the people than to give them TV sets."

Bunker shook his head disbelievingly, and I felt, watching him, that he was wondering how this young upstart dared to utter such nonsense. But then Bunker no doubt believed in Napoleon's dictum that an army marches on its stomach, and saw no reason why civilians should be any different. But they were.

Among my first priorities when I became prime minister was to introduce some form of social revolution, a term I later amended to "social justice." My aims, my hopes, were very simple: I wanted my people to get a proper reward for their efforts. I wanted a man working eight hours a day to receive twice as much as a man working four hours a day. It takes very little to make the Vietnamese happy.

From Nguyen Cao Ky, *Twenty Years and Twenty Days,* 1976, Stein & Day. Reprinted with permission of Nguyen Cao Ky.

Our needs are simple because we are Asians; we are influenced by the sayings of Confucius. We are not interested in material gain like Westerners; commercial success does not attract us as it does Americans, so we can be happy with little. On the other hand, we do not like to feel exploited, and there lay the root of our problem.

For above all else, the Communist cadres, infiltrating from the North; exploited our corruption and black marketeering as they tried to win over puzzled (yet at heart loyal) peasants to the cause of Ho Chi Minh. They were diabolically clever, for they made no spectacular promises; they held out no bribes. Like Churchill, they offered nothing but blood, sweat, toil, and tears, but they were able to build up the image of a simple, Spartan leader as great in his way as Churchill, and contrast it with our squabbling, corrupt politicians, as squalid in their way as the French politicians in 1940 who bickered among themselves while the Germans streamed across their land.

Yet we had one ace in our hand, if only we could play the hand properly, an ace that did not even exist in the Communist deck of cards. It was freedom, the world's most precious—yet most elusive—treasure. The freedoms that Roosevelt had preached, not only the freedom from fear and want, but the freedom for us to choose our leaders, and the freedom to boot them out if they proved unworthy of the trust reposed in them.

I felt we had to start at the top—and at the bottom. We needed to establish free elections at all levels—in the village tribunal as well as the presidential palace. We needed to introduce fair systems of compensation, provisions for social welfare— all things that are taken for granted in the West.

We achieved more than we were given credit for, though all our efforts were made against a backdrop of a bitter fight for survival. The draft continued in Vietnam until virtually the end, and at the height of the fighting every family in the country had one member, if not two or three, in uniform.

But if we held an ace, we also held a deuce. For while I was preaching the need for freedom, I was not always free myself. True, we were not puppets, yet we never achieved the standing or appearance of an independent, self-governing country. The Americans criticized us for not having a highly developed system of government, but how could we have that when every Vietnamese in Saigon referred to the American ambassador as "the Governor General"?

The Americans did not seek this; they were not colonists, but South Vietnam had been a colony until the defeat of the French, and in many ways it remained virtually a colony, though without the restrictions imposed by the French. We still lacked our own identity.

We never produced a leader to unite the country with its many religious and political factions. The North had one in Ho Chi Minh; rightly or wrongly, the Communists believed in him and fought and died for him. He had a charisma that won many supporters even in the West and not all of them were Communists. Neither Diem, nor Thieu—both backed by the Americans—won the hearts of even the South Vietnamese.

The Americans controlled the fighting of the war. American aid financed the country; without it we could not survive. Americans selected or influenced the selection of our politicians and leaders, even at village level, and had a natural tendency to pick the most compliant rather than the most gifted. American culture—its films, television, and advertising—swamped our own.

Conscious of their dollar-bought superiority, the Americans patronized us at all levels. GIs thoughtlessly but hurtfully referred to Vietnamese as Dinks and Gooks, Slants and Slopes. (Charlie, Chuck, and Claude were reserved for the Viet Cong.)

Their contemptuous attitude was typified by an announcer on the American Forces Radio in 1970: "For those of you staying on in 'Nam, here's a little advice regarding our Vietnamese friends. As you know, they're kind of jumpy now, so please remember the golden rule. Never pat a Vietnamese on the head. Stand on low ground when you talk to them. They kind of resent looking up to you. Okay?"

Certainly the Vietnamese resented being patted on the head. The battle for the hearts and minds of the people was more fundamental to success even than air power or fire power. Yet someone, presumably a GI, painted in white letters on an old warehouse by the river in Saigon the legend: "Just grab the Gooks by the balls and their hearts and minds will follow.". . .

Once more I reiterate that we needed America; we could never have fought the Communists alone. But how much better it would have been if the Americans had never appeared in the picture and we had combined patience with American economic aid and expertise to improve the lot of the average Vietnamese family and the skill of our fighting men. I am convinced that slowly but surely we could have won the war, simply because all the people would have been behind us once the social revolution had been won.

4. Nguyen Van Thieu's Address to the National Assembly, 1969

Today, in this forum, I wish to solemnly confirm once more to the world, to our allies, to our fellow countrymen, and to our enemy that in our constant search for a constructive solution to the conflict, we consider that the following six points constitute a reasonable and solid basis for the restoration of peace in Viet-Nam:

1. Communist aggression should stop.

Communist North Viet-Nam should give up its attempts to conquer the RVN by force. It should stop violating the DMZ and the frontiers of the RVN, and stop its wanton attacks against the innocent population of the RVN.

2. Communist North Vietnamese and auxiliary troops and cadres should be completely withdrawn from the Republic of Viet-Nam.

As the military and subversive forces of Communist North Viet-Nam are withdrawn, infiltration ceases, and the level of violence thus subsides, the RVN will ask its allies to remove their forces, in accordance with the Manila joint-communique of seven nations in October, 1966.

3. The territories of the neighboring countries of the RVN should not be violated and used by Communist North Viet-Nam as bases and staging areas for aggression against the RVN.

U.S. Senate, 93rd Cong., 2nd Sess., December 1974, *Background Information Relating to Southeast Asia* (Washington, 1974).

Communist North Vietnamese troops and cadres illegally introduced and stationed in Laos and Cambodia should be withdrawn from these countries. Communist North Viet-Nam military installations in these countries should be dismantled.

4. The RVN adopts the policy of National Reconciliation.

Those now fighting against us, who renounce violence, respect the laws, and faithfully abide by the democratic processes, will be welcomed as full members of the National Community. As such, they will enjoy full political rights and assume the same obligations as other lawful citizens under the National Constitution.

5. The reunification of the two Viet-Nams is to be decided by the free choice of the entire population of Viet-Nam through democratic processes.

To establish the atmosphere conducive to national reunification, after peace has been reestablished, modalities of economic and cultural exchanges between the two Viet-Nams and other countries of this area, can be actively explored, together with other intermediary measures of peaceful coexistence so that, pending reunification, the two Viet-Nams can participate more fully and more constructively in the various undertakings of the international community.

6. There must be an effective system of international control and reliable international guarantees against the resumption of Communist aggression.

The control mechanisms should be freed from the paralyzing effects of the Veto system. It should have sufficient personnel and adequate means to detect any violation of peace agreement. When violations are committed, and aggression is renewed, there should be prompt and effective response from a reliable system of international guarantees, otherwise any peace agreement will be only a sham device used by the Communists to weaken our system of defense, and not a basis for long lasting peace and stability for this part of the world.

5. An American Serviceman's View of the South Vietnamese Army, 1987

Probably the first two months I was there, I spent out in the bush. Out there the war was easy in a way because there was no ambiguity. Anybody you met out there was hard core NVA regular. No "good guy, bad guy" problem. Later, when we came back to work the coastal area where there were villages and refugees, that's when things started to go "wait a second." Cam Lo, which is one I remember very well, was a refugee village where people had been taken from another place called Gio Linh, ten or fifteen miles away. I didn't understand it then, but for Vietnamese villagers, their rice paddy and their little ancestral burial ground defines their universe. You take them away as we did and you've totally disrupted what they relate to. And in Cam Lo what I experienced was just hatred in the eyes of people.

The Vietnamese did not like us and I remember I was shocked. I still naively thought of myself as a hero, as a liberator. And to see the Vietnamese look upon us with fear or hatred visible in their eyes was a shock. The only thing we were good for is to sell us something. And frankly every time we operated around Cam Lo we got fucked with. Any patrol, any operation, any convoy passing by would get a smack. So the people that I thought would regard us as heroes were the very people that we were fighting, and all of a sudden my black-and-white image of the world became real gray and confused.

Then I came into contact with the ARVN and that was all the more absurd. First there were some joint operations and then I went with MACV as an advisor and worked with three different ARVN battalions and that's when everything just went screwy in my head. Every night I slept with the battalion commander. We had personal bodyguards and the reason was that a good percentage of the guys in the ranks were VC or even North Vietnamese. The bodyguards were to protect us against getting blown away by the guys we were fighting with. We went out into the A Shau valley for what was supposed to be a ten-day operation and it wound up being ten weeks, and we lost a good number of guys not because of firefights but because they took as much rice as they could carry and they split. The A Shau was badlands. It was not a friendly place. And when you leave your unit out in the A Shau you ain't leaving to go bring in the crops back at the farm. You're leaving because you're joining the other side.

It was a joke. The enemy was a tough, hard, dedicated fucking guy, and the ARVN didn't want to hear about fighting. It was LaLa Land. Every, every, every, *every* firefight that we got into, the ARVN broke, the ARVN fucking ran. I was with three different battalions and the story never changed. I almost fell over laughing once. I had an Australian I was working with, and this NVA unit had just ambushed us. We had two companies of ARVN, and finally they got on line to counterattack, and the company commanders give the order to move and nobody moves. And they have to run up and down line with little sticks, beating these guys and kicking them in the fucking rear end to get them up out of their holes. And the Aussie and I look at each other, and we know then and there that this ain't going to work.

✗ *E S S A Y S*

Gabriel Kolko of York University (Toronto) investigates the inherent structural limitations of the South Vietnamese regime in the opening essay. He sees a government hopelessly dependent on American aid and reliant on a pervasive system of corruption for its survival. Such a regime, Kolko argues, had little prospect for widening its narrow political base or blunting the communist appeal to the peasantry.

In the second essay, Bui Diem, former South Vietnamese ambassador to the United States, acknowledges many of the government's shortcomings while insisting that South Vietnam could have evolved into a viable state. Under the most difficult circumstances, real accomplishments were made; others were possible, including the development of a more democratic political system. The United States, he contends, must bear considerable responsibility for failing to use its leverage as a catalyst for reform and for the arrogant manner with which it treated its ally. Bui Diem now serves as a member of George Mason University's Indochina Institute.

A Doomed Dependency

GABRIEL KOLKO

The war's economic and social impact on South Vietnam between 1965 and 1970 was decisive to its eventual military conclusion. The accumulated effects of war produce their own internal dilemmas and contradictions as well as unintended consequences which may prove far more consequential to a war's outcome than anyone's conscious desires, thereby fixing the boundaries of historical possibilities. The U.S. intervention in Vietnam produced such ironies from the inception, but by the late 1960s their impact was decisive and irreversible.

These economic and social trends appeared less than critical to American leaders, and measured in the form of numbers—the only index available to men whose values preclude empathy—they were quite elusive. Even today, information on South Vietnam's demography, the class structure, or the economy is poor and masks unconscionably the enormous human drama and suffering of fully one-half of a nation. It offends the sense of real human experiences to attempt to reduce such events to aggregate, measurable proportions, but to fathom their meaning and importance is to understand, as fully as frail human capacities allow, controlling factors in war and history, the forces which decide the outcome of the more easily described, much more closely studied world of battles or of decision making.

The nature of South Vietnamese society was not incidental to the U.S. effort, but a critical factor, by itself sufficient to determine whether Washington's fate would be victory or defeat. It explains not only the sources of the Revolution's initial efforts in the south but also the subsequent directions imposed upon it, the nature of its triumph, and the peace that followed. The strength, fragility, and evolution of the U.S. dependent determined the very viability of its undertaking and the extent of the obligation the Americans assumed in their naive optimism.

Firepower shaped the demography of South Vietnam after 1964, reducing the issue for a substantial portion of the peasantry to one of physical survival. At the core of the vast panorama of events emerging from this protracted conflict were men and women whose commitments and lives were ceaselessly affected by innumerable challenges and travails. Their responses ranged across the whole spectrum of possible individual reactions, from heroism and conscious efforts to resolve their problem through collective action against foreign invaders to an elemental decision to survive physically as a person by whatever means necessary. To comprehend that process of constant choice for most of the adults is quite impossible, because the destruction, grief, and physical anguish around them, the extremes of human bravery and human degradation, defy description.

The United States in Vietnam unleashed the greatest flood of firepower against a nation known to history. The human suffering was monumental. The figures on all aspects of this enormous trauma are inadequate, and between 1968 and 1970 the refugee reporting system alone underwent three major revisions. The Pentagon's

From Gabriel Kolko, *Anatomy of a War: Vietnam, the United States, and the Modern Historical Experience* (New York: Pantheon, 1985). Copyright © 1985 by Gabriel Kolko. Reprinted by permission of the author.

final estimate of killed and wounded civilians in South Vietnam between 1965 and 1972 ran from 700,000 to 1,225,000, while Senate numbers for the same period were 1,350,000. Deaths in these two assessments ranged from 195,000 to 415,000; "enemy" killed were 850,000 minimum, and a substantial part of these were civilians. The Revolution's figures are much higher. In a nation of about 18 million people in 1970, the war exacted an immensely high toll in killed and wounded.

Munitions was the primary cause of casualties, and the vast bulk of it was employed by the United States and the ARVN which accounted for nearly all the artillery and 100 percent of that delivered by air. In 1969, internal U.S. discussions admitted, "the information available . . . on the overall scale and incidence of damage to civilians by air and artillery . . . is less than adequate." They did know, however, that in the single month of January 1969 over four million people, nearly a quarter of the population, had one or more air strikes within three kilometers of their hamlet. The U.S. and RVN pacification programs sought to empty the NLF-dominated regions of their population, not merely by firepower but also by defoliation, forced removals into strategic hamlets, and other means of separating the peasants from their land. While the reasons for this vast population displacement were both political and military, American officials also considered it "desirable" in making available the huge labor pool they required for their own bases and logistics. And once displaced, the peasants had to be kept, the Americans believed, from returning home. For all these reasons, [Robert] Komer said in April 1967, the United States should "[s]tep up refugee programs deliberately aimed at depriving the VC of a recruiting base."

In essence, a substantial part of the peasantry was consciously forced off the land against its will, permanently transforming the nature of South Vietnamese society. The most conservative estimates are that at least half of the peasants were pushed into refugee camps or urban settings one or more times, many repeatedly. The statistics are, again, far from precise, not least because the United States was hardly inclined to expend the effort to document accurately the brutal consequences of its policies. Senate figures for 1964–72 give only 5.8 million persons as refugees, but additional data show that provinces under the NLF, primarily north of Saigon, and in the Mekong as well, generated the largest proportion of refugees. The correlation between firepower and population displacement is very close. RVN numbers on refugees or war victims during 1965–72 are substantially higher than U.S. figures, about 7 million people, or about one-third of the population or well over half the peasantry. Once in refugee camps, the peasants saw their standard of living drop by about two-thirds, and their psychic loss was incalculable. The result was the urbanization of a rural society in a manner unique in this century, for it was far more brutal and disorienting to the population than any that a large Third World nation has ever experienced.

Urban Vietnam before 1960 had been remarkably comfortable, its cities scarcely more than colonial enclaves. The French had controlled them until 1954, of course, but the Chinese also were always vital economically and physically. Even in 1966 one-fifth of South Vietnam's urban population, comprising about a million persons, was Chinese. The virtual Chinese monopoly over important economic activities left little space for newcomers, whose commerce was really marginal subsistence. A portion of them made up the most dynamic, entrepreneurial sector, and were in the best position to amass the benefits of the new foreign presence. Into this turbulent world came millions of peasants after 1964.

In 1960, 20 percent of South Vietnam's population lived in urban areas. The proportion had reached 26 percent by 1964, 36 percent by 1968, and 43 percent by 1971—a growth rate of five times that of all less developed nations during the same decade. Saigon's expansion, though great in the surrounding suburbs, was astonishingly small in the metropolitan area, and far less than that of such provincial towns as Can Tho, Danang, Bien Hoa, Hue, and cities closer to actual combat. Danang and Nha Trang grew fourfold between 1960 and 1971, mainly after 1964, while Can Tho's population tripled. . . .

Forced urbanization not only produced a wholly untenable RVN economy but also created a profoundly disturbed human order, fraught with immense political implications. Looked at objectively, the United States in less than a decade did more damage to an entire society than other colonial nations or the urbanization process elsewhere accomplished over generations. No one, the Revolution included, at first fully perceived the magnitude of this cultural assault, which touched the basic question of the nature of politics and individual commitments in a social context of personal and family crisis. By necessity, this experience can affect people in various ways, one of which is egoism, personalism, and *attentisme* or apathy toward politics. The adult peasantry forced into cities became profoundly alienated from a culture and society succumbing to Americans who devoured their sons and daughters, patronized successive juntas, and wreaked havoc on Vietnamese lands and traditions. One split in urban society which emerged was between those who had absorbed the officially sanctioned urban mores and those who remained rural and traditional in either their economic lives or their values. More dangerous, the newly arrived city dwellers were alienated from their children. . . .

A critical problem for the NLF was whether the former peasantry's involuntary rupture with its rural origins and the Revolution was irreversible, but the decisive question for the United States and the RVN was whether it would ever leave its cocoon of private concerns to sustain the RVN in some effective fashion. For while the Revolution had other means of struggling, without a measure of support from the urban population the RVN would remain politically unstable and the cities only a fatal economic burden.

The social order that urbanization created was ultimately the functional outcome of many policies, and though the new society was largely incremental and ad hoc in nature, aspects of it were certainly planned. Urbanization was the unavoidable logic of the high-firepower war, and its cultural form was strongly influenced by the over two million GIs who passed through the country. Many in America and Saigon regarded population reconcentration as both an opportunity and a hidden blessing. That Washington did not understand the critical economic and political implications of the war's demography until it was too late was one of its great miscalculations in the war.

Thousands of Americans were involved in "nation building" projects, including social scientists eager to test their wares in practice. These ranged from the surrounding of air bases with civilians they attempted to make happy with subsidies of every kind so that they would not aid the NLF (a policy that failed dismally) to an effort to write a Vietnamese equivalent of the song "God Bless America" to win over the masses. The radio propaganda that incessantly swept the nation had very little impact, even in the opinion of the RVN's experts, and the most powerful tool that both the United States and the RVN had to consolidate their influence among the masses was the dollar—a weapon which worked best among the youth on the streets but proved also to be finite both in quantity and in effectiveness.

The dollar's assault on the culture, whether traditional or Revolutionary, profoundly alienated a significant element of the older urban dwellers, particularly the students and intelligentsia who had the leisure to observe and think about it. Secondary school and university enrollment increased over ten times between 1954 and 1970, when the RVN claimed there were about 680,000 in the two categories. The children of the petite bourgeoisie, merchants, and even civil servants and RVN functionaries, many transcended their class position and related to their own peer culture in much the same way the children of uprooted peasants did.

The intellectuals, too, were as fragile in South Vietnam as they are anywhere, full of moods, variations, and typical equivocations, but many became increasingly sympathetic to the NLF as they observed what the United States was doing to the nation and its culture, though a significant portion always did what those in power demanded. Many among them, particularly teachers, were poorly paid. The students, especially, reacted to the nightmare of human degradation around them, and some preserved their capacity for action, even as many retreated into their privileged private worlds. Among people in these social categories, the NLF certainly increased its influence as a by-product of the American cultural offensive, and a significant portion of this crucial social stratum was always alienated from the RVN and the United States.

The final test was less the alienated urban intelligentsia's relationship to the Revolution than its willingness to make those commitments and sacrifices necessary to maintain the existing order in power, and the effects of urbanization prevented this from occurring. As a physical solution to the problem of cooperation between the Revolution and peasantry, the urbanization of the south appeared sensible to the United States. Despite its immediate advantages, however, it was by the late 1960s increasingly alienating the expanding urban population, leaving a growing political, economic, and psychological void. France's struggle against the Communists had not altered the rural society's structure, character, and values in any basic way. Even during its entire colonial reign, only a small minority of the people had been affected ideologically. But the American style of war was far more damaging to the population's identity and existence. The reconciliation of the economic and political contradictions in its policies was almost immediately beyond Washington's abilities. Ultimately, the cumulative effects of urbanization on the RVN's economic, political, and military system immeasurably aided its total collapse.

The Communist Party's virtual monopoly on the opposition to French and American imperialism reflected the impact of colonialism on the Vietnamese class structure and its evolution. All of its potential challengers were too divided, too sectarian, or too ambitious to fill the void in the political system, and religious differences, especially in the south, gravely weakened the non-Marxist opposition. Chinese domination of the economy meant that the stratum with the most to gain from the status quo was unable directly to relate politically to the rest of the system and was mobile, should need arise, and no other potential class-based leadership existed. This vacuum in power and politics was institutionalized for most of the RVN's brief life in the hands of two men, producing hybrid ruling elites without an autonomous class constituency and dependent ultimately on foreign support. Diem's nearly decade-long rulership at the inception of the RVN's twenty-two-year existence, with his systematic attacks on the fragile French bureaucratic legacy and class-based elites, the Chinese particularly, further narrowed the social basis of rulership, reducing it essentially to his clique and the military—the only large institutional force he could not abolish or decrease in functional power. Put simply, the military was the only non-Communist stratum able to succeed Diem and to aspire to power.

The RVN was very much in the same position as many non-Asian Third World states dependent on foreign aid or created in a vacuum to perform a comprador role for a foreign imperialism, and the military in this context traditionally serves as the political arena and instrument of political succession, even though the sponsoring state—the United States in this case—hopes also to utilize it primarily as a way of transferring the techniques of violence and administration necessary to maintain foreign influence. Should the army's political function become its dominant preoccupation, then its tools of violence will ultimately be crucial only within the military establishment's political process, for arms will become the only real or potential means of political change—making its concern for external threats to the state quite secondary. And where the militarized political structure defines the nature and boundaries of economic development and accumulation to a critical extent, corruption drastically erodes its fighting capacities. In brief, politics neutralizes military capabilities decisively by making all purely military considerations subordinate to the control of political and economic power. The state, the economy, and military and political power all become integrated. The overcoming of this contradiction is the United States' main dilemma every time it creates a dependency on which it in turn becomes dependent to attain its own national objectives.

Such a context makes the social nature and function of the officers a fundamental issue, their class origins and linkages being facts of potentially great significance to their definition of their social and economic role as well as their personal aspirations. This is especially true when the military in underdeveloped nations with a vacuum in institutional power is the dominant mechanism within which rulership is determined. The marginality or stability of a class society at its various levels is critical where a cohesive opposition exists, and it becomes a crucial factor in determining how wars are concluded.

The officers in the RVN's armed forces, some 25,000 by 1967, as well as the tiny elite of senior officers at the rank of major or higher, were homogenous to an astonishing degree. The junior officers, composing 95 percent of the total number of officers, were very young. Since they had to have at least a high school diploma, they were overwhelmingly urbanized and born into families that could afford to educate their children. Soldiers could not rise through the ranks to become officers. A quarter were born in the north, and the percentage of Catholics was double South Vietnam's average, which meant that the military was an important avenue of social mobility for displaced refugees coming from the DRV after 1954. Economically, though, the profession was poorly paid, second lieutenants earning but $55 monthly in 1967 and enjoying few legal perquisites. For the majority who were married and had families, this fact became critical to their real functions. At least one major

distinction between officers was their training academy and their year of graduation. Without a definable class or ideological differentiation among the officers, the
"school tie" became inordinately important. The National Military Academy at
Dalat produced 13 percent of the officers in the military in 1967, but 30 percent of
the general-ranking officers graduated from it, while Thu Duc academy graduated
two-thirds of the officers and a mere 5 percent of the generals and 30 percent of the
field-grade officers. Catholics accounted for a third of the generals.

Of a sample of sixty generals in 1972, one-third were the sons of landowners,
another quarter of government officials, and over a quarter of officers and urban
professionals and middle- and upper-class elements. They were upwardly mobile;
their families were not yet important but at a point where they might aspire to be,
and this profoundly affected their use of power. Thieu, for example, was the son of
a small landlord, and he graduated from Dalat. A scant majority were graduates of
Dalat academy, 14 percent of Thu Duc. Nearly all had begun their careers under
the French. The military, given the role of war in the French and the RVN's priorities,
was the chief channel of social and economic mobility for an important sector of
the marginalized middle classes ready to work for the dominant colonial power.

The motive of the senior officers after Diem's death was simple: power in the
form of careers and money. This was just as true of the congeries of civilian mini-
parties, factions, or religious sects who were always moving in and out of various
coalitions or plotting on the sidelines. Where neither coherent class interest nor
ideology exists, there is no basis of collective action and responsibility, and personal
welfare becomes the motive of politics, resulting in individual corruption as an institutionalized dimension of society.

The Americans always watched this charade with the utmost cynicism. Perhaps the most dangerous aspect of this period was the effort of civilians to link up
with military factions and encourage them, which was a guarantee of continuous
turmoil and, by mid-1966, of various degrees of warlordism in the four military
regions into which the RVN was divided, particularly MR I in the north. Indeed, as
the successive military juntas passed through Saigon, mutual suspicions justifiably
became axiomatic among those in the perpetual imbroglio the United States was
sustaining. As they conspired and as membership in the ruling juntas changed, the
system was made ripe for a superior political fixer, and in Nguyen Van Thieu the
senior officers met their master.

Thieu was surely the ablest politician to emerge in the RVN's history, and
his conversion from Buddhism to Catholicism to advance his career proved he
was supremely flexible. He was a member in the June 1965 junta representing
the "Young Turks" with no close past ties to the French and Diem. From there he
moved unobtrusively to find ways of maneuvering around potential opponents and,
above all, to try to find the price or weakness of any who might resist him. Unlike
Diem, he had no serious ideological pretensions, and the initial key to his success
was his readiness co-optively to share the spoils. Thieu was much more interested
in obtaining stable control over power rather than a monopoly of it, and not until
1973 was he to seek total authority in his own hands.

In the wake of Diem's death, one of the most important factors in his rise to
power was the aid he obtained from the Chinese business elite. Thieu's sister-in-law
married Ly Luong Than, who was already one of the richest Chinese in Saigon, held

a U.S. passport in his traditionally abundant collection, and was a key figure in the Fukienese *bang* [Chinese merchant organizations]. Than brought Thieu together with Francis Koo, first secretary of the Taiwanese embassy in Saigon and a senior figure in SEATO intelligence circles. Koo decided Thieu would serve the embattled Chinese community well and provided him funds and contacts to advance his career. When Nguyen Cao Ky, his main rival, in early 1966 excoriated speculators and had one Chinese publicly executed as a warning to the others, the still nervous Chinese elite gave Thieu massive financial backing and intervened on his behalf with U.S. officials. Thieu was a shrewd operator in his own right, but his access to funds also smoothed his way. He had far more tact and cash to employ than Ky did. The United States' obsessive desire to see military unity was the single most important element in bringing Thieu to power, but his Chinese connection undoubtedly shaped the regime's distribution of economic benefits.

Thieu in 1967 was the sole general with sufficient talent to survive the chaos of Saigon politics and create a powerful political machine. In June 1967 he had the junta nominate him for the new presidency, after he promised to abide by the will of a collective leadership. Even when he was most powerful, Thieu neutralized, co-opted, and pressured many of his military and civilian elite rivals far more gently than Diem did, trying to divide the rewards of office widely to gain time to enjoy the prerogatives of power and, above all, to prevent any threats to his increasingly durable machine from the other senior military commanders. As for the Chinese, one of his first acts in 1967 was to allow them to reestablish their *bangs* and to return their associations' confiscated property.

The moment he came to office, in September 1967, Thieu embarked on building a largely private power machine which integrated the military, the political structure, and the economy in numerous formal and informal ways. Complex in certain aspects and baldly simple in others, his system assured that the RVN's destiny after 1968 would become synonymous with Thieu's ambitions, his power, and, ultimately, his weaknesses.

In an underdeveloped class structure traumatized by the effects of Diem's own power machine, the demography of the war, a subsidized war economy, and an enormous American presence, Thieu temporarily and partially remolded the elastic class system to suit his interests. He unified ambitious, essentially marginal class elements and the rich Chinese around only one common denominator: money and access to privilege. As a Rand Corporation summation of the views of twenty-seven high RVN officers and officials after the war said, " A central feature of the South Vietnamese regime . . . was corruption." His integrative effort encompassed a variety of approaches, ranging from a vast number of people brought into the RVN's employment to a higher elite which was incorporated into the war economy formally and informally, together sharing the main prerogatives of power. The fluid RVN power structure possessed intersecting economic, political, and military components in varying degrees, according to the people and elements involved, but it was never fully formalized before it collapsed both from its own contradictions and from the pressures the Revolution as well as the United States imposed on it.

The analysis of transitional and dependent social orders is potentially misleading if one attributes excess coherence and form to constantly evolving relationships. The task in Vietnam is made all the more difficult because the senior officers, Chinese capitalists, and civilian Vietnamese politicians were each internally divided, and only from 1969 to 1973 (but not later) did Nguyen Van Thieu sufficiently control power to make the structure susceptible to some generalizations. Thieu used his family as much as possible, of course, but his real strength was his ability to find and reward generals ready to cooperate with him loyally in running both the military and the civil administrations. Such a co-optive strategy was successful so long as there was enough to share. It was the sheer enormity of the American economic impact which defined the parameters of the RVN's class development and the political life intimately linked with it.

Both the Revolution and the U.S. government had a handful of analysts who tried to assess the structure of power within the RVN. Their work, as well as that of former RVN officials who have written postmortems, was remarkably parallel in both methods and conclusion. All assigned special significance to the Chinese capitalists in the running of the RVN system. Yet one cannot attribute causal power to them, because it was the French and later the Americans who ultimately controlled the collaborationist system. Without them, Thieu could not have undertaken so much, so well and so quickly. But while it is true that the Chinese by the 1960s were a traditional elite and the generals a distinctly new one, the political leverage the generals possessed made the Chinese highly dependent on their favors. A huge amount of money could be made in the economy and in the state's operations, and the Chinese obtained the major share in the former and a significant proportion of the latter. Opportunities for corruption available from direct control of state positions were vast, and officers and key bureaucrats dominated them.

Thieu was ultimately the functional master of the whole order during four years. His access to money was crucial to political cohesion in the military elite, and it kept most senior civil servants docile until 1973. The hybrid power structure which emerged was really a very personalized synthesis of Thieu and his coalition of loyal generals as well as a Chinese elite, and it is futile to try to determine their relative importance since each without the other was inconceivable. Getting rich was the common consensus which united them, and as Thieu manipulated their avarice, his machine possessed all of the subjective, arbitrary qualities one associates with the accumulation of capital by political means and corruption during a war which was sponsored entirely by a foreign power. Ultimately, the RVN's existence was improvised in an environment of chicanery, desperation, and tragedy which made absurdity and audacity common coin, with marginalized gangsters the mainstay of the social order the United States was attempting to keep in place.

A crucial aspect of America's funding for Thieu's system was mass employment and the perquisites that went with it. When Diem was overthrown, there were 121,000 civilian employees working for the RVN; by 1965 the number had grown to 179,000, increasing very slowly until 1968 (when Thieu took full command of the state administrative apparatus). From 208,000 government employees in 1968, the bureaucracy bounded to 337,000 in 1972 (the police composed 38 percent of this number), its share of the labor force having more than doubled since the early 1960s. The civil service had been fickle and inept in the stormy sea of post-Diemist politics, and Thieu sought to make it a reliable instrument of his power. Although their nominal salaries were low and kept falling, he allocated to them a whole panoply of corrupt practices to deepen his hold on their loyalties. The most common were bribes to obtain essential papers, ranging from normal legal transactions or identification documents to draft deferments, plus numerous petty forms of boodle. Corruption suffused and financially lubricated the state bureaucratic system at all levels.

The junior officer corps also became a major source of support for Thieu, for he satisfied their ambitions far more than any of his predecessors did. The regular military grew rapidly from 1961 to 1965, but the junior officer appointments failed to keep pace with it. When Thieu took power, he increased the number of first lieutenants from 8,764 in 1968 to 17,353 two years later and that of captains from 4,793 to 10,654, at a time when the regular military grew by less than a fifth. They too, of course, were allocated a share of condoned corruption as a supplement to their low salaries, and they often received their appointments because they were beholden to some senior officer for critical recommendations or, more simply, because they bought his favor. Their rackets were generally petty, ranging from the collecting of rice rations and salaries for dead or deserted soldiers to the funneling of military gasoline and supplies into the local markets, some of which the NLF purchased. Along with political officials, some participated in local usury, which during the Thieu period was 50 to 90 percent monthly. Together they could enforce their claims if necessary.

Higher-level officers were far more important, and their appointments were treated more seriously, since they alone could challenge Thieu's growing hegemony. Success in combat or purely military competence was increasingly ignored in senior appointments; political tendencies and personal ambition were far more critical. This made staff rather than combat officers ever-more preponderant at the upper ranks. Friends and relatives were very important. All appointments at the level of major or above had to be carefully approved by one of Thieu's closest allies in Saigon. He alone chose every general officer. There were only 40 generals in 1967, and 82 colonels, and it was to these men that Thieu turned his attention as he consolidated power. Shunting some of them off to powerless positions and avoiding any challenges to powerful generals' corruption, Thieu increased his control over the military apparatus by enlarging the number of generals to 73 and that of colonels to 200 in 1972, but the senior officer corps, in various degrees, remained seriously underbilleted after 1967, as Thieu cautiously filled the higher positions primarily with political appointees and assigned the lower officers duties which far exceeded both their rank and their abilities. Such a bottom-heavy officer corps was designed essentially to prevent a coup d'etat. Those at the top were repaid for their devotion with a significant share of the state's diverse economic resources, ranging from normal commerce to sanctioned corruption of every variety, from larceny and graft to import licenses. "We would be left with practically no one to fight the war," Thieu's vice-president, Tan Van Huong, admitted, "if all corrupt commanders were to be prosecuted and relieved." Thieu's genius was to deflect the ambitions of his select group of senior officers from a desire for real political power and to make them, as two former generals recalled, "motivated by money." By the most cautious estimates, fully two-thirds of all generals and colonels were corrupt. . . .

The RVN's military and political machinery increasingly merged in Thieu's hands and could not operate without him, and this fact was far more important to its eventual destiny than the issue whether it was trained to fight conventional or guerilla warfare. The military establishment's primary function was to maintain

Thieu's power, and the United States' ability to fight a counterrevolutionary war depended on the durability of a regime which was, in the words of one of Thieu's generals after the war, "intrigue-ridden, dictatorial, and repressive." American officials knew by 1971 what was not fully revealed until spring 1975—that Thieu's talent as a military leader was mediocre at best. His role was political, and Washington supported him for this reason.

Thieu understood that by permitting corruption, indeed even encouraging it, he could win loyalty: "The best way of avoiding coups d'etat . . .," as one of his aides quoted him. But the fundamental dilemma of such an order for America's anti-Communist crusade remained. The various constituencies Thieu drew into his expanding system were usually linked to him informally rather than institutionally, a fact which somewhat disturbed U.S. officials, although not enough to alter their overwhelming wish to see stability maintained. Elections were, as Nguyen Cao Ky aptly phrased it from his own experience as the victorious vice-president in 1967, "a loss of time and money. They were a joke. They have served to install a regime that has nothing in common with the people—a useless, corrupt regime." The National Assembly, which Diem himself created, had no significant powers, and Thieu ignored it. Even the most sympathetic American analysts thought that at least one-third of its members were fortune seekers—and Thieu let them enjoy this search often. . . .

The general dilemma confronting the United States' efforts to expand the military's power and role in numerous underdeveloped nations since 1950 has been the senior officer class' utilization of American support to assume far greater political power. And given the weak economic elite in most nations, the military's political role quickly dominates and exploits the nation's economic development, which ultimately produces instability and crisis politics and thwarts genuine development. In the end, the militarization of the RVN not only monopolized politics but also catalyzed social and human transformations which gravely eroded the coherence and future of the non-Revolutionary ideologies and followers. Those strata of South Vietnamese society without political links could scarcely compete for a large share of the new riches, even though a small number of individuals, mainly Chinese, managed to succeed in the highly fluid context in one way or another. The urban masses lived on the narrowest margins, and even some brothels and bars belonged to the elite that was forming from officers, key bureaucrats, and the Vietnamese and Chinese elements directly allied to them.

American officials always saw clearly the role of the new RVN elite in making vast private gains from political power. They were often informed by various senior generals currying U.S. favor that "corruption exists everywhere, the rich get richer while the mass of the poor Vietnamese see little hope of improvement"—as Marshall Ky told American leaders in July 1965, while jockeying for a greater share of it himself. Far worse than corruption, in American eyes, was tension among the generals and political instability. This consideration caused Washington increasingly to support Thieu, until the officer corps rightly came to believe that he was their surest, perhaps only, link to the Yankee cornucopia. "Patterns of existent political alignments are greatly affected by corruption because of its endemic character in GVN and RVNAF functioning," the National Security Council's early 1969 review of the war concluded. Since reformers could only upset Thieu's cohesive and firmly managed dictatorship, American interest in reform never went beyond occasional subtle changes palatable to Thieu in the aid program.

In this sense, the Americans knew they were ultimately responsible for the Thieu regime, for without their money the RVN would not be able to buy allies who assured stability. The economic basis of its very existence would vanish. "Moreover," the NSC acknowledged in early 1969, "it is natural that many Vietnamese will hold the United States responsible for not controlling its aid so that corruption will not flourish." This relationship was the critical linkage in the social and class structure in the south after 1965; and all else would ultimately prove secondary. Conversely, since the United States now correctly saw that its entire mission was contingent on the RVN's stability, which only Thieu was able to provide, it in turn was wholly dependent on Thieu's remaining in power, a fact he perceived and exploited ruthlessly. Ironically, who was master and who was puppet was increasingly blurred with time.

Analyzed structurally, the apex of the Thieu system was a narrow clique of officers and key civilian officials, not more than several thousand. Immediately below them was a far more numerous set of lower-ranking officials and officers. Directly allied with this elite were various merchants, entrepreneurs in service industries, and businessmen, including a small group of landlords, who collectively channeled money to and from the higher levels via contracts, kickbacks, licenses for imports, and the like. While they never estimated its size, the AID's experts on the upper echelons of this system concluded, "Many of the larger industries in South Vietnam are currently controlled by a small number of coalitions of Chinese businessmen who are allied with strategic Vietnamese government personnel." The Fukienese, according to American officials, were by far the most powerful, Ly Luong Than was their most important leader, and they controlled or had major shares in textiles, scrap metal, construction, banking, insurance, food processing, and imports. Chinese from Swatow were congregated in banking, insurance, diverse manufacturing, and textiles.

All of the analyses of the dominating persons in this system number in the hundreds the officers and senior politicians and officials involved, and their capitalist allies—the large majority being Chinese—could not have been more than one or two thousand. This tiny but critical element accounted for the bulk of the accumulated capital and capital flight. Most of the capitalists had been wealthy before the war, but not on a remotely comparable scale. Directly beneath them was an altogether new group of largely politically based rich whose primary power lay in access to the state's largesse, and these were paralleled by entrepreneurs, mainly Chinese, but with a growing number of Vietnamese, who simply made money in conventional ways inevitable with the boom the American forces brought. . . .

Thieu, of course, never attempted seriously to create a broad class foundation for his regime, but the cumulative effect of Thieu's system was to create a congenial if fickle constituency out of those who were the direct or indirect beneficiaries of the American-funded society. There was never a class base for the Thieu regime in the true sense of class as an institutionally stable and broad element of society. The disintegration of the French legacy and the marginalization of the educated elements who had earlier been ideologically or economically predisposed to anti-Communist politics continued, inevitably conditioning a substantial portion of them for anti-Thieu coalition politics with virtually anyone, including the NLF. The shallow privileged class residues inherited from the French era continued to narrow, especially as inflation after 1965 began to whittle away at the economic resources of all except the Chinese.

The very context in which Thieu's regime developed convinced most of its new elite that it could not endure, and this especially affected its Chinese members, who had traditionally been mobile, prone to keeping wealth highly liquid, and often linked to families and interests elsewhere in Southeast Asia. Between the Chinese and the officers, the basic paradox of the Thieu regime was the opportunism of its most powerful and favored supporters, which took the form of a vast flight of capital, an exodus of children, and a reluctance to invest in long-term economic development. The Chinese capitalists were by definition the weakest class on which the military elite could rely. And precisely because they knew that the generals were vulnerable and transitional, they tried to make certain that their options outside the country were always ready. The Chinese, American officials in Saigon accurately concluded in 1972, for the most part "do not consider themselves a part of the nation in which they live. For the large entrepreneurs, the business decision to invest here or transfer funds abroad is made on business calculations and not on any consideration of national need—exactly, in fact, like any foreign investor does."

The fragile class structure that the French had created and Diem eroded now became even weaker in the flotsam and jetsam of demography, social disintegration, and changes far too rapid to be absorbed coherently. The new lumpen element of war profiteers destroyed the final vestiges of the national and the petite bourgeoisies, plunging them into economic and moral crises which compromised some and radicalized others. And being wholly dependent on American money and support for the very existence of the RVN, the new profiteers had no nationalist or cultural legitimacy for their politics, a fact they could not alter. The underdevelopment of a possible conservative class characterized the pre-Revolutionary order until its end. Both the French and the American colonial legacies made this ephemeral, fluid class development inevitable by their reliance on the Chinese and on dependent, obsequious arriviste generals whose only loyalty in serving comprador roles was ultimately to their own, personal welfare.

Though South Vietnam's economy under Diem was wholly dependent on American aid, after 1964 it was far more fragile. The intensified war and the exponential growth of American GIs posed potentially catastrophic economic challenges to the United States' ambition. For agriculture was being uprooted and the population displaced into cities wholly unable to absorb them with local resources.

The purpose of American economic policy was to stanch the immense economic wounds the war was inflicting long enough to allow its vague military objectives to be attained at a time, as the Agency for International Development later ruefully admitted, when "no one thought the war would last ten years, let alone that we would lose it." The cost to the United States could, if its military assumptions were valid, remain tolerable only for a short period. But to cut its losses was tantamount to military surrender, which was unthinkable. Meanwhile, Washington's temporary economic solutions produced fabulous opportunities for growing corruption, becoming the key to Thieu's political consolidation and, to a lesser degree, the maintenance of more social stability among the masses than would otherwise have been possible. In effect, the RVN's very existence was linked to sufficient economic and military aid, surpassing in importance the outcome of battles or diplomacy, for the very artificiality of the economy and the war's impact left it vulnerable to countless potentially fatal problems.

In retrospect, the AID accurately concluded in 1975, the "period 1965–67 in Viet Nam was unlike anything ever experienced by an underdeveloped country." While the various mechanisms the United States employed may seem complicated to nonspecialists, in essence they were merely manifestations of a simple policy. An escalating war was destroying the existing economy, and Washington made the decision that it was vital to prevent inflation, which could only further radicalize the people and make defeat more certain. The Korean War, which was much smaller in terms both of troops and of areas affected at any one time, had created a runaway inflation, the memory of which was still fresh in Washington in 1964. To combat inflation, the United States decided to maximize imports, neutralizing the vast inflow of dollars accompanying its half a million soldiers, the American expansion of bases and military construction, and the ruination of South Vietnam's traditional productive economic sector. The RVN's seeming prosperity, so illusory for the majority of the nation, was based wholly on this strategy.

Agricultural production by 1968 was a quarter below the already low 1961–65 average. Not until 1970 did it finally surpass it, although per capita output never equaled it. Industrial production, mainly to service U.S. troop demands and provide supplies for construction, rose during 1964–67, dropping sharply in 1968. In 1964–67 imports increased over 100 percent, and imports during 1969–71 exceeded exports by a factor of over fifty-five. By 1967 about 40 percent of the RVN's gross national product was composed of imports entirely dependent on U.S. aid, and by 1970 nearly 50 percent was. Proportionately, the share of gross domestic product devoted to manufacturing dropped dramatically throughout this period—making South Vietnam the only major nation of Asia to experience this form of deindustrialization and leaving it with the lowest proportion in manufacturing of any of them. The South Vietnamese economy was sharply diverted from the production of goods, the only basis of real economic development, into the provision of services, making it structurally very weak and vulnerable to an economic crisis the moment the Americans started to withdraw.

A Viable State

BUI DIEM

Except for the special circumstances that put me close to the center stage of the war in Vietnam, and except for the sheer luck that spared me much of the suffering endured by others, I am not different from other Vietnamese of my generation. In terms of dreams and aspirations, frustrations and disappointments, my life story is essentially theirs.

Vietnamese of my generation came of age in the early forties with the hope that after almost a century as second-class citizens in their own country, they would

From *In the Jaws of History* by Bui Diem and David Chanoff, pp. 334–343. Copyright © 1987 by Bui Diem and David Chanoff. Reprinted by permission of Houghton Mifflin Company.

have a chance to recover their dignity and achieve their independence from France. They dreamed also of peace and a decent life for themselves and their children. It was their misfortune that instead of independence, peace, and a decent life, they saw only revolution, war, and destruction. For three decades they existed in the maelstrom. And even now, when Vietnam no longer has to deal with foreign invaders, their misery continues. Theirs has been a tragedy of historic proportions.

In an interview with Walter Cronkite in 1963, President John Kennedy said, "In the final analysis, it's their war and they are the ones who will either win it or lose it." Much as we might like to, there is no getting away from Kennedy's judgment. The South Vietnamese people, and especially the South Vietnamese leaders, myself among them, bear the ultimate responsibility for the fate of their nation, and to be honest, they have much to regret and much to be ashamed of. But it is also true that the war's cast of characters operated within a matrix of larger forces that stood outside the common human inadequacies and failings. And it was these forces that shaped the landscape on which we all moved.

First among these root causes was the obduracy of France, which in the late forties insisted on retaining control of its former colony rather than conceding independence in good time to a people who hungered for it. Second was the ideological obsession of Vietnam's Communists. Not content with fighting to slough off a dying colonialism, they relentlessly sought to impose on the Vietnamese people their dogma of class warfare and proletarian dictatorship. Finally came the massive intervention by the United States, inserting into our struggle for independence and freedom its own overpowering dynamic. These three forces combined to distort the basic nature of Vietnam's emergence from colonialism, ensuring that the struggle would be more complex and bloodier than that of so many other colonies which achieved nationhood during mid-century.

Caught in the midst of these powerful forces, Vietnam's nationalists found themselves in a succession of precarious situations. In most cases they were forced to choose among unpalatable alternatives; often, indeed, they saw no choice at all. With their survival at stake, they were forced to take refuge in a series of uneasy and uncomfortable compromises that little by little eroded their legitimacy. From one experience to another—first with the French and Bao Dai, then with Ngo Dinh Diem, then with the Americans and the military—they tried to carve out a role for themselves and establish their influence. But always they were pushed to the periphery, and the influence they wielded was never enough to affect the ultimate course of events. To myself and others, for a time it seemed we might be able to develop the nation's economy and build a functioning democracy, even while waging war. But eventually the room to make this kind of contribution diminished, and in the end, against a mechanized North Vietnamese invasion army equipped by the Soviets, all that remained was an alley fight for survival. By then Vietnam's nationalists had been forced to take their place alongside all the other Vietnamese who could only stand by and watch their fate unfold in front of them.

As I look back on the external forces that shaped our lives, it is the American intervention that stands out. French colonialism, after all, is dead and gone, a subject for historians who prefer the inert remains of the past to the passions of the present. As for Vietnamese communism, no one but the fervid or the blind any longer argues the merits of a system that has brought in its wake only war and deprivation and mass flight. (Not that having been right comforts us as we house our refugees and send what sustenance we can back to our families.) But American intervention is a living issue. In the train of failure in Vietnam, and in the face of hard choices elsewhere, the questions of its correctness and its morality still inform American foreign policy debates. Americans still seek to learn the lessons of intervention, and so do America's smaller allies, who cannot help but see in the fate of Vietnam intimations of their own possible futures.

For critics of the Vietnam War, the original decision to intervene was wrong, a result, as one of them put it, of a "steady string of misjudgments." It was wrong because American policymakers in the sixties failed to assess correctly the vital interests of the United States, because they exaggerated the geopolitical importance of Vietnam, and because they had an inflated concept of American capabilities.

Although it is neither my business nor within my competence to pass judgment on how the United States defined its interests at that time, it is my impression that such arguments are made on a distinctly *a posteriori* basis. I remember vividly the political atmosphere in the United States in the summer of 1964, the summer of the Tonkin resolution and Barry Goldwater's nomination, when I first visited this country. At that time the Johnson administration and practically the entire Congress were in favor of the commitment to defend Vietnam (the resolution passed in the Senate, 98 to 2, and in the House, 416 to 0). And so, *mirabile dictu,* were the national news media.

Moreover, the context of international affairs in that period provided good reasons for this nearly unanimous opinion, reasons that went beyond the specific perception of North Vietnamese aggressiveness. It was then the aftermath of the Communist attack in Korea, and China's Communist leaders were broadcasting the most belligerent and expansionistic views, even as they attempted to establish a Peking-Jakarta axis with Indonesia's pro-Communist President Sukarno. For the fragile governments of Southeast Asia the situation seemed serious indeed. Although twenty-five years later it became fashionable among some Americans to belittle Communist threats to the region's stability, among the responsible governments at the time there was deep anxiety.

Even for those South Vietnamese who thought they saw the inherent dangers in American intervention, there was still nothing illogical about it. The American interest in Vietnam, even its land intervention, seemed a natural extension of U.S. policies in Europe (the Marshall Plan, the Berlin airlift, Greece) and Asia (Korea) aimed at preventing the expansion of combined Soviet and Chinese power (at least until the early 1960s, no one could imagine that the two Communist giants would become antagonists). And for the Europeans who were able to rebuild their countries and save their democratic institutions, for the Germans in Berlin, for the Greeks, and for the South Koreans, those policies were not wrong. Nor were they based on misjudgments of geopolitical realities. In Vietnam the policy failed. But that is not to say that it was wrong there either. The disastrous mistakes that were made were mistakes in implementation rather than intention. But the thrust of the policy of containment and protection, that I do not think can be faulted. It is, on the contrary, something for Americans to be proud of.

The more vocal critics of the war in the sixties and seventies characterized the intervention, not just as wrong, but also as immoral. Their charge was based primarily on the theory that the war in Vietnam was a civil war, and that consequently American intervention was an act of aggression against people who were fighting to free themselves from an oppressive regime and unify their country in accord with the aspirations of the great majority of decent-minded Vietnamese.

It is my own belief that this theory held the field for so long primarily because it was a powerful attraction to the many Americans who were angry at their own government and society and were looking for issues to hang their anger on. Certainly, the facts that refuted it were readily available. From early on, both Saigon and Washington knew beyond a doubt that the National Liberation Front—the Vietcong—was a creation of the Communist party, and that without North Vietnamese organization, leadership, supplies, and, starting in 1964, without the North Vietnamese regular army, there would have been no revolution to speak of and no war. It was one of my greatest frustrations that our firm knowledge of this—both from widespread and incontrovertible evidence and also from personal experience among many of us of communist "front" techniques—made no impact on popular understanding in the West. Regardless of what was there to be seen, people saw only what they wished.

After the war, when propaganda no longer mattered, the party dropped its pretense. "Our Party," said Le Duan in his 1975 victory speech, "is the unique and single leader that organized, controlled, and governed the entire struggle of the Vietnamese people from the first day of the revolution." During the war, the North Vietnamese never openly admitted they had troops in South Vietnam. (Le Duc Tho even kept up the pretense with Henry Kissinger, although Kissinger knew the situation as well as he knew his own name, and Tho, of course, knew that he knew it.) But afterward the party treated this subterfuge simply as an excellent piece of public relations and its own role as a matter of intense pride. As the North Vietnamese general Vo Ban told French television interviewers in 1983, "In May 1959 I had the privilege of being designated by the Vietnamese Communist Party to unleash a military attack on the South in order to liberate the South and reunify the fatherland."

During the heyday of the antiwar movement, I marveled at the innocence of its spokesmen in believing something different from this. I wonder even now if they ever feel shame for their gullibility and for their contribution to the tragedy. But they are not heard from. It was, after all, only one chapter in their lives, as it was only a chapter in the book of American history.

The issue of morality, then, comes down to whether it was moral for the United States to have supported an admittedly flawed South Vietnamese regime in its attempt to survive against a totalitarian antagonist. Here, too, the answer seems to me self-evident. However unpalatable leaders like Nguyen Van Thieu might have been, South Vietnam was full of pluralistic ferment and possibilities for change and development. It was a place where good people could hope for something better to evolve, where they could even fight for it, as so many strong-minded opposition politicians, intellectuals, and writers did. None but ideologues can compare such a place with the chilling police state that destroyed it. And none, I think, can fairly question the morality of the effort to prevent its destruction.

To my mind, the lessons of American intervention in Vietnam have to do not so much with the geopolitical or moral underpinning of the war, but rather with the way the intervention was implemented. The real question was not whether to intervene, but how to intervene effectively.

. . . The salient feature of [the] confused and unclear process (as Bill Bundy characterized it) [by which the Johnson administration decided to bring an American land army to Vietnam] was not that it was ill planned and based on no comprehensive strategy. It was the startling attitude of American decision makers toward their ally. At the top levels of the administration, the State Department, and the Pentagon, there is no evidence to suggest that anyone considered the South Vietnamese as partners in the venture to save South Vietnam. In a mood that seemed mixed of idealism and naivete, impatience and overconfidence, the Americans simply came in and took over. It was an attitude that would endure throughout the remainder of the conflict. The message seemed to be that this was an American war, and the best thing the South Vietnamese could do was to keep from rocking the boat and let the Americans get on with their business.

The military consequences of this orientation were that the United States took the entire burden on itself instead of searching for ways to make a decisive impact while limiting its exposure. Had the South Vietnamese been consulted in early 1965, it is likely they would have preferred either no intervention or a limited effort sufficient to stabilize the military situation and block the infiltration routes from North Vietnam. An agreement among the United States, South Vietnam, and Laos, allowing U.S. troops to be stationed along the seventeenth parallel as a barrier, would have been quite feasible at the time. With that done, an immediate Vietnamization program could have been undertaken to strengthen and upgrade the South Vietnamese army.

Could such a simple strategy have worked? That is one of the "what if" questions with which the Vietnam War abounds. Colonel Harry Summers, in *On Strategy,* his uncompromising review of American military planning, concludes that it would have, that in fact, isolating the South Vietnamese battlefield from North Vietnamese reinforcement and resupply was the only logical objective for American arms. Whatever the imponderables of war, this approach would at least have had the virtue of establishing the United States as a peace-keeping force protecting South Vietnam from outside aggression. It would have reduced American casualties and precluded the involvement of American firepower in the disconcerting people's war that was such a nightmare for the GIs to fight and that created such powerful antagonism in the arena of international public opinion.

On the political level, too, this American failure to regard the South Vietnamese as people worthy of partnership had destructive results. It meant that the United States never pursued a consistent policy aimed at encouraging the development of a viable democracy in South Vietnam. Certainly, such a thing was possible. Between 1965 and 1967 the South Vietnamese drafted and adopted a constitution, elected a president, vice president, and legislature, and successfully held many local elections—all of this in the middle of a war. It was a substantial achievement, but it would not have happened except that during those years the impulse toward democracy in South Vietnam and the objectives of the Johnson administration coincided.

Unfortunately, thereafter "stability" became the American watchword. As long as the Saigon government demonstrated a modicum of equilibrium, that was all that was asked of it. Several years of progress toward decent government might erode, corruption and autocracy might swell, but these things were not a primary American concern. By 1969 Henry Kissinger and Richard Nixon had embarked on a complex chess game, manipulating big-power diplomacy, military force, and secret negotiations in an attempt to extricate the United States from its quagmire. Amidst this constellation of variables, they needed a government in Saigon that was stable and predictable. If Thieu provided them with that, then whatever else he might do was essentially irrelevant.

It was a fatal error on two counts. First, stigmatized as undemocratic and corrupt, South Vietnam was deemed unworthy of support by an ever-increasing percentage of the American public and Congress. Second, within South Vietnam itself, the unpopular nature of the regime produced apathy, cynicism, and finally, in the anti-corruption movement, outrage. Charles Mohr, veteran correspondent of the *New York Times,* summed it up succinctly in a seminar at the American Enterprise Institute. "We lost the war in Vietnam," he said, "not because we did not bring enough pressure to bear on our enemy, but because we did not bring sufficient pressure on our ally." Admittedly, bringing pressure for reform and democracy is a delicate business. But in situations where the United States has significant leverage, the role of catalyst for change, of prodding contending factions toward consensus, beckons to American diplomacy.

To successfully play such a role, there are two prerequisites. One is the will to carry out a strong and consistent advocacy. The other is the determination to accept the consequences if in the end American pressure proves unavailing. The United States must find a way to say to a Ngo Dinh Diem or a Nguyen Van Thieu (or a Ferdinand Marcos or an Augusto Pinochet), "We have no alternative but to stand by our own values. If for your own reasons you find you cannot bring yourselves toward conforming with them, then we are very sorry, but we will have no choice but to leave you to your own devices." With all its power and prestige, the United States simply cannot allow itself to yield to the tyranny of the weak, to authoritarians who believe their importance is so vast that the United States cannot help but support them. If Vietnam has one single lesson to teach, it is that people cannot be saved in spite of themselves. Far better to get out and cut losses before ensnaring treasure, lives, prestige, and all in the service of those whose rule means violent discord and social breakdown.

In Vietnam I always believed that among decent and reasonable people there could be no disagreement about things like corruption, economic and social reforms, and democratic procedures. I believe the same is true elsewhere. Another *New York Times* man, A. M. Rosenthal, in reflecting on his decades of covering American diplomacy, had this to say: "What should our policy be? Simply to act in our belief and interest. Our belief is political freedom and our interest is political freedom. We will not be able to achieve them for others all of the time or even much of the time. But what we can do is stand up for what we believe in, all of the time. . . . That requires two things: vision and constancy. Haitians, Filipinos, Koreans, Afghans seem to have no great confusion about what they really seek from us. Neither do the Czechoslovaks or the Poles." Neither, he might have added, did the South Vietnamese.

The experience of Vietnam suggests that a policy such as Rosenthal recommends would not be simple idealism. After Vietnam it is natural to question the extent to which the United States can sustain any major commitment to a foreign nation unless that nation is capable of eliciting moral support from an idealistic and essentially antimilitaristic American public. The suggestion is that geopolitical considerations by themselves constitute an insufficient grounding for stable, long-term policy. From this perspective, a democratic commitment in foreign policy is not mere idealism; it is also pragmatic self-interest.

From 1965 through 1967, Lyndon Johnson's administration acted according to this concept of idealistic pragmatism. From time to time other administrations did too, but never consistently and never strongly. For all the rhetoric, the American commitment to democracy in South Vietnam was a timid and wavering and some-time thing. That is another way of saying that in South Vietnam American policy neglected the human dimension. It did not accord its allies their requisite dignity as human beings. (I am not speaking here of the thousands of Americans who worked devotedly alongside the Vietnamese.) At the decision-making level, Vietnam was regarded primarily as a geopolitical abstraction, a factor in the play of American global interests. That was true about the way the United States intervened in the war with its land army. It was true about the way the United States conducted the war. And it was especially true about how the United States left the war.

Of all the successive phases of U.S involvement—the intervention of 1965, the Americanization of the war, then its Vietnamization, and finally the disengagement—it is the disengagement that will stick longest in the minds of the South Vietnamese. Major mistakes were made during the war by everyone concerned. But the manner in which the United States took its leave was more than a mistake; it was an act unworthy of a great power, one that I believe will be remembered long after such unfortunate misconceptions as the search and destroy strategy have been consigned to footnotes.

It was not that the leave-taking itself was a disgrace. The United States fought long and hard in Vietnam, and if in the end circumstances required that it withdraw, it may be considered a tragedy but hardly an act of shame. The same cannot be said, however, for the manipulative and callous manner with which the American administration and the American Congress dealt with South Vietnam during the last years of the war. It was not one of America's finest hours, and there are plenty of lessons in it for both the United States and for other nations, particularly small ones that must rely on the United States for their defense.

As for Henry Kissinger, the architect of the Paris agreement, one can sympathize with his desire for "flexibility," that is, for control. Kissinger was in the middle, attempting to maneuver disparate and obstinate parties (including the North Vietnamese, South Vietnamese, Soviets, Chinese, even, on occasion, his own president) toward the same end. But he had taken on himself an awesome responsibility, negotiating not just for the global interests of the United States but for the existence of South Vietnam. In this context, he and Richard Nixon avoided holding frank discussions on common strategies with the South Vietnamese. They knew that Nguyen Van Thieu could do nothing without American support, yet they chose the unnecessary expedient of keeping developments to themselves until the last moment, then bringing to bear the heavy tactics of promises and threats. They treated a dependent ally of twenty years with finesse and then brutality, instead of with the openness the relationship required.

The fact that Kissinger and Nixon may have believed they had a viable agreement, or at least the best they could get, does not in my view justify their conduct toward South Vietnam. But at the same time, as unique as the Nixon administration's diplomatic style was, it was in effect just another aspect, another face of the American policy that had obtained in Vietnam from the beginning, informed by worthy motives but without an understanding of the human beings who would be affected by its geopolitical goals.

The congresses that in 1973, 1974, and 1975 washed their hands of Vietnam shared fully in this same guilt. Although senators and representatives talked a good deal then about credibility and moral obligation, in fact what they did was to make a geopolitical decision on the basis of what they saw as American self-interest. They did so in callous disregard of the consequences their actions would have on a nation of twenty million people, and they did so although it was no longer a matter of American blood, but only of some hundreds of millions of dollars.

"Is it possible for a great nation to behave this way?" That was the question an old friend of mine asked me in Saigon when news came in August of 1974 that Congress had reduced the volume of aid. He was a store owner whom I had gone to school with in North Vietnam, a totally nonpolitical person. "You are an ambassador," he said. "Perhaps you understand these things better than I do. But can you explain this attitude of the Americans? When they wanted to come, they came. And when they want to leave, they leave. It's as if a neighbor came over and made a shambles of your house, then all of a sudden he decides the whole thing is wrong, so he calls it quits. How can they just do that?" It was a naive question from an unsophisticated man. But I had no answer for it. Neither, I think, would William Fulbright, or George McGovern, or the other antiwar congressmen.

In the end, though, the culpability is hardly theirs alone. So many thought they knew the truth. The newsmen—as arrogant as any—Kissinger, Thieu, Nixon, myself as well. But none of us knew the truth or, knowing it, took it sufficiently to heart. Not we, and certainly not the implacable and ruthless ideologues who were our enemies. The truth is in the millions of Vietnamese families that have suffered the most horrible tragedies, people who understood what was happening only in the vaguest way. The truth of this war lies buried with its victims, with those who died, and with those who are consigned to live in an oppressed silence, for now and for the coming generations—a silence the world calls peace.

✗ *F U R T H E R   R E A D I N G*

Bloodworth, Denis. *An Eye for the Dragon* (1970).
Bouscaren, Anthony. *The Last of the Mandarins: Diem of Vietnam* (1965).
Elliott, David. *The Vietnamese War: Revolution and Social Change in the MeKong Delta* (2001).
Fall, Bernard B. *The Two Vietnams* (1967).
FitzGerald, Frances. *Fire in the Lake* (1972).
Goodman, Allan E. *Politics in War: The Bases of Political Community in South Vietnam* (1973).
Grinter, Lawerence E. "Bargaining Between Saigon and Washington: Dilemmas of Linkage Politics During War," *Orbis,* 18 (1974), 837–67.

Herring, George C. "'Peoples Quite Apart': Americans, South Vietnamese, and the War in Vietnam," *Diplomatic History,* 14 (1990), 1–23.

Hickey, Gerald C. *Village in Vietnam* (1964).

McT. Kahin, George, and John W. Lewis. *The United States in Vietnam* (1969).

Komer, Robert W. *Bureaucracy Does Its Thing* (1972).

Lacouture, Jean. *Vietnam Between Two Truces* (1966).

Lancaster, Donald. *The Emancipation of French Indochina* (1961).

Race, Jeffrey. *War Comes to Long An* (1972).

Scigliano, Robert. *South Vietnam: Nation Under Stress* (1964).

Scigliano, Robert, and Guy Fox. *Technical Assistance in Vietnam* (1965).

Shaplen, Robert. *The Road from War* (1970).

Trullinger, James. *Village at War* (1980).

Thai, Nguyen. *Is South Vietnam Viable?* (1962).

Warner, Denis. *The Last Confucian* (1963).

Richard M. Nixon's Strategy for Withdrawal

✕

Richard M. Nixon assumed the presidency in January 1969 with a clear mandate to end America's commitment to Vietnam. Convinced that a precipitous withdrawal of American troops would jeopardize South Vietnam's prospects for survival as well as America's global prestige and credibility, he opted for a strategy of Vietnamizing the war: withdrawing American forces gradually while turning over the conduct of the war to the South Vietnamese.

Twice Nixon widened the war at least temporarily, in order, he believed, to hasten its end. In April 1970 he ordered U.S. and South Vietnamese troops into Cambodia in an effort to rout enemy bases there and buy time for Vietnamization. One of the most controversial moves of his presidency, the Cambodian incursion met with passionate opposition, especially on college campuses. Then in February 1971 he approved a major ground operation into Laos.

Nixon simultaneously moved on the diplomatic front. His special assistant for national security affairs, Henry A. Kissinger, began secret negotiations with Le Duc Tho, his North Vietnamese counterpart, in Paris early in 1969. After several years of talks, those efforts appeared ready to bear fruit in 1972 toward the end of Nixon's first term. The president, however, considered it necessary to apply additional military pressure on Hanoi—the controversial "Christmas bombings" of 1972—in order to conclude a negotiated settlement. On January 27, 1973, a peace agreement was finally signed in Paris that allowed the total withdrawal of American combat forces.

Although much documentary evidence regarding the Nixon years remains closed to researchers, public and scholarly interest in the president's Vietnam policy has been strong. Interpreters of the Nixon record have differed over such critical matters as the underlying rationale for Vietnamization; the reasons for and consequences of the Cambodian invasion; the relationship between U.S. actions in Vietnam and a global strategy centered on détente with the Soviet Union and normalization of relations with China; and the nature of the Paris peace settlement. Critics on the left have accused Nixon of needlessly prolonging the fighting for a settlement that could have been achieved years earlier; critics on the right have charged him with sacrificing an American ally on the altar of expediency and global interests. The documents and essays in this chapter address these issues.

✗ *D O C U M E N T S*

In Document 1, Henry Kissinger offers his retrospective assessment of the challenges that the continuing war in Vietnam posed for the Nixon administration. He argues that the conflict remained a fundamental obstacle to the administration's search for stability and order abroad—and at home. In early January 1969 Kissinger's National Security Council staff circulated a series of questions about Vietnam policy to concerned agencies within the executive branch. The answers were summarized in National Security Study Memorandum No. 1, dated January 21, from which extracts are printed as Document 2. In Document 3, Trinh Duc, a Vietcong guerrilla, describes the difficulties that American firepower caused for the communist insurgents during 1969 and 1970.

Document 4 is drawn from a nationwide address by Richard Nixon, delivered on November 24, 1969, in which the president outlined his Vietnamization strategy and appealed to the "silent majority" for support. In Document 5, reprinted from Nixon's televised national address of May 11, 1970, the president explained and defended his decision to order U.S. and South Vietnamese troops into Cambodia. Document 6 contains extracts from Kissinger's news conference of January 26, 1972, in which he discussed previously secret negotiations with North Vietnam, emphasizing the remaining points of contention between the two sides. On September 11, 1972, the Provisional Revolutionary Government (the title formally adopted by the National Liberation Front in 1969) released a statement that laid out its negotiating position; it is reprinted as Document 7.

1. Henry A. Kissinger Reflects on the Nixon Administration's Dilemma in Vietnam (1969), 1979

In my view, Vietnam was not the cause of our difficulties but a symptom. We were in a period of painful adjustment to a profound transformation of global politics; we were being forced to come to grips with the tension between our history and our new necessities. For two centuries America's participation in the world seemed to oscillate between overinvolvement and withdrawal, between expecting too much of our power and being ashamed of it, between optimistic exuberance and frustration with the ambiguities of an imperfect world. I was convinced that the deepest cause of our national unease was the realization—as yet dimly perceived—that we were becoming like other nations in the need to recognize that our power, while vast, had limits. Our resources were no longer infinite in relation to our problems, instead we had to set priorities, both intellectual and material. In the Fifties and Sixties we had attempted ultimate solutions to specific problems; now our challenge was to shape a world and an American role to which we were permanently committed, which could no longer be sustained by the illusion that our exertions had a terminal point.

Any Administration elected in 1968 would have faced this problem. It was a colossal task in the best of circumstances; the war in Vietnam turned it into a searing and anguishing enterprise. . . .

I cannot yet write about Vietnam except with pain and sadness.

When we came into office over a half-million Americans were fighting a war ten thousand miles away. Their numbers were still increasing on a schedule established by our predecessors. We found no plans for withdrawals. Thirty-one thousand had already died. Whatever our original war aims, by 1969 our credibility abroad, the reliability of our commitments, and our domestic cohesion were alike jeopardized by a struggle in a country as far away from the North American continent as our globe permits. Our involvement had begun openly, and with nearly unanimous Congressional, public, and media approval. But by 1969 our country had been riven by protest and anguish, sometimes taking on a violent and ugly character. The comity by which a democratic society must live had broken down. No government can function without a minimum of trust. This was being dissipated under the harshness of our alternatives and the increasing rage of our domestic controversy.

Psychologists or sociologists may explain some day what it is about that distant monochromatic land, of green mountains and fields merging with an azure sea, that for millennia has acted as a magnet for foreigners who sought glory there and found frustration, who believed that in its rice fields and jungles some principle was to be established and entered them only to recede in disillusion. What has inspired its people to such flights of heroism and monomania that a succession of outsiders have looked there for a key to some riddle and then been expelled by a ferocious persistence that not only thwarted the foreigner's exertions but hazarded his own internal balance?

Our predecessors had entered in innocence, convinced that the cruel civil war represented the cutting edge of some global design. In four years of struggle they had been unable to develop a strategy to achieve victory—and for all one can know now such a strategy was not attainable. They had done enough to produce a major commitment of American power and credibility but not enough to bring it to a conclusion. In the last year of the Johnson Administration the Communists had launched a massive countrywide offensive. Few students of the subject question today that it was massively defeated. But its scale and sacrifice turned it into a psychological victory. Under the impact of the Tet offensive we first curtailed and then ended our bombing of the North for no return except the opening of negotiations which our implacable adversary immediately stalemated. Public support was ebbing for a war we would not win but also seemed unable to end.

And in our country, opposition grew. It was composed of many strands: sincere pacifists who hated to see their country involved in killing thousands of miles away; pragmatists who could discern no plausible outcome; isolationists who wished to end American overseas involvement; idealists who saw no compatibility between our values and the horrors of a war literally brought home for the first time on television. And these groups were egged on by a small minority expressing the inchoate rage of the 1960s with shock tactics of obscenity and violence, expressing their hatred of America, its "system" and its "evil." All these groups had combined to produce the bitter chaos of the Democratic Convention of 1968, the campus violence, and the confusion and demoralization of the leadership groups that had sustained the great American postwar initiatives in foreign policy.

Richard Nixon inherited this cauldron. Of all choices he was probably the least suited for the act of grace that might have achieved reconciliation with the responsible members of the opposition. Seeing himself in any case the target of a liberal conspiracy to destroy him, he could never bring himself to regard the upheaval caused by the Vietnam war as anything other than a continuation of the long-lived assault on his political existence. Though he sympathized more with the anguish of the genuine protesters than they knew, he never mustered the self-confidence or the largeness of spirit to reach out to them. He accepted their premises that we faced a mortal domestic struggle; in the process he accelerated and compounded its bitterness.

Fairness compels the recognition that he had precious little help. After all, Hubert Humphrey, whose entire life was a reach for reconciliation, had been treated scarcely better during his campaign for the Presidency. And after Nixon took office those who had created our involvement in Vietnam moved first to neutrality and then to opposition, saddling Nixon with responsibility for a war he had inherited and attacking him in the name of solutions they themselves had neither advocated nor executed when they had the opportunity.

The Nixon Administration entered office determined to end our involvement in Vietnam. But it soon came up against the reality that had also bedeviled its predecessor. For nearly a generation the security and progress of free people had depended on confidence in America. We could not simply walk away from an enterprise involving two administrations, five allied countries, and thirty-one thousand dead as if we were switching a television channel. Many urged us to "emulate de Gaulle"; but they overlooked that it took even de Gaulle four years to extricate his country from Algeria because he, too, thought it important for France to emerge from its travails with its domestic cohesion and international stature intact. He extricated France from Algeria as an act of policy, not as a collapse, in a manner reflecting a national decision and not a rout.

Such an ending of the war was even more important for the United States. As the leader of democratic alliances we had to remember that scores of countries and millions of people relied for their security on our willingness to stand by allies, indeed on our confidence in ourselves. No serious policymaker could allow himself to succumb to the fashionable debunking of "prestige" or "honor" or "credibility." For a great power to abandon a small country to tyranny simply to obtain a respite from our own travail seemed to me—and still seems to me—profoundly immoral and destructive of our efforts to build a new and ultimately more peaceful pattern of international relations. We could not revitalize the Atlantic Alliance if its governments were assailed by doubt about American staying power. We would not be able to move the Soviet Union toward the imperative of mutual restraint against the background of capitulation in a major war. We might not achieve our opening to China if our value as a counterweight seemed nullified by a collapse that showed us irrelevant to Asian security. Our success in Middle East diplomacy would depend on convincing our ally of our reliability and its adversaries that we were impervious to threats of military pressure or blackmail. Clearly, the American people wanted to end the war, but every poll, and indeed Nixon's election (and the Wallace vote), made it equally evident that they saw their country's aims as honorable and did not relish America's humiliation. The new Administration had to respect the concerns of the opponents of the war but also the anguish of the families whose sons had suffered and died for their country and who did not want it determined—after the fact—that their sacrifice had been in vain.

2. National Security Study Memorandum No. 1, 1969

The responses to the questions posed regarding Vietnam show agreement on some matters as well as very substantial differences of opinion within the U.S. Government on many aspects of the Vietnam situation. While there are some divergencies on the facts, the sharpest differences arise in the interpretation of those facts, the relative weight to be given them, and the implications to be drawn. In addition, there remain certain areas where our information remains inadequate.

There is general agreement, assuming we follow our current strategy, on the following—

1. The GVN and allied position in Vietnam has been strengthened recently in many respects.

2. The GVN has improved its political position, but it is not certain that GVN and other non-communist groups will be able to survive a peaceful competition with the NLF for political power in South Vietnam.

3. The RVNAF alone cannot now, or in the foreseeable future, stand up to the current North Vietnamese–Viet Cong forces.

4. The enemy have suffered some reverses but they have not changed their essential objectives and they have sufficient strength to pursue these objectives. We are not attriting his forces faster than he can recruit or infiltrate.

5. The enemy is not in Paris primarily out of weakness.

The disagreements within these parameters are reflected in two schools in the government with generally consistent membership. The first school, which we will call Group A, usually includes MACV, CINCPAC, JCS and Embassy Saigon, and takes a hopeful view of current and future prospects in Vietnam within the parameters mentioned. The second school, Group B, usually includes OSD [Office of the Secretary of Defense], CIA and (to a lesser extent) State, and is decidedly more skeptical about the present and pessimistic about the future. There are, of course, disagreements within agencies across the board or on specific issues.

As illustration, these schools line up as follows on some of the broader questions:

In explaining reduced enemy military presence and activities, Group A gives greater relative weight to allied military pressure than does Group B.

The improvements in RVNAF are considered much more significant by Group A than Group B.

Group A underlines advancements in the pacification program, while Group B is skeptical both of the evaluation system used to measure progress and of the solidity of recent advances.

In looking at the political scene, Group A accents recent improvements while Group B highlights remaining obstacles and the relative strength of the NLF.

Group A assigns much greater effectiveness to bombing in Vietnam and Laos than Group B.

National Security Study Memorandum No. 1, January 21, 1969, reprinted in *Congressional Record,* May 10, 1972, pp. E4977–E4981.

Following is a summary of the major conclusions and disagreements about each of six broad areas with regard to Vietnam: the negotiating environment, enemy capabilities, RVNAF capabilities, pacification, South Vietnamese politics and U.S. military operations. . . .

Negotiating Environment

There is general U.S. government agreement that Hanoi is in Paris for a variety of motives but not primarily out of weakness; that Hanoi is charting a course independent of Moscow, which favors negotiations, and of Peking, which opposes them; and that our knowledge of possible political factions among North Vietnamese leaders is extremely imprecise. There continues wide disagreement about the impact on Southeast Asia of various outcomes in Vietnam.

Various possible North Vietnamese motives for negotiating are discussed, and there is agreement that the DRV is in Paris for mixed reasons. No U.S. agency responding to the questions believes that the primary reason the DRV is in Paris is weakness. All consider it unlikely that Hanoi came to Paris either to accept a face-saving formula for defeat or to give the U.S. a face-saving way to withdraw. There is agreement that Hanoi has been subject to heavy military pressure and that a desire to end the losses and costs of war was an element in Hanoi's decision. The consensus is that Hanoi believes that it can persist long enough to obtain a relatively favorable negotiated compromise. The respondents agree that the DRV is in Paris to negotiate withdrawal of U.S. forces, to undermine GVN and USG [U.S. government] relations and to provide a better chance for FV victory in the South. State believes that increased doubt about winning the war through continued military and international political pressure also played a major role. Hanoi's ultimate goal of a unified Vietnam under its control has not changed.

There continues to be a sharp debate between and within agencies about the effect of the outcome in Vietnam on other nations. The most recent NIE [National Intelligence Estimate] on this subject (NIB 50–58) tended to downgrade the so-called "domino theory." It states that a settlement which would permit the Communists to take control of the Government in South Viet-Nam, not immediately but within a year or two, would be likely to bring Cambodia and Laos into Hanoi's orbit at a fairly early state, but that these developments would not necessarily unhinge the rest of Asia.

The NIE dissenters believe that an unfavorable settlement would stimulate the Communists to become more active elsewhere and that it will be difficult to resist making some accommodation to the pressure than generated. They believe, in contrast to the Estimate, these adjustments would be relatively small and insensitive to subsequent U.S. policy. . . .

The Enemy

Analyses of various enemy tactics and capabilities reveal both significant agreements and sharp controversies within the Government. Among the major points of consensus:

A combination of military pressures and political tacts explains recent enemy withdrawals and lower levels of activity.

Under current rules of engagement, the enemy's manpower pool and infiltration capabilities can outlast allied attrition efforts indefinitely.

The enemy basically controls both side's casualty rates.

The enemy can still launch major offensives, although not at Tet levels, or, probably, with equally dramatic effect.

Major controversies include:

CIA and State assign much higher figures to the VC Order of Battle than MACV, and they include additional categories of VC/NLF organization.

MACV/JCS and Saigon consider Cambodia (and specifically Sihanoukville) an important enemy supply channel while CIA disagrees strongly. . . .

It is generally agreed that the NVN/VC manpower pool is sufficiently large to meet the enemy's replenishment needs over an extended period of time within the framework of current rules of engagement. . . .

The South Vietnamese Armed Forces

The emphatic differences between U.S. agencies on the RVNAF outweigh the points of agreement. There is consensus that the RVNAF is getting larger, better equipped and somewhat more effective. And all agree that it could not now, or in the foreseeable future, handle both the VC and sizable NVA forces without U.S. combat support. On other major points there is vivid controversy. The military community gives much greater weight to RVNAF statistical improvements while OSD and CIA highlight remaining obstacles, with OSD being the most pessimistic. Paradoxically, MACV/CINPAC/JCS see RVNAF as being less capable against the VC alone than does CIA. . . .

Pacification

Two well-defined and divergent views emerged from the agencies on the pacification situation in South Vietnam. One view is held by MACV and Embassy Saigon and endorsed by CINCPAC and JCS. The other view is that of OSD, CIA and State. The two views are profoundly different in terms of factual interpretation and policy implications. Both views agree on the nature of the problem, that is, the obstacles to improvement and complete success. What distinguishes one view from the other is each's assessment of the magnitude of the problem, and the likelihood that obstacles will be overcome.

The first group, consisting of MACV JCS Saigon, maintains that "at the present time, the security situation is better than any time during period in question," i.e., 1961–1968. MACV cites a "dramatic change in the security situation," and finds that the GVN controls three-fourths of the population. JCS suggests that the GVN will control 90% of the population in 1969. The second group, OSD CIA State, on the other hand, is more cautious and pessimistic, their view is not inconsistent with another Tet-offensive-like shock in the countryside, for example, wiping out the much-touted gains of the 1968 Accelerated Pacification Program, or with more gradual erosion. Representing the latter view, OSD arrives at the following conclusions:

(1) "The portions of the SVN rural population aligned with the VC and aligned with the GVN are apparently the same today as in 1962 [a discouraging year]: 5,000,000 GVN aligned and nearly 3,000,000 VC aligned.

(2) "At the present, it appears that at least 50% of the total rural population is subject to significant VC presence and influence."

CIA agrees, and State (INR) [Bureau of Intelligence and Research] goes even further, saying: "Our best estimate is that the VC have a significant effect on at least two-thirds of the rural population."

The Political Scene

This section on the political situation can be boiled down to three fundamental questions: (1) How strong is the GVN today? (2) What is being done to strengthen it for the coming political struggle with the NLF? (3) What are the prospects for continued non-Communist government in South Vietnam?

The essence of the replies from U.S. agencies is as follows: (1) Stronger recently than for many years but still very weak in certain areas and among various elites. (2) Some steps are being taken but these are inadequate. (3) Impossible to predict but chancy at best.

Within these broad thrusts of the responses there are decided differences of emphasis among the agencies. Thus MACV/JCS and Saigon, while acknowledging the problems, accent more the increasing stability of the Thieu regime and the overall political system; the significance of the moves being made by the GVN to bolster its strength; and the possibility of continued non-Communist rule in South Vietnam given sufficient U.S. support. CIA and OSD on the other hand, while acknowledging certain progress, are decidedly more skeptical and pessimistic. They note recent political improvements and GVN measures but they tend to deflate their relative impact and highlight the remaining obstacles. State's position, while not so consistent or clear-cut, generally steers closer to the bearishness of OSD and CIA. . . .

U.S. Military Operations

The only major points of agreement with the U.S. Government on these subjects are:

The description of recent U.S. deployment and tactics;

The difficulties of assessing the results of B-52 strikes, but their known effectiveness against known troop concentrations and in close support operations;

The fact that the Soviets and Chinese supply almost all war material to Hanoi and have enabled the North Vietnamese to carry on despite all our operations.

Otherwise there are fundamental disagreements running throughout this section, including the following:

OSD believes, the MACV/JCS deny, that there is a certain amount of "fat" in our current force levels that could be cut back without significant reduction in combat capability.

MACV/JCS and, somewhat more cautiously CIA ascribe much higher casualty estimates to our B-52 strikes.

MACV/JCS assign very much greater effectiveness to our past and current Laos and North Vietnam bombing campaigns than do OSD and CIA.

MACV/JCS believe that a vigorous bombing campaign could choke off enough supplies to Hanoi to make her stop fighting, while OSD and CIA see North Vietnam continuing the struggle even against unlimited bombing.

3. A Guerrilla Leader Remembers 1969
as "The Worst Year" (1969), 1986

Early in 1970 I was ambushed along with eight others in a jungle clearing. The nine of us were walking single file across a vegetable field that the villagers had carved out of the jungle, on our way from one hamlet to another. It was a cloudy night. The moon was partially covered over and no one could see much. I knew I should have taken the line around the clearing, keeping to the jungle, but I was in too much of a hurry. Toward the middle of the clearing there was a clump of banana trees. Just as I pulled even with them, I realized there were some shapes in the trees. They saw me at exactly the same instant, and instinctively I flattened to the ground.

Just at that moment claymore mines fired off on the path behind me, huge explosions. The instant they stopped I crawled back along the path right over where they had gone off. As I crawled I felt some of the bodies, then squirmed off at a right angle toward the jungle. Firing was going on all around. At least two bullets hit my backpack before I got to the tree line. I had to leave the bodies there in the field. I kept thinking how demoralizing it would be for the peasants when they came out in the morning.

So many killed in 1969 and 1970. There was no way we could stand up to the Americans. Every time they came in force we ran from them. Then when they turned back, we'd follow them. We practically lived on top of them, so they couldn't hit us with artillery and air strikes. During those years I had to reorganize my unit three times. Twice, the entire unit was killed. Each time I reorganized, the numbers were smaller. It was almost impossible to get new recruits.

Worse than the Americans were the Australians. The Americans' style was to hit us, then call for planes and artillery. Our response was to break contact and disappear if we could, but if we couldn't we'd move up right next to them so the planes couldn't get at us. The Australians were more patient than the Americans, better guerrilla fighters, better at ambushes. They liked to stay with us instead of calling in the planes. We were more afraid of their style. . . .

There's no doubt that 1969 was the worst year we faced, at least the worst year I faced. There was no food, no future—nothing bright. But 1969 was also the time I was happiest. I destroyed several American tanks from the "Flying Horses" tank battalion that was stationed in Suoi Ram. I did it with pressure mines that our bomb makers made from unexploded American bombs. Each mine had seven kilos [fifteen pounds] of TNT. I was given an award as a champion tank killer.

The year 1969 was also the period when the true heroism of the peasants showed itself. Although we were isolated from the villagers, many of them risked their lives to get food to us. They devised all sorts of ingenious ways to get rice through the government checkpoints. Their feeling for us was one of the things that gave me courage to go on.

Another thing was the conviction the Americans couldn't last. In 1969 they began to pull out some of their troops. We believed that eventually they would have to withdraw altogether. We knew that even though we faced tremendous difficulties, so did they. They had terrible problems, especially at home. We didn't think their government could stand it in the long run. That gave me heart.

4. Richard M. Nixon on Vietnamization, 1969

Good evening, my fellow Americans: Tonight I want to talk to you on a subject of deep concern to all Americans and to many people in all parts of the world—the war in Viet-Nam.

I believe that one of the reasons for the deep division about Viet-Nam is that many Americans have lost confidence in what their Government has told them about our policy. The American people cannot and should not be asked to support a policy which involves the overriding issues of war and peace unless they know the truth about that policy.

Tonight, therefore, I would like to answer some of the questions that I know are on the minds of many of you listening to me.

How and why did America get involved in Viet-Nam in the first place? How has this administration changed the policy of the previous administration?

What has really happened in the negotiations in Paris and on the battlefront in Viet-Nam?

What choices do we have if we are to end the war?

What are the prospects for peace?

Let me begin by describing the situation I found when I was inaugurated on January 20.

- The war had been going on for 4 years.
- 31,000 Americans had been killed in action.
- The training program for the South Vietnamese was behind schedule.
- 540,000 Americans were in Viet-Nam, with no plans to reduce the number.
- No progress had been made at the negotiations in Paris and the United States had not put forth a comprehensive peace proposal.
- The war was causing deep division at home and criticism from many of our friends, as well as our enemies, abroad.

In view of these circumstances there were some who urged that I end the war at once by ordering the immediate withdrawal of all American forces.

From a political standpoint this would have been a popular and easy course to follow. After all, we became involved in the war while my predecessor was in office. I could blame the defeat which would be the result of my action on him and come out as the peacemaker. Some put it to me quite bluntly: This was the only way to avoid allowing Johnson's war to become Nixon's war.

But I had a greater obligation than to think only of the years of my administration and the next election. I had to think of the effect of my decision on the next generation and on the future of peace and freedom in America and in the world.

Nixon speech, November 3, 1969, U.S. Department of State *Bulletin,* 61. (November 24, 1979), 437–443.

Let us all understand that the question before us is not whether some Americans are for peace and some Americans are against peace. The question at issue is not whether Johnson's war becomes Nixon's war.

The great question is: How can we win America's peace?

Let us turn now to the fundamental issue. Why and how did the United States become involved in Viet-Nam in the first place?

Fifteen years ago North Viet-Nam, with the logistical support of Communist China and the Soviet Union, launched a campaign to impose a Communist government on South Viet-Nam by instigating and supporting a revolution.

In response to the request of the Government of South Viet-Nam, President Eisenhower sent economic aid and military equipment to assist the people of South Viet-Nam in their efforts to prevent a Communist takeover. Seven years ago President Kennedy sent 16,000 military personnel to Viet-Nam as combat advisers. Four years ago President Johnson sent American combat forces to South Viet-Nam.

Now, many believe that President Johnson's decision to send American combat forces to South Viet-Nam was wrong. And many others, I among them, have been strongly critical of the way the war has been conducted.

But the question facing us today is: Now that we are in the war, what is the best way to end it?

In January I could only conclude that the precipitate withdrawal of American forces from Viet-Nam would be a disaster not only for South Viet-Nam but for the United States and for the cause of peace.

For the South Vietnamese, our precipitate withdrawal would inevitably allow the Communists to repeat the massacres which followed their takeover in the North 15 years before.

• They then murdered more than 50,000 people, and hundreds of thousands more died in slave labor camps.

• We saw a prelude of what would happen in South Viet-Nam when the Communists entered the city of Hue last year. During their brief rule there, there was a bloody reign of terror in which 3,000 civilians were clubbed, shot to death, and buried in mass graves.

• With the sudden collapse of our support, these atrocities of Hue would become the nightmare of the entire nation—and particularly for the million and a half Catholic refugees who fled to South Viet-Nam when the Communists took over in the North.

For the United States, this first defeat in our nation's history would result in a collapse of confidence in American leadership not only in Asia but throughout the world.

Three American presidents have recognized the great stakes involved in Viet-Nam and understood what had to be done. . . .

For the future of peace, precipitate withdrawal would thus be a disaster of immense magnitude.

• A nation cannot remain great if it betrays its allies and lets down its friends.

• Our defeat and humiliation in South Viet-Nam without question would promote recklessness in the councils of those great powers who have not yet abandoned their goals of world conquest.

• This would spark violence wherever our commitments help maintain the peace—in the Middle East, in Berlin, eventually even in the Western Hemisphere.

Ultimately, this would cost more lives. It would not bring peace; it would bring more war.

For these reasons I rejected the recommendation that I should end the war by immediately withdrawing all our forces. I chose instead to change American policy on both the negotiating front and the battlefront. . . .

It has become clear that the obstacle in negotiating an end to the war is not the President of the United States. It is not the South Vietnamese Government.

The obstacle is the other side's absolute refusal to show the least willingness to join us in seeking a just peace. It will not do so while it is convinced that all it has to do is to wait for our next concession, and our next concession after that one, until it gets everything it wants.

There can now be no longer any question that progress in negotiation depends only on Hanoi's deciding to negotiate, to negotiate seriously. . . .

At the time we launched our search for peace, I recognized we might not succeed in bringing an end to the war through negotiation.

I therefore put into effect another plan to bring peace—a plan which will bring the war to an end regardless of what happens on the negotiating front. It is in line with a major shift in U.S. foreign policy which I described in my press conference at Guam on July 25.

Let me briefly explain what has been described as the Nixon doctrine—a policy which not only will help end the war in Viet-Nam but which is an essential element of our program to prevent future Viet-Nams. . . .

. . . I laid down in Guam three principles as guidelines for future American policy toward Asia:

•   First, the United States will keep all of its treaty commitments.

•   Second, we shall provide a shield if a nuclear power threatens the freedom of a nation allied with us or of a nation whose survival we consider vital to our security.

•   Third, in cases involving other types of aggression, we shall furnish military and economic assistance when requested in accordance with our treaty commitments. But we shall look to the nation directly threatened to assume the primary responsibility of providing the manpower for its defense.

After I announced this policy, I found that the leaders of the Philippines, Thailand, Viet-Nam, South Korea, and other nations which might be threatened by Communist aggression welcomed this new direction in American foreign policy.

The defense of freedom is everybody's business—not just America's business. And it is particularly the responsibility of the people whose freedom is threatened. In the previous administration we Americanized the war in Viet-Nam. In this administration we are Vietnamizing the search for peace.

The policy of the previous administration not only resulted in our assuming the primary responsibility for fighting the war but, even more significantly did not adequately stress the goal of strengthening the South Vietnamese so that they could defend themselves when we left.

The Vietnamization plan was launched following Secretary [of Defense Melvin R.] Laird's visit to Viet-Nam in March. Under the plan, I ordered first a substantial increase in the training and equipment of South Vietnamese forces.

In July, on my visit to Viet-Nam, I changed General Abrams' orders so that they were consistent with the objectives of our new policies. Under the new orders, the primary mission of our troops is to enable the South Vietnamese forces to assume the full responsibility for the security of South Viet-Nam. . . .

We have adopted a plan which we have worked out in cooperation with the South Vietnamese for the complete withdrawal of all U.S. combat ground forces and their replacement by South Vietnamese forces on an orderly scheduled timetable. This withdrawal will be made from strength and not from weakness. As South Vietnamese forces become stronger, the rate of American withdrawal can become greater. . . .

If the level of infiltration or our casualties increase while we are trying to scale down the fighting, it will be the result of a conscious decision by the enemy.

Hanoi could make no greater mistake than to assume that an increase in violence will be to its advantage. If I conclude that increased enemy action jeopardizes our remaining forces in Viet-Nam, I shall not hesitate to take strong and effective measures to deal with that situation.

This is not a threat. This is a statement of policy which as Commander in Chief of our Armed Forces I am making in meeting my responsibility for the protection of American fighting men wherever they may be.

My fellow Americans, I am sure you can recognize from what I have said that we really only have two choices open to us if we want to end this war:

•   I can order an immediate, precipitate withdrawal of all Americans from Viet-Nam without regard to the effects of that action.

•   Or we can persist in our search for a just peace, through a negotiated settlement if possible or through continued implementation of our plan for Vietnamization if necessary—a plan in which we will withdraw all of our forces from Viet-Nam on a schedule in accordance with our program, as the South Vietnamese become strong enough to defend their own freedom.

I have chosen this second course. It is not the easy way. It is the right way. It is a plan which will end the war and serve the cause of peace, not just in Viet-Nam but in the Pacific and in the world.

In speaking of the consequences of a precipitate withdrawal, I mentioned that our allies would lose confidence in America.

Far more dangerous, we would lose confidence in ourselves. Oh, the immediate reaction would be a sense of relief that our men were coming home. But as we saw the consequences of what we had done, inevitable remorse and divisive recrimination would scar our spirit as a people. . . .

I have chosen a plan for peace. I believe it will succeed.

If it does succeed, what the critics say now won't matter.

If it does not succeed, anything I say then won't matter.

I know it may not be fashionable to speak of patriotism or national destiny these days. But I feel it is appropriate to do so on this occasion.

Two hundred years ago this nation was weak and poor. But even then, America was the hope of millions in the world. Today we have become the strongest and richest nation in the world. The wheel of destiny has turned so that any hope the world has for the survival of peace and freedom will be determined by whether the American people have the moral stamina and the courage to meet the challenge of free-world leadership.

Let historians not record that when America was the most powerful nation in the world we passed on the other side of the road and allowed the last hopes for peace and freedom of millions of people to be suffocated by the forces of totalitarianism.

And so tonight—to you, the great silent majority of my fellow Americans—I ask for your support.

I pledged in my campaign for the presidency to end the war in a way that we could win the peace. I have initiated a plan of action which will enable me to keep that pledge.

The more support I can have from the American people, the sooner that pledge can be redeemed; for the more divided we are at home, the less likely the enemy is to negotiate at Paris.

Let us be united for peace. Let us also be united against defeat. Because let us understand: North Viet-Nam cannot defeat or humiliate the United States. Only Americans can do that.

5. Nixon Explains the Cambodian Incursion, 1970

Good evening, my fellow Americans. Ten days ago, in my report to the Nation on Viet-Nam, I announced a decision to withdraw an additional 150,000 Americans from Viet-Nam over the next year. I said then that I was making that decision despite our concern over increased enemy activity in Laos, in Cambodia, and in South Viet-Nam.

At that time, I warned that if I concluded that increased enemy activity in any of these areas endangered the lives of Americans remaining in Viet-Nam, I would not hesitate to take strong and effective measures to deal with that situation.

Despite that warning, North Viet-Nam has increased its military aggression in all these areas, and particularly in Cambodia.

After full consultation with the National Security Council, Ambassador Bunker, General Abrams, and my other advisers, I have concluded that the actions of the enemy in the last 10 days clearly endanger the lives' of Americans who are in Viet-Nam now and would constitute an unacceptable risk to those who will be there after withdrawal of another 150,000.

To protect our men who are in Viet-Nam and to guarantee the continued success of our withdrawal and Vietnamization programs, I have concluded that the time has come for action.

Tonight I shall describe the actions of the enemy, the actions I have ordered to deal with that situation, and the reasons for my decision.

Cambodia, a small country of 7 million people, has been a neutral nation since the Geneva agreement of 1954—an agreement, incidentally, which was signed by the Government of North Viet-Nam.

Nixon speech, April 30, 1970, U.S. Department of State *Bulletin,* 62 (May 18, 1970), 617–621.

American policy since then has been to scrupulously respect the neutrality of the Cambodian people. We have maintained a skeleton diplomatic mission of fewer than 15 in Cambodia's capital, and that only since last August. For the previous 4 years, from 1965 to 1969, we did not have any diplomatic mission whatever in Cambodia. And for the past 5 years, we have provided no military assistance whatever and no economic assistance to Cambodia.

North Viet-Nam, however, has not respected that neutrality.

For the past 5 years . . . North Viet-Nam has occupied military sanctuaries all along the Cambodian frontier with South Viet-Nam. Some of these extend up to 20 miles into Cambodia. The sanctuaries . . . are on both sides of the border. They are used for hit-and-run attacks on American and South Vietnamese forces in South Viet-Nam.

These Communist-occupied territories contain major base camps, training sites, logistics facilities, weapons and ammunition factories, airstrips, and prisoner of war compounds.

For 5 years neither the United States nor South Viet-Nam has moved against these enemy sanctuaries, because we did not wish to violate the territory of a neutral nation. Even after the Vietnamese Communists began to expand these sanctuaries 4 weeks ago, we counseled patience to our South Vietnamese allies and imposed restraints on our own commanders.

In contrast to our policy, the enemy in the past 2 weeks has stepped up his guerrilla actions, and he is concentrating his main forces in these sanctuaries . . . where they are building up to launch massive attacks on our forces and those of South Viet-Nam.

North Viet-Nam in the last 2 weeks has stripped away all pretense of respecting the sovereignty or the neutrality of Cambodia. Thousands of their soldiers are invading the country from the sanctuaries; they are encircling the Capital of Phnom Penh. Coming from these sanctuaries, . . . they have moved into Cambodia and are encircling the capital.

Cambodia, as a result of this, has sent out a call to the United States, to a number of other nations, for assistance. Because if this enemy effort succeeds, Cambodia would become a vast enemy staging area and a springboard for attacks on South Viet-Nam along 600 miles of frontier, a refuge where enemy troops could return from combat without fear of retaliation.

North Vietnamese men and supplies could then be poured into that country, jeopardizing not only the lives of our own men but the people of South Viet-Nam as well. . . .

In cooperation with the armed forces of South Viet-Nam, attacks are being launched this week to clean out major enemy sanctuaries on the Cambodian-Viet-Nam border.

A major responsibility for the ground operations is being assumed by South Vietnamese forces. . . .

There is one area, however, . . . where I have concluded that a combined American and South Vietnamese operation is necessary.

Tonight American and South Vietnamese units will attack the headquarters for the entire Communist military operation in South Viet-Nam. This key control center has been occupied by the North Vietnamese and Viet Cong for 5 years in blatant violation of Cambodia's neutrality.

This is not an invasion of Cambodia. The areas in which these attacks will be launched are completely occupied and controlled by North Vietnamese forces. Our purpose is not to occupy the areas. Once enemy forces are driven out of these sanctuaries and once their military supplies are destroyed, we will withdraw. . . .

A majority of the American people, a majority of you listening to me, are for the withdrawal of our forces from Viet-Nam. The action I have taken tonight is indispensable for the continuing success of that withdrawal program.

A majority of the American people want to end this war rather than to have it drag on interminably. The action I have taken tonight will serve that purpose.

A majority of the American people want to keep the casualties of our brave men in Viet-Nam at an absolute minimum. The action I take tonight is essential if we are to accomplish that goal.

We take this action not for the purpose of expanding the war into Cambodia, but for the purpose of ending the war in Viet-Nam and winning the just peace we all desire. We have made and we will continue to make every possible effort to end this war through negotiation at the conference table rather than through more fighting on the battlefield. . . .

My fellow Americans, we live in an age of anarchy, both abroad and at home. We see mindless attacks on all the great institutions which have been created by free civilizations in the last 500 years. Even here in the United States, great universities are being systematically destroyed. Small nations all over the world find themselves under attack from within and from without.

If, when the chips are down, the world's most powerful nation, the United States of America, acts like a pitiful, helpless giant, the forces of totalitarianism and anarchy will threaten free nations and free institutions throughout the world.

It is not our power but our will and character that is being tested tonight. The question all Americans must ask and answer tonight is this: Does the richest and strongest nation in the history of the world have the character to meet a direct challenge by a group which rejects every effort to win a just peace, ignores our warning, tramples on solemn agreements, violates the neutrality of an unarmed people, and uses our prisoners as hostages?

If we fail to meet this challenge, all other nations will be on notice that despite its overwhelming power the United States, when a real crisis comes, will be found wanting.

During my campaign for the presidency, I pledged to bring Americans home from Viet-Nam. They are coming home.

I promised to end this war. I shall keep that promise.

I promised to win a just peace. I shall keep that promise.

We shall avoid a wider war. But we are also determined to put an end to this war. . . .

No one is more aware than I am of the political consequences of the action I have taken. It is tempting to take the easy political path: to blame this war on previous administrations and to bring all of our men home immediately, regardless of the consequences, even though that would mean defeat for the United States; to desert 18 million South Vietnamese people who have put their trust in us and to expose them to the same slaughter and savagery which the leaders of North Viet-Nam inflicted on hundreds of thousands of North Vietnamese who chose freedom when the Communists took over North Viet-Nam in 1954; to get peace at any price now, even though I know that a peace of humiliation for the United States would lead to a bigger war or surrender later.

I have rejected all political considerations in making this decision.

Whether my party gains in November is nothing compared to the lives of 400,000 brave Americans fighting for our country and for the cause of peace and freedom in Viet-Nam. Whether I may be a one-term President is insignificant compared to whether by our failure to act in this crisis the United States proves itself to be unworthy to lead the forces of freedom in this critical period in world history. I would rather be a one-term President and do what I believe is right than to be a two-term President at the cost of seeing America become a second-rate power and to see this nation accept the first defeat in its proud 190-year history.

6. Henry A. Kissinger Reveals the U.S. Negotiating Position, 1972

As you remember from the many briefings that we have had on Viet-Nam, there has been no issue of greater concern to this administration than to end the war in Viet-Nam on a negotiated basis. We have done so because of what we felt the war was doing to us as a people and because we felt that it was essential that whatever differences that may have existed about how we entered the war and how we conducted the war, that we ended it in a way that showed that we had been fair, that we had been reasonable, and that all concerned people could support.

We have not approached these negotiations in order to score debating points. We have not conducted these negotiations in order to gain any domestic benefits. . . .

On the political evolution, our basic principle has been a principle we have been prepared to sign together with them, that we are not committed to any one political structure or government in South Viet-Nam. Our principle has been that we want a political evolution that gives the people of South Viet-Nam a genuine opportunity to express their preferences.

We have pointed out, in innumerable meetings, that we recognize that this is a tough problem. We have indicated with extraordinary repetitiveness, as those of you who have heard me will not challenge, with extraordinary repetitiveness, that we know that Vietnamese traditions are different and that we are prepared to listen to their version of what a free political process might be like.

We have searched our souls to try to come up with a proposal that seems free to us; and after all, the agreement by the existing government—to have a commission comprising the people that wish to overthrow them run, organize, and supervise the

Kissinger news conference, January 26, 1972, U.S. Department of State *Bulletin* 66 (February 1972), 191–194.

election, to put the election under international supervision, and to resign a month before the election—is not just a trivial proposal.

The North Vietnamese position has been that they want us to agree with them, first, on replacing the existing government and, secondly, on a structure in which the probability of their taking over is close to certainty.

They want us, in other words, to do in the political field the same thing that they are asking us to do in the military field, to negotiate the terms of the turnover to them, regardless of what the people may think. . . .

They have said that they want a government composed of people who stand for peace, neutrality, and independence. There is another magic word which eludes me at the moment. And Americans cannot object to this proposal. The only thing is, they are the only ones who know who stands for peace, neutrality, and independence.

Whenever in these negotiations we have said, "All right, you don't like Thieu. How about this fellow, or that fellow, or that fellow?" there is almost no one that we know who they believe stands for peace, neutrality, and independence.

So I would like to express this to you. The issue is to us: We are prepared, in all conscience and in all seriousness, to negotiate with them immediately any scheme that any reasonable person can say leaves open the political future of South Viet-Nam to the people of South Viet-Nam, just as we are not prepared to withdraw without knowing anything at all of what is going to happen next. So we are not prepared to end this war by turning over the Government of South Viet-Nam as part of a political deal.

We are prepared to have a political process in which they can have a chance of winning, which is not loaded in any direction. We have given our views of what this political process might be. We are prepared to listen to their views of what that political process might be. And we said in both notes of last fall, notes that were not intended for publication, at a time when we were hoping to be able to step before you with an agreement, that we are prepared to listen to their points.

Now, there has been some question of, "Did they ask us to replace or overthrow"—or whatever the word is—"the existing government in South Viet-Nam?"

We have every interest in stepping before you with total honesty. They have asked two things of us:

One, an indirect overthrow of the government; that is to say, that we have to withdraw. The way they phrase it, we would have to withdraw all American equipment, even that which the South Vietnamese Army has. They have asked us to withdraw all equipment, all future military aid, all future economic aid; and the practical consequence of that proposal, while they are receiving close to $1 billion worth of foreign aid, would be the indirect overthrow of the Government of South Viet-Nam, something about which there can be no question.

But they have further asked us, and we do not want to be forced to prove it, to change the government directly, generously leaving the method to us, and, therefore, the President's statement was true and is supportable.

We have no interest in engaging in a debate with the North Vietnamese that would force any more of this record into the open. We do have an interest that the American public understand exactly what is at issue today.

7. Negotiating Position of the Provisional Revolutionary Government, 1972

The provisional Revolutionary Government of the Republic of South Vietnam solemnly declares as follows:

If a correct solution is to be found to the Vietnam problem, and a lasting peace ensured in Vietnam, the U.S. Government must meet the two following requirements:

1. To respect the Vietnamese people's right to true independence and the South Vietnamese people's right to effective self-determination; stop the U.S. war of aggression in Vietnam, the bombing, mining and blockade of the Democratic Republic of Vietnam; completely cease the "Vietnamization" policy; and all U.S. military activities in South Vietnam; rapidly and completely withdraw all U.S. troops, advisors, military personnel, technical personnel, weapons and war materials and those of the other foreign countries in the U.S. camp from South Vietnam; liquidate the U.S. military bases in South Vietnam; end all U.S. military involvement in Vietnam; and stop supporting the Nguyen Van Thieu stooge administration.

2. A solution to the internal problem of South Vietnam must proceed from the actual situation that there exist in South Vietnam two administrations, two armies, and other political forces. It is necessary to achieve national concord. The sides in South Vietnam must unite on the basis of equality, mutual respect and mutual nonelimination. Democratic freedoms must be guaranteed to the people. To this end, it is necessary to form in South Vietnam a provisional government of national concord with three equal segments to take charge of the affairs in the period of transition and to organize truly free and democratic general elections.

✗ E S S A Y S

In the opening essay Melvin Small of Wayne State University offers a pointed critique of Richard Nixon's Vietnam policies. He contends that, despite public boasts to the contrary, Nixon had no new Vietnam strategy when he entered office and never truly developed one. Rather, he adapted the Vietnamization approach developed by his predecessors in the Johnson administration while improvising a series of ad hoc, and often contradictory, responses to unfolding military and political events. Nixon's determination to forge what he called a peace with honor, one that would preserve America's credibility as a global power, led the president to delay needlessly a final peace settlement— at the cost, according to Small, of tens of thousands of American and hundreds of thousands of Vietnamese lives.

Retired Army officer Lewis Sorley, the author of several works of military history and a former instructor at both West Point and the Army War College, focuses on the continuing war on the ground in the next selection. He argues that, under the capable leadership of General Creighton W. Abrams, U.S. forces radically revised their tactical approach to the war after 1968. The results proved remarkably successful: by late 1970,

---

Provisional Revolutionary Government statement, September 11, 1972, reprinted in U.S. Senate, Committee on Foreign Relations, *Background Information Relating to Southeast Asia and Vietnam* (Washington, 1974), p. 648.

Sorley insists, the United States and its South Vietnamese allies had largely won the war, with pacification by then a reality throughout most of South Vietnam. Yet political and budgetary pressures at home, he laments, would subsequently turn victory into defeat.

Nixon's Flawed Search for Peace

MELVIN SMALL

Nixon considered the negotiation of a speedy and honorable end to the Vietnam War his first order of business, and here he thought that linkage politics would be decisive. That is, if the Soviet Union wanted progress in other areas of mutual interest, it would use its influence to prod the North Vietnamese to be more forthcoming at the bargaining table.

Henry Kissinger, once a supporter of U.S. involvement in Southeast Asia, later called the war in Vietnam a "nightmare" and "a Greek tragedy. We should have never been there at all." But the United States was there on 20 January 1969, with 530,00 troops in the field and no immediate end to the war in sight. The previous year had been the bloodiest for Americans, who suffered 14,600 battle deaths. Nixon knew that it was essential to end the war that had cost the nation so much in human and financial treasure and had led to unprecedented domestic turbulence and the alienation of a good part of the next generation. He had to end the war as quickly as possible so that he could launch dramatic diplomatic initiatives that, if successful, might avert future Vietnams.

But Nixon was "convinced that how we end this war will determine the future of the U.S. in the world." He had to obtain what he would characterize as "peace with honor"; he could not just "cut and run," leaving the 17 million people of South Vietnam to be taken over by the communist North Vietnamese. Much like his predecessors, beginning with Truman, Nixon saw U.S. credibility at stake in Southeast Asia. Washington had to hold the line to demonstrate its willingness to pay a steep price to defend its interests. All the architects of postwar American policy, including Nixon, were influenced by the experience of the thirties, when, they believed, the lack of will of the democratic states encouraged aggressors to launch World War II.

Nixon and Kissinger were also certain that how the United States ended the war in Vietnam would influence upcoming negotiations with the Russians and Chinese. Relations with the communists could not be stabilized unless the United States left Vietnam with dignity.

Nixon had always been hawkish on Vietnam, from his advocacy of U.S. intervention to assist the French in 1954 to his criticism of Lyndon Johnson's graduated escalatory policies in 1965 and 1966. By 1967, and certainly 1968, however, he came to understand that the war was unwinnable in a conventional sense. During the summer of 1968, he promised an end to the war if elected, although he never said directly that he had a "secret plan" to accomplish that goal. In fact, when he and his colleagues began to organize the transition at the Hotel Pierre in December, it became clear that he had no plan, not even a general strategy, to end the war. Melvin Laird later insisted, "I don't care what anybody else told you. He had no plan." Laird boasted, somewhat inaccurately, "I developed the plan."

During those discussions in New York before the inauguration, Nixon and his advisers quickly rejected escalation, including invading North Vietnam, blockading its ports, using tactical nuclear weapons, or bombing its dike system. In effect, the president accepted the general strategy of the lame-duck Johnson dministration— the United States would not send any more troops to Vietnam, would continue to observe the bombing pause, would trust that the Paris peace talks and Soviet assistance could produce an acceptable arrangement, and would hope that the South Vietnamese could make the needed economic and military progress to confront the North with a formidable opponent. The last bit of strategy and the one that set the nation on a new path, "Vietnamization," was based on a program developed in Johnson's Pentagon by Assistant Secretary of Defense for International Security Affairs Paul Warnke that had, in effect, begun to be implemented in 1968. Vietnamization marked a return to the early sixties, when the Kennedy administration hoped that a massive buildup of Saigon's economic and military infrastructure would enable the South Vietnamese to defend themselves against the National Liberation Front (NLF).

In the definitive history of the administration's Vietnam policy, historian Jeffrey Kimball concludes that Nixon had no new Vietnam policy when he took office and never really developed one, as he and Kissinger constructed ad hoc and often contradictory strategies in reaction to military and political events. The closest Nixon came to establishing anything resembling a consistent approach to Vietnam was his so-called madman strategy.

Whatever it was, Nixon and Kissinger held their Vietnam policy close to their vests in January 1969, as they would throughout the first term. Although demanding a thorough review of the situation in Southeast Asia in NSSM-1, they had decided on their course of action before the agencies submitted their final reports. It was just as well, for the CIA and the Defense Department not only disagreed with each other but were both critical of White House policies. The CIA reported that bombing North Vietnam and Laos had not been successful and that the domino theory did not apply to that theater. The Defense Department had little confidence in Vietnamization, and throughout the first two years of that program, the military command in Vietnam consistently opposed Nixon's troop withdrawals, arguing that Washington overestimated the quality of the South Vietnamese army.

The limited patience of the American people affected all [of] Nixon's Vietnam strategies from 1969 through 1973. By the spring of 1968, a majority of Americans thought that getting involved in Vietnam had been a mistake. They did not call for an immediate withdrawal—only a small minority of Americans ever favored that option—but they desired an end to the war and the unprecedented societal dislocation that had come with it. The administration had to demonstrate a slow but steady commitment to bringing all the boys home. As Secretary [of State William] Rogers wrote to W. Averell Harriman, who was finishing up his work at the Paris peace talks, "it was essential to reduce American casualties and get some of our troops home in order to retain the support of the American people."

The administration's hands were tied. It could escalate only covertly, since almost all Americans demanded that the war wind down on Nixon's watch. During the campaign, Americans had expressed greater confidence in Nixon's ability to end the war than in Humphrey's by a two-to-one margin. When Nixon took office, 40 percent of the population considered the war to be the nation's most serious problem. In addition, many Democrats in Congress, who had previously supported Johnson's policies, no longer confronted a Democratic president armed with the powers of patronage. They could begin coming out of their dovish closets, posing a variety of threats to Nixon's policies on Capitol Hill.

Nixon also had to worry about the antiwar movement and antiwar sentiment among Americans in general, which had contributed to Johnson's decision on 31 March 1968 not to seek the presidency again. For example, the administration was rocked in June 1969 when the popular, mainstream *Life* magazine printed pictures of the 242 young Americans who had died in Vietnam during the previous week. As a State Department official later recalled, "The fact of the matter is that we were continually trying to calm down the opposition—in Congress, the press, and the demonstrations, the academic circles—by making unilateral concessions" in the peace talks.

Like all presidents, Nixon began to think about his second term almost as soon as he took office. Daniel Patrick Moynihan wrote to him on 5 January 1969 that his would be a one-term presidency unless the war in Vietnam soon ended. Nixon had to be concerned about the political implications of the way the war ended. Although a speedy peace agreement would please almost all Americans, what would happen if the South Vietnamese government fell to communism before the 1972 election? Could even such a reputed hard-line anticommunist as Nixon survive the Democratic catcalls, "Who lost Vietnam?" Although no hard evidence suggests that the president thought about his reelection prospects as he fashioned his Vietnam policy—few presidents have ever admitted that domestic politics affected their foreign policies—he undoubtedly had his eye on a second term throughout his first term.

Despite the potential political problem posed by "losing" Vietnam, Nixon was optimistic about obtaining an honorable peace in a short time. The previous summer, he had told dovish Michigan congressman Donald Riegle, then a Republican, that "if we're elected we'll end this war in six months." Kissinger later used that same six-month time frame. Even considering his constraints, as well as the previous administration's failure to extricate itself from Vietnam, Nixon confidently believed that he could end the war on favorable terms through Vietnamization and by employing Moscow to convince Hanoi to be more flexible in negotiations. Haldeman affirms that Nixon "had fully expected that an acceptable, if not totally satisfactory, solution would be achieved through negotiation within the first six months." As he told his aide, "I'm not going to end up like LBJ, holed up in the White House afraid to show my face on the street. I'm going to stop that war. Fast."

Nixon overestimated Moscow's influence with Hanoi. He failed to understand that the Soviet Union had limited control over anti-Western Marxist regimes and revolutions around the world, few of which were more independent than the venerable Vietnamese nationalist movement led by Ho Chi Minh. In many ways, the Soviet Union's inability to coerce North Vietnam to accept its "advice" mirrored the United States' inability to coerce its own "puppet" in Saigon.

From 1965 through November 1968, one of the sticking points to opening negotiations was the North Vietnamese precondition that the United States stop bombing them. Once the United States conceded this point, the two key issues that would be negotiated from 1969 through 1973 involved the withdrawal of "foreign" forces from South Vietnam and the nature of the postwar regime in Saigon. The U.S. position, which the Nixon administration inherited and initially supported, was that the North Vietnamese army was a foreign force that had to withdraw from South Vietnam when the Americans withdrew. The North Vietnamese, in turn, insisted on U.S. withdrawal from South Vietnam, refusing to acknowledge that they had a military presence in the South. They also demanded a coalition government in Saigon to replace the pro-Western regime of President Nguyen van Thieu. Once the United States committed itself to no further escalation, and once the Nixon administration began its phased withdrawal, the North Vietnamese had little incentive to make a speedy peace, since there would come a day when the last American combat soldier would leave Vietnam. In addition, they felt that they had been burned twice in previous negotiations (in 1946 with the French and in 1954 at the Geneva Conference) when they had accepted compromise agreements that their enemies violated. Kissinger, who did the most important negotiating with the North Vietnamese, was frustrated by their "maddening dictatorial style" and the way "Vietnamese history and Communist ideology combined to produce almost morbid suspicion and ferocious self-righteousness." The communists, in turn, were frustrated by his condescending attitude and carrot-and-stick approach.

Quickly discovering what he was up against, Nixon hoped to obtain his peace with honor by employing covert escalations and diplomatic pressure. He also had to demonstrate to Hanoi that, unlike Johnson, protesters in the streets and dissenters in Congress would not influence his policies.

The prisoner of war (POW) issue was the new element introduced by the Nixon administration during the peace negotiations. No peace would be made until the communists accounted for all American POWs and promised to return them once the war was over. The National League of Families of American Prisoners and Missing in Southeast Asia, founded by relatives and supporters of American prisoners and those still listed as missing in action (MIA), pressured the administration to do something about this cause. By the fall of 1969, Nixon opportunistically adopted the cause as his own, declaring a National Day of Prayer for the POWs on 9 November and meeting with organization leaders in December. . . .

Nixon finally obtained peace with the communists on 27 January 1973. But South Vietnam fell to communism in 1975. During Nixon's four years, the United States lost more than 18,000 of its more than 58,000 battle deaths during the entire war. Most of these deaths occurred in 1969. As U.S. casualties declined from that year to 1973, the pressures to end the war eased. All the same, considering Nixon's earlier conviction that he had to end the war with dispatch to reestablish domestic tranquility and to free himself internationally, his ability to maintain support for his policies over four years and win reelection by a landslide in 1972 was a more remarkable feat than ending the war itself.

Although most Americans were unhappy about the war, they were even more unhappy with what they perceived to be an unruly and revolutionary antiwar movement. Considering the movement "a brotherhood of the misguided, the mistaken, the well-meaning, and the malevolent," Nixon used the public anger at the "hippies" in the streets to buy support for his policies. The president believed that "many leaders of the antiwar movement were hard-core militants of the New Left who hated the United States," and many of their followers opposed the war not out of "moral conviction" but "to keep from getting their asses shot off." He was especially upset about the antiwar movement's "encouragement to the enemy" that "prolonged the war."

Hanoi did count on the American public, influenced by antiwar critics, to tire of the war just as the French public had. One prominent Vietnamese diplomat later explained that his government believed that the antiwar movement was more important under Nixon's than Johnson's presidency because it help constrain Nixon from reescalating the war.

Like his predecessor, Nixon ordered the CIA and FBI to identify the alleged foreign connections of the antiwar movement's leaders, and like Johnson, he was incredulous when they could not do so. The intelligence services' apparent failure in this realm was one reason Nixon contemplated establishing the secret White House intelligence organization envisioned in the Huston Plan.

But Nixon did not need the foreign connection to rally most Americans to his side. Disorder on the campuses and in the streets continued into 1969. Most Americans easily conflated the increasingly violent revolutionary splinter groups with the mainstream antiwar movement, thus playing into the president's hands. Between 1 January 1969 and 15 April 1970, authorities recorded over 8,000 bombings or threats of bombings, and during the academic year 1969–70, 7,200 young people were arrested for violent acts on college campuses, a number almost double that of 1968–69. Many Americans who saw disheveled and foul-mouthed protesters carrying Vietcong flags on the nightly news concluded that if those are the sort of people who oppose Nixon, then we must be on his side.

Seven times from 1969 through 1971, the president preempted primetime television programs to ask the nation to support his foreign policies as part of the offensive against his critics. That offensive also led to an intensification of the intelligence agencies' surveillance and harassment of antiwar opponents, activities that came back to haunt him during the Watergate investigations.

But the movement was quiescent when Nixon took office in 1969. Like the rest of the nation, it was giving the new president time to enact his "plan." Although Nixon and Kissinger knew that victory in Vietnam was no longer possible, they still thought that tough military action might convince the North Vietnamese to make concessions at the peace table. The president encouraged the U.S. commander in Vietnam, General Creighton Abrams, to maintain the pressure on the communists while his diplomats saw what they could extract from them.

For their part, the North Vietnamese and the NLF were still recovering from the battering they took during the Tet offensive of the previous year. Consequently, in 1969, they retreated from the massive, conventional attacks of that offensive and returned to small-unit guerrilla warfare. Their leaders instructed cadres to concentrate their fire on U.S. troops to keep American body counts high, thus increasing the pressure on Nixon. This strategy succeeded. During Nixon's first six months in office, Americans suffered approximately 8,000 battle deaths, making it the second most lethal six-month period of the war. Especially disconcerting to the administration was a three-week offensive launched on 22 February in response in part to U.S. offensive activities. Washington asserted that the communists' offensive, which resulted in 1,100 American battle deaths, violated the November 1968 bombing agreement because it also targeted civilians.

Barely a month into his term, Nixon decided to show the North Vietnamese that they could not push him around. First, he took advantage of a loophole in the 1968 agreement that permitted the United States to launch "protective reaction" strikes against antiaircraft sites in the North whenever their radar locked on to American reconnaissance flights. Under the guise of protective reaction, the administration ordered thousands of "legal" bombing raids against the North. It also stepped up covert cross-border raids into Laos and continued the bombing of that country begun under the Johnson administration. By the fall of 1969, American military activities in Laos had produced 600,000 refugees out of a population of 3 million. Nixon's decision in February 1970 to increase the brutal B-52 bombing runs in Laos made matters even worse. To its misfortune, Laos was home to hundreds of miles of the Ho Chi Minh Trail system through which North Vietnam supplied its cadres in the South.

Eastern Cambodia was an even more important part of that supply system. Although the American military had earlier recommended bombing the trails in neutral Cambodia, Johnson had rejected that option, despite the fact that Special Forces units had performed small-scale ground operations in the area. To Nixon, Cambodia seemed the perfect place to weaken the communists and to demonstrate to them that he could secretly escalate without suffering domestic political damage. Secretary of State Rogers and Secretary of Defense Laird worried about the possible repercussions if Americans learned about the proposed Cambodian bombing, but Nixon and Kissinger were not dissuaded by their arguments. Throughout 1969 and 1970, Rogers and Laird generally opposed the president's escalations.

Nixon obtained the informal approval of Cambodian leader Prince Norodom Sihanouk, who opposed North Vietnamese use of his country to infiltrate material and soldiers into South Vietnam. He was also disturbed by Hanoi's support for a small communist insurgency, the Khmer Rouge. Sihanouk warned the Americans, however, that if they made the bombing public, he would disavow it.

Accordingly, the president developed a system to keep Americans, including some of the brass in Vietnam, in the dark about the bombing. He accomplished this by ordering the tampering with the computerized navigational systems on the B-52s and by maintaining two sets of flight plans—one that reported that the bombers in question had hit targets in South Vietnam, and the other, sent to the NSC, that revealed the true targets. Even the secretary of the air force was not immediately informed about Operation Menu, which began on 18 March 1969 and continued through April 1970 with Operations Breakfast, Lunch, Dinner, Supper, and Snack. Over the fourteen months of its existence, Menu operations involved 3,875 sorties dropping 108,823 tons of bombs. In a vague way, Nixon shared the secret of Menu with several key hawkish congressional leaders.

The bombing of Cambodia made it more difficult for the North Vietnamese to deliver material to the South. But it produced two far more important consequences. For one thing, it pushed the North Vietnamese further inland, along with their Khmer Rouge allies, thereby increasing popular support for indigenous anti-Western forces who profited politically from the civilian casualties and the destabilization of normal life caused by the bombing.

Even more important, on 9 May 1969, *New York Times* reporter William Beecher revealed the bombing. . . .

On 14 May 1969, the president told the nation about a new eight-point peace plan that featured an American withdrawal six months after the North Vietnamese had left South Vietnam. Having "ruled out attempting to impose a purely military solution" as well as a "one-sided withdrawal," he called for mutual withdrawals of Americans and their allies and North Vietnamese from South Vietnam and free elections in the South under international supervision. He also called for support from "the American people united behind a generous and reasonable peace offer."

Despite Hanoi's rejection of the U.S. terms, Nixon began the process of Vietnamization on Midway Island on 8 June when he met with an unhappy President Nguyen van Thieu. Announcing the imminent withdrawal of 25,000 U.S. troops, Nixon promised more withdrawals, depending on the progress of Vietnamization, movement at the peace table, and enemy activity. From this point on, Nixon periodically addressed the nation to announce the latest withdrawal of American troops. He had no options. An aide recalled, "We were under immense domestic pressure to give an appearance of a kind of steady diminution of the American role."

When the North Vietnamese did not respond positively to his initiative, Nixon sent a private letter to Ho Chi Minh on 15 July calling for action on his proposals. If the North Vietnamese leader was not willing to compromise, he could face "measures of great consequence and force," later referred to by Kissinger as a "savage, punishing blow." The letter may have induced the North Vietnamese to request secret peace talks, which the United States had sought. Kissinger first met with Xuan Thuy on 4 August, at which point he informed the North Vietnamese diplomat that if his government did not respond positively to Nixon's 15 July message by 1 November, the United States would adopt new military measures.

As part of Nixon's new "go-for-broke" strategy, NSC staffers began working on Duck Hook, feasibility studies of escalatory measures, including the use of tactical nuclear weapons, blockading the ports of Hanoi and Haiphong, and bombing the North's flood-control system. Kissinger could not believe "that a fourth-rate power like North Vietnam doesn't have a breaking point." . . .

While Nixon was developing his new, more assertive strategies, the somnolent antiwar movement began to move into action once again. By the summer of 1969, many doves had become convinced that Nixon was not doing all that he could to bring the war to a speedy end. Antiwar moderates who formed the Vietnam Moratorium Committee (VMC) at the end of June devised a new tactic for their sometimes unpopular movement. This time, they would not call for the traditional mass march in one or two cities on a weekend. Instead, on Wednesday, 15 October (two weeks before Nixon's ultimatum, of which they were unaware), citizens around the country would take time off from work or school to attend rallies, ceremonies in cemeteries, and other symbolic activities to signal their dissatisfaction with the pace of troop withdrawals from Vietnam. Should the war continue, the VMC intended to organize further moratoriums, adding a day each month to the protests.

The battle lines were drawn. Nixon told his cabinet in September that he would not be the "first American President to lose a war," because the "first defeat in history would destroy the confidence of the American people in themselves." As the moratorium gained momentum, especially among middle-class adults, Nixon went on the offensive. On 16 September, he announced a troop withdrawal of 35,000. Four days later, he announced the reassignment of General Lewis Hershey, the outspoken chief of the Selective Service System. In addition, at a press conference on 26 September, referring to the upcoming protest, he declared, "under no circumstances will I be affected whatever by it." Finally, two days before the moratorium, Nixon replied publicly to a letter from a student, explaining that "to allow government policy to be made in the streets would destroy the democratic procedure. It would give the decision not to the majority . . . but to those with the loudest voices."

Despite the administration's counteroffensive, the moratorium turned out to be the most successful antiwar demonstration in history, involving over 2 million people in over 200 cities. It was decorous enough that people such as W. Averell Harriman and Defense Secretary Laird's college-student son participated. The media emphasized the peaceful and middle-class nature of the telegenic rallies and prayer vigils. Yet the majority of Americans still supported the president. In one poll taken on 16 October, more than 68 percent of the respondents approved of the way Nixon was handling the war. All the same, the moratorium had shaken the administration. The 1 November deadline came and went without movement form Hanoi or retaliation from Washington. Years later, Nixon blamed the moratorium, complaining that it had "undercut the credibility of the ultimatum" and, by encouraging the North Vietnamese that they could count on support in the American population, had "destroyed whatever small possibility may still have existed to end the war." He decided not to retaliate because Duck Hook planners had concluded that their contemplated escalations would not work. In addition, the death of Ho Chi Minh on 2 September may have made it difficult for the new regime in Hanoi to take any bold negotiating initiative.

Concerned about the renewed strength of the antiwar movement and its apparent effect on Hanoi, Nixon developed a strategy to mobilize the majority of Americans who did not take part in or sympathize with the moratorium. He needed them for the long haul but, more immediately, to dampen enthusiasm for the second moratorium scheduled for 13–14 November. The key component would be his 3 November "Silent Majority" speech, which he began working on almost immediately after the first moratorium. Nixon considered this speech, which he wrote himself, the most important of his career. He worked through twelve drafts, sometimes spending entire days on them, until he was satisfied. He received advice, especially on the way to rally support, from former secretary of state Dean Acheson, a Democrat.

In his televised address, seen by as many as 80 million Americans, Nixon outlined his Vietnamization program; revealed his secret letter to Ho, but not the ultimatum; and explained why the United States could not cut and run. He then appealed to "the great silent majority" to support him and warned, "North Vietnam cannot humiliate the United States. Only Americans can do that." He had thrown down the gauntlet to the antiwar movement.

A major part of this new offensive involved neutralizing the media, which he felt favored the doves. . . .

The appeal to a silent majority and the companion assault on the eastern liberal media resonated with many Americans who despised the counterculture and the radicals and worried about the political and social changes they had experienced over the past few years. The president who promised to bring the nation together relied on a polarizing strategy to regain the upper hand in the battle for the hearts and minds of the American people. . . .

After more than a year in office, Nixon still appeared to be a long way from bring the war to a peaceful and honorable conclusion. The situation seemed to improve somewhat on 18 March 1970, when pro-Western General Lon Nol, backed by the Cambodian National Assembly, led a coup that overthrew Prince Sihanouk's neutralist regime. Although American intelligence agents knew about the coup in advance and informed the plotters that they would assist them once they deposed the erratic Sihanouk, this was not a CIA operation.

When Lon Nol demanded that the North Vietnamese leave his country and then closed the port of Sihanoukville through which much of their war material flowed, Washington was pleased. From the earliest days of the war, the Pentagon had wanted to deny Cambodian border areas to the enemy. But Lon Nol was a weak leader of a weak country who needed assistance to defend himself against both the 40,000 North Vietnamese troops and the lesser numbers of Khmer Rouge rebels who, by the middle of April, controlled one-third of Cambodia.

To assist its new ally, the United States began sending military and economic aid to Phnom Penh. Through 1975, the amount of such aid totaled $2.3 billion. The more immediate problem was how to help Lon Nol's forces against the better-armed and better-trained North Vietnamese with whom they had become involved in combat.

Despite Cambodia's shift from neutrality to the U.S. camp, April 1970 was not a good month for Richard Nixon. The secret Paris peace talks between Kissinger and Le Duc Tho had broken off, new Soviet military advisers appeared in Egypt in the midst of the undeclared War of Attrition with Israel along the Suez Canal, talks with Moscow about a summit were on hold, the *Apollo 13* moon shot was aborted, and advisers informed the president that he could not attend daughter Julie's graduation from Smith College and son-in-law David's from Amherst College that spring because of inevitable student hostility. Anticipating problems the previous fall, he had asked Haldeman "to plan some sort of trip out of the country at the time of Julie's graduation." Above all, on 8 April, the Senate rejected his Supreme Court nomination of G. Harrold Carswell, after having rejected Clement F. Haynsworth in November. On 13 April, Nixon told Kissinger, "Those senators think they can push Nixon around on Haynsworth and Carswell. Well I'll show them who's tough."

It is too simple to say that Nixon decided to send American and South Vietnamese troops into Cambodia on 30 April because of his domestic travails. Such an invasion had long been on the Pentagon drawing boards. He felt that he owed the North Vietnamese a response after they had called his bluff the previous November. Nonetheless, Nixon's anger and frustration influenced his decision making in April. . . .

Nixon informed only a few people about his decision to approve a joint United States–South Vietnamese invasion of Cambodia. Lon Nol himself did not find out about it until the last minute. Nixon did consult Chairman of the Joint Chiefs [Thomas] Moorer but kept Secretary of Defense Laird and Secretary of State Rogers in the dark until virtually the eleventh hour. The president knew that Laird and Rogers would oppose it, and he was right. When hearing about the plan on 27 April, the usually dignified Rogers groaned, "This will make the students puke." At Langley,

CIA analysts considered the invasion impractical, but CIA director Richard Helms did not offer their arguments to Nixon because he did not want to anger him. . . .

On the evening of 30 April, Nixon went before the nation to announce his surprising escalation. He referred to the invasion as an "incursion" needed to defend Cambodia against North Vietnamese aggression and also to capture the enemy's Central Office for South Vietnam (COSVN). He concluded, "If when the chips are down the world's most powerful nation acts like a pitiful helpless giant, the forces of totalitarianism and anarchy will threaten free nations and free institutions throughout the world."

Almost immediately, the antiwar opposition exploded. Students poured out of college dormitories to launch the most widespread series of campus protests in American history. By the time the crisis ended in mid-May, 89 percent of all private universities and 76 percent of all public universities had experienced demonstrations. At least 448 colleges experienced strikes or closures, with some even shutting down for the academic year because it was no longer possible to conduct classes. Nixon did not aid his cause when on 1 May, while walking through the Pentagon, he criticized the "bums . . . blowing up the campuses." He was referring to a few specific cases of recent violence, including the firebombing of the Center for Advanced Study in the Behavioral Sciences in Stanford, California, the previous week, but many students thought he was labeling all youthful dissenters bums.

Because of the Cambodian incursion, Roger Morris, Anthony Lake, and William Watts resigned from the NSC, and 250 foreign service officers sent a protest note to Secretary Rogers. Learning of this protest on 1 May, Nixon called the undersecretary of state in a rage: "This is the president. I want you to make sure all those sons of bitches are fired first thing in the morning." The president's orders were ignored.

Secretary of the Interior Walter Hickel, not one of Nixon's favorites, publicly expressed his criticism of an administration that lacked "appropriate concern for . . . our young people," as did Commissioner of Education James Allen. Nixon removed Allen from office twenty days after his offensive remarks. He waited until November before firing his "adversary" Hickel, who not only became popular because of his protest but also was a champion of the environmentalists.

Having expected some reaction over what many would deem a widening of the war, Nixon was confident that he could weather this storm—but not after 4 May. On that day, four young people were killed and fourteen wounded at Kent State University after poorly trained and jittery National Guradsmen fired into crowds of students; some were demonstrating against the war, but others were merely going to class. Although the Kent State campus had experienced violence in the previous days, including the burning of a Reserve Officers' Training Corps (ROTC) building, and although a handful of stones may have been thrown at the guardsmen on the fateful day, to some Americans, especially college students, it appeared that the government had deliberately murdered dissenters. On 15 May, two students were killed and eleven wounded under similar circumstances at the predominantly black Jackson State University in Mississippi.

In the ensuing days, a shaken Nixon and his staff met with college presidents, academics, and governors in an attempt to calm what one aide called the "absolute public hysteria." Although the VMC itself had disbanded earlier that month, antiwar leaders hastily put together a Washington protest for the weekend of 9–10 May that drew 100,000 activists. In the most bizarre incident of that weekend, after making more than fifty telephone calls from 10:35 P.M. to 3:50 A.M. (Kissinger eight times, Haldeman seven times) an anxious and depressed Nixon left the White House without telling anyone, accompanied only by his valet, to visit the area around the Lincoln Memorial where young demonstrators were encamped. With the Secret Service quickly following after him, the president tried to explain to sleepy and incredulous students that he understood their concerns. Although many of his conversations dealt with serious subjects, albeit not much on Vietnam, he also talked about the students' football teams and foreign travel, and that sort of frivolous banter is what appeared in newspaper accounts of the strange visitation.

Julie Nixon, who would soon be subject to "Fuck Julie" chants at her Smith College graduation, reported that the White House that weekend was like "a tomb." Charles Colson compared the "besieged" White House to a presidential palace in a Central American country during a coup; a battalion of the 81st Airborne, hidden in the EOB, prepared to deploy to protect a White House surrounded by district transit buses. The demonstration was peaceful, however.

Nixon took solace in the fact that more than a majority of those polled supported his Vietnam policies during the period of the Cambodian invasion, but he did not command a majority of the elite media or those on Capitol Hill. In a dramatic challenge to presidential authority in wartime, the Senate passed the Cooper-Church Amendment to cut off all funds for the Cambodian operation after 30 June. The vote was fifty-eight to thirty-seven with sixteen Republicans joining the majority. In a symbolic action that June, the Senate also repealed the 1964 Gulf of Tonkin Resolution. Although the House rejected the Cooper-Church Amendment, Nixon announced that he was going to withdraw the troops by 30 June anyway, claiming that they did not need any more time to accomplish their task of clearing out a twenty-one-mile-deep area. After Kissinger's assistant Alexander Haig informed Lon Nol of the pullout, the Cambodian leader began to cry.

When the president went before the American people on 30 June, he claimed a great victory. The allied forces had captured as much as 40 percent of all enemy arms in Cambodia, including 22,892 individual weapons, 15 million rounds of ammunition, 14 million pounds of rice, 143,000 rockets and mortars, and almost 200,000 antiaircraft rounds. Nixon did not talk about COSVN, the presumed reason for invading Cambodia. COSVN was a mobile field headquarters that was easily moved out of harm's way once the North Vietnamese learned of the invasion. The invasion did damage the communists' ability to conduct military operations in South Vietnam and disrupted their supply lines. Nixon later claimed that he was able to be more flexible on peace terms and also to announce the withdrawal of another 40,000 troops in November because of the blow he had dealt the enemy in May. Left unsaid was the fact that the invasion forced the communists further inland, where they began to pose more of a threat to the survival of the pro-Western regime in Phnom Penh.

The administration's support for Cambodian participation in the war, which included increased bombing further inland from the Vietnamese border, had the unintended consequence of increasing the popularity and effectiveness of the once marginal communist Khmer Rouge rebels. When the United States pulled out of Southeast Asia in 1975, the Khmer Rouge took over their country and proceeded to institute one of the most brutal revolutionary systems in history. During the three years they controlled Cambodia, they killed or permitted to die from starvation or disease as much as 20 percent of the population. Nixon's Cambodian policy of 1969 and 1970 was partly responsible for the rise to power of the murderous Khmer Rouge. Naturally, no one in the United States or the rest of the world in the spring of 1970 could have imagined such an outcome of the Cambodian invasion. . . .

. . . The North Vietnamese, who watched patiently as more and more American combat troops went home, refused to budge in negotiations. They were heartened when the Senate mustered thirty-nine votes in early September for the McGovern-Hatfield Resolution, which demanded the recall of all American troops from Vietnam by 31 December 1971. Unprepared to accept anything but their maximum terms at this point, the North Vietnamese believed that if they continued to delay, despite the heavy punishment from "protective reaction" bombings, a time would come when the American public would demand that the last American combat soldier leave Vietnam. In the fall of 1970, they began to plan for their next major offensive to be launched in the spring of 1972, when the South Vietnamese might have to go it alone against them.

Nonetheless, on 7 October, Nixon announced a "new initiative for peace," with the centerpiece being a cease-fire in place. He did not mention a mutual troop withdrawal in that address. However, at a press conference the next day, he returned to mutual withdrawal as a major element in U.S. peace proposals, thus undercutting the apparent 7 October breakthrough. Critics suggested that Nixon had presented the "new initiative," which turned out to be not all that new, as a cynical appeal to those concerned about the war who would soon cast their ballots in the congressional elections. In much the same way, the announced withdrawal of 40,000 additional troops on 12 October was geared to those elections. As he told Americans while on the campaign trail on 17 October, "I can say confidently that the war in Vietnam is coming to an end, and we are going to win a just peace in Vietnam." . . .

Despite the troop withdrawals and continued opposition to further escalation, Nixon had to maintain pressure on the North Vietnamese both to help the South Vietnamese and to demonstrate to Hanoi that the United States could still punish it. For those reasons, the administration began planning Lam Son 719, an incursion into Laos similar to the previous spring's incursion into Cambodia, in another attempt to disrupt the Ho Chi Minh Trail supply system. Domestic considerations made it impossible for the president to employ American troops this time; Lam Son 719 would be an all–South Vietnamese operation. The operation, according to Kissinger, which was "conceived in doubt" and "assailed by skepticism," "proceeded in confusion."

The invasion, which began on 8 February 1971, was a disaster. The North Vietnamese knew that the South Vietnamese were coming and were well dug in, and the South Vietnamese withdrew before achieving their goals. President Thieu had committed only 17,000 soldiers to the incursion—far fewer than the number recommended by the American high command—fearing that he could lose his crack troops in the campaign into which Nixon had dragooned him. Kissinger railed against the Saigon leadership: "Those sons of bitches. It's their country and we can't save it for them if they don't want to."

The South Vietnamese lost 8,000 men and the North Vietnamese 12,000; the communists downed between 100 and 200 helicopters and damaged 600. Fifty-five Americans, performing support roles, died in the operation. Nixon had told congressional leaders two days into the incursion that Lam Son 719 would prove that Vietnamization was working. Instead, Americans saw shocking films on the nightly newscasts of South Vietnamese clinging to helicopters taking them out of Laos. An embarrassed Nixon ordered Haldeman, "Have Agnew blast T.V. for the distorted coverage." He told a press conference on 17 February that everything "has gone according to plan" and that General Abrams had assured him that the South Vietnamese "are fighting . . . in a superior way." On 4 March, at another press conference, he announced that the South Vietnamese army had "come of age" and reported that Abrams had concluded that "the South Vietnamese by themselves can hack it."

Privately, Nixon, Kissinger, and Abrams knew that the incursion demonstrated that the South Vietnamese were not ready to go it alone. Moreover, it showed the North Vietnamese that the United States was hesitant to commit its own troops to such operations. They were further encouraged when the "success" of Vietnamization permitted Nixon to announce on 7 April the withdrawal of another 100,000 personnel, bringing total withdrawals to 365,000.

Spring 1971 was not a good period for President Nixon. Washington was rocked by "The Selling of the Pentagon," a CBS documentary revealing that the Department of Defense spent $190 million annually on public relations. In addition, Lieutenant William Calley went on trial for ordering the My Lai massacre, the antiwar movement mounted one of its largest demonstrations, and the *New York Times* and *Washington Post* published sections of the Defense Department's classified history of the war, the *Pentagon Papers.* . . .

While dealing with these difficult problems during the spring of 1971, Nixon made the most important concession to date in the peace talks. On 31 May, the United States, albeit in a vague manner, informed the North Vietnamese that its demand for a mutual withdrawal was no longer a sine qua non. That is, although all U.S. troops would leave South Vietnam, the North Vietnamese would not necessarily have to leave. With this concession, the key stumbling block to settlement became the nature of the postwar regime in the South.

Until the fall of 1972, the North Vietnamese held firm to their demand that Thieu would have to resign or otherwise be rendered politically ineffective before they would accept a peace agreement. They even allegedly suggested to Kissinger that he have the CIA assassinate Thieu. Refusing to alter his position significantly despite U.S. concessions, North Vietnamese negotiator Le Duc Tho told Kissinger in September 1971, "I really don't know why I am negotiating with you. I have just spent several hours with [South Dakota] Senator [George] McGovern and your opposition will force you to give me what I want." Between April and July 1971 alone, Congress had voted seventeen times on measures to restrict Nixon's actions in Southeast Asia. These activities contributed to Kissinger's pessimism in the fall of 1971. Hanoi, he wrote to Nixon, had "every incentive to wait for the interreacting [*sic*] combination of unrest in South Vietnam and an American domestic squeeze to topple [Thieu's government] . . . and pave the way for their eventual control."

To please the United States, Thieu submitted to the holding of an election that he won handily on 3 October 1971. Even so, the administration had been unable to encourage a serious opponent to run against him in what turned out to be another stacked South Vietnamese election. The CIA even offered the popular general Duong Van Minh a sizable bribe to ensure that he would remain in the race to preserve the illusion of a democratic choice. Nixon admitted the problem at a 16 September press conference: "We would have preferred to have a contested election in South Vietnam. We, however, cannot get people to run when they do not want to run." Despite this disappointment on the political front, the generally low level of enemy activity permitted the president to announce a further troop withdrawal of 45,000 on 12 November. This proved to be the lull before the storm as the North Vietnamese continued their buildup in a prelude to a full-scale offensive in four months.

With the U.S. presidential election less than one year away, Nixon worried about the ramifications of the failure of his diplomatic efforts to end the war. Hoping to shore up public support for his policies, he launched a propaganda blitz in January 1972. . . .

While Nixon was attempting to win the hearts and minds of the American people, the North Vietnamese were preparing their largest offensive since Tet. Although American intelligence analysts expected the offensive, they were taken aback by its scale and by the fact that it was a conventional and not a guerrilla operation. In an attempt to occupy large areas of South Vietnam, bloody Saigon's army, and weaken President Thieu, thereby paving the way for a coalition government in the South, fourteen divisions and twenty-six independent regiments of North Vietnamese regulars, employing two hundred Soviet T-54 tanks and a host of modern weapons they had just received from Moscow, took part in the offensive that began on 30 March. Virtually all North Vietnamese regulars participated in a three-pronged attack that resulted in the communist capture of Quang Tri on 1 May, despite Nixon's contention that South Vietnam had created "a formidable fighting force." With almost all U.S. combat troops out of the fray, the North Vietnamese rather easily cut through the well-equipped but poorly trained and poorly motivated South Vietnamese.

The United States saved the South Vietnamese from defeat with the massive use of tactical airpower in the South and B-52 bombing of Hanoi and Haiphong in the North. On 16 April, American planes hit four Soviet merchant ships anchored in Haiphong harbor, an action that could have jeopardized the long-awaited Soviet-American summit in Moscow scheduled for May. The next month, in the midst of the offensive, Nixon announced the withdrawal of another 20,000 troops.

When on 2 May General Abrams reported that the South Vietnamese were still in desperate shape, and Kissinger reported an especially bitter session in Paris with Le Duc Tho on the same day, Nixon made another daring decision. He would mine, from the air, the harbors of Hanoi and Haiphong, severely limiting the North's ability to obtain supplies. The Pentagon had recommended such mining as early as October 1966. The president also announced the resumption of large-scale bombing attacks on the North with over 40,000 sorties from May through October. An angry Nixon warned, "The bastards have never been bombed like they're going to be bombed this time." Whatever his intentions, he soon became "thoroughly disgusted" with the air force's "pusillanimous" performance in the North, which was not as devastating as he had hoped.

Most of Nixon's advisers feared that the mining decision, announced on 8 May, would force the Russians to cancel the summit. Nixon wrote to Kissinger the next day that North Vietnam "has gone over the brink *and so have we.* We have the power to destroy his war making capacity. The only question is whether we have the will to use that power. What distinguishes me from Johnson is that I have the *will* in spades."

With Kissinger ambivalent about the move, only Haig, Connally, and Agnew initially supported the mining decision. Nixon was not happy about possibly having to forgo the summit, but he wanted to punish the Soviet-backed North Vietnamese. He had concluded that although the Russians would protest vigorously in public, the odds were fifty-fifty that they would not cancel the summit; they needed it more than the United States, especially since Nixon had concluded a very successful summit with their arch-enemies, the Chinese, in February. The president was correct, although it was a near thing in Moscow, with several important members of the Politburo calling for cancellation of the summit, an action that might have hurt Nixon in the presidential election.

Nixon was buoyed by public-opinion polls that showed that at least 60 percent of the population supported the minings and by his reception of 22,000 favorable telegrams at the White House. Many of those had been generated by Republican operatives. His operatives also fixed a *Washington Star* and a local television poll by "stuffing" the ballot boxes. These operations were unnecessary, because a majority of Americans supported Nixon's actions, especially since he had made good on his promise to bring their boys home. The last ground combat forces, the Third Battalion of the 21st Infantry, left Vietnam on 23 August 1972.

By August, Hanoi acknowledged that its offensive had failed and American retaliatory blows had taken their toll. Both the Russians and Chinese, intent on improving their relations with the United States, had been pressuring the North Vietnamese to bring the war to an end by offering compromises. Finally, North Vietnamese officials read the U.S. presidential polls, and with Nixon's reelection appearing to be a certainty, they concluded that he would be less likely to make peace on terms favorable to them after the election than before. Toward the end of August they began to back away from their long-held position that Thieu would have to leave office before they would agree to peace. . . .

Could the peace Nixon achieved in 1973 have been obtained in 1969? During the four years that his administration prosecuted the war in Vietnam, the United States lost over 18,000 troops, the South Vietnamese at least 107,000 and the communists perhaps as many as half a million. Had Nixon surrendered the principle of mutual withdrawal in 1969 instead of in 1972, the North Vietnamese might have compromised on political issues, and the war could have been brought to a much speedier end, with the concomitant saving of hundreds of thousands of Asian and American lives.

A Better War

LEWIS SORLEY

Soon after Tet 1968 General Westmoreland was replaced as U.S. commander in Vietnam by General Creighton W. Abrams, renowned as a troop leader since World War II, when he commanded a battalion of tanks in the drive across Europe, en route breaking through to the 101st Airborne Division where it was encircled at

Bastogne during the Battle of the Bulge, and winning two Distinguished Service Crosses and a battlefield promotion to colonel in the process.

Abrams joined Ambassador Ellsworth Bunker, a patrician Vermonter and international businessman-turned-diplomat, recently acclaimed for dextrous handling of a volatile situation during U.S. intervention in the Dominican Republic. Bunker had settled into the Saigon post the previous spring, thereby ending a long series of frequent ambassadorial changes.

Soon these men were joined by Ambassador William E. Colby, a career officer of the Central Intelligence Agency who had earlier been the Agency's Chief of Station, Saigon, then Chief of the Far East Division at CIA Headquarters. Building a brilliant intelligence career on World War II service with the Office of Strategic Services, service that saw him decorated for valor after parachuting behind enemy lines. Colby arrived to take over American support of the pacification program.

In the wake of Tet 1968, the tasks confronting the new leadership triumvirate were challenging indeed. America's long buildup of forces was at an end, soon to be supplanted by a progressive reduction in the forces deployed. Financial resources, previously abundant, were becoming severely constrained. Domestic support for the war, never robust, continued to decline, the downward spiral fueled in reinforcing parts by opponents of the war and others deploring inept prosecution of it. Lyndon Johnson had in effect been driven from office by these escalating forces, while Richard Nixon's tenure would of necessity constitute an extended attempt to moderate and adapt to them without losing all control.

Whatever the mood of the country, for those in Vietnam the war still had to be fought, and the new leadership went about doing that with energy and insight. Shaped by Abrams's understanding of the complex nature of the conflict, the tactical approach underwent immediate and radical revision when he took command. Previously fragmented approaches to combat operations, pacification, and mentoring the South Vietnamese armed forces now became "one war" with a single clear-cut objective—security for the people in South Vietnam's villages and hamlets. And under a program awkwardly titled "Vietnamization," responsibility for conduct of the war, largely taken over by the Americans in the earlier period, was progressively turned back to the South Vietnamese.

Most of the better-known treatments of the Vietnam War as a whole have given relatively little consideration to these later years. Stanley Karnow's *Vietnam: A History,* for example, does not get beyond Tet 1968 until page 567 out of 670, and indeed Karnow does not even list Abrams, who served in Vietnam for five years and commanded U.S. forces there for four, in his "Cast of Principal Characters."

George Herring's admirable academic treatment of the conflict, *America's Longest War,* is similarly weighted toward the early years, with 221 pages devoted to the period through Tet 1968 and 60 pages to the rest of the war. William J. Duiker's *Historical Dictionary of Vietnam* likewise emphasizes the early stages, with entries for Lodge, Taylor, and Westmoreland, but none for Bunker, Abrams, or Colby.

The most pronounced example of concentration on the earlier years is Neil Sheehan's Pulitzer Prize–winning book *A Bright Shining Lie.* Sheehan devotes 725 pages to events through Tet 1968 and only 65 pages to the rest of the war, even though John Paul Vann, the nominal subject of his book, lived and served in Vietnam for four years after the Tet Offensive. And of course the famous *Pentagon Papers,* first made public in June 1971, cover the war only through the end of Defense Secretary Robert McNamara's tenure in 1968. William Colby once observed that, due to the prevalence of such truncated treatments of the Vietnam War, "the historical record given to most Americans is . . . similar to what we would know if histories of World War II stopped before Stalingrad, Operation Torch in North Africa and Guadalcanal in the Pacific." To many people, therefore the story of the early years seems to be the whole story of the war in Vietnam, a perception that is far from accurate.

Bunker, Abrams, and Colby, and the forces they led in the later years of American involvement in Vietnam, brought different values to their tasks, operated from a different understanding of the nature of the war, and applied different measures of merit and different tactics. They employed diminishing resources in manpower, matériel, money, and time as they raced to render the South Vietnamese capable of defending themselves before the last American forces were withdrawn. They went about that task with sincerity, intelligence, decency, and absolute professionalism, and in the process came very close to achieving the elusive goal of a viable nation and a lasting peace. . . .

There came a time when the war was won. The fighting wasn't over, but the war was won. This achievement can probably best be dated in late 1970, after the Cambodian incursion in the spring of the year. By then the South Vietnamese countryside had been widely pacified, so much so that the term "pacification" was no longer even used. Four million members of the People's Self-Defense Force, armed with some 600,000 weapons, represented no threat to the government that had armed them; instead they constituted an overt commitment to that government in opposition to the enemy.

South Vietnam's armed forces, greatly expanded and impressively equipped, were substantially more capable than even a couple of years earlier. Their most impressive gains were in the ranks of the territorial forces—the Regional Forces and Popular Forces—providing close-in security for the people in the countryside. The successful pacification program, one repeatedly cited in enemy communications as a threat that had to be countered, was extending not only security but also elected government, trained hamlet and village officials, and economic gains to most of the population.

In Military Region 3, the critical complex of provinces surrounding Saigon, recalled General Michael Davison, "it is fair to say that by the winter of 1970–1971 the VC had virtually been exterminated and the NVA, which had endeavored to go big time with divisional size units, had been driven across the border into Cambodia." And by 1971," recalled Colby, "I could go down the canals in the Delta in the middle of the night." And he could—and did—drive out in the countryside around Hue, just two unarmed jeeps in convoy, to show the British ambassador around. They saw people standing guard where three years before divisions had been fighting. "I mean," said Colby, "the hell with the numbers. I don't know about the numbers either, but by God I did it." . . .

Not only was the internal war against subversion and the guerrilla threat won, so was that against the external conventional threat—in the terms specified by the United States. Those terms were that South Vietnam should, without help from U.S. ground forces, be capable of resisting aggression so long as America continued to provide logistical and financial support, and—of crucial importance later, once a cease-fire agreement had been negotiated—renewed application of U.S. air and naval power should North Vietnam violate the terms of that agreement.

The viability of such arrangements would be demonstrated in 1972, when the enemy's Easter Offensive was met and turned back after heavy fighting by just that combination of South Vietnamese and American forces and resources. So severely were the invading forces punished that it was three years before they could mount another major offensive, and that despite the complete withdrawal of all U.S. troops in the meantime. At that later fateful juncture, as will be seen, the United States defaulted on all three elements of its promised support and, unsurprisingly, the war was no longer won.

Later, after the war had been lost, Stephen Young observed in a conversation with his former boss, Ambassador Bunker, that "in effect the population was seized away from the enemy, that about 90 percent of the population came under GVN control during 1969, and that in 1970 and 1971 the figure stayed about that level." Young asked Bunker whether General Abrams's strategy had made "it possible to in effect win the war by seizing the population during 1969." Without a pause Bunker answered simply, "I think so, yes."

From his first days as commander, Abrams had clamped down on excessive use of force, especially in populated areas, reserving to himself authority to permit the use of heavy weapons in cities. Likewise he cut back sharply on unobserved artillery fire. In late August 1970, Abrams again discussed this aspect of the war with his senior field commanders. "I think that there're areas around here in Vietnam right now where the question should be asked whether artillery, gunships, tac air, and all that kind of stuff, whether it ought to be used *at all.* Out here to try to get four guerrillas— three air strikes, and 155s and 105s, and two helicopter gunship runs—."

General [George] Brown suggested it was necessary to do such things to keep the system viable. "This has got to be *examined,*" Abrams insisted. "I don't want to be just out here banging up the goddamn country in order to keep the *system* going. I don't think it's too *soon* to start thinking of some places around here where you just don't *do* any of that stuff. Now I didn't ring this up on the basis of saving ammunition," he added. "I'm thinking about the Vietnamese people, the whole atmosphere of political and economic and a healthy attitude toward the government and all that kind of stuff!"

These concerns led to a study titled "Where Do We Let Peace Come to Vietnam?" It began with consideration of the application of tactical airpower within South Vietnam, then expanded to consider artillery as well. Seventh Air Force was tasked to conduct the study, which was to look at "conditions under which the application of air power produces undesirable consequences, and where that application may be unproductive." Barry Horton, a brilliant Air Force captain who was also a skilled systems analyst, headed it up. General Lucius Clay, who by this time had taken command of Seventh Air Force, told the young officer, "General Abrams is really uncomfortable that we are doing more harm than good."

Horton's study was designed to identify conditions under which application of air power produced undesirable consequences for the people supposedly being defended, especially those living in rural areas. Even before the study was fairly under way, however, Abrams's expressed concern began having an effect. For one thing Lieutenant General Michael Davison, commanding U.S. forces in Military Region 3, had his staff analyze the use of tac air strikes in his area of responsibility.

Since Cambodia, he found, they had been running twenty-five to thirty-five preplanned air strikes a day and ten to twenty immediates, these latter strikes called in on targets of opportunity developed during an operation. Davison's staff analyzed the targets being struck and the bomb damage assessment they were getting from forward air controllers. "And then we just sort of came to some gross conclusions that we had too many preplanned strikes," said Davison, so they cut back to twelve a day and were doing fine, along with maybe ten immediates. The next step was to influence the South Vietnamese along the same lines.

When, a few months later, the results of Seventh Air Force's study were ready to be briefed, it was anticlimactic. By then, influenced by Abrams's concern, field commanders had already modified their operations to cut back on the use of air and artillery in populated areas, and the analysts had seen that reflected in the data. "We were running out of examples to analyze," said Horton. "We'd had the results without actually having to publish the study."

By 1970, concluded George Jacobson, a fundamental change had taken place, one that had a great deal to do with the success of pacification. In the early 1960s "people had regard for the VC, and I believe that—had free elections been possible—they would have won by a very considerable percentage. I *now* believe that, in those areas where they do not have control, the Viet Cong exert their influence by sheer naked terror, and by little else." Thus, "I think if a free election could be held now, the VC would lose. You can't get popular throwing grenades into marketplaces and blowing up school buses." Despite this apparently obvious conclusion, the enemy's devotion to terrorism continued unabated. In the first week of April 1970, Jacobson reported, "the total number of victims was 1,427, which was the highest we've ever had since Tet of 1968, when they were so high we couldn't even keep *track* of them."

When Secretary Laird and General Wheeler made their next visit, Colby discussed pacification statistics. "We have our questions as to the absolute veracity of the HES figures," he said candidly, "but I think the key thing is the change. Approximately three million people, and 2,600 hamlets, last year moved from the something less than 'C' category up to the C or above. What the absolute level of security is, is another question, but the fact they moved is really not in much doubt. Security *did* expand during 1969." And Colby cited President Thieu's strong emphasis on the People's Self-Defense Force as a base point on which to build the rest of the security structure, calling it "both a paramilitary and a political force for the future." The thrust during 1970 would be on consolidation of security gains, because expansion had gone about as far as it was going in most places.

President Thieu set pacification goals for 1970 at very ambitious levels—100 percent at 'C' or better by the end of the year, and of that 90 percent at 'A' or 'B,' then saw them very nearly achieved. "If 1968 was a year of military contest, and if 1969 was a year of expansion of security," observed Colby, "1970 is going to be a process of economic and political and security consolidation. It's beginning to really solidify." One reason was agreement on the mission at hand. In late September 1969

Abrams had convened his field commanders and their senior pacification advisors for extensive discussions. "And when we got all through," he recalled, "I think it was the unanimous opinion of everyone who was here that the place to put your money now, in terms of energy, effort, imagination, and all the rest of it is into this pacification program—enhancing the security, enhancing the effectiveness of government out among the people. This is not the B-52 league, and it's not the tac air league. It's really not the maneuver battalion league so much. It's all of the little things that you can do in there to push this along."

The key to the whole thing was the people, said Abrams, "that's what both sides are struggling for." That meant that "instead of talking about offensives, we've got to get into the RF/PF, PSDF, NP/NPFF, all that stuff, and we've got to put a lot of effort up there so that pacification continues to march and continues to consolidate. That's the *nature* of the *beast!* Instead of toying around about whether you ought to move another brigade of the 4th Division, something like that. That's *not* the *real* answer!"

Progress in pacification was now being reflected in very practical ways—reduction in VC extortion of "taxes," a decrease in enemy food supplies taken from the villagers, and less in-country recruiting by enemy forces. "If you ever needed any proof that it's just one war after all—pacification, combat operations, Vietnamization—that it's all one thing," observed Abrams, "it's the effect it has on the infrastructure. It makes it tougher for them. The more that advances, the more—." During a visit to Long An Province, Abrams had been shown a very interesting chart, a tabulation by year of kilometers of road open and in use, bridges functioning and serviceable, and so on. "You could kind of trace the war," he said. "You start at the 1963 level, which is when things were in pretty good shape, bustling and all that. Then as you go 1964, 1965, 1966, 1967, 1968 the kilometers of road and the number of bridges just keep going down and down and down. *Then* it starts back up, and in September of 1970 they passed the 1963 level, and are considerably above it now."

Colby visited various places in the countryside twice a week or more, usually staying overnight, a routine that gave him a current and authentic feel for the situation. Frequently he invited one or another of the Saigon press corps to go along. Flying back to Saigon after one such visit, Colby asked the newsman of the day what he thought about the situation. "Nothing much going on," the fellow replied. Colby pondered that for a moment. "Well," he ventured, "you're right. We weren't mortared, nobody attacked us while we slept. People were farming, the school was in operation, some refugees had returned to their homes. Nothing very dramatic, except the *contrast* with how things were there three years ago."

General George Brown, an airman par excellence, understood not only his craft but also pacification and its importance to the outcome in Vietnam. "There's no question in my mind but what we'll make work the thing that most people understand Vietnamization to be—that is, we'll form the units, equip them, train them," he affirmed early in 1970. "But, in the time remaining, we're not going to create a force that will take the place of the force that's here now. So what you've got to do is trim the security problem to a dimension that that force you create can handle. That's pacification, and that means continuing our presence over here until that pacification reaches the point." It was a race, and everybody working in Vietnam knew it, a desperate race to shape what was left to manageable proportions before all the Americans were pulled out.

Pacification in its broadest meaning thus had another crucially important purpose, freeing ARVN divisions from static security missions so they could undertake mobile operations against enemy main forces. Colby described the situation very graphically for the visiting Richard Helms: "Of your total force here of roughly 500,000 PSDF weapons, 500,000 RF and PF, 500,000 ARVN, and 500,000 Americans, you're going to drop out the last one. You're going to *cut* your force by a quarter, and it's the strongest quarter and the quarter that's been contributing most. ARVN's got to be freed of everything else so it can replace *that. That's* your real *gap.*"

If it was difficult for Abrams to convince some of his senior officers that population security and pacification were the essence of the war, so much more so was it—in his view, at least—to get the press to understand this, let alone report it. Looking at the situation in Cambodia, where the enemy was mimicking his earlier actions in South Vietnam by building up a political structure, establishing an infrastructure, and undermining the mechanisms of government, Abrams saw that as sailing right over the heads of reporters. "You see, the cosmetics of the thing—you've got the press reporting a raging battle, preparations for the assault on Phnom Penh. Christ, even these young chaps, they've got to get it into sort of a World War II context. Otherwise, you can't report it. And that's *not* what's going on over there. It just *isn't.*" But that seemed to be the only way the press knew how to explain it. "Christ," Abrams complained, "talk about the *traditionalists.* They're not among *us,* it's these young chaps *reporting.* And this movie on *Patton,* you see—it comes at the wrong time. It just *reinforces* all that. You've got a war on, that's about the only way you can run it."

Abrams was on to something here, and it wasn't confined to Cambodia or any other single aspect of what was happening in Southeast Asia. In these later years the press simply missed the war. Maybe it wasn't exciting enough, maybe it wasn't graphic enough for television, maybe it was too difficult to comprehend or to explain, maybe it ran counter to preconceived expectations or even wishes. Probably some part of this was also due simply to war weariness in the United States, meaning that developments in Vietnam were not news in the same way they had been earlier. Admittedly much of what now constituted the most important aspects of the war was difficult to dramatize or portray. Hamlets in which the population remained secure, refugees who were able to return to their villages, distribution of land to the peasantry, miracle rice harvests, roads kept open for farm-to-market traffic, and the election and training of village governments were less dramatic than whatever fighting still went on, but they were also infinitely more important in terms of how the war was going. . . .

Even as the cumulative effect of the "one war" approach was reaching a peak, influences were at work that would eventually undermine much of what had been accomplished. In the United States, these included further erosion of political support for the war, growing budgetary pressures on support for the U.S. forces still in Vietnam and for the South Vietnamese alike, and the influence of both on the pace of withdrawal. Clearly the time would come, and sooner rather than later, when American ground forces could no longer play any significant part in prosecution of the war.

✕ *F U R T H E R   R E A D I N G*

Aitken, Jonathan. *Nixon: A Life* (1994).

Ambrose, Stephen E. *Nixon* (vols. 1–3) (1987–1991).

Andradé, Dale. *America's Last Vietnam Battle: Halting Hanoi's 1972 Easter Offensive* (2001).

Brandon, Henry. *The Retreat of American Power* (1974).

Bundy, William. *A Tangled Web* (1998).

Burr, William, ed. *The Kissinger Transcripts* (1999).

Caldwell, Dan, ed. *Henry Kissinger* (1983).

Clarke, Jeffrey J. *Advice and Support: The Final Years,* 1965–1973 (1988).

Garthoff, Raymond. *Détente and Confrontation* (1985).

Garver, J. W. "Sino-Vietnamese Conflict and Sino-American Rapprochement," *Political Science Quarterly,* 96 (1981), 445–61.

Goodman, Allan E. *The Lost Peace* (1978).

Hersh, Seymour M. *The Price of Power* (1983).

Isaacs, Arnold R. *Without Honor: Defeat in Vietnam and Cambodia* (1983).

Isaacson, Walter. *Kissinger* (1992).

Kalb, Marvin and Bernard. *Kissinger* (1974).

Kimball, Jeffrey. *Nixon's Vietnam War* (1998).

Kissinger, Henry. *Diplomacy* (1994).

———. "The Vietnam Negotiations." *Foreign Affairs,* 47 (1969) 211–34.

———. *Years of Upheaval* (1983).

Litwak, Robert S. *Détente and the Nixon Doctrine* (1984).

Morris, Roger. *Uncertain Greatness: Henry Kissinger and American Foreign Policy* (1977).

Nixon, Richard M. "Asia After Vietnam," *Foreign Affairs,* 46 (1967), 111–25.

———. *RN: The Memoirs of Richard Nixon* (1978).

Osgood, Robert E. *Retreat from Empire?* (1973).

Parmet, Herbert S. *Richard Nixon and His America* (1990).

Schell, Jonathan. *The Time of Illusion* (1975).

Schulzinger, Robert D. *Henry Kissinger* (1989).

Shawcross, William. *Sideshow: Kissinger, Nixon and the Destruction of Cambodia* (1979).

Stoessinger, John. *Kissinger: The Anguish of Power* (1976).

Szulc, Tad. *The Illusion of Peace* (1978).

Turley, G. H. *The Easter Offensive* (1985).

The Antiwar Movement
and Public Opinion

✕

The American people overwhelmingly supported government policy in Vietnam during the early years of the U.S. military buildup, much as they had other post–World War II foreign policy commitments. Even after Johnson's major escalation of 1965, dissent remained muted, with the exception of vocal protests by a handful of isolated student and intellectual groups. But as the war dragged on inconclusively and American casualties mounted throughout 1966 and 1967, protest marches and demonstrations proliferated. A symbolic march on the Pentagon in the fall of 1967 drew tens of thousands of antiwar protesters. Following the Tet offensive of early 1968, the ranks of the antiwar movement swelled.

Despite the persistence of stereotypes perpetuated in part by the media, antiwar dissidents were not confined to the young, radicals, intellectuals, and the disaffected. Indeed if one defines the antiwar movement more broadly to encompass all who came to question the efficacy of the U.S. commitment to Vietnam, by 1968 it included many powerful individuals within the business and financial communities, the media, and the government itself. Public-opinion polls conducted during the late 1960s and early 1970s revealed a steady erosion of popular support for U.S. policy. Many observers at the time noted that the war had polarized American society more than any other event since the Civil War.

The nature of the antiwar movement—its origins, purposes, and ultimate impact on policy—has long been a subject of heated controversy. Perhaps of equal importance, albeit less frequently studied, is the aggregate domestic response to Vietnam, measurable by public-opinion surveys. Who opposed the war? Why did they oppose it? What impact did antiwar activities, or changes in levels of public support, have on the actions of the Johnson and Nixon administrations?

✕ D O C U M E N T S

Students for a Democratic Society (SDS), an organization that by the mid-1960s had become a leading voice for the student protest movement and the New Left, announced its opposition to the war in 1965. A public statement explaining its position, issued to the press in October 1965, is Document 1. Document 2 gives excerpts from a speech by SDS president Carl Oglesby during a protest march in Washington, D.C., on November 27 of that year. Widely circulated, the address reproached not only the war but the system that had produced it. Martin Luther King, Jr., the preeminent civil-rights leader and Nobel Peace Prize recipient, declared his opposition to America's involvement in Vietnam on April 4, 1967. Portions of King's controversial speech, delivered as a sermon at New York's Riverside Church, are printed as Document 3.

The military draft quickly emerged as a focus of antiwar activity. Document 4, a call to resist the draft, was issued by Women Strike for Peace, the leading women's antiwar organization. It was publicized during an anti-draft rally in Washington, D.C. on September 20, 1967, that culminated in a demonstration in front of the White House. Document 5, issued in the fall of 1967 by the Antidraft Resistance, led to federal prosecution of five of its signers, including famed pediatrician Benjamin Spock and Yale University chaplain William Sloane Coffin, Jr. In Document 6, author and former White House speechwriter James Fallows reflects on the class inequities of the draft. Document 7 features a veteran's anguished memories of how antiwar civilians mistreated him upon his return from service in Vietnam.

Former student activist Todd Gitlin, now a sociology professor at New York University, in Document 8 recalls the New Left's infatuation with the Vietcong and other Third World revolutionary movements. In Document 9, John Kerry, a leader of Vietnam Veterans Against the War, bitterly attacks government policy. Now a Democratic senator from Massachusetts, Kerry condemned the duplicity that underlay American policy at a congressional hearing on April 22, 1971.

1. SDS States Opposition to the War, 1965

Students for a Democratic Society wishes to reiterate emphatically its intention to pursue its opposition to the war in Vietnam, undeterred by the diversionary tactics of the administration.

We feel that the war is immoral at its root, that it is fought alongside a regime with no claim to represent its people, and that *it is foreclosing the hope of making America a decent and truly democratic society.*

The commitment of SDS, and of the whole generation we represent, is clear: we are anxious to build villages; we refuse to burn them. We are anxious to help and to change our country; we refuse to destroy someone else's country. We are anxious to advance the cause of democracy; we do not believe that cause can be advanced by torture and terror.

We are fully prepared to volunteer for service to our country and to democracy. We volunteer to go into Watts to work with the people of Watts to rebuild that neighborhood to be the kind of place that the people of Watts want it to be—and when we say "rebuild," we mean socially as well as physically. We volunteer to help the Peace Corps learn, as we have been learning in the slums and in Mississippi, how to energize the hungry and desperate and defeated of the world to make the big decisions. We volunteer to serve in hospitals and schools in the slums, in the Job

---

Public statement issued to the press, October 1965.

Corps and VISTA, in the new Teachers Corps—and to do so in such a way as to strengthen democracy at its grass-roots. And in order to make our volunteering possible, we propose to the President that all those Americans who seek so vigorously to build instead of burn be given their chance to do so. We propose that he test the young people of America: if they had a free choice, would they want to burn and torture in Vietnam or to build a democracy at home and overseas? There is only one way to make the choice real: let us see what happens if service to democracy is made grounds for exemption from the military draft. I predict that almost every member of my generation would choose to build, not to burn; to teach, not to torture; to help, not to kill. And I am sure that the overwhelming majority of our brothers and cousins in the army in Vietnam would make the same choice if they could—to serve and build, not kill and destroy. . . .

Until the President agrees to our proposal, we have only one choice: we do in conscience object, utterly and wholeheartedly, to this war; and we will encourage every member of our generation to object, and to file his objection through the Form 150 provided by the law for conscientious objection.

2. Carl Oglesby Denounces the "Liberals' War," 1965

Seven months ago at the April March on Washington, Paul Potter, then President of Students for a Democratic Society, stood in approximately this spot and said that we must name the system that creates and sustains the war in Vietnam—name it, describe it, analyze it, understand it, and change it.

Today I will try to name it—to suggest an analysis which, to be quite frank, may disturb some of you—and to suggest what changing it may require of us.

We are here again to protest against a growing war. Since it is a very bad war, we acquire the habit of thinking that it must be caused by very bad men. But we only conceal reality, I think, to denounce on such grounds the menacing coalition of industrial and military power, or the brutality of the blitzkrieg we are waging against Vietnam, or the ominous signs around us that heresy may soon no longer be permitted. We must simply observe, and quite plainly say, that this coalition, this blitzkrieg, and this demand for acquiescence are creatures, all of them, of a government that since 1932 has considered itself to be fundamentally *liberal*.

The original commitment in Vietnam was made by President Truman, a mainstream liberal. It was seconded by President Eisenhower, a moderate liberal. It was intensified by the late President Kennedy, a flaming liberal. Think of the men who now engineer that war—those who study the maps, give the commands, push the buttons, and tally the dead: Bundy, McNamara, Rusk, Lodge, Goldberg, the President himself.

They are not moral monsters.
They are all honorable men.
They are all liberals.

Oglesby speech, November 27, 1965, reprinted in *Monthly Review,* 17 (January 1966), 21–30.

But so, I'm sure, are many of us who are here today in protest. To understand the war, then, it seems necessary to take a closer look at this American liberalism. Maybe we are in for some surprises. Maybe we have here two quite different liberalisms: one authentically humanist, the other not so human at all.

Not long ago, I considered myself a liberal. And if someone had asked me what I meant by that, I'd perhaps have quoted Thomas Jefferson or Thomas Paine, who first made plain our nation's unprovisional commitment to human rights. But what do you think would happen if these two heroes could sit down now for a chat with President Johnson and McGeorge Bundy?

They would surely talk of the Vietnam war. Our dead revolutionaries would soon wonder why their country was fighting against what appeared to be a revolution. The living liberals would hotly deny that it is one: there are troops coming in from outside, the rebels get arms from other countries, most of the people are not on their side, and they practice terror against their own. Therefore, *not* a revolution.

What would our dead revolutionaries answer? They might say: "What fools and bandits, sirs, you make then of us. Outside help? Do you remember Lafayette? Or the 3,000 British freighters the French navy sunk for our side? Or the arms and men we got from France and Spain? And what's this about terror? Did you never hear what we did to our own loyalists? Or about the thousands of rich American Tories who fled for their lives to Canada? And as for popular support, do you not know that we had less than one third of our people with us? That, in fact, the colony of New York recruited more troops for the British than for the revolution? Should we give it all back?"

Revolutions do not take place in velvet boxes. They never have. It is only the poets who make them lovely. What the National Liberation Front is fighting in Vietnam is a complex and vicious war. This war is also a revolution, as honest a revolution as you can find anywhere in history. And this is a fact which all our intricate official denials will never change.

But it doesn't make any difference to our leaders anyway. Their aim in Vietnam is really much simpler than this implies. It is to safeguard what they take to be American interests around the world against revolution or revolutionary change, which they always call Communism—as if that were that. In the case of Vietnam, this interest is, first, the principle that revolution shall not be tolerated anywhere, and second, that South Vietnam shall never sell its rice to China—or even to North Vietnam.

There is simply no such thing now, for us, as a just revolution—never mind that for two thirds of the world's people the twentieth century might as well be the Stone Age; never mind the terrible poverty and hopelessness that are the basic facts of life for most modern men; and never mind that for these millions there is now an increasingly perceptible relationship between their sorrow and our contentment.

Can we understand why the Negroes of Watts rebelled? Then why do we need a devil theory to explain the rebellion of the South Vietnamese? Can we understand the oppression in Mississippi, or the anguish that our Northern ghettos make epidemic? Then why can't we see that our proper human struggle is not with Communism or revolutionaries, but with the social desperation that drives good men to violence, both here and abroad? . . .

Let's stare our situation coldly in the face. All of us are born to the colossus of history, our American corporate system—in many ways, an awesome organism.

There is one fact that describes it: with about 5 percent of the world's people, we consume about half the world's goods. We take a richness that is in good part not our own, and we put it in our pockets, our garages, our split-levels, our bellies, and our futures.

On the *face* of it, it is a crime that so few should have so much at the expense of so many. Where is the moral imagination so abused as to call this just? Perhaps many of us feel a bit uneasy in our sleep. We are not, after all, a cruel people. And perhaps we don't really need this super dominance that deforms others. But what can we do? The investments are made. The financial ties are established. The plants abroad are built. Our system *exists*. One is swept up into it. How intolerable—to be born moral, but addicted to a stolen and maybe surplus luxury. Our goodness threatens to become counterfeit before our eyes—unless we change. But change threatens us with uncertainty—at least.

3. Martin Luther King, Jr., Declares His Opposition to the War, 1967

Since I am a preacher by trade, I suppose it is not surprising that I have seven major reasons for bringing Vietnam into the field of my moral vision. There is at the outset a very obvious and almost facile connection between the war in Vietnam and the struggle I, and others, have been waging in America. A few years ago there was a shining moment in that struggle. It seemed as if there was a real promise of hope for the poor—both black and white—through the Poverty Program. Then came the build-up in Vietnam, and I watched the program broken and eviscerated as if it were some idle political plaything of a society gone mad on war, and I knew that America would never invest the necessary funds or energies in rehabilitation of its poor so long as Vietnam continued to draw men and skills and money like some demonic, destructive suction tube. So I was increasingly compelled to see the war as an enemy of the poor and to attack it as such.

Perhaps the more tragic recognition of reality took place when it became clear to me that the war was doing far more than devastating the hopes of the poor at home. It was sending their sons and their brothers and their husbands to fight and to die in extraordinarily high proportions relative to the rest of the population. We were taking the young black men who had been crippled by our society and sending them 8000 miles away to guarantee liberties in Southeast Asia which they had not found in Southwest Georgia and East Harlem. So we have been repeatedly faced with the cruel irony of watching Negro and white boys on TV screens as they kill and die together for a nation that has been unable to seat them together in the same schools. So we watch them in brutal solidarity burning the huts of a poor village, but we realize that they would never live on the same block in Detroit. I could not be silent in the face of such cruel manipulation of the poor.

My third reason grows out of my experience in the ghettos of the North over the last three years—especially the last three summers. As I have walked among the

King speech, reprinted in *Ramparts* (May 1967), 33–37.

desperate, rejected and angry young men, I have told them that Molotov cocktails and rifles would not solve their problems. I have tried to offer them my deepest compassion while maintaining my conviction that social change comes most meaningfully through non-violent action. But, they asked, what about Vietnam? They asked if our own nation wasn't using massive doses of violence to solve its problems, to bring about the changes it wanted. Their questions hit home, and I knew that I could never again raise my voice against the violence of the oppressed in the ghettos without having first spoken clearly to the greatest purveyor of violence in the world today—my own government.

For those who ask the question, "Aren't you a Civil Rights leader?" and thereby mean to exclude me from the movement for peace, I have this further answer. In 1957 when a group of us formed the Southern Christian Leadership Conference, we chose as our motto: "To save the soul of America." We were convinced that we could not limit our vision to certain rights for black people, but instead affirmed the conviction that America would never be free or saved from itself unless the descendants of its slaves were loosed from the shackles they still wear.

Now, it should be incandescently clear that no one who has any concern for the integrity and life of America today can ignore the present war. If America's soul becomes totally poisoned, part of the autopsy must read "Vietnam." It can never be saved so long as it destroys the deepest hopes of men the world over.

As if the weight of such a commitment to the life and health of America were not enough, another burden of responsibility was placed upon me in 1964; and I cannot forget that the Nobel Prize for Peace was also a commission—a commission to work harder than I had ever worked before for the "brotherhood of man." This is a calling that takes me beyond national allegiances, but even if it were not present I would yet have to live with the meaning of my commitment to the ministry of Jesus Christ. To me the relationship of this ministry to the making of peace is so obvious that I sometimes marvel at those who ask me why I am speaking against the war. Could it be that they do not know that the good news was meant for all men—for communist and capitalist, for their children and ours, for black and white, for revolutionary and conservative? Have they forgotten that my ministry is in obedience to the One who loved His enemies so fully that He died for them? What then can I say to the Viet Cong or to Castro or to Mao as a faithful minister of this One? Can I threaten them with death, or must I not share with them my life?

And as I ponder the madness of Vietnam, my mind goes constantly to the people of that peninsula. I speak now not of the soldiers of each side, not of the junta in Saigon, but simply of the people who have been living under the curse of war for almost three continuous decades. I think of them, too, because it is clear to me that there will be no meaningful solution there until some attempt is made to know them and their broken cries. . . .

What do the peasants think as we ally ourselves with the landlords and as we refuse to put any action into our many words concerning land reform? What do they think as we test out our latest weapons on them, just as the Germans tested out new medicine and new tortures in the concentration camps of Europe? Where are the roots of the independent Vietnam we claim to be building?

Now there is little left to build on—save bitterness. Soon the only solid physical foundations remaining will be found at our military bases and in the concrete of the concentration camps we call "fortified hamlets." The peasants may well wonder if we plan to build our new Vietnam on such grounds as these. Could we blame them for such thoughts? We must speak for them and raise the questions they cannot raise. These too are our brothers.

Perhaps the more difficult but no less necessary task is to speak for those who have been designated as our enemies. What of the NLF—that strangely anonymous group we call VC or communists? What must they think of us in America when they realize that we permitted the repression and cruelty of Diem which helped to bring them into being as a resistance group in the South? How can they believe in our integrity when now we speak of "aggression from the North" as if there were nothing more essential to the war? How can they trust us when now we charge *them* with violence after the murderous reign of Diem, and charge *them* with violence while we pour new weapons of death into their land?

How do they judge us when our officials know that their membership is less than 25 per cent communist and yet insist on giving them the blanket name? What must they be thinking when they know that we are aware of their control of major sections of Vietnam and yet we appear ready to allow national elections in which this highly organized political parallel government will have no part? They ask how we can speak of free elections when the Saigon press is censored and controlled by the military junta. And they are surely right to wonder what kind of new government we plan to help form without them—the only party in real touch with the peasants. They question our political goals and they deny the reality of a peace settlement from which they will be excluded. Their questions are frighteningly relevant.

Here is the true meaning and value of compassion and non-violence—when it helps us to see the enemy's point of view, to hear his questions, to know of his assessment of ourselves. For from his view we may indeed see the basic weaknesses of our own condition, and if we are mature, we may learn and grow and profit from the wisdom of the brothers who are called the opposition. . . .

Somehow this madness must cease. I speak as a child of God and brother to the suffering poor of Vietnam and the poor of America who are paying the double price of smashed hopes at home and death and corruption in Vietnam. I speak as a citizen of the world, for the world as it stands aghast at the path we have taken. I speak as an American to the leaders of my own nation. The great initiative in this war is ours. The initiative to stop must be ours.

This is the message of the great Buddhist leaders of Vietnam. Recently, one of them wrote these words: "Each day the war goes on the hatred increases in the hearts of the Vietnamese and in the hearts of those of humanitarian instinct. The Americans are forcing even their friends into becoming their enemies. It is curious that the Americans, who calculate so carefully on the possibilities of military victory, do not realize that in the process they are incurring deep psychological and political defeat. The image of America will never again be the image of revolution, freedom and democracy, but the image of violence and militarism."

If we continue, there will be no doubt in my mind and in the mind of the world that we have no honorable intentions in Vietnam. It will become clear that our minimal expectation is to occupy it as an American colony, and men will not refrain from thinking that our maximum hope is to goad China into a war so that we may bomb her nuclear installations.

The world now demands a maturity of America that we may not be able to achieve. It demands that we admit that we have been wrong from the beginning of our adventure in Vietnam, that we have been detrimental to the life of her people.

In order to atone for our sins and errors in Vietnam, we should take the initiative in bringing the war to a halt. I would like to suggest five concrete things that our government should do immediately to begin the long and difficult process of extricating ourselves from this nightmare:

1. End all bombing in North and South Vietnam.
2. Declare a unilateral cease-fire in the hope that such action will create the atmosphere for negotiation.
3. Take immediate steps to prevent other battlegrounds in Southeast Asia by curtailing our military build-up in Thailand and our interference in Laos.
4. Realistically accept the fact that the National Liberation Front has substantial support in South Vietnam and must thereby play a role in any meaningful negotiations and in any future Vietnam government.
5. Set a date on which we will remove all foreign troops from Vietnam in accordance with the 1954 Geneva Agreement.

Part of our ongoing commitment might well express itself in an offer to grant asylum to any Vietnamese who fears for his life under a new regime which included the NLF. Then we must make what reparations we can for the damage we have done. We must provide the medical aid that is badly needed, in this country if necessary.

Meanwhile, we in the churches and synagogues have a continuing task while we urge our government to disengage itself from a disgraceful commitment. We must be prepared to match actions with words by seeking out every creative means of protest possible. . . .

I am convinced that if we are to get on the right side of the world revolution, we as a nation must undergo a radical revolution of values. When machines and computers, profit and property rights are considered more important than people, the giant triplets of racism, materialism, and militarism are incapable of being conquered.

A true revolution of values will soon cause us to question the fairness and justice of many of our past and present policies.

4. "Women's Statement of Conscience," 1967

Increasing numbers of young Americans are finding that the Vietnam war so outrages their deepest moral and religious sense that they cannot serve in the Armed Forces while it continues.

As Americans they have been taught respect for the rights of others and to stand up for their belief in justice.

Amy Swerdlow, *Women Strike for Peace: Traditional Motherhood and Radical Politics in the 1960s* (Chicago: University of Chicago Press, 1993), p. 177.

They now refuse to violate these principles. They refuse to be sent to Vietnam to kill men, women and children who have never harmed them and who have never threatened our country.

As mothers, sisters, sweethearts, wives, we feel it is our moral responsibility to assist these brave young men who refuse to participate in the Vietnam war because they believe it to be immoral, unjust and brutal.

Too many men have died. Too many more will die, unless they have the courage to say "No!" We can help give them that courage by giving them our support.

We believe that support of those who resist the war and the draft is both moral and legal. We believe that it is not we, but those who send our sons to kill and be killed, who are committing crimes. We do, however, recognize that there may be legal risks involved, but because we believe that these young men are courageous and morally justified in rejecting the war regardless of consequences, we can do no less.

5. Proclamation of the Antidraft Resistance, 1967

To the young men of America, to the whole of the American people, and to all men of goodwill everywhere:

1. An ever growing number of young American men are finding that the American war in Vietnam so outrages their deepest moral and religious sense that they cannot contribute to it in any way. We share their moral outrage.

2. We further believe that the war is unconstitutional and illegal. Congress has not declared a war as required by the Constitution. Moreover, under the Constitution, treaties signed by the President and ratified by the Senate have the same force as the Constitution itself. The Charter of the United Nations is such a treaty. The Charter specifically obligates the United States to refrain from force or the threat of force in international relations. It requires member states to exhaust every peaceful means of settling disputes and to submit disputes which cannot be settled peacefully to the Security Council. The United States has systematically violated all of these Charter provisions for thirteen years.

3. Moreover, this war violates international agreements, treaties and principles of law which the United States Government has solemnly endorsed. The combat role of the United States troops in Vietnam violates the Geneva Accords of 1954 which our government pledged to support but has since subverted. The destruction of rice, crops and livestock; the burning and bulldozing of entire villages consisting exclusively of civilian structures; the interning of civilian non-combatants in concentration camps; the summary executions of civilians in captured villages who could not produce satisfactory evidence of their loyalties or did not wish to be removed to concentration camps; the slaughter of peasants who dared to stand up in their fields and shake their fists at American helicopters;—these are all actions of the kind which the United States and the other victorious powers of World War II declared to

---

Reprinted in *Vietnam and America: A Documented History,* Marvin E. Gettelman, et al., eds. (New York: Grove Press, 1985), pp. 304–305.

be crimes against humanity for which individuals were to be held personally responsible even when acting under the orders of their governments and for which Germans were sentenced at Nuremberg to long prison terms and death. The prohibition of such acts as war crimes was incorporated in treaty law by the Geneva Conventions of 1949, ratified by the United States. These are commitments to other countries and to Mankind, and they would claim our allegiance even if Congress should declare war.

4. We also believe it is an unconstitutional denial of religious liberty and equal protection of the laws to withhold draft exemption from men whose religious or profound philosophical beliefs are opposed to what in the Western religious tradition have been long known as unjust wars.

5. Therefore, we believe on all these grounds that every free man has a legal right and a moral duty to exert every effort to end this war, to avoid collusion with it, and to encourage others to do the same. Young men in the armed forces or threatened with the draft face the most excruciating choices. For them various forms of resistance risk separation from their families and their country, destruction of their careers, loss of their freedom and loss of their lives. Each must choose the course of resistance dictated by his conscience and circumstances. Among those already in the armed forces some are refusing to obey specific illegal and immoral orders, some are attempting to educate their fellow servicemen on the murderous and barbarous nature of the war, some are absenting themselves without official leave. Among those not in the armed forces some are applying for status as conscientious objectors to American aggression in Vietnam, some are refusing to be inducted. Among both groups some are resisting openly and paying a heavy penalty, some are organizing more resistance within the United States and some have sought sanctuary in other countries.

6. We believe that each of these forms of resistance against illegitimate authority is courageous and justified. Many of us believe that open resistance to the war and the draft is the course of action most likely to strengthen the moral resolve with which all of us can oppose the war and most likely to bring an end to the war.

7. We will continue to lend our support to those who undertake resistance to this war. We will raise funds to organize draft resistance unions, to supply legal defense and bail, to support families and otherwise aid resistance to the war in whatever ways may seem appropriate.

8. We firmly believe that our statement is the sort of speech that under the First Amendment must be free, and that the actions we will undertake are as legal as is the war resistance of the young men themselves. But we recognize that the courts may find otherwise, and that if so we might all be liable to prosecution and severe punishment. In any case, we feel that we cannot shrink from fulfilling our responsibilities to the youth whom many of us teach, to the country whose freedom we cherish, and to the ancient traditions of religion and philosophy which we strive to preserve in this generation.

9. We call upon all men of good will to join us in this confrontation with immoral authority. Especially we call upon the universities to fulfill their mission of enlightenment and religious organizations to honor their heritage of brotherhood. Now is the time to resist.

6. James Fallows Reflects on
the Draft's Inequities (1969), 1975

Many people think that the worst scars of the war years have healed. I don't. Vietnam has left us with a heritage rich in possibilities for class warfare, and I would like to start telling about it with this story:

In the fall of 1969, I was beginning my final year in college. As the months went by, the rock on which I had unthinkingly anchored my hopes—the certainty that the war in Vietnam would be over before I could possibly fight—began to crumble. It shattered altogether on Thanksgiving weekend when, while riding back to Boston from a visit with my relatives, I heard that the draft lottery had been held and my birthdate had come up number 45. I recognized for the first time that, inflexibly, I must either be drafted or consciously find a way to prevent it.

In the atmosphere of that time, each possible choice came equipped with barbs. To answer the call was unthinkable, not only because, in my heart, I was desperately afraid of being killed, but also because, among my friends, it was axiomatic that one should not be "complicit" in the immoral war effort. Draft resistance, the course chosen by a few noble heroes of the movement, meant going to prison or leaving the country. With much the same intensity with which I wanted to stay alive, I did not want those things either. What I wanted was to go to graduate school, to get married, and to enjoy those bright prospects I had been taught that life owed me.

I learned quickly enough that there was only one way to get what I wanted. A physical deferment would restore things to the happy state I had known during four undergraduate years. The barbed alternatives would be put off. By the impartial dictates of public policy I would be free to pursue the better side of life.

Like many of my friends whose numbers had come up wrong in the lottery, I set about securing my salvation. When I was not participating in antiwar rallies, I was poring over the Army's code of physical regulations. During the winter and early spring, seminars were held in the college common rooms. There, sympathetic medical students helped us search for disqualifying conditions that we, in our many years of good health, might have overlooked. Although, on the doctors' advice, I made a half-hearted try at fainting spells, my only real possibility was beating the height and weight regulations. My normal weight was close to the cut-off point for an "underweight" disqualification, and, with a diligence born of panic, I made sure I would have a margin. I was six-feet-one-inch tall at the time. On the morning of the draft physical I weighed 120 pounds.

Before sunrise that morning I rode the subway to the Cambridge city hall, where we had been told to gather for shipment to the examination at the Boston Navy Yard. The examinations were administered on a rotating basis, one or two days each month for each of the draft boards in the area. Virtually everyone who showed up on Cambridge day at the Navy Yard was a student from Harvard or MIT.

"What did You do in the Class War Daddy?" by James Fallows from *The Washington Monthly,* October, 1975. Reprinted with permission from *The Washington Monthly.* Copyright by The Washington Monthly Company, 1611 Connecticut Avenue, NW, Washington, D.C. 20009.

There was no mistaking the political temperament of our group. Many of my friends wore red arm bands and stop-the-war buttons. Most chanted the familiar words, "Ho, Ho, Ho Chi Minh/NLF is Gonna Win." One of the things we had learned from the draft counselors was that disruptive behavior at the examination was a worthwhile political goal, not only because it obstructed the smooth operation of the criminal war machine, but also because it might impress the examiners with our undesirable character traits. As we climbed into the buses and as they rolled toward the Navy Yard, about half of the young men brought the chants to a crescendo. The rest of us sat rigid and silent, clutching x-rays and letters from our doctors at home.

Inside the Navy Yard, we were first confronted by a young sergeant from Long Beach, a former surfer boy no older than the rest of us and seemingly unaware that he had an unusual situation on his hands. He started reading out instructions for the intelligence tests when he was hooted down. He went out to collect his lieutenant, who clearly had been through a Cambridge day before. "We've got all the time in the world," he said, and let the chanting go on for two or three minutes. "When we're finished with you, you can go, and not a minute before."

From that point on the disruption became more purposeful and individual, largely confined to those whose deferment strategies were based on anti-authoritarian psychiatric traits. Twice I saw students walk up to young orderlies—whose hands were extended to receive the required cup of urine—and throw the vial in the orderlies' faces. The orderlies looked up, initially more astonished than angry, and went back to towel themselves off. Most of the rest of us trod quietly through the paces, waiting for the moment of confrontation when the final examiner would give his verdict. I had stepped on the scales at the very beginning of the examination. Desperate at seeing the orderly write down 122 pounds, I hopped back on and made sure that he lowered it to 120. I walked in a trance through the rest of the examination, until the final meeting with the fatherly physician who ruled on marginal cases such as mine. I stood there in socks and underwear, arms wrapped around me in the chilly building. I knew as I looked at the doctor's face that he understood exactly what I was doing.

"Have you ever contemplated suicide?" he asked after he finished looking over my chart. My eyes darted up to his. "Oh, suicide—yes, I've been feeling very unstable and unreliable recently." He looked at me, staring until I returned my eyes to the ground. He wrote "unqualified" on my folder, turned on his heel, and left. I was overcome by a wave of relief, which for the first time revealed to me how great my terror had been, and by the beginning of the sense of shame which remains with me to this day.

It was, initially, a generalized shame at having gotten away with my deception, but it came into sharper focus later in the day. Even as the last of the Cambridge contingent was throwing its urine and deliberately failing its color-blindness tests, buses from the next board began to arrive. These bore the boys from Chelsea, thick, dark-haired young men, the white proles of Boston. Most of them were younger than us, since they had just left high school, and it had clearly never occurred to them that there might be a way around the draft. They walked through the examination lines like so many cattle off to slaughter. I tried to avoid noticing, but the results were inescapable. While perhaps four out of five of my friends from Harvard were being deferred, just the opposite was happening to the Chelsea boys.

We returned to Cambridge that afternoon, not in government buses but as free individuals, liberated and victorious. The talk was high-spirited, but there was something close to the surface that none of us wanted to mention. We knew now who would be killed.

As other memories of the war years have faded, it is that day in the Navy Yard that will not leave my mind. . . .

We have not, however, learned the lesson of the day at the Navy Yard, or the thousands of similar scenes all across the country through all the years of the war. Five years later, two questions have yet to be faced, let alone answered. The first is why, when so many of the bright young college men opposed the war, so few were willing to resist the draft, rather than simply evade it. The second is why all the well-educated presumably humane young men, whether they opposed the war or were thinking fondly of A-bombs on Hanoi, so willingly took advantage of this most brutal form of class discrimination—what it signifies that we let the boys from Chelsea be sent off to die.

The "we" that I refer to are the mainly white, mainly well-educated children of mainly comfortable parents, who are now mainly embarked on promising careers in law, medicine, business, academics. What makes them a class is that they all avoided the draft by taking one of the thinking-man's routes to escape. These included the physical deferment, by far the smartest and least painful of all; the long technical appeals through the legal jungles of the Selective Service System; the more disingenuous resorts to conscientious objector status; and, one degree further down the scale of personal inconvenience, joining the Reserves or the National Guard.

7. A Veteran Remembers His Bitter Homecoming, 1981

The day I got discharged, I flew into Philadelphia Airport. I got two and a half rows of ribbons. I'm very proud. I'm a meritorious sergeant and I got an honorable discharge. How do you like that shit?

I got off the plane and I went into a bar. The only thing I knew how to do was drink. I order a shot of CC and a beer and I'm standing there with a big smile on my face. There was a guy over at a table with two kids and a woman. The kids were about my age—nineteen or twenty.

"Home on leave, are you," the guy says to me.

"Nope, just got discharged."

"You just got back from where," one of the kids says.

"Vietnam."

"How do you feel about killing all of those innocent people?" the woman asks me out of nowhere.

I didn't know what to say. The bartender got a little uptight. But, I didn't say anything. They told me when I got discharged that I was going to get this shit. But, I didn't believe them.

"Excuse me," I called the bartender over. "Could I buy them all a drink?" I felt guilty. I *did* kill. I tried to make amends somehow.

"We don't accept any drinks from killers," the girl says to me. Now I'm pissed. The bartender tells me to take it easy and goes over and chews out this girl. She says, "How does it feel being in the Army?"

"He's not in the Army, he's a Marine," the bartender said.

"You bet your fucking ass, I'm a Marine."

"Oh, you going to get nasty now?" They were harassing me right in the fucking bar. I paid for my drinks, left the bartender a tip and walked out. Forgot all about it. I got in the car with my brother and his wife and I was just too happy being home to let that bother me. But now it does.

Later when we got home, my brother said, "Don't wear your uniform." What kind of shit was that? I wanted to wear the fucking thing. I had my ribbons. I was proud of what I'd done. I'm a king. That didn't hurt me then, but it hurts me now.

8. Todd Gitlin Recalls the New Left's Revolutionary Romanticism, 1987

As the war became more militant, so did the antiwar movement—in demands, in spirit, in tactics. Between 1965 and 1967, as American troops in Vietnam doubled and redoubled and redoubled twice more, most antiwar movers and shakers shook off their leftover faith in negotiations and endorsed immediate withdrawal. When doubters asked, "How can we get out of Vietnam?" the quick answer was: on boats. But the New Left wing, young and sick at heart at what it reasonably took to be empire flexing its muscles, moved beyond rebellion against American foreign policy. Much of the leadership, and some of the rank and file—it is hard to say exactly how many—slid into romance with the other side. To wear a button calling for "Victory to the National Liberation Front," to wave an NLF flag or shout, "Ho, Ho, Ho Chi Minh/The NLF is gonna win," meant more than believing that the NLF was the most popular force in South Vietnam, or that Vietnamese had flocked to it for compelling reasons, or that it represented the least bad practical alternative for Vietnam—all defensible propositions. It meant feeling the passion of the alignment and placing it at the heart of one's political identity. It meant finding heroes where the American superstate found villains and pointed its guns. It meant imagining comrades riding to *our* rescue.

This was *a* tendency, not the only one, not final or unopposed even in SDS [Students for a Democratic Society]. Its significance was certainly inflated by the prowar Right and by the attentions of a demagogic press. Although almost always greatly outnumbered by American flags turned to patriotic antiwar use, NLF flags seized a disproportionate share of the media spotlight at the giant antiwar marches. And so a too-uncomplicated endorsement of Third World revolutions—and revolutionary organizations—built a firebreak around the New Left part of the antiwar movement, sealing it off from the underbrush sympathy of the unconvinced. Surely

From *The Sixties* by Todd Gitlin. Copyright © 1987 by Todd Gitlin. Used by permission of Bantam Books, a division of Random House, Inc.

those NLF flags were part of the explanation for one of the stunning political facts of the decade: that as the war steadily lost popularity in the late Sixties, *so did the antiwar movement.* At the growing edge of the New Left, it was as if there had to be a loyalty oath for working against the war, or American dominion in general. The napalm had to be stopped for the correct reasons. Strategy-minded antiwar liberals rudely reminded us that we were forfeiting the respect of Americans who were turning against the war but were unwilling to do so at the price of their own sense of patriotism. But the hell with them! Which side were they on, anyway?

The consequence of the New Left's Third World turn—both product and impetus of our isolation—was yet more isolation. But the reporters had not invented those NLF flags out of proverbial whole cloth. Desperate for moral companionship—America having forfeited our love—a part of ourselves looked with respect, even awe, even love, on an ideal version of ourselves who we thought *existed*—had to exist—out there in the hot climates. We needed to feel that someone, somewhere in the world, was fighting the good fight and winning. Better: that the world's good guys formed a solid front. Even better: that out of the rubble, someone, somewhere, might be constructing a good society, at least one that was decent to the impoverished and colonized. If the United States was no longer humanity's beacon—and if the movement was not building a new society itself—the light had to be found outside. The melodrama of American innocence was alive and well in the anti-American left. Henry Luce [of *Time-Life*] had been deluded when he anticipated "the American Century"; we thought this was going to be the *anti*-American Century, just as pure, just as irresistible, with a different although equivalently happy ending.

And always there was the war, which we took to be the definitive moral test of America's intentions toward the vast poor and dark-skinned world. The Third Worldist movement route began in McComb, Mississippi, and led to the Mekong Delta. With the United States pulverizing and bullying small countries, it seemed the most natural thing in the world to go prospecting among them for heroes. Their resistance was so brave, their enemies so implacable, their nationalism so noble, we could take their passions, even their slogans and styles of speech, even—in fantasy— their forms of organization for our own. And so we identified with victims who were in the process of repossessing their homelands, as we were straining to overcome our own sense of homelessness. We loved them for what we took to be their struggle for independence, as we were struggling—no mere hackneyed word—for our own. We started out feeling the suffering of peasants, defending their right to rebel, and ended up taking sides with the organizations and leaders who commanded the rebellion—all the while knowing, in anguish, that guerrilla organizations usurp the freedom which rebels are willing to die for, yet also knowing, also in anguish, that without organization (even, often, the wrong organization: dictatorship in embryo) all the bravery in the world is squandered. Some of us took seriously the dreadful histories that Communist groups had imposed, and some didn't, but the New Left tendency was to agree that American occupation was so clear and present an evil—a *homegrown* evil—that the other side would have to be forgiven its crimes. Even the movement's antiutopians thought the future of "the other side," and the morality of guerrilla war, were questions to be left until later, luxuries, or, worst of all, potential weapons in the hands of the napalmers, the question for the present being simply whether the guerrillas, or the enemy nation (the two were often confused), were entitled to have any future of their own. The issue became *how we felt* more than *what would end the war.* We would settle for nothing less than a cleaning of the historical slate.

And so, increasingly, we found our exemplars and heroes in Cuba, in China, in the Third World guerrilla movements, in Mao and Frantz Fanon and Che and Debray, most of all—decisively—in Vietnam. It no longer felt sufficient—sufficiently estranged, sufficiently furious—to say no to aggressive war; we felt driven to say yes to revolt, and unless we were careful, that yes could easily be transferred onto the Marxism-Leninism which had commandeered the revolt in the interest of practicality. Apocalypse was outfitted with a bright side. If the American flag was dripping napalm, the NLF flag was clean. If the deluded make-Vietnam-safe-for-democracy barbarism of the war could be glibly equated with the deliberate slaughter of millions in Nazi gas chambers—if the American Christ turned out to look like the Antichrist—then by this cramped either-or logic the Communist Antichrist must really have been Christ. America had betrayed us; the war, Carl Oglesby movingly said in 1965, "broke my American heart." Only true-blue believers in the promise of America could have felt so anti-American. Ours was the fury of a lover spurned. But a fury so intense, left to itself, would have consumed us. "Don't you want somebody to love?" as the Jefferson Airplane sang. So we turned where romantics have traditionally turned: to the hot-blooded peoples of the subtropics and the mysterious East. The Manichaean all-or-nothing logic of the Cold War was conserved, though inverted, as if costumes from Central Wardrobe had been rotated.

9. A Vietnam Veteran Opposes the War, 1971

Thank you very much, Senator Fulbright, Senator Javits, Senator Symington, Senator Pell. I would like to say for the record, and also for the men behind me who are also wearing the uniform and their medals, that my sitting here is really symbolic. I am not here as John Kerry. I am here as one member of the group of 1,000 which is a small representation of a very much larger group of veterans in this country, and were it possible for all of them to sit at this table they would be here and have the same kind of testimony. . . .

I would like to talk on behalf of all those veterans and say that several months ago in Detroit we had an investigation at which over 150 honorably discharged, and many very highly decorated, veterans testified to war crimes committed in Southeast Asia. These were not isolated incidents but crimes committed on a day to day basis with the full awareness of officers at all levels of command.

It is impossible to describe to you exactly what did happen in Detroit—the emotions in the room and the feelings of the men who were reliving their experiences in Vietnam. They relived the absolute horror of what this country, in a sense, made them do.

Kerry statement, April 1971, in U.S. Senate, Committee on Foreign Relations, *Legislative Proposals Relating to the War in Southeast Asia: Hearings* (Washington: U.S. Government Printing Office, 1971), 180–210.

They told stories that at times they had personally raped, cut off ears, cut off heads, taped wires from portable telephones to human genitals and turned up the power, cut off limbs, blown up bodies, randomly shot at civilians, razed villages in fashion reminiscent of Genghis Khan, shot cattle and dogs for fun, poisoned food stocks, and generally ravaged the countryside of South Vietnam in addition to the normal ravage of war and the normal and very particular ravaging which is done by the applied bombing power of this country.

We call this investigation the Winter Soldier Investigation. The term Winter Soldier is a play on words of Thomas Paine's in 1776 when he spoke of the Sunshine Patriots and summer time soldiers who deserted at Valley Forge because the going was rough.

We who have come here to Washington have come here because we feel we have to be winter soldiers now. We could come back to this country, we could be quiet, we could hold our silence, we could not tell what went on in Vietnam, but we feel because of what threatens this country, not the reds, but the crimes which we are committing that threaten it, that we have to speak out.

I would like to talk to you a little bit about what the result is of the feelings these men carry with them after coming back from Vietnam. The country doesn't know it yet but it has created a monster, a monster in the form of millions of men who have been taught to deal and to trade in violence and who are given the chance to die for the biggest nothing in history; men who have returned with a sense of anger and a sense of betrayal which no one has yet grasped.

As a veteran and one who feels this anger I would like to talk about it. We are angry because we feel we have been used in the worst fashion by the administration of this country.

In 1970 at West Point Vice President Agnew said, "Some glamorize the criminal misfits of society while our best men die in Asian rice paddies to preserve the freedom which most of those misfits abuse," and this was used as a rallying point for our effort in Vietnam.

But for us, as boys in Asia whom the country was supposed to support, his statement is a terrible distortion from which we can only draw a very deep sense of revulsion, and hence the anger of some of the men who are here in Washington today. It is a distortion because we in no way consider ourselves the best men of this country; because those he calls misfits were standing up for us in a way that nobody else in this country dared to; because so many who have died would have returned to this country to join the misfits in their efforts to ask for an immediate withdrawal from South Vietnam; because so many of those best men have returned as quadriplegics and amputees—and they lie forgotten in Veterans' Administration Hospitals in this country which fly the flag which so many have chosen as their own personal symbol—and we cannot consider ourselves America's best men when we are ashamed of and hated for what we were called on to do in Southeast Asia.

In our opinion, and from our experience, there is nothing in South Vietnam which could happen that realistically threatens the United States of America. And to attempt to justify the loss of one American life in Vietnam, Cambodia or Laos by linking such loss to the preservation of freedom, which those misfits supposedly abuse, is to us the height of criminal hypocrisy, and it is that kind of hypocrisy which we feel has torn this country apart.

We are probably much more angry than that, but I don't want to go into the foreign policy aspects because I am outclassed here. I know that all of you talk about every possible alternative for getting out of Vietnam. We understand that. We know you have considered the seriousness of the aspects to the utmost level and I am not going to try to dwell on that. But I want to relate to you the feeling that many of the men who have returned to this country express because we are probably angriest about all that we were told about Vietnam and about the mystical war against communism.

We found that not only was it a civil war, an effort by a people who had for years been seeking their liberation from any colonial influence whatsoever, but also we found that the Vietnamese whom we had enthusiastically molded after our own image were hard put to take up the fight against the threat we were supposedly saving them from.

We found most people didn't even know the difference between communism and democracy. They only wanted to work in rice paddies without helicopters strafing them and bombs with napalm burning their villages and tearing their country apart. They wanted everything to do with the war, particularly with this foreign presence of the United States of America, to leave them alone in peace, and they practiced the art of survival by siding with whichever military force was present at a particular time, be it Viet Cong, North Vietnamese or American.

We found also that all too often American men were dying in those rice paddies for want of support from their allies. We saw first hand how monies from American taxes were used for a corrupt dictatorial regime. We saw that many people in this country had a one-sided idea of who was kept free by our flag, and blacks provided the highest percentage of casualties. We saw Vietnam ravaged equally by American bombs and search and destroy missions, as well as by Viet Cong terrorism, and yet we listened while this country tried to blame all of the havoc on the Viet Cong.

We rationalized destroying villages in order to save them. We saw America lose her sense of morality as she accepted very coolly a My Lai and refused to give up the image of American soldiers who hand out chocolate bars and chewing gum.

We learned the meaning of free fire zones, shooting anything that moves, and we watched while America placed a cheapness on the lives of orientals.

We watched the United States' falsification of body counts, in fact the glorification of body counts. We listened while month after month we were told the back of the enemy was about to break. We fought using weapons against "oriental human beings." We fought using weapons against those people which I do not believe this country would dream of using were we fighting in the European theater. We watched while men charged up hills because a general said that hill has to be taken, and after losing one platoon or two platoons they marched away to leave the hill for reoccupation by the North Vietnamese. We watched pride allow the most unimportant battles to be blown into extravaganzas, because we couldn't lose, and we couldn't retreat, and because it didn't matter how many American bodies were lost to prove that point, and so there were Hamburger Hills and Khe Sanhs and Hill 81s and Fire Base 6s, and so many others.

Now we are told that the men who fought there must watch quietly while American lives are lost so that we can exercise the incredible arrogance of Vietnamizing the Vietnamese.

Each day to facilitate the process by which the United States washes her hands of Vietnam someone has to give up his life so that the United States doesn't have to admit something that the entire world already knows, so that we can't say that we have made a mistake. Someone has to die so that President Nixon won't be, and these are his words, "the first President to lose a war."

We are asking Americans to think about that because how do you ask a man to be the last man to die in Vietnam? How do you ask a man to be the last man to die for a mistake? But we are trying to do that, and we are doing it with thousands of rationalizations, and if you read carefully the President's last speech to the people of this country, you can see that he says, and says clearly, "but the issue, gentlemen, is communism, and the question is whether or not we will leave that country to the communists or whether or not we will try to give it hope to be a free people." But the point is they are not a free people now under us. They are not a free people, and we cannot fight communism all over the world. I think we should have learned that lesson by now. . . .

We wish that a merciful God could wipe away our own memories of that service as easily as this administration has wiped away their memories of us. But all that they have done and all that they can do by this denial is to make more clear than ever our own determination to undertake one last mission—to search out and destroy the last vestige of this barbaric war, to pacify our own hearts, to conquer the hate and the fear that have driven this country these last ten years and more, so when 30 years from now our brothers go down the street without a leg, without an arm, or a face, and small boys ask why, we will be able to say "Vietnam" and not mean a desert, not a filthy obscene memory, but mean instead the place where America finally turned and where soldiers like us helped it in the turning.

Thank you.

✗ E S S A Y S

The opening essay considers the evolution of the antiwar movement from the mid-1950s to the mid-1970s. In it, Charles DeBenedetti, a professor of history at the University of Toledo until his death in 1987, and Charles Chatfield, a professor of history at Wittenberg University, locate the origins of the movement in the earlier opposition of a small group of liberal protesters to atmospheric nuclear testing. The ranks of the antiwar activists expanded exponentially with the escalation of America's involvement in Vietnam after 1965. DeBenedetti and Chatfield examine the shifting composition, amazing diversity, tactical differences, and ever expanding social, political, and cultural agenda of the antiwar movement. They emphasize that, although it failed to achieve many of its stated purposes, the peace movement of the Vietnam era both challenged and changed American society in fundamental ways.

In the middle essay, Rhodri Jeffreys-Jones, a professor of history at Edinburgh University, analyzes the seminal contribution that women made to the antiwar movement. Protest by women against the Vietnam War, he demonstrates, was extensive, multi-faceted, and effective. Opposition to the war was, in fact, greater among women than men; and, from 1970 on, Jeffreys-Jones claims, female activists helped legitimize the peace movement within the general public.

The final selection presents a more critical assessment. Adam Garfinkle, resident scholar at Philadelphia's Foreign Policy Research Institute, aims to debunk a series of myths that he believes have come to envelop the antiwar activism of the Vietnam War era. Not only did it fail to stop the war, Garfinkle asserts, the antiwar movement actually helped prolong it. Further, he contends that its chief impact was felt not in Southeast Asia but in the United States. Garfinkle concludes that, on balance, the antiwar movement should be recognized as a well-intentioned but ultimately ineffectual phenomenon.

The Antiwar Movement and American Society

CHARLES DEBENEDETTI AND CHARLES CHATFIELD

A darkening cloud of war gathered almost imperceptibly in the decade after 1955, and the storm broke before its magnitude was recognized. Its center was in Indochina, but it engulfed America. For ten years more it churned across the nation, charging every internal conflict with high tension and obscuring the issues which defined national identity. In the roiling darkness a Catholic priest wrote from hiding that America was "hard to find."

The priest was part of the antiwar movement, an amorphous and pervasive social current that connected the war in Vietnam to domestic struggles. The movement was both a cultural and a political phenomenon, and in that duality lay its central paradox: its cultural power compromised its political effectiveness. It gave cultural dissonance a political import more surely than it affected public policy. Nonetheless, it was part of the political process, for it was locked in a struggle with the government over how the people would define their values, institutions, and destiny.

. . . As a whole more antiwar than peace-seeking, [this] movement was a loose alignment of elements which changed in style, tactics, and thrust during the era. It altered partly in response to political and international circumstances and partly in relation to the personal ethos of its participants as they wrestled with the meaning of the war and the society.

The movement involved only a few dozen organizations in 1960, over twelve hundred a decade later. Most of them were local and ephemeral. Numbers never were an accurate index of the antiwar movement, either in organizations or in demonstrations. Although antiwar dissent gained continuity from a core of activists, insofar as it was organized at all, its components were not primarily membership organizations. There never was a single directing agency, common leadership, or ideology. Only at a few points was there even a formal coalition, and then it was but partial. Highly eclectic, protesters employed tactics ranging from letter writing to bombings, from prayer vigils to self-immolations. Improvisational, they experimented with organized lobbying, electoral politics, mass demonstrations, teach-ins, vigils, and nonviolent civil disobedience. The measure of the movement was its influence, not the number of its adherents. Probably the very diversity of dissent increased its outreach, for its leadership permeated the society from the most elite and conventional to the most antisocial elements.

The American antiwar movement was at once a product of history and a process that made history. As a process, the movement was a highly charged force for change that galvanized some American citizens to challenge their government's

From Charles DeBenedetti and Charles Chatfield, *An American Ordeal: The Antiwar Movement of the Vietnam Era.* (Syracuse: Syracuse University Press, 1990), pp. 1–5, 388–399, 401–405, 408. By permission of the publisher.

nuclear weapons testing and then its policy in Southeast Asia. As a product, the movement was the latest expression of a long tradition of citizen peace activism that was organized around issues such as international disarmament and opposition to great-power interventionism. The Vietnam War was the catalyst for changes in peace advocacy, as well as in the nation, but in order to appreciate this fact it is necessary to locate the movement's prewar sources and to follow its course beyond the formal termination of war in 1973. Otherwise, we are left with only the stereotypes formed in the period of most intense conflict—images that obscure the continuity between seeking peace and confronting war.

In 1955 the movement appeared as a fresh form of peace advocacy familiar in American history. Seizing on the perceived threat from nuclear testing in order to advocate alternatives to Cold War confrontation, a coalition of liberal internationalists and radical pacifists developed new organizations and tactics. By the time of the nuclear test-ban treaty of 1963, the coalition had been influenced also by a revitalized radicalism, identified in the North with the New Left and in the South with civil rights activists. By then it had acquired the internal differences and the distinctive ethos which would characterize opposition to war in Indochina.

With the government's escalation of military involvement in Vietnam in the first half of the 1960s, the coalition was gradually transformed into an antiwar movement. It defined the issues on which policy would be debated for a decade. It provided a focus for citizens who felt uneasy about the war, and it attracted new constituencies of discontent which strengthened the movement's left-wing cast. When President Lyndon Johnson definitively committed the nation to war in 1965, he faced a loosely organized opposition ready to contest him for the support of the nation's political center.

As the war expanded in scope, intensity, and cost over the next two years, antiwar dissidents improvised a wide range of actions which forced the war issue into the public arena, generated organized opposition to intervention, pressed the administration to make ever-larger claims for the war, and fragmented the movement itself. Protest moved into the streets. Early in 1968 the ferocity of the communist Tet offensive triggered a change of war strategy and imposed limits on U.S. military commitment. In the midst of mounting domestic disorder, antiwar liberals pressed the war issue in electoral politics; but their chosen vehicles, the McCarthy and Kennedy campaigns, collapsed and left them on the political margin. About the same time, radicalism as a driving force of organized protest began to wane, and militant extremism spun off on the periphery.

The antiwar movement declined early in the Nixon presidency, but it regrouped to mount massive demonstrations in the fall of 1969. Exhausted and fragmented, though, it was unable to capture or mobilize the widespread public protest evoked by the administration's invasion of Cambodia the following spring. The politics of confrontation seemed to have played out, despite a brief resurgence in the spring of 1971. Although war dissenters still challenged government policy, they increasingly worked within established political institutions responding to war-weariness among the public.

Gradually leadership returned to political liberals until, with the 1972 presidential campaign of George McGovern, the war issue was brought fully within the political system. By the end of the year, Congress itself appeared ready to confront the

Nixon administration. That contest was preempted by the Paris peace accord of January 1973, but shortly afterward the issue of presidential authority emerged as the Watergate syndrome. Antiwar dissidents linked the constitutional issue to the war, first on behalf of withdrawal from military engagement and, after the peace agreement, in opposition to a widening air war over Indochina and continued aid to the regime in Saigon.

The shifts in the emphasis and tactics of antiwar protest were largely a result of its intersection with political institutions. In particular, stridency and militancy in protest were related to the obduracy of the Johnson and Nixon administrations: confrontation was a product of the interaction of committed dissent and an unresponsive government. Insofar as the political system accommodated criticism in electoral and congressional politics, protest tended to flow within established channels.

Rapid transformations in organized protest were also a product of its relationship to American society. Like the larger culture of which it was a part, the antiwar movement of 1955–1975 was a diverse and dynamic enterprise that changed dramatically in its composition, assumptions, and purposes. Especially in the 1960s the United States experienced sharp challenges to important cultural norms—traditional religious beliefs, scientific objectivity, white and male dominance, adult standards of behavior, the assumption that poverty was a normal part of society, the notion of a Cold War mission, and the liberalism of consensus. As each of these became organized, it added to a plethora of social movements which were related to one another only tenuously, if at all. The demand to end the war and the concomitant challenge to established authority aligned several of these dissident elements.

On the one hand, the vision of a broad coalition for social change provided the antiwar movement with an incisive, radical cutting edge. Leading activists believed that national values and institutions had been distorted by a Cold War emphasis on maintaining order by force, which in turn was repressing pressures for social justice, whether in the Third World or in the United States. It was in this sense that the antiwar movement was related to other social and cultural protests of the decade. On the other hand, the eclecticism of antiwar protest made it especially vulnerable to fragmentation. Its leaders disagreed over whether to pursue a single-minded challenge to war or to develop a broad coalition for social change. They were divided by the eddies of controversy carried in the cultural currents that fed into the antiwar movement. They were burdened by stereotypes grounded in the reality of their uneasy association with radicals and counterculture figures, fixed in popular mythology by the media, and exploited by the supporters of administration policy. Thus, the organized movement developed a dual identity that was the source of its strength as well as its weakness. As a cultural force it vibrated with resilience and adaptability, energizing people with ideas, criticisms, political alternatives, and values. As a political force it remained embarrassingly weak, and this contributed to its disillusionment and despair. In spite of its appeal among church people, organized women, traditional peace workers, intellectuals, students, and assorted leftists, it remained largely on the political periphery. Movement leaders helped to rally a shattering cultural rebellion that altered the course of American politics and foreign policy; but the society for which many of them yearned remained "hard to find."

Fundamentally, the war was always about America. From start to finish in the arguments over intervention, the welfare of the Vietnamese people was secondary. Pro-war citizens maintained that the war was necessary to contain Asian communism far from America's shores. Policymakers referred to Vietnam as a "showcase" of nation building, a "proving ground" of successful counterinsurgency, or a "test" of America's will to prevail in the greater Cold War. Although critics of the war, on the other hand, argued that intervention thwarted the emergence of an independent Third World and many of them showed a poignant concern for the people of Indochina, even they argued mainly that the war effort hurt the United States. Antiwar activists habitually charged that the war weakened prospects for Soviet-American détente, destabilized the international order, smeared the nation's image as a positive force, wasted chances for domestic reform, and subverted national values and institutions. The war was in Indochina, but the ordeal for the antiwar movement and the citizens it sought to mobilize was in and over America. . . .

Bernard Fall once observed that there were many wars in Vietnam—multiple dimensions to the conflict. Similarly, there were many antiwar movements in America. Protest had many masks, so different that some observers contended that there was no such thing as an antiwar movement. William Stringfellow doubted its existence in 1969, and he opposed the war. Shortly after the November Mobilization, he wrote in *Christianity and Crisis* that "the war protests of the past few years have been spasmodic, haphazard, frustrated, fatigued and incoherent." They were all of that. Antiwar activists did not establish a single directing organization, coordinated leadership, or ideology. They drew on varied constituencies. They offered contradictory critiques of American society and foreign policy. They argued among themselves almost as bitterly as they excoriated those they held responsible for the war. As Stringfellow knew, however, his observation was a reflection of the character of the peace and antiwar movement rather than a denial of its existence.

There was after 1955, in fact, a definable body of Americans who sought new initiatives in disarmament and the international order that would reverse the nuclear arms race and reduce Soviet-American tensions. Drawing on established peace societies such as the American Friends Service Committee, the Fellowship of Reconciliation, the Women's International League for Peace and Freedom, and the War Resisters League, peace advocates added specialized campaigns such as SANE [National Committee for Sane Nuclear Policy] and CNVA [Committee for Non-Violent Action] (and also Women Strike for Peace and the Student Peace Union), whose primary achievement was to draw attention to the issue of atmospheric nuclear testing. After 1965 many of these same people sought to reverse Washington's military involvement in Vietnam. Few foreign policy dissidents dared hope at the outset to assemble a massive campaign against intervention. They were joined nonetheless by countless citizens who improvised an identifiable antiwar movement of disparate groups, leaders, followers, and tendencies. It was more assembled than it was organized. It functioned as a movement of movements.

Its constituent organizations were national, regional, and local, with only loose connections among the levels or the groups. Many of them were nuclei of people within professional or civic bodies. Most were ephemeral, leaving only traces of their activity. The size of the movement is very difficult to estimate, since only a few

national organizations had definable memberships. Their combined known membership probably was between forty and eighty thousand people in 1962 and increased
to three or four hundred thousand a decade later. Most of that growth came from
the addition of new organizations such as Vietnam Veterans Against the War,
Clergy and Laity Concerned [CALC], and Another Mother for Peace [AMP]. The
figure does not include coalitions, covert groups such as the Resistance, or political
ones like the Socialist Workers Party. Moreover, the total number includes groups
as different as CALC and AMP: the former was a network for specific projects, the
latter a largely nominal grouping. The memberships themselves were not particularly
significant (although changes in any definable group were instructive) because dissent grew at mostly local levels, often spontaneously, and faded there. In this broad
sense, probably several million citizens were involved in antiwar activity. The assem-
bling of increasingly large crowds through 1969 was impressive, but even so, the
impact of public demonstrations depended more on media coverage than on mere
numbers. Most important, especially after 1971, dissatisfaction with war policy was
multiplied and channeled through a labyrinth of citizen networks.

Liberals and leftists, men and women, blacks and whites, students and established intellectuals, clergy and laity: countless citizens passed in and out of the
antiwar movement. Its core was indelibly middle class and well educated. It was a
typically American reform effort—a voluntary crusade attracting adherents and
impelling them to act out of a felt personal responsibility for social wrongs. The tendency to define political obligation in terms of personal morality, and the assumed
value of action per se, contributed to the movement's persisting problems with poor
organization, lack of discipline, and intermittent participation. It proved very difficult to mount sustained political pressure, and the temptation to attribute frustration
in this regard to the system itself or to the government only exacerbated a sense of
moral isolation from society. On the other hand, this same personal and moral quality
gave the movement the fluidity, adaptability, and irrepressibility that enabled it to
survive and metamorphose in a struggle that none of the dissidents had anticipated.

Building on small, established groups, the resurgent peace movement of
1955–1963 was essentially a form of public advocacy. It focused attention on atmospheric testing, and it organized through a liberal coalition. Political liberals in SANE,
for instance, sponsored conferences, developed newspaper advertisements, popularized expert testimony, and organized letter-writing campaigns. Even the radical
pacifists in the CNVA applied non-violent direct action mainly for its symbolic value
in dramatizing the nuclear arms issue. The great majority of actions were low-key
and informational, although gradually the movement became more aggressive and
turned to mass demonstrations, prayer vigils, and nonviolent civil disobedience.
Then, with the signing of the 1963 test-ban treaty, the coalition began to dissolve.

By that time, intensified civil rights campaigns, heightened sensibility to the
Third World, and the rise of a new and youthful left began to shift the weight of
elements in the peace movement, motivating activists to put themselves on the line
for their beliefs. Some peace advocates joined early critics among the articulate
elite to criticize U.S. intervention in Vietnam, but the movement did not undergo a
significant change until 1965. Then the sudden escalation of military involvement
in Vietnam precipitated an abrupt change in focus from the generalized Cold War
to the specific conflict. As American intervention assumed massive proportions,

the peace movement rapidly evolved an antiwar thrust and offered leverage to the gathering dissent.

The tactics of the movement changed, but not suddenly. At the outset they represented an extension of the antinuclear campaign, emphasizing persuasion (as in teach-ins) and political pressure. Between 1965 and 1967 protest remained largely respectful, its tactics designed to build an antiwar consensus. Facing hostile prowar majorities, most activists talked, taught, and marched without disruption. A few burned their draft cards—or, in extreme cases, themselves—in symbolic demonstrations of their willingness to atone for their country's alleged wrongdoing.

Almost from the outset, however, there was a sharp note of disillusionment with Lyndon Johnson, who had campaigned against Goldwater on a peace platform and had identified himself with the social programs of the Great Society. Congressional reluctance to confront the issues in Vietnam and evidence of official dissimulation served to heighten the frustration. In the face of a war escalating indefinitely and an apparently unresponsive political system, dissidents challenged the credibility and implacability of the government. The tone of protest became sharper, even theatrical, like that of the concurrent civil rights and black power movements. The emphasis of dissident strategy turned from an attempt to influence key policy-shapers to the mobilizing of massive demonstrations.

By 1967 the weight and initiative in the antiwar movement had shifted to the left. It was attracted there by the social turbulence that now swirled around the war issue, and it was driven there by the apparent inflexibility of national policy. By the fall of 1968, opponents of the war were afflicted with despair (encouraged by political responses in the spring, they felt disillusioned in the summer). Anguish deepened through the next two years. There seemed to be no recourse, nothing that had not been tried. The dissenting judgment on the war appeared to have been vindicated—Vietnamization was a response to popular disaffection—and yet the devastation continued, even expanded, with no indication that the United States was about to abandon its original political objectives. Distorted judgment in that period was not limited to antiwar activists; it was a national malaise.

Between 1967 and 1971 dissidents aligned sporadically in attempts to reverse U.S. military policy in Vietnam, but they could not agree on what that implied. Their purpose was clear; their direction was not. The war and the protest against it alike became tokens of what was wrong in America. Public policy debate was freighted with symbolism, and rising disaffection was diffused. The antiwar movement reacted, expanded, or contracted in intensity as U.S. policy in Indochina varied. It appeared to abandon its function as an advocate to alternative policy and emerged in an adversarial role.

There was a self-conscious shift "from protest to resistance," although it was never as aggressive as it was portrayed. The overwhelming majority of antiwar actions remained peaceable and restrained. Dissidents mainly petitioned, prayed, marched, picketed, published, and worked through the political system. Quite plainly, however, a notable minority of activists escalated their protest in nonviolent sit-ins, occupation of draft boards and ROTC installations, and organized draft resistance. The number of draft-card burnings rose to a few thousand, and there were a few dozen recorded instances of flag-burning. Nonetheless, tactics remained in general both nonviolent and symbolic.

With the country trapped between a racial crisis at home and military failure abroad, a relatively small number of extremists resorted to physical attacks on the institutions and representatives of domestic authority. Infatuated with the romantic anarchism of yippies or the rebel mystique of the Weathermen, some militants called for mass disorder and street actions, and a few argued for outright violence. Whenever possible, they attached themselves to the periphery of the antiwar movement. Such was the air of moral crisis that a few radical pacifists courted confrontation on the assumption that it could be kept nonviolent. To a surprising degree it was, but the exceptions made the media—notably in Chicago in 1968 and at the MayDays of 1971. Although the great majority of antiwar activists condemned violence and continued to pray and petition, a very small number of extremists sought to "bring the war home," detonating bombs, attacking police, and committing vandalism. The pseudorevolutionary fantasy played itself out, but not before it had been attached to the public image of the antiwar movement.

The revolutionary rhetoric of radical leftists, the actions of militant extremists, a counterculture fringe, nonviolent civil disobedience, and organized draft resistance: protesting the war increasingly meant resisting authority, and it was portrayed as being more confrontational than it actually was. In particular, the Nixon White House deliberately heightened and exploited confrontation. The administration's carefully crafted strategy of attacking critics while withdrawing troops, combined with the exhaustion of the radical left—and the nation—seemed to brake the momentum of opposition. Countless dissidents drifted off into other reform endeavors or became passive. Ironically, the dispersal of street dissidence facilitated antiwar efforts within Congress and the Democratic party, even though it left many protesters with a sense of failure.

The movement never regarded itself as exclusively adversarial, of course. The ADA, SANE, and Allard Lowenstein's campaign to dump Johnson functioned within the political system. Even as confrontation reached its apogee in the streets of Chicago in 1968, critics within the Democratic convention hall challenged the war through conventional strategies of persuasion and electoral politics. Nixon's winning campaign that year was predicated on his achieving peace, and Humphrey's loss intensified efforts to reform the Democratic party. The Moratorium of the following year was an essentially liberal strategy. By that time a broad grouping of antiwar liberals and elite policy critics was in a position to bring the movement more fully into the political mainstream. It was not only that radicalism had disintegrated; the political system had become more responsive.

This could be seen throughout the country, where independent local groups were organized on political lines. They were not tabulated in the declining memberships that so distressed national peace organizations. Rather, they reflected pervasive discontent with the war. Gradually, this was directed into congressional politics. Through the McGovern candidacy it was normalized in the Democratic party. With the demand for withdrawal by a specific date, it was pursued in the legislature. In 1973 activists on the national level developed a systematic lobbying effort around the issue of military assistance for Saigon. They helped to link war-related corruption and arbitrary policies such as the bombing of Cambodia to the issue of presidential unaccountability, which reached its nadir in the Watergate scandal. So enmeshed with other national issues was the war, and so integrated with other advocacy groups were Vietnam dissidents, that the antiwar movement became all but invisible.

These shifts in composition and approach were matters of emphasis. The personalized and heterogeneous peace and antiwar movements of 1955–1975 encompassed a wide range of tactics, from polite letter-writing to terrorist bombings, from quiet prayer vigils to horrific self-immolations, from reasoned analysis to fiery rhetoric. Lacking any central direction or agreed-upon strategy, the choice of action was determined mostly by personal impulses; but it was strongly influenced by the political conduct of the war and the degree to which the political system itself accommodated protest.

Antiwar activists contributed to the growth of public disaffection with the war and helped to give it focus, but they were unable to harness it. At least prior to the 1973 peace accord, they did not establish themselves as a positive reference point for the many politicians and millions of people whose early support of the war turned into resentful neutrality. The opportunity certainly seemed to be there. According to public opinion polls, domestic opposition to Washington's Vietnam policies consistently spread through parts of American society. On the one hand, there existed a small but vibrant antiwar movement, extremely articulate and politically active. On the other hand, there was a much larger body of people (some analysts estimated that it was sixty times the organized antiwar movement) who opposed U.S. military engagement but refused to make their dissent public.

The two groups differed with respect to class and culture. Organized opposition to the war came mainly from middle-class, college-educated whites, materially comfortable and motivated by largely moral considerations. Politically liberal and sympathetic to social justice causes, antiwar activists were also tolerant of changes in popular culture, sexual mores, and race relations. In contrast, the great majority of Americans favoring disengagement from Vietnam were a people apart. According to public opinion analysts, the greatest number of them were in the lower economic class, often women and blacks, with grade-school educations and low-prestige jobs. Politically inarticulate and generally isolationist, these disaffected citizens opposed the war as a waste of men and money and had little confidence in the democratic sensibilities of the Vietnamese people, North or South. Suspicious of most authority, they seemed ambivalent in the face of cultural change, but they made no secret of their dislike for active protesters and street demonstrators.

The connection with civil rights groups was a special case. It antedated and stimulated the organized antiwar movement. In the early 1960s, SNCC [Student Nonviolent Coordinating Committee] inspired radical activists; but it was ruptured by an internal crisis, and the emphasis on black power precluded any real cooperation with that organization. Martin Luther King, Jr., *briefly* became a cementing force in the movement, but the connection was very much weakened by his assassination. In any case, civil rights groups had political problems and agendas of their own.

Middle-class antiwar activists made some lackluster attempts to rally working-class Americans to their side. Although they repeatedly tried to organize around the idea of a coalition of the disaffected, radical sectarianism and self-interest invariably proved to be disruptive, and in any case cooperation was limited to specific antiwar actions. . . .

Potential supporters of the antiwar movement may have been alienated by qualities they associated with militant radicals who, although not representative, got much media exposure: a kind of romantic egoism, political indiscipline, an orientation toward action regardless of consequences, argumentative sectarianism, and disdain for venerated national symbols. The movement was most visible between 1967 and 1971 when it was least conventional and, therefore, least acceptable to many Americans. Antiwar activists took to the streets in impressive numbers then. They even penetrated government offices and corporate boardrooms, but they failed to mobilize the American laboring class or even the middle class. . . .

Abuse of revered national symbols did accompany opposition to the war, although it occurred mainly on the periphery of organized activity and was misunderstood. It took forms such as street theater, unfurling Vietcong flags, spilling blood on Selective Service files, burning draft cards, and even some violence against war-related public property. Predictably, this cultural agitprop infuriated large numbers of Americans and antagonized some elements of the movement. It was counterproductive insofar as it did not take seriously the myths and symbols that defined America, doubtless conveying a sense that the war and the national ordeal were not taken seriously either. That was deeply offensive to many people who anguished over Vietnam.

In a more profound and almost certainly more usual sense, the denigration of popular symbols reflected the activists' own indignation—even anger—that patriotism was draped around an unjust war. If so-called Americanism itself had not been used as a cultural weapon, it could have been put in quotation marks to describe antiwar rhetoric: anti-"Americanism." Draft-card burning clearly had this force, particularly after it was made a federal offense. The connotation was similar to the occasional inversion of the flag, an international signal of distress.

Unfortunately for activists, distress was generic in the 1960s. Symbolism was used to challenge social and cultural conformity in general, and it offered no distinction between rejection of a dominant, even if oppressive, lifestyle and a specific, if repressive, foreign policy. This left the antiwar movement vulnerable to extraneous attack, since the contest over the war was waged more on the level of symbols than on issues. The recognizable peace sign itself was subjected to tortuous exegesis designed to convert it from an affirmative to a negative image. Moreover, it proved very difficult to condemn the war as immoral without impugning the morality of the nation, or the leadership as distinct from the people. The problem was aggravated by activists' pervasive concern with popular anomie (the motif of moral numbness) and complicity (the Eichmann motif). "Madness is an infection in the air," Daniel Berrigan wrote, and it obscured all distinctions.

Negative images were indiscriminately associated with dissent itself, especially those of violence and disorder. In reality, violence was seldom employed in antiwar protests. It was used mostly by local right-wing activists or police, especially prior to 1967. In that year disruptive street actions and attacks on draft board property began to increase in frequency and, more important, in notoriety. Concurrently the country experienced worsening racial crisis and campus unrest. Governing authorities, growing apprehensive about the relation of domestic violence and Vietnam, made serious attempts to infiltrate security agents in the antiwar movement, both for surveillance and harassment. Not until 1968–1971 did the connection between violence and the antiwar movement become salient in American politics. Militancy did increase then. With the disintegration of the radical left and the rise of groups such as the Weathermen, some dissidents detonated bombs, set fire to buildings, and attacked police. Still, it is difficult to correlate the actual growth of antiwar violence with the sharp rise in official concern at the time. According to a 1970 study conducted by Treasury Department officials Eugene Rossides and G. Gordon Liddy, there were 4,358 bombings in the United States from January 1969 to April 1970, of which 36 percent could be attributed to specific sources and 20 percent to antiwar dissidents. Otherwise, there are no federal figures which attribute violence to the war issue.

In spite of lacking concrete evidence, the Nixon administration consistently identified antiwar protest with domestic violence and terrorism, particularly after it failed to link the movement to communism. Ironically, some administration officials used agents provocateurs to incite antiwar activists to violence or encouraged prowar enthusiasts to inspire citizen attacks on dissidents. The Nixon White House made a determined effort to discredit and destroy the antiwar movement, and it identified dissent with violence so effectively that it made the legitimacy of protest itself a political issue.

Government officials and prowar partisans also routinely attacked antiwar activists as being either communist-inspired or a source of encouragement to Vietnamese communists and, thus, a force prolonging the war. Doubtless some radical leaders naïvely romanticized Hanoi (as the White House knowingly romanticized Saigon); but despite their most energetic efforts, investigative agencies failed to find any evidence to the charge that dissenters were either inspired or manipulated by communists. Exhaustive studies prepared for both Johnson and Nixon concluded instead that even radical elements in the movement were indigenous American idealists, however perverse they might seem. Indeed, by the 1970s the word "commie" conveyed cultural and social deviance more than political subversion.

Similarly, there is no evidence that protest prolonged the war. Certainly the war continued despite dissident attempts to end it. The fact that Vietnamese communists periodically proclaimed their appreciation of the antiwar movement does not mean that they depended on it. To suppose so is to confuse cause-and-effect with parallel causes and to perpetuate the underestimation of Vietnamese will and capacity which itself contributed to American defeat. The charge that the movement prolonged the war rests on the assumption that it sapped the will of the nation to fight (or that the Vietnamese thought it did) and that the contest could otherwise have been won. In fact, it seems likely that most Americans concluded that the effort was futile and counterproductive, and withdrew their support accordingly. In this sense, it was the people themselves who were "no longer so naïve" about the war.

Nonetheless, the antiwar movement was vulnerable to unwarranted charges of abetting violence and communism. It was extraordinarily large and diverse. It was organized to attract dissidents, not to discriminate among them. Included in its number were a relatively few who were prepared to emulate the violent acts of what Fred Halstead aptly called "plate glass revolutionaries" and others who proffered a romantic version of Maoist revolution. Moreover, its public image was formed when those elements were most visible and domestic confrontation most intense. . . .

The significance of the antiwar movement depends upon what it is measured against, of course, and evaluation is laden with anomalies. Leading activists never believed that they could literally stop the war, and yet they did not relent in their struggle to do so. Indeed, they even cultivated the impression that public opposition could reverse official policy. The Johnson and Nixon administrations insisted that they would not respond to protest, and yet both adapted their policies to pressure from dissenters. Public opinion surveys indicated that the American people consistently resented the antiwar movement but increasingly agreed with its arguments and conclusions.

The very contradictions in the movement and in reactions to it suggest dissonance. Probably it helped to transform the war in Southeast Asia into a protracted domestic struggle which, when compounded by related social turmoil, produced a crisis in the American social and political order. Certainly antiwar activists confronted their people and leaders with fundamental questions about democratic politics and national interest. . . .

From 1955 on, more and more citizens were learning from related experiments in social change. By the early 1960s a resurgent peace movement converged with political liberalism, radicalism revitalized in a New Left, and a civil rights movement imbued with an interfaith revival of the social gospel. Reform efforts created a base of material resources, adaptable ideas, experienced organizers, and networks of supporters. Together they animated a lively sense of idealism: they contributed to the range, tone, energy, and momentum of the opposition which crystalized around escalating intervention in Vietnam.

Although interaction with other social reform impulses contributed synergistic power to the antiwar movement, it also aggravated an inherent division there. Nominally, the split was between liberals and radicals, but those labels do not convey a sense of the issues because both wings were in flux, and neither was fixed by a governing ideology or stable constituency. Still, there was an irreducible difference in the ways they approached the Vietnam War. Some activists fresh from peace and civil rights campaigns viewed American intervention in Indochina as a mistake, an aberration that had to be corrected through public education and electoral action so that the United States could resume its quest for international order and domestic reform. They were in this measure liberals. Other activists, especially from the Old and New Left, viewed Vietnam as a counterrevolutionary war of American aggression that sprang from the elitist and self-interested culture of American capitalism, which they wanted to transform for the sake of social and international justice. Their approach was at least in this sense radical.

Together, antiwar liberals and radicals believed that American military intervention in Vietnam was wrong and that Washington bore the principal responsibility for effecting a peace settlement. Beyond that basic agreement they divided. Often their difference was expressed in strategic quarrels on the relative merits of immediate or negotiated withdrawal, of organization around the single issue of the war or on multiple social issues, and of various techniques for effecting change, such as persuasion, conventional politics, mass demonstrations, or confrontation. Prolonged and often esoteric quarrels over strategy only obscured the main line of division. Antiwar liberals saw the war as a policy issue, antiwar radicals as a means toward revolutionary social change. The former tried to de-escalate and then end U.S. military involvement, while the latter challenged intervention in an attempt to transform the distribution of power and privilege in America. One side saw Vietnam as a crisis in a democracy that it wanted to save; the other viewed the war issue as an opportunity to redeem society from falseness and corruption. The lines were not neat (there were liberals, after all, who also wanted to redistribute power and privilege), the alternatives not necessarily exclusive. Nonetheless, antiwar rhetoric often masked a debate over America.

For the most part, that division was understood only by a small core of activists. The antiwar movement provided a focal point for large numbers of Americans who for one reason or another opposed the war but were not involved in protest organizations. Organized activism related millions of otherwise disconnected people to a single issue. This was its raison d'être: to mobilize public opposition to the war.

The opposition to this war was also linked to the liberalization of popular culture. Wars tend to breed cultural conformity and conservative politics, but the Vietnam War was different. In varying measure, the antiwar movement aligned the organized disaffection of blacks, women, and students. It also competed with these groups and others, such as environmentalists. It included a few activists who thought themselves the harbingers of a counterculture, many who emphasized individual autonomy and alternative group loyalties, and a majority that questioned authority at a root level. . . .

The most distinctive quality of organized opposition to the war was its moral thrust. Vietnam intensified the dissatisfaction with pragmatic liberal realism and the anxiety over moral numbness which had surfaced with respect to nuclear arms. The war was widely condemned as immoral, not only on the universal grounds of pacifism but in terms of "just war" ethics—by Reinhold Niebuhr as much as A. J. Muste, by Hans Morgenthau as well as Daniel Berrigan. Policy was challenged on moral grounds, especially after 1968 when military victory was implicitly abandoned. As American troops were withdrawn, Indochinese became the only combatants—and civilians—at risk. For those who followed events, the question was more clearly what U.S. policy was doing to others. The issue of war-related public morality was brought home in the latter years of the Nixon administration when the events surrounding Watergate joined it to the issue of accountability. Throughout the period the moral criterion was the only common denominator in the antiwar movement, where it was pressed incessantly.

Calling the war "immoral" was a form of rhetoric—an abstract shorthand for "terribly wrong." The administration countered that the conflict was a matter of honor and obligation: hence moral. Offsetting ethical claims tended to undercut the force of abstractions. To that extent the nation lost familiar value-laden reference points. Words such as communism, containment, democratic government, free world, peace, and victory became too obviously manipulative, and too often contradicted by reports from Southeast Asia. Notions such as patriotism, loyalty, and national honor were imbued with ambivalence as the antiwar movement associated them with dissent. It was little wonder, then, that the public was benumbed by abstract words naming alternative moralities. In this environment it was hardly ironic that skepticism about war was extended to exhortations for peace. It was appropriate for *Commonweal* to advise the graduating class of 1975 that its fight would be against cynicism.

The obverse of public ethics was the morality of personal responsibility. Whatever its sources in American culture, this was a strong current in the 1960s. Early in the decade it impelled black students to take repression upon their own shoulders, and some white students perceived racism as a shared responsibility. The sense of personal accountability for social injustice surfaced in the Peace Corps and community service. It was extended to Vietnam. Especially among the pacifist and youthful elements of the antiwar movement, it was joined to an ethics of action: the notion that belief must find expression in behavior, that decision is the epitome of morality, that to witness outweighs results.

This attitude was characteristic of the so-called romantic radicalism of the period. Its attraction was felt mainly among young people, although it was also inherent in radical pacifism. Doubtless it was profoundly therapeutic when activists were oppressed by the apparent futility of their efforts. Apparently relegated to the periphery of their society and alienated from their government, they could at least [be] witness to the truth as they knew it: *at least it was something to do.*" Still, the emphasis on personal morality aggravated the problems of already isolated activists. It could not only motivate activism but also rationalize withdrawal from politics. To the extent that action justified itself, the test of political impact was eroded. To the extent that the transformation of character became an all-absorbing goal, the organizational bonds required for sustained public action were snapped.

Such moralism never dominated the antiwar movement as a whole. Liberals, including leading pacifists, and even radicals in the Communist party and Socialist Workers party did try to mount politically effective campaigns, although they might rely on mass demonstrations to do so. Again they faced the difficulty of coalition politics. Theirs was a hydra-headed movement. The established peace groups had to reconcile differences not only among themselves but also with a series of ephemeral groupings, each with its own floating constituency. More or less together, they reacted to whatever crisis promised to unify them and give them access to the public. Under circumstances beyond their control, activists often appeared to be leaderless, their movement politically unstable. Nonetheless, at the core there was staying power and remarkable persistence, due in part to a coterie of dedicated, even professional, organizers and in part to the intractable fact of the war itself.

The problems associated with building a coalition against the war thus derived partially from the diversity and intensity with which individuals gathered in the hope of improving the quality of American society. In the midst of a despondent reflection on the fragility of the movement in 1973, an activist noted that someone had counted seven hundred volunteer groups in Massachusetts that were dedicated to various causes. What a dynamic society, she thought! The antiwar movement was a part of that dynamism.

The fabric of American society was dramatically rewoven in the two decades after 1955. Racism was at least mitigated. Student life-styles and curricula were altered. The status of women was reexamined. The Democratic and Republican coalitions began to realign. The executive branch was constrained by the 1973 War Powers Act. A large number of new peace organizations were formed which continued after the war, such as SANE, the Council for a Livable World, the World Without War Council, the Center for War/Peace Studies, the Fund for Peace and its project centers, and the Campaign to Stop Funding the War (under various names). Those concerned themselves mainly with foreign policy. Clergy and Laity Concerned and Common Cause bridged over to domestic issues. A number of other organizations stimulated peace research and education, or international exchange. All of them were complemented by a plethora of associations address-ing civil rights, environmental, and feminist issues, or by cells of socially con-cerned professionals—civil servants, business people, physicians, psychologists, scientists, entertainers, educators, historians. Throughout the period there seemed to be a cycle of social consciousness, protest, campaigns, and long-term organization for concrete goals. The process was accompanied by turbulence, as old social patterns were rent and refashioned.

Whatever forces were acting elsewhere in American society, the war had at least two major effects on it. First, the war touched all domestic conflicts, charging them with high tension and obscuring the issues around which national identity was being redefined. Second, the antiwar movement interacted with the process of social reconstruction. Voluntarism in opposition to the war mushroomed, especially on the local level. Often it was only loosely connected to national organizations—perhaps to receive information, raise funds, or send demonstrators to a mobilization. Indeed, local activists sometimes resented the fact that their resources were drained to support national actions. All this citizen activity suggests that the movement in the broadest sense was not so peripheral to the American mainstream as its leaders feared. Its history on the national level reflected efforts in the American interior—in church meetings, college teach-ins, congressional offices, city street actions, curbside vigils, and divided families—where most Americans struggled among themselves over Vietnam. . . .

Martin Luther King, Jr., and many other activists observed, when confronted with allegations of protest violence, that in objective terms the United States was employing devastating and indiscriminate violence in Indochina. It was imposing its will as though that were a goal in itself: this was the point of their opposition to the war. But those were not objective times, and it still is difficult to reflect on King's words without raising extremely painful questions that go to the heart of national identity and purpose. It was, and perhaps still is, easier to pretend that dissent was merely the rhetorical expression of malcontents whose tactics contradicted or ob-scured their plea for peace—to treat the challenge of antiwar dissidents as willful or trivial rather than to answer it.

There gathered in the United States between 1955 and 1975 the largest domestic opposition to a warring government in the history of modern industrial society. Orig-inating in a small-scale protest against Washington's Cold War policies, specifically against the atmospheric testing of nuclear weapons, it exploded after 1965 into a sustained challenge to military intervention in Indochina. Overwhelmingly, antiwar dissidents regarded the decision on Vietnam as a definition of American purpose. They were idealists, and they identified their ideals with their nation. This is why they tried so desperately to reach the public. It is also why they were so vulnerable to popular rejection and apathy. They felt intensely that they shared the ordeal of the war—for the nation. They argued that the core issue was not the future of democracy in Vietnam: that they insisted, was beyond the purview of the United States. The critical issue was the purpose of the American people. The antiwar movement did not force the United States to quit the war. Its political significance was, instead, that it persistently identified that choice as the essential issue of American foreign policy and national identity.

Women and Antiwar Activism

RHODRI JEFFREYS-JONES

Women were effective opponents of the Vietnam War. They supplied the antiwar movement with literary luminaries like Mary McCarthy, [movie] stars like Jane Fonda, and publicity-capturing organizations like Women Strike for Peace (WSP). They were especially important in helping to legitimize the antiwar movement from 1970 on, with Congresswoman Bella Abzug to the fore in cutting off the funds that sustained the U.S. military effort in Indochina. Whereas students started the antiwar campaign and African Americans took up the standard two years later, it fell to women to make the final charge.

The pronounced affinity of women with the legitimization movement arose from their minority mentality and their ambitions for political breakthrough. Here, however, some serious qualifications must be borne in mind. Women were a majority of the population. Some women deeply resented being labeled members of a minority group, and a few, prominent in voluntary organizations and drawn from the upper classes, thought of themselves as insiders having an influence on policy by indirect means.

Against this may be set evidence indicating that women had long played the outsider's role in politics. The sociologist Gunnar Myrdal had in 1944 identified "striking similarities" between the predicament of women and that of African Americans. There can be few more graphic illustrations of the power of the outsider concept than the following extract from Shirley Chisholm's campaign book, *Unbought and Unbossed* (1970). Chisholm was the first African American congresswoman. "Women," she wrote, "are a majority of the population, but they are treated like a minority group. . . . Of my two 'handicaps,' being female put many more obstacles in my path than being black."

Yet, and this is an important qualification, it was precisely because women felt they were excluded from full participation in the American democratic process that it was tempting for them to try to improve their acceptability by supporting the Vietnam War. Antimilitarism was all very well in peacetime, but not in wartime. A character in Mary McCarthy's novel *The Group* (1963) noted the distinction, declaring that "in *peacetime* . . . she was a pacifist." Some women thought that they would have to become politically indistinguishable from their more belligerent menfolk before they could break through to a position of full equality. One did not have to be a feminist to think this way. Many women abhorred the stridency of feminism but wanted political equality. According to this line of reasoning, the new woman, to shed her minority status and capitalize on her demographic advantage, would have to be an Amazon in foreign policy.

This point of view prevailed among women in the early stages of the war. But after a while, they turned against it, becoming, in effect, wartime pacifists. They resolved the conflict between the desire to protest and the desire to win political

From Rhodri Jeffreys-Jones, *Peace Now! American Society and the Ending of the Vietnam War,* Yale University Press. Copyright © 1999 Yale University Press. Reprinted with permission.

legitimacy by inventing a tactical synthesis: they legitimized protest. Their prefer-ence for political and legislative means of opposing the war went hand in hand with legitimization of women in politics.

In accomplishing the dual goals of protest and progress, women had an advan-tage over African Americans and students: they were able to turn against the war without incurring a major backlash. Women had suffered from backlash in the past and suffered from it again in the future. One reason for their escape in the sixties may have been that students and African Americans took the heat. Another reason for the underdeveloped backlash was the slow pace of sixties feminism. There was no great reaction against women in the sixties because they did not achieve a great deal in that decade and did not discomfit the male world. Women even went backward in some respects. For example, they started the decade with twenty members in Congress and ended it with eleven. Between 1957 and 1970 the number of women in the U.S. Foreign Service declined from 8.9 to 4.8 percent of the total; women made up three-fourths of State Department personnel but supplied less than 4 percent of its senior officials. According to India Edwards, director of the women's division of the Demo-cratic National Committee, women were a "at a lower ebb in the political life of this country" in 1969 than they had been at any point in her long career. There had been a particular deterioration under Presidents Kennedy and Johnson.

On the one hand, women faced a power deficit. On the other, given their slow and even negative record, the foreign policy establishment was taken unawares when women rebelled against the war. The establishment had neglected to build the apparatus of backlash. They had no law and order issue or Southern strategy to launch against women. This lack of response encouraged women to proceed with their protest and allowed them to do so without effective political retribution.

At first, women were behind the war. As ever, support for a war was one way an outsider group could climb the greasy pole of status advancement. There were other reasons, too. Prowar female newspaper reporters and women in politics were, of course, influenced by the same arguments as men were, but in the early stages of the war an additional element in the standard anticommunist arguments appealed especially to women: the apparent link between totalitarianism—with its accom-plishment of objectives through coercion—and physically based male misrule of women. Democracy was inherently attractive to women. The lack of democracy in the U.S. ally, South Vietnam, was upsetting, but the promise of reform there and the argument that the fight in the Mekong delta was the essential element in the fight to contain the spread of international communism did resonate with women. They saw a gender-specific ideological reason for supporting any war against communism, and Vietnam seemed to fit the case.

Prowar feeling among women retained its strength throughout the peak years of student and black protest. Women serving in Vietnam in the military, for example, voiced few significant political protests until the end of the sixties. One reason may have been that they were barred from combat and failed to experience the full horror of war at first hand. Another was their small number: between 1962 and 1973, only 7,500 women served on active military duty in Vietnam. The highest estimate for the total number of military and civilian women serving in Vietnam is 55,000, an eleven-year aggregate figure that includes nurses, air traffic controllers, photographers, cartographers, clerks and secretaries, intelligence specialists, missionaries, teachers, journalists, and flight attendants. . . .

Strong though their loyalty may have been, the women who supported the war lacked a gender-specific reason for supporting the hostilities in Vietnam as distinct from other wars in other places at other times. In contrast, women who opposed the war had both general and gender-specific reasons for doing so.

Debate is heated over the gender difference on the war-and-peace issue. Some feminists are incensed by the hypothesis that women oppose war because of their nurturing instincts. They object to the idea that they are innately or essentially different from men and to its corollary that they will in perpetuity be lumbered with caregiving activities of the type that carry a menial status. Other discussion focuses on the notion that it is men, not women, whose beliefs and behavior differ from the rational, peaceful norm; women simply have the advantage of being free from male conditioning. Still another theory holds that women should oppose war because war perpetuates patriarchy. This argument helped to give a special edge to women's critique of the Vietnam War, for the new feminism of the sixties looked beyond women's-rights issues and offered a more fundamental critique of male-dominated society.

In general, though not always by a wide margin, American women have been more antiwar than American men have. Depending on their viewpoint, they have advanced various reasons for their distinctively peaceful stance: their maternal instinct, their objection to war-induced inflation, their conviction that war is an artifact of male domination. In relation to the Vietnam War, women's opposition to price escalation was probably the weakest of these factors. By the 1960s, changing expenditure patterns within the family meant that women were no longer the unpaid guardians of the American pocketbook, as they had been in the 1920s. But consumerism may still have been a residual factor—in 1967, Denver housewives protested against war-induced price rises.

The sharpness of women's critique of the Vietnam War derived from the nature and impact of that conflict in the sixties. Women had long argued that war demeaned them, being a men's game, and the declining status of women in public life in the sixties seemed to underline the point. The very fact of the war, it could be argued, was a symptom of women's loss of power in the United States, and its effect was the reinforcement of male hegemony. Gender aspects of the war played into the hands of its American opponents, especially in light of the contrast with the Vietnamese Communists. In Vietnam, Confucianism and polygamy had subordinated women for centuries. But the communist leader Ho Chi Minh emphasized the principle of gender equality. In June 1969 the South Vietnamese Provisional Revolutionary Government appointed a woman, Madame Nguyen Thi Binh, as foreign minister.

The Communist-nationalists thus appeared to be fighting for women as well as against Saigon and the Americans. Vietnamese women rallied to the cause and, depending on geographic area, could compose up to one-third of the fighting force of the Viet Cong. In contrast, the American and South Vietnamese governments restricted women to ancillary roles. Prostitution further reinforced the sexist image of the American cause. Prostitution was, in fact, rife in Hanoi as well as Saigon, but it had a higher profile in South Vietnam, plus official encouragement, and offended American women because the prostitutes served American men. Finally, the racial overtones of the war were conspicuous, not least because of the publicity that arose from the antiwar activities of African Americans. The women's rights movement had been allied to the fight against racial discrimination ever since the antislavery crusade. All these factors meant that the campaign against the Vietnam War had, potentially, a special appeal for American women.

But the nascent female opposition to the war had certain weaknesses. No critique of the war attained the status of a universal article of faith among American women. Consciousness of gendered aspects of the war affected minorities of women in different ways and reached a lower plane in the sixties than in the seventies. Another weakness was the problem of male chauvinism in the antiwar movement. Women activists complained widely that men in the movement excluded them from decisionmaking and allocated them to menial tasks like food preparation—women at Berkeley cooked until 1968—typing, and the provision of sex. . . .

Male chauvinism in the peace movement alienated women and caused division in their ranks. But chauvinism and its consequences must be kept in perspective. Male chauvinism was hardly peculiar to the peace movement. It was to be found in the civil rights and, notably, the Black Power movements. And it was especially a feature of the war machine, from officers' clubs in Vietnam to the White House. President Johnson observed of a male dove in his administration: "Hell, he has to squat to piss!" His attitude appealed to men who despised peaceniks and looked down on women. Norman Mailer—although he had once stabbed his own wife—drew attention to the actions of "working class" soldiers in breaking up the 1967 Pentagon demonstration: they singled out women to beat and humiliate. The predominantly middle-class feminists took note.

Also, there is another side to the charge that male-chauvinist antiwar leaders engaged in sexual exploitation. Women connived at, if they did not invent, the effective antidraft slogan Girls Say Yes to Boys Who Say No. When, in 1967, the singer Joan Baez posed with two other women for a resistance poster bearing that caption, she did so of her own volition, even if her act did provoke a storm from "women's libbers." The reputation of the peace movement for chauvinism arose in part from heightened expectation; a male antiwar protester was expected to be revolutionary in every respect, and his failure to be a New Man was commensurably disappointing. Distorted expectations could mask the change that was taking place. Years later, [Tom] Hayden claimed that although only a few movement men had read Simone De Beauvoir in 1963, Betty Friedan's book was on their reading list as soon as it appeared that year. If the New Man had not quite arrived, he was about to.

Male chauvinism impaired the peace movement in some ways. Yet it was less extreme than might be supposed, and it did stimulate feminist debate. Far from preventing the construction of the platform from which women launched their effective post-sixties protest, chauvinism in the antiwar movement may even have contributed some planks. Most important, it paled into insignificance compared with the gender chauvinism of war supporters. It was the chauvinism of the hawks that goaded the peace feminists into action.

Women's protest against the war was extensive and came in many varieties. It ranged from the activities of communist partisans like Anna Louise Strong, Bettina Aptheker, and Angela Davis to more conservative protests like the "Fuck the Army" rebellion by some military women at the end of the sixties. Tactically, it embraced individual acts, like the self-immolation of a solitary Quaker mother in Detroit, and great collective enterprises, like the production of antiwar newsletters with circulations running into tens of thousands. Yet the volume and variety of protest is no more than one might expect in a country that prides itself on individualism and libertarianism and contains a large population of women. To appreciate more fully the way that sixties women built a platform for successful resistance to the war, it is helpful to review their contributions systematically in terms of organizations, personalities, and dramatic episodes.

According to one strain of New Left reasoning, anti-oppression organizations are incapable of effecting significant social change, because being structured destines them to become part of the opposing power elite. It has further been observed that women's antiwar organizations were not always capable of commanding attention in the media, the prerequisite for political impact. But the sixties threw up new women's organizations that were too immature to be incorporated into any power structure. The most important of them, WSP, contributed to major media-grabbing demonstrations, repeatedly commanded attention in its own right, and supplied a new generation of women with political training.

The children's book illustrator Dagmar Wilson and three of her suburban neighbors in Washington, D.C., established WSP in 1961. The name of the organization, Women Strike for Peace, derived from the housewives' "strike" and accompanying marches organized for November 1, 1961. They progressed to other types of demonstration, backing the campaign for an atmospheric nuclear test ban treaty so effectively that they won tacit recognition from President Kennedy, who made strong appeals to mothers and grandmothers in whipping up support for enactment of the treaty in 1963. They built up a network of contacts through two existing organizations. The Women's International League for Peace and Freedom (WILPF), established in 1919, had been formidable in the 1920s and 1930s and agitated against the Vietnam War in its own right. It was a source of contacts, even if early WSP supporters regarded it as bureaucratically constipated. The National Committee for a Sane Nuclear Policy (SANE) was another resource, even if it was dominated by men and had made enemies by purging itself of left-wingers. The WSP itself was post-McCarthy and could even be regarded as precociously post–Cold War. Although it contained a contingent of "red diaper" women—the progeny of an earlier generation of radicals—its members were typically respectable, suburban, middle-class mothers worried about their children's prospects in a nuclear world. Wilson was an Englishwoman with an upper-class accent; attempts by congressional red-baiters to label her a puppet of Lower East Side radicals fell flat. Amy Swerdlow, the WSP press officer and in later years a historian, argues that WSP "helped to legitimize a radical critique of the Cold War and U.S. militarism."

WSP expressed concern about Vietnam from its earliest days and in 1965 made the war the main focus of its protest activities. In the spring of that year, after the United States began to bomb North Vietnam, Mary Clarke and Lorraine Gordon of WSP visited Hanoi, the first representatives of the U.S. peace movement to do so.

At home, the WSP contributed to the mass demonstrations against the war, giving a gendered twist to the doves' dialogue. In a manner consistent with the "nurturant motherhood" outlook of its early days, it drew attention to the fate of children in the war. In 1966, WSP protested the indiscriminate American use of defoliants that had resulted in horrifying injuries to Vietnamese children by trying to block the napalm shipments of the Dow Chemical Company from San Jose, California. These "housewife terrorists" and "napalm ladies"—so dubbed in the newspapers— were arrested and convicted. In January of the next year 2,500 angry WSP marchers hammered on the locked doors of the Pentagon. This, too, was worth publicity, and women began to rival students as image makers. They proved adept at coining memorable slogans. Their paper daisies heralded "flower power." They delivered to the office of General [Lewis] Hershey, head of the selective service, a coffin in- scribed with the words "Not Our Sons, Not Your Sons, Not Their Sons."

An organism more than an organization, the early WSP was spontaneous and chaotic. Reliable estimates of its numerical strength and support are well-nigh im- possible to obtain. Fifty thousand women were reported to have taken part in the original housewives' strike in 1961, but a more carefully researched estimate by Amy Swerdlow suggests that they numbered twelve thousand at most. Women- only demonstrations were imaginative and colorful and attracted publicity once the antiwar movement gathered momentum, but direct-action episodes did not draw large numbers of participants. There appears, however, to have been a wider residual sympathy for the WSP and its goals. On December 10, 1965, President Johnson received 100,000 cards with this appeal: "For the sake of our sons . . . for the sake of our children . . . give us peace in Vietnam." That many cards did not mean that many activists, but it did mean dedicated women with widespread support. In May 1966 a WSP delegation from New York turned up in Washington to present one of Senator Javits's staff with a petition. It consisted of four yellow sheets of paper with 112 signatures and some remarks. One of the remarks, by Rose Hochman of Bayside, New York, gives an impression of WSP's cumulative outreach: "In several one hour periods on weekends I have been getting 40–50 signatures on WSP peace pledges. The people have no confidence in this war and will not support those in the Congress who do not stop the war."

The message also indicated that a change was taking place in WSP. Members were taking an interest in the legislative process. Their interest was a prelude to the legitimization of the women's campaign against the war. It also signaled the arrival of a new feminism. The women who personified these processes was Bella Abzug.

A distinguished civil rights lawyer, Abzug had been involved in the WSP since the beginning and was its political action coordinator. She was determined to give the organization more legislative power and to link that goal to the achievement of feminist objectives—"I wanted an end to nuclear testing for *women,* for us ourselves, not just for our kids." By the mid-sixties, Abuzg's most important political objec- tive was the ending of the war in Vietnam. At the outset, few WSP women had been either feminist or politically minded, but their involvement in the peace movement gradually made significant numbers of them more conscious of women's rights and congressional politics. From 1965 on, WSP women, numbered in their "thousands" according to Swerdlow, worked in the Democratic Party to promote peace candidates and to work for the Dump Johnson movement. They later provided the core of sup- port for Abzug's 1970 congressional bid, in aid of which 235 WSP volunteers worked at her campaign headquarters.

In the meantime, the formation of Another Mother for Peace (AMP) in March 1967 had ensured that pure and simple motherists would never be without a home in the antiwar movement. AMP was the creation of Barbara Avedon and fourteen other women associated with the Hollywood film industry. Run from Beverly Hills, it was nonpartisan and endorsed no candidates. It demanded an end to the war and the establishment of a cabinet-level secretary for peace. It appealed to the idea of nurturant motherhood, arguing that women were by nature more peaceful than men because they were responsible for the seeds of life. AMP had a gift for coining images and slogans. Lorraine Schneider designed its best-known logo: a message, "War is not healthy for children and other living things," arranged around a flower. Madison Avenue could only struggle to match this and another of its slogans: "All the flowers of all the tomorrows are in the seeds of today."

One of AMP's first actions was to print a thousand Mother's Day cards for sympathizers to send to their respective members of Congress. The cards contained a poem demanding, in the name of motherhood, peace, not "candy or flowers." The verse was execrable by AMP's literary standards, but it was a huge success and had to be reprinted over and over again until 200,000 cards had been sent in all. AMP now started producing peace Christmas cards, and the combined total printed and sent was half a million by the end of the year. By 1968, AMP was thought to have a membership of around 100,000, about the same as WSP, although that did not mean a combined total of 200,000, because there was some overlap. By 1971 the AMP newsletter reached an estimated 240,000, and by the following year a further 10,000 had been added to its mailing list. . . .

. . . The evidence points overall to a greater opposition among women than among men. Data collected by the Harris poll organization in 1971 presents a complex picture but does confirm women's relatively greater disposition to oppose. In 1970, of the women polled, 63 percent thought that antiwar pickets did more harm than good, but they also tended to think that troop withdrawals from Vietnam were progressing too slowly. In 1972, Harris conducted several polls aimed at women. Compared with men, these women were, if anything, unconcerned at the inflationary and other economic costs of the war. But they favored an end to the war more strongly than men did; withdrawal from Vietnam was the top political priority for 49 percent of female respondents, compared with 44 percent of the males. Sixty percent of both men and women thought that President Nixon was doing an excellent or pretty good job of "working for peace in the world." But both sexes thought that "when it comes to getting us out of Vietnam . . . women in public office could do a better job than men . . . or just as good a job as men."

Movement Myths

ADAM GARFINKLE

This [essay] argues three propositions about the Vietnam antiwar movement: One concerns its impact on American decision making during the war, a second is about the sources of the era's youthful radicalism, and a third focuses on the movement's longer-term impact on American political culture. The three are linked historically by the obvious fact that they all concern the Vietnam War and its times. They are linked, too, in that the state of the American commonwealth, the condition of the hearts and minds of its citizens, and relationships between public opinion and policy making remain, one hopes, issues of contemporary interest. Last, all three are liable to strike many readers as counterintuitive and give rise to some skepticism. It is my hope that, upon reflection, skepticism will give way to an appreciation of paradox, so often the subtle garb of truth in political life.

The first thesis is this: Contrary to the great weight of common knowledge, the Vietnam antiwar movement at its radical height was counterproductive in limiting U.S. military operations in Southeast Asia. It was not decisively counterproductive; other factors strongly drove American public opinion against the war: mounting casualties, mounting costs, the failure to win, the credibility gap, shifts in administration policy, and more besides. But the antiwar movement, at least between 1966 and 1969, was not among these factors. It did not help stop the war but rather helped prolong it.

My fuller argument on this point holds that the antiwar movement moved through three phases along with the war itself. In the first phase, before 1966, opposition to expanding the U.S. role in Vietnam was predominantly liberal in inspiration, was well represented inside both the Kennedy and Johnson administrations, and was strongly held by many of those in the press and elsewhere to whom principals of those administrations listened. In this very broad constellation it was effective too in limiting U.S. military activity: The escalation of the war in 1965 might have taken place in 1962, 1963, or 1964. The rationale for escalation in these years was not different in kind, only in degree, from the one that propelled American action in 1965.

In the second phase, between 1966 and 1968–69, the antiwar movement's center of gravity grew increasingly radical and counterproductive to its goal of stopping U.S. military activity in Southeast Asia. At the very time when the war's unpopularity was growing in the country at large, the image of irresponsibility and willful antipatriotism conveyed by the antiwar movement had the general effect of muting the expression of disaffection. Lyndon Johnson made his famous March 31, 1968, speech on national television reversing American policy and admitting personal political weakness not because the movement had taken to the streets, but despite the fact that it had.

The antiwar movement's impact in this phase was doubly hurtful because U.S. military activity in Southeast Asia was itself unwittingly counterproductive to American war aims at this stage of the war. The antiwar movement's inadvertent role in bolstering the Johnson administration's own stasis thus not only helped prolong the war but also contributed to losing it.

In the third phase of the war and the antiwar movement, from 1969 to the fall of Saigon in 1975, the redomesticated, more liberally centered movement was again moderately effective in limiting U.S. military activity in Southeast Asia, mainly through actions taken by Congress designed to hem in the Nixon administration militarily and politically. But electoral dynamics were mainly responsible for the movement's renewed effectiveness in its return to mainstream American politics. Democrats were now in the opposition, and their reluctance to criticize the war evaporated when Vietnam became Nixon's and the Republicans' war instead of their own. The great tumult within the party in 1968, of course, had primed the Democrats well for this new role.

But this phase of the antiwar movement was injurious too, because, after the Tet offensive, the war entered a postinsurgency phase for which U.S. military power, operating under a reconceived strategy, was much better suited. Had the political situation in the United States allowed it, the U.S. military, acting as a deterrent to conventional aggression, probably could have achieved the main task at hand: building a shield to protect the construction of a self-sustaining non-Communist government in Saigon. This could have been done in more or less the same way that such a government was constructed in Seoul under the wing of U.S. military protection after the Korean armistice in 1953.

The failure to proceed along such lines during the Nixon administration does not rest mainly—as most believe—on the antiwar movement's influence over the Congress, which is beyond doubt. The Congress was unhelpful, but ultimately it was the Nixon administration itself that elected not to take the time or spend the political capital necessary to save South Vietnam. Strong congressional opposition to helping Saigon was less important than the administration's broader global foreign policy vision, which required putting the war behind and moving on. There was Watergate too and the ever-present impact of electoral politics: Richard Nixon's determination to win the 1972 election and subsequently choose his own successor for 1976. Just as fear of the electorate had restrained Democrats in the White House before 1964, the same fear restrained Republicans after 1969.

These utterly normal contours of American politics—together, of course, with the battlefield situation—better explain American decisions about escalation and de-escalation in Vietnam than anything the antiwar movement did in the streets either before or after Richard Nixon became president. Those observers, such as historian Tom Wells, who still believe the antiwar movement "played a major role in constraining, de-escalating and ending the war," are wrong.

[This essay's] other two theses may also seem counterintuitive to some. The first is that while the war in Vietnam was the main catalyst for 1960s radicalism, especially among selected groups of youth, it was not the cause. The real causes lay in the generic difficulties of coping with the revolutionary social life of post–World War II America—even in the supposedly somnambulistic 1950s—and the result was to produce what, for want of a better term, was a religious movement among youth. Human beings are meaning-making animals. Postwar youth, affluent and idealistic beyond prior generations, sought a new godhead in the face of the subtle but pervasive banishment of the sacred from everyday life in the on-rushing technetronic age. That chiliastic search turned to politics, where the impulse to the sacred has often come to reside in modern times, even if it has often done so incognito. In some respects, the antiwar movement was a modern children's crusade, with similarly depressing consequences.

The final thesis is that the main impact of the antiwar movement was not felt in Southeast Asia but in the United States. The impact has also transcended politics as conventionally construed, for the antiwar movement cannot be analyzed apart from larger trends in American culture. Relatedly, the impact of the movement cannot be discussed entirely in the past tense. As time passes and one set of experiences is overlaid by others, sifting the effects of moments frozen in time 25 years ago is a delicate task. Perceptions and accounts that have come down to us today about both the war and the antiwar movement are necessarily influenced by ideas, events, and edited memories from well after the fall of Saigon. When we speak today about the impact of the Vietnam War and the antiwar movement, we have to mean not only what happened between 1964 and 1975 but also what has been said and written about it since and even subsequent actions taken on the basis of those sayings and writings. Grasping this mixed class of phenomena is quite difficult. . . .

To evaluate the effect of the antiwar movement on the prosecution of the war and its final outcome is difficult business. We can sum up our argument as follows: To the modest extent that the antiwar movement ever worked to limit U.S. involvement in Vietnam, it did so *before* the election of Lyndon Johnson and *after* the election of Richard Nixon, particularly after U.S. ground troops had been withdrawn and U.S. prisoners of war returned in early 1973. In between, and particularly in the period between 1965 and 1970—and possibly up to the 1972 election—the movement achieved nothing concrete according to its own measure and probably helped the sitting administrations to manage the broadest segments of American public opinion into relative quiescence. Its counterproductive impact may have been modest—as modest as its limiting impact before and after this core period—but that was its direction.

It is clear that the Johnson administration was *self-restrained* from sharp escalation, not restrained because of public opinion, which was more hawkish than the administration much of the time, or because of the antiwar movement, which was marginal to the decision-making process throughout. Antiwar demonstrations mounted and populated by radicals stifled at least as much if not more nonradical dissent against the war than they stimulated. Most Americans, while concerned about a war seemingly without end or prospect of clearcut victory, were more prepared to suffer in silence than to associate themselves with lurid leftists and yelping Yippies.

And when the Johnson administration changed course in March 1968, it did so through a calculation of various costs and benefits in which the antiwar movement counted as only one of several factors and certainly not as a major one. Nor can the changed views of the Wise Men, as they revisited the problem in February and March of that year, be ascribed to the antiwar movement in any simple way. Their changed views appear to have been predicted not only on erroneous assumptions about public opinion after the Tet offensive, but also on account of a confluence of other, more fundamental factors than what they referred to euphemistically as division in the nation. Even then, to the Wise Men, those divisions probably meant divisions in establishment opinion, division among Democratic politicians and opinion leaders, not the dissent represented by radicals in the streets.

The antiwar movement succeeded eventually in limiting U.S. military involvement only to the extent that antiwar sentiment became reliberalized through the Democratic Party and its post-1969 Moratorium youth contingent. At that point, only after the fizzled incandescence of the New Left in the 1968–69 period, the movement affected marginally the timing and perhaps the tone of the decision to negotiate withdrawal, and this was done in consort with the Congress—hardly an extra-parliamentary phenomenon over all. The movement was not responsible for the overthrow of policy itself; that rested first with Lyndon Johnson's decision to change U.S. policy aims and then with Richard Nixon's decision to limit them further in deference to broader foreign and domestic policy goals.

We mustn't forget, too, while the movement moved back toward and into the Democratic Party between 1970 and 1974, that party never had a chance to freely pursue its own plans for withdrawal from Vietnam. This is because the Republicans won the White House in the 1968 election. In other words, another layer, or filter— a Republican White House—interposed itself between the flow of antiwar sentiment into mainstream politics and actual executive branch decisions about the war. President Nixon did shape his administration's diplomatic and military policies over Vietnam to what he thought domestic political traffic would bear, but that isn't the same as claiming that the movement had a direct restraining influence on administration policy. Rather, the deradicalized movement merged with growing broad public antiwar sentiment, which pushed the Democrats, and the Democrats pushed the Republicans, who, as practicing politicians, were already looking toward the next midterm and presidential elections. Such dynamics describe what radical movement activists used to refer to derisively as "working through the system." It is hardly heroic, and hardly the stuff of which many antiwar radicals were proud then and are still proud of today.

As antiwar sentiment became more firmly ensconced in the Congress, it contributed to the cutoff of U.S. aid to South Vietnam, undermined Saigon's confidence, and contributed to its fall to the Communist regime in Hanoi. This might not have happened had the Nixon administration taken a different approach to the Paris Accords and to foreign policy priorities generally. That is to say: The White House made the essential decision to disengage using the Paris Accords as a means to create a "decent interval." It was a decision not to find out if Vietnamization would work if it took 10 or 12 years instead of 2 or 3. There was nothing inevitable about this decision, but, with a new global foreign policy to unfurl and an election to win in 1972, Richard Nixon made it. To blame the Congress entirely for the fall of South Vietnam is unfair. To blame—or credit—the antiwar movement isn't justified in the least.

The antiwar movement neither lost the war nor caused the subsequent bloodbath in Southeast Asia. In the broadest sense, the war was lost because the American ship of state itself had lost its bearings. The expansion of containment to Asia and its post–Korean War militarization merged with a rapidly expanding economic base to produce a level of American hubris that was bound to send its ship of state onto the rocks sooner or later. However morally motivated, the U.S. commitment to Vietnam was strategically unsound; thus, even had the war been won the costs might well have exceeded any strategic benefits. But the war was not won because U.S. administrative, diplomatic, and especially military strategies failed. In other words, even beyond a flawed decision to commit itself, which flowed from the lack of a realistic strategy for containing polycentric Communism in the geostrategic peripheries of the Cold War, the Vietnam War was lost by some combination of the U.S. military's inability to adapt to politico-military counterinsurgency warfare, ill-advised micromanagement of the war by Pentagon civilians, and maladroit meddling in South Vietnam's stygian political system. None of these sources of American defeat was set in motion or significantly worsened either by antiwar activism or by fear of it in Washington.

What happened to the Vietnamese and Cambodian people happened because the war was lost, but, again, the antiwar movement did not play a major role in that. The only way to argue otherwise is to assume that the movement bolstered Hanoi's morale to a decisive degree as it contemplated the "correlation of forces." No doubt the antiwar movement did boost morale in Hanoi to some degree—how could it not?—but no evidence suggests it was decisive.

Even if we assume the war was unwinnable, it still does not follow that the antiwar movement can take credit for driving that point home. The Wise Men and their bureaucratic allies made their decisions after the Tet offensive in light of their own sense of limits. After all, by March 1968 the United States had already gone beyond its self-imposed restrictions and still not won, and it had to contemplate the possibility of causing still greater damage to American life and squandering still more of its treasure without victory. Such a specter was quite sufficient to generate a change of view; it required no help from the street.

About the essential decision to fight in Vietnam, the antiwar movement was right but for the wrong reasons. The war's sources had nothing to do with the sinister face of corporate capitalism, but the war *was* a mistake. The Johnson administration *was* pursuing policies that, even though well-intended, were incoherent and unwise. Public dissent against those policies was a reasonable response to such unwisdom. There is, after all, nothing sinister about protesting either a futile war or the steely hubris of a government that cannot recognize or admit that it has erred.

The antiwar movement was not responsible for the basic flow of American government judgments about Vietnam, and what minor influence it did have tended to reinforce policy stasis during the Johnson period and to quicken modestly the reduction of military activity during the Nixon period. How does this affect common arguments about the merit, the guilt, and the responsibility that the antiwar movement should bear for what happened in Southeast Asia after 1975?

Few can doubt that a horrific bloodbath took place in Southeast Asia after 1975, and that millions of people who suddenly wanted desperately to escape their homeland did so for good reason. Doves have tended to argue that the antiwar movement saved American lives but did not sacrifice Asian ones because the war was unwinnable, and what was going to happen was going to happen eventually anyway. American participation in the war made what happened worse, they claim, especially in Cambodia, but it never could have made anything better. Most hawks have claimed the reverse, blaming what happened directly on the loss of the war, and the loss of the war on the antiwar movement and other related maladies on the home front. What are we to make of these judgments in light of the analysis brought here?

One way to answer this question is to divide our thinking into consideration of intentions and consequences. Judging intentions alone is often fruitless because the world rarely abets the simple transformation of intentions, whether good or evil, into intended consequences. Judging consequences alone, however, can suggest the premise that history proclaims its own meaning—that what happened was meant to happen—but it doesn't.

What goes for the antiwar movement goes for the war itself. Even if we discount the impact of the movement, it is still no simple matter to determine how much of what happened in Southeast Asia after 1975 was the fault of the United States. Would South Vietnam have survived without American intervention in 1964–65? If not, did all the United States achieve amount to a delay of a decade? Was that worth 58,000 American lives? Would Cambodia have been spared Pol Pot and then a Vietnamese occupation had the Nixon administration not bombed and invaded the country? Or doesn't it follow instead that a quicker Communist victory in Vietnam would have brought the Khmer Rouge to power sooner rather than later? So in consideration of intentions and consequences it is best to consider those of the antiwar movement and the government it opposed together.

As to intentions, the great majority of those active in the antiwar movement clearly felt themselves to be patriotic Americans. The movement cannot be fairly characterized as having been made up of primarily individuals who were self-hating, psychologically aberrant, or sociopathic. Acts of self-sacrifice, powerful idealism, and a deep love of country characterized the antiwar movement at least in part throughout its existence.

The U.S. government was also well-intended. It wished to stop Communism because it believed it to be wrong, and it wanted to help the Vietnamese achieve self-determination because it believed that to be right. There was no hidden agenda of economic exploitation, of seeking bases in order to wage aggressive war against China, of fighting mainly to generate profits for a military-industrial complex.

But good intentions are not always useful measures for judgment because everyone except the pathologically ill is well-intended at least on an abstract level. When parts of the antiwar movement came to believe that love for country required destroying all existing social structures and norms, it adopted the same dubious logic (dubiously) attributed to a U.S. military commander who said that a certain Vietnamese village had to be destroyed in order to be saved. When the Johnson administration went to war, it did almost everything wrong, from undermining the Saigon government instead of building it up to pushing peasants and intellectuals both into the arms of the Vietcong instead of the other way around. Instead of being flexible enough to recognize error, the U.S. military pursued its counterproductive behavior to a virtual point of no return, politically if not literally, on the battlefield. So much for good intentions.

When one speaks of consequences, on the other hand, the first thing to remember is that ethics is a serious discipline. Several popular but blithe judgments that have been made about Vietnam slide off the low end of the logic scale. Some have argued, for example, that the war effort was worth it, despite the loss of South Vietnam, because it bought a decade's worth of time for the rest of Southeast Asia to mobilize and develop, and for ASEAN (the Association of Southeast Asian Nations) to consolidate. Is this really what 58,000 Americans died for?

Others have argued that since Communism is dead anyway, and since Vietnam is a basket case, it proves that even bothering to stop Communism in Southeast Asia was a stupid thing to do in the first place. Mickey Kaus of *The New Republic* argued that the best case against Communism in the area is Vietnam's economic failure, a case that never could have been made had the United States won the war: "Vietnam may even (in the long run) be better off for the Communists' victory. In power they discredited themselves in a way that never would have been possible if they'd remained a Philippine-like guerrilla opposition."

This is a worthwhile line of reasoning if only because it makes nonsense of Frances Fitzgerald's prophecies about the "cleansing effects" of the Vietnamese revolution. The only thing that the Vietnamese revolution cleansed, or should have cleansed, was the foolish idea that Third World revolutions are cleansing. But Kaus never mentions costs: the re-education camps; the boat people who left, risking or giving their lives in the process; and the millions living in deepening poverty and fear under Hanoi's iron fist since 1975. Is scoring a rarefied debating point about Asian Communism worth it to those who have paid the price? Too bad Kaus never bothered to ask them.

Clearly, justifying the war post hoc on the basis of "results" that were neither primary nor explicit is not very compelling. Neither is justifying opposition to the war based on information no one could possibly have had at the time; obviously, it isn't much of an achievement to conclude that the war was unwinnable after one already knows the outcome. Just because something is hard to do—such as bringing ethics to bear on a war after the fact—is no reason to be satisfied with arguments like these.

Moral judgment is always a problem but always a necessity. So I make mine: Both the government and the antiwar movement were well-intentioned, and both failed to translate good intentions into good consequences. The same can probably be said for both South and North Vietnamese leaders. Simply put, what happened both here and in Southeast Asia is that the mistakes of the powerful overwhelmed the mistakes of the weak. Is it so, as Nietzsche said, that "the errors of great men are venerable because they are more fruitful than the truths of little men"? No, they are only more horrible. The antiwar movement never came close to doing the sort of harm that the failed policies of the U.S. government did. Unfortunately, it seems fairly clear that neither movement nor government did anybody in Vietnam any good at all.

✗ F U R T H E R   R E A D I N G

Anderson, Terry H. *The Movement and the Sixties* (1995).

Bacciocco, Edward I. *The New Left in America* (1974).

Baskir, Lawrence M., and William A. Strauss. *Chance and Circumstance* (1978) (on the draft).

Berman, William C. *William Fulbright and the Vietnam War* (1988).

Burstein, Paul, and William Fredenberg. "Changing Public Policy: The Impact of Public Opinion, Anti-War Demonstrations, and War Costs on Senate Voting on Vietnam War Motions," *American Journal of Sociology,* 84 (1978), 99–122.

DeBenedetti, Charles. *The Peace Reform in American History* (1980).

———. "On the Significance of Citizen Peace Activism: America, 1961–1975," *Peace and Change,* 9 (1983), 6–20.

Dellinger, David. *From Yale to Jail* (1993).

Franklin, H. Bruce. *Vietnam and Other American Fantasies* (2000).

Gottlieb, Sherry Gershon. *Hell No We Won't Go: Resisting the Draft during the Vietnam War* (1991).

Hall, Mitchell K. *Because of Their Faith: CALCAV and Religious Opposition to the Vietnam War* (1990).

Halstead, Fred. *Out Now* (1978).

Hatcher, Patrick Lloyd. *The Suicide of an Elite: American Internationalists and Vietnam* (1990).

Hayden, Tom. *Reunion* (1988).

Heineman, Kenneth H. *Campus Wars: The Peace Movement at American State Universities in the Vietnam Era* (1993).

Hodgson, Godfrey. *America in Our Time* (1976).

Hunt, Andrew. *The Turning: A History of Vietnam Veterans Against the War* (2001).

Katz, Milton S. "Peace Liberals and Vietnam: SANE and the Politics of 'Responsible' Protest," *Peace and Change,* 9 (1983), 21–39.

Kendrick, Alexander. *The Wound Within* (1974).

Levy, David W. *The Debate over Vietnam* (1991).

Lunch, William L., and Peter W. Sperlich. "American Public Opinion and the War in Vietnam," *Western Political Quarterly,* 32 (1979), 21–44.

Matusow, Allen I. *The Unraveling of America* (1984).

Miller, James. *"Democracy is in the Streets"* (on SDS) (1987).

Moser, Richard R. *The New Winter Soldiers* (1996).

Nicosia, Gerald. *Home to War: A History of the Vietnam Veterans' Movement* (2001).

Powers, Thomas. *Vietnam: The War at Home* (1973).

Rorabaugh, W. J. *Berkeley at War: The University of California in the 1960s* (1989).

Rosenberg, Milton, Sidney Verba, and Phillip Converse. *Vietnam and the Silent Majority* (1970).

Sale, Kirkpatrick. *SDS* (1973).

Schalk, David L. *War and the Ivory Tower: Algeria and Vietnam* (1991).

Small, Melvin. *Johnson, Nixon, and the Doves* (1988).

Small, Melvin, and William D. Hoover, eds. *Give Peace a Chance: Exploring the Vietnam Antiwar Movement* (1992).

Stacewicz, Richard, ed. *Winter Soldiers: An Oral History of the Vietnam Veterans Against the War* (1997).

Tomes, Robert R. *Apocalypse Then: American Intellectuals and the Vietnam War* (1998).

Vickers, George R. *The Formation of the New Left: The Early Years* (1975).

Viorst, Milton. *Fire in the Streets* (1979).

Vogelgesang, Sandy. *The Long Dark Night of the Soul: The American Intellectual Left and the Vietnam War* (1974).

Weinstein, James. *Ambiguous Legacy: The Left in American Politics* (1975).

Wells, Tom. *The War Within* (1994).

———. *Wild Man* (on Daniel Ellsberg) (2001).

Woods, Randall B. *Fulbright* (1995).

Young, Nigel. *An Infantile Disorder?: The Crisis and Decline of the New Left* (1977).

Zaroulis, Nancy, and Gerald Sullivan. *Who Spoke Up?* (1984).

The Paris Peace Accords
of 1973 and the
Fall of South Vietnam

✕

The Paris Peace Accords left many fundamental problems unresolved. North Vietnam had not abandoned its long-held objective of unifying the country under its direction. Nor had South Vietnam abandoned its goal of maintaining a government free of communist influence. Given those irreconcilable ambitions, it should not be surprising that the Paris agreements never brought peace to Vietnam. In fact, in the weeks immediately following the signing ceremony in January 1973, both sides were guilty of flagrant truce violations, which worsened throughout 1973 and 1974.

The United States continued to provide massive economic and military support to the Thieu regime. But with the spreading Watergate scandal, Congress reasserted its constitutional role in foreign affairs, denying or limiting many Nixon administration requests for aid to South Vietnam. Congress's hand was strengthened when the Watergate revelations forced Richard M. Nixon to resign as president in August 1974. His successor, Gerald R. Ford, faced an increasingly activist Congress that was reluctant to undertake any new commitments in Vietnam.

When North Vietnam launched a major military offensive in the spring of 1975, officials in Hanoi were evidently as stunned as those in Washington by the rapidity of South Vietnam's disintegration. Congress refused to comply with the Ford administration's last-minute request for emergency aid. On April 30, the South Vietnamese government formally capitulated. Ten years after the introduction of U.S. combat forces, and nearly thirty years after Ho Chi Minh's declaration of independence, the struggle for Vietnam was over. The triumphant northerners quickly gave Saigon a new name—Ho Chi Minh City.

This final phase of the Vietnam War has sparked much political and scholarly controversy. Why did the peace agreement break down so quickly? Which side bears primary responsibility for failing to fulfill its provisions? Why did South Vietnam collapse so swiftly in the face of North Vietnam's offensive? What role did the United States play in these events? Did Washington abandon its ally at a critical moment?

*Might additional American aid or military support have enabled Saigon to survive?
And finally, how is the communist victory best explained?*

✗ D O C U M E N T S

In a letter of January 5, 1973, Richard M. Nixon tried to reassure Nguyen Van Thieu
about the future of his regime. One of a series of letters exchanged between the two
leaders before the signing of the Paris Peace Accords, it is reprinted here as Document 1.
Key sections of the multilateral part of those accords follow. They were signed in Paris
on January 27, 1973, by representatives of the United States, North Vietnam, South
Vietnam, and the Provisional Revolutionary Government. On April 15, 1975, Secretary
of State Henry A. Kissinger appealed to Congress to provide emergency aid to South
Vietnam, then reeling from North Vietnam's military offensive; his request is reprinted
as Document 3.

The remaining documents are reminiscences. Secretary of Defense James R.
Schlesinger, Jr., recalls the advice that he gave President Ford as South Vietnam
appeared on the verge of collapse. Next, a member of the South Vietnamese air force
and a sixteen-year-old civilian give their personal recollections of South Vietnam's
final days. Then, General Van Tien Dung offers a North Vietnamese perspective on the
fall of Saigon. Finally, in Document 8, excerpted from his memoirs, Nixon places the
blame for South Vietnam's fall on Congress.

1. Richard M. Nixon Reassures
Nguyen Van Thieu, 1973

This will acknowledge your letter of December 20, 1972.

There is nothing substantial that I can add to my many previous messages, including my December 17 letter, which clearly stated my opinions and intentions.
With respect to the question of North Vietnamese troops, we will again present
your views to the Communists as we have done vigorously at every other opportunity in the negotiations. The result is certain to be once more the rejection of our
position. We have explained to you repeatedly why we believe the problem of North
Vietnamese troops is manageable under the agreement, and I see no reason to repeat
all the arguments.

We will proceed next week in Paris along the lines that General [Alexander]
Haig explained to you. Accordingly, if the North Vietnamese meet our concerns on
the two outstanding substantive issues in the agreement, concerning the DMZ and
the method of signing, and if we can arrange acceptable supervisory machinery,
we will proceed to conclude the settlement. The gravest consequences would then
ensue if your government chose to reject the agreement and split off from the United
States. As I said in my December 17 letter, "I am convinced that your refusal to
join us would be an invitation to disaster—to the loss of all that we together have
fought for over the past decade. It would be inexcusable above all because we will
have lost a just and honorable alternative."

Letter from Nixon to Thieu, January 5, 1973, reprinted in *New York Times,* May 1, 1975, p. 16.

As we enter this new round of talks, I hope that our countries will now show a united front. It is imperative for our common objectives that your government take no further actions that complicate our task and would make more difficult the acceptance of the settlement by all parties. We will keep you informed of the negotiations in Paris through daily briefings of Ambassador Lam.

I can only repeat what I have so often said: The best guarantee for the survival of South Vietnam is the unity of our two countries which would be gravely jeopardized if you persist in your present course. The actions of our Congress since its return have clearly borne out the many warnings we have made.

Should you decide, as I trust you will, to go with us, you have my assurance of continued assistance in the post-settlement period and that we will respond with full force should the settlement be violated by North Vietnam. So once more I conclude with an appeal to you to close ranks with us.

2. The Paris Peace Accords, 1973

The Parties participating in the Paris Conference on Viet-Nam,

With a view to ending the war and restoring peace in Viet-Nam on the basis of respect for the Vietnamese people's fundamental national rights and the South Vietnamese people's right to self-determination, and to contributing to the consolidation of peace in Asia and the world.

Have agreed on the following provisions and undertake to respect and to implement them:

Chapter I   The Vietnamese People's Fundamental National Rights

Article I.   The United States and all other countries respect the independence, sovereignty, unity, and territorial integrity of Viet-Nam as recognized by the 1954 Geneva Agreements on Viet-Nam.

Chapter II   Cessation of Hostilities—Withdrawal of Troops

Article 2.   A cease-fire shall be observed throughout South Viet-Nam as of 2400 hours G.M.T., on January 27, 1973.

At the same hour, the United States will stop all its military activities against the territory of the Democratic Republic of Viet-Nam by ground, air and naval forces, wherever they may be based, and end the mining of the territorial waters, ports, harbors, and waterways of the Democratic Republic of Viet-Nam. The United States will remove, permanently deactivate or destroy all the mines in the territorial waters, ports, harbors, and waterways of North Viet-Nam as soon as this Agreement goes into effect.

The complete cessation of hostilities mentioned in this Article shall be durable and without limit of time.

Article 3.   The parties undertake to maintain the cease-fire and to ensure a lasting and stable peace.

U.S. Treaties and Other International Agreements, 1 USC 112A, v. 24, pt. 1.

As soon as the cease-fire goes into effect:

a. The United States forces and those of the other foreign countries allied with the United States and the Republic of Viet-Nam shall remain in-place pending the implementation of the plan of troop withdrawal. The Four-Party Joint Military Commission described in Article 16 shall determine the modalities.

b. The armed forces of the two South Vietnamese parties shall remain in-place. The Two-Party Joint Military Commission described in Article 17 [not included here] shall determine the areas controlled by each party and the modalities of stationing.

c. The regular forces of all services and arms and the irregular forces of the parties in South Viet-Nam shall stop all offensive activities against each other and shall strictly abide by the following stipulations:

• All acts of force on the ground, in the air, and on the sea shall be prohibited;

• All hostile acts, terrorism and reprisals by both sides will be banned.

Article 4. The United States will not continue its military involvement or intervene in the internal affairs of South Viet-Nam.

Article 5. Within sixty days of the signing of this Agreement, there will be a total withdrawal from South Viet-Nam of troops, military advisers, and military personnel, including technical military personnel and military personnel associated with the pacification program, armaments, munitions, and war material of the United States and those of the other foreign countries mentioned in Article 3 (a). Advisers from the above-mentioned countries to all paramilitary organizations and the police force will also be withdrawn within the same period of time.

Article 6. The dismantlement of all military bases in South Viet-Nam of the United States and of the other foreign countries mentioned in Article 3 (a) shall be completed within sixty days of the signing of this Agreement.

Article 7. From the enforcement of the cease-fire to the formation of the government provided for in Article 9 (b) and 14 of this Agreement, the two South Vietnamese parties shall not accept the introduction of troops, military advisers, and military personnel including technical military personnel, armaments, munitions, and war material into South Viet-Nam.

The two South Vietnamese parties shall be permitted to make periodic replacement of armaments, munitions and war material which have been destroyed, damaged, worn out or used up after the cease-fire, on the basis of piece-for-piece, of the same characteristics and properties, under the supervision of the Joint Military Commission of the two South Vietnamese parties and of the International Commission of Control and Supervision.

Chapter III   The Return of Captured Military Personnel and Foreign Civilians, and Captured and Detained Vietnamese Civilian Personnel

Article 8

a. The return of captured military personnel and foreign civilians of the parties shall be carried out simultaneously with and completed not later than the same day as the troop withdrawal mentioned in Article 5. The parties shall exchange complete lists of the above-mentioned captured military personnel and foreign civilians on the day of the signing of this Agreement.

b. The Parties shall help each other to get information about those military personnel and foreign civilians of the parties missing in action, to determine the location and take care of the graves of the dead so as to facilitate the exhumation and repatriation of the remains, and to take any such other measures as may be required to get information about those still considered missing in action.

c. The question of the return of Vietnamese civilian personnel captured and detailed in South Viet-Nam will be resolved by the two South Vietnamese parties on the basis of the principles of Article 21 (b) of the Agreement on the Cessation of Hostilities in Viet-Nam of July 20, 1954. The two South Vietnamese parties will do so in a spirit of national reconciliation and concord, with a view to ending hatred and enmity, in order to ease suffering and to reunite families. The two South Vietnamese parties will do their utmost to resolve this question within ninety days after the cease-fire comes into effect.

Chapter IV   The Exercise of the South Vietnamese People's Right to Self-Determination

Article 9.   The Government of the United States of America and the Government of the Democratic Republic of Viet-Nam undertake to respect the following principles for the exercise of the South Vietnamese people's right to self-determination:

a. The South Vietnamese people's right to self-determination is sacred, inalienable, and shall be respected by all countries.

b. The South Vietnamese people shall decide themselves the political future of South Viet-Nam through genuinely free and democratic general elections under international supervision.

c. Foreign countries shall not impose any political tendency or personality on the South Vietnamese people.

Article 10.   The two South Vietnamese parties undertake to respect the cease-fire and maintain peace in South Viet-Nam, settle all matters of contention through negotiations, and avoid all armed conflict.

Article II.   Immediately after the cease-fire, the two South Vietnamese parties will:
•   achieve national reconciliation and concord, end hatred and enmity, prohibit all acts of reprisal and discrimination against individuals or organizations that have collaborated with one side or the other;
•   ensure the democratic liberties of the people: personal freedom, freedom of speech, freedom of the press, freedom of meeting, freedom of organization, freedom of political activities, freedom of belief, freedom of movement, freedom of residence, freedom of work, right to property ownership, and right to free enterprise.

Article 12

a. Immediately after the cease-fire, the two South Vietnamese parties shall hold consultations in a spirit of national reconciliation and concord, mutual respect, and mutual non-elimination to set up a National Council of National Reconciliation and Concord of three equal segments. The Council shall operate on the principle of unanimity. After the National Council of National Reconciliation and Concord has assumed its functions, the two South Vietnamese parties will consult about the formation of councils at lower levels. The two South Vietnamese parties shall sign an agreement on the internal matters of South Viet-Nam as soon as possible and do their utmost to accomplish this within ninety days after the cease-fire comes into effect, in keeping with the South Vietnamese people's aspirations for peace, independence and democracy.

b. The National Council of National Reconciliation and Concord shall have the task of promoting the two South Vietnamese parties' implementation of this Agreement, achievement of national reconciliation and concord and ensurance of democratic liberties. The National Council of National Reconciliation and Concord will organize the free and democratic general elections provided for in Article 9 (b) and decide the procedures and modalities of these general elections. The institutions for which the general elections are to be held will be agreed upon through consultations between the two South Vietnamese parties. The National Council of National Reconciliation and Concord will also decide the procedures and modalities of such local elections as the two South Vietnamese parties agree upon.

Article 13. The question of Vietnamese armed forces in South Viet-Nam shall be settled by the two South Vietnamese parties in a spirit of national reconciliation and concord, equality and mutual respect, without foreign interference, in accordance with the postwar situation. Among the questions to be discussed by the two South Vietnamese parties are steps to reduce their military effectiveness and to demobilize the troops being reduced. The two South Vietnamese parties will accomplish this as soon as possible.

Article 14. South Viet-Nam will pursue a foreign policy of peace and independence. It will be prepared to establish relations with all countries irrespective of their political and social systems on the basis of mutual respect for independence and sovereignty and accept economic and technical aid from any country with no political conditions attached. The acceptance of military aid by South Viet-Nam in the future shall come under the authority of the government set up after the general elections in South Viet-Nam provided for in Article 9 (b).

Chapter V   The Reunification of Viet-Nam and the Relationship Between North and South Viet-Nam

Article 15. The reunification of Viet-Nam shall be carried out step by step through peaceful means on the basis of discussions and agreements between North and South Viet-Nam, without coercion or annexation by either party, and without foreign interference. The time for reunification will be agreed upon by North and South Viet-Nam.

Pending reunification:

a. The military demarcation line between the two zones at the 17th parallel is only provisional and not a political or territorial boundary, as provided for in paragraph 6 of the Final Declaration of the 1954 Geneva Conference.

b. North and South Viet-Nam shall respect the Demilitarized Zone on either side of the Provisional Military Demarcation Line.

c. North and South Viet-Nam shall promptly start negotiations with a view to reestablishing normal relations in various fields. Among the questions to be negotiated are the modalities of civilian movement across the Provisional Military Demarcation Line.

d. North and South Viet-Nam shall not join any military alliance or military bloc and shall not allow foreign powers to maintain military bases, troops, military advisers, and military personnel on their respective territories, as stipulated in the 1954 Geneva Agreements on Viet-Nam.

3. Henry A. Kissinger Appeals to Congress for Emergency Aid, 1975

The long and agonizing conflict in Indochina has reached a tragic stage. The events of the past month have been discussed at great length before the Congress and require little additional elaboration. In Viet-Nam President Thieu ordered a strategic withdrawal from a number of areas he regarded as militarily untenable. However, the withdrawal took place in great haste, without adequate advance planning, and with insufficient coordination. It was further complicated by a massive flow of civilian refugees seeking to escape the advancing North Vietnamese Army. Disorganization engendered confusion; fear led to panic. The results, as we all know, were tragic losses—of territory, of population, of material, and of morale.

But to fully understand what has happened, it is necessary to have an appreciation of all that went before. The North Vietnamese offensive, and the South Vietnamese response, did not come about by chance—although chance is always an element in warfare. The origins of these events are complex, and I believe it would be useful to review them briefly.

Since January 1973, Hanoi has violated—continuously, systematically, and energetically—the most fundamental provisions of the Paris agreement. It steadily increased the numbers of its troops in the South. It improved and expanded its logistics system in the South. It increased the armaments and ammunition of its forces in the South. And as you know, it blocked all efforts to account for personnel missing in action. These are facts, and they are indisputable. All of these actions were of course in total violation of the agreement. Parallel to these efforts, Hanoi attempted—with considerable success—to immobilize the various mechanisms established by the agreement to monitor and curtail violations of the cease-fire. Thus, it assiduously prepared the way for further military actions.

South Viet-Nam's record of adherence to the agreement has not been perfect. It is, however, qualitatively and quantitatively far better than Hanoi's. South Viet-Nam did not build up its armed forces. It undertook no major offensive actions—although it traded thrusts and probes with the Communists. It cooperated fully in establishing and supporting the cease-fire control mechanisms provided for in the agreement. And it sought, as did the United States, full implementation of those provisions of the agreement calling for an accounting of soldiers missing in action.

Kissinger testimony, April 17, 1975, U.S. Department of State *Bulletin,* 72 (May 1975), 583–586.

But perhaps more relevant to an understanding of recent events are the following factors.

While North Viet-Nam had available several reserve divisions which it could commit to battle at times and places of its choosing, the South had no strategic reserves. Its forces were stretched thin, defending lines of communication and population centers throughout the country.

While North Viet-Nam, by early this year, had accumulated in South Viet-Nam enough ammunition for two years of intensive combat, South Vietnamese commanders had to ration ammunition as their stocks declined and were not replenished.

While North Viet-Nam had enough fuel in the South to operate its tanks and armored vehicles for at least 18 months, South Viet-Nam faced stringent shortages.

In sum, while Hanoi was strengthening its army in the South, the combat effectiveness of South Viet-Nam's army gradually grew weaker. While Hanoi built up its reserve divisions and accumulated ammunition, fuel, and other military supplies, U.S. aid levels to Viet-Nam were cut—first by half in 1973 and then by another third in 1974. This coincided with a worldwide inflation and a fourfold increase in fuel prices. As a result almost all of our military aid had to be devoted to ammunition and fuel. Very little was available for spare parts, and none for new equipment.

These imbalances became painfully evident when the offensive broke full force, and they contributed to the tragedy which unfolded. Moreover, the steady diminution in the resources available to the Army of South Viet-Nam unquestionably affected the morale of its officers and men. South Vietnamese units in the northern and central provinces knew full well that they faced an enemy superior both in numbers and in firepower. They knew that reinforcements and resupply would not be forthcoming. When the fighting began they also knew, as they had begun to suspect, that the United States would not respond. I would suggest that all of these factors added significantly to the sense of helplessness, despair, and, eventually, panic which we witnessed in late March and early April.

I would add that it is both inaccurate and unfair to hold South Viet-Nam responsible for blocking progress toward a political solution to the conflict. Saigon's proposals in its conversations with PRO [Provisional Revolutionary Government] representatives in Paris were in general constructive and conciliatory. There was no progress toward a compromise political settlement because Hanoi intended that there should not be. Instead, North Viet-Nam's strategy was to lay the groundwork for an eventual military offensive, one which would either bring outright victory or at least allow Hanoi to dictate the terms of a political solution.

Neither the United States nor South Viet-Nam entered into the Paris agreement with the expectation that Hanoi would abide by it in every respect. We did believe, however, that the agreement was sufficiently equitable to both sides that its major provisions could be accepted and acted upon by Hanoi and that the contest could be shifted thereby from a military to a political track. However, our two governments also recognized that, since the agreement manifestly was not self-enforcing, Hanoi's adherence depended heavily on maintaining a military parity in South Viet-Nam. . . .

The present situation in Viet-Nam is ominous. North Viet-Nam's combat forces far outnumber those of the South, and they are better armed. Perhaps more important, they enjoy a psychological momentum which can be as decisive as armaments in battle. South Viet-Nam must reorganize and reequip its forces, and it must restore the morale of its army and its people. These tasks will be difficult, and they can be performed only by the South Vietnamese. However, a successful defense will also require resources—arms, fuel, ammunition, and medical supplies—and these can come only from the United States.

Large quantities of equipment and supplies, totaling perhaps $800 million, were lost in South Viet-Nam's precipitous retreat from the northern and central areas. Much of this should not have been lost, and we regret that it happened. But South Viet-Nam is now faced with a different strategic and tactical situation and different military requirements. Although the amount of military assistance the President has requested is of the same general magnitude as the value of the equipment lost, we are not attempting simply to replace those losses. The President's request, based on General Weyand's [Gen. Frederick C. Weyand, Chief of Staff, United States Army] assessment, represents our best judgment as to what is needed now, in this new situation, to defend what is left of South Viet-Nam. Weapons, ammunition, and supplies to reequip four divisions, to form a number of ranger groups into divisional units, and to upgrade some territorial forces into infantry regiments will require some $326 million. The balance of our request is for ammunition, fuel, spare parts, and medical supplies to sustain up to 60 days of intensive combat and to pay for the cost of transporting those items. These are minimum requirements, and they are needed urgently.

The human tragedy of Viet-Nam has never been more acute than it now is. Hundreds of thousands of South Vietnamese have sought to flee Communist control and are homeless refugees. They have our compassion, and they must also have our help. Despite commendable efforts by the South Vietnamese Government, the burden of caring for these innocent victims is beyond its capacity. The United States has already done much to assist these people, but many remain without adequate food, shelter, or medical care. The President has asked that additional efforts and additional resources be devoted to this humanitarian effort. I ask that the Congress respond generously and quickly.

The objectives of the United States in this immensely difficult situation remain as they were when the Paris agreement was signed—to end the military conflict and establish conditions which will allow a fair political solution to be achieved. We believe that despite the tragic experience to date, the Paris agreement remains a valid framework within which to proceed toward such a solution. However, today, as in 1973, battlefield conditions will affect political perceptions and the outcome of negotiations. We therefore believe that in order for a political settlement to be reached which preserves any degree of self-determination for the people of South Viet-Nam, the present military situation must be stabilized. It is for these reasons that the President has asked Congress to appropriate urgently additional funds for military assistance for Viet-Nam.

I am acutely aware of the emotions aroused in this country by our long and difficult involvement in Viet-Nam. I understand what the cost has been for this nation and why frustration and anger continue to dominate our national debate. Many will argue that we have done more than enough for the Government and the people of South Viet-Nam. I do not agree with that proposition, however, nor do I believe that to review endlessly the wisdom of our original involvement serves a useful purpose now. For despite the agony of this nation's experience in Indochina and the substantial reappraisal which has taken place concerning our proper role there, few would deny that we are still involved or that what we do—or fail to do—will still weigh heavily in the outcome. We cannot by our actions alone insure the survival of South Viet-Nam. But we can, alone, by our inaction assure its demise.

The United States has no legal obligation to the Government and the people of South Viet-Nam of which the Congress is not aware. But we do have a deep moral obligation—rooted in the history of our involvement and sustained by the continuing efforts of our friends. We cannot easily set it aside. In addition to the obvious consequences for the people of Viet-Nam, our failure to act in accordance with that obligation would inevitably influence other nations' perceptions of our constancy and our determination. American credibility would not collapse, and American honor would not be destroyed. But both would be weakened, to the detriment of this nation and of the peaceful world order we have sought to build.

4. James R. Schlesinger, Jr., Recalls the Collapse of South Vietnam (1975), 1987

My first inkling that we had lost came when the North Vietnamese began to make maneuvers toward the end of 1974 and in January of 1975 and we did not respond. They were testing us. They did not really believe that they were getting away with what they were getting away with. But given the constraints under which we had to operate, I knew they were going to get away with it. Then of course came the attack in the Central Highlands and the total collapse of the ARVN divisions. At that point it was all over. I had been making menacing sounds in public whenever the subject of North Vietnam had come up—they'd just better beware, and so forth. But the congressional restraints that had been established in the summer of '73 wouldn't permit our taking effective countermeasures.

Now, many of the people who were with me were people who had served there, and they had emotional ties to the country, and they just could not—and I understand it, and I'm not criticizing them—back off and say "We did our best, but it is now hopeless." They kept seeing hope where hope did not exist. [General] Fred Weyand, for example, whom Ford had sent out to Southeast Asia, was tied to Thieu and to the Vietnamese with bonds of loyalty. He came back and reported to the President, that six hundred and fifty million bucks is needed.

Before Mr. Ford asked for additional assistance in Vietnam we had a meeting of the NSC, and I said "Mr. President, it's all over." He was kind of rankled by that, quite indignant. I got sort of the Michigan fight song. And I said "Mr. President, you should go up to the Hill tomorrow and say we have suffered a severe setback, call for blood, sweat, and tears, and a national effort to deal with the consequences, but there's no way that you can persuade anybody that Vietnam is salvageable."

5. A South Vietnamese Pilot Reflects on His Country's Defeat (1975), 1990

My parents moved to the South in 1954, when the country was partitioned and the Communists took over the North. I was just one year old at the time. My parents knew the Communists and did not want to live under their government. So they came south to freedom.

I joined the Air Force and went to flight school. I got out of flight school in early April of 1975. By that time, when pilots flew they never had enough fuel. We had to take some planes apart in order to get parts for other planes. And we never had enough bullets. We had to count the bullets for the planes. We wanted to fight. But how could we fight without weapons?

Some of us in the Air Force talked to each other about the possibility of losing the war. But when we talked like that we were afraid because we thought maybe we had heard too much Communist propaganda. We knew that we had good generals at the top. As long as we had good generals, how could we lose?

I was at Tan Son Nhut on April 28 when North Vietnamese pilots bombed us. They came over in A-37s and dropped bombs on us. It didn't frighten me at all. In 1968 during Tet, the Communists had come into the city, too, and we pushed them out. So this was nothing new to us. But then, on April 29, we heard that our generals had run away. We couldn't believe it. We—the young ones—we expected to continue fighting. But how could we fight when there were no generals to lead us any more?

On the morning of April 30 all of the pilots were talking about a message they had heard on the emergency radio channel. They said that the American fleet had told all Vietnamese pilots to bring their aircraft out to the ships so that they would not fall into Communist hands. Many of the pilots took helicopters filled with people out to the American fleet after they heard that message.

I wasn't yet sure that I wanted to leave. So I didn't go out on a helicopter. I knew that there were still soldiers fighting in the Delta. So I thought maybe I would go south and join them. But then, late in the morning, I heard that the government had already surrendered to the Communists. Only then did I decide to leave.

I went with a friend down to the Saigon River. There was a boat that was just leaving, so we decided to get on it. We were feeling bad about leaving, but when the government surrendered, there was no more hope. People in Saigon were celebrating because they had been fooled by the Communists. They thought that when the Communists took over there would be no more war. But now they would have to learn.

When our boat went down the Saigon River no one fired at us. There were more than 3,000 people on the boat—men, women and children. We had no food or water on board and we did not know what would happen once we got into the South China Sea. But we believed that we could not stay and live under Communism.

We all looked at Vietnam for the last time as we left. The last thing we saw was the beautiful beach at Vung Tau. It was a nice day. The sun was shining. And everyone was crying.

After we saw Vung Tau for the last time, a soldier on the boat took his own gun and put it under his chin and shot himself to death. And some people jumped over the side of the ship and disappeared in the sea. I watched two men jump over the side.

We were in the South China Sea for three days without food or water. On the third day a Danish ship found us. They took the women and children off and took them to Hong Kong. Then they gave us food and water so we wouldn't die at sea and they told us how to get to Hong Kong. During the rest of the journey we didn't talk to each other because we were so sad about losing our country.

6. A South Vietnamese Civilian Remembers His Last Days in Saigon (1975), 1990

Every night I cry for Vietnam. I remember and I cry. In the darkness my memories turn into tears. There are tears for my dad and my mom and for my brother and my sisters, and for all of the people who ran away from Vietnam and for all of those who could not run away. I don't want my memories to be lost, like tears in the rain. . . .

I was sixteen in the spring of 1975. At that time in school kids were starting to worry about the Communists taking over. Some of them talked about leaving the country. Some days, on the way home from school, I saw long lines of people trying to get papers or trying to change their money so they could leave the country.

My brother came home from college. My dad told my brother and me that he wanted us to leave the country for a while. "You are young," he said. "You have a future. And when everything is safe again you can come back." He thought we should go to the United States to study. Then when we returned to Vietnam we would have a better future. But it was very difficult to get out of Vietnam, and for a long time we did not believe we would be able to leave.

My best friend's name was Nguyen Quang. His sister, Nguyen Huong, worked as a clerk at the American Embassy. He told us that she might be able to get us out of the country. The Americans told her that they would fly her and her relatives out of Vietnam. All she had to do was type our names on a list. So we said that would be all right. She told her boss—who was also Vietnamese—that she had two young men who wanted to get out of Vietnam and that they were not relatives. But she said she wanted to put the two names on her list. And her boss said that was okay.

After our names were on the list she called us and said that we had to be ready to leave at any time, day or night. She said she would tell us where to go when we were scheduled to leave.

Then at ten in the morning on April 28, she came to our house and said, "Sonny, you had better get ready, because you will be leaving in one hour." She told us where we were supposed to go. A bus was going to pick us up there and take us to the airport. We could only bring one bag each for clothes. We did not have much time to say goodbye. I only had time to say, "Dad, I love you. I have to leave now." Mom and Dad cried a lot that morning. They told my brother, "Take good care of Ut."

From *Tears Before the Rain: An Oral History of the Fall of South Vietnam* by Larry Engelmann. Copyright © 1990 by Larry Engelmann. Used by permission of Oxford University Press, Inc.

Dad then drove us to where a bus was to pick us up. We had no special papers and we really didn't know if we would be asked for any. We drove to a big building that had a fence around it. We knocked on the gate and a man let us in. He had a list of names. Our names were on his list. When we got inside the fence I was surprised because there was a large courtyard and it was filled with people who were waiting. The people had come from all over the country—from central Vietnam and from the northern cities. There were about a thousand people there. I asked some of them, "Where did you come from?" I didn't see anybody I knew. And they told me, "We came from Danang," or, "We came from Nha Trang." So many people from so many different cities. And there seemed to be nobody there from Saigon but my brother and me.

I felt happy at that moment. I was young and I would not have to live under the Communists. I could go to school in the United States and then when the Communists had been driven out I could come back to Saigon.

We had not been in the courtyard of the building very long when they called our names. My brother and I went to the gate again and a bus driver was standing there with a list and he checked off our names. We got on the bus. I could hardly believe it. We were the first ones to leave the courtyard. We were each carrying just one bag. My brother and I had no money. My dad told us to call him when we got to the U.S. and then he would send us some money. We were going to stay with a friend in California.

We were driven to the airport. It was really crowded. We had to get off the bus and stand outside. There was a big field with people in it and the sun was very hot. There were loud-speakers paging people and vendors trying to sell food and drinks and trying to exchange money. Lots of people were crying and lots of them were shocked because they didn't really know what was happening or where they were going.

We really didn't know what would happen. Then all of a sudden they called our names over the loudspeaker. I was very surprised because I had asked some of the other people, "How long have you been waiting here?" and some of them said, "One week already." Others had been waiting two or three days. I thought at first that my brother and I would never get on a plane, but then they called our names. We were taken into the terminal with other people. They searched us there and searched our luggage. Then they asked us to stand in a long line. After a little time they led us out to an airplane. Outside the plane there were two Vietnamese MPs standing and watching the people. They wanted to prevent deserters from leaving the country. They looked at everyone carefully. They didn't stop us or question us and we got on the plane.

I thought it would be a nice airplane. It was a big C-130. We walked up the back ramp. When we got inside we saw that there were no seats. We just had to get in and sit on the floor—like sardines. When I saw that I thought, "Oh, my God, are we going to take this all the way to the United States without seats? And packed so close together?" But nobody was saying anything so I didn't say anything about it, either. I just thought that thought.

As they were loading us—it was very late in the afternoon—all of a sudden I heard a lot of explosions outside, around the plane. And thought, "Oh, my God, what is happening out there?" The door was still open and I saw an explosion right behind the plane. A big explosion. Then the airplane started to move with the door still open. I was looking out the door and I saw people running around in all directions shooting crazily into the air. They seemed to be in a panic. People all around me on the airplane started screaming and crying. Some of them started praying very loudly. I grabbed my brother and I said, "I hope we don't crash."

They didn't even have time to close the door. They just went down the runway with the door open. As we took off, all of us could see out the back, and on the ground it looked like there were hundreds of explosions and fires and people were running in all directions. It looked like the whole airport was going crazy.

Then right behind us another C-130 came up—it took off on another runway only a few seconds after we did. I think we were the last two planes to take off from Tan Son Nhut. We were very lucky.

As we left Saigon, there was an American soldier standing at the back door of the plane, and he was shooting at the ground. He just kept shooting as we pulled away. And people were still crying inside the plane. I watched the soldier shooting and I wondered what he was shooting at. I think he was just trying to show American power one last time. I think he was trying to say with his gun, "Don't shoot at our airplane. Don't mess around with this airplane. We've got guns on board. We're Americans. Stay away. Leave us alone." But I can only guess. I don't think he knew what was happening, either. We were all confused.

Anyway, that was my last look at my country. I saw Vietnam as we flew away and at the back door of the plane was a soldier with a gun shooting at it.

We landed in the Philippines at Clark Field. We were taken to a big warehouse. The Americans had everything very well organized for us. We were surprised. They put us all in a big waiting area. We had televisions and beds. The next day they told us that the Communists had taken over Saigon. We were shocked. We did not know what would happen. "What about our family?" we asked. "What about Mom and Dad? What will happen to us now when we get to the United States?" We had nothing but questions.

We watched the news on television. We saw the Communists in Saigon. A lot of people cried when they saw that. My brother and I cried, too. Our family was still in Vietnam. And we looked at each other and asked, "What will happen to us tomorrow?"

7. A North Vietnamese Commander Celebrates the "Great Spring Victory" (1975), 1977

When it was almost light, the American news services reported that [U.S. Ambassador Graham] Martin had cleared out of Saigon in a helicopter. This viceregal mandarin, the final American plenipotentiary in South Vietnam, beat a most hasty and pitiful retreat. As it happened, up until the day he left Saigon, Martin still felt certain that the quisling administration could be preserved, and that a ceasefire could be arranged, so he was halfhearted about the evacuation, waiting and watching.

Van Tien Dung, *Our Great Spring Victory: An Account of the Liberation of South Vietnam,* translated by John Spragens, Jr. Copyright © 1977 by Cora Weiss. Reprinted by permission of Monthly Review Foundation.

He went all the way out to Tan Son Nhut airfield to observe the situation. Our barrage of bombs and our fierce shelling had nearly paralyzed this vital airfield, and the fixed-wing aircraft they had intended to use for their evacuation could no longer operate. The encirclement of Saigon was growing tighter by the day. The Duong Van Minh card which they had played far too late proved useless. When Martin reported this to Washington, President Ford issued orders to begin a helicopter evacuation. Coming in waves for eighteen hours straight, they carried more than 1,000 Americans and over 5,000 of their Vietnamese retainers, along with their families, out of the South. Ford also ordered Martin to evacuate immediately "without a minute's delay."

The American evacuation was carried out from the tops of thirteen tall buildings chosen as landing pads for their helicopters. The number of these landing pads shrank gradually as tongues of fire from our advancing troops came closer. At the American embassy, the boarding point for the evacuation copters was a scene of monumental confusion, with the Americans' flunkies fighting their way in, smashing doors, climbing walls, climbing each other's backs, tussling, brawling, and trampling each other as they sought to flee. It reached the point where Martin, who wanted to return to his own house for his suitcase before he fled, had to take a back street, using the rear gate of the embassy. When "Code 2," Martin's code name, and "Lady 09," the name of the helicopter carrying him, left the embassy for the East Sea, it signaled the shameful defeat of U.S. imperialism after thirty years of intervention and military adventures in Vietnam. At the height of their invasion of Vietnam, the U.S. had used 60 percent of their total infantry, 58 percent of their marines, 32 percent of their tactical air force, 50 percent of their strategic air force, fifteen of their eighteen aircraft carriers, 800,000 American troops (counting those stationed in satellite countries who were taking part in the Vietnam war), and more than 1 million Saigon troops. They mobilized as many as 6 million American soldiers in rotation, dropped over 10 million tons of bombs, and spent over $300 billion, but in the end the U.S. ambassador had to crawl up to the helicopter pad looking for a way to flee. Today, looking back on the gigantic force the enemy had mobilized, recalling the malicious designs they admitted, and thinking about the extreme difficulties and complexities which our revolutionary sampan had had to pass through, we were all the more aware how immeasurably great this campaign to liberate Saigon and liberate the South was. . . .

The most extraordinary thing about this historic campaign was what had sprouted in the souls of our cadres and fighters. Why were our soldiers so heroic and determined during this campaign? What had given all of them this clear understanding of the great resolution of the party and of the nation, this clear understanding of our immeasurably precious opportunity, and this clear understanding of our unprecedented manner of fighting? What had made them so extraordinarily courageous and intense, so outstanding in their political acumen in this final phase of the war?

The will and competence of our soldiers were not achieved in a day, but were the result of a continuous process of carrying out the party's ideological and organizational work in the armed forces. And throughout our thirty years of struggle, there had been no campaign in which Uncle Ho had not gone into the operation with our soldiers. Going out to battle this time, our whole army had been given singular, unprecedented strength because this strategically decisive battle bore his name: Ho Chi Minh, for every one of our cadres and fighters, was faith, strength, and life. Among the myriad troops in all the advancing wings, every one of our fighters carried toward Ho Chi Minh City the hopes of the nation and a love for our land. Today each fighter could see with his own eyes the resiliency which the Fatherland had built up during these many years, and given his own resiliency there was nothing, no enemy scheme that could stop him.

Our troops advanced rapidly to the five primary objectives, and then spread out from there. Wherever they went, a forest of revolutionary flags appeared, and people poured out to cheer them, turning the streets of Saigon into a giant festival. From the Binh Phoc bridge to Quan Tre, people carrying flags, beating drums and hollow wooden fish, and calling through megaphones, chased down the enemy, disarmed enemy soldiers, neutralized traitors and spies, and guided our soldiers. In Hoc Mon on Route 1, the people all came out into the road to greet the soldiers, guide them, and point out the hiding places of enemy thugs. Everywhere people used megaphones to call on Saigon soldiers to take off their uniforms and lay down their guns. The people of the city, especially the workers, protected factories and warehouses and turned them over to our soldiers. In all the districts bordering the city—Binh Hoa, Thanh My Tay, Phu Nhuan, Go Yap, and Thu Duc—members of the revolutionary infrastructure and other people distributed leaflets, raised flags, called on enemy soldiers to drop their guns, and supplied and guided our soldiers. Before this great army entered the city, the great cause of our nation and the policies of our revolution had entered the hearts of the people.

We were very pleased to hear that the people of the city rose up when the military attacks, going one step ahead, had given them the leverage. The masses had entered this decisive battle at just the right time, not too early, but not too late. The patriotic actions of the people created a revolutionary atmosphere of vast strength on all the city's streets. This was the most precious aspect of the mass movement in Saigon-Gia Dinh, the result of many years of propaganda, education, organizing, and training by the municipal party branch. When the opportune moment arrived, those political troops had risen up with a vanguard spirit, and advanced in giant strides along with our powerful main-force divisions, resolutely, intelligently, and courageously. The people of the city not only carried flags and food and drink for the troops, but helped disperse large numbers of enemy soldiers, forced many to surrender, chased and captured many of those who were hiding out, and preserved order and security in the streets. And we will never forget the widespread and moving images of thousands, of tens of thousands of people enthusiastically giving directions to our soldiers and guiding them as they entered the city, and helping all the wings of troops strike quickly and unexpectedly at enemy positions. Those nameless heroes of Saigon-Gia Dinh brought into the general offensive the fresh and beautiful features of people's war.

As we looked at the combat operations map, the five wings of our troops seemed like five lotuses blossoming out from our five major objectives. The First Army Corps had captured Saigon's General Staff headquarters and the command compounds of all the enemy armed services. When the Third Army Corps captured Tan Son Nhat they met one wing of troops already encamped there—our military delegation at Camp Davis; it was an amazing and moving meeting. The Fourth Army Corps captured Saigon's Ministry of Defense, the Bach Dang port, and the radio station. The 232nd force took the Special Capital Zone headquarters and the Directorate-General of Police. The Second Army Corps seized "Independence Palace," the place where the quisling leaders, those hirelings of the United States, had sold our independence, traded in human blood, and carried on their smuggling. Our soldiers immediately rushed upstairs to the place where the quisling cabinet was meeting, and arrested the whole central leadership of the Saigon administration, including their president, right on the spot. Our soldiers' vigorous actions and firm declarations revealed the spirit of a victorious army. By 11:30 A.M. on April 30 the revolutionary flag flew from "Independence Palace"; this became the meeting point for all the wings of liberating troops.

At the front headquarters, we turned on our radios to listen. The voice of the quisling president called on his troops to put down their weapons and surrender unconditionally to our troops. Saigon was completely liberated! Total victory! We were completely victorious! All of us at headquarters jumped up and shouted, embraced and carried each other around on our shoulders. The sound of applause, laughter, and happy, noisy, chattering speech was as festive as if spring had just burst upon us. It was an indescribably joyous scene. Le Duc Tho and Pham Hung embraced me and all the cadres and fighters present. We were all so happy we were choked with emotion. I lit a cigarette and smoked. Dinh Duc Thien, his eyes somewhat red, said, "Now if these eyes close, my heart will be at rest." This historic and sacred, intoxicating and completely satisfying moment was one that comes once in a generation, once in many generations. Our generation had known many victorious mornings, but there had been no morning so fresh and beautiful, so radiant, so clear and cool, so sweet-scented as this morning of total victory, a morning which made babes older than their years and made old men young again.

8. Nixon Blames Congress for the Fall of South Vietnam (1975), 1978

For more than two years after the peace agreement the South Vietnamese had held their own against the Communists. This proved the will and mettle of the South Vietnamese people and their desire to live in freedom. It also proved that Vietnamization had succeeded. When Congress reneged on our obligations under the agreements, the Communists predictably rushed in to fill the gap. The congressional bombing cutoff, coupled with the limitation placed on the President by the War Powers Resolution in November 1973, set off a string of events that led to the Communist takeover in Cambodia and, on April 30, 1975, the North Vietnamese conquest of South Vietnam.

Congress denied first to me, and then to President Ford, the means to enforce the Paris agreement at a time when the North Vietnamese were openly violating it. Even more devastating and inexcusable, in 1974 Congress began cutting back on military aid for South Vietnam at a time when the Soviets were increasing their aid to North Vietnam. As a result, when the North Vietnamese launched their all-out invasion of the South in the spring of 1975, they had an advantage in arms, and the

---

Excerpted from the memoirs of Richard M. Nixon.

threat of American action to enforce the agreement was totally removed. A year after the collapse of South Vietnam, the field commander in charge of Hanoi's final offensive cited the cutback in American aid as a major factor in North Vietnam's victory. He remarked that Thieu "was then forced to fight a poor man's war," with his firepower reduced by 60 percent and his mobility reduced by half because of lack of aircraft, vehicles, and fuel.

The war and the peace in Indochina that America had won at such cost over twelve years of sacrifice and fighting were lost within a matter of months once Congress refused to fulfill our obligations. And it is Congress that must bear the responsibility for the tragic results. Hundreds of thousands of anti-Communist South Vietnamese and Cambodians have been murdered or starved to death by their conquerors, and the bloodbath continues.

✗ E S S A Y S

In the first essay, Larry Berman, a professor of Political Science at the University of California, Davis, and director of the University of California's Washington Center, blasts Nixon and Kissinger for engineering a cynical betrayal of South Vietnam. Berman characterizes the Paris peace accord as a"Jabberwocky agreement" that was riddled with vague and contradictory provisions and backed by promises to the Saigon regime that the United States proved unable to keep.

This chapter's other essay focuses on the events and forces that led to the North Vietnamese-NLF topping of the Saigon regime. Robert K. Brigham, a professor of history at Vassar College, emphasizes that neither the North Vietnamese nor the NLF displayed any willingness to abandon their central objective of a reunified, communist Vietnam in the wake of the Paris peace agreement. He details the policy debates and divisions that occurred within and between the Hanoi leadership and the southern insurgency prior to the successful final offensive in the Spring of 1975.

The Betrayal of South Vietnam

LARRY BERMAN

Signed at the International Conference Center in Paris on Saturday morning, January 27, 1973, the essential elements of the Agreement on Ending the War and Restoring Peace on Vietnam included the cessation of hostilities and the withdrawal of American troops. The United States would halt all air and naval actions against North Vietnam and dismantle or deactivate all mines in North Vietnam's waters. Within 60 days after the signing of the agreement, all United States forces, as well as all forces of foreign nations allied with the United States, would withdraw from Vietnam. The United States was prohibited from reintroducing new war materials or supplies into Vietnam and was required to dismantle all military bases in South

Reprinted and edited with the permission of The Free Press, an imprint of Simon & Schuster Adult Publishing Group, from *No Peace, No Honor: Nixon, Kissinger and the Betrayal in Vietnam* by Larry Berman. Copyright © 2001 by Larry Berman.

Vietnam. The armed forces of the two South Vietnamese parties were permitted to remain in place, but the cease-fire prohibited accepting the introduction of troops, military advisers, and military personnel, including technical military personnel, armaments, munitions, and war material from the North or anywhere else. The disposition of Vietnamese armed forces in South Vietnam would be settled by the two South Vietnamese parties in a spirit of "national reconciliation and concord." The two South Vietnamese parties were permitted to make periodic replacement of armaments, munitions, and war material that had been destroyed, damaged, or used up on a one-for-one basis under international supervision and control.

The agreement further called for the return of all captured military personnel and foreign civilians during this same 60-day period. The return of Vietnamese civilians would be left to the two South Vietnamese parties. The United States and North Vietnam pledged to respect the principles of self-determination for the South Vietnamese people, including free and democratic elections under international supervision. To this end, the two South Vietnamese parties would create the National Council for National Reconciliation and Concord. The United States was prohibited from intervening in the internal affairs of South Vietnam.

In spite of this, there was not supposed to be a coalition government in South Vietnam. The existing government in Saigon would remain in office. Yet no national boundary would formally separate North and South Vietnam, meaning that two governments were running one country. The agreement identified the military demarcation line between the two zones, the 17th parallel, as "the only provisional and not a political or territorial boundary." Both North and South Vietnam were required to respect the DMZ on both sides of the Provisional Military Demarcation Line.

If that was not extraordinary enough, for implementing and monitoring compliance with the provisions on withdrawal, cease-fire, base dismantling, return of POWs, and exchange of information on those missing in action, the treaty provided for the Four-Party Joint Military Commission to be constituted by the four signatories. An International Commission of Control and Supervision (ICCS), composed of representatives from Canada, Hungary, Indonesia, and Poland, would oversee the agreement and report violations. A Two-Party Joint Military Commission, consisting of representatives from the two South Vietnamese parties, would be responsible for overseeing the implementation of provisions specific to the two parties, such as determining the areas controlled by each party, modalities of stationing, and the return of civilian detainees. This Two-Party JMC would continue operations after the 60-day period.

"The Jabberwocky" is the strange, nonsense poem of gibberish from Lewis Carroll's *Through a Looking Glass and What Alice Found There*. It contains words of nonsense, or as Alice put it, "It seems very pretty, but it is rather hard to understand. Somehow it seems to fill my head with ideas—only I don't know what they are! However, somebody killed something; that's clear, at any rate." The peace treaty written in Paris was indeed a Jabberwocky agreement.

Not a moment of peace ever came to Vietnam. Hoping to establish the province city of Tay Ninh as their new capital, the Vietcong immediately launched an assault to capture the city. Two separate communist delegations to the Two-Party JMC, one arriving from Hanoi and the other from Paris, looked out their airplane windows in hopes of seeing PRG flags flying over that city. Sir Robert Thompson reported that Vietcong delegates "flying by Air France from Paris asked to be diverted over Tay Ninh on their way to Saigon so that they could admire the PRG flag flying over their new capital. But they were disappointed to find the town firmly in Government hands and South Vietnamese flags waving strongly in the wind." . . .

In his address to the nation marking the beginning of the cease-fire, President Thieu urged his countrymen not to let down in their vigilance against the communist enemy. He warned that the current atmosphere of international détente should not lead to a false sense that citizens were safe from communists in their midst. Thieu described the agreement as "a ceasefire in place, no more, no less, which would develop into a true and lasting peace depending on four factors: (1) The degree to which the communists respect the ceasefire in the coming months; (2) The sincerity of the communists in the coming talks with the GVN: specifically, whether or not the communists would use the talks as a delaying tactic behind which they would make preparations for a renewal of the war; (3) The attitude shown by the communists, particularly whether or not they remained in South Vietnam and threatened the freedom necessary to ensure the right of self-determination for South Vietnamese people by engaging in violence and assassinations; (4) The attitude of the communists toward the results of an election in which they might achieve only a minority."

A day earlier Thieu was quoted in *Le Monde* as saying, "If the communists dare put a foot in our zones, we will kill them." This warning was consistent with the instructions that were being distributed to South Vietnamese on how to implement the agreement. . . .

Days before the cease-fire, the blue and red NLF flag was erected in areas of communist control, and the red-striped yellow flag of the RVN was displayed in areas of their control. The RVN flag was painted on rooftops and houses and on every car and motorbike. Troops were given flags and told to wave them wherever they went. All of this made it virtually impossible for the ICC to determine who controlled an area and who initiated a violation. There was frenzied competition by both sides to remove enemy flags and plant their own.

Donald Kir reported walking with Don Tate of Scripps Howard through the borderline between the liberated zone of the PRG territory and territory controlled by the ARVN. Virtually all of the hooches had flags flying at the top of bamboo polls: "a minimal sign of loyalty to one side or another." Some had signs scribbled in Vietnamese, "Peace and welcome." Yet as soon as the GVN spotted VC flags, they came and burned down those hooches. "Across the road, South Vietnamese troops fan out toward another tree line over which hang several more VC flags. Suddenly a woman screams uncontrollably, 'My home is destroyed. Ten people in my hamlet have been killed. Peace, peace, they promised us peace.'"

In a private meeting with French president Pompidou on the day of the signing, Secretary of State William Rogers was asked "if the U.S. had a commitment from North Vietnam on the withdrawal of their forces from the South." Secretary Rogers duly responded that "there was no specific commitment in the agreement itself and that it would have been difficult to obtain because Hanoi refused to admit that North Vietnamese troops were in the South." Meanwhile, violence continued.

Article 1 of the Paris agreement was, to the Vietnamese, what the essence of the war was all about: "The United States and all other countries respect the independence, sovereignty, unity, and territorial integrity of Vietnam as recognized by the 1954 Geneva Agreements on Vietnam." This wording, as Thieu understood all too well, was virtually identical to the NLF's Ten Points of May 1969: "The U.S. must respect the Vietnamese people's fundamental national rights, i.e. independence, sovereignty, unity, and territorial integrity, as recognized by the 1954 Geneva Agreements."

Throughout October, November, and December, President Thieu had fought for better and more improved language to soften Article 1. He wanted language that would guarantee Saigon's sovereignty over South Vietnam, since there really were two countries in Vietnam, not one. To the extent that there was only one, Thieu knew it would be controlled by Hanoi. He wanted the 17th parallel to be recognized as an international political boundary. Thieu knew that if he could get these additions, the DRV and PRG would be defeated diplomatically.

In the end, Kissinger was able to mollify Thieu with references in the agreement (Articles 14, 18(e), and 20) regarding "respect for the sovereignty of South Vietnam" pending reunification, but because the agreement specifically stipulated "two South Vietnamese parties" as governments, Thieu could not claim sole sovereignty there. The agreement left two rival parties in the South to contest political power. Nonetheless, President Nixon publicly stated that "the United States will continue to recognize the Government of the Republic of Vietnam as the sole legitimate government in Vietnam." For the same reason, the DRV and PRG delegation to the Four-Party JMC had refused to fill out Saigon forms before debarking from their planes.

The status of the DMZ and the 17th parallel was also a victory for the communists. According to the Paris agreement, pending reunification, "the military demarcation line between the two zones at the 17th parallel is only provisional and not a political or territorial boundary, as provided for in paragraph 6 of the Final Declaration of the 1954 Geneva Conference." Compare this with the almost identical wording of the NLF's ten points of May 1969: "The military demarcation line between the two zones at the 17th parallel, as provided for by the 1954 Geneva Agreements, is only of a provisional character and does not constitute in any way a political or territorial boundary."

Finally, the North Vietnamese troops would remain in the South. The agreement provided only for future discussions between the two South Vietnamese parties on the subject of demobilization. General Cao Van Vien and Lieutenant General Dong Van Khuyen in their monograph, *Reflections on the Vietnam War,* concluded that "the Paris Agreement of January 1973 served only the immediate purposes of the United States and North Vietnamese." The Paris agreement "offered North Vietnam the favorable conditions to pursue its conquest of South Vietnam with success. . . . In South Vietnam, the NLF was given a legitimate national status. It now had an official government, an army, and a national territory of its own. In all respects, the NLF had become a political entity equal in power to the GVN. . . . Never since 1954 had the communists enjoyed such a strong political and military posture."

Comparing the NLF's ten-point program of 1969 and the 1973 final agreement, it is striking how much of the former remained intact in the latter; in fact, the wording is almost identical on key points. Articles 9, 10, and 11 of the Paris agreement are the actual text of the NLF proposal with respect to the political components of the agreement. The National Council, while not a coalition government, was everything that President Thieu feared it would be. Its functions, as specified by the Paris agreement, were to implement the agreement; prohibit all acts of reprisal and discrimination against individuals or organizations that had collaborated with one side or the other; ensure democratic liberties; decide the procedures and modalities of these general elections; and organize the free and democratic general elections. It was hardly the "joke" that Haig and Kissinger presented it as to Thieu and the South Vietnamese. As Le Duc Tho said on January 25, 1973, "In the end, we reached an agreement not to use the term 'structure of power' or 'administrative structure' but to call it directly the National Council of Reconciliation and National Concord, for the importance of the body lies in its way of proceeding in its work."

With such insignificant difference between the 1969 proposal and the 1973 deal, we can only conclude that many tens of thousands died for very little, or simply while waiting for Thieu to give in because Nixon had allowed him to remain in office because Nixon believed that there was no acceptable American alternative to Thieu. Nixon feared that anyone else would not accept the American guarantee of continuous war under the guise of a paper peace. Thieu was their man to punch the ticket for the return of the B-52s. In the end, Thieu was betrayed not just by Watergate but by the men who kept him in power and made him sign the so-called peace agreement.

Vice President Ky later reflected on the Paris agreement, "In fact, the Paris agreement gave the world an entirely wrong impression. Though it was the end of the war for America, it was never regarded as the end of the war by Hanoi. . . . The North Vietnamese seized on one fact: that the U.S. was not really concerned with peace at all; it was only concerned with getting out of Vietnam."

It is true that both sides made concessions in order to produce the final accord. That Thieu remained in power was the major concession of the communists. "We thought that an agreement that left him in office, and in which he was legitimized by the North Vietnamese, was such a spectacular success that he would not pay attention to all the other surrounding circumstance," is how Kissinger explained it two decades later.

But the concessions made by the United States were much greater and far more detrimental. The United States abandoned the principle of mutual withdrawal, which allowed the North Vietnamese to pursue their long-range goals of unification. It also botched the implementation completely. Because of Kissinger's and Nixon's suspicion of the bureaucracy and dedication to secrecy, there was no agreed on position with the government for implementing and enforcing a cease-fire in place. The accord became a protocol for the disengagement of U.S. troops and the return of the POWs, but not for a sustained peace.

For the 60 days immediately following the agreement, the JMC, composed of representatives from four parties, the U.S., PRG, DRV, and GVN, was responsible for overseeing the implementation of the agreement and related issues of securing the peace. After 60 days, provided that all U.S. and allied troops were withdrawn and all military and foreign civilian prisoners were released, the DRV and U.S. teams would terminate their roles. The Two-Party JMC of Saigon and PRG representatives would supersede the four-party group.

The American team in Saigon, which had been working in absolute secrecy imposed by Kissinger, had five major goals to accomplish in the 60 days. The most central was the return of POWs, followed by the orderly and safe withdrawal of all remaining troops, including the sizable number of outside forces. The third goal was to reduce the level of fighting in Vietnam, the fourth to stabilize the conflict as much as possible by creating a forum for talks, and the fifth to provide the South Vietnamese with a reasonable chance to survive on their own. The official historian of the U.S. delegation, Lieutenant Colonel Walter Scott Dillard, concluded that in "pursuing this last goal, the United States violated the spirit of the provisions of the Paris agreement and protocols. Article 6 of the basic agreement required the dismantlement of the American military bases in South Vietnam within 60 days of the signing of the agreement. By no stretch of the imagination can the argument be sustained that these bases were dismantled. . . . A subterfuge was invented in which the US transferred and the South Vietnamese accepted ownership of the bases. . . . Appropriate documents were subsequently signed formalizing the transfer but, until their actual physical withdrawal, American forces retained the same rights and privileges they had enjoyed before, as if ownership had been retained—occupancy, complete control, reentry, use of all facilities." Nonetheless, the U.S. did very little to slow the Northern encroachment. . . .

. . . In fact, the ambiguities in the details of the agreement virtually guaranteed that the Vietnamese parties themselves would reach no agreement, and that once it was violated, the terms of Nixon's secret assurances would be activated.

The U.S. delegation succeeded admirably in the area of prisoner returns and troop withdrawals, but they lacked power to enjoin all three Vietnamese parties to implement, much less enforce, a complete and effective cease-fire. "This failure cannot be emphasized too strongly. It meant that the war would continue unabated and unchecked until one Vietnam conquered the other," observed Dillard in the official military history of the period.

The North Vietnamese wanted the United States out of Vietnam, so on the one issue most important to the Americans, return of the POWs, Hanoi cooperated with the United States because jeopardizing the safety or release of the POWs would result in a brutal response. . . .

Five days before he had been sworn in for his second term as the nation's thirty-seventh president, Nixon had written in his diary, "It is ironic that the day the news came out stopping the bombing of North Vietnam, the Watergate Four plead guilty." Unbeknown to anyone, as Henry Kissinger was negotiating with Le Duc Tho in Paris, "Watergate was changing from amber to red," recalled Admiral Zumwalt. "The private commitments made by Nixon to Thieu were unraveling alongside Nixon's presidency."

More than a private commitment was at stake; a secret plan was being overtaken by events. By April 30, Nixon had told the country that he accepted responsibility for the Watergate incident, but he also denied any personal involvement in either the break-in or cover-up. He said that he had been misled by subordinates who had made an "effort to conceal the facts." Nixon announced the nomination of Elliot Richardson as attorney general and that Richardson would have authority to appoint a special prosecutor. The White House also announced that the president had accepted the resignations of Ehrlichman, Haldeman, Attorney General Richard Kleindienst, and the president's counsel, John Dean. As Kissinger later told Stanley Karnow, "After June 1973 I did not believe that the cease-fire would hold. I certainly did not after July 1973. Watergate was in full strength. We had intelligence documents from North

Vietnam decoded that Nixon could not honor his pledge and do what he had done in 1972 because of domestic situations."

Watergate would have another effect. Kissinger later stated that this was a "different Nixon. He approached the problems of the violations in a curiously desultory fashion. He drifted. He did not home in on the decision in the single-minded, almost possessed manner that was his hallmark. The rhetoric might be there, but accompanied this time with excuses for inaction. In retrospect, we know that by March, Watergate was boiling."

There is no question now, nor was there then, that Watergate sapped any resolve that Nixon may have had to bomb again. For decades, Henry Kissinger has used that fact to justify his argument that the administration—including himself—never intended to abandon South Vietnam. Yet something is hard to swallow in that argument. Nixon, the die-hard anticommunist, may have convinced himself that the American people would support South Vietnam in the face of the new—and newly illegal—Northern aggression no matter what. But most Americans were weary of the war, and the public no longer held the same zeal for anticommunism that it had had in the late 1940s and 1950s.

Could Kissinger, the realist, the pragmatist, have failed to see this? Indeed, two newly released records of conversations at meetings suggest a more devious plan. The first, a meeting with Lee Quan Yew, prime minister of Singapore, on August 4, 1973 reveals, in Kissinger's own words, the belief that bombing was the only way to make certain that the South would not fall.

The secret meeting occurred in the Captain's Conference Room of the New York Port Authority Policy Building at Kennedy Airport. The euphoria of January's peace with honor was now a distant memory. Lee had just returned from meeting Nha.

Kissinger told Lee that "[Nha] dislikes me intensely!"

"That is not important—personal likes and dislikes. The important thing is the job to be done. I told him it would be useful if Thieu met me. He said, 'why not just meet me?'"

"What is your impression of Nha?" asked Kissinger.

"He is bright, ambitious. With full confidence that what he says will carry weight with the President," said Lee.

"That is true. He is also immature. Emotional," concluded Kissinger.

But Kissinger had come to talk about Watergate and Vietnam, not Mr. Nha. "Our objectives are still the same. We have suffered a tragedy because of Watergate. . . . We were going to bomb North Vietnam for a week, then go to Russia, then meet with Le Duc Tho. Congress has made it impossible." Then Kissinger made the tell-tale confession of his dashed hopes: "In May and June I drew the conclusion that the North Vietnamese were resigning themselves to a long pull of 5-to-6 years. . . . And it would have been a certainty if we had given them one blow." In other words, a little bombing now might have slowed them down, which would be a decent interval before losing the South. Nixon and Kissinger would not be directly tied to it.

One more blow was a far more realistic expectation on Kissinger's part. Kissinger told Lee that "the last three months were the most difficult period for us. We couldn't say anything because we could never be sure what some junior aide would say next. But as soon as the hearings are over, we will go on the counteroffensive. We are already in the process. While we are in these difficulties, we have to stay cool. But we won't give up our foreign policy. We will regain the initiative. In Southeast Asia, we haven't gone through all this for four years to abandon it. Sixty-one percent voted in November 1972 not to abandon Southeast Asia. It was a clear issue."

The meeting ended with Lee Kuan Yew's saying how important it was that South Vietnam survive through 1976. "My concern is to have it last through 1976 so that you will have a strong President. If it falls, you will have a new President who says, 'that's what tore American society apart.'"

Kissinger must have been reassured, because he told Lee, "You are an asset to us in that part of the world and we have no interest in destroying you. We won't leave any documents around. They stay in my office."

A little more than a month later, on September 26, Kissinger met with Nguyen Phu Duc in the Waldorf Towers in New York. Kissinger was now secretary of state, and Duc asked Kissinger what the United States planned to do with respect to the North's violations of the Paris Accord. "If it were not for domestic difficulties, we would have bombed them. This is now impossible. Your brothers in the North only understand brutality," said Kissinger. The secretary then spoke about how the Congress had acted "irresponsibly" by cutting off support for bombing, but North Vietnamese "suspiciousness is playing into our hands. They don't completely understand the restrictions placed on us by Congress. President Nixon has fooled them so often that they are probably more concerned that you believe. It is important that you show confidence and behave strongly." He ended with a joke: "Treat them like you treat me."

The conversation then got much more revealing. Kissinger made a startling admission: "I came away from the January negotiations with the feeling that we would have to bomb the North Vietnamese again in early April or May." He did not say, "If the North violated the accord, we would bomb." He confirmed what Haig had told Phouma, what Nixon had said to Thieu and what Zumwalt had concluded in November 1972 at the JCS meeting: it was a sham peace held together with a plan to deceive the American public with the rhetoric of American honor. He knew the North would cheat and was planning on resuming the bombing.

As Kissinger toasted Le Duc Tho with words of peace in January 1973 and as Richard Nixon addressed the nation with news of an honorable peace in Vietnam, both men knew that as soon as the last American POW was home, the bombing would be renewed. For Nixon, the bombing would continue right through 1976, and for Kissinger, just long enough to pick up his Nobel Peace Prize.

Writing in the *Wall Street Journal* on April 27, 1975, William Buckley noted that Watergate had derailed the president's plan to pulverize Hanoi and that Nixon at the time was too emotionally unstable to renew the bombing: "What would Nixon, under Kissinger's prodding, have done, if his reactions had been healthy, when only a few weeks after the Paris Accord was executed, North Vietnam began its blatant disregard of it. My own information is that it was planned, sometime in April, to pulverize Hanoi and Haiphong," wrote Buckley. Indeed, the plans were made even earlier. . . .

Kissinger later acknowledged that he had misjudged the willingness of the American people to defend the agreement. "But I admit this: we judged wrong. And what we judged wrong above all was our belief that if we could get peace with honor, that we would unite the American people who would then defend an agreement that had been achieved with so much pain. That was our fundamental miscalculation. It never occurred to me, and I'm sure it never occurred to President Nixon, that there could be any doubt about it, because an agreement that you don't enforce is a surrender; it's just writing down surrender terms."

The North Vietnamese-NLF Triumph

ROBERT K. BRIGHAM

The Paris agreements did little to stop the war in Viet Nam. Neither of the southern protagonists was willing to abandon its objectives, and by mid-1974 the Thieu regime had declared the opening of the "Third Indochina War." During the last two years of the conflict, the NLF skillfully combined its military and diplomatic struggle movements to precipitate a political crisis in Saigon. The political crisis and southern pressure led the Party to use military force to bring down the Saigon regime. Postwar studies emanating from Hanoi, however, have emphasized the North's role in the final victory of the southern revolution. In 1988, for example, Le Duc Tho, the DRV's chief negotiator at the Paris talks and one of the Political Bureau's most powerful members, explained that the liberation of Saigon was made possible by large contingents of regular forces from the DRV army. As PAVN tanks rolled south, however, they carried NLF flags, a gesture not soon forgotten by southerners after the war. In reality, there was considerable conflict within the Lao Dong concerning the use of revolutionary violence to end the war. As in the debate that had preceded the formation of the Front, some northern officials worried that armed force in the South threatened northern objectives.

This conflict began when NLF diplomats walked out of negotiations with the Saigon regime at La Celle St-Cloud, a French estate outside of Paris. On March 19, 1973, the two southern adversaries met in direct discussions for the first time in an attempt to settle the political issues of the Paris peace accord. Article 12 had called on the parties to reach agreement on the "internal matters of South Viet Nam as soon as possible and to do their utmost to accomplish this within ninety days after the cease-fire went into effect." The Front's representative, a revived Nguyen Van Hieu, hoped to secure a standstill cease-fire that would stop the RVN's southern offensives. Thieu, for his part, had viewed the Paris peace agreement not as an end to the war but, according to Gareth Porter, as "the start of a new war under ground rules which he hoped would be advantageous to Saigon." Indeed, the Saigon regime used new shipments of American war matériel to launch major territory-grabbing campaigns in early 1973. In Long Khanh, Tay Ninh, and Hau Nghia provinces, the RVN relied on air power to retake key hamlets after the cease-fire. The cost in civilian lives was tremendous, but the RVN justified the attacks on the ground that it was recapturing territory illegally gained by the NLF just before the cease-fire went into effect.

The NLF sincerely believed that it could force the Thieu regime to abide by the Paris agreement, and Hieu hoped he could use these direct negotiations to end the fighting. "I think we can show the Saigon government that the world wants peace," Hieu explained before leaving for Paris, "but we are also prepared to defend ourselves should Thieu continue to violate the Paris agreement." For its part, the RVN sent Nguyen Luu Vien as its delegate and suggested an extended agenda for the first round of discussions. These items included the election of a national president, the makeup of the Council of National Reconciliation, and the removal of all foreign troops (including North Vietnamese) from the South. The NLF countered with its own agenda, proposing to discuss a cease-fire, the return of all political prisoners, and civil freedoms for opposition candidates. The Front also included the need to discuss the character and nature of the Council of National Reconciliation. The council was supposed to supervise national elections and oversee the implementation of all political agreements between the two parties. The proposed agendas, then, differed in substantial ways, with the makeup of the reconciliation council the only agreed-upon topic. This impasse represented the limited impact of the Paris agreement on events on the ground in the South.

In a lengthy press conference on April 20, Hieu criticized the Saigon government's agenda, claiming that it was premature to discuss elections while the war dragged on. "The house is burning, threatening everything inside," he explained. "We propose to extinguish the fire. The other side pretends not to see the fire, and suggests that we discuss how to decorate the living room." The Thieu regime, he reported, wanted the NLF to make significant sacrifices without surrendering any of its own political control. "The Thieu government has used terror to crush all democratic opposition," Hieu complained. "It now wants to use the peace process to ensure this stranglehold on the people of South Viet Nam." He vowed not to return to the negotiating table until the Saigon regime altered its agenda.

Hieu informed Hanoi of the deadlock and threatened to walk out of the talks unless the Saigon regime ended its military offensives. He urged the Military Commission of the Lao Dong's Political Bureau to consider an all-out military campaign to overthrow the RVN. Party leaders warned, however, that "opposition to the enemy will not win victory unless there is a change in the ratio of military forces between us and the enemy." The only way to accomplish this shift, Hanoi insisted, was to attack Thieu politically. The Communists hoped to use the talks "to exploit the growing contradiction between the Thieu regime and the southern Vietnamese people." The Political Bureau in Hanoi ordered Hieu back to the negotiating table and urged him to exploit the enemy's political weakness. Hieu complied, but confided to friends privately that the Political Bureau's decision perhaps delayed an end to the war.

On April 25, the NLF and RVN presented their formal peace proposals. The Saigon regime submitted a ten-point plan that outlined, in the broadest terms, its conditions for a settlement. They included the election of an "organ representing the people of South Viet Nam" within four months. From the very beginning, Saigon had wanted an early election date to take advantage of a DRV withdrawal from South Viet Nam and to limit the opposition's ability to organize. Thieu correctly assumed that the DRV would be incapable of mobilizing troops for a southern campaign (or unwilling to do so) after they had crossed the DMZ. The RVN planned to loosen its restrictions on civil freedoms only months before the election, making it impossible for the opposition to organize a nationwide crusade. Furthermore, Thieu's proposal included no guarantees that he would release political prisoners before the election.

The Thieu regime was under no illusion that the NLF would accept such a proposal; its hope was that its offer of a quick election and its promise of political reform would put the Communists in an awkward position. The Front would refuse to accept the conditions for elections, Saigon officials predicted, and then Thieu could exploit the NLFs recalcitrance in the West. "The United States Congress was eager for us to settle the conflict through political elections," one Saigon official later commented. "We knew that the Communists would never agree to an open election, so we pressed the issue immediately for our advantage." The Thieu government also believed that few people would actually read the detailed provisions of its proposal, so that it would appear more acceptable than it actually was.

To counter Saigon's election ploy, the NLF released its own six-point program for peace. The Front proposed that the two sides settle each of the political issues separately and that the negotiators not move forward to the next item on the list until the last had been satisfactorily resolved and the solution implemented. Only after the settlement of all of the political considerations would the NLF agree to elections, and only for a national constitutent assembly, not the presidency, as the RVN had proposed. NLF strategists correctly feared that the Saigon regime would continue to use American military support to prolong the war unless each issue was settled individually. After careful consideration, each side rejected the other's proposal.

As the talks at La Celle St-Cloud continued with no apparent results in the spring of 1973, an impatient NLF began to urge the Lao Dong's Political Bureau to revise its postwar strategy. Shortly after signing the Paris agreement, the Military Commission and the Political Bureau met in Hanoi and approved a policy that granted primacy to the political struggle. Many northern Lao Dong leaders feared that the renewal of main force warfare would give the Nixon administration an excuse to resume bombing North Viet Nam. In early 1973, Hanoi therefore decided to consolidate its gains and force Thieu from power by applying tremendous political pressure. "We wanted a strict interpretation of the Paris agreement," a Lao Dong leader explained, "because we correctly believed that the Saigon regime would never allow a fair election and that its failure to do so would erode its base of support throughout the South and promote a universal movement against Thieu." Shortly after signing the January 1973 compact, Party leaders in Hanoi issued a directive that outlined the new phase of the southern struggle: "Cadres are to mobilize the masses to create basic conditions to guarantee the implementation of the agreements, maintain peace, and enable the revolution to continue its march forward." Some southerners have also suggested that Hanoi believed it could secure American reconstruction aid if it did not violate the spirit of the accord.

The Lao Dong's defensive posture angered many southerners, who remembered too well Diem's anticommunist sweeps from 1954 to 1959. "Hanoi was asking us to return to the pre-NLF days," one angry NLF cadre later commented, "when we were told to avoid the use of armed force altogether. That policy led to disaster, and only the formation of the Front and the reliance on the military struggle saved southerners from complete annihilation." The Front's diplomatic corps once again drew parallels to Geneva. One former NLF cadre insisted that the key to lasting peace in the South rested with a battlefield victory over the RVN. Another NLF leader complained, "We were making the same mistakes all over again. We left the enemy in the field and in control in Saigon and retreated to a defensive posture." Even General Tran Van Tra, the military commander in Nam Bo, the southernmost region of Viet Nam, argued later, "We sincerely did not want a recurrence of the grievous naiveté of the 1954–1959 period." Hanoi's policy was based on the knowledge that the puppet government in Saigon would not negotiate in good faith," complained one cadre. "It was as if we were used for bait."

Several southern Lao Dong officials supported the NLF's calls for a more aggressive military policy and the Front's intransigence at La Celle St-Cloud. Beginning in April, Le Duan, the Party's secretary general, argued that Hanoi's protracted war strategy and its defensive posture must give way to tactics more sensitive to southern revolutionary requirements. He understood the demoralizing impact of the Saigon regime's military offensives and worried that southern cadres thought that "the enemy was stronger than we were, that the balance of forces on the battlefield had changed in favor of the enemy, and that the revolution was in danger." In an emotional speech before the Political Bureau, Le Duan read a letter from a southern cadre who criticized the Party's defensive posture: "How could we sink any lower?" The secretary general had always been one of the most flexible Lao Dong leaders, willing to change overall policy as long as it led to victory and reunification with the South.

In mid-April, at a secret meeting of the Central Committee, Le Duan asked Lao Dong officials to consider several points for discussion at the regular Central Committee meeting the following week. The Paris peace agreement had been a victory, he said, but the enemy "still had a large army with a full complement of equipment." He asked if the southern revolution had shifted to a new phase with new requirements and how the Party might build up the local armies in the South. Clearly, Le Duan was preparing the Lao Dong for more aggressive action in the South. When the Central Committee reconvened the following week, on April 19, it had concluded that the "possibility of American intervention had diminished" and that the time had come "to build up our military forces . . . because only with a powerful punch by the main force could we launch our general counteroffensive."

On May 24, 1973, the Political Bureau met to discuss the Central Committee's conclusions. Representing the South was Tran Huu Duc, from Tri-Thien province; Vo Chi Cong and Chu Huy Man, from the Fifth Military Zone; the southern Party leaders Nguyen Van Linh, Senior General Tran Van Tra, Tran Nam Truong, Vo Van Kiet, and Nguyen Minh Duong; and General Hoang Van Thai. Le Duan presided over the conference and carefully outlined the Central Committee's thinking on the future of the southern revolution. The secretary declared that "now that the U.S. and its agents were blatantly sabotaging the Paris Agreement and obviously committed to continuing the war, there was no alternative in South Viet Nam but to use revolutionary violence to oppose them." Premier Pham Van Dong concurred, adding, "If we want to force the enemy to de-escalate, we must use violence, to strike them repeatedly, wearing them out in order to defeat them step by step." On June 1, after several weeks of discussion, Le Duan reported, "The heated debate and its results underline the complete unanimity of views among the leadership on many crucial questions. It reflects another step in the maturing of our Party through the realities of struggle."

Despite Le Duan's optimistic remarks about Party unity, tactics and strategy in the South were still subjects of debate. Throughout the summer, therefore, the

Military Commission and the Political Bureau met to "determine the direction and policies with regard to fulfilling the people's democratic national revolution, liberating the South, and unifying the homeland." One participant described the meetings as "animated" and "very tense," and reported that "there was a clashing of many different opinions and interpretations regarding the developments on the battlefields." The main protagonists once again were Le Duan and Truong Chinh. The two were old rivals, and Chinh still harbored great bitterness over the fact that Le Duan had replaced him as Party secretary. During the first few weeks of discussion, Truong Chinh, the leader of the DRV's National Assembly, reminded Lao Dong leaders that the Americans could unleash a bombing campaign at any minute and that the revolution had always had twin objectives: "building socialism in the North and carrying out a national democratic revolution in the South. We cannot sacrifice one goal for the other . . . we must continue to attend to our economic policies in the North." In an interview with a reporter from the *Far Eastern Economic Review* in July, Chinh revealed the nature of the conflict within the Party when he emphasized the need to "strictly respect and scrupulously implement the Paris Agreement on Vietnam."

Although Le Duan had significant support within the military, most political leaders accepted Chinh's argument. "If we use our forces to smash the Saigon army it would open the possibility of a renewed war with the United States," cautioned Hoang Tung, a Lao Dong Central Committee official. "That is why our efforts are to try to keep the war on a small scale and to force the other side to implement the Paris Agreement and have real peace." Another Party strategist had explained earlier in the Lao Dong's theoretical journal, "We cannot exterminate imperialism at one time and in a single battle; we drive it back step by step and destroy it part by part."

With the debate raging in Hanoi, NLF diplomats left for Algiers and the conference of nonaligned nations. Front strategists correctly predicted that they could use these meetings to influence the Party's deliberations. "We understood that international support and recognition of the PRG were very important to future strategy considerations concerning the South," one NLF official later explained. "If we wanted to have any impact in Hanoi, we had to show that the progressive peoples of the world supported our right to exist and to fight back." On August 31, Nguyen Thi Binh and Nguyen Huu Tho left for Algiers to launch the Front's new diplomatic initiative. On the first day of the conference, the delegates of the seventy-five represented nations approved a motion offered by Algeria to grant the NLF full status as the third Vietnamese state. Despite an angry protest from the Thieu regime, all but three nations voted to approve the resolution.

The conference also provided Tho with the first opportunity to express NLF goals and aspirations in the post-Paris period. "We ask you to assist in the application of the Paris cease-fire agreement," Tho said, "but we also need your support should the Saigon government refuse to end the war through negotiations and national elections." Since talks between Nguyen Van Hieu and the RVN representatives had already stalled and the prospects of a political settlement appeared dim, Tho was warning the Saigon regime that the NLF intended to launch a counteroffensive soon. He also hoped that support from the nonaligned nations would shift Hanoi toward a more forceful policy.

The NLF's official report to the Lao Dong's Central Committee arrived in Hanoi on September 10, as the Party was preparing resolutions discussed at the Twenty-first

Plenum, in June. Tho apparently authored the summary, which reported that the non-aligned nations supported the Communists' wish to abide by the conditions of the Paris agreement, but clearly understood that further military action might be needed to "force the enemy to strictly implement them." The report also said that the Saigon regime's land-grabbing offensives in the spring were a direct violation of the peace compact and that the Front therefore had "the right to punish the enemy." The NLF's report seems to have had an impact on the resolutions approved in October.

Indeed, the Lao Dong passed a resolution, number 21, confirming the use of military force to keep Saigon off balance and deter truce violations; it also confirmed that "the path of the revolution in the South is the path of revolutionary violence." The manifesto concluded that "whatever the situation, we must maintain the offensive strategy line." Le Duan and Tran Van Tra were instrumental in forcing the policy shift. As southerners, they were no doubt sympathetic to conditions in the region and were perhaps influenced by the NLF's report from Algiers. Records from the plenum indicate a dramatic shift in thinking among policy elites when Duan said that Southern forces were stronger now than they had been at any time since 1954. This had not been the feeling among a majority of the northern officials when the Military Commission first met in the late spring. Also, as Le Duc Tho noted in 1988, "southern cadres fought back, in spite of orders to the contrary by northern cadres," and as a result, "the Central Committee was forced to meet in October 1973 and authorized the revolutionary fighters in the South to strike back against encroachments by Saigon."

Resolution 21 had an immediate impact on the conduct and outcome of the war in the South. The shift in military policy allowed NLF main force units to attack RVN rear base units and other selected targets. The main emphasis of the counter-offensives was the destruction of the Saigon regime's pacification program and the liberation of previously held territory. Within weeks of its passage, Resolution 21 had shifted the balance of the war. The Front regained significant territory and sent the message that it would no longer be a passive actor in South Viet Nam's future. More important, the ability to launch counterattacks made the NLFs diplomatic and political struggle movements more effective. "The combination of military, political, and diplomatic pressure made it possible to exploit the internal contradictions within the Saigon regime," One NLF official reported, "and this is what caused its eventual collapse."

The Saigon regime used the NLF counterattacks approved in Resolution 21 to move another step toward the complete rejection of the Paris agreement and total reliance on a military solution. Declaring that the "Third Indochina War" had begun, Thieu urged his troops to forget about the peace accord and carry out operations "in areas where their army is now stationed." He warned, "As far as the armed forces are concerned, I can tell you the war has restarted." The Saigon government had expected all along that the United States would continue to support the war in Indochina. Thieu hoped that these new attacks against NLF territory would provoke a severe Communist reaction and force the United States to accept Saigon's rejection of the Paris agreement. Thieu had long feared that direct negotiations with the NLF at La Celle St-Cloud gave the Communists added prestige and created the perception that there were indeed two southern governments. By launching new attacks, he believed, he could end the negotiations and renew the war.

Thieu had not been a good student of events in the United States, however, and the NLF quickly exploited the political situation. In July 1973, the U.S. Congress had passed a resolution to end all bombing in Indochina and prohibit any future military action there without prior congressional approval. In November, it approved the War Powers Act, requiring the president to notify the appropriate congressional committees within forty-eight hours of the deployment of American troops abroad and obligating him to withdraw them within sixty days unless Congress specified otherwise. Furthermore, the Watergate scandal was now front-page news and the Nixon administration was under siege. By February 1974, the NLF realized that the United States would not reenter the war and that any further aggressive action by the Saigon regime opened it to the possibility of a complete political collapse. "We understood clearly that Saigon wanted to do away with the Paris agreement and settle the conflict on the battlefield," commented one Vietnamese general, "but the balance of forces was shifting in our favor because of our superior political and moral position."

By March 1974, the NLF recognized that it could maintain enough military pressure on the Saigon government to cause a complete political collapse. "The Thieu regime had relied on military strength and technological superiority to hide its political weakness," explained a former military official in 1995, "but by March 1974 we had taken away that advantage and left the Saigon administration open for political attack from within." Front strategists correctly predicted that internal political pressure was mounting against Thieu and that only fear and terror had kept it from exploding before 1974. The goal, therefore, was to combine military campaigns with political agitation to foster the domestic dissent.

The result of the combined domestic political and military struggle was total chaos in Saigon. The absence of the Americans left the southern economy in a shambles. During the war, neither the United States nor Saigon had concentrated on developing a commercial foundation for the South's urban areas. The influx of refugees had turned the cities into powder kegs ready to blow as more and more of them failed to find employment. At the same time, the worldwide inflation caused by the Middle East oil embargo had a tremendous negative impact on the southern economy. By midsummer, more than 90 percent of the RVN's forces claimed that their pay was not enough to support their families. Desertion rates increased dramatically and former soldiers began to blame their commanding officers for the economic crisis. According to one Western journalist, "Corruption was not exceeding all bounds as commanders robbed payrolls and embezzled other funds."

In the spring of 1974, Thieu urged his armed forces to do their utmost to enforce a blockade to defeat the NLF by "starving them out." This blockade, labeled the "rice war" by several Western reporters, restricted the transportation of rice from one village to the next, prohibited the milling of rice except in government-run facilities, and outlawed the sale of rice to anyone other than an approved government buyer. The result was widespread starvation. In Thua Thien province alone, over 20,000 people died of hunger as a result of Thieu's blockade.

By mid-July 1974, Thieu's economic blockade had created a major economic depression and had contributed significantly to the political unrest in the South's cities. Demonstrators demanding jobs and food filled the streets daily, and even conservative Saigon newspapers condemned Thieu's policies. By the end of August, veterans' groups threatened to take over several towns to protest the lack of food and jobs. On September 21, workers in Cholon walked off their jobs, demanding food and temporary economic relief. The blockade had caused suffering in Saigon as well, where only a quarter of the population had enough to eat. According to several Saigon newspapers, most families could afford only one meal of steamed rice a day.

By late summer, the Thieu regime faced opposition from every quarter, including the United States. In late August, Tran Huu Thanh, a Catholic priest and former lecturer at the RVN's military command school, began an anticorruption campaign that led many former Thieu supporters to call for his ouster. Thanh had the support of the U.S. Central Intelligence Agency, and by early September the American embassy in Saigon called for a coalition of conservative forces to replace Thieu. Ironically, several members of Thieu's own National Assembly supported Thanh, and throughout the fall they abandoned the president. Eventually the American embassy, aware of the damage caused by its own actions, issued a statement denying that it had supported any opposition group and renewing its commitment to Thieu. By that time, however, the damage had been done.

By late September, the Lao Dong realized that the Thieu regime could no longer resist a major military offensive. During a policy review meeting of the Political Bureau, the Party discussed the impact of the political, diplomatic, and military struggle movements in the South. Party leaders concluded that "the present opportunity is most favorable" to liberate the South militarily. This decision, known as COSVN Directive 08 in the West, committed the Lao Dong to a major military action within the next several months. From September 30 until October 8, the General Staff of the Military Commission prepared for a strategic offensive. On October 8, the Political Bureau unanimously approved the General Staff's plan to liberate the South in 1975 and 1976 with a campaign to begin in the Central Highlands. The two-year, two-step crusade called for main force units to mount continuous attacks in 1975, paving the way for a general offensive and uprising in 1976. Military leaders warned the Political Bureau not to expect an uprising until the ARVN "had been smashed. Only then could favorable conditions be created for uprisings by the urban masses." Le Duan heralded the Political Bureau's decisions. "This is an event of paramount importance, a very courageous decision. This decision is the outcome of the collective wisdom of the Politburo, and the result of a long weighing up process based on the experience of several decades of fighting, on the implementation of revolution on the battlefield, on the balance of forces in our country and throughout the world."

Naturally, the NLF's diplomats fired the first shot in the Party's new military campaign. On the same day that the Lao Dong approved the two-year offensive, Madame Binh announced that the Front was breaking off all negotiations with the Saigon regime until Thieu was removed from office. Conditions in the South had deteriorated so rapidly that even Thieu's supporters urged him to reach a political settlement. The only hope of attaining this goal, of course, lay in a continued dialogue with the Front. When the NLF called off the talks, therefore, it precipitated a political crisis in Saigon. Several conservative newspapers called for Thieu to step down immediately to avoid an all-out war. "We can no longer match the Communists with U.S. aid so unpredictable," one paper editorialized in late October, "and new enemy divisions have crossed the border into South Viet Nam." Although the press was wrong on both counts, the NLF's action had created the proper conditions for the military offensive.

When the campaign began in early January, even the most optimistic Lao Dong cadre could not have foreseen the events of the next four months. In its initial plan, the General Staff in Hanoi envisioned a three-phased offensive. The first phase was to begin in January and end in late February, with main force units confining their attacks to the western portion of the B-2 theater, the southernmost region of Viet Nam. The next phase was to extend from March until June and encompass the entire country. Beginning in July, the military strategy shifted to small-scale encounters to prepare the urban areas for the general uprisings and the grand offensive. With the first attacks on ARVN forces in Phuoc Long province, northeast of Saigon, it appeared as if the Party might have to speed up its timetable.

On January 9, officials of the Lao Dong's Military Commission and General Staff met with the COSVN commander, Vo Chi Cong, to select the first target in the Central Highlands offensive. The generals finally concluded that the seizure of Ban Me Thuot would isolate the ARVN from the other principal cities in the highlands (Play Ku and Kontom) and would make it difficult for the Saigon forces to control movement in the region. On March 10, combined NLF and DRV forces attacked the city and within twenty-four hours it was in Communist hands. Spurred on by their relatively easy victory, revolutionary forces pursued ARVN troops as they retreated to Play Ku. After two weeks of fierce fighting, the ARVN commander, Pham Van Phu, ordered a complete withdrawal from the highlands.

On March 16, after inflicting several costly defeats on the ARVN, Van Tien Dung, the commander in charge of the final southern offensive, sent a report to the Political Bureau "reviewing the situation and proposing follow-up action to win decisive victory in this current dry season." The report recommended that the Lao Dong consolidate its victories in the Central Highlands by launching a two-pronged military offensive. The first group of attacks would be eastward and the second into the Fifth Military Zone, northeast of Saigon. Senior General Vo Nguyen Giap and the Military Commission accepted Dung's proposals and urged the armed forces "not to let the enemy withdraw safely and conserve their forces. You have to move right away and cut the enemy's retreat along Highway 1. . . ." When Le Duan read Dung's report, he predicted that victory was at hand.

With the highlands secured, Communist forces attacked the coastal cities of Quang Tri and Hue. Using Soviet-made tanks and taking advantage of the lack of U.S. air support, DRV and NLF forces routed the ARVN's elite First Division. Within weeks the Communists had isolated Da Nang, the second largest city in the South. President Thieu had ordered his troops to hold on to the city at all costs, but the flood of refugees from the highlands, reportedly a million strong, made it impossible to defend. On March 29, three DRV divisions entered the city unopposed.

In just three weeks, Communist forces had captured twelve provinces and the ARVN had lost nearly half of its troop strength. Optimistic Saigon generals predicted that the Communists would be incapable of sustaining the offensive and urged their troops to remain in the field. By the end of March, however, hundreds of officers had left their commands and thousands of troops had abandoned their units. NLF flags prominently displayed in the majority of homes along National Highway 1 welcomed the combined regular force units as they marched south toward the RVN's capital city.

In early April, the Political Bureau met to assess the results of the military campaign. It concluded that "with regard to both strategy and political-military forces, we have sufficient strength to overwhelm the enemy troops. The U.S. has proved to be completely impotent, and even if it increases its aid, it cannot save the puppets from collapse." The decision was therefore made to grasp the strategic opportunity and end the war by May 1, 1975. Responding to the Political Bureau's resolution, Communist forces rushed toward Saigon. It was only a matter of days before the city was completely surrounded by NLF and DRV troops.

On April 19, Vo Dong Giang, speaking for the NLF, warned the RVN that if Thieu were not removed immediately, the Communists would take the city by force. Two days later, under pressure from Ambassador Graham Martin, Thieu resigned. In a television speech on April 22, Thieu blamed the Ford administration for refusing to rescue its ally, as it had promised to do. Thieu escaped to Taiwan, apparently with a substantial amount of the RVN treasury, and named Vice President Tran Van Huong as his replacement. The NLF rejected Huong, however, and demanded that Saigon accept a leader who would support the Paris agreement. On April 28, the National Assembly turned power over to Big Minh. Two days later, at 11:30 A.M., Minh ordered RVN troops to abide by a cease-fire and urged the Communists to accept a peaceful transfer of power to avoid further bloodshed. With Minh's surrender on April 30, the Second Indochina War had finally come to an end.

✗ F U R T H E R   R E A D I N G

Brown, Weldon A. *The Last Chopper* (1976).
Burchett, Wilfred. *Grasshoppers and Elephants: Why Vietnam Fell* (1977).
Butler, David. *The Fall of Saigon* (1985).
Dawson, Alan. *55 Days: The Fall of South Vietnam* (1977).
Dillard, Walter Scott. *Sixty Days to Peace* (1982).
Duiker, William J. *The Communist Road to Power in Vietnam* (1981).
Ford, Gerald R. *A Time to Heal* (1979).
Goodman, Allan E. *The Lost Peace* (1978).
Haley, P. Edward. *Congress and the Fall of South Vietnam and Cambodia* (1982).
Herrington, Stuart A. *Peace with Honor?* (1983).
Hosmer, Stephen T., et al. *The Fall of South Vietnam* (1980).
Hung, Nguyen Tien, and Jerrold L. Schecter. *The Palace File* (1986).
Kimball, Jeffrey. *Nixon's Vietnam War* (1998).
Kissinger, Henry. *Years of Renewal* (1999).
LeGro, William E. *Vietnam from Cease-Fire to Capitulation* (1981).
Pilzer, John. *The Last Day* (1976).
Porter, Gareth. *A Peace Denied* (1975).
Snepp, Frank. *A Decent Interval* (1977).
Szulc, Tad. "How Kissinger Did It: Behind the Vietnam Cease-Fire Agreement," *Foreign Policy,* No. 15 (1974), 21–61.
Terzani, Tiziano. *Giai Phong! The Fall and Liberation of South Vietnam* (1976).
Tra, Tran Van. *Ending the Thirty Years' War* (1982).
Zasloff, Joseph J., and MacAlister Brown, eds. *Communism in Indochina* (1975).

CHAPTER

15

Legacies and Memories

of a War

✕

Although over twenty-five years have elapsed since the conclusion of the Vietnam War, the debate over the war's meaning continues to rage. The proliferation of novels, memoirs, films, and television programs about Vietnam testifies to the war's continuing hold on the American people. A veritable explosion of scholarly and political accounts of the Vietnam conflict has paralleled the remarkably diverse out-pourings of popular culture. Yet the picture that emerges from those diverse efforts remains hazy.

What have been the war's consequences—on America, on Asia, and on the rest of the world? How should we read the lessons of the war? Why do Americans remain divided over how to remember the Vietnam experience? Those fundamental questions have inspired a variety of conflicting answers. The documents and essays in this chapter explore those issues, continuing the debate introduced in Chapter 1 about the broader meaning of the war.

✕ D O C U M E N T S

In Document 1, an excerpt from a presidential press conference of June 9, 1975, President Gerald R. Ford responds to questions about the lessons he has learned from America's experience. In Document 2, Ford's successor, President Jimmy Carter, describes the profound moral crisis that he believes the war created for America. His comments formed part of a major foreign-policy address delivered at Notre Dame University on May 22, 1977. In a book published in 1985, part of which is reprinted as Document 3, Richard M. Nixon reflected on the lessons of Vietnam, charging that Saigon's fall represented one of the Soviet Union's greatest victories. Document 4 is an address delivered by President Ronald Reagan at the 1988 Veterans' Day ceremony. He made his remarks, celebrating the nobility and sacrifice of Vietnam veterans, at the Vietnam Veterans' Memorial in Washington. Document 5 includes excerpts from President Bill Clinton's public remarks after announcing the normalization of diplomatic relations with Vietnam on July 11, 1995.

Documents 6, 7, and 8 comprise personal reflections from American veterans deeply affected by the war. First, John Ketwig explains the powerful emotions that the unveiling of the Vietnam War memorial stirred in him. Then Stephen A. Howard, an African-American draftee, explains why his experiences in Vietnam have left such painful psychological scars. Finally, Lily Adams, an Army nurse in Vietnam, describes her own troubled adjustment after the war, concluding with a personal assessment of the war's contradictory legacy.

1. Gerald R. Ford on the Lessons of Vietnam, 1975

The President. I think . . . there are a number of lessons that we can learn from Vietnam. One, that we have to work with other governments that feel as we do— that freedom is vitally important. We cannot, however, fight their battles for them. Those countries who believe in freedom as we do must carry the burden. We can help them, not with U.S. military personnel but with arms and economic aid, so that they can protect their own national interest and protect the freedom of their citizens.

I think we also may have learned some lessons concerning how we would con-duct a military operation. There was, of course, from the period of 1961 or 1962 through the end of our military involvement in Vietnam, a great deal of controversy whether the military operations in Vietnam were carried out in the proper way, some dispute between civilian and military leaders as to the proper prosecution of a mili-tary engagement. I think we can learn something from those differences, and if we ever become engaged in any military operation in the future—and I hope we don't— I trust we've learned something about how we should handle such an operation.

Q. Does that mean that you would not conduct a limited war again with a certain amount of restraint on the part of our bombers and so forth ?

The President. I wouldn't want to pass judgment at this time on any hypothetical situation. I simply am indicating that from that unfortunate experience in Vietnam, we ought to be able to be in a better position to judge how we should conduct our-selves in the future.

2. Jimmy Carter Sees a "Profound Moral Crisis," 1977

For too many years, we've been willing to adopt the flawed and erroneous principles and tactics of our adversaries, sometimes abandoning our own values for theirs. We've fought fire with fire, never thinking that fire is better quenched with water. This approach failed, with Vietnam the best example of its intellectual and moral poverty. But through failure we have now found our way back to our own principles and values, and we have regained our lost confidence.

Excerpt from a presidential press conference, June 9, 1975.

Excerpt from address delivered at Notre Dame University, May 22, 1977.

By the measure of history, our nation's 200 years are very brief, and our rise to world eminence is briefer still. It dates from 1945, when Europe and the old international order lay in ruins. Before then, America was largely on the periphery of world affairs, but since then, we have inescapably been at the center of world affairs.

Our policy during this period was guided by two principles: a belief that Soviet expansion was almost inevitable but that it must be contained, and the corresponding belief in the importance of an almost exclusive alliance among non-Communist nations on both sides of the Atlantic. That system could not last forever unchanged. Historical trends have weakened its foundation. The unifying threat of conflict with the Soviet Union has become less intensive, even though the competition has become more extensive.

The Vietnamese war produced a profound moral crisis, sapping worldwide faith in our own policy and our system of life, a crisis of confidence made even more grave by the covert pessimism of some of our leaders.

In less than a generation, we've seen the world change dramatically. The daily lives and aspirations of most human beings have been transformed. Colonialism is nearly gone. A new sense of national identity now exists in almost 100 new countries that have been formed in the last generation. Knowledge has become more widespread. Aspirations are higher. As more people have been freed from traditional constraints, more have been determined to achieve, for the first time in their lives, social justice.

The world is still divided by ideological disputes, dominated by regional conflicts, and threatened by danger that we will not resolve the differences of race and wealth without violence or without drawing into combat the major military powers. We can no longer separate the traditional issues of war and peace from the new global questions of justice, equity, and human rights.

It is a new world, but America should not fear it. It is a new world, and we should help to shape it. It is a new world that calls for a new American foreign policy—a policy based on constant decency in its values and on optimism in our historical vision.

3. Richard M. Nixon Reads Vietnam's Lessons, 1985

Today, after Communist governments have killed over a half million Vietnamese and over 2 million Cambodians, the conclusive moral judgment has been rendered on our effort to save Cambodia and South Vietnam: We have never fought in a more moral cause. Assertions in the antiwar news media that life in Indochina would be better after our withdrawal served to highlight in a tragic way the abysmally poor level of their reporting throughout the war. But of all their blatantly inaccurate statements over the years, none was more hideously wrong than that one.

"If wise men give up the use of power," de Gaulle once said, "what madmen will seize it, what fanatics?"

When we abandoned the use of power in Indochina, we also abandoned its people to grim fate. When the American ambassador to Cambodia, John Gunther Dean, was about to be evacuated from Phnom Penh, he offered Lon Nol's closest colleague, Sirik Matak, asylum in the United States. The former Premier responded in a letter:

> Dear Excellency and Friend,
>
> I thank you very sincerely for your letter and for your offer to transport me toward freedom. I cannot, alas, leave in such a cowardly fashion. As for you, and in particular your great country, I never believed for a moment that you would have this sentiment of abandoning a people which has chosen liberty. You have refused us your protection, and we can do nothing about it.
>
> You leave and my wish is that you and your country will find happiness under this sky. But mark it well, that if I shall die here on the spot and in the country I love, it is too bad, because we are all born and must die one day. I have only committed this mistake of believing you.
>
> Sisowath Sirik Matak

It was a fittingly noble, if tragically sad, epitaph for his country, his people, and himself. He was among the first whom the Khmer Rouge executed.

After we abandoned the use of power, it was seized by the North Vietnamese and Khmer Rouge Communists. Our defeat was so great a tragedy because after the peace agreement of January 1973 it was so easily avoidable. Consolidating our gains would not have taken much to accomplish—a credible threat to enforce the peace agreement through retaliatory strikes against North Vietnam and a sufficient flow of aid to Cambodia and South Vietnam. But Congress legislated an end to our involvement. It also legislated the defeat of our friends in the same stroke.

A lesson that our adversaries should learn from our intervention in Vietnam is that the United States, under resolute and strong leadership, will go to great lengths and endure great sacrifices to defend its allies and interests. We fought in Vietnam because there were important strategic interests involved. But we also fought because our idealism was at stake. If not the United States, what nation would have helped defend South Vietnam? The fact is that no other country would have fought for over a decade in a war half a world away at great cost to itself in order to save the people of a small country from Communist enslavement.

One lesson we must learn from Vietnam is that if we do not exercise power for the good, there are plenty of men like Ho Chi Minh, Le Duan, Khieu Samphan, and Pol Pot who will gladly exercise it for evil purposes. Our armed intervention in the Vietnam War was not a brutal and immoral action. That we came to the defense of innocent people under attack by totalitarian thugs is no moral indictment. That we mishandled it at times in no way taints the cause. South Vietnam and Cambodia were worthy of our help—and the 3 million people who were killed in the war's aftermath deserved to be saved. Our abandonment of them in their moment of greatest need was not worthy of our country.

Another lesson we must learn is that in the real world peace is inseparable from power. Our country has had the good fortune of being separated from our enemies by two oceans. Others, like our friends in Indochina, did not enjoy that luxury. Their enemies lived just a few miles away up the Ho Chi Minh Trail. Our mistake was not that we did too much and imposed an inhumane war on peace-loving peoples. It was that in the end we did too little to prevent totalitarians from imposing their inhumane rule on freedom-loving peoples. Our cause must be peace. But we must recognize that greater evils exist than war.

Communist troops brought peace to South Vietnam and Cambodia—but it was the peace of the grave.

The Third World war began before World War II ended. Saigon's fall ten years ago was the Soviet Union's greatest victory in one of the key battles of the Third World war. No Soviet soldiers fought in Vietnam, but it was a victory for Moscow nonetheless because its ally and client, North Vietnam, won and South Vietnam and the United States lost. After we failed to prevent Communist conquest in Vietnam, it became accepted dogma that we would fail everywhere. For six years after Vietnam, the new isolationists chanted "No more Vietnams" as the dominoes fell one by one: Laos, Cambodia, and Mozambique in 1975; Angola in 1976; Ethiopia in 1977; South Yemen in 1978; Nicaragua in 1979.

4. Ronald Reagan Calls Vietnam a Noble and Just Cause, 1988

We're gathered today, just as we have gathered before, to remember those who served, those who fought, those still missing, and those who gave their last full measure of devotion for our country. We're gathered at a monument on which the names of our fallen friends and loved ones are engraved, and with crosses instead of diamonds beside them, the names of those whose fate we do not yet know. One of those who fell wrote, shortly before his death, these words: "Take what they have left and what they have taught you with their dying and keep it with your own. And take one moment to embrace those gentle heroes you left behind."

Well, today, Veterans Day, as we do every year, we take that moment to embrace the gentle heroes of Vietnam and of all our wars. We remember those who were called upon to give all a person can give, and we remember those who were prepared to make that sacrifice if it were demanded of them in the line of duty, though it never was. Most of all, we remember the devotion and gallantry with which all of them ennobled their nation as they became champions of a noble cause.

I'm not speaking provocatively here. Unlike the other wars of this century, of course, there were deep divisions about the wisdom and rightness of the Vietnam war. Both sides spoke with honesty and fervor. And what more can we ask in our democracy? And yet after more than a decade of desperate boat people, after the killing fields of Cambodia, after all that has happened in that unhappy part of the world, who can doubt that the cause for which our men fought was just? It was, after all, however imperfectly pursued, the cause of freedom; and they showed uncommon courage in its service. Perhaps at this late date we can all agree that we've learned one lesson: that young Americans must never again be sent to fight and die unless we are prepared to let them win.

Public Papers of the Presidents: Ronald Reagan, 1988–1989, 2, pp. 1495–1496.

But beyond that, we remember today that all our gentle heroes of Vietnam have given us a lesson in something more: a lesson in living love. Yes, for all of them, those who came back and those who did not, their love for their families lives. Their love for their buddies on the battlefields and friends back home lives. Their love of their country lives.

This memorial has become a monument to that living love. The thousands who come to see the names testify to a love that endures. The messages and mementos they leave speak with a whispering voice that passes gently through the surrounding trees and out across the breast of our peaceful nation. A childhood teddy bear, a photograph of the son or daughter born too late to know his or her father, a battle ribbon, a note—there are so many of these, and all are testimony to our living love for them. And our nation itself is testimony to the love our veterans have had for it and for us. Our liberties, our values, all for which America stands is safe today because brave men and women have been ready to face the fire at freedom's front. And we thank God for them.

Yes, gentle heroes and living love and our memories of a time when we faced great divisions here at home. And yet if this place recalls all this, both sweet and sad, it also reminds us of a great and profound truth about our nation: that from all our divisions we have always eventually emerged strengthened. Perhaps we are finding that new strength today, and if so, much of it comes from the forgiveness and healing love that our Vietnam veterans have shown.

For too long a time, they stood in a chill wind, as if on a winter night's watch. And in that night, their deeds spoke to us, but we knew them not. And their voices called to us, but we heard them not. Yet in this land that God has blessed, the dawn always at last follows the dark, and now morning has come. The night is over. We see these men and know them once again—and know how much we owe them, how much they have given us, and how much we can never fully repay. And not just as individuals but as a nation, we say we love you.

5. Bill Clinton Announces the Normalization of Diplomatic Relations with Vietnam, 1995

Thank you very much. I welcome you all here, those who have been introduced and distinguished Members of Congress and military leaders, veterans, others who are in the audience.

Today I am announcing the normalization of diplomatic relationships with Vietnam.

From the beginning of this administration, any improvement in relationships between America and Vietnam has depended upon making progress on the issue of Americans who were missing in action or held as prisoners of war. Last year, I lifted the trade embargo on Vietnam in response to their cooperation and to enhance our efforts to secure the remains of lost Americans and to determine the fate of those whose remains have not been found.

Public Papers of the Presidents: Bill Clinton, 1995, II, pp. 1073–1074.

It has worked. In 17 months, Hanoi has taken important steps to help us resolve many cases. Twenty-nine families have received the remains of their loved ones and at last have been able to give them a proper burial. Hanoi has delivered to us hundreds of pages of documents shedding light on what happened to Americans in Vietnam. And Hanoi has stepped up its cooperation with Laos, where many Americans were lost. We have reduced the number of so-called discrepancy cases, in which we have had reason to believe that Americans were still alive after they were lost, to 55. And we will continue to work to resolve more cases.

Hundreds of dedicated men and women are working on all these cases, often under extreme hardship and real danger in the mountains and jungles of Indochina. On behalf of all Americans, I want to thank them. . . .

Never before in the history of warfare has such an extensive effort been made to resolve the fate of soldiers who did not return. Let me emphasize, normalization of our relations with Vietnam is not the end of our effort. From the early days of this administration I have said to the families and veterans groups what I say again here: We will keep working until we get all the answers we can. Our strategy is working. Normalization of relations is the next appropriate step. With this new relationship we will be able to make more progress. To that end, I will send another delegation to Vietnam this year. And Vietnam has pledged it will continue to help us find answers. We will hold them to that pledge.

By helping to bring Vietnam into the community of nations, normalization also serves our interest in working for a free and peaceful Vietnam in a stable and peaceful Asia. We will begin to normalize our trade relations with Vietnam, whose economy is now liberalizing and integrating into the economy of the Asia-Pacific region. Our policy will be to implement the appropriate United States Government programs to develop trade with Vietnam consistent with U.S. law.

As you know, many of these programs require certifications regarding human rights and labor rights before they can proceed. We have already begun discussing human rights issues with Vietnam, especially issues regarding religious freedom. Now we can expand and strengthen that dialog. The Secretary of State will go to Vietnam in August where he will discuss all of these issues, beginning with our POW and MIA concerns.

I believe normalization and increased contact between Americans and Vietnamese will advance the cause of freedom in Vietnam, just as it did in Eastern Europe and the former Soviet Union. I strongly believe that engaging the Vietnamese on the broad economic front of economic reform and the broad front of democratic reform will help to honor the sacrifice of those who fought for freedom's sake in Vietnam.

I am proud to be joined in this view by distinguished veterans of the Vietnam war. They served their country bravely. They are of different parties. A generation ago they had different judgments about the war which divided us so deeply. But today they are of a single mind. They agree that the time has come for America to move forward on Vietnam. All Americans should be grateful especially that Senators John McCain, John Kerry, Bob Kerrey, Chuck Robb, and Representative Peter Peterson, along with other Vietnam veterans in the Congress, including Senator Harkin, Congressman Kolbe, and Congressman Gilchrest, who just left, and others who are out here in the audience have kept up their passionate interest in Vietnam but were able to move beyond the haunting and painful past toward finding common ground for the future. Today they and many other veterans support the normalization of relations, giving the opportunity to Vietnam to fully join the community of nations and being true to what they fought for so many years ago.

Whatever we may think about the political decisions of the Vietnam era, the brave Americans who fought and died there had noble motives. They fought for the freedom and the independence of the Vietnamese people. Today the Vietnamese are independent, and we believe this step will help to extend the reach of freedom in Vietnam and, in so doing, to enable these fine veterans of Vietnam to keep working for that freedom.

This step will also help our own country to move forward on an issue that has separated Americans from one another for too long now. Let the future be our destination. We have so much work ahead of us. This moment offers us the opportunity to bind up our own wounds. They have resisted time for too long. We can now move on to common ground. Whatever divided us before let us consign to the past. Let this moment, in the words of the Scripture, be a time to heal and a time to build.

Thank you all, and God bless America.

6. An American Veteran Helps to Dedicate the Vietnam War Memorial (1982), 1985

November of 1982 brought a tidal wave of emotions and long-suppressed memories into my life, all centered around a shaded corner of the mall in Washington, D.C., where a Vietnam Memorial was being constructed. A television camera scanned the vast wall of names, my eyes recognized a ghost from the past, and I burst into tears. I didn't know he hadn't made it. The children were upset at the sight of their daddy crying. We hustled them into the car and drove to Washington. The memorial was surrounded by snow fence and security guards, waiting quietly to be dedicated the following weekend. Television hadn't prepared me for the power of those huge, black walls; it takes a lot of space to print 57,939 names. We stood on a small knoll beneath the naked branches of hickories in winter dress. Perhaps a hundred strangers were scattered around us, many sobbing, none ashamed. My eyes were watering uncontrollably when the children spotted a squirrel and rescued me with their delighted chatter. . . .

The parade started at ten. We stood on the curb, hunched against the wind. Not long ago, I swore I would never come to the memorial, let alone a parade. Now I needed to be there, to see it and be a part of it, but from a distance. State by state, the waves of veterans came. Phalanxes of wheelchairs, ragged clusters out for a stroll, paunchy, nearing middle age, often irreverent. Clad in three-piece suits, jungle fatigues, green berets, and Indian war bonnets. Jeans and T-shirts. On crutches and canes. There was a disproportionate amount of long hair, as if overcompensating. Orange banners defying America to admit to Agent Orange, and black banners remembering POWs and MIAs. Too often, someone broke ranks to rush to the curb and share a hug and a tear with a ghost come to life. I strained my eyes when the

Ohio contingent passed. Perhaps it's best I didn't recognize the barrel chest and wavy blonde hair I had known for less than a day. I called Archie's name, and no one answered.

I was expecting the end of the parade when I saw an approaching solution to years of regret. They looked like all the others, except some carried outrageous signs.

> I am a Vietnam Veteran.
> I like the memorial.
> And if it makes it difficult
> To send people into battle again . . .
> I'll like it even more!

I could hear them now, chanting as they must have chanted in 1969 when I had stayed home. "HELL NO, OUR KIDS WON'T GO!" I hesitated, as I had hesitated in 1969. No, I couldn't wait another thirteen years! I pulled Carolynn off the curb and into the midst of them. I added my voice to theirs, fighting back years of emotion and frustration that threatened to crack my throat. I was amazed as people stepped from the curb to shake our hands or slap our backs.

Someone thrust a cassette recorder to my face and asked what I was feeling. I was too emotional. "We can't allow this to be the end of it. The war isn't over. We can't allow Vietnam to be swept under the rug as past history, because many of the men responsible for Vietnam are right over there," I pointed to the Pentagon, "hard at work, trying to involve us in Nicaragua, or El Salvador, or Libya, or Angola, or anywhere they can try out their terrible toys. It's not past history. It's a terrible, terrible threat, and we have children of our own now. We don't want to raise them to die in some swamp for no reason!" The recorder disappeared, and Carolynn worried that it might have been some form of government surveillance. I didn't care; I had an American right to my opinion, and to voice it. It was a free and glorious feeling, and we followed along to the memorial amid overwhelming joy and sadness. Rain had left the lawn a shambles. Behind us, a pathetic voice declared, "Nice of them to provide all this mud to make us feel at home." A worn guitar hung neck-down from a backpack. A wrinkled old man welcomed us home, his World War I uniform immaculate and proud.

I didn't need speeches to remember The Nam. Carolynn and I lunched on crepes and wine at the Smithsonian Associates' restaurant, enjoying a rare meal without bibs or potty breaks. By the time we returned to the memorial, it was dedicated. The crowd was enormous, and I tugged Carolynn into the midst of it. These were my peers, my generation. I didn't know them, but I wanted to soak up their company. Just being here, I was making a statement I had been unable to make for many years.

Finally the sun faded, the November chill returned, and we headed home. We walked hand in hand under Lincoln's stony gaze, through the trees where the antiwar protesters had been beaten and teargassed. To our right the bronze image of Thomas Jefferson watched us retreat; to our left the White House glowed in the glare of electric lights. Carolynn asked if I was okay.

Behind us, there were no proud sabers or prancing horses. There was only a black wall with 57,939 terrible reminders of the American blood shed in The Nam. Every morning, members of Congress would see it, feel it. It stood out, black and somber, and it couldn't be ignored. I was fine.

In early January of 1983, a group of "scholars and analysts," many from the Defense Department and the Army War College, met at the Smithsonian Institution in Washington, D.C. Officially known as The Smithsonian Institution's Wilson International Center For Scholars, they hoped to define "the lessons of Vietnam." The conference lasted two days. The Baltimore Sun reported, "There was disagreement and criticism, but little in the way of raw emotion." Half a mile away, a veteran stood before a black wall and shivered . . . and a hard rain fell.

7. An African-American Draftee Reflects on the War's Impact, 1984

When I got out, I applied for disability. But they didn't give me 10, 20, 30, 90 percent. Nothin'. They said I was physically fit for service. But for years I had to exercise, exercise to tone back the stomach and pelvic muscles. And even today, if I don't follow a perfect game plan eating proper foods, I get congestion in my intestines. And, at first, sex was a problem, but then it became a mental thing. At least there is no more of that to worry about.

I started to free-lance. And I was rolling in this industrial photography, doing the whole deal when they were building the Washington subway. But the contracts dried up. I am a highly skilled photographer, but I can't get a job. And my art is becoming more and more sophisticated, becomin' computerized. And I'm still on the outside looking in. I know that if I go someplace and I tell this employer I'm a Vietnam vet, it don't mean shit. Pardon the expression.

You know, I was sitting in my apartment with Carolyn. We weren't married yet. And I picked up the Washington *Post,* and it said Saigon had fallen. I said, "What the F was I there for?" I mean what was the whole purpose? All of a sudden you—your—your mechanism said, Hey, you don't have to worry about it. It cuts off. You don't think about Vietnam. That's the way it was.

Then about two years ago, one day, I decided that I'm not out to lunch. I'm null and void. I am not getting up today for no reason. And not getting up today for any reason is not justifiable in our society. See, you can't quit our society.

I don't have the flashbacks and the nightmares. It's the depression. And you can't identify what the depression is. Plenty of times I just wouldn't come home. All day, you know. And 30 minutes not coming home in my house is a long time. Or you walk into your house one night, take all the clothes out of your closet, and stack 'em up on the floor.

We came back totally fucked up in the head. But it took ten years for our bodies to catch up to where our heads were. All of a sudden you feel this psychological pain become physical pain. Then if you're lucky, which I was, somebody come up and pull your coat and say, "Hey, you need some help." 'Cause if my old lady hadn't decided I needed some help, I would probably either be dead or in jail today.

I went to Walter Reed first. They put me in a situation with about 34 people in a room. How in the hell are you gonna talk to me about my problems with 34 other problems in your face? I went to the VA hospital in Baltimore, and they gave me two aspirins and told me to go to bed and call in the morning. By my wife havin' a job that she could have Blue Cross and Blue Shield, I got a private shrink gettin' me through the moment. But I don't understand why we gotta pay this guy $90 an hour when I gave you three years, four months, five days, and twelve hours of the best of my life.

This psychological thing, we try to suppress it. But it kills us quicker than if somebody just walked up to you and put a bullet in your head. 'Cause it eats away at your inner being. It eats away at everything that you ever learned in life. Your integrity. Your word. See, that's all you have.

Vietnam taught you to be a liar. To be a thief. To be dishonest. To go against everything you ever learned. It taught you everything you did not need to know, because you were livin' a lie. And the lie was you ain't have no business bein' there in the first place. You wasn't here for democracy. You wasn't protecting your homeland. And that was what wear you down. We were programmed for the fact as American fighting men that we were still fighting a civilized war. And you don't fight a civilized war. It's nothing civilized about—about war.

Like this day, they took this water buffalo from the farmers. Either paid them off or killed them. It didn't matter. Whichever was best.

They lifted it with the Huey about 300 feet. Nobody paid much attention. 'Cause you on a chopper base. You see helicopters liftin' off with all kinds of strange things.

So he flew the chopper up, just outside Bien Hao. The game plan was to drop it. And when you drop a water buffalo 300 feet, it has a tendency to splatter. So that meant the farmers around knew that you were almighty. That you would take their prized possession. That we'll come and get your shit.

So we dropped it in the middle of a minefield. Set off a whole bunch of 'em.

I know the Vietnamese saw it. They watched everything we did.

I think we were the last generation to believe, you know, in the honor of war. There is no honor in war.

My mama still thinks that I did my part for my country, 'cause she's a very patriotic person.

I don't.

8. A Former Army Nurse Considers the War's Impact, 1987

I get on the bus [after returning from Vietnam]. Everyone is staring at me. I mean, they're looking at me like I just killed somebody. I'm sitting there thinking something must be wrong with my uniform, that they're critical of me because I'm not shipshape—I really did not have any idea what it was all about. So I get off the bus. People are giving me dirty looks all over the place. Still, I can't figure it out. I had heard in Vietnam from letters back that people in the World were negative about us,

Excerpted from *In the Combat Zone: An Oral History of American Women in Vietnam* (Little, Brown), edited by Kathryn Marshall. Copyright © 1987 Kathryn Marshall. Reprinted by permission of Melanie Jackson Agency, L.L.C.

only it didn't make any sense to me. Why would they be negative about us when we're saving lives backward and forward? Anyhow, I go inside, change into my jeans, and go down to my friend's house. When I get there I take my uniform out of my bag, throw it on the floor and say, "Burn it!" "You sure you don't want to save this? Just look at all the medals! What did you get the medals for?" "I don't want to talk about it—just burn it!"

So I moved into an apartment in San Francisco, on the edge of Chinatown. I lived alone and was very angry and very hostile, only I didn't know what I was angry and hostile about. I didn't know if I was angry at the country for being angry at me. I didn't know if I was angry because all that work in Vietnam was for nothing—I mean, I was very, very confused. That's why I ended up going to bars looking for Vietnam vets. . . .

What do I tell my kids about Vietnam? The truth. The confusion. I've explained to Erika about one kid who had one leg missing, one arm missing, and one eye missing. When he came in to us he yelled, "You bitches leave me alone!" The captain got on his case, said, "You don't talk to them like that—they're women and you don't say those words to them!" Well, the kid had been hanging around with GIs and didn't know *bitch* was a bad word. He was a toughie, a real toughie, that kid. He ended up getting very attached to me and used to cry whenever I'd leave him. Well, I resisted getting attached to him—I resisted and resisted and felt real guilty for not allowing myself to give him what I wanted to give him. Because I didn't want to get attached, not to anybody. So I explained to Erika that this kid haunted me. That I did everything I should have done, that there was no way I could have adopted him—yet he got to me. That kid really got to my defenses.

Yeah, I had problems with children. Last Christmas is the first one I survived without going totally bananas at the sight of crowds of children. And that's because I'm really very well healed. I went to Salute One [the dedication ceremonies for the Vietnam Veterans Memorial in Washington], dealt with my grief at the Wall, and left a hundred pounds lighter.

Vietnam taught me a lot. It taught me that war is not the practical way of dealing with disagreements among countries, and it taught me that the men and women who served in Vietnam are very special people.

When I discuss Vietnam I find myself discussing the negative stuff. War is negative, and most of the time Vietnam was negative. But I want to emphasize that, as a nurse in a war zone, I found myself performing beyond my limits—as a result, I have more self-confidence, know that I can tackle any task, that nothing is impossible if you want it bad enough. I'm really proud to have served in Vietnam. No one can take that away from me or from the other vets.

I was lucky enough to witness the special friendship between men that you rarely see in so-called real life. I learned that men can be gentle, tender, and loving with each other. I learned that men and women can work together with mutual respect and admiration. But no matter what positive experiences we had over there, I know war is not the answer to anything. That's why I'll continue to work on peace issues for the rest of my life.

Soldiers aren't the only ones who die in wars. Like I tell my kids, grandmas, grandpas, mommies, daddies, and babies die in wars, too.

✗ *E S S A Y S*

In the first essay, Paul Kennedy, a Yale University historian, assesses the Vietnam War's impact on the international power system. The author of a highly acclaimed book on the rise and fall of the great powers over the past five hundred years, from which this selection is drawn, Kennedy argues that the war's practical and symbolic consequences have been profound for the United States and for the rest of the world. Historian Marilyn B. Young of New York University explains why the Vietnam War has become a political and cultural touchstone for Americans, despite their inability to reach a consensus on the conflict's meaning, in the middle essay. Indeed, she argues that it will likely remain indefinitely "a zone of contested meaning." Young also probes why the war in Vietnam has left such a powerful—and often tragic—imprint on the men and women who served there. Finally, Arnold R. Isaacs, who covered the conflict as a correspondent for the *Baltimore Sun* from 1972 to 1975, ruminates on the continuing struggle within American society over how to remember the Vietnam War. "The war and its ghosts," he writes, "continue to hover over the national life and spirit."

The Impact of Vietnam on America's World Role

PAUL KENNEDY

In so many ways, symbolic as well as practical, it would be difficult to exaggerate the impacts of the lengthy American campaign in Vietnam and other parts of Southeast Asia upon the international power system—or upon the national psyche of the American people themselves, most of whose perceptions of their country's role in the world still remain strongly influenced by that conflict, albeit in different ways. The fact that this was a war fought by an "open society"—and made the more open because of revelations like the Pentagon Papers, and by the daily television and press reportage of the carnage and apparent futility of it all; that this was the first war which the United States had unequivocally lost, that it confounded the victorious experiences of the Second World War and destroyed a whole array of reputations, from those of four-star generals to those of "brightest and best" intellectuals; that it coincided with, and in no small measure helped to cause, the fissuring of a consensus in American society about the nation's goals and priorities, was attended by inflation, unprecedented student protests and inner city disturbances, and was followed in turn by the Watergate crisis, which discredited the presidency itself for a time; that it seemed to many to stand in bitter and ironic contradiction to everything which the Founding Fathers had taught, and made the United States unpopular across most of the globe; and finally that the shamefaced and uncaring treatment of the GIs who came back from Vietnam would produce its own reaction a decade later and thus ensure that the memory of this conflict would continue to prey upon the public consciousness, in war memorials, books, television documentaries, and personal tragedies—all of this meant that the Vietnam War, although far smaller in terms of casualties, impacted upon the American people somewhat as had the First World War upon Europeans. The effects were seen, overwhelmingly, at the *personal* and *psychological* levels; more broadly, they were interpreted as a crisis in American civilization and in its constitutional arrangements. As such, they would continue to have significance quite independent of the strategical and Great Power dimensions of this conflict.

But the latter aspects are the most important ones for our survey, and require further mention here. To begin with, it provided a useful and sobering reminder that a vast superiority in military hardware and economic productivity will not always and automatically translate into military *effectiveness*. . . . Economically, the United States may have been fifty to one hundred times more productive than North Vietnam; militarily, it possessed the firepower to (as some hawks urged) bomb the enemy back into the stone age—indeed, with nuclear weapons, it had the capacity to obliterate Southeast Asia altogether. But this was *not* a war in which those superiorities could be made properly effective. Fear of domestic opinion, and of world reaction, prevented the use of atomic weapons against a foe who could never be a *vital* threat to the United States itself. Worries about the American public's opposition to heavy casualties in a conflict whose legitimacy and efficacy came increasingly under question had similarly constrained the administration's use of the conventional methods of warfare; restrictions were placed on the bombing campaign; the Ho Chi Minh Trail through neutral Laos could not be occupied; Russian vessels bearing arms to Haiphong harbor could not be seized. It was important not to provoke the two major Communist states into joining the war. This essentially reduced the fighting to a series of small-scale encounters in jungles and paddy fields, terrain which blunted the advantages of American firepower and (helicopter-borne) mobility, and instead placed an emphasis upon jungle-warfare techniques and unit cohesion—which was much less of a problem for the crack forces than for the rapidly turning over contingents of draftees. Although Johnson followed Kennedy's lead in sending more and more troops to Vietnam (it peaked at 542,000, in 1969), it was never enough to meet General Westmoreland's demands; clinging to the view that this was still a limited conflict, the government refused to mobilize the reserves, or indeed to put the economy on a war footing.

The difficulties of fighting the war on terms disadvantageous to the United States' real military strengths reflected a larger political problem—the discrepancy between means and ends (as Clausewitz might have put it). The North Vietnamese and the Vietcong were fighting for what they believed in very strongly; those who were not were undoubtedly subject to the discipline of a totalitarian, passionately nationalistic regime. The South Vietnamese governing system, by contrast, appeared corrupt, unpopular, and in a distinct minority, opposed by the Buddhist monks, unsupported by a frightened, exploited, and war-weary peasantry; those native units loyal to the regime and who often fought well were not sufficient to compensate for this inner corrosion. As the war escalated, more and more Americans questioned the efficacy of fighting for the regime in Saigon, and worried at the way in which all this was corrupting the American armed forces themselves—in the decline in morale, the rise in cynicism, indiscipline, drugtaking, prostitution, the increasing racial sneers at the "gooks," and atrocities in the field, not to mention the corrosion of the United States' own currency or of its larger strategic posture. Ho Chi Minh had declared that his forces were willing to lose men at the rate of ten to one—and when they were rash enough to emerge from the jungles to attack the cities, as in the 1968

Tet offensive, they often did; but, he continued, despite those losses they would still fight on. That sort of willpower was not evident in South Vietnam. Nor was American society itself, increasingly disturbed by the war's contradictions, willing to sacrifice everything for victory. While the latter feeling was quite understandable, given what was at stake for each side, the fact was that it proved impossible for an open democracy to wage a halfhearted war successfully. This was the fundamental contradiction, which neither [Secretary of Defense Robert] McNamara's systems analysis nor the B-52 bombers based on Guam could alter.

More than a decade after the fall of Saigon (April 1975), and with books upon all aspects of that conflict still flooding from the presses, it still remains difficult to assess clearly how it may have affected the U.S. position in the world. Viewed from a longer perspective, say, backward from the year 2000 or 2020, it might be seen as having produced a salutory shock to American global hubris (or to what Senator [J. William] Fulbright called "the arrogance of power"), and thus compelled the country to think more deeply about its political and strategical priorities and to readjust more sensibly to a world already much changed since 1945—in other words, rather like the shock which the Russians received in the Crimean War, or the British received in the Boer War, producing in their turn beneficial reforms and reassessments.

At the time, however, the short-term effects of the war could not be other than deleterious. The vast boom in spending on the war, precisely at a time when domestic expenditures upon Johnson's "Great Society" were also leaping upward, badly affected the American economy. . . . Moreover, while the United States was pouring money into Vietnam, the USSR was devoting steadily larger sums to its nuclear forces—so that it achieved a rough strategic parity—and to its navy, which in these years emerged as a major force in global gunboat diplomacy; and this increasing imbalance was worsened by the American electorate's turn against military expenditures for most of the 1970s. In 1978, "national security expenditures" were only 5 percent of GNP, lower than they had been for thirty years. Morale in the armed services plummeted, in consequence both of the war itself and of the postwar cuts. Shakeups in the CIA and other agencies, however necessary to check abuses, undoubtedly cramped their effectiveness. The American concentration upon Vietnam worried even sympathetic allies; its methods of fighting in support of a corrupt regime alienated public opinion, in western Europe as much as in the Third World, and was a major factor in what some writers have termed American "estrangement" from much of the rest of the planet. It led to a neglect of American attention toward Latin America—and a tendency to replace Kennedy's hoped-for "Alliance for Progress" with military support for undemocratic regimes and with counterrevolutionary actions (like the 1965 intervention in the Dominican Republic). The—inevitably—open post–Vietnam War debate over the regions of the globe for which the United States would or *would not* fight in the future disturbed existing allies, doubtless encouraged its foes, and caused wobbling neutrals to consider re-insuring themselves with the other side. At the United Nations debates, the American delegate appeared increasingly beleaguered and isolated. Things had come a long way since Henry Luce's assertion that the United States would be the elder brother of nations in the brotherhood of man.

The War's Tragic Legacy

MARILYN B. YOUNG

The course of the Vietnam War challenged all the axioms of the post–World War II world, and the ideological conviction the United States needs to pursue its global domination has yet to be recovered, if it ever can be. The Vietnam War remains today and is likely to remain for the foreseeable future a zone of contested meaning; and the struggle over its interpretation is central to contemporary American politics, foreign and domestic, and of American culture as well.

A fundamental axiom of U.S. foreign policy had been that this nation is always on the side of freedom and justice. "When I got to Saigon I was twenty-two," Richard Holbrooke remembered, "and I believed everything I had been told by the United States government. I believed that the commitment was correct—freedom of choice, self-determination, save the country from Communism—and that we were doing the right thing because the U.S. government *did* the right thing. In those days you didn't question it." Vietnam seriously weakened that automatic response for Holbrooke and for much of his generation; many Americans born during the decade of the war grew up not believing *anything* their government told them.

If axiomatic American goodness was brought into question by the war, so too was the axiomatic evil of the government's designated enemies. Everything that had been used to characterize the enemy—his indifference to human life, his duplicity, his ruthlessness—had at various times during the war been seen to characterize the United States as well. And while this might have been a surmountable problem in the name of a cause fervently embraced by a majority of Americans, it had become a very serious problem in the absence of such a cause.

Nor have American policymakers been able to appeal to the experience of Munich quite as confidently as in the past, although the Bush administration repeatedly did so during the Iraq crisis. For the post–World War II generation of voters, Vietnam has replaced Munich as their foreign policy paradigm.

Popular revulsion from the Vietnam War has been a sufficiently serious constraint on foreign policy to merit special designation by pro-war publicists and politicians: "the Vietnam syndrome." Thus pathologized, its symptoms—grave reluctance to send American troops abroad, close questioning of administration interventionist appeals, consistent poll results indicating that an overwhelming majority judge the Vietnam War to have been not simply a mistake but fundamentally wrong—require a cure, a pacification program. As in Vietnam itself, pacification is both military and civilian. Reagan's 1983 invasion of the tiny island of Grenada—in which 6,000 elite troops won 8,700 medals in the course of an exceedingly brief war against the Grenadian militia and a small group of Cuban advisers—was designed to make Americans "stand tall" again, confident in their capacity to exercise force when their government deems it necessary. Similarly, in 1986 Reagan met the problem of international terrorism by terror-bombing Muammer el-Qadaffi's headquarters in Libya.

And in 1989, the Bush administration invaded Panama to remove a former ally who had fallen out of favor. In the summer of 1990, President Bush's rapid military buildup in Saudi Arabia seemed directed not only at Iraq but also at a war-phobic American public.

Militarists, both civilian and in the armed forces, took comfort from the positive response of the public to these actions. But Pentagon analysts were also quick to note the speed and secrecy with which these interventions were launched and, more to the point, terminated. Reagan administration efforts to enlist popular support for American armed intervention in Nicaragua, on the other hand, received little encouragement.

On the civilian front, postwar pacification addresses itself to the restoration of the belief in the essential benevolence of U.S. actions, or, if not always its actions, then certainly its intentions. Jimmy Carter's human rights policy was an effort to achieve the restoration of America's good name, to give the world, in [National Security Adviser Zbigniew] Brzezinski's words, "greater respect for the moral meaning of America . . . and for the President himself as the personal expression of the fundamentally spiritual message of America." The policy required certification of good behavior before congressional appropriations could be approved for regimes whose human rights violations had reached a sufficient level of abuse to come to general international attention. The policy was more rhetorical than real, for whenever serious policy choices had to be made, human rights invariably took second place. In El Salvador in 1979 and 1980, for example, tens of thousands of citizens were being killed by U.S.-trained and -funded military death squads (30,000 between 1979 and 1981; double that number by 1985). Shortly before his assassination, in February 1980, Archbishop Oscar Romero appealed to Carter to end military aid to El Salvador, and he was ignored.

Ronald Reagan jettisoned Carter's human rights policy and set out on a more direct and less expensive approach to healing spiritual wounds: he renamed them. The United States invasion of Vietnam was a "noble cause," the American-paid mercenaries in Nicaragua were "freedom fighters." In one press conference, he rewrote the history of Vietnam itself, informing reporters that it had always been two countries that France had liberated after World War II and whose possible reunification was disrupted by Ho Chi Minh's refusal to participate in elections.

Another postwar necessity has been the development of a satisfactory approach to popular insurgencies or governments in the Third World, a task both complicated and made urgent by the ongoing impact of Vietnam on the United States: "Our failure in Vietnam still casts a shadow over U.S. intervention anywhere," a Reagan administration report warned. Unless the pessimism engendered by Vietnam is overcome and an interventionist policy restored, "America's ability to defend its interest in the most vital regions, in the Persian Gulf, the Mediterranean and the Western Pacific" will be undermined. In this area too there has been renaming, from the "counterinsurgency" of the 1960s to "low intensity conflict."

The phrase "low intensity conflict" may do more than rename, however. As Michael Klare has pointed out, "for U.S. policymakers and war planners . . . low-intensity conflict . . . represents a strategic reorientation of the U.S. military establishment, and a renewed commitment to employ force in a global crusade against Third World revolutionary movements and governments." It is a "broad concept that spans the spectrum of conflict from relative peace to conventional war." Perhaps this is the major departure from the past: low-intensity conflict frankly embraces a policy of permanent war.

The Reagan report identified a monolithic Third World forever poised on the brink of change as the permanent enemy in this permanent war. Communist-led or not, change uncontrolled by the United States endangers its interests. In the report, all the countries of the Third World look alike, all peasants are either passive or terrorized into support for guerrilla movements, and all guerrillas are the same: outsiders supported by the Soviet Union or its regional surrogates. On the other side, all legitimate governments are also alike: modernizing elites, prevented from achieving reasonable reforms by the need to first defeat Communist-inspired popular movements from below, while all revolutionary governments are also the same: totalitarian minorities kept in power by force and Soviet support.

None of the above was true. But acting as if it were sometimes made it so, or effectively so—self-fulfilling prophecies, which exacted a terrible cost on the countries involved. Nicaragua, Angola, Mozambique, have each been blocked from exploring the larger possibilities of their revolutions in order to defend their countries against U.S.-funded mercenary armies. In this way, insurgencies were punished, their example tarnished, and American interests, as recent administrations have defined them, safeguarded. . . .

Over 26 million American men came of draft age during the Vietnam War; 2.15 million of them went to Vietnam, 1.6 million were in combat. Those who fought the war and died in it were disproportionately poor, badly educated, and black. (A high school dropout who enlisted had a 70 percent chance of being sent to Vietnam, a college graduate only 42 percent; until 1971, student deferments protected the majority of students from the draft altogether.) It was also a teen-aged army—over 60 percent of those who died in Vietnam were between the ages of seventeen and twenty-one, and the average age of those who served was nineteen, five to seven years younger than in other American wars.

Between 1966 and 1972, a special Great Society program—Project 100,000—scooped up over 300,000 young men previously considered ineligible for the military because of their low test scores. Project 100,000, Secretary of Defense Robert McNamara declared, was the "world's largest education of skilled men." With lower admissions scores, the "subterranean poor" would have an opportunity to serve their country in Vietnam; simultaneously, the program had the advantage of avoiding the politically unpleasant alternative of requiring students or reservists to do the same. The benefits, especially to young black men, were said to be especially striking. As Daniel Patrick Moynihan pointed out, the military was "an utterly masculine world. Given the strains of disordered and matrifocal family life in which so many Negro youth come of age, the armed forces are a dramatic and desperately needed change, a world away from women, a world run by strong men and unquestioned authority, where discipline, if harsh, is nonetheless orderly and predictable, and where rewards, if limited, are granted on the basis of performance." In its first two years of operation, 41 percent of those brought into the military through Project 100,000 were black, 80 percent had dropped out of high school, 40 percent could read at less than sixth-grade level, and 37 percent were put directly into combat. Court-martialed at double the usual rate, over eighty thousand of these veterans left the military without the skills and opportunities McNamara assured them would be theirs. and many of them with service records that would make civilian life far more difficult than if they had never served at all.

Each young man who went to war had an individual tour of duty, 365 days, and then home, on his own, with no effort on anyone's part to prepare for the shock of return, to help make the transition from war to peace, from the privileging of violence to its prohibition, from the sharp edge death brings to the life of a soldier to the ordinary daily life of a civilian, which denies death altogether. They had spoken always of coming back "to the world," counting each day "in country" which brought them closer to the end of their tour. But the homecoming was harder than any of them had expected. Later, many veterans would tell stories of having been spat upon by anti-war protesters, or having heard of veterans who were spat on. It doesn't matter how often this happened or whether it happened at all. Veterans *felt* spat upon, stigmatized, contaminated. In television dramas, veterans were not heroes welcomed back into the bosom of loving families, admiring neighborhoods, and the arms of girls who loved uniforms; they were psychotic killers, crazies with automatic weapons. It was as if the country assumed that anyone coming back from Vietnam would, even should, feel a murderous rage against the society that had sent him there. The actual veteran—tired, confused, jet-propelled from combat to domestic airport—disappeared. Or rather, he became a kind of living hologram, an image projected by conflicting interpretations of the war: a victim or an executioner, a soldier who had lost a war, a killer who should never have fought it at all.

Of course there were also just the daily bread-and-butter problems of finding work in an economy far less open than it had been when the war was young. Today, from one quarter to one third of the homeless (between one quarter and three quarters of a million men) are Vietnam-era veterans. Without training or skills, without any public sense that the country owed them anything at all, many Vietnam veterans found themselves not only unrewarded but even disadvantaged by their service records. The war had begun to unravel even as it was being fought, so that by 1971 dissent and disobedience within the armed forces were endemic. The result was a tremendous increase in the number of less than honorable discharges—"bad paper"— which have followed the 500,000 to 750,000 men who received them ever since, making it difficult for them to get and keep jobs, and depriving them of educational and even medical benefits.

The lack of skills, the bad service records, the war wounds, have been only part of the difficulty many veterans face. At first, the widespread appearance of psychological problems was named "postwar trauma" and assimilated to the literature on the problems of veterans of other wars. It soon became clear, however, that Vietnam veterans were not like veterans of other wars. As early as 1970, Vietnam Veterans Against the War organized "rap sessions," sometimes attended by sympathetic psychiatrists, to help returning soldiers deal with their experiences. Even the Veterans Administration, obviously reluctant to single out Vietnam veterans as having any particular difficulties (especially in the light of the meager benefits accorded them), reported a "greater distrust of institutions" and a "bitterness, disgust and suspicion of those in positions of authority and responsibility."

More disturbing was the persistence—or sudden onset ten or even fifteen years after the war—of symptoms of acute distress, accompanied by flashbacks, severe sleep problems, depression, and rage. "Postwar trauma" was renamed "post-traumatic stress disorder" and assimilated not to battle fatigue or shell shock but to what people experience as survivors of floods or earthquakes. A V. A. doctor estimates that as many as 700,000 veterans suffer from some form of "post-traumatic stress disorder" (or PTSD). A massive study of Vietnam-era veterans revealed that those who had been "exposed to significant amounts of combat and/or witnessed or were participants in abusive violence [against prisoners, civilians, etc.] demonstrate long-term problems" with disabling memories of the war.

Veterans of other American wars, Robert Jay Lifton argued in his book *Home from the War,* had come to terms with the absurdity and evil of war by believing that *their* war "had purpose and significance beyond the immediate horrors [they] witnessed." But "the central fact of the Vietnam War," Lifton wrote in 1973 while it was still going on, "is that no one really believes in it." Although it is possible to challenge Lifton and demonstrate that soldiers in World War II also had difficulty discerning significance beyond the immediate horror of their situation, it is nevertheless true that when they got home, the purpose and significance of what they had done was universally affirmed and most were able to accept it. This was not the situation of Vietnam veterans, for even those who came home to families or communities who approved of the war were aware of those who protested against it. Moreover, the announced goals of the war—to repel an outside invader, to give the people of South Vietnam the chance to choose their own government—were daily contradicted by the soldier's sense that in fact he was himself the invader, and that "the government he had come to defend [was] hated by the people and that he [was] hated most of all."

"What kind of a war is it?" Larry Rottman, poet and veteran, asked in a poem written during the war,

> where you can be pinned down
> all day in a muddy rice paddy
> while your buddies are being shot
> and a close-support Phantom jet
> who has been napalming the enemy
> wraps itself around a tree and explodes
> and you cheer inside.

"To have been in a war does not mean you understand the memories of it," Gloria Emerson has written. In published and unpublished novels, memoirs, poems, Vietnam veterans have tried to understand their memories.

For women veterans the problem was compounded by the initial inability of anyone, including themselves, to acknowledge that they too were combat veterans. No one seems to have kept close count of their numbers. The Department of Defense says 7,500 women were on active military service in Vietnam during the war; the Veterans Administration lists 11,000 women as having served there. Together with civilians working for the Red Cross or other voluntary services, the general estimate is that a total of between 33,000 and 55,000 women worked in Vietnam during the war. Like the young men who fought the war, the young women who nursed their wounds, or tried to "take their minds off the war," were confused, often defensive, almost always pained by their memories. "Our job was to look them [wounded soldiers] in the eye and convince them that everything was all right." It took practice, but "you finally built up a facade and could literally look at somebody dying and smile like Miss America or whatever we personified to them." The war gave many women responsibilities and a sense of power actually denied them in civilian life. But this new status too was confusing and even distressing in that there was no way to extricate it from the death and dehumanization that were its occasion. One nurse resisted having to treat wounded Vietnamese until one day she was forced to take care of an infant and broke down: "How, I wondered, could I ever come to believe I hated a baby?"

Lynda Van Devanter tried to join a VVAW demonstration when she returned from Vietnam, but was told, "This demonstration is only for vets." "I am a vet," she explained. "I was in Pleiku and Qui Nhon. . . ." "I . . . don't think you're supposed to march," came the answer. "But you told me it was for vets." "It is. . . . But you're not a vet."

In 1982, the Veterans Administration acknowledged that women were truly Vietnam vets: for the first time groups were established for women suffering from post-traumatic stress disorder. "She is afraid to trust again," Marilyn McMahon says in her poem "Wounds of War":

> Her days are haunted
>   by the texture of blood
>   the odor of burns
>   the face of senseless death;
> friends known and loved
>   vanished
>   abandoned.
> She sits alone in the darkened room
>   scotch her only hope.

"The war is never over," one homeless man explained to a reporter in 1987. "You drink one too many beers and it pops up. . . . Sometimes, I hope to settle down some-where where I won't be reminded of what I've seen. But I really don't see a future for myself." Being unable to imagine a future often precludes having one. More veterans have committed suicide since the war than died in it—at least sixty thousand. Nor is the connection between their war experience and their death at all obscure. Steven L. Anderson's parents, for example, found this note next to the body of their dead son: "When I was in Vietnam, we came across a North Vietnamese soldier with a man, a woman and a three- or four-year old girl. We had to shoot them all, I can't get the little girl's face out of my mind. I hope that God will forgive me."

In May 1971, Medal of Honor winner Dwight W. Johnson was shot dead by the owner of a store he was attempting to rob. In Vietnam, Johnson killed "five to 20 enemy soldiers, nobody knows for sure," when the tank crew he was trying to rescue blew up in front of his eyes. "When he ran out of ammunition," his obituary continues, "he killed one with the stock of his machine gun." Unskilled and jobless in Detroit, Skip Johnson's fortunes turned when he was awarded the Medal of Honor for his heroism that day. Civic notables showered him with gifts and the Army persuaded him to return to the service as a recruiter in Detroit's predominantly black high schools. But his wife noticed some changes in him, as she had in other veterans she knew: "They get quiet. It's like they don't have too much to say about what it was like over there. Maybe it's because they've killed people and they don't really know why they've killed them."

Eventually Skip Johnson went AWOL from his recruiter's job and ended up in Valley Forge VA Hospital, where the head psychiatrist reached a preliminary diagnosis: "Depression caused by post-Vietnam adjustment problem." Later, the doctor observed Johnson's guilt over having survived the tank ambush and over "winning a high honor for the one time in his life when he lost complete control of himself. He asked: 'What would happen if I lost control of myself in Detroit and behaved like I did in Vietnam?' The prospect of such an event apparently was deeply disturbing to him." The psychiatrist refrained from answering Johnson's question; but a store manager in the western end of Detroit was more forthcoming: " I first hit him with two bullets," the manager . . . said later. "But he just stood there, with the gun in his hand, and said, 'I'm going to kill you. . . .' I kept pulling the trigger until my gun was empty."

Johnson's mother, thinking about her son's life and death after he was buried at Arlington National Cemetery with full military honors, wondered whether he had simply "tired of this life and needed someone else to pull the trigger."

And many of those who have not tired of their lives, nor suffered from "post-traumatic stress disorder," who have homes, jobs, families, ambitions, nevertheless find the war somehow remains central to their lives. . . .

After the Korean War, the poet Thomas McGrath memorialized the American war dead—"brave: ignorant: amazed: Dead in the rice paddies, dead on the nameless hills." In November 1982, the brave, ignorant, amazed dead of Vietnam were remembered at the dedication of a Vietnam Veterans Memorial. Money for the memorial had been raised by the veterans themselves; the winning design, by Maya Ying Lin, provided for two black granite walls bearing the names of the Americans who died in Vietnam. There was a protest by those who deemed the design insufficiently patriotic, and so a life-size statue of three GIs, two white, one black, was added to the original conception. Maya Ying Lin protested that it was like "drawing a moustache" on her design, but in the event, the statues have a different impact, as unpredictable as that of the wall itself.

Unlike the commemoration of the flag raising at Iwo Jima, these soldiers are flagless and exhausted. They seem to be waiting for something, but the only thing visible in the direction in which they look are the giant slabs with the names of their dead comrades. At first Bruce Weigl wondered why he had come to the dedication ceremony in Washington on Veterans Day, 1982. "I think we came," he wrote later,

> without really knowing it, to make the memorial our wailing wall. We came to find the names of those we lost in the war, as if by tracing the letters cut into the granite we could find what was left of ourselves. It turns out that, beyond all the petty debates over the monument, no veteran could turn his back on the terrible grace of Maya Lin's wall and the names of the 57,939 who died or disappeared in Vietnam from July 1959 to May 1975: America's longest most vicious sin.

What militarists deplore as the Vietnam syndrome can better be understood as a relatively unique event in American history: an inability to forget, a resistance to the everyday workings of historical amnesia, despite the serious and coordinated efforts of the government and much of the press to "heal the wounds" of the war by encouraging such forgetting, or what comes to the same thing, firm instructions on how to remember. At the dedication of the Vietnam Memorial, President Reagan announced that the time had come to move on, "in unity and with resolve, with the resolve to always stand for freedom, as those who fought did, and to always try to protect and preserve the peace." Harry Haines, a Vietnam veteran, terms Reagan's call the "administrative version of Vietnam memory." According to Reagan, in Vietnam Americans stood for freedom "as Americans have always stood—*and still do.*" The Vietnam War, Haines observes, is thus "normalized, the deaths are made rational, and the veterans are whole once again, stronger for their expiated burden."

To Harry Haines, the design of the memorial is ambiguous, able to contain Weigl's meaning but also that of a veteran who shouted at a group that attempted to hold a vigil for peace at the memorial: "No, not here. . . . These people died fighting against communism and for freedom. Those people [the vigil group] have no right. It's the same thing that went on with Vietnam, saying we don't belong in El Salvador." How the memorial is interpreted is part of an *ongoing* political struggle. Its meaning, Haines insists, lies "not so much in how the dead are remembered by those of us who survived Vietnam at home or abroad, but in how that remembrance is used by power to explain—to justify—sacrifices in future Vietnams."

What distinguishes many Vietnam veterans from those who fought in other U.S. wars, Peter Marin has written, is their exceptional "moral seriousness," emerging from a "direct confrontation not only with the capacity of others for violence and brutality but also with their own culpability, their sense of their own capacity for error and excess." When a friend asked Marin, as those faced with the morally serious so often do, "Well, what is it [the veterans] really want?" Marin found himself answering spontaneously, "'Justice.' That is what they want, but it is not justice for themselves—though they would like that too. They simply want justice to exist for there to be justice in the world. . . ." Which is why, perhaps, Tim O'Brien insists that a "true war story is never moral. It does not instruct, nor encourage virtue, nor suggest models of proper human behavior. . . . If a story seems moral do not believe it. If at the end of a war story you feel uplifted, or if you feel that some small bit of rectitude has been salvaged from the larger waste, then you have been made the victim of a very old and terrible lie. There is no rectitude whatsoever. There is no virtue."

Michael Herr, a reporter who breathed the war in as deeply as any combat soldier, wrote that it "took the war to teach it, that you were as responsible for everything you saw as you were for everything you did. The problem was that you didn't always know what you were seeing until later, maybe years later, that a lot of it never made it in at all, it just stayed stored there in your eyes." Vietnam has remained stored in the eyes of America; very slowly it is becoming possible to know what we have seen. To figure out what it might mean, to accept responsibility for it, will take much longer.

Competing Memories

ARNOLD R. ISAACS

"Dear Michael: Your name is here but you are not. I made a rubbing of it, thinking that if I rubbed hard enough I would rub your name off the wall and you would come back to me. I miss you so."

No one leaves notes or offerings at the rest of Washington's many monuments. But the Vietnam Veterans Memorial is different. From the moment of its dedication, the wall, with its 58,209 names inscribed on slabs of polished black granite, has seemed to give physical form to a whole nation's feelings of pain and loss. The names unify, while other words about the war continue to divide. "It doesn't say whether the war was right or wrong," a man whose son was wounded in Vietnam, but survived, said about the wall. "It just says, 'Here is the price we paid.'"

The memorial's emotional power is easier to describe than to explain. In part it comes from the names, which make the war's loss personal and concrete and immediate instead of distant and abstract. In part it comes from the reflecting surface, where those looking at the wall can also see the sky and trees and their own faces mirrored in the black stone behind the names of the dead.

There is a kind of mystery in those reflected images. It is as if the stone surface really became what its creator, Maya Ying Lin, imagined: a meeting place "between the sunny world and the quiet dark world beyond, that we can't enter." That sense of closeness between the dead and the living may explain why visitors so often do not just look, but touch, as if they can send their messages of sorrow and love through their fingertips. At the memorial, communication with the dark world seems possible. Thus, along with tears and touching, the wall of names became a place for tokens of remembrance: not only letters but also photographs, old dog tags and decorations, flags, religious medals, birthday and Christmas cards, faded scraps of uniforms and military equipment, souvenirs of war and high school and childhood.

These offerings expressed love and grief for the dead and often something more: a laying down of burdens, a release from the past. People came there to make peace with their memories—like a former marine sergeant named Frederick Garten, who left a ring and a note: "This wedding ring belonged to a young Viet Cong fighter. He was killed by a Marine unit in the Phu Loc province of South Vietnam in May of 1968. I wish I knew more about this young man. I have carried this ring for eighteen years and it's time for me to lay it down. This boy is not my enemy any longer."

Lin's design, selected when she was only twenty-one years old and studying architecture at Yale University, was at first bitterly denounced by those favoring a more conventionally patriotic monument. Opponents didn't like her design and some of them didn't like her, either: a young Chinese American woman who had only been in her early teens when the war ended, had no connection with it, hadn't even known anyone who had served in it.

When the U.S. Fine Arts Commission met to give final approval to the plan, Tom Carhart, a twice-wounded West Point graduate who had been one of the original fund-raisers for the memorial, arrived wearing his two Purple Hearts pinned on his suit jacket to tell the commissioners his reaction:" "A black gash of shame and sorrow. . . . Black walls, the universal color of sorrow and dishonor. Hidden in a hole, as if in shame." (Later, Carhart told a television interviewer: "We want something that will make us feel a part of America.") If Carhart and many like him were outraged because the memorial wasn't heroic enough, a few others were bitter for exactly the opposite reason. "I didn't want a monument," wrote the poet Bill Ehrhart, who also came home from Vietnam with a Purple Heart, "not even one as sober as that / Vast black wall of broken lives. . . . / What I wanted / Was an end to monuments."

Eventually, in an attempt to make the memorial less "antiheroic," as Tom Carhart called it, Lin's austere plan was modified by adding a U.S. flag and a statue, sculpted by Frederic Hart, naturalistically representing three GIs and carrying the inscription: "Our nation honors the courage, sacrifice and devotion to duty and country of its Vietnam veterans."* Not all critics were reconciled, even then. But by the time Hart's statue was completed, two years after the wall was dedicated, the initial criticisms of the memorial had long since been overwhelmed by the public's reaction. The controversy over the design, which had attracted a good deal of coverage before the memorial's dedication, quickly faded from view, to be replaced by images of veterans, children, parents, and other visitors shedding healing tears and finding solace in the sight and touch of the names. The wall quickly became one of the most-visited of all Washington's attractions, and certainly the most emotionally compelling. Some veterans still wouldn't go, but others found themselves returning again and again. "It is exactly the right memorial," said a retired three-star general, "for that war."

Powerful as it was, though, the wall did not close the book on America's confusion and pain about Vietnam. The war and its ghosts continued to hover over the national life and spirit. Rather than becoming a historical event that would automatically recede into the past, Vietnam lingered as a symbol, a metaphor for everything that troubled Americans in the closing years of what had once been called the American Century.

It was the war that "cleaves us still," as George Bush once said. Presumably, Bush was referring to the obvious divisions: between those who supported the policy and those who opposed it, between those who served and those who didn't, between those who denounced the United States and its symbols and those who put flag pins in their lapels and bumper stickers on their cars proclaiming "America—Love it or Leave it."

But the country's division over Vietnam could also be something more elusive and profound. I think, for example, of the only time I had a serious discussion about our respective wars with my father, who was a war correspondent in the China-Burma-India theater in World War II—and had, as a young man a decade earlier, also seen the early stages of Japan's brutal war in China. (He was also in Vietnam shortly after the Japanese surrender in 1945, at the very start of the Viet Minh uprising

---

*In 1993, a second sculpture was erected, honoring women veterans.

against French rule. It is a curious bit of family history that my father, who reported on some of the first skirmishes of that long conflict, lived to see his son cover the end, three decades later.)

From childhood, I knew that my father accepted none of the sentimental myths of war. He saw, as clearly as anyone I have known, the waste and degradation and cruelty. Probably that is why I assumed for years that he had come out of his war, in some fundamental way, with the same vision that I took from mine: that war, at its dark, bloody heart, is insanity. In Vietnam, from time to time during the nearly three years I spent reporting there, I would feel myself waking up, as if from a dream, thinking, *Who's the lunatic who invented this? Who figured out that this is how we decide what color bit of cloth will be fluttering in the morning over this village or that crossroads?* And whoever it was, I wondered, why wasn't he in an asylum, where he belonged?

That feeling came only intermittently, in what I came to think of as lucid moments. The truth is that the landscape of war was so completely familiar to my generation, the children of World War II, that most of the time it didn't seem crazy at all, but quite normal and sane. When I first arrived in Vietnam, in fact, one of the surprises was how much of the scenery and sensations felt familiar and well known: not everything, but a lot. But there was a kind of clarity in those moments of seeing the war as insane. I couldn't make the feeling last—it was like catching a fish with your bare hands and then having it slip away. Yet it was in those fleeting intervals that I thought I had grasped the truth of what I was experiencing. It had never occurred to me that my father didn't feel the same way. But that evening when we talked about it, the year before he died, ten years after my war ended and forty years after his, I learned—to my amazement—that I was wrong. His war was ugly and degrading, even tragic, but not absurd. It was necessary. The Japanese had to be beaten, and there wasn't any other way to do it. With all its cruelty and waste, it was still sane.

I was so surprised by that realization that I don't remember much of what we actually said to each other. I do remember thinking that I now understood in a new way just how profoundly, and in how many different ways, Vietnam had split this country apart. My father and I had no serious disagreements on Vietnam itself. But our generations' different experiences divided us on a much deeper level than that. Vietnam taught me (and, I think, most Americans who were there) that the world is, ultimately, absurd. World War II taught my father and his generation that the world may contain vast terror and evil—but also rationality and, even, a rough and approximate kind of justice. Between those two visions lay a gulf that was, and remains, almost impossible to cross.

The abyss between Americans whose lives were shaped by the great crusade of World War II and their children who grew up in the Vietnam era emerged clearly in a major survey of the baby boom generation conducted in 1986. Reporting on the survey, the writer William Greider wrote:

> The victory in World War II was not only a glorious triumph for the nation, but it taught deeper lessons about what one could expect in life. The United States could stand up for just causes, and if everyone pulled together, it could win. . . . The Sixties experience taught the opposite, . . . that the structure itself was corrupt, that individuals must follow their own moral compass and that they could not expect much moral leadership from above. The nation's framework, the sense of larger purpose and possibilities inherited

from their parents' era, collapsed for this generation. It no longer seemed believable. And nothing has happened since to restore it.

It did not occur to me until many years after that conversation with my father that it didn't just have to do with America after Vietnam. It revealed something about our history during Vietnam, too. The men who made the choices that got the United States into the war, and who decided how to fight it, were also my father's age, sharing his experiences if not his particular knowledge or views about Vietnam. It was a generation whose vision of the world was shaped largely by the experience of World War II and the great triumph achieved by American resources and technological skill in that war. "A generation of men who believed that the world makes sense," one journalist wrote in an article about former Defense Secretary Robert S. McNamara. "That human events could be mastered. That if enough planes drop enough bombs on a backward Asian country, victory must follow."

The same article, whose subject was McNamara's long-delayed apologia for the war in his 1995 book *In Retrospect,* quoted one of its "lessons" from Vietnam: "We failed to recognize," McNamara acknowledged, "that in international affairs, as in other aspects of life, there may be problems for which there are no immediate solutions. For one whose life has been dedicated to the belief and practice of problem solving, this is particularly hard to admit. But at times, we may have to live with an imperfect, untidy world."

To which the reporter added a one-word comment: "May?"

The Vietnam War was not the only thing that changed America. It was probably not even the most important. A vast windstorm of changes in technology, in economic and family life, in racial and ethnic relations, and—possibly most profound of all— in matters of gender and sexual identity, gathered strength and speed during the last third of the twentieth century, swirling away old certainties, making everyone's world a more confusing, unstable, and uncertain place. Looking back, it's possible to trace the beginnings of the storm back far before Vietnam: taking shape in the huge turbulence of World War II, like a tropical storm forming in unseen air currents far out at sea; gently ruffling the seemingly placid air of the 1950s before reaching gale force in the following decades.

Even if the United States had never gone to war in Vietnam, the old system of racial segregation would still have been challenged, and fallen, and new racial tensions would have arisen. Women would still have assumed new roles, inside and outside the home, and men would still have felt troubled and threatened by challenges to old, deeply rooted concepts of masculinity. Suburbs would have provided unprecedented green comfort for millions while also dividing Americans ever more sharply by income and class. Tides of immigrants would still have arrived, making this a much more varied, multicolored society, with correspondingly more jostling and conflict as different groups vied for a place in their new country. Global business trends and technology would have wiped out traditional industrial jobs, transforming the occupational landscape and stranding millions of less-skilled, less-educated workers in poorly paid, unsatisfying, and impermanent jobs. Television would still have transformed the ways in which Americans saw themselves, and revolutionized the political process and the way we debate and decide national policies. And with all of these changes, old rules and traditions and standards of taste and conduct would have weakened; more people would have experimented with more freedoms, and, inevitably, more would also feel deeply threatened and anguished by the pace and wrenching nature of change.

Erase Vietnam from our history and one can reasonably speculate that America in the 1990s would still probably look much the same as it does: fragmented, self-doubting, cynical about its leaders, uncertain of its future, confused about its standards and beliefs. But, of course, Vietnam did happen, and became the era's most powerful symbol of damaged ideals and the loss of trust, unity, shared myths, and common values. Like a magnet, which draws steel shavings scattered on a sheet of paper into a particular form and pattern, Vietnam gave visible shape to the great cultural changes sweeping over American society, defining, more than any other event, the era and its pains.

Perhaps because it was such an exact reverse image of America's epic victory in World War II, Vietnam—the "bad war"—had an extraordinarily shattering effect on the national spirit. World War II ("the last good war," American officers in Vietnam often called it, in tones ranging from sour to sardonic to wistful) had become in many ways the culminating myth of the American experience and national character. It was "such a triumph of American resources, technology, and industrial and military genius," as the author Neil Sheehan put it, that during the next twenty years of unprecedented prosperity at home and military and economic dominance abroad, Americans came to think the success of their society was guaranteed.

Following World War II, the country's military and political leaders and "the greater part of the political, academic, and business leadership" as well, Sheehan wrote, took their supremacy for granted: "the elite of America had become stupefied by too much money, too many material resources, too much power, and too much success." The country that marched into Vietnam in the mid-1960s, two decades after the great crusade against Germany and Japan, had forgotten that it could fail. America's generals of the sixties "assumed that they would prevail in Vietnam simply because of who they were," Sheehan wrote. The same could have been said of American society as a whole.

There had been the ambiguous Korean War, of course. But as the nation gradually stepped up its effort in Vietnam, the towering triumph in World War II was still the dominant image in the imagination of most Americans—and their soldiers, as well. The great majority of men who fought in Vietnam were born between 1945 and 1953, growing up in the sunlit, high noon of postwar prosperity and national self-confidence. A large number were certainly the sons of World War II veterans. Virtually everything in their culture—novels, movies, family stories, childhood games, schoolbooks, the traditional patriotic rhetoric of Veterans Day speeches and graduations and political campaigns—conditioned young men entering military service in the mid-1960s to think of Vietnam as their generation's turn to be, as one veteran said, "the good guys against the bad guys."

If their war was on a smaller scale, they still imagined it—at least in the first few years—as essentially the same experience as World War II, the memory of which was now softened and sentimentalized by twenty years of heroic legends. And when Vietnam turned out to be such a different and disappointing war, the contrast with their fathers' experience made the disillusionment even sharper. One veteran, in a poem that may not have been great literature but achieved a kind of eloquence in its sadness, closed with these lines: "I want to say out loud, had we been in your war, dad, we would have made you proud."

Perhaps because it struck at such powerful myths, Vietnam acquired a mythical nature of its own. The word became a synonym for all kinds of national failure or frustration, as when the mayor of one crime-ridden city referred to the failed war on drugs as "a domestic Vietnam." The country seemed unable to shake its memories of the war or the cultural and political divisions associated with it.

The moral confusion of the war was mirrored in the postwar debate over how to remember it. "We want to give ourselves absolution," one journalist wrote, "although we remain deeply divided—as individuals and as a people—over what it is we need to absolve (whether it is what we did fighting the war in Indochina or what we did protesting it at home)." In fact, the more one examines it, the more one comes to feel the issue lingered so long because it wasn't really about how we fought or protested the war, after all, but something much more profound. America's continuing divisions about Vietnam reflected, more than anything else, an unfinished argument about who we are—about just who it is, when we look at our reflected selves in the black granite of the wall of names, that we really see.

✗ *F U R T H E R   R E A D I N G*

Allen, Douglas, and Ngo Vinh Long, eds. *Coming to Terms: Indochina, the United States, and the War* (1991).

Beattie, Keith. *The Scar that Binds: American Culture and the Vietnam War* (1999).

Brown, T. Louise. *War and Aftermath in Vietnam* (1991).

Canh, Nguyen Van. *Vietnam Under Communism, 1975–1982* (1983).

Capps, Walter H. *The Unfinished War* (1982).

Chanda, Nayan. *Brother Enemy: The War After the War* (1986).

Duiker, William J. *Vietnam Since the Fall of Saigon* (1980).

Franklin, H. Bruce. *M.I.A. or Mythmaking in America* (1993).

Goldman, Peter. *Charlie Company: What Vietnam Did to Us* (1980).

Greene, Bob. *Homecoming* (1989).

Hass, Kristin Ann. *Carried to the Wall* (1998).

Hellman, John. *American Myth and the Legacy of Vietnam* (1986).

Hendin, Herbert, and Ann P. Haas. *Wounds of War: The Psychological Aftermath of Combat in Vietnam* (1985).

Hoffman, Stanley, et al. "Vietnam Reappraised," *International Security,* 6 (1981), 3–26.

Holsti, Ole, and James N. Rosenau. *American Leadership in World Affairs: Vietnam and the Breakdown of Consensus* (1984).

Kaiser, David E. "Vietnam: Was the System the Solution?" *International Security*, 4 (1980), 199–218.

Kolko, Gabriel. *Vietnam: Anatomy of a Peace* (1997).

LaFeber, Walter. "The Last War, the Next War, and the New Revisionists," *Democracy,* 1 (1981), 93–103.

Lake, Anthony, ed. *The Vietnam Legacy* (1976).

Lembcke, Jerry. *The Spitting Image: Myth, Memory, and the Legacy of Vietnam* (1998).

Lifton, Robert Jay. *Home from the War* (1973).

McMahon, Robert J. "Contested Memory: The Vietnam War and American Society, 1975–2001," *Diplomatic History,* 26 (Spring 2002).

MacPherson, Myra. *Long Time Passing: Vietnam and the Haunted Generation* (1984).

Morris, Richard J., and Peter C. Enrenhaus, eds. *Cultural Legacies of Vietnam* (1990).

Nardin, Terry, and Jerome Slater. "Vietnam Revised," *World Politics,* 33 (1981), 436-448.

New, Charles, ed. *After Vietnam: Legacies of a Lost War* (2000).

Paterson, Thomas G. "Historical Memory and Illusive Victories: Vietnam and Central America," *Diplomatic History,* 12 (1988).

Podhoretz, Norman. *Why We Were in Vietnam* (1982).

Ravenal, Earl C. *Never Again* (1978).

Rowe, John Carlos, and Rick Berg, eds. *The Vietnam War and American Culture* (1991).

Salisbury, Harrison E. *Vietnam Reconsidered: Lessons from a War* (1984).

Sheehan, Neil. *After the War Was Over* (1991).

Stevens, Robert Warren. *Vain Hopes, Grim Realities: The Economic Consequences of the Vietnam War* (1976).

Sturken, Marita. *Tangled Memories* (1997).

Thompson, W. Scott, and Donaldson D. Frizzell, eds. *The Lessons of Vietnam* (1977).

Turner, Fred. *Echoes of Combat: The Vietnam War in American Memory* (1996).

Wheeler, John. *Touched with Fire: The Future of the Vietnam Generation* (1984).

Young, Marilyn B. "Revisionists Revised: The Case of Vietnam," *The Society for Historians of American Foreign Relations Newsletter;* 10 (1979), 1–10.